Judyth Vary Baker #100

1994424

Lee Harvey Oswald and Me

The Weaponization of Cancer
The Monkey Virus

and

The Kennedy Assassination

Judyth Vary Baker

Lee Harvey Oswald and Me

Lee Harvey Oswald and Me

Published by Silver Bullet Publications, LLC

US Office 2501 Pearl St.
Austin, TX 78705
1-800-980-3509 Silver.bullet.publications@gmail.com
Library of Congress Control Number TBA

Baker, Judyth Vary,

Lee Harvey Oswald and Me:
The Weaponization of Cancer, the Monkey Virus and the Kennedy Assassination
Revised 2nd Edition (former title: "Me & Lee: How I Came to know, love and lose Lee Harvey Oswald)
Includes references and index.
Hardcover print (ISBN-13) 978-1953848000
Epub (ISBN-13) 978-1953848017

1.Oswald, Lee Harvey 2. Kennedy, John F (John Fitzgerald) 1907-1963 – Assassination 3.Baker, Judyth Vary. 4. Cancer - United States – Polio Vaccine (1954 -1963) 5. Castro, Fidel. 6. New Orleans Mafia 1950 – 1963. 7.Marcello, Carlos. 8.SV-40 Monkey Virus 1955 – 1965. 9. Haslam, Edward T. 10.Dr. Mary's Monkey. II.Title 12. Biological Weapons 1955 – 2020 13. Cancer – United States – Research 14. Politics and Government- History. 15.Memoir, Baker, Judyth Vary. I6. Title 17. David Ferrie

2nd Edition, Revised and Retitled 10 9 8 7 6 5 4 3 2 -

Printed in the USA

Dedication

To Lee Harvey Oswald, my dearest friend, who gave his life for President John F. Kennedy, and to his family, who need to know that their husband and father was a brave, good man, a patriot, and a true American hero of whom they can be proud. Vast numbers of people now agree and honor his memory.

Special Thanks **To Gilles Lauzon**, who had faith in me. Thank you, my good and thoughtful friend, for your unwavering support that made this new hardcover edition possible. **To Mark Mueller**, who gave me medical help and a roof over my head during COVID, making this hardcover edition possible. **To R. A. 'Kris' Millegan**, who, recognizing my medical problems, released me from obligations so I could gain more financial relief by using a new publisher for the 2nd Edition. **To Robert Tanenbaum, Ray Hale** and **Lukas Ettlin**, for their steadfast support and assistance after honestly investigating my account and evidence. **To Dan Storper**, who seeks unity in the research community. **To Phil Nelson**, who defended me against lies, misrepresentations and libel. **To Phil Singer**, who fed me when hungry, in exile in Europe. **To Don Ratliff, Sara Pirie** and **Robert Freeman**, whose faithful help often made all the difference to my survival; and finally, **to my faithful oldest son**, **my oldest daughter, my sister, brother-in-law, cousins, and beloved friends in Sweden**: I can only say to all of you, that you have my eternal love and gratitude.

To My Precious Internet Friends and The Board of Directors for JFK Conferences, LLC
It is impossible to properly thank my Board of Directors, and the thousands of friends and supporters who have brought *Me & Lee* --and this revised, re-titled 2nd edition--, *Lee Harvey Oswald and Me*), to the world. You have saved the truth.

To Those Who Have Passed On... Jim Marrs, Dennis David, Hubert Clark, Gerry Patrick Hemming, the *Sixty Minute* team of Don Hewitt, Phil Scheffler, Mike Wallace, and Howard Liebengood; Edward Sherry, Edward I. Schwartz, Col. Dan Marvin, William "Mac" McCullough, Anna Lewis, Evelyn Hall, Martha Rose Crow, Col. Phillip Ware, Mavinee Black and Al Maddox.

Acknowledgments and Thanks (In Random Order) Rev. Ken Hughes, Edward T. Haslam, Robert F. Kennedy Jr., Dick Russell, Dr. Cyril Wecht, Oliver Stone, Abraham Bolden, Judge Jim Botelho, Edgar Tatro, David Denton, Larry Rivera, Robert Groden, Vincent Palamara, Saint John Hunt, Barbara Honegger, Dr. John deLane Williams, Dr. Wm. H. Warrick, Dr. James Campbell, Dr. John Hughes, Randolph Benson, Peter Hymans, Dr. Jim Fetzer, Marty Eichler, Dr. Kathy Santi, Dr. Howard Platzman, Tom Rozoff, Ole Dammegard, David Neal, Damon Ise, Pat Hall, Beverly Oliver, Robert Kelly,

Ryan M. Jones, Victoria Powell Sulzer, Claudia and Vicki [Rodick family], Kelly Thomas Cousins, Anita Langley, Tim Rian, Steve Zubco, Thom Whitehead & Sydney Wilkinson, Allan Mattsson, Kjell Berglund, Ing-Marie Ohlson, Garrett Ten-have Chapman, Dave Evans, Jesse Ventura, George Freund, Lee Forman, Carol Sloan, Johnny C. Smith, Karen Walk, Kathryn Giddens, Ron Bean, Geoff Meollard & family, Hy McEnery, Shane O'Sullivan, Dr. David Mantik, Paul Kuntzler, Paul Wilson, Tyrel Ventura, Sean Stone, Zack Shelton, Mary Morgan J., Pam Dennis, John B. Wells, Jack Roth, Annette Carr, Gary Fannin, J. Christer, Andrew Kreig, Harold Trischman, Jason Goodman, Richard Bartholomew, Jeffrey Holmes, Jason Trachtenburg, Lisa Soland, Gary Severson, Tony Bonn, Arturo Tudury, Nate Geigner, Roland Tremblay, Ed Bishop, Steve Cameron, William M. Law, Dr. Jack Kruse, Greg Lewis, Gary Shaw, Pastor Roy Johnson, Tom Truel, Cathy Soo, Garrett Ten-Have Chapman. Please forgive me if your name is missing!

Select Commentary About the Author of Me & Lee

"We all owe Judyth Baker a huge debt and much thanks for her courage, forbearance, tenacity and grit in bringing to us all her very personal and revelatory story. A journey that has been beset with the trials and tribulations of exposing unwelcome truths."
R.A. 'Kris' Millegan Publisher, Trine Day, July 19, 2010

"This story is thick with political intrigue, but it is also about something softer, but stronger... that invisible force called "love." A stubborn and enduring love, spiced with anger, frustration and yes, revenge. This is the story of the 20-year-old girl who screamed as she watched the man she loved murdered on national television, who saw him summarily convicted of the very crime she knew he gave his life trying to stop. Judyth hid in silence for decades, afraid that she, too, would be murdered. But love eventually overcame fear. And love is ultimately the reason this woman decided to risk her life to tell the iconoclastic tale you are about to read." **Edward T. Haslam** Editor. Author of *Dr. Mary's Monkey* Nov. 2009

"Will anyone in the government finally tell the truth about the Kennedy assassination? It is highly unlikely. But can we ever really know the truth? I say yes, by studying the wide array of information now available, thinking for ourselves, and listening to the impassioned, unflinching voice of Judy Vary Baker. For once, I agree with one of her constant critics, who wrote, "If Judyth Vary Baker is telling the truth, it will change the way we think about the Kennedy assassination." For those who know the facts behind her story, I think it already has." **Jim Marrs** Journalist and author of the best-selling book *Crossfire: The Plot that Killed Kennedy* (basis for the film "JFK' by Oliver Stone.) Nov. 2009

Oliver Stone: "I believe this good woman." Remarks, before live audience, the 7th Annual JFK Assassination Conference, Dallas, TX, Nov. 2019

Edward T. Haslam, Judyth Vary Baker, Oliver Stone, Edgar Tatro

Table of Contents

FOREWORD by Robert K. Tanenbaum

In October '76 I received a telephone call from Richard A. Sprague (RAS). At the time, I was an Assistant District Attorney (ADA) in New York County (Manhattan) hired by legendary D.A. Frank S. Hogan and had been Bureau Chief of the Criminal Courts, ran the Homicide Bureau and was in charge of the legal training of the staff. I had also prosecuted to verdict several hundred cases and never lost a trial wherein a felony was charged. RAS informed me that he was appointed Chief Counsel and staff director of the recently formed Congressional Committee entitled House Select Committee on Assassinations (HSCA) regarding the assassinations of President Kennedy and the Reverend Dr. Martin Luther King. He asked me if I would be interested in leading the subcommittee investigation into the JFK assassination. Since RAS and I had never met or ever spoken to one another, I said, "why me?" He replied that I was recommended to him and that he had checked out my credentials during my ADA tenure.

Shortly thereafter, RAS and I met on several occasions which resulted in my appointment as Deputy Chief Counsel in charge of the Kennedy probe. During my initial meeting with Congressional members of the HSCA, I suggested that the Committee not hire me. At best, I opined, Congress is

well-served by compromise. I made it quite clear to the HSCA that in my view, one should not compromise during search for truth. The Committee members present assured RAS and me that they would not interfere with the fact-finding investigation. Several months later, RAS and I would

regrettably learn otherwise, which necessitated our resignations. Both the Warren Commission (WC) and the HSCA alleged probes were downright dishonest and gut wrenchingly misleading. A brief case on point: by invitation, I represented the "people's case" including Lee Harvey Oswald (LHO) against the Government in a JFK "mock trial" conducted at the South Texas College of Law – Houston on Thursday, November 16, 2017. During my ADA experience, I had been accustomed to debunking beyond doubt so-called conspiracy theories proffered by defense attorneys during major, high profile murder cases. Many of those types of cases and trials are the subject matters in my thirty-two published books (29 Butch Karp/Marlene Ciampi thrillers and 3 non-

fiction dramas). Confoundingly disappointing, at the Houston mock trial, the Government's case was a
putatively pathetic regurgitation of the Government's false narrative that it has propounded for the past 58 years. In fact, the Government's evidence has been indelibly rendered scientifically invalid and otherwise inherently unworthy of belief. Of significance, the jury, of course, did not convict LHO. During my presentation, I offered no opinions, inclinations, wishes or conspiracy theories, only those "stubborn things" --immutable facts-- which inexorably validate search for truth. An important portion of my case was that LHO could not have fired the fatal shot that blew out the back of JFK's head where occiptal and parietal bones locate at the resulting avulsive injury.

To more fully understand the true nature of Lee Harvey Oswald, read the passionately presented Judyth Vary Baker memoir, *Lee Harvey Oswald and Me* – you will not be disappointed. She graphically describes her experience with Lee Harvey Oswald with ample corroboration, particularly during the New Orleans 1963 summer. She presents Lee Harvey Oswald as a government patsy, an innocent individual who was unjustly accused. In my opinion, I do not believe any fair-minded jury would convict him. Quite a conclusion, I understand, but one based on the evidence and the embarrassing lack thereof by the Government! Read this book and decide for yourself.

Respectfully submitted by
Robert K. Tanenbaum
6/14/21

A Great Man Has Weighed In, On Lee Harvey Oswald's Side

Beyond what he's done for Lee's cause, this article tells you more about this author of 32 books. In 2013: "Author and criminal prosecutor **Robert K. Tanenbaum** hosted a launch party for his new nonfiction *Echoes of My Soul* (Kensington) earlier this month in

the shadow of the Manhattan courthouse at Forlini's Restaurant, a favorite haunt among those in New York's legal scene. Attendees included State Supreme Court Justice **Bob Seewald**, Federal District Court Judge **John Keenan**, author and former prosecutor **Linda Fairstein** (right), former Supreme Court Justice **Herb Adlerberg**, former D.A. and special prosecutor for the Knapp Commission **Maurice Nadjari**, and Kensington Publishing execs Steven Zacharius and Laurie Parkin. **After speaking about the personal and historical significance of the Wylie-Hoffert case covered in *Echoes of My Soul*--the murders that helped lead to the Supreme Court's Miranda Rights ruling and helped end the death penalty in New York State**--Tanenbaum signed copies of the book."

Chapter One
Tender Years

Few people remember much of their lives before the age of five, but I certainly remember my fifth year clearly, for I nearly died. I got very ill: I had a fever and couldn't keep anything in my stomach. An intense pain developed in my abdomen, but my mother, the youngest in her own big family, had little experience with sick children, and no patience with weakness. Her remedy was to send me to bed.

Busy hosting a family party that night at our home, she didn't realize I had a ruptured appendix. There I was until midnight, when my Grandpa Whiting decided to check on me.

"My God!" he cried, "she's burning up!" My mother began to cry as he scooped me up in his arms, hurried to his car, and drove us to Pawating Hospital. It was cold outside, and Grandpa had my mother hold my head out the window to cool me down. Doctors later said that may have saved my life, but just barely. I was operated on immediately, but the situation was dire. The ruptured appendix had caused a festering gangrene to spread everywhere. Penicillin had just become available: it was pumped into my body in massive amounts, along with blood transfusions. When they thought I had stopped breathing, I was rolled out of the operating room and our family priest, Father Rose, began giving me Last Rites, surrounded by my weeping family. I could see them, as I was out of my body, walking toward a great White Light. In that light I could see many people urging me to "Go back, go back!" Reluctantly, I did so – and sat up!

My mother screamed, and the doctors, seeing I was still alive, rushed me back into the operating room

(L) Grandparents George & Jessie Vary - Germans (R) Grandma Anna Nemeth Hoffer Whiting – born in Hungary w/ Grandpa Jesse E. Whiting – English

When they ran out of Type O blood, my Uncle Leo, the Black Sheep of the family, who had my blood type, stepped forward. He was laid on a bed beside me. I saw his dark blood transfused directly into my arm.

Somehow, I made it through the night, but there would be more operations to come. Surgery after surgery, they cut away infected tissues and even portions of my intestines. I remembered the words: peritonitis, gangrene, abscesses, bowel obstruction, anemia... A hole developed in my stomach. Stomach acids leaked into the upper part of my torso. Unable to eat, I was fed sugar water with a tube down my nose. Another tube in my nose sucked out bloody material from my stomach. Tubes were also in my arms, to add fluids, while tubes in my belly and bladder drained fluids away.[1] When the veins in my arms collapsed, the needles connecting them were moved to my hands, my ankles, even my head.

(L) My fierce mother, Gloria (R) Donald W. Vary & Gloria W. Vary 1946: Sisters: Lynda (L), Judy w/Santa. 1949: School, 1950: hair is a rat's nest after months of illness. (R) Judy, age 8.

[1] Penicillin had just reached small hospitals in small towns, previously being available only for troops during WWII. Steroids and penicillin slowly healed me.

There is no describing the pain and helplessness. I would gaze at a picture of the Virgin – *Stella Matutina* – on the hospital wall, wishing I could return to the beautiful White Light of love and peace, before all those shining figures there told me, *"Go back!"* Nuns from Notre Dame's St Mary's College had brought the picture in, and learning that I begged for Communion, though I was only five, priests came and celebrated Communion with me for months. It was with nuns and priests that I learned to pray. Most of the time, I was totally dependent upon the care of the nursing staff. They called me their "Little Angel" and would hold up magazines for me to read. When they ran out of children's books, and I asked them to find some *Popular Mechanics* and *Scientific Americans*, they start calling me their "Little Genius." If I had not been confined to bed, no doubt I would have been reading very little, but in the hospital, I had caught glimpses of amazing medical and scientific magazines, and I yearned to read them.

After realizing that I knew how to read but was too weak to hold a big magazine in my hands, Dr. Prichard, who visited me every day, contrived a little stand to hold magazines, and with a slit straw between my teeth, I was able to turn pages. After I'd been there for months, I was offered my first solid food: it was Thanksgiving, and I was asked to try some chopped turkey and dressing. But somehow, a piece of sharp bone had fallen into the small dish, and I swallowed it. Great damage was done, ripping the hole in my stomach open again. I survived after yet another blood transfusion, and additional months in the hospital. By now, my busy parents had grown tired of visiting me, atop their long hours running two TV stores and a TV station. Priests and grandparents, cousins, aunts and uncles took turns visiting me, but there were many lonely hours. Dr. Prichard and the nurses, nuns and priests made them more bearable. Since I didn't complain much, when I finally asked a nurse for some chewing gum, longing to be able to have something in my mouth, she walked half a mile to find some.

And when my Aunt Elsie, concerned that I was reading too many medical and science magazines, and missing out on childhood, asked if there was any toy I might like, I told her I'd love to have a doll with red hair and a blue dress. After searching everywhere for such a doll, Auntie Elsie finally found one in Chicago, and brought it triumphantly to my bedside. "What will you name her?" my aunt asked. "I will call her Margaret!" I replied.

After playing with the doll for a day, my next idea was to ask for all kinds of surgical instruments and tubes and hypodermic needles so I could do unto poor Margaret as the doctors had done unto me. I gave up when the nurses said that Margaret had nothing inside her but cotton, and to have mercy on her. Instead, they brought me take-apart models of parts of the human body, and let me assemble a real preserved skeleton. They also brought in a Gilbert's chemistry set and an Erector Set for Christmas. I was soon building noisy little engines that took turns dumping chemicals together to produce interesting little explosions. It made a mess of my bedside table, but that's what happens when nurses and doctors become your playmates! By the time I was able to go home, my extremely fine hair had grown so matted, from months in bed, that it had become like felt. Nobody could get a comb through it. Nobody wanted to shave my head, perhaps because the specter of the Holocaust was so fresh in everyone's memory, and the fact that I was practically a skeleton.

I had missed a lot of school, but since I'd started early, technically, I had never been held back, for I was now with children my own age. There would be more operations when I turned ten, at which time a nun, Sister Mary Hugh, objected to my being allowed to pass to the next grade (hers). I was not a favorite. When only a 2nd grader, I had argued with her about the nature of mathematics and we had sparred about the nature of God.

Her red face and glaring eyes, when we argued, gave me a clue that I had crossed a line in her belief system. I had even demanded the right to be allowed to spell "with" as w-**h**-i-t-h, because **wh**at, **wh**ich, **wh**y, **wh**en, **wh**o, **wh**ile, etc. were all spelled with the 'h' added. I had walked out of kindergarten when that teacher introduced the class to "the number seven" with a cute little train. So when I arrogantly told Sister Mary Hugh I could calculate numbers faster than she could, she was determined to teach me some humility.

Recovering at the hospital from an operation to correct internal adhesions, I had missed a lot of school. The Sister saw her chance and came storming into my room. "You've missed all your exams," she announced, "and I refuse to give you any more days of absence. You are to be held back a year." Fortunately, Dr. Prichard was nearby. Overhearing her sharp tone, he stepped into my room.

Seeing the tears in my eyes, he snapped, "She doesn't have to take any exams! Hell, she's ready for high school." This was the first time I had heard anybody say that I was intelligent: it just wasn't said in front of children at the time I was growing up. But my family knew. I had already built a few TV sets for my father to experiment on in his electronics lab.

I even did Dad's income tax returns. The adults in my family also used me to settle squabbles about "who said what," trusting my precise memory. But they also worried that I spent too much time reading. My grandparents on both sides sent me outside to play and have fun in "the real world" with my many friends and cousins. But in the evenings, I had access to their many books. At the same time, my dad obtained adult reading privileges for me at the Niles Public Library, even though the librarian was quite upset when my first selection, at age seven, was

Tobacco Road by Erskine Caldwell, described by one critic as late as 2006 as "a greasy hairball of a novel - one of the sickest and most lurid books to have emerged from the literature of the American South." Attending high school at age ten with big kids, as Dr. Prichard intimated, had no appeal.

I did not want to lose my friends. Nor did I want to be held back a year and be forced to sit with my sister in her classroom!

Seeing that I did not dare speak in this nun's formidable presence, Dr. Prichard asked her to return the next day, at which time he promised to give her proof that I should not be held back. Then he turned to me. "You need to eat what you can, to get some strength," he said.

All that day and the next morning, I was carefully given extra jello, crackers, and tea. Finally, I had some wonderful ice cream. Then I dozed in a morphine cloud of painkillers into a medicated sleep. The next morning, Dr. Prichard spoke to my concerned parents, then sat down at my bedside.

"Young lady," he said, "in a few hours, the lady in black and white will return. It took some doing, but I have figured out a way to make sure you will not be held back. Will you agree to take an IQ test? All your classmates took it this year, but you were too sick. If you take it now, they will not be able to hold you back. But you can't have any more painkillers today, or you won't be alert enough."

After warning me that it was a long test, and that I could stop at any time if it became too much for me, Prichard left me alone to rest. About an hour later, in came Sister Mary Hugh, smiling and calm, for she believed that her sacrilegious student would soon be a mere unpleasant memory: kindly Sister Mary Albert would suffer my presence, instead of her. Surprised that I was about to take an IQ test, she was asked to wait for the results.

I took the Weschler. In pain. In bed, with an IV in my arm. It was different from anything I'd encountered. But as the questions became more interesting, something clicked in my brain. I forgot my pain and began sailing through the questions. Only near the end I lay back, exhausted, and said, "That's all I can do."

"Do you want a shot?"

"Yes." The pain in my abdomen had become too intense to be ignored, but Prichard said I'd done enough. He had brought in a specialist from nearby Notre Dame, who scored the test and handed the results to the waiting nun. "136," he said. "The highest in the school. And she didn't even finish it."[2] Sister Mary Hugh had to keep me!

---

[2] Scores on IQ tests have risen every decade, a phenomenon known as "the Flynn effect." Better nutrition, more years of schooling, and test experience contributed to higher scores. My IQ scores ranged 136-160 (several 160's). In 2001 Geico paid for a Weschler after a concussion in an "accident" affected my short-term memory (lower IQ scores). I scored 142. In 2006, a Weschler of 155 indicated recovery of most my cognitive abilities.

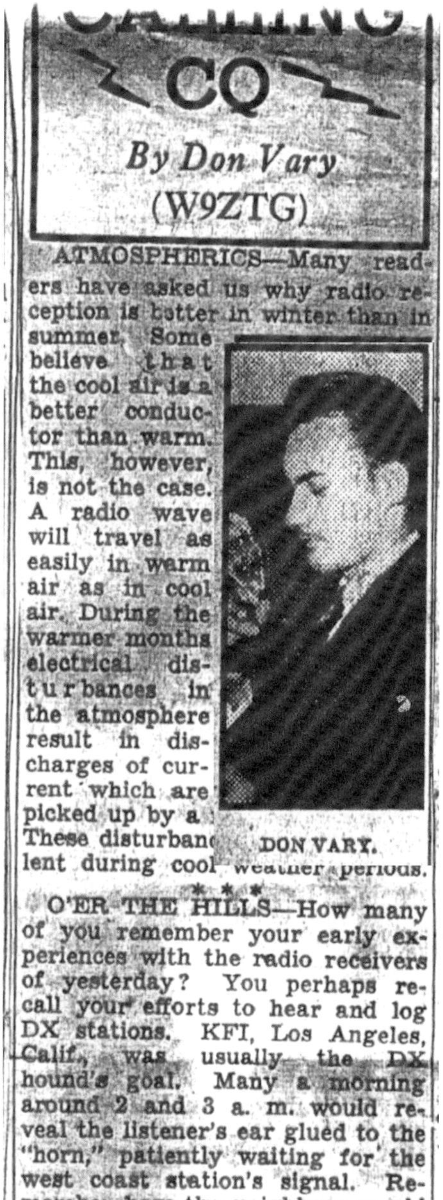

CQ

By Don Vary
(W9ZTG)

ATMOSPHERICS—Many readers have asked us why radio reception is better in winter than in summer. Some believe that the cool air is a better conductor than warm. This, however, is not the case. A radio wave will travel as easily in warm air as in cool air. During the warmer months electrical disturbances in the atmosphere result in discharges of current which are picked up by a [illegible] These disturban[illegible] lent during cool weather periods.

DON VARY.

* * *

O'ER THE HILLS—How many of you remember your early experiences with the radio receivers of yesterday? You perhaps recall your efforts to hear and log DX stations. KFI, Los Angeles, Calif., was usually the DX hound's goal. Many a morning around 2 and 3 a. m. would reveal the listener's ear glued to the "horn," patiently waiting for the west coast station's signal. Remember how the neighbors would gather around the set and wonder how the signal could go right through the mountains? Today we know that the signal doesn't go through the mountains, but jumps over them. The wave uses two gigantic surfaces for it's reflecting units—the earth, and the so-called Kennelly-Heaviside layer, to throw itself in a zigzaging path around the world.

* * *

Only then did she start awarding me "A" grades, except in math. That would never change.

I was born in Epworth Hospital in South Bend, Indiana on May 15, 1943, fifteen months before my only sibling, Lynda. It was at the height of WWII. The hospital was so crowded with wounded soldiers that I was born in its corridor. My mother was only 17, but had already been married two years. Their marriage was based on my father's reaction to a truly bizarre event.

Don Vary, before his marriage, was popular on local radio as a weekend deejay. He had his own newspaper column "Calling CQ" about ham radio. And he led a motorcycle club called "The Steeds of Steel." But at age 16, Don leg was broken in a motorcycle accident. Described in a news article as if he were to blame, the car he 'hit' had made a sudden left turn in front of him, then kept on going, dragging him by his leg, which was caught in the bumper, for a quarter of a mile. A 3-inch piece of bone was removed from his shattered leg, but the multiple bone fractures never properly healed. Ashamed that he was unable to serve as a soldier, Dad decided to use his talents in TV and radio-electronics to serve his country. After impressing Bendix Corp. with his improvements to their electric washing machine dials, he was transferred to their Aviation Research Division, where his true talents began to shine. Don began a career inventing various radio, television and aircraft devices. But it was Don's leadership in the popular Steeds of Steel motorcycle club, which met at his home, and his muscular physique as a former Golden Glove champion boxer that dazzled the girls, who took little notice of his brilliance. That is, until Gloria Whiting came along. She was only 15, but she stood out. Gloria was the only one of Don's female admirers who had a true interest in his complex life.

Furthermore, she asked Don to teach her Morse Code. She wanted to be a ham radio operator, just like him. Atop that, Gloria was fearless, eager to ride any motorcycle on the planet.

Impressed with her courage and charmed by her wit and flaring temper, 21-year-old Don had come to visit Gloria on his big Harley-Davidson motorcycle very early in the morning, after learning that her friends said Gloria was in big trouble.

The night before, Gloria, whose friends in town missed her after her parents were forced to move to one of their farms (it was during the Great Depression), had picked her up in an over-crowded Coup for an evening of fun. Things turned sour when they all began smoking, and Gloria refused. They finally drove her home late, where, ominously, her parents [my grandparents] stood waiting for her. When they smelled cigarette smoke on her clothes, my angry grandmother said, "You're going to get a switching for that!" Despite the protests of her friends, Grandma turned to a big willow tree, where she broke off a long branch and began to peel it. Seeing that, Gloria's friends backed their car out of the driveway and fled. Now, in the fog of early morning, Don drove as close as he dared to the farm, shut off his motorcycle, and walked up the driveway, trying to decide what to do. That's when he heard somebody coughing in the barn. It was Gloria. She was kneeling on a heap of old corncobs, shivering in the cold. There were long, red welts on her arms and legs. My usually kind, affectionate grandparents had harshly punished her. Concerned that they were losing control of their rebellious daughter, they had decided to lay down the law.

When she arrived home late, smelling like cigarette smoke, they decided to give her a lesson she wouldn't forget, with a willow switch. And if she stopped kneeling on the corncobs before they called her to breakfast, they said she would never see her friends again. Full of hot anger, my father carried Gloria to his motorcycle, telling her, "I love you! I will protect you!"

When she protested that her parents would never let him see her again if she rode away with him, my father got on his knees and said, "Gloria, will you marry me?" It would not be a marriage made in heaven. The hasty elopement was condemned by the families on both sides.

WIFE, 17, MISSING OVER TWO WEEKS

Seventeen-year-old Mrs. Gloria Ann Vary, 602 Klinger street, has been missing since Sept. 2, her father, J. Edward Whiting, rural route No. 4, Niles, Mich., has informed police.

Her husband, Donald Vary, aged 24, told police the last he saw her was at the Bendix Aviation corporation gate No. 4 about 3:30 p. m.; on Sept. 1 when he gave her $11. Vary filed charges for divorce four days later and is staying with his parents at 545 North Sunnyside avenue.

Months later, Aunt Elsie arranged a discrete Catholic marriage for the errant pair at a side altar in St. Joseph's Church, South Bend. Dutifully, my father began attending Mass every Sunday with the Whitings, the Vargo's and the Hoffers, but the Lutheran Vary side remained hostile to his Catholic wife. Headstrong, fiery and fierce, my mother often battled Dad fist to fist. At the same time, she proved to be a smart woman in her own right. [3]

On most weekends, we lived with our grandparents Whiting and life was good. Sometimes we had a good weekend with my parents, too, and had fun, but all too often, when they drank too much, they would start fighting, and we were often whipped with a belt just for existing in the same house. Later, they sometimes apologized. But we still had the sore bodies, bruises and marks after they sobered up. Of course, we were not to tell our grandparents. In the end, the two lovebirds always reconciled.

However, they came close to divorce more than once.

The article "Wife, 17, Missing..." only hints at their worst fight. Dad hit Mother in the mouth and broke off her two front teeth after she kicked his sore, infected leg in a fit of anger. It took two weeks to get her teeth capped. During that time, my grandparents hid their daughter's whereabouts from her half-crippled husband. I was conceived shortly after they reconciled.

Despite the fights, my parents worked well together, making money in the big TV boom. Mother encouraged Dad to take courses in electronics, though he never got a degree: he was too busy inventing stunning new technology for Raytheon, Bendix, Whirlpool and finally, Zenith, working on color TV development, new TV tubes, and frequency tuning inventions with Austria-born Robert Adler in Chicago, co-inventor of the TV Remote Control.

My father with one of his inventions.

Perhaps my grandmother's Hungarian family, who once lived close to Vienna, knew his family. So familiar was my family with 'Adler' that when I asked my sister in 2020 if she remembered the name 'Adler,' she replied, "Yes, I remember Bob." Dad had a crew, led by a man called 'Snooks'[4] to install TV towers for better reception for wealthy clients. As Dad developed improvements in fringe area reception for both Adler and WGN in Chicago, Raytheon proudly advertised that Dad could get good TV reception "71 miles from Chicago."

---

[3] My mother was a ham operator both in her youth and again in her 70's.

[4] Snooks, a poor laborer, nevertheless taught me how to write the cursive letter "S."

"He invented special TV tubes," "aspects of color TV" and an idea for "a synchronizing circuit which could achieve demonstrably greater stability in fringe areas of television reception." As half-owner of a local TV station, Dad tested his TV-related ideas and inventions there. The photo shows him holding a synchronizer. My parents also enjoyed singing duets and doing commercials on camera at their TV station, and my sister and I became minor celebrities, singing duets in cute costumes on live TV. When Dad went to Chicago, sometimes he took me along.

We stayed at the elegant Drake Hotel, for Adler always treated my father well. [5] But we were not as wealthy as we might have been: a tornado almost destroyed our home, taking off the roof, a devastating car crash hospitalized my mother, and my parents' love of luxuries constantly drained their bank account. My illnesses didn't help matters, either, but graciously, my parents never said a word about the many Florida vacations Dr. Prichard took on my father's dime. After all, they would fly to The Bahamas whenever they wanted, to renew their stash of Planter's Punch! While their love for new cars, gadgets and travel strained their bank account, I remember best the raging tornado that ripped the roof right off our house. I was only four. We were eating breakfast when it happened. My father's quick actions saved our lives.He pulled us under our huge marble-topped oak table, which was so heavy that we all survived. Luckily, Grandpa George Vary was a skilled carpenter and boatwright with his own construction company located in nearby South Bend.

A kind and wonderful Grandpa, he moved in and cared for us while my parents worked, supervising the rebuilding of our house. With his own hands, he crafted fine, new cabinets for our kitchen. But it wasn't cheap. Fortunately, though Adler claimed all the patents for the ideas and discoveries Dad presented, he always gave Dad all the royalty money.

When I was almost eleven, Dad had enough base income[6] to aim for his dream career: to become a rocket scientist. Then Dad got a security clearance and began work as an electrical engineering consultant at the Chrysler plant in Warren, Michigan. That's where Chrysler produced the Redstone Missile. They sold the store in South Bend and my mother handled the remaining TV store at the State Line. A manager was hired for the TV station. Then Dad got his big break: Sandia Corp. wanted him. Sandia handled the engineering for Los Alamos National

---

[5] https://www.technologyintegrator.net/article/robert-adler-co-inventor-remote-control-dies-93-47584/all/ Dad is holding one of his inventions, for which Adler got the credit. "Adler... began his six-decade career with Zenith Electronics in 1941..."

[6] My father enjoyed semi-retirement in Florida when he was only 38. The payments continued until the patents finally expired in the 1980's. "Geoff Wilson... of Elo Touch Systems was well acquainted with Robert Adler's intellectual honesty to champion the best idea regardless of who came up with the idea." http://www.bswd.com/CNSV-1303- AdlersTouchscreenInventions.pdf

Laboratory, home of the atomic bomb. Since the government planned to use the Bomb in rockets, the guidance system needed perfecting. A post card dated June 29, 1955 shows Mother's notes about our trip to New Mexico to check out the site. It was an isolated compound, set in the midst of a blazingly hot desert. "Where are we to live?" my mother demanded.

We learned that we would be staying in a trailer park until we could rent a suitable house, for which there was a long waiting list. We were advised not to buy a house because Dad could be transferred at any time to Sandia's labs at Livermore, California. He also would not be allowed to speak a word about his work, which was classified, and sometimes he could be exposed to a lot of radiation. Since the Cold War was heating up, Dad was also warned that the scientists and engineers working in his specialty might require tighter security measures, which could force our family to live in a compound behind barbed wire. When my mother heard that, she informed my father that she was not going to raise their children in a prison surrounded by barbed wire. It was an ultimatum made by a strong-willed woman who loved freedom. My father had to choose between his dream career and his family. He chose family. It was a decision that haunted him the rest of his life. We drove on, to Livermore, California. After waiting a few months in California, hoping Livermore would accept my father without the preliminary training required, my parents gave up and chose to move to Florida.

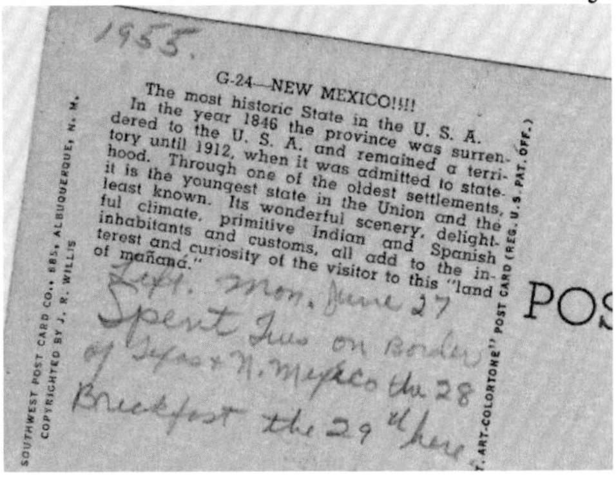

Meanwhile, my health had improved so much, while they'd enjoyed a new, easy-going life no longer consumed by hours of hard work, my parents decided to move to Florida and semi-retire. My mother's brother, Jerry Whiting, observing my return to full health, believed that Barbie, his youngest child who had severe bronchitis every winter, would also do better.

That began the exodus of our Hungarian side of the family to St. Petersburg, Florida. Our homes in Niles and South Bend were quickly sold at bargain prices in auctions, but everyone had extra money due to years of wise financial decisions. Only my dear Hungarian grandma understood the true gravity of this decision.

She wept as her priceless antiques and peerless possessions from the Old World went for scant dollars on the auction block. Even so, having our family stay together meant more to her than living up north without us. Auntie Elsie, Uncle Emery and their last son at home, Ronnie, also joined us. All was well, at first, when we moved into our beautiful new homes. The men enjoyed fishing together in the Gulf, the women enjoyed making *kolach* and getting acquainted with their new Catholic parish, and we lived only steps from each other. Everybody had a good job. Then came disaster. The builder, a Mr. Pontius, vanished with our money.

The subcontractors, demanding their pay, took us to court and were awarded our homes. Our Florida dream was in tatters. To survive, Uncle Jerry and his family had to go back north. Elsie, Emery and Ronnie would follow. Meanwhile, my precious Grandma developed a fever, then some serious pain. She was dying of breast and lung cancer.

When we learned she was dying, everyone hid from her the harrowing fact that soon, we would all be homeless. Every day, I'd get off the school bus and visit her. I'd write down some of our family's history from her lips, and at other times prayed the rosary with her. She was my "Nanitsa," and I begged God, in my prayers, to save my grandma's life. How could mere words convey how beloved this woman was to us? She had shepherded her big, diverse family through all the moral, physical and financial trials of World War I, the Great Depression, World War II, to this final crisis that we hid from her, as she failed and weakened.

She was not a beautiful woman, but her character, impeccable honesty and kindness left an indelible imprint on our lives.

My children say I lose too much by being so honest. But I will always follow my grandmother's stellar example. I'll always try to do what is right, in honor of her. Educated in a convent in Budapest, making seven ocean trips from Indiana to Europe to be so educated, my Nanitsa could speak six languages,[7] loved classical music and the arts, and enjoyed international travel. She was an independent woman, the family

[7] She spoke English, French, German, Hungarian, Polish, and Czech and could read Latin. She had books in all those languages. I still have one of her books, in Polish.

matriarch whose love, wisdom and cultural standards held us all together.

Then, she was gone. As I looked down into my Grandma's coffin, into all that sudden stillness and loss, a deep hatred for cancer took root in my soul. I had been helpless to stop the insidious growth inside her that took her life. That would change. This is where our story really begins.

After Nanitsa ("little Nancy") died on Oct. 6, 1956, for months, I cared about nothing. I wrote dark poems about death, painted morbid pictures, and avoided attending Southside Jr. High. That September, when Grandma had been so very ill, they had wanted me to skip two grades. Instead, I asked to take all the 8th grade exams when classes began.

I passed them all with high scores, including plane geometry, simply to be able to skip classes. By now, I hated math and wanted it out of my life. Acing the geometry final exam the first week of school, they gave me credit for the course and allowed me to take Glee Club instead, taught by a true genius named David Wilcox. Schools without sports, music and art can be prisons for kids.

In my sorrows, when Grandma died, I sang my heart out, and Mr. Wilcox recognized that passion. He sometimes let me sing a solo in a public presentation. Singing would become a path to healing. If it hadn't been for that Glee Club class, I may have dropped out of school for good, from sheer depression. But thanks to Wilcox, and a nearby Youth Center, where my sis and I began doing gymnastics together, life improved. I began singing, played basketball and volleyball, and studied art.

My dear grandparents were happily married almost thirty years when, at a nuptial Mass, they renewed their vows. Promises were required: my Grandma promised not to hit Grandpa anymore with a slipper. My sociable, bar-hopping grandpa promised he would stop drinking and would be baptized Catholic. He kept that promise until she died.

The day came when an elderly Russian at the Youth Center taught me to play chess. That's when my brain came alive again! I became fascinated with bewhiskered Sergei, my brilliant Russian mentor, and with his native country. He began teaching me not only chess, but also introduced me to Russian books, art and music. Chess helped keep me from thinking about how much our family's lives had changed. Our family was scattered, my grandpa was heart-broken, my dad's dream to be a rocket scientist was forever lost, and my parents were fighting and drinking more than ever, now that Nanitsa was gone.

But with my mind re-awakened through chess, I realized that I had dishonored my grandmother's memory by skipping so much school. I'd even stolen some comic books. What would she have thought of that?

Determined to learn more about cancer, I returned to reading medical magazines. I had lost so much time! I resumed all my classes at school, saving my grades, when suddenly, we had to move again. Despite every appeal, we, too, had lost our beautiful home and had to vacate. But our finances were back on track: my father had invented an improvement for water softeners. Once again he "made a patent deal," this time through an old friend back in Michigan, where the patent rights were sold to the whole industry. An article on the next page explains what Dad invented succinctly. He was also given a big area contract by a water conditioning company. I later learned the Mafia was involved. The water conditioning industry got Dad's electrical control valves for free, while Dad gained inventory.He was given dozens of free water conditioners to start his business. It would be my father's last invention. Our fortunes once more on the rise, we moved to 'Le Chalet' in Bradenton and took the whole second story of that remarkable old mansion. Bradenton was a smaller town then, nestled between the palm-lined banks of the Manatee River and the white sand beaches of the Gulf of Mexico.

Dad's business now began to boom.[8] I enrolled in 8th grade, at Walker Jr. High, cancer research on my mind. My mother was concerned when I started dissecting all kinds of fish, more concerned when I dissected a road-killed turtle, then was horrified when I began dissecting wild mice. "Those things are full of disease!" she snapped. "Get rid of them!" I told her I was using plenty of alcohol to soak the mice before dissecting them, and that they were perfectly safe. My mother said she would make sure: she was going to contact a family friend who was a genius, Dr. James Reyniers.He was famous for raising germ-free chickens and guinea pigs at Notre Dame. "He would know all about germs on rats," she said. "He came to Grandma's wedding," she went on. "You were little, you probably don't remember." My mother soon forgot about contacting Dr. Reyniers, but I did not. When Mrs. DePew, my new art teacher, assigned our class to paint a landscape, I packed an easel and some oil paints and sallied forth. I chose a site near Ware's Creek Bridge and began painting. Before long, a woman came walking by, who stopped to look at my work. "Who taught you to paint?" she asked. I told her that my "Uncle Tubby" (Harold Vary), was a professional artist. Trained in Chicago, and one of only a few professional artists in upper

---

[8]"The Evolution of the Water Conditioning Control Valve," was written by a relative of Dad's Michigan friend:http://wcponline.com/2020/03/15/the-evolution-of-the-water-conditioning-control-valve/"Into the mid-1950's, water conditioners "still retained the simplified manual controls... by the mid-1950s, the electromechanical control valve was introduced to the industry... "The Mafia individual involved in the deal was Nicholas Scaglione of the Trafficante Crime Family, Tampa. He attended my father's funeral in Bradenton, FL in 1977.

Indiana, he was an overworked man, in demand by dozens of RV trailer companies in and around Elkhart. The ad seen here is typical of his work. "Uncle Tubby" – known for taking daily baths-- created and designed ads, catalogs, billboards, and the interiors of RV's. He did almost all the ads, art and interior design work for the famous Gulfstream Cavalier.

When Mrs. DePew, my new art teacher, assigned our class to paint a landscape, I packed an easel and some oil paints and sallied forth. I chose a site near Ware's Creek Bridge and began painting. Before long, a woman came walking by, who stopped to look at my work. "Who taught you to paint?" she asked. I told her that my "Uncle Tubby" (Harold Vary), was a professional artist. Trained in Chicago, and one of only a few professional artists in upper Indiana, he was an overworked man, in demand by dozens of RV trailer companies in and around Elkhart. The ad seen here is typical of his work. "Uncle Tubby" – known for taking daily bahs-- created and designed ads, catalogs, billboards, and the interiors of RV's. He did almost all the ads, art and interior design work for the famous Gulfstream Cavalier. It was built in Nappanee, Indiana. At its debut, huge billboards appeared across the nation showing a French Cavalier my uncle painted, in full regalia.[9] Despite his weariness from a heavy workload, my kind Uncle, recognizing my talent, gave me art lessons every summer. As this dignified lady and I continued to talk, I learned her name was **Georgianna Watkins** (my sketch), the Director of the area chapter of the American Cancer Society. She not only knew Mrs. DePew, my art teacher, but the two women held poster contests at Walker Jr. High to make kids aware of the warning signs of cancer.

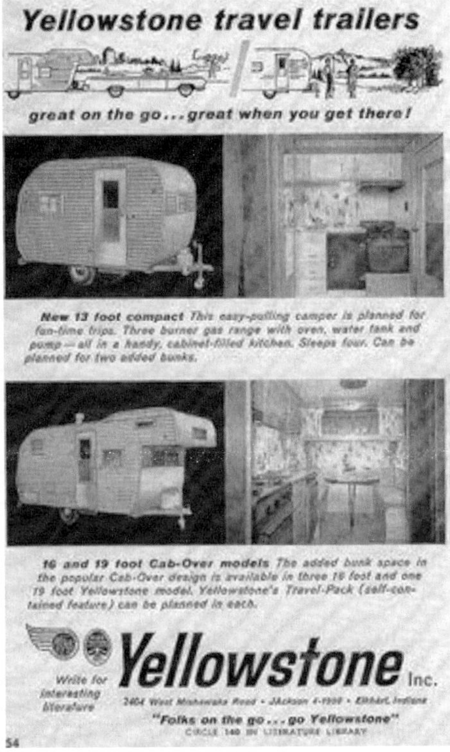

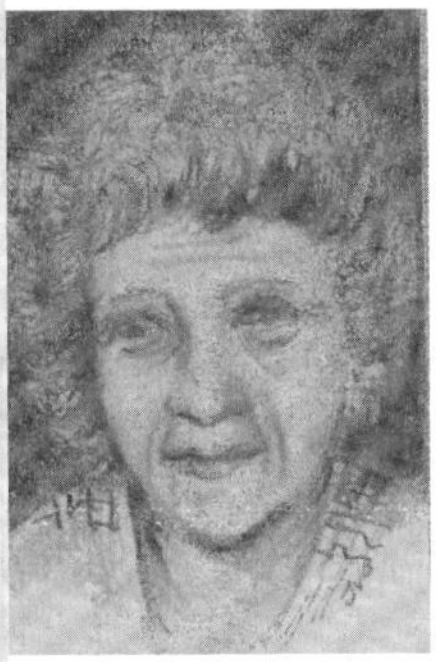

[9] "National press clippings show Elkhart as the 'Trailer Capital of the World'...100 companies were building trailers in and around Elkhart County." The Yellowstone ad shows that Yellowstone, Inc. was headquartered in Elkhart. REF: insideindianabusiness.com/story/32117836/thursday-how-elkhart-became-the-rv-capital-of-the-world.

I told Mrs. Watkins how I wished my family had known the warning signs. It might have saved my grandma's life. In no time we became fast friends. resembled my Grandma Vary. Not only did I end up designing posters for the local American Cancer Society, but I practically moved into her home. Mrs. Watkins lived only blocks from Le Chalet, in a house dedicated to fighting cancer. There were rows and stacks of books about cancer, rare diseases and nursing, plus piles of donated bandages and medical supplies that she was constantly sorting and delivering to patients with cancer. A widow who lived alone, she provided opportunities for me to meet doctors, technicians and cancer patients. Was this a mere coincidence? To me, it was the Hand of God. At home, my pal and constant companion was my sister Lynda. Our parents had sometimes sent us to "Camp Woodland," a Catholic summer boarding camp in Comstock, Michigan. But now we were older, and were allowed to do as we pleased. They gave us fancy English bikes and plenty of money to spend whole days at
skating rinks, gyms, and swimming pools. Soon, Lynda and I, who had trained at the Lake Maggiore Youth Center in gymnastics, were invited to further train at the Sarasota Summer Circus, held every summer for young athletes (Sarasota was the winter home of Ringling Bros. Circus). There we trained on trapeze, low wire, high wire and trampoline. By summer's end, Lynda and I had an impressive little acrobatic act. Our goal was to help area charities such as Sarasota's Happiness House. The handicapped kids there enjoyed our live performances.

Mischievous, spirited, and a gifted athlete, Lynda enjoyed the hard work and discipline it took to present a good show. To combat the pain caused by the stress on our bodies, as we had entered gymnastics later than most kids, we tried some hypnosis techniques. I'd learned them from one of Mrs. Watkins' medical contacts. He explained that hypnosis helped cancer patients who had intractable pain. To demonstrate its efficacy, he tried to hypnotize me, but try as he might, he couldn't do it.

Because he tried so many ways to put me under, I remembered some of them. When I asked Lynda if I could hypnotize her, to my amazement, my sister could be hypnotized in moments! That turned out to be handy for our act, as it helped Lynda to take the pain that came from such a late start in gymnastics. In a matter of weeks, Lynda accomplished feats that should have taken months to master. I was proud of her. The grumpy look on my face in the photo of us with our mother, taken right after a performance, suggests how my body felt!

Lynda also won trophies in baton twirling and became a majorette – a bubbly portrait of wholesome normalcy.

Meanwhile, I was being seduced by science's new frontiers. Even though I had lots of friends, and enjoyed football games, sock hops, joyrides to the beaches and pajama parties with my girlfriends, another side of me hungered to learn. The hunger grew, not to be denied.

The world's great thinkers, scientists, authors, and poets were waiting for me, with Russian art, culture, music and literature at the top of the list. That's when my parents started calling me 'Juduffski.' Meanwhile, thanks to Mrs. Watkins, I had extra lab privileges after school. I even won a first-place science fair award in biology for a study of gibberellin, a powerful plant growth hormone. My question was, 'Would gibberellin help or harm live cells taken from my mouth?' Even today, little research exists about the toxicity of gibberellin and my clumsy project did nothing to help. I still had lots to learn.

Now 15 years old, in the 9th grade, I was given another IQ test. I was also tested on reading skills and clocked at 1,600 words/minute with highest comprehension and 3,400 words/minute as my limit.[10] It came in handy. Bored in school, and yearning to learn at my own pace, I was allowed to read the high school's *Encyclopedia Britannica* on a daily basis. By the 10th grade I had completed all 24 volumes of the 1956 edition.[11] I also became fascinated by what I found in "The New Age Bookstore," where I was allowed to read both *Urantia* and *The Last Temptation of Christ,* a book banned by the Catholic Church. Then, on October 4, 1957, at 7:28 PM, almost a year after Nanitsa died, the world became a more dangerous place: Sputnik was launched. Suddenly, the Russians were ahead of America in the Space Race. Our government reacted by seeking to identify and train the nation's brightest.

---

[10] This was reported in a 1960 *Sarasota Herald-Tribune* article written about me.

[11] I skipped entries about "the Catholic church" which I thought I already knew.

All too soon, though I didn't know it yet, my life and future would be in the hands of others. But right now, in 1957, I still enjoyed the life of a basically normal young teen, and Bradenton was still a small, peaceful southern city. Bradenton boasted a shopping center, a courthouse, a fine library, and a thriving downtown section full of busy stores. Sometimes my friends and I would go shopping there after school. One time, after we were let out early from a football rally, we went downtown, first stopping at Walgreens for root-beer floats. Next, we went to Woolworth's, the classic five-and-dime where we knew we could buy the latest **Tangee** lipstick color. We also wanted the newest Elvis record. Then, I spotted some small, black tropical fish for sale. They were mollies, and viviparous (they bore their young alive). I was in luck: one of the mollies was pregnant. My parent had a big tank full of angelfish and other exotica, but they had nothing like mollies.

Mollies are special because they give birth to clones of themselves. That is, all molly DNA comes from just the mother. There is no father-- the males that are born merely stimulate females to produce young, but their sperm is never part of the deal. With every mollie identical to their mother, they are purebreds, perfect for cancer experiments. So I put back the Elvis record I'd bought and got Miss Molly, some of her friends, and a cooperative male instead. After a few days, when it was time to give birth, Mollie's babies started popping out one by one. But instead of some fifty babies, only twenty or so were born, though Miss Molly still had a big lump. What was the matter with her? Our vet, who took care of Mother's poodles, had an opinion: it could be a melanoma tumor. He said mollies often got melanoma, the same kind of cancer humans could get. *What*? Humans and fish could get the *same* kind of cancer? This was worth looking into.

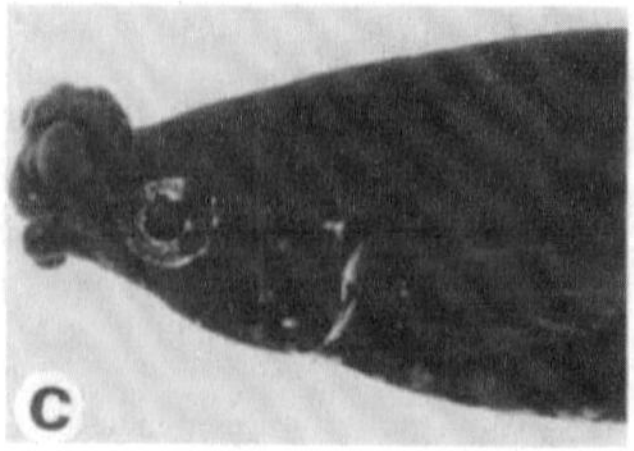

A black mollie suffering from an oral cancer.

"She'll never survive another pregnancy," he predicted. Sure enough, as her time to give birth again drew near, little Miss Molly struggled to swim, gasping for breath. It was clear that she was dying. As she sank to the bottom of the tank, all I could think of were the tiny babies she carried within her heaving body. Every one of them would surely die! Taking a razor, and with tears blurring my vision, I quickly cut off her head, then slit her open.

Quickly washing her living babies into a watch-glass full of warm water, six of the eight babies survived. It was my first 'operation' on an animal sacrificed for a good cause, but it would not be the last.

It did not take long to dissect out the tumor that killed her. I preserved the tumor in 70% isopropyl alcohol, much to the dismay of my mother. "She was a pet. She should have been buried!" she told me. My mother was right about one thing: did I respect my pet enough to give her the dignity of a burial? I removed Miss Molly from her alcohol bath and buried her in the back yard. But I kept the tumor. Raw curiosity, and a new microscope – a gift from my parents – made me cross the Rubicon. I had to find out what normal tissues looked like in a molly. With resolve, I scooped up one of my trusting, healthy mollies who had come eagerly to the tank's surface to be petted and fed, and cut off her head.

Exposing her internal organs and tissues, I compared them to sections of the tumorous mass saved from Miss Molly, using the microscope. It was my first 'cancer experiment.' A few weeks later, I noticed an alarming development. Every molly related to Miss Molly had tumors. I considered the fact that every molly lived long enough to give birth before the tumors got big enough to kill. If it was a virus, it had adapted to grow slowly enough not to run out of hosts, developing only after a new generation was born.

Then I thought of all the old people who were dying of cancer, compared to other age groups. It was my first foray into theorizing a cause of cancer. What if some cancers might be carried around in our bodies for years, which could become active after our reproductive ability ended? Did a balancing act exist between deadly cancers and their hosts, to keep them both going? For the first time, I became frightened. So little was known about cancer! What if my mother and sister and I carried cancer as a virus from Grandma, hidden inside? A time bomb that would explode when we got old? What if handling these tumors with my bare hands could pass on what was killing the mollies to me and my family? But maybe it wasn't cancer. I had just read about an enormous, benign tumor removed from a woman before it killed her. What if the mollies' tumors were benign, simply taking too much energy from the fish? It was time to talk to Mrs. Watkins.

Since moving from Le Chalet to a small house, (our big new home was being built on Snead Island) it was harder to visit and show her the mollies. But this was important! Intrigued at what she saw, Mrs. Watkins encouraged me to record everything in a journal. So I recorded diet, date of birth, weight at time of death, length, and the weights and colors of the tumors. I must use rubber gloves, she said, and remember not to touch my face. Now a 9th grader, with boys on my mind instead of cancerous fish, my science fair project about fish tumors only won third prize in the biology division. For good reason: I had failed to get a professional to confirm that these pitiful fish actually had cancer. I was ashamed. I had been distracted by handsome Albert Waite Freeman, who had built me a telescope so we could view Mars together in the moonlight.

That wasn't all. I'd also been studying osculation [kissing!] in the same moonlight. There had been a few other interesting science experiments going on with Al, but realizing I was not ready for that kind of research, I turned to Mrs. Watkins. Could I be a volunteer with her again? Assist her when she visited hospitals and homes?

So that summer, when an invitation to attend the dedication of Watson Clinic, a new critical care hub, came into Mrs. Watkins' hands, she naturally asked me to come with her. "Dr. Alton Ochsner will be there, to lay the cornerstone of the new clinic," she told me. "I want you to meet him."

She instructed me to prepare a means to transport my mollies. With luck, Ochsner, the great cancer researcher, might be persuaded to take a look at them. One fine morning, we transferred some of the most advanced cases to a Heinz pickle jar and set off for Lakeland. Florida. A website tells us, "Dr. Watson had retired four years earlier, but he was nevertheless front and center during the dedication ceremony of the Main Clinic location in 1958" attended by "distinguished residents and business leaders in the area." The guest of honor was **Dr. Alton Ochsner**, "Founder of the renowned Ochsner Clinic in New Orleans." He "was there to lay the cornerstone of the building." Mrs. Watkins, whose

name sounded like "Watson," made use of it to meet, greet, and introduce the "young scientist" who was carrying a big pickle jar full of small black fish. Curious about the fish, people began to ask Dr. Ochsner to look at them. One of Georgianna's contacts introduced her as an American Cancer Society local official. Dr. Ochsner was not only the founder of Ochsner Clinic in New Orleans; he was also a former President of the American Cancer Society. After greeting Mrs. Watkins, Ochsner turned his attention to the inhabitants of my pickle jar. I pointed out the tumors swelling up every molly's belly, explained that they were all related and asked, Did they have cancer? Ochsner looked closely at the fish, asked a few questions about their diet and environment, and then gave his opinion. "Miss Vary," he said, "you need to move up from fishes to mammals for your next investigation." He gave me a wink. "A first-class experiment," he went on, "would be to try to pass your fishes' cancer on to mice." Then, with the warmth and sparkle of the charismatic professional that he was, Dr. Ochsner turned to the many others surrounding him who sought his attention. My epiphany came when Dr. Ochsner delivered his keynote speech about smoking and lung cancer. The man could have had horns growing out of his head and I would not have cared; Ochsner was fantastic. His ground-breaking observations on smoking and cancer were stunning.[12] Yes, people were dying from lung cancer, but almost always because they smoked. What had once been a very rare disease was becoming a global epidemic. I still remember Dr. Alton Ochsner's closing statement: "My friends and I who have seen the light are doing our best to prove that smoking tobacco kills people." Then Ochsner declared, with a booming voice, "In our hospital, we have banned smoking. We hope that every clinic and hospital in the nation will soon do the same." As I listened, my thoughts began racing. What if mice could get cancer from smoking, too? Both humans and mice are mammals, and I knew that mice had some of the same kinds of problems fighting cancer that people had. If I could give mice lung cancer, I'd be able to use them for experiments on ways to fight lung cancer, and that could lead to a cure for humans. Dr. Ochsner didn't know it, but he had given me a clear road to follow. I believed the time would come when we would meet again.

Chapter Two
Whiz Kid

In October, 1957, Russia shocked the world by launching a 184 pound ball of polished steel into space. [13] Senator Lyndon Johnson summed up our fears in one sentence: "The Communists could drop atom bombs on our heads if they wanted to." The CIA had given us no warning. Our reply to the USSR was weak. Our 'Explorer' weighed 30.8 pounds.[14] It did not go into orbit until 1958. The CIA, the Office of Naval Intelligence and other agencies had not informed us of these spectacular advances.

---

[12]Two items are restored in this edition: note: (1) I easily hynotized Lynda. She could not hypnotize me. (2) The name "Watson" identifying the Clinic wasn't named in *Me & Lee*. Plus(correction) the clinic had not yet been built.

[13] The media reported Sputnik's weight as 30.66 pounds. Its true weight was 30.8 pounds:*"Sputnik and the Dawn of the Space Age". NASA History.* NASA. (2008-02-13).

[14] REF: https://www.history.com/this-day-in-history/sputnik-launched

They needed to work harder to improve the spy system that had failed them. A year later, on October 17, 1959, another extraordinary event occurred. A 19-year-old Marine named Lee Harvey Oswald 'defected' to the Soviet Union. What kind of teenager would choose to live in Communist Russia, a land of oppression, over life in America, where we enjoyed so many freedoms? He would be called a traitor. But was he? I was just a few years younger than Lee Oswald, still leading an almost normal life. But that was about to change. Sputnik also had an impact on my father. He was ashamed that he had turned down a chance to serve his country against the Soviet threat. When two of the next four Explorers failed to reach orbit, Dad felt as if those failures were his own. His troubles began when a tragic motorcycle accident mangled his leg. He was only 16. It stopped him from joining the Navy. Now Dad, his dreams shattered when my mother refused to move to Sandia's compound,, was spending a lot of time drinking. That's when a real-life hero became my 'father figure.' His name was 'Canute Michaelson.'

17, 1958 Page Th

Norwegian Scientist Visits MHS Classes

Dr. Canute Michaelson, research scientist and professor genetics (science of heredity) at Oslo University, Oslo, Norw visited various MHS classes last week. Dr. Michaelson is in No America for the annual Congress of Genetics and the Congress of Radiation. While in the U.S. he will visit several universities to study American methods of teaching and to collect material for a book.

Dr. Michaelson, who recently returned from a trip to Russia, was active in the underground during World War II, was captured by the Nazis and condemned to death, but managed to escape at the last possible moment. Among other things, he has taught the children of the King of Norway.

Speaking in Mrs. Dudley Key's college preparatory English class, he stressed Darwin's theory and the theory of mutation. In answering student questions, he stated that according to genetics and biology, there is a racial difference. He said, however, that there is no known intelligence differences in the races, but mainly a cultural difference. He explained briefly about the background of the races.

Western scientists, he said, believe that mutations are accidential, while Russian scientists say that they are not. In this way, he explained, the Russians have invented a biological excuse for Communism in that if all people lived in a Communistic environment, all would change or mutate to the Communist way of life.

While stating his theories on mutation caused by radiation, which is his special field, he said that ninety percent of the mutation caused by radiation is nonbeneficial to life. The lethal mutation causes death of the individual. That is the reason that geneticists are fighting for a ban on nuclear tests.

Educational T To Start Here On Channel 3

Educational television is sch uled to start October 27 at Ma tee High on channel 3.

Television sets will be availa to Mrs. Paul Parrish, Mrs. Le McLaughlin, and Miss Elizab Sloan's sixth period English cla es.

To Set Up Control Classes

Control classes will be set up test the effectiveness of this p gram. These classes will taught in much the same way l without the use of television se

Manatee County is one of sev counties participating in this p gram. The other counties are H dy, Polk, Pinellas, Sarasota, Hil borough, and Pasco.

All programs telecast by t station will fall into one of fo categories: pre-school progran in-school programs, adult edu tion, and civic and public servi programming.

Teacher Is Still Important

The teacher of the classro which is participating in any te vision lesson is the most importa factor for success. Educational is not designed to replace t classroom teacher.

School superintendents, leade of business and civic affairs, a the heads of the colleges in o area, through their own tim founded the board of directors the Florida West Coast Educatio

Mrs. Key had invited him to speak to her Advanced English class. It was an odd place to find a top scientist, just arrived in the U.S. He said he was on his way to New York, where he would soon attend conferences in radiation and genetics. So why did he come to an English class? It seems there may have been a reason that was kept a bit quiet, for he quickly centered his attention on three students: me, David Tracy and Dave Deitrich. At least, that's what he told me. We were the school's science stars. We met the first time when my science teachers brought Michaelson from a classroom to meet me. On October 10, 1958, my biology teacher, Mrs. Grace McCarty and Col. Doyle, my physics teacher, asked me to meet 'Dr. Canute Michaelson,' a brilliant scientist from Norway. It was probably not his real name: I can find no such name in the records. Once a spy for the OSS in WWII, he had posed as a Nazi, but paid a high price, as his own people then saw him as a traitor. That meeting would change my life.

It was lunch time, so they found me easily, for at lunchtime I was always in the library, either playing chess with friends or reading the encyclopedia. Dr. Michaelson at once made me feel comfortable. He was not just a stuffy scientist. He told me that he had been a real spy, pretending to be a Nazi while secretly opposing Hitler.

His fellow Norwegians had condemned him as a despicable man who had turned against his own country, but the Nazi's, learning the truth, eventually captured and tortured him. By clever means, he managed to escape. Now a hero, and a Professor of Genetics at Oslo University, he said he had even given science lessons to the children of the King and Queen of Norway. What was awesome is that he wanted to talk to me. But why? After spending some time questioning me and reviewing my cancer research project, Dr. Michaelson dropped a bombshell.

He said I had scored the highest IQ in the state of Florida (160). That was a shock. He said "everyone" would make sure I would get whatever I needed for any science projects I was working on.[15] I met with this geneticist and radiation expert twice more before he and his name vanished from all the records. What I do know is that suddenly our school had money—enough to start construction of a brand-new Science Building. Col. Doyle also created the Science Research Seminar, the brain-child of school geniuses David Tracy and Dave Deitrich. They were also the most handsome guys in school. That was fine with us girls -- Helen Neel, Anne Estrup, and me, who had those cute guys (and about sixteen more) to ourselves! I especially loved being around Bob Pope, Tony Lopez-Fresquet, Larry Jerome, Buce Korth, Charles Throckmorton, and Albert Freeman. We had to choose a personal research project.

[15] I had only Michaelson's statement until The Mackle Brothers tested students and adults in Melbourne, Florida in 1960, at which time I again scored 160. The link to the Mackle Brothers and the government was their huge land development project at Cape Canaveral. Their 1960 Annual Report describes it as a 5,400 acre "planned community" for the "nearby Air Force Missile Test Center" that employed "47,500 persons."

We were also given access to specialists and professors from New College and elsewhere. I took four mind-blowing semesters. In 1959, due to Michaelson's comments that I should have a private workspace, a small, personal lab area was created for me in the new Science Building's chemical storage room. This private space, plus the Science Seminars, gave me the time and means to develop two research projects that would receive national attention. I had previously moved my cage of brown mice (to my mother's relief!) to school, but let them all go when a shipment of 50 white mice arrived from The Rockefeller Foundation. Even so, mice don't last long in cancer research, and I was always begging for more, against opposition from some of the teachers.They were worried about cancer as a danger to the school. To quell their fears, ultraviolet lights were installed in the science building. The purple glow was there every night until I left Manatee High for good. At this time, Milton Sharer, my chemistry teacher and a former industrial chemist, hoped I would choose a career in chemical engineering. He lent me a book --*The Story of Magnesium*. It was fascinating. Magnesium was not only "an important metal in alloys used in the manufacture of aircraft, rockets, and space satellites," but "1,272 pounds of magnesium were hidden, ready to extract, in a cubic mile of sea water."

Excited, I asked Mr. Sharer, "Do we have the equipment for a project like this?" [16]

"I just don't know if it's possible to get the pure metal itself," he answered.

"This is just a high school," he went on. "You'd need a refinery if you got that far." Recalling my Nanista's saying, 'Where there's a will, there's a way,' I persuaded Mr. Sharer to drive me to the beach. There we collected five gallons of seawater into clean plastic jugs. Long hours in the chemistry lab, and in books, came next. Finally, I was ready to start some experiments. First, a local welder constructed two tabletop furnaces (in case one would leak or blow up, there was a backup). He made them from scraps found in a junkyard. They had to withstand high temperatures. They had to be air-tight. A small leak of air inside could cause an explosion. If it was easy to build the smelting furnaces, it was much harder to get the argon gas needed to blanket the melting magnesium inside, as it cooked: no oxygen could enter the furnace, or bye-bye Judy and half a dozen windows. It was an anxious time. What if somebody got hurt? Also, the German process I chose required

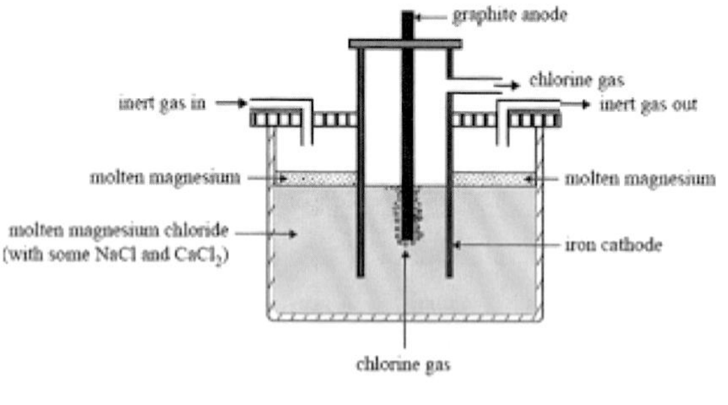

[16]https://www.britannica.com/technology/magnesium-processing/The-metal-and-its-alloys

platinum. – an expensive catalyst-- but very efficient. Then I had an idea: could I find a substitute for the platinum? And if I did, would the catalyst work as well?

But there were a lot of German chemists and engineers in Germany. What if they already had a substitute for platinum? Mr. Sharer guessed not, because there was no magnesium plant operational in Germany. By February, 1960, I had a solution on paper, but had to prove it. First, I created a flux to cover the magnesium extract and keep explosive gases from reaching it so it could be safely smelted.[17] The inert gas to blanket the flux and the molten magnesium chloride under it, was to be handled with absolutely reliable valves and pumps, to pressurize the argon gas, even at extremely high temperatures (a minimum of 1,202°F). My father, anxious that I would not end up in a hospital, showed me how to assemble the system, which he tested. Next, instead of platinum-coated cathodes, I tried out special coatings, and after lots of trials and errors, found one to cover the carbon rod cathodes. I do not own the right to disclose this formula, which Dow Chemical appropriated, but when Mg was drawn to the cathodes by eletricity, it didn't stick, saving the cathodes from corrosion. The next problem was handling boron and other impurities that could ruin the diodes. After some time, that problem was solved, too.

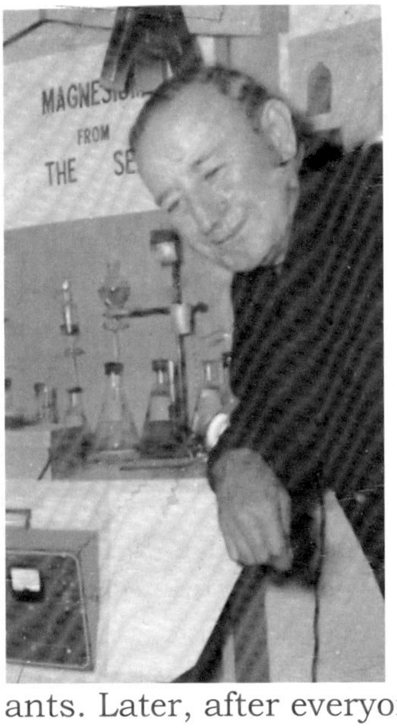

I was truly lucky that nobody got hurt. While the project was potentially dangerous my small improvement to a German process nobody used in America was at best a minor discovery. When "Magnesium from the Sea" won top honors at Manatee High's Science Fair, I was surprised. When it won Best Physical Science Entry and Best of Show at the Manatee County Science Fair, I was thrilled! So was my grandfather. You can see the rosette over my proud grandpa's head in the photo.

Next was the State Science Fair. On April 7, 1960, Col. Doyle drove Mrs. McCarty, Dave Dietrich, Bob Pope, Larry Jerome and me to Melbourne for the 2-day event. At a souvenir shop next to our motel, flush with a generous allowance, I bought a box of chocolate-covered ants. Later, after everyone enjoyed a crunchy piece, I revealed the contents! The motel was upscale, with a luxurious swimming pool.Doyle had worked hard to raise the funds needed for us to compete in these fairs, and we lacked nothing. The next morning, Mrs. McCarty, my chaperone (I was only 16) fixed my hair. Then we entered the huge hall, which was crammed with exhibits.

[17] The covering flux was approx. $MgCl_2$: 40%; KCl:40%; CaF_2:8%. $BaCl_2$:8% and aluminum particles, melting at about 700 F.

A crowd of reporters followed the judges around. What surprised me was the interest my project raised. There were many interviews. Was there a chance to win a ribbon? “They are amazed that you got actual magnesium metal!” McCarty told me. The pure metal itself was not on display because it had been classified as an explosive, so I’d converted a second batch into magnesium oxide, which was perfectly safe. It sat in a test tube on a rotating display with red and blue floodlights and all the lab equipment used (except the furnaces, which were too heavy to transport with all the other projects in Doyle’s car).

The weight of recovered Mg was precisely what was calculated to be found in exactly one gallon of seawater. We sat up in the balcony of a big hall, looking down at the stage, when the award ceremony began. As prize after prize was announced, and recipients came forward, my heart sank. First prizes, second prizes, third prizes, fourth prizes... The boys with me all won ribbons, but there was nothing for me. Then, when the ceremony was almost over, I heard my name, and was asked to come to the stage below.

“Judy, I think you’ve won it all!” Col. Doyle said softly. In shock, Doyle and I made our way downstairs, past cheering rows of students, teachers, parents and reporters, with camera flashes blinding our vision. I’d won the State Championship in the Physical Sciences and would represent The Florida Foundation for Future Scientists at the International Science Fair in Indianapolis. But the big news was that Indiana was my home state!

A huge ache in my heart, caused by life in Florida far from everyone I had loved and known all my life, turned into a surge of joy. I had won a chance see my grandparents, aunts, uncles and cousins again! This is why I cried when the big purple rosette for the Most Outstanding Exhibit was placed in my shaking hands. Pleased as I was with all the cash prizes and awards, there were two sour notes: the Navy refused to give me their much-advertised 5-day cruise on an aircraft carrier. Why? Because I was female! All previous winners in the Physical Sciences had been males. Instead, they gave me a (useless) *World Book Encyclopedia.*

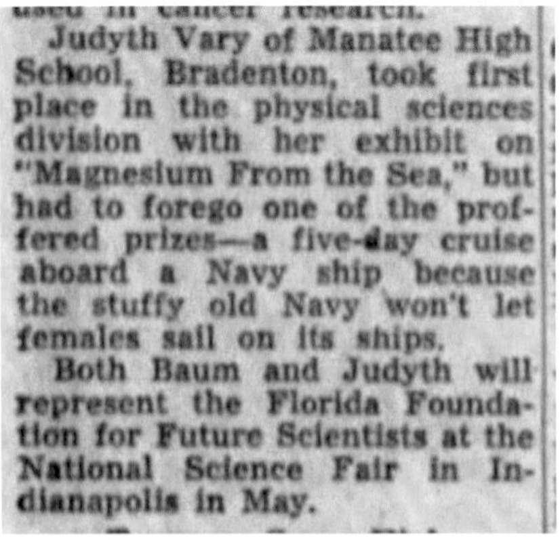
used in cancer research.
Judyth Vary of Manatee High School, Bradenton, took first place in the physical sciences division with her exhibit on "Magnesium From the Sea," but had to forego one of the proffered prizes—a five-day cruise aboard a Navy ship because the stuffy old Navy won't let females sail on its ships.
Both Baum and Judyth will represent the Florida Foundation for Future Scientists at the National Science Fair in Indianapolis in May.

The 1960 International Science Fair made a NASA engineer out of Homer Hickam, a coal miner’s son, who trained the first Japanese astronauts. His best-selling 1998 memoir, *Rocket Boys,* became the 1999 film *October Sky*. We would both meet Wherner Von Braun in Indianapolis. As a female, it was harder to have my work recognized. I was the first girl to win top honors in the Florida State Science Fair’s Physical Science Division.

Then Dow Chemical, who actually mined magnesium from the sea, had me step behind the curtains on the stage with my Grandpa Whiting, who had come up to Melbourne to surprise me. That's when I learned that big corporations sent scouts to big science fairs, and they would steal ideas.

I could accept a $200 "finder's fee" or try for a patent. We were told how much a patent search would cost, and that any patent we managed to get could be altered slightly by Dow or anybody else, making our patent worthless. My small discovery was worth something only to Dow Chemical. We reluctantly signed the release (my parents did not attend). By the time we got home, the story of my big win had hit the newspapers, which led to a series of talks to various civic groups to keep funding the Science Seminar. Of course, I mentioned my need for more mice, cages and equipment!

With the Magnesium from the Sea exhibit ready to go to national competition, I had time to return fulltime to my cancer project. With all the publicity, another carton full of pedigree mice arrived from an anonymous donor.[18] Sadly, these mice became the victims of a common but cruel "cancer research" experiment. Dyes were used to identify each group: if any got loose, we'd know which cage they belonged to. I then followed the traditional steps to induce cancer, dousing the mice in oily, caustic carcinogens extracted from cigarette butts, which they helplessly tried to lick off their little bodies. That created mouth sores, trembling, and diarrhea. Then they were barraged with x-rays to produce cancer.

It worked. But for what? My grandma had not died from skin cancer, nor did any of these mice develop an internal cancer. Injecting them with even small doses of nicotine-based materials killed them. Dr. Ochsner himself had stated that smoking caused lung cancer. But how do you get mice to smoke? I was ashamed. I had wasted the lives of innocent animals.

The cancers were only topical. Oncologists from Manatee Memorial checked it out. Soon afterward, I received 100 Webster-Swiss pedigree mice from Palmetto Savings and Loan, thanks to bank president Fred Langford. This time, I didn't have to beg for replacements when the mice died. In a lucky accident, one of the mice shipped to me was a male! (He had been one happy fellow, with all those girls!) Only female mice are used in the majority of experiments. News articles would say I had "99 mice," but there were always a couple of nests of baby mice, kept in my large, former aquarium, thanks to my little Romeo. Meanwhile, another class would create another link to the military, through the famous writer MacKinlay Kantor – author of the Pulitzer Prize-winning historical novel *Andersonville.*

Versatile Suncoast

How can one become a writer? "Write!" If you must keep asking "how" you shouldn't be writing.

[18] The "donor" later identified themselves once more as The Rockefeller Foundation.

He came to lecture our English Club. He read to us from his small book, *The Voice of Bugle Ann*. Then, after the class ended, Miss Dalrymple, our teacher, introduced me and gave him some of my writings. Maybe it was because I had been carrying love notes between Miss Dalrymple and my civics teacher, Mr. Schork, for some time, and they had grown fond of me. Kantor and I chatted a bit, and that was that, until he called my parents about a week later. Would it be okay, he asked, if he could give me some writing lessons? He had read some of my short stories and liked them.

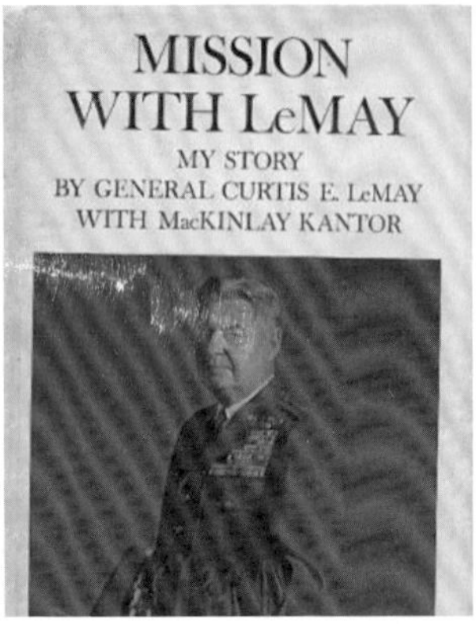

The caption in the MHS 1960-1961 yearbook says: "How can one become a writer? If you must keep asking 'how' you shouldn't be writing." **So says MacKinlay Kantor, Pulitzer prize-winning author who addressed the Lanier English Club." Kantor would be hard on me, but he must have liked what I wrote, because he took the time to mentor me.**

Miss Dalrymple sometimes drove me to Kantor's lovely Sarasota beachside home on Saturdays. She also gave me rides to school on Saturdays so I could feed and water my mice, on days my father couldn't. I didn't enjoy the lessons Kantor gave me. He'd sit me down and proceed to severely criticize my writing. It was devastating. After I rewrote what he wanted, he became kinder, inviting me to carry his tape recorder as he walked along the beach. "Listen how I do it!" he demanded. "Read the words you write out loud," he commanded, "so you'll hear what's wrong with them." I thus heard Kantor dictate notes for the biography of General Curtis LeMay, a famous man I decided I did not like. Kantor said progress was slow with LeMay's book. "His book is taking forever to write," he complained. "You think I am hard on you? LeMay is even harder on me." Kantor did praise one thing I'd written, a poem about the American flag called "First Lady," which he told me he sent to General LeMay.[19]

Though busy with writing, art, and other classes, I was still stubbornly trying to give mice cancer. You can't cure cancer without some cancer. About this time, a prankster flipped open my big cage of control mice, not used in experiments). Unafraid of people, they soon invaded the biology lecture room, where they began climbing up pantlegs and jumping into purses, as laughter, shrieks and screams filled the room. These were perfectly healthy white controls. Their rumps weren't dyed pink, blue or yellow, as were the mice suffering from skin cancer or keratotic lesions, but horrified parents and School Board officials demanded a more secure location at once. They found one: under the high school stadium! Cement flooring was quickly poured inside half of a dirt-floor room available there.

[19]LeMay's 1965 autobiography was co-written with MacKinlay Kantor,.

Steel mouse cages and a big library display case with screened sides (to hold the healthy control mice) were installed on the side that had the dirt floor. Plenty of sawdust was brought in from Manatee High's woodshop. A strong door opened to the second half of the room, with its cement floor. It was equipped with a vent, fans, ultraviolet lights and running water. This made everyone feel safer about cancerous mice at school. My work was now being supervised by four radiologists and doctors. Two of them – Drs. Shively and Roggenkamp--are not only specifically named in news stories about my work in 1960 and 1961, but both had been recently trained in preclinical studies (tissue cultures) at Oak Ridge, under the watchful eye of the CIA.[20] Things went well until I was accidentally exposed to too much radiation while x-raying mice at Manatee Memorial Hospital,'[21] in their bare-bones oncology center, with a powerful new x-ray machine that was improperly calibrated. Things had previously proceeded safely at the Professional Building, where Dr. Roggenkamp had administered supposedly ¼ lethal x-rays. They had been calculated properly, but the doses were underweighted. The x-rays were weaker than what the dials read. The machine needed to be re-calibrated. Thus, all we got were precancerous keratoses. That's why I switched to the new, powerful machine at the hospital, with disastrous results. All the exposed mice died, and I fell ill. I was probably glowing in the dark. The calibration for the new machine wasn't right, either. It was delivering more powerful doses than the dials read. After that disaster, I stayed as far from the machines as possible. I taped each mouse down onto the cars of a toy train that could roll each individual mouse under the machine without exposing myself to as many x-rays. Radiation was a killer, but if used wisely, it cured some cancers. It had cured my Auntie Elsie of uterine cancer, but at a cost. Her radiation wounds refused to heal and continued to discharge blood and fluids for the rest of her life. [22] Questions swarmed in my head. What if an anabolic steroid, for example, injected under a cancerous breast tumor, such as my grandma had developed, could save a breast?

S' — Admiring Judy Vary's science pr

[20] Documents on special training my doctors received are in the Appendix.

[21] Manatee Memorial was actually called Manatee Veterans Memorial Hospital until 1963.

[22] As late as 1994, inaccuracies in X-ray machines tested in Texas were as high as 30%. https://pubmed.ncbi.nlm.nih.gov/8058911/ "X-Ray Machines: a study of failure rates" Radiol Technol May-Jun 1994;65(5):291-5;

Reflecting x-rays back through the cancerous tissues, rather than allowing them to pass all through the body would mean less exposure! I wanted to test the theory, but needed cancers to test it on. I used the tarry extracts of cigarettes, high in nicotine sulphate and other carcinogens, and induced skin cancer in dozens of white mice, but now it was time to induce cancer to mice internally – specifically, lung cancer—using the same carcinogens. The idea was to force mice to breathe toxic fumes strong enough to induce cancer without poisoning them. To test my ideas, we needed more than a few used cigarette filters and stubs: we needed thousands! My sister and our friends helped: we collected ten pounds of cigarette butts from all over town. I already had the "gas chamber" from the magnesium project. After creating the extracts, the same chamber could reliably hold mice. A deadly aerosol would be pumped in, full of distilled tars suspended in smoke. I'd burn end up burning many test tubes of the stuff. The mice would be forced to breathe it, and eventually, lung cancer should develop. The big factor was time. I had to do it as fast as possible, so I would have lots of cancerous lungs to test my theory. At least, that was the plan, if Col. Doyle and his military friends would approve. Fortunately, they did. These military people were interested in my future. Others weren't so supportive.

On April 12, 1960, when a newspaper article gushed that "her own hard work after school hours, even on Saturdays and holidays, had been responsible for her prize-winning project, 'Magnesium from the Sea'," I was ordered to hand over the keys to the building. Why? Because I had no employee insurance!

When my parents refused to get involved because of a water treatment contract, things were tense until Col. Doyle and his military friends agreed to pay for the insurance. Then I got the keys back.

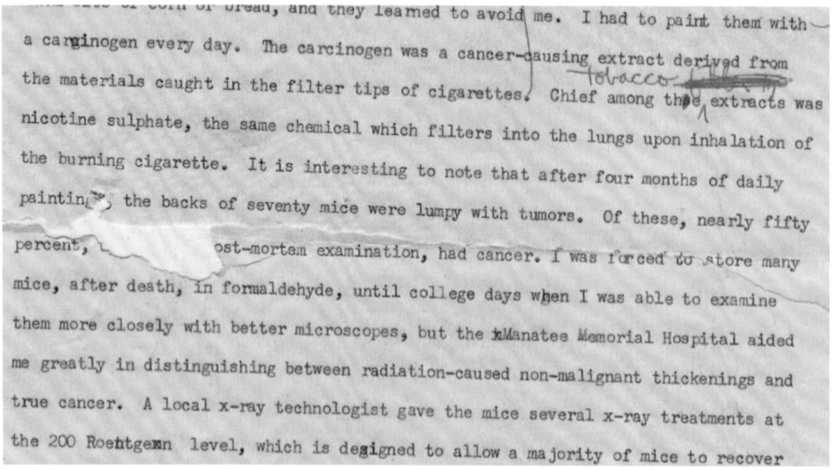
... bread, and they learned to avoid me. I had to paint them with a carginogen every day. The carcinogen was a cancer-causing extract derived from tobacco the materials caught in the filter tips of cigarettes. Chief among these extracts was nicotine sulphate, the same chemical which filters into the lungs upon inhalation of the burning cigarette. It is interesting to note that after four months of daily painting, the backs of seventy mice were lumpy with tumors. Of these, nearly fifty percent, [illegible] post-mortem examination, had cancer. I was forced to store many mice, after death, in formaldehyde, until college days whhen I was able to examine them more closely with better microscopes, but the kManatee Memorial Hospital aided me greatly in distinguishing between radiation-caused non-malignant thickenings and true cancer. A local x-ray technologist gave the mice several x-ray treatments at the 200 Roehtgemn level, which is degigned to allow a majority of mice to recover

Part of my first draft of a report to Science News Service, 1960. In 1958, Congress mandated that the latest science news should be available to all. Vandals damaged many of my documents in 2001 in Dallas. I was given a fine microscope later, but had no time to return to these first batches of preserved mice. Their cancers were common and predictable.

Earlier that year, learning from Mr. Schork, my civics teacher, that I "loved all things Russian," the same military officers --friends of Col. Doyle-- asked if I'd like to take a course in Russian at Manatee Jr. College. They were concerned because the Russians, who were ahead in the Space Race, could also be ahead in cancer research! Since I couldn't attend a class in Russian during the day. Dr. T. Concevitch, a retired Russian professor, was asked to teach a new evening class. Some 25 college students signed up. The class "made," so I quietly began attending, though I was only in 11th grade.[23] Thanks to the Russian classes, I was able to get the gist of science articles about cancer printed in Russian. Better yet, I learned to speak some Russian. My life was getting busy!

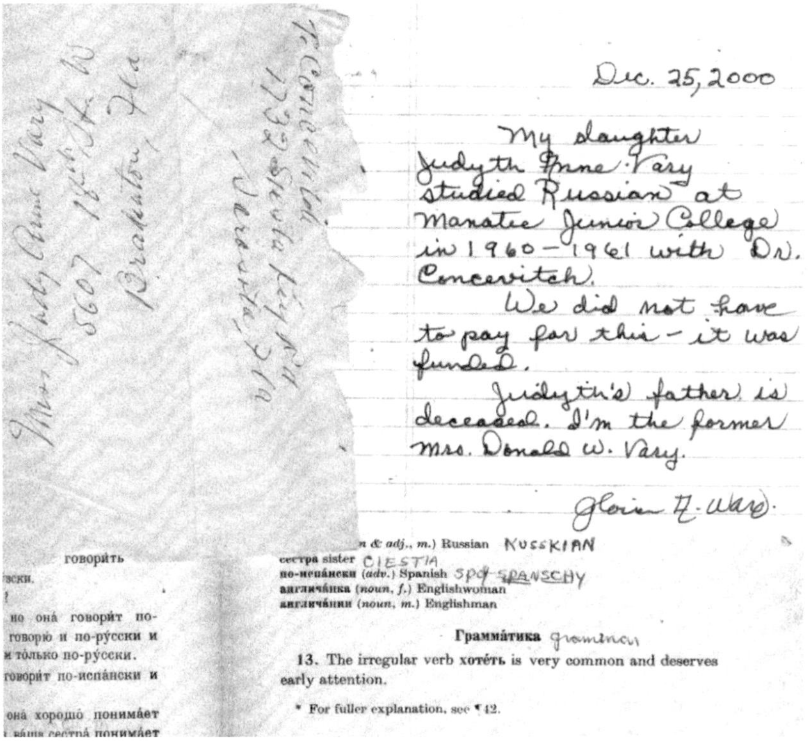
Dec. 25, 2000

My daughter Judyth Anne Vary studied Russian at Manatee Junior College in 1960 – 1961 with Dr. Concevitch.

We did not have to pay for this – it was funded.

Judyth's father is deceased. I'm the former Mrs. Donald W. Vary.

Gloria H. Ward

Envelope from Dr. Concevitch

Note from my mother that the course was "funded"

Portion of my Russian textbook

At this time, letters of congratulations were pouring in, including hand-signed letters from Senator George Smathers and Governor LeRoy Collins. I was sure Robert Baum, the other winner (in biological sciences) got the same letters. So, I thought little of it all until I was called out of P.E. class to the Dean's Office to take a phone call. What was the matter? Was somebody hurt? When I got to the office, smiles were all around as the staff watched me pick up the phone. In a minute, the Senator himself was congratulating me for my Science Fair win.

---

[23] Today "AP" classes are common, but back in 1960, they were almost unheard-of outside special college prep schools. Manatee Jr. College, two years old, had just moved onto its own property. Our Russian class met in one of a half-dozen temporary buildings sitting on cement blocks in an empty lot.

UF was his *alma mater*, he said, and he wanted Florida's top students to go there. He not only offered me a full scholarship, he also said he had set up a local bank account for me to which my friends and supporters could donate. He didn't know my address, so he used my school as the address (see envelope, here, which was saved due to chemistry notes on it!) Smathers, a close friend of President Kennedy, was not only lobbying to get Florida's top students in science and medicine to come to the University of Florida, his alma mater; he was also funding dozens of research projects, including the construction of UF's brand-new hospital. On April 19, my first bank deposit receipt was mailed to me from the First National Bank in Bradenton. [24] Before hanging up, Smathers also said he would call Governor Collins and ask him to look into my helping Florida's magnesium extraction industry. I was excited that day because Dr. Richard Moran, who helped me calculate radiation

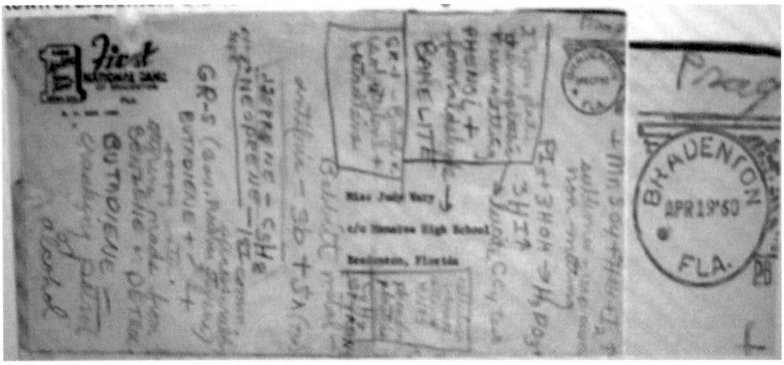

dosage, had called me the night before with fabulous news: Dr. James Reyniers, the Notre Dame bacteriologist who had created germ-free animals, had moved to Tampa.

A furnace similar to one made for my Mg project was modified to provide a sterile chamber for germ-free mice to live in.

When Dr. Moran called Reyniers to welcome him, he learned that Reyniers was breeding germ-free mice. Since such mice had an immune system status of zero, theoretically, they should be able to get lung cancer quickly. When Dr. Moran told him about me, Reyniers, recognizing my unusual last name, asked for our family's phone number. My mother, of course, would want to talk to Reyniers first, about mutual friends. Then I'd have a chance to try to convince him to give me some of his precious germ-free mice. They were arguably the most expensive

[24] **Smathers:** "I was on the board of the Pan-American Banks. I was on the board of the Winn-Dixie Grocery Company. I was on the board of one private high school, and one University of Florida group, and that sort of thing. I was on the board of a commercial bank, and I owned two other banks that I bought after I got out of the Senate, and made a little money, one in Ocala and one in Bradenton, and so on." See George Smathers, oral history interview with Donald Ritchie, October 17, 1989, Senate Historical Office. https://rowman.com/WebDocs/Dark_Quadrant_Appendix.pdf

domesticated rodents in the world. Would Reyniers trust a high school kid with his rare and special mice? I was not yet 17.

The 2nd photo shows a small smelting furnace, similar to what a welder made for me from junkyard scrap metal. I had two of them, built for the magnesium project. Luckily, both had cleaned up nicely.

They would be able to be used as germ-free chambers. I adapted air pumps for aquariums, purchased from a pet store, plus filters donated by Tropicana Laboratories, to set up the "atmosphere." With big hopes of germ-free mice on the way, imagine what I thought when told to come to the office for an important phone call! Of course, I thought it was Dr. Reyniers. Instead, it was Governor LeRoy Collins. I'd called the Governor's office earlier because his letter mentioned that he wanted to hear from me, but the Governor had been in a meeting. Days went by, so this call was unexpected. Now Collins himself was soon on the line. First, he mentioned scholarships the state of Florida could offer me. "We keep losing our best to the Ivy League schools," he said. "But we are the future." Then he said he'd like me to tour a plant in Port St. Joe that was trying to deal with chemical by-products such as magnesium.

I expressed how much the scholarships meant to me, but as for the tour of the plant at Port St Joe, I couldn't do that until after the National Science Fair and final exams were over. I realized that I was just a lucky high school student. A decision by busy science fair judges had made all the difference. The attention of politicos would be repeated with my cancer work in 1961. Most important were my contacts, such as Col. Doyle, his friends, my supportive doctors, Mrs. Watkins, and people such as Dr. Reyniers. Thinking like that saved me much grief when it was time to go to Indianapolis for the national event, for when that time came, there was a crisis. My mother refused to let me board the plane!

My parents had experienced a hard landing that almost tipped their plane over, and no longer made flights anywhere. Despite my pleadings and tears, my project was packed up and Mr. Sharer, my chemistry teacher, took off without me. With my cautious mother at the wheel, driving hundreds of miles at a snail's pace, by the time we reached Butler University's arena, the Fair was well underway. I never got a chance to speak to any of the first rounds of judges.

As for Mother, she dropped me off with my suitcase and drove away, for she was anxious to visit her friends and relatives. I didn't see her again until the event was over. Thanks to Mr. Sharer, my project was set up, but he was nowhere to be found. Sadly, I took my notebooks from the suitcase and shoved the suitcase under my ignored exhibit. But then I saw who was standing across the aisle and cheered up. It was Robert Strom! At age 11, Rob, who was now a handsome young teen, had won $192,000 (worth $1.8+ million today) on TV, on *The $64,000 Dollar Question*. He was very nice to me, and on top of that, he had a superior exhibit for the Fair. He methodically explained his project to me: a computerized trajectory program that could plot how a rocket from earth could swing around the moon in an orbit.

Tweaked, I think he could calculate how to land a rocket on the moon. Everything had to be calculated—the speed of the earth, its rotation, the speed of the moon and its imperfect orbit, etc.

Rob was way ahead of his time in using calculators and the simple computers available to work on these concepts. I hoped to talk more to Rob, but presently, he was not alone. With most of the judging now finished, a group of reporters, CIA scouts, military officers and scientists descended on the young genius, asking him questions. These people were hyper-patriotic: Indianapolis was where the John Birch Society, a militant right-wing anti-communist organization, had been recently founded.

When Rob, by his own admission in an email, displayed "leftist leanings," these super-patriots were not happy. One of the military officers turned away and, seeing me standing there, growled, "Well young lady, do *you* love America, and our great military, and our great American flag?" In reply, I boldly recited my "First Lady Poem." MacKinlay Kantor had sent it to General Curtis LeMay. It ended with these lines: *"Oh, precious, dear First Lady, to thee do we give our love / For you are the Flag of the United States, streaming on high above!"*

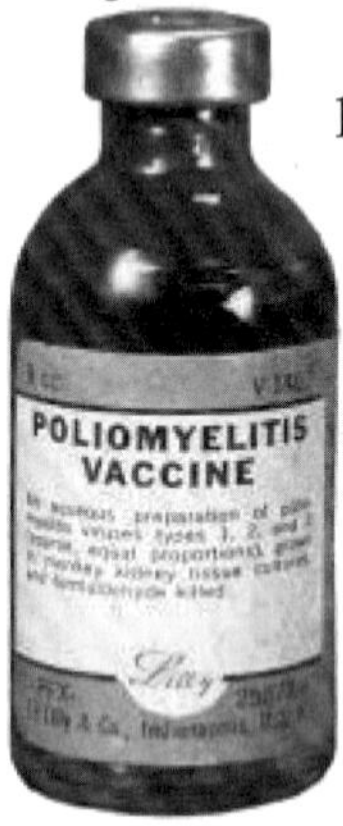

With a nod of approval, the officer said, "I've heard that poem before. It's been passed around." Then he invited me to spend the day with his group. From their speech and actions, I guessed that I'd be perfectly safe. These people could have been in a war movie, they were so vocal about their love for America. They stressed the greatness of our military, America's need for scientists, and the importance of "beating the Reds." With Mr. Sharer nowhere in sight, I agreed to come along. Let the adventure begin! They rounded up about ten of us, to be shepherded to various sites. Our first stop was Eli Lilly.

This tour was on the published schedule, which one could sign up for, but not with these military officers and scientists as guides! The Eli Lilly tour began with how polio vaccines were made. Eli Lilly was a major pharmaceutical company headquartered in Indianapolis. Its huge manufacturing facility sold products worldwide, including not only polio vaccines, but also antibiotics and insulin. I did not know that seven years earlier they had synthesized LSD-25 for the CIA, which ordered millions of doses of LSD for use in secret experiments. I did not know at this time about the CIA's massive mind control project, MK-ULTRA, which used LSD in many illegal ways on unwitting victims. After learning that Lilly's first product to treat cancer, called vinblastine, was to be released in 1961, I was anxious to show my cancer research notebooks and photographs to one of the speakers there.

In 2002 Marrs and Dankbaar filmed my Science Fair files.

In response, he handed me some Indiana University brochures. "I hope you'll think about going to the University of Indiana," he said. "We could sponsor you. Why stay in Florida?" he teased. "You're an Indiana girl. You belong here with us!" We were then taken to a room that had walls that reminded me of my dad's TV station's sound-proofed "green" room. Maybe this was where Lilly made TV commercials. Here, a few of us were asked to sit down and fill out some papers about ourselves, so we could be considered for Lilly scholarships. I only clearly remember one item: I was required to sign a loyalty oath. To me, a staunch patriot, it was an insult. A subversive, a terrorist or a Communist would lie, and sign, while people of conscience who cherished freedom of speech would not. I finally signed, but that inch of ink turned me sour about plans to attend a state university in my beloved Indiana. Two important things happened next: first, after touring some chemistry labs, we were given a stern lecture about serving our country in these perilous times. We were the country's future, we were told. Then a few scientists, accompanied by an Army Colonel, began to ask us questions about our science projects, and I got a chance to speak. I asked for technical help for my cancer research project. I'd had a lot of practice, by now, speaking to civic groups with Col. Doyle to raise money to pay for our new Science Building. I gave them my address, which the Colonel scribbled down, as well as copies of my cancer research.

They received my project ideas and outlines of some of the experiments I'd been working on. [25] I would eventually receive a response from Walter Reed Army Institute of Research (WRAIR), who would supply me with powerful chemicals to test on mice with and without cancer. Then, while the rest of the group went on without me, a doctor and the Colonel asked to look at my notebooks. When they gave me some names to contact at both Oak Ridge and Walter Reed Army Institute of Research (WRAIR), I was thunderstruck. Help from Oak Ridge came quickly, beginning with tiny radioactive pellets that could be implanted in mice[26] and a pair of lead gloves to protect my hands from x-rays. In September, 1960, WRAIR also stepped in, sending me hard-to-get experimental chemicals. I sent two or three reports back to WRAIR's section called "MEDEC-ZOA" with no idea what "MEDEC" meant. It was the US Army's "**Me**dical Research and **De**velopment **C**ommand," "headquartered at Fort Detrick," America's lethal combat research and biological warfare center.

---

[25]Years later I understand that Cold War paranoia fueled the oath requirement between the years of 1958 and 1961, and I had landed smack in the middle of those years. The State of Indiana required loyalty oaths for their NDEA loans. It was hinted that if I didn't sign the oath, many scholarships to Indiana's state universities would be out of reach.

[26] Regulations prohibiting radioactive substances to civilians were not yet in place.

Since I would be asking for help from the U.S Army, the Colonel also asked me to write to the President, offering my services to my country. It was another indication of the heated anti-communist atmosphere that was so powerfully on display. Though I eventually wrote the letter, I put it off until President Kennedy was in office. The letter was read, for it has some underlining on it. I received a hand-signed reply from JFK's close aide, Ralph Dungan. My letter and a carbon copy of his reply are in the National Archives (see Appendix). [27] At one point during this tour, at University of Indiana Medical School, we were assembled for photos on a staircase next to a human cadaver on a gurney. I was the only one who agreed to use a scalpel on the cadaver (you can't be a doctor if you're squeamish!). The doctor asked if I could locate the trigeminal nerve on the cadaver's face. I was able to do so, since I had studied this nerve. It had caused my grandmother considerable pain.

The doctor was impressed, but I was just lucky. Fortunately, the photo didn't get published in the paper. After a hectic late lunch, full of introductions to more scientists and men in black, we returned to the University of Indiana's School of Medicine, which was receiving a lot of funding from the National Institute of Health. The tour ended by watching an operation on a grown man.

The size and scope of the 11th National Science Fair-International (1960) held at Butler University, spurred on by Cold War and Space Race obsessions, was impressive. Of course, the military and CIA were there.

I returned so late to my project that I only had a chance to speak to one judge (a nun) on her final round. She asked why I used the Haber process in the exhibit. She obviously knew a lot about Mg, so I told her that the Haber process could make enough ammonia from the leftover "slag," rich in Mg Chloride, to make the

[27] I was pilloried when I first spoke out, for saying I was asked to write to 'President Kennedy' -instead of Eisenhower-as if this disqualified me from ever being a credible witness! The point was that I was asked to write the letter, when I did, it was to JFK.

magnesium production cost-competitive. And that's all the 'judging' my exhibit got. At least I had a chance to chat with Bob Strom again: we even started a game of chess because traffic slowed down so much. Years later, Rob, now a stellar figure at IBM, wrote that he remembered me (his wife, he told me, was also named 'Judy.'). The next day, prize ribbons began appearing on the exhibits. Mine got a 4th place ribbon. I was satisfied: I was afraid my project would get nothing! For example, Mr. Sharer had 'cleaned up' my display by choosing to bring the backup smelting furnace I had not used, which "looked nicer.' But it would not have convinced a judge that I had actually refined magnesium myself. That made me lose points, I heard, with the judges.

When Mother finally picked me up, she apologized for not coming, but she had a surprise: she drove us up to Bremen, Indiana, where my grandparents Vary, Uncle Tubby (Harold), Auntie Grace and cousins David and Sharon welcomed me! I had missed my Jr. Prom to attend the Fair, but Mother had brought along my sea-green Taffeta and chiffon gown. Everyone asked me to put it on. Then came photos, and requests for me to sing. I sang "I Believe." I hadn't been singing much in the past year and it didn't go well: my voice broke on a high note, but everybody pretended I did just fine! In the "prom dress" photo, behind me, you can see a long, white building. It was separated into two parts.

Uncle Harold ("Tubby") lived in the front part of the building. Inside his cottage was the kind of compact furniture you'd find in the interiors of RV's. His spotless home could have been inside an R.V. in a magazine. On the walls were paintings of horses, wolves, dogs, deer, birds and other wildlife. On the wooden mantel over the brick fireplace were sculptures of horses, dogs, and carved duck decoys.

The back half of the white building was Grandpa's a workshop, where Grandpa Vary, now retired, was building his very last shining mahogany boats, similar to the boat in this photo. He had six of them suspended from the rafters and was working on their sharp keels. Grandpa obtained the mahogany wood from a nearby Kris Kraft facility.

As we sat together on the back porch swing, looking over the beautiful park-like gardens he and Grandma worked on together, Grandpa told me his secret for getting along with her. "She thinks I'm deaf," he said. "It saves me a lot of trouble." He told me how they had both decided, one being Republican and the other a Democrat, not to vote at all, after which he sneaked out on a bicycle, instead of using his car, and voted for Truman. He planned to do the same for Kennedy. The next day, my cousins and I decided to hike around Lake of the Woods on a densely wooded trail five miles long. Our spunky grandmother, age 83, hiked right along with us! The forests had been kept intact, alongside pristine farms lovingly cared for by the Amish. All too soon, it was time to leave. On the way back to Florida, Mother stopped at a riding school and I got to ride a nice horse. The attention from "Magnesium from the Sea" continued: I had scholarship offers from MIT, UC-Berkeley, Purdue University, Indiana State U, Michigan State, Rutgers, Duke, University of Florida, New College, and St. Francis College, a small Catholic college in Indiana. I never applied to any of them in the traditional sense. Sailing blissfully along on daydreams about my future, it would take some harsh reality to teach me some basic common sense. Later that summer, I rode a bus to Florida's panhandle near Pensacola to take the tour of "the St. Joe Facility." There, the plant manager introduced me to **U.S. Rep. Robert Sikes**. Sikes was no ordinary politician. He was of that contingent of "Mr. Pork Barrel" Sen. Robert Byrd, and Sen. Lyndon Johnson, who flooded their respective states with lucrative government contracts. As Chair of the Subcommittee for Military Construction for the U.S. House Appropriations Committee, Sikes constructed 14 military bases in just one Florida district—his. What nobody told me was that Port St. Joe's "chemical plant" was a paper mill. The mill's greed for trees had denuded every green branch for miles, eradicating endless acres of native longleaf pines and many other kinds of trees and their diverse animal life. The native trees were replaced with endless rows of slash pines. Millions of gallons of pristine water from Florida's aquifer were pumped in, to wash away the toxic wastes. Then it was pumped out again as a steaming potion, replete with cadmium, lead, arsenic, and other deadly chemicals. The stench from the paper mill came from towers expelling tons of toxic, carcinogenic waste products into the clouds. And we were breathing it.

It was such a contrast to the Amish-style of life surrounding Lake O' the Woods, where my Grandparents Vary lived! Rep. Sikes said he hoped I had some ideas on how St. Joe could make higher profits from the heavy-metal by-products they currently sold to three companies.

That would mean "continued prosperity for the workers in the area," he stressed. "His" workers here were paid better than anywhere else in the Panhandle. Unwilling to give the paper company any more help in tearing apart its corner of the world, I told Sikes a fib. Perhaps they should consider making phosphite, I told him. Florida had more lightning strikes than any other state. If the plant had strike towers to attract lightning to their phosphate-rich, toxic slurry dumps, free electrical energy would be generated to produce phosphites, a rare form of phosphate which helps makes a superior fertilizer. What I didn't tell Sikes was that a single rusting car can make more phosphite than dozens of lightning strikes. Back in Bradenton, inspired more than ever to honestly serve my country, I worked hard to improve my Russian, even after classes ended, using dual English-Russian books and plowing through scientific papers about cancer written in Russian, which were supplied by Col. Doyle and his friends. I basically understood them, but my ability to speak Russian just stumbled along, with nobody to talk to.

Col. Doyle and I continued to give fund-raising speeches to help pay for our new Science Building, to which many civic groups responded with big checks. Both Tropicana Orange Juice in Bradenton and Bausch & Lomb in Sarasota also responded. From then on, Tropicana and B & L let me come by for "scraps," such as throwaway test tubes and glass rods, which we could cleanse and use again in our chemistry classes. Later that year, Bausch and Lomb began experimenting with colored contact lenses.

When they heard I had lost a contact lens at the hotel swimming pool in Melbourne, and that my friend Larry Jerome had spent an hour diving, trying to find it for me, they gave me a free pair! But that wasn't the end of their generosity. They also gave Manatee High 25 new microscopes. Then in December 1960, they saw the big newspaper article about me in the Sarasota paper, where I pleaded for a better microscope. That's when Bausch & Lomb gave me a professional microscope that I treasured. At that time, B & L had a product development lab in Sarasota.

For some time, movie stars had been using colored contact lenses. Now the company was researching the idea for the general public (Eventually, B & L would invent the soft contact lens.). Suffering from severe myopia that developed when I first became ill as a child, my contact lenses were much thicker than average. Their question was, *'If she wears a very thick, blue-colored contact lens, will she see the world too blue?'*

After several tries, they found the right level of tint, and I got to keep the lenses. Eventually, they also tested green and brown lenses that I was allowed to keep, too.

As summer ended, I was wearing contact lenses again, and was anxiously awaiting the start of my senior year. Football ga mes! The Prom! Homecoming! Dances! I also received my first advanced cancer research package, with a letter, from Walter Reed Army Institute of Research (WRAIR). My expectations had been low; I'd written a long report on my work, in as much detail as possible, such as what I had sent to Oak Ridge, with statistics, photos and graphs. But there hadn't been a quick response. Oak Ridge had helped, but I needed chemicals, not lead shielding, radioactive pellets or Geiger counters, all of which Oak Ridge had been so willing to send. Would I get a polite letter from WRAIR, saying how nice it was that I was interested in cancer? Or was it hopeless? In fact, Dr. David Jacobus himself responded. He was the head of WRAIR's Radiobiology Department, run by the Army and U.S. Government. This department worked with the lethal effects of radiation on human bodies.

Jacobus' letter carefully explained his thoughts about the field. He also sent two small boxes with vials of sophisticated chemicals, with instructions on how to use them.

With my mice, of course. I'd been trying everywhere to get one of them – mercaptoethylamine [MEA].

He wrote that Walter Reed was conducting work similar to my own in hypothermia. I didn't have the nerve to write back and tell him that I wasn't studying hypothermia anymore. Instead of slowing cancer down, as I'd hoped, by making the mice live in an icebox, their cancer spread faster than ever. I'd put them all to sleep with ether. New supplies arrived a month later, including a third chemical, an anabolic steroid not mentioned in Jacobus' long letter, called 2-α-methyl-dihydrotestosterone propionate. Recently declassified documents show that Dr. Jacobus' research was so advanced that in 1964 he protected a group of monkeys from dying of lethal doses of radiation by giving them some of the same chemicals he had sent to me.[28]

Walter Reed also sent some published and unpublished articles, along with the dates and locations of upcoming scientific meetings and conferences. I marked one of them: an important cancer research symposium was coming to nearby St. Petersburg in the spring. That would be interesting to attend, I thought to myself. Armed with exotic new chemicals and inspired by Walter Reed's interest and support, I plunged into months of work with a vengeance! I had a real laboratory now, with high-quality Webster Swiss mice, anti-radioactive chemicals,

[28] From research conducted by Edward T. Haslam.

and expert guidance. I often prayed on my knees, thanking God for the doors opening for me, just because of the Space Race and the Russians.

My friend Albert Freeman had no support because his field was in astronomy and there were no astronomers nearby to help him. He made big, magnificent telescopes, hand-grinding their lenses, but he never got a chance to go to college. All his extra time was spent mowing lawns before and after school, under the thumb of a tyrannical father, to help his mother. Our own father was becoming unreasonable about our dating boys. He trusted me, but because Lynda was flirtatious, so he didn't trust her, even though she was chaste and innocent. It was so unfair. Meanwhile, my horizons were expanding. Dear Col. Doyle no longer had to drive to the medical libraries of big hospitals to hunt up information for me, either. Now, they all let me in! I even traveled to UF's libraries in Gainesville, where I access edthe latest journals in the University's new Teaching Hospital (It opened in October, 1958, thanks to Senator Smathers.). I was a peripatetic teenage pioneer in President Kennedy's New Frontier, with one goal in mind: I wanted Dr. Reyniers' mice for my cancer research! So far, he had given me only one mouse pup to care for. He was wisely unwilling to risk losing a big batch to a teenage *wunderkind.* While the pup was originally healthy, all the equipment and procedures needed to keep the pup alive stymied me. It soon died.

The World of Tony Lopez-Fresquet

All this time, I was dating a few great boys. Some of them would sweetly carry my books for me all the way to Manatee Memorial Hospital.

We would sometimes stop at the Shake Pit, or A & W's on the way, after school. Life was still normal. But then I began dating a handsome, wealthy Cuban refugee. His name was Antonio Lopez-Fresquet. To me, he was just 'Tony.'

He and his brothers had fled Cuba after Fidel Castro took over. He spoke excellent English and immediately became popular. Their American mother, Helen, also fled, no longer feeling safe in the new Communist regime. But Tony's dad, Rufo, was still Castro's Finance Minister. His name was on Cuba's money. Tony worried about him every day. He had a right to be worried. His father was secretly CIA.

Tony and his two brothers had been attending the prestigious American school, Ruston Academy, in Havana, Cuba. They fled just before the CIA started up a secret project. It began at Ruston itself and was called "Operación Pedro Pan." This involved an unprecedented ship-out of Cuban children in "a clandestine mass exodus of over 14,000 unaccompanied Cuban minors, ages 6 to 18, to the United States over a two-year span from 1960 to 1962."[29] The Catholic Church worked with the CIA to get emergency visas to spirit of these children out of Cuba, but they had to leave their parents behind to face the music.[30] Their parents thought their children would be safer.

They were convinced that a civil war was imminent and that Castro would soon be overthrown. That was a dangerous political position to hold at this time. But in the end, these parents believed they would get back their old life and would be re-united with their kids. It didn't work out that way. Instead, Castro became firmly entrenched, as he brutally eliminated his enemies. Some of these exiled Cuban children would never see their parents again. Tony and his brother Vince were both friendly and good-looking, with almost no accent, so they fit right in. During the summer, Tony and I went joyriding from time to time in his fancy convertible.

On one such occasion, we found an interesting part of Snead Island called Emerson Point, with an Indian mound to explore. It was only accessible by means of a narrow, unpaved dirt road. It was full of deep potholes. Even today, the road still exists at Emerson Point. The photo resembles what the road was like in 1960. That's when Tony suddenly stopped the car. "Would you like to have a driving lesson, Lady J?" he asked. When I foolishly said 'yes,' he switched seats with me, and as I began to steer, he jumped onto the hood of his car. "If you make a mistake," he laughed, "you can kill me, so be very careful to do what I tell you!" Tony's driving lesson taught me a lot – fast! I learned very quickly how to steer Tony's expensive car. As Tony stood confidently looking down at me, his hands on his hips, I strove not to kill either one of us by avoiding the potholes, the deep ditches, and the tangles of mangrove swamp roots that invaded both sides of the narrow road.

[29] https://en.wikipedia.org/wiki/Operation_Peter_Pan The article is inaccurate.
[30] https://www.wbur.org/npr/131449904/carlos-eire-a-cuban-american-searches-for-roots "operation Peter Pan Ruston academy...Carlos Eire was one of 14,000 children who were airlifted out of Cuba to the U.S. after Castro took power. Their parents were not allowed to leave Cuba."

I learned how to gently use the accelerator, how to properly apply the brakes, and how to use my first curse words.

Another time, Tony stopped the car and pointed at some horses grazing peacefully in a field. "I know you love horses, Lady J," he announced, "so I will get one for you to ride, right now!" With that, he walked into the field, stole up behind a pretty chestnut mare, and grabbing her by the mane, he leaped on her back. The horse would have none of it and promptly bucked him off. Tony pretended he wasn't hurt a bit, but I kissed his bleeding elbow.

"Oh, Tony, why did you do that?" I asked, hugging him. He gave me one of his enchanting smiles. "In my world, it's called *machismo*, being a real man," Tony replied. "You know, if we fell in love and got married," he went on, "I would still have to act *macho*. As the son of an important man, I would have to have a mistress. It's part of the show." Then he asked, "Would that upset you?"

"Thank you for the warning," I told him.

Handsome as he was, that was more than I wanted to know. We happily shared classes such as Physics and Science Seminar together, and sometimes, after school, Tony would stay late to help me, such as when I burned cigarette products to make aerosol bases for cancer experiments, for I was forbidden to work alone in the lab whenever I used open fire or a dangerous chemical.

There was never a question about an improper situation, perhaps because I sometimes asked my heavily-panting boyfriends with wandering paws to pray with me for God's guidance as to our future. This prayer session was short and usually happened in the interior of an automobile. One time, I was burning aerosols and distilling them, using a Bunsen burner, when Tony grabbed the Bunsen burner and stuck it under his armpit. I pulled the Bunsen burner away from him. Then I

slapped away at the fire that started in the cloth under his arm.

"Why in heck did you do that, Tony?" I asked, as I turned the burner off. As I began unbuttoning his shirt, anxious to treat his burn, he murmured, "You don't know what it's like, Judy. Nether did I. But now I do."

"What do you mean?" I asked, as I applied some petroleum jelly onto his burned armpit. He leaned close to me and softly said, "Some of my friends..." He closed his eyes and said their names in Spanish. "Castro was sure they were CIA. He sent one off to a work camp, to be a slave..."

"...But he took the other two, hung them up, and had them tortured with a blowtorch, under their arms." I never forgot the look of anger and hatred in Tony' eyes when he told me this. As he began to cry, we held each other tight. Stories such as these made me hate Castro. In 1961, my parents finally let me have parties, and Tony came to all three. First, there was a Polar Bear party on Jan. 9, 1961, as seen in the news clipping and photo where I wear a striped bathing suit. Tony also came to a swim party on my birthday, May 15. Tony can be seen in the upper-right of the Polaroid photo made at that time. Finally, he came to a 'surprise' party held for me in early September to celebrate the successful outcome of my hard work at Roswell Park, for good reports had preceded me from Drs. Moore and Diehl to the Suncoast. (I think Tony flew in from California). Tony's desire to kill Fidel Castro had a profound effect on me. How far should one go, [31] if given the chance to save people from a tyrant? I would be tested on that very point only two years later.[32] In spring, 1961, I was named one of eleven students representing Florida in the Westinghouse Science Talent Search. I had spent hours studying for the national test, focusing on the Science Service's *Science Newsletter*. Our eleven had tested highest in the state, beating thousands of applicants. To show you how tough the competition was, all eleven of us had tied with perfect scores. We also submitted our science projects to qualify for the tests. This award would attract a phone call that would change my life. A *Sarasota Herald-Tribune* reporter, Jane Kolb, called, planning to write a small news article. My sister Lynda, who had memorized the official name of my project, answered the phone.

Judith Vary Has 'Polar Bear' Swim Party

Judith Vary, daughter of Mr. and Mrs. D. W. Vary, entertained a group of friends from Manatee High School Saturday afternoon at the Vary residence on Pompano Drive, Snead's Island, with a Polar Bear swimming party.

Decorations for the party, which began as a dare to go swimming on winter's coldest day in an unheated pool, were polar bears used at various points around the house.

By way of entertainment Margaret Stanford gave a pantomime show using puppets and Bruce Korth read a number of his original poems. Later in the evening the time was spent dancing.

Those attending were Bobby Bennett, Bruce Korth, John Leedy, Pete Marine, Jim Richeson, Danny Underwood, Kay Whidden, Judy Wang, Don Wilson, Bob Pope, Tony Lopez-Fresquet, Bob Conner, Beth Champagne, Barbara Ridgsdill, Nicky Kosco, Sara Haile, Sandy Smith, Margaret Stanford, Barry Stewart, Charles Throckmorton, Mary Hinnis and Lynda Vary.

SPEED QUEEN
Sales and Service
WASHERS & DRYERS
McCRANIE'S
828 9th Avenue, West
Phone 3-8423

A POLAR BEAR swim party was a novel affair at which Judith Vary entertained over the weekend and pictured just before taking dip in the icy water were Sandy Smith, left, Charles Throckmorton, Bob Pope and Judith Vary. (Herald photo by King)

[31] Editors of *Me & Lee* linked the wrong date to the Polaroid photo. The swimsuit in the newspaper article was striped red and white, with spaghetti string ties. Tony's name is mentioned among the guests for the Polar Bear party. In the May 15, 1960 Polaroid photo, where Tony is at top right, I'm wearing a dark green swimsuit with thick straps.

[32] I tried for years to find Tony again. Then, in 2006, the Ruston Academy published a list of deceased students online: both Tony and his youngest brother were on the list.

I'll try to reconstruct their conversation:

Reporter: Is your sister available?

Lynda: She'll be home in an hour.

Reporter: Well, I have a deadline. Would you happen to know the name of your sister's science project?

Lynda: Which one?

Reporter: The one about mice.

Lynda: Oh, that one? Yes, I know its name. Do you have a pencil?

Reporter: You can just go ahead and tell me the name.

Lynda: OK. It's called "Studies on the Chemotherapeutic Action of Aminoethylisothiourea Bromide Hydrobromide, Mercaptoethylamine as the Hydrochloride, and Two-alpha-methyldihydrotestosterone Propionate on the Normal and Irradiated Tissues in White Mice of the Webster-Swiss Strain."

Reporter: I'm coming over.

MHS Senior Gives Time To Cancer Project

Judy Vary, a friendly, dark-haired, dynamic worker, devotes the greater part of her time, energy, and money to a job any adult scientist would be proud of.

Reading all summer yielded Judy, a senior at Manatee High, one sentence which gave her the key to the exciting project. Because of her great concern for the preservation of life, Judy is attempting to find a method which may lead to a cure for cancer.

Irradiation is often used in the treatment of cancer, because it destroys carcinomous (cancer) growths. However, the radioactive bombardment frequently has adverse effects upon normal cells which cause them to become cancerous. Judy believes that antiradioactive agents plus nontoxic stearates injected subcutaneously (beneath the cancers) may retard the movement of the cancer to other parts of the body (metastasis) and also protect normal tissue from injury.

Mice Due Any Day

One hundred white mice (99 males!), to be used in her research, are due to arrive any day now. The big problem is cages! At present Judy has accommodations for only 15 mice, and it will just not do to have the biology and chemistry stockrooms overrun with them.

Defining a mouse cage as "anything a mouse can't get out of but I can get my hand into" (such as a half-gallon pickle jar with its lid), Judy says that she will be very grateful for any cages students could donate.

Mr. Fred Langford, executive vice-president of Palmetto Federal Savings and Loan Association, is giving Judy the mice. They will be treated with a substance from cigarette filters which has been proven to cause cancer. When cancers have developed Judy will try to destroy them by her new method.

Walter Reed Dr. Aids

Dr. David Jacobus, of the Walter Reed Army Medical Center in Washington, D.C., has given Judy $60.00 worth of chemicals. He will continue to back her in this research, provided that she sends him a monthly report of her progress.

Col. Philip Doyle, physics teacher, and Mr. Milton Scharer, chemistry teacher, assist Judy in many ways. Dr. John Shively, of Bradenton and a Sarasota doctor, are giving her information on biocultures, and the use of hospital equipment, such as x-rays.

Her parents contribute immeasurably to her work, but Judy does as much as she can to pay her own way. She paints

The story ended up taking more than half a page in the Dec. 6, 1961 edition of Sarasota's biggest Sunday newspaper. Small excerpts are shown here. The first excerpt shows the impact of my vocabulary on the reporter. She picked up the concept, hardly known at the time, that radiation to treat cancer could backfire, causing new cancers. That had to stop! She captured many details, such as my speed-reading abilities and my habit of running rather than walking (to save time). Best of all, she caught the vision: I was determined to cure cancer! By now, I was running low on mice again, despite Mouse Romeo's heroic efforts. Because I was using young mice, they developed skin cancer faster than adults. But they were also weaker. Forced to live in the smoke chamber, they died rapidly, but not from cancer. Tar deposits in their lungs poisoned them. A new problem to solve! By the time the article was published, I'd solved the 'too large for mice' x-ray problem by taping the mice to toy railroad cars, and moving the cars electronically to distribute even x-ray doses.

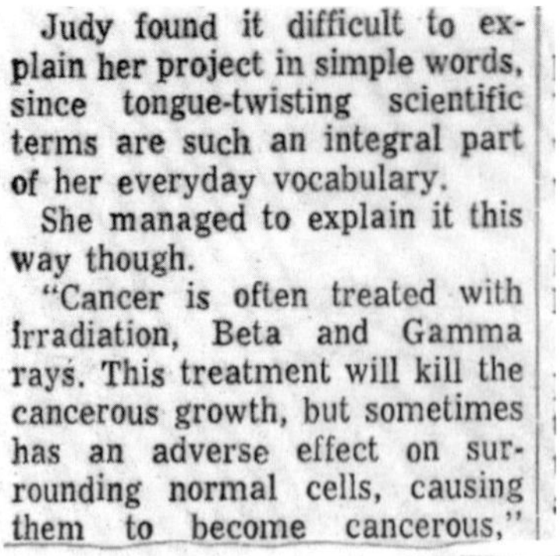

Judy found it difficult to explain her project in simple words, since tongue-twisting scientific terms are such an integral part of her everyday vocabulary.

She managed to explain it this way though.

"Cancer is often treated with irradiation, Beta and Gamma rays. This treatment will kill the cancerous growth, but sometimes has an adverse effect on surrounding normal cells, causing them to become cancerous,"

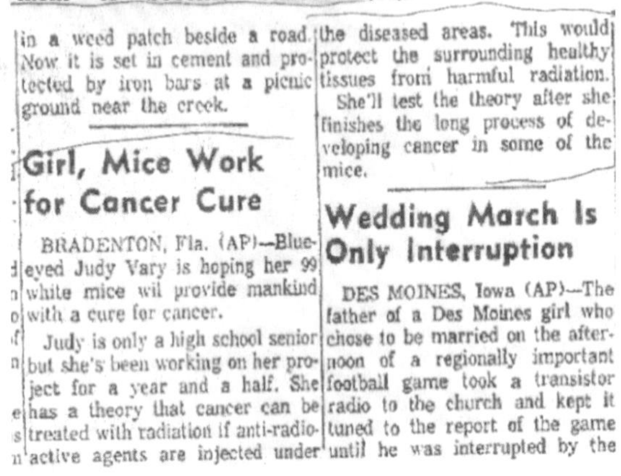

in a weed patch beside a road. Now it is set in cement and protected by iron bars at a picnic ground near the creek.

Girl, Mice Work for Cancer Cure

BRADENTON, Fla. (AP)—Blue-eyed Judy Vary is hoping her 99 white mice wil provide mankind with a cure for cancer.

Judy is only a high school senior but she's been working on her project for a year and a half. She has a theory that cancer can be treated with radiation if anti-radioactive agents are injected under the diseased areas. This would protect the surrounding healthy tissues from harmful radiation.

She'll test the theory after she finishes the long process of developing cancer in some of the mice.

Wedding March Is Only Interruption

DES MOINES, Iowa (AP)—The father of a Des Moines girl who chose to be married on the afternoon of a regionally important football game took a transistor radio to the church and kept it tuned to the report of the game until he was interrupted by the

It was Kolb's only technical error in the article. The reporter got the drift of my experiments[33] and expressed my hope to access a more suitable x-ray machine. She learned of my getting x-ray overdoses. She posted my big wish: to get a top-notch microscope. She described the dyes (pink, blue, yellow) used on the mice to identify each group tested. She interviewed teachers, friends, doctors. Then a photographer showed up. I was working on six varieties of nicotine-rich extracts at the time, visible in six test tubes. I brought Romeo out to join the fun. As the only mouse not involved in experiments, he was quite tame. Then, on Sunday, the phone began to ring. Things moved quickly after that. Dr, Reyniers called and told me he would be delivering a dozen germ-free mice, with sterilized food pellets and other items. Further, he would show me how to handle them. I managed to not shout with joy! For the next nine months, between Jan. 24, 1961 and Sept. 15, 1961, The Associated Press ran a short version of the story in some 100 newspapers across the country. Prior to the largely accurate story in the Sarasota newspaper written by Kolb, my school newspaper printed a story too, with a glaring inaccuracy: it said 99 male mice were on the way, instead of 99 female mice! Quite a difference! Meanwhile, messages kept arriving from celebrities such as Arthur Godfrey, Billy Graham, and Lord Bertrand Russell. My father ripped up Bertrand Russell's telegram. He let me know Russell was an atheist and a Communist. The Damon Runyon Cancer Fund also sent me money.

The ongoing attention was because the story "Girl, Mice Work for Cancer Cure" was published all over America. [34] In Jan. 1961, another important article was published in *The Bradenton Herald*, followed in

[33] Kolb was told the Palmetto Bank had provided 99 mice (plus 1 male!) but didn't know the Rockefeller Foundation had "anonymously" sent a 2nd batch.

[34] 32 of 100 newspapers that carried the story were located by Edward T. Haslam.

Feb. by a photo and article in our school newspaper. With lots of cages now, germ-free mice to work with, and fresh ideas to implement, I began making some real progress. Little did I realize that I had embarked on a road of no return.

(arrows) Col. Doyle w/ Slinky...Tony Lopez-Fresquet...Judy w/other end of Slinky...Albert Freeman

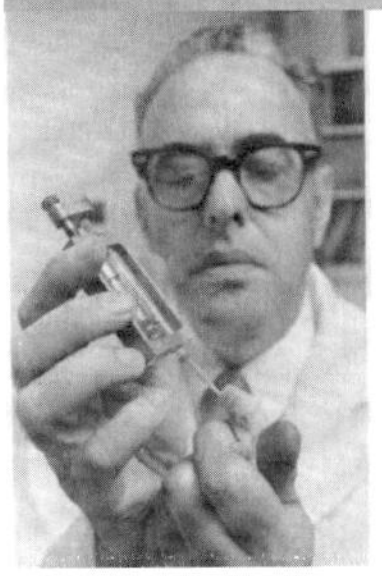

Manatee High gave us great mentors such as. Col. Phillip V. Doyle and Marion Brady, plus access to real scientists, doctors & retired military officers

Dr James Reyniers

Chapter Three
To Conquer Cancer

Scholarship offers were pouring in. I did not have to apply for any of them. The ones I remember were from MIT, UC at Berkley, U of Texas at Austin, Rutgers, Duke, Purdue, University of Indiana, Michigan State, Stanford U, Syracuse U, Amherst College, and St. Francis College in Fort Wayne, Indiana. What was missing was an offer from the University of Chicago. My counselor failed to tell me that they expected an application. With my heart set on returning to Indiana, I wrote to my grandparents and Uncle Tubby in Bremen, Indian and sent Purdue an acceptance letter. School life went on: we created a mock city-state. Bruce Korth, Peter Rowe, Gene Courson, Mastin Overstreet, Burton Eppel and Barbara Rigdel were some of the members.

The wonderful Mr. Marion Brady was Grand Vizier. He barely kept us under control. Our irreverent slogan was “Up, toga!” It was our flippant answer to “the Red Scare.” Russia was far away, but we were safe, far away, across the ocean. Or were we? As 1960 came to an end, we weren’t so sure. The arms race continued to escalate like an out-of-control poker game.

Both sides were bristling with tanks, submarines, supersonic aircraft, and nuclear bombs and missiles. Each side defied the other with new generation of powerful hydrogen bombs. These radioactive super-weapons promised a blast equivalent to a hundred million tons of dynamite -- large enough to obliterate a huge city, while leaving a cloud of radioactive fallout to enshroud the earth and sicken every form of life. Hopes for a “Peace Summit” in Paris collapsed in bitter disarray a few days after the Russians shut down America’s U2 spy plane. It had been flying over Soviet airspace on May Day (their equivalent of our Fourth of July), 1960. Raising the stakes further, our Polaris and Minute Man missiles were trotted out, ready to strike the Soviets, as the names implied, at a moment’s notice. But if we could do it to them, they could do it to us. Peace on earth hung on a thread, based on the official strategy of two super-powers, cynically labeled MAD – Mutual Assured Destruction. The generals on our side seemed anxious to get it over with, led by **Curtis LeMay**. The movie, *Dr. Strangelove* [1964] reflected LeMay’s “bomb ‘em to hell’ attitude. At the same time, the new, untested young President, John F. Kennedy, was looked upon as “soft on Communism” – a man who might not push the red button in time to save us, if Russia attacked first. History’s verdict on who was right was long in coming. In 2013, *The Atlantic* argued that “President Kennedy faced a foe more relentless than **Khrushchev**, just across the Potomac...
the bellicose Joint Chiefs of Staff argued for the deployment of nuclear weapons and kept pressing to invade Cuba. Kennedy's success in fending them off may have been his most consequential victory.”[35]

The argument to crush Russia before Russia crushed us was powerful: the American “Hawks” cited worldwide Soviet aggression, and their rhetoric about Soviet communism could not have been sharper. It was a totalitarian dictatorship fixated on total control -- cradle-to-grave –internally, as well as global dominion externally.

[35]https://www.theatlantic.com/magazine/archive/2013/08/jfk-vs-the-military/309496/

The Soviet leadership saw America as a reckless bully, destroying the delicate balance between the two superpowers with tough talk and banks of nuclear missiles. The American media portrayed Soviet Premiere **Nikita Khrushchev** as a crude, dangerous man who beat his shoe on the podium during crucial UN meetings. *Time Magazine* presented the Soviet leader grimacing in front of a mushroom cloud to emphasize that the Soviets had resumed testing nuclear weapons.
They were planning to develop a new 100-megaton bomb, a weapon twice as powerful as anything in the American arsenal.

America's President, Dwight D. Eisenhower, a 5-star General famed for his leadership in World War II, had tried to maintain peace in the tense years that followed. Now, on Jan. 17, 1961, he gave the nation his famous farewell speech, filled with prophetic warnings. It has been repeated by concerned citizens ever since. A threat to our democratic way of life had emerged, he said, which was "new" in the American experience. *"In the councils of government,"* he warned, *"we must guard against the acquisition of unwarranted influence, whether ought or unsought, by the military-industrial complex. The potential for the disastrous use of misplaced power exists, and will persist."*

It was a wake-up call that would come to haunt us. Three days later, JFK was sworn in, greeting the world with a new vision. "Let the word go forth. from this time and place, to friend and foe alike," he proclaimed, "that the torch has been passed to a new generation of Americans, born in this century, tempered by war, disciplined by a hard and bitter peace, proud of our ancient heritage and unwilling to witness or permit the slow undoing of those human rights to which this nation has always been committed, and to which we are committed today at home and around the world." He reminded us that "Man holds in his mortal hands the power to abolish all forms of human poverty, and all forms of human life." Soon after, JFK announced the formation of the Peace Corps to bring much-needed technical assistance to alleviate poverty in the undeveloped third world, and The Alliance for Progress to bring economic development to Latin America in our own hemisphere. Somehow, under Kennedy's leadership, this new vision of hope surfaced to live side by side with the nightmare of thermonuclear war, which had become part of our daily lives.

For my family in Florida, the threats of the Cold War and Communism were closer than the evening news reports. 90 miles off the Florida coast, the revolution in Cuba that threw out Fulgencio Batista and his corrupt government was right next door. A flood of angry, wealthy political refugees swarmed into Florida, convinced that soon enough, our government would intervene and get their country back. When the new Cuban president, Fidel Castro, made it clear that the big, corrupt American companies, the Mafia's lavish casinos and brothels, and the good ole boy bribery systems that had overrun his country were no longer welcome, shock and disbelief set in. As CIA contract agent Frank Sturgis put it, the Mafia was stunned.

Castro turned down millions in payoffs![36] The angry reaction of the US government, spurred on by American companies, Cuban millionaires and the Mafia, pushed Castro into the welcoming paws of the Russian bear. President Kennedy would soon be drawn into this conflict. The plot to invade Cuba and restore it to its former condition began before JFK took office, but these efforts were stymied when Eisenhower refused to let the CIA kill Castro. The CIA remained unhappy when Kennedy began probing into their growing power and questionable activities.

To be brief, the CIA realized that if the pre-planned invasion failed under the new president's watch, the CIA and the military could then use public opinion to force the young President to invade Cuba and take back the island "for Democracy." Kennedy would have to go along with the plan if he didn't want to be labeled a weak, pro-Red coward. It could be very profitable for the military-industrial complex, because Russia would react to such U.S interference with their Cuban ally, and a full-blown war could occur. That would make fortunes for the right people. Of course, if the war went nuclear, there would be millions of deaths, but America – though in ruins, and covered with radiation that would sicken and kill many millions more -- would end up "winning" -- because America had more nuclear weapons.

To fool JFK, the CIA and his military advisors told him that the oppressed Cuban people would rise up and support the anti-Castro invaders. That was a lie. The Cubans were willing to give Castro a chance, not wanting Batista or any other American-backed dictator to return.

On April 15, 1961, things came to a head. Kennedy refused to bomb Havana and other key areas when the invaders landed on a swampy beach on the south side of Cuba known as the Bay of Pigs, where the Cuban military and their Russian advisors, responding to "leaks" that an invasion was coming, were waiting for them. Kennedy, refusing to grant the full military support that he knew could cause World War III, infuriated the anti-Castro Cubans, the CIA, the bankers, and the military-industrial complex by his perceived inaction. Most of the 1500-man invasion force was captured, imprisoned, and tortured. The rest died on the beach. Most of these inner problems were totally unknown to the American people at the time.

The Bay of Pigs fiasco embarrassed the US in the eyes of the world and strained relations with the Soviets almost to the breaking point. While JFK publicly accepted the blame for the defeat, he privately realized that the CIA had set a trap for him. To make sure the CIA would think twice about fooling him again, the CIA's top three CIA officers were

[36] CIA no-# doc released 2017: Tatel: 8/4/76 Sturgis phone calls– Fonzi collection

fired or forced to retire. At least two of them – **Allan Dulles** and Gen. Charles Cabell – the two top CIA officers--would play for high stakes to rid themselves of JFK. Behind the scenes, the CIA's system maintained its ties to their former leaders.

Allan Dulles

The Cuban Missile Crisis Over the next few years, the CIA would continue to oppose Kennedy. Sometimes they ignored or refused to follow the President's orders. The CIA regarded Kennedy as a naïve and dangerous intruder who needed to be removed from office before he dismantled the Agency.

Political analyst Chris Matthews tells us that when "...Nikita Krushchev, the Soviet leader...secretly deployed 90 nuclear missiles in Cuba..." he had a back-up plan in place." If the United States decided to attack the weapon sites, Soviet Premiere Khrushchev wrote, "I knew the United States could knock out some of our installations, but not all of them. If a quarter or even a tenth of our missiles survived—even if only one or two big ones were left—we could still hit New York..."

Mathews tells us, "Only one man stood between testing Khrushchev's backup plan and a nuclear holocaust: President Kennedy." He "improvised a jerry-built policy that included an embargo on further shipment of Soviet missiles and a demand that all such weapons in Cuba be removed. Khrushchev turned back his cargo ships and removed his missiles. In this eyeball-to-eyeball conflict, he appeared to "blink" while his counterpart, President John F. Kennedy stood firm... All around Kennedy were men arguing that the only safe action by the United States, once the nuclear missile sites were discovered, was to destroy them before the missiles became operational."

It took years to realize what JFK accomplished behind the scenes. Air Force chief of staff Curtis LeMay had tried to force the President to strike before Russia struck us. National Security Advisor McGeorge Bundy, staffers led by Dean Acheson and JFK's own brother Bobby pushed for an immediate air attack on the Cuban missiles.

JFK's Generals, Cabinet, advisors, and brother Bobby, the Attorney General, also wanted to bomb Havana. The generals advised that the next step would be to go to war against the USSR if the Russians decided to retaliate. The Bay of Pigs had triggered a similar crisis: now it was back. The argument now was stronger: such a war would wipe out the Communists' plans to take over the world. The threat to America, 90 miles from its borders, would be over. The price would be high, but it would be a quick war. An estimated seventy million people would die, but more Russians than Americans would be incinerated, and so, we would "win."

Ignored was the fact that there would be enough radioactive fallout to kill off the rest of the world's population a dozen times over.

Only people who worked with radiation, such as myself, fully realized that a nuclear war would destroy all life on the planet. Only Kennedy seemed to understand the dire consequences.

Chris Matthews summed up our base fears: "*To many of us growing up in the early Cold War, a nuclear war was taught as a real possibility...*

On a regular basis, the Sisters of Mercy at St. Christopher's drilled us on it, ordering us to squeeze ourselves under our desks. Fifteen minutes, we were told. That would be the time it took for the missiles to drop, the warning we'd each get to say our prayers. Next would come the "flash of light" that would mark the greatest and no doubt final conflagration in the history of mankind: the end of the world... World War II had us taught that the most unthinkable catastrophes could easily become reality... if one wasn't careful."

But World War II in Europe also taught another lesson: "shows of weakness" could encourage a stronger side to dare to wage war anyway, believing that significant opposition would not develop. Hitler did just that, taking country after country, until he was almost undefeatable.

Kennedy's dilemma rested on that fact: he had to avoid a nuclear war, but in the process, he had to avoid looking weak to the Soviets.

What if they accepted the offer and then went on to peremptorily strike the US anyway? JFK "had a first-hand reason to believe that Khrushchev was just the man to pull the trigger. At their meeting in Vienna the prior year, Mathews wrote, this was made stunningly clear. "I talked about how a nuclear exchange would kill seventy million people in ten minutes," Kennedy later told *Time's* Hugh Sidey, "and he just looked at me as if to say, 'So what?' My impression was that he just didn't give a damn if it came to that."

If Khrushchev ordered Castro to give the missiles back to Russia, to avoid an attack on Cuba by the US, what could the US give Khrushchev in return, to save his reputation? At the 11th hour, JFK used his brother to quietly approach a back-channel contact, a trusted old friend of Khrushchev, who was also unwilling to see the world go up in flames. And so, a deal was made. If Cuba returned its nuclear warheads to the USSR, the US would remove its [obsolete] Jupiter missiles deployed in Turkey that were armed with nuclear warheads aimed at Russia.

The deal would have outraged Kennedy's generals. JFK would have been accused of being a "pinko" that catered to the Communists.

But JFK gave Khrushchev a way out that saved face. The only other option was to proceed to war. Khrushchev later wrote,[37][38] "The climax came after five or six days, when our ambassador to Washington, Anatoly Dobrynin, reported that the President's brother, Robert Kennedy, had come to see him on an unofficial visit. Dobrynin's report

---

[37] CIA no-# doc released 2017: Tatel: 8/4/76 Sturgis phone calls– Fonzi collection

[38] https://nsarchive2.gwu.edu/nsa/cuba_mis_cri/moment.htm [*Khrushchev Remembers*, intro., commentary, and notes by Edward Crankshaw, trans. and ed. by Strobe Talbott (Boston: Little, Brown, 1970; citation from paperback edition, New York: Bantam, 1971), pp. 551-52]

went something like this: "Robert Kennedy looked exhausted. One could see from his eyes that he had not slept for days. He himself said that he had not been home for six days and nights. 'The President is in a grave situation,' Robert Kennedy said, 'and does not know how to get out of it.

We are under very severe stress. In fact, we are under pressure from our military to use force against Cuba. Probably at this very moment the President is sitting down to write a message to Chairman Khrushchev. We want to ask you, Mr. Dobrynin, to pass President Kennedy's message to Chairman Khrushchev through unofficial channels. President Kennedy implores Chairman Khrushchev to accept his offer and to take into consideration the peculiarities of the American system. Even though the President himself is very much against starting a war over Cuba, an irreversible chain of events could occur against his will. That is why the President is appealing directly to Chairman Khrushchev for his help in liquidating this conflict. If the situation continues much longer, the President is not sure that the military will not overthrow him and seize power. The American army could get out of control.'"

Khrushchev accepted the trade, writing, "It was a step that [Kennedy] knew threatened to render him finished politically...he did it anyway, keeping the deal a secret...If he hadn't done this all the other gutsy steps of those valiant "13 days" wouldn't have avoided war. It was not enough that JFK didn't blink when the Soviet ships neared the "quarantine" line patrolled by the U.S. Navy; it was Kennedy's willingness to cut a deal, under the table, with the enemy that saved the day and, really, the planet...Kennedy's deal with Khrushchev would lead to the first treaty of the Cold War: the 1963 limited nuclear test ban treaty."[39]

Florida's exile community, most of them located in Miami, were not pleased.

They felt they had been betrayed by the Bay of Pigs fiasco. They distrusted Kennedy. Because of my interest in defeating Castro, thanks to Tony Lopez-Fresquet, I now sided with the anti-Castroites.

Though I'd written a letter praising the new President and offering my services to my country, a letter that was answered personally by JFK's Latin American advisor and close friend, Ralph Dungan,[40] I didn't know what this great President had done to save us. Instead, my admiration for Kennedy had faded. By 1963, I hated the President for allowing Cuba to suffer so much under the hands of a tyrant. The name of the person who changed my mind might surprise you: his name was Lee Harvey Oswald.

---

[39] Chris Matthews, host of *Hardball* and author of *Jack Kennedy: Elusive Hero.* https://newrepublic.com/article/108575/how-john-f-kennedys-appeasement-strategy-averted-nuclear-holocaust He also commented: "Kennedy didn't see the Cuban crisis as a test of his manhood. He'd already passed such a test back in the Solomons as a sailor in World War II when he swam for four hours with a badly-burnt engineer on his back, when he'd kept his crew alive after his PT boat had been rammed by a Japanese destroyer."

[40] See my letter and Dungan's reply in the Appendix, which letters can also be found in The National Archives. Portions of my letter were underlined.

But in 1961, I was still in Bradenton. Manatee High was a warehouse of hormones, teeming with dreams, crowded with cliques, littered with romances, contaminated with rumors and decorated with the pageantry of sports teams, Drill Team, ROTC, marching bands, cheerleaders and screaming crowds in the football stadium.

Friday nights were a spectacle to behold. Though our big new house, with its pool and personal dock was on Snead Island, in a different school district, and my sister was transferred over, I was allowed to remain at Manatee High. It was a busy time. I was in no more class plays, as in my sophomore year, since my research consumed so many hours, but I stayed active in many clubs and committees.

There was the National Honor Society, science club, English club, art club, Tri-Hi-Y, the Prom Committee and *Societas Latina.* I would get the Art Award for my artwork in the school newspaper, *The Macohi,* and for winning top awards in state art competitions.[41] I got along well with most of my teachers and had fun dating, of course.

I even took some time to have some dates with Bob S____, a tall, shy underclassman who was on the track team. My friends couldn't believe I was dating an underclassman! But I had a reason: despite how sweet and tall and smart Bob was, he couldn't get a date, simply because he had a large, unsightly mole on his forehead. That was so wrong! He took me bowling a lot. Because he did, I would go on to get an athletic award in bowling at the University of Florida. Bob told me he had been adopted, which also made him feel shy. Later, Bob's mole was successfully removed. I think he had no more problems getting dates after that!

By New Year's, 1960, I had induced lung cancer in weanling white mice, but without enough time to test any of my hypotheses. Giving mice cancer had taken up the whole project! As a *St. Petersburg Times* article noted, four doctors, Dr. Milton Roggenkamp, Dr. Richard Meaney, Dr. James Moran, and Dr. John Shively assisted me when they could, and could verify I was working with mice and radiation. But I would make a disastrous error that would destroy all chances of winning big in the upcoming science fairs. I had been air-mailing tissue samples and dead mice to Oak Ridge, with dry ice. At the time, the scientists at Oak Ridge's "Mouse House" had a pioneer mentality that was not as stifled by regulations as were other parts of the "Secret City."

Mouse radiation wheel, Oak Ridge. (~1960)

[41] Manatee High had "Study Day" was held once a month so students could attend club meetings all day, if they didn't need tutoring due to por grades. It was a wonderful incentive to keep good grades. My friends and I joined lots of clubs together. These kinds of activities made us more well-rounded socially.

Manatee Hi Senior Hunts Cancer Cause
Senior Attends National Meet With Scientists
With two Nobel Prize winners, and leaders in cancer research, Judy Vary, Manatee High School senior, recently attended the National American Cancer Society Seminar for 1961 in St. Petersburg.
Dr. Howard Moore, head of the Roswell Park Memorial Institute for Cancer Research in Buffalo, New York, was so impressed by Judy and her cancer project that he offered her transportation to and from the Institute, room and board, plus $150 a month, to continue her research this summer in Buffalo.
She's Going
Judy is going; she's delighted! Of her work, she explains, "It's never been done before, and that's the reason these people are so interested." And "It's so encouraging," she adds, meaning the definite and positive results of her experiments. What Judy is trying to do is
DON'T WIGGLE — Judy Vary, top-notch MHS science student who has recently been honored in the Westinghouse Science Talent Search, administers cancer inducing materials into her white mouse — an important part of her cancer research project.

The Oak Ridge geneticists there were able to quickly identify lung cancers in my mice. Their sole interest was in what genetic damage was done to murine (mouse) lungs by tobacco-derived aerosols. My sponsoring doctors could have written statements that both my white mice and my black germ-free mice had developed lung cancer, but perhaps the biggest news was how fast the germ-free mice, in particular, had developed it. An even bigger problem was that my local doctors had not witnessed the miracle. Both batches of mice developed lung cancer within a week of each other and had to be shipped just as quickly to Oak Ridge for analysis. I thought Dr. Reyniers could replace them quickly, but Reyniers, thinking I'd be busy for months with the mice he'd given me, had no more to offer. All I had left were a few control germ-free mice, and about forty white control mice. The germ-free control mice had been exposed to radiation, but not to the aerosol, and were very ill. Worse, the title of my project -- experimenting with three exotic chemicals to see how they would protect normal cells when nearby cancerous cells were subjected to radiation-- meant nothing if I couldn't conduct the experiments. This was a blow. What could I do? Not much. Even so, I kept working.

My sponsoring doctors could have written statements that both my white mice and my black germ-free mice had developed lung cancer, but perhaps the biggest news was how fast the germ-free mice, in particular, had developed it. An even bigger problem was that my local doctors had not witnessed the miracle. Both batches of mice developed lung cancer within a week of each other and had to be shipped just as quickly to Oak Ridge for analysis. I thought Dr. Reyniers could replace them quickly, but Reyniers, thinking I'd be busy for months with the mice he'd given me, had no more to offer. All I had left were a few control germ-free mice, and about forty white control mice. The germ-free control mice had been exposed to radiation, but not to the aerosol, and were very ill. Worse, the title of my project -- experimenting with three exotic chemicals to see how they would protect normal cells when nearby cancerous cells were subjected to radiation-- meant nothing if I couldn't conduct the experiments. This was a blow.

What could I do? Not much. Even so, I kept working.

After all, I'd found a rapid way to produce lung cancer in mice without a functional immune system. It had not been easy. Germ-free mice required a lot of work to keep them alive and healthy. It took so much time that on Senior Photo Day, there was no chance to even fix my hair to look nice for the yearbook! In the photo, you can see my hair looking strangely flattened down. That's because I was wearing a hair net! I had also been collecting urine samples from four groups of mice, three of them living in smoke chambers. The photo shows how it's done—drop by drop. To obtain urine, I'd use a large eye-dropper to stimulate the urethral opening. A drop of urine would usually enter the eye-dropper. Urine from a dozen mice would make just enough to test. Paper chromatographs gave me a lot of data. The photo shows that this method is still being used today to collect mouse urine. I also

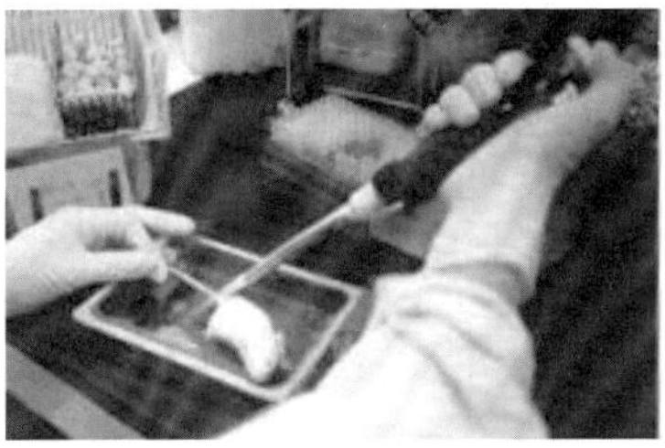

inspected urine drops under a microscope, looking for metastasized cancer cells. [42] It was time-consuming, but I was checking for the chemical **cotinine**, which helped give me an idea of how much nicotine was entering the lungs of my mice.

If I found a lot of WBCs or suspicious cells, I would kill the mouse to see if it had bladder cancer.[43] One time, in Mrs. Key's English class, when it was raining, she let me borrow her raincoat. I had been delayed and had to run to my lab under the stadium to remove mice from their smoke chamber.
In my haste, I knocked over some mouse urine from the control mice onto her raincoat. I tried to hose it off, but no luck.The stench was still heavy. Some kids, seeing my skirt so wet in one spot, thought I pee'd my pants! As for Mrs. Key, she was furious! She said she had to replace her raincoat. From then on, she hated me. She picked on me in her classroom, ending by giving me a "D" in English. To have been a pupil of MacKinlay Kantor, who had tutored me because he thought I was a talented writer, and then to receive a "D" in Mrs. Key's English class, was devastating. That "D" took me from Salutatorian (#2) to #21 in our class of ~495 students. But an even bigger concern was looming. All my work could soon be lost. I would move away to college, and then what? I'd even lose my network of doctors. My parents, consumed with their own problems, hoped I'd never leave. They wanted me to help run Dad's business so they could spend more time fishing and traveling.

Then, I had an idea. I recalled the list of conferences coming up that had been sent to me-- and there it was: the long-awaited meeting of the 4th Annual Science Writers Seminar, sponsored by the American Cancer Society, was imminent. Some of the best cancer research scientists in the world, including six Nobel Prize winners, were to reveal their latest findings and opinions to the world.

The most qualified medical news writers in America would be attending. *I had to go!* When Col. Doyle told me that no outsiders were allowed at this kind of professional event, I thanked him and went to Miss Dalrymple, who sometimes picked me up on weekends and drove me to school so I could take care of my mice. But she was going to visit her family with Mr. Schork for the weekend: Mr. Schork planned to ask her father for her hand in marriage.

---

[42] "Urine concentrations are generally much higher than those in plasma or saliva [18], and for this reason urine analyses can provide greater sensitivity for assessing low level exposure." [to nicotine] I also used column chromatography.
https://www.ncbi.nlm.nih.gov/pmc/articles/PMC3050598/)

The two lovebirds invited me to meet them after school for a coke at The Shake Pit, to talk things over, but there was never a more worthless meeting than that one! They could think of nothing but each other, holding hands under the table and once even kissing, right in public, even though they were teachers. I was glad for them, but still had no ride.

The Conference began the next day –Saturday! I called all four of my doctors, hoping one of them had been invited to the conference, but none had the status to attend. I called Dr. Reyniers, but he was out of town. As for my parents, they had a big fight that night after drinking too much rum and coke. They both took off in their brand-new cars in opposite directions. It was quiet and sad in our home: Lynda and I waited tensely, not knowing when they might return.

Our gardener didn't work on weekends, and Kateen, our maid, didn't drive. Saturday morning crawled by with no sign of our parents.

Then Lynda was picked up to go to a baton twirling training camp. It would last all weekend. Saturday was long gone when Burton Eppel showed up for a date. One of the rich kids in town, he had a Jaguar. First, we took care of my mice, and then, after discussing religion over a nice dinner (Burton said he wished to become a minister) we went to the movies. Always funny and joking, Burt really wanted to help me, but then he got a speeding ticket, and he knew he was going to get grounded.

Even so, as Saturday turned into Sunday, I held onto a thread of hope. We usually went to Mass on Sunday and met Grandpa there (He had no phone). Maybe my parents would finally show up. They didn't. We lived on a deserted island, with no bus or neighbors. It was Kateen's day off, and my sister was still gone at the twirling camp. Angrily, I paced the floor, raging that I was only 17 and so helpless. I swam lap after lap in the pool, our anxious poodle, Zsa Zsa, following me back and forth.

About 5 AM Monday morning, my parents finally showed up. They had reconciled and had been partying all night. My dad, just before he crashed, told me the gardener could drop me off at school early – his only concession to my pleadings. It was now the third day of the 5-day Conference. No more time could be wasted! On Sunday night I'd asked Tony, Burton Eppel and Bruce Korth to meet me early at school to help me. Thank God, they did, and I showed them how to take care of my mice for the next two days. Mastin Overstreet had brought over a lot of sawdust from the woodshop for bedding, so that was taken care of, too.

As the school bells rang, armed with my high school newspaper press pass and a stack of research records, I headed on foot for the Science Writers Seminar. It was March 20, 1961.

Behind me, I heard the tardy bell ring. All my friends were now in their seats in their Home Rooms: in a few minutes, the trumpet would be playing Reveille over the Intercom, the Pledge of Allegiance would follow, the morning's Scripture would be read, and then the school would report me missing. As I
jogged, I began calculating. How long would it take to get to reach St. Petersburg? My destination was 18.4 miles north, at The Doctor's Motel, an elegant resort on a white sand beach studded with palms, just off the Sunshine Skyway. I was athletic and determined. If a good Marathon runner could cover 26 miles in a few hours, I could jog 75% as far! My destiny was in the balance! After jogging three hours, I had covered 14 ½ miles and was seriously short of breath. The Skyway Bridge came to view, towering over the waves of Tampa Bay. Ahead were miles of causeways and bridges. At first, I was discouraged.

Then it hit me: why walk when I could ride? The highway was full of vehicles rushing by, headed in the right direction. I could hitch-hike there! As I pondered the obvious dangers for a lone young female in a vehicle with a total stranger, I spotted a Trailways bus coming up the highway and decided to try a trick inspired by a photo of my mother.

I raised the hem of my skirt high enough to show a little thigh. It worked. The driver stopped and let me on. I sat in the front and talked to him as we crossed the causeways, ascended the high bridge itself, then plunged back down to cross over yet more causeways.

When he heard I was headed for the Doctors Motel, he said, "Why, that's just a hop, skip and a jump from the highway! You can see the Skyway from there!"

It was such great luck, for I could get lost going around a corner! He dropped me off within sight of the long, stretched-out building. After crossing the ugly parking lot, I found the lobby and entered a hall so crowded with the Seminar's guest writers that they never noticed me. They were talking, arguing, patting each other on the back. I'd arrived during a break, which was coming to a close. The writers were now hurrying inside, into an already dark and silent meeting room.

As the doors began to close, I thrust myself between a pair of late-comers and flashed my high school press pass at the doormen, who waved me in with the others. *I made it!*

But once inside, it was hard to conceal the fact that I was a teenage girl in a room populated primarily by mature, grave-looking men in business suits. I hunted for an empty seat, as newsmen, scientists and doctors turned to stare at me. Finding a seat at last, I put my head down, as if that made me less visible, and nervously took out my notebooks. I was crashing their meeting, and everybody knew it. The next presentation began with an air of routine. Slides began flashing on the screen at the front of the room, but the whispers and pointing fingers continued. Maybe walking straight in wasn't such a good idea after all. Suddenly the slideshow came to a halt.

Several men in suits approached me, with a uniformed police officer. Busted! What could I do? Well, nothing.

The officer grabbed my elbow and was steering me up from my seat when a white-haired gentleman seated on the stage stood up and motioned with his hand to bring me forward. He had no idea who I was, but he was intrigued. This young person had dared intrude on the meeting! As I reached the base of the stage, a couple sitting to his right began whispering to him. Then the gentleman leaned down toward me and smiled. Without a word, he dismissed the security guard. Everything was OK. I was now his guest! An extra chair was brought to the foot of the stage and placed at the main off-stage table, where an elderly lady greeted me with a smile. The murmurs in the room faded away as the lights went down again, and the slide show resumed. Coincidentally, it was about a discovery at Notre Dame about tagging cancer cells with fluorescent dyes so they would glow in the dark and could be counted. The white-haired gentleman, I soon learned, was none other than Dr. Harold Diehl, the Senior Vice President in charge of research for the American Cancer Society. He was also in charge of the entire Conference. When he later left the stage and sat beside me, he gave me a stack of conference papers to hold. As I thanked him, he smiled and put a finger to his lips, so I began taking notes. During the break that followed, Dr. Diehl questioned me. Why had I crashed his Seminar? His attention increased when he heard that I had been conducting my own research on smoking and cancer, which he said he'd been keenly interested in since his days as the Dean of the University of Minnesota medical school. Reaching into his pocket, he gave me his business card. Then he introduced me to the Robinsons, who had encouraged Diehl to intervene on my behalf.

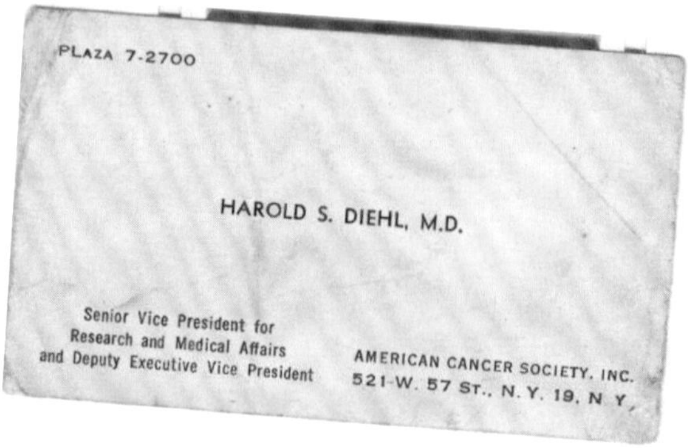

It took a while to realize that this was ***the* Sir Robert Robinson**, who had won the Nobel Prize in Chemistry. He was arguably the most famous organic chemist in the world and had been Knighted by the Queen of England. Learning about my Magnesium from the Sea project, Dr. Diehl would soon introduce me to another of his friends, also a Nobel Prize winner in Chemistry —Dr. Harold Urey**.** I knew of him, too, because of his work developing the atomic bomb, but when I first met him, all of that escaped me.

I was simply too bedazzled by everything. It wouldn't sink in until the next day, when we were in the car together on the way to my high school, that this was ***the real* Dr. Harold Urey!**

As we talked, I discovered that he was born in Indiana and that his grandparents were German, just like my Grandparents Vary. With his first degree in zoology, he was interested in cancer as well as math and physics. But when I first met him, Dr. Urey was just a stern man who asked a lot of questions. Before more presentations started, I was invited to a late lunch with the Robinsons, Dr. Urey, and Mr. and Mrs. Diehl. The table was just big enough for six. At lunch, I was a novelty with these scientists, who were curious as to what research I'd done.

Dr. Diehl[44] examines a science fair project: cigarette smoke collected and pumped into flasks, as judges look on. My project went on to use such smoke to induce lung cancer in mice.

My notebooks were passed around, but of course there wasn't time to delve into them. However, I was being asked many questions, so I replied, using all the medical terminology at my command to show them what I knew. I told them it all began with my dear Grandma dying of cancer. Next, I met Mrs. Watkins, and Dr. Ochsner, who after examining my line of cancerous fish, encouraged me to do research with mammals. His speech at Watson Clinic, declaring cigarette smoking led to lung cancer, gave me the path to follow.

---

[44] In 1962, Dr. Diehl invited the controversial Nobelist Linus Pauling to head the seminar. He was ultimately in charge of who could come and who couldn't. http://scarc.library.oregonstate.edu/coll/pauling/calendar/1962/02/index.html

Finally, when I described the aerosol I developed from cigarette products that had produced lung cancer in my mice in as few as seven days, Dr. Diehl got up and said, "I'm going to call Ochsner." When Dr. Diehl returned from his phone call, he told us he had asked if Dr. Ochsner could fly in to meet me. He was waiting for a call back. Dr. Diehl also brought another star in the anti-cancer galaxy with him to our table. His name was **Dr. George E. Moore**, the Director of the oldest cancer research center in the world, Roswell Park Memorial Institute for Cancer Research (RPMI) in Buffalo, New York. Moore, a genial man devoid of pretense, ran a staff of over 1,800 researchers and support teams.

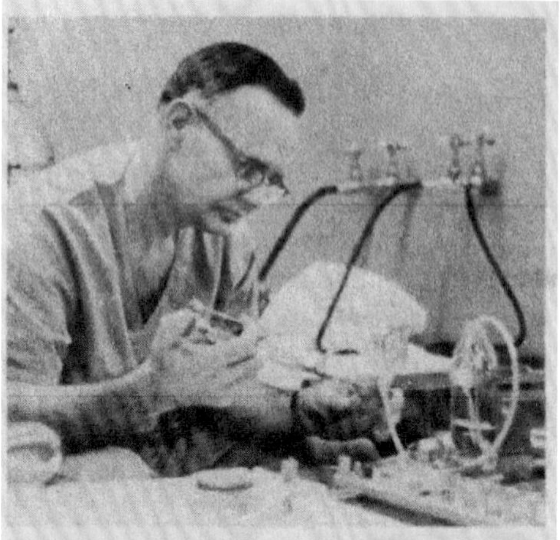
Dr. George E. Moore, Institute Director, shown here in his characteristic scrub suit, does surgery, administration, laboratory research, fund raising, public relations and flies his own plane to medical meetings—all with unique skill.

It turned out that Dr. Diehl, Dr. Ochsner and Dr. Moore had often testified together at hearings against various tobacco companies, arguing that smoking caused lung cancer. Therefore, all three doctors were highly interested in my work. RPMI was the first hospital in the United States to ban cigarette vending machines from its buildings. As we talked, at one point I mentioned my germ-free mice, and Dr. Moore almost jumped from his chair. "How did you get germ-free mice?" he asked. "We have just started to raise our own. It was the very devil to get them."

"I got them from Dr. Reyniers," I told him.

"She knows Reyniers," Diehl said.

"I heard that," Moore replied.

"And how long did you say it took you to develop lung cancer in your mice?" Dr. Diehl inquired, for the second or third time.

"The last time, it took only seven days," I replied.

"And you insist on that."

"Yes, I do."

The great scientists looked at each other and fell silent. Then Dr. Diehl gently informed me that only a select number of very sophisticated research labs in the country were able to give lung cancer to mice at all, and that it took months to do it. "Let me see your notebooks again," he commanded. I handed them over, only to see Diehl, Moore and Urey walk off with them. Mrs. Robinson, a lovely woman dressed in a business suit, saw my anxiety and took my hand. "They are quite enthralled with you," she said softly. "Don't be afraid." Just then, the afternoon sessions resumed. Once again, I sat at Dr. Diehl's table, and this time, Mrs. Diehl took her turn to comfort me. "If it took a hundred days to give your mice cancer, they would still be pleased, my dear," she assured me.

Noticing how swollen Mrs. Diehl's arms were, and because she was so charming and gracious, I felt comfortable asking her if she felt well. "Would you like to help me up to my room?" she asked. Of course, I would!

Once inside their suite, Mrs. Diehl explained that both her breasts had been removed due to cancer, and with them, the lymph nodes under both arms. This meant that fluids kept collecting in her arms, until it seemed her very skin might burst. To counter the swelling in her hands, she wore pressure gloves. It was hard for her to brush her own hair, so when Mrs. Diehl sat down before the bathroom mirror and tried to brush it, I did it for her, finishing up with a comb to separate out her curls. Then she removed her blouse to show me the scars from her surgery.

As I viewed the wasteland of scars across her chest, I recalled the sufferings of my Nanitsa. Then Mrs. Diehl talked at length of her long battle to stay alive, while frustration and anger arose in me all over again. This was the wife of one of the top cancer research scientists in the world. Was this the best they had to offer? Nothing but radiation, crude surgery and amputations? After Mrs. Diehl rested for half an hour, with her forearms in the air, flat on her back, the swelling was reduced enough so we could return to the Seminar, at which time she introduced me to two more Nobel Prize winners. They seemed to be everywhere! Dr. Diehl then called me to a phone. He had Dr. Ochsner on the line.

After teasing Ochsner that he had caused all this trouble by telling a girl to do cancer research after glancing at some black fish, Dr. Diehl handed me the phone. Dr. Ochsner, who barely remembered me, began asking questions. Then he said bluntly, "I've heard enough. Let me talk to Harold." I gave the phone back: a gesture from Dr. Diehl told me I was to return to the hall. Only later did I learn from Dr. Moore that Dr. Diehl told Ochsner that "George" (Dr. Moore) "had flown in for the Seminar." Moore could come get him! It turned out that Dr. Moore was a pilot, with his own plane. New Orleans was only two hours away. After Ochsner agreed to come, Dr. Diehl returned to his table and whispered to me, "If your records are correct and Col. Doyle and your doctors support your claim" I could count on the "team" of Diehl, Moore, Ochsner, Urey and Robinson to guide me into a stellar career in cancer research. "But first," he said, "we'll have to visit your school. Tomorrow." Full of tension, I forced myself to listen to more presentations, taking notes at a furious pace. I've already described who Dr. Moore was, but it was only at dinner that I learned that information for myself. He was incredibly important! And kind. This incredible man offered to get up at 5 am to fly to New Orleans to get Dr. Ochsner. At 7 PM, a medical news writer from *The San Francisco Examiner* drove me home, but the doctors kept my notebooks. As soon as I got home, I called Mrs. Watkins and told her the news. Learning that I knew Dr. Diehl's hotel room number, she called him at once, asking him to make me an "official guest writer" on behalf of the local American Cancer Society.

Then I could write articles for local newspapers, which would be good publicity. Next, I told my sister about the day's adventures, but there was no chance to talk to Mother and Dad: they had gone to Tampa "to meet an insurance broker" for Dad's business. I was uncomfortable about that.[45] When Dad booked TV shipments to his stores from Chicago, the Mafia stepped in. To make sure his TV sets would arrive safely, he had to meet "an insurance broker" and pay "an insurance premium." A different news writer picked me up early the next morning, and once again, I sat with Mrs. Diehl, taking notes. A badge stuck to my blouse proclaimed that I was a "guest writer" for the local ACS. One presentation got my full attention: Dr. Ludwik Gross, on concluding his lecture on the origins of cancer, offered that most malignancies, in his opinion, arose from cancer-causing viruses. *What? Most cancers were caused by viruses?* As my mind tuned over this frightening thought, Dr. Ochsner entered the hall, causing everyone's head to turn. After shaking a few hands, Ochsner spotted the only girl in the hall – me- and came over to our table. "So it's you, again!" he rumbled. "We want to take a look at your experiments." He then left the table to sit somewhere else.

Senior Attends National Meet With Scientists

With two Nobel Prize winners, and leaders in cancer research, Judy Vary, Manatee High School senior, recently attended the National American Cancer Society Seminar for 1961 in St. Petersburg.

Dr. Howard Moore, head of the Rosewell Park Memorial Institute for Cancer Research in Buffalo, New York, was so impressed by Judy and her cancer project that he offered her transportation to and from the Institute, room and board, plus $150 a month, to continue her research this summer in Buffalo.

She's Going

Judy is going; she's delighted! Of her work, she explains, "It's never been done before, and that's the reason these people are so interested." And "It's so encouraging," she adds, meaning the definite and positive results of her experiments. What Judy is trying to do is to protect normal tissue from the adverse efefcts of irradiation while this radioactive bombardment destroys cancerous tissue, and to retard the movement of the cancer to other parts of the body. She has tried her theories with white mice, keeping exact records and pre-

The seminar ended at about noon, after which Dr. Ochsner, Dr. Diehl, Dr. Urey and I were taken by car to Bradenton. The school office could not detain me for being absent and tardy without a note from my parents when I entered with three distinguished-looking men in business suits. When Col. Doyle met them, they asked to see my laboratory. I was told to wait as the four men crossed the street, heading to the stadium. After some time, they returned, and I was asked to follow them into Col. Doyle's empty classroom. It was time for a talk.

"It's never been done before, and that's why these people are so interested." - jvb

I was asked to bring out my hundreds of microscope slides and preserved lung

[45] To observe how deeply the Mafia had infiltrated Florida, see http://documents.theblackvault.com/documents/fbifiles/Wackenhut_Corp.-Tampa-2_text.pdf

cancer specimens. They were carefully inspected with the microscope Bausch & Lomb had given me. Then I was asked to leave the room.
As I stood in the hall, my friend Bruce Korth came by. “Dammit, Judy,” he said, “what in hell is going on in there?”

Bruce liked being irreverent and used curse words as his way of rebelling, which got him suspended from school once. But he was a brilliant thinker who eventually became a clinical psychologist. I told him my fate was being decided by three men I hardly knew. I was soon called back in, to a flood of compliments and praise. What an excellent project! What a well-designed project! It was brilliant, they agreed. I had indeed produced lung cancer in mice faster than anyone else, in a poorly-equipped lab under a stadium, with a dirt floor. Then the tone changed. There wasn't enough time to contact all my doctors about this project, they said gravely, but they definitely would. There were some serious safety issues, involving radiation and cancer viruses. I did not anticipate what was about to happen next. After some discussion of the many dangers my experiments invited, they concluded that no high school student should be allowed to do this kind of research. It should not happen again. I had been playing with fire. To be more precise, they were shutting it down. I had knocked myself out to get these experts to come to our school and look at my research, and, *for what?*
Now this had happened! In what should have been the Colonel's hour of triumph, the most powerful and respected cancer research scientists in the country were insisting that my laboratory must be dismantled at once. Time to take a deep breath and think. A good chess player always thinks several moves ahead.

While extremely unhappy about the order to shut down my lab, I kept control of my reactions, realizing that their intent was not to punish me. These people had just praised my work. But these eminences saw the dangers clearly. As for me, I had learned about the possibility of triggering cancer-causing viruses by radiation only this morning. I had no way to anticipate this sudden decision.

But high school was nearly over: I would be graduating in 6 weeks. What would happen to the lab then? Would I show up at college dragging hundreds of mice in cages along with me? I'd accomplished part of my dream. Some of the top cancer scientists in the country knew me now. They had acknowledged the value of my work before telling me to shut it down. To ameliorate some of the pain, I was now made privy to the good news: I was invited to get fast-track training at Dr. George Moore's Roswell Park Memorial Institute! While it was too late to apply for a spot in RPMI's competitive international Summer Training Program for students, teachers and med students, Dr. Moore had arranged for me to join the program anyway, by placing me as a college student in his own private laboratory there (I qualified, having been accepted by several universities as a college freshman in the Fall). I would also attend weekly seminars held by Dr. Edwin Mirand, who ran the competitive summer program that was already closed to new applicants.

Most of my time would be spent with Dr. Moore and his friend, Dr. James T. Grace, who was doing world-class work with irradiated cancer-causing viruses. At last, I was on my way to fulfill my life's goal– to cure cancer! Little did I realize how that dream would be used to destroy lives – not to save them.

Chapter Four
Roswell Park

On April 6, 1961, Mr. Sharer drove 8 science seminar students, including me, to Lakeland Florida to compete in the State Science Fair. I had won First Prizes at the high school and county level, but there would be no grand prize this time for Judy. Forbidden to bring my cancerous mice to the fair, I didn't have the stars of the show with me. I could only display control animals, journals, and stacks of X Rays and slides. The busy judges, upon being told that my lab had been shut down over safety concerns, were not impressed. I did receive a collection of small scholarships and minor awards from organizations like the ACS, the American Medical Association and the Florida Medical Association.

But I felt that I'd let my school down. Still, there was one more event - the Westinghouse Science Talent Search Competition--for which hundreds gathered. During my presentation, questions were thrown at me from every possible angle by a panel of scientists who had studied my paper and statistics. They were truly qualified to judge my work. However, my statistics were 'off' due to 24 missing germ-free mice that could not be mentioned due to their possible contamination by a cancer-causing virus.

Even so, my doctors had verified that I'd induced lung cancer in my Webster Swiss mice, and I received The Award of Excellence. Upon our return, the school newspaper ran an article about my adventures that spring, including the ACS Science Writer's Seminar.

Distracted by the Bay of Pigs invasion that upset Tony so much, I didn't get around to writing the news story that Mrs. Watkins had asked for as "guest writer" at the American Cancer Society's Science Writer's Seminar, [46] so when Mrs. McCartney, my former biology teacher, asked if I had written anything, I decided to contact Dr. Urey and Sir Robert Robinson. They had asked me to keep in touch. I was able to call both men to get information on some of the talks I'd missed. By that time, both Urey and Robinson had read copies of my Science Talent Search paper, and now they took the time to offer advice on how to pre-plan my next research projects. Both men gave me over an hour of time mentoring me on how to design cancer research projects.

They stressed the advantages of teamwork, and how I should find like-minded researchers. Dr. Urey went a step further, promising that if I went to college in Indiana, especially at the University of Chicago, he would be on call, even though he was now living in California. [47] We both shared an inordinate love for Indiana.

---

[46] See the Appendix for this article and a few others that were saved.

[47] When Dr. Urey died, he was buried in DeKalb County, Indiana, where he'd been so happy as a boy, living on the family farm. He understood why I loved Indiana!

he Robertson said they hoped to see me one more time before they left for London. They were visiting relatives of Sir Robert's wife near Buffalo, New York. Recalling that my mother wouldn't let me fly, the Robinsons promise to buy train tickets for me. When I told Mrs. Watkins about the free train ride, not wanting me to travel all the way to New York alone, she volunteered to come most of the way. Her health had been declining recently, and I was worried about her, but my precious friend insisted. "I want to visit relatives in Philadelphia," she said. "What if I ride the train with you as far as Penn Station? Then later, when I come up to Roswell Park, you can introduce me to Dr. Moore."

That's when I learned that Mrs. Watkins had made an appointment to see if anything could be done about her advanced pancreatic and stomach cancer. I was shocked. Stunned. Why would God let somebody like Georgianna Watkins, who helped so many people recover from cancer operations, who raised countless thousands to provide free treatment for cancer patients, get cancer herself? Unfair! Horrible! I went home and cried myself to sleep.

The failure of the Bay of Pigs invasion in Cuba happened next. It devastated Tony, who blamed President Kennedy. At that time, Senator Smathers' secretary called to remind me that the Senator had donated to my college fund again and had a full scholarship waiting for me at the University of Florida. I told her I was grateful but hadn't decided. Perhaps with the news of the Bay of Pigs (April 17-21) fresh on his mind, the Senator then took the phone to inquire "about the Lopez-Fresquet boys." I told him they were unhappy about it, but otherwise, they were fine. A welcome relief from politics and cancer came with an art award. On April 18th. *The Bradenton Herald* published a story about my winning a state art competition in sculpture. I also won in watercolor, with a war theme. "Woman of War" was part of my anti-war art series (1960-1965). Art and poetry were a source of welcome relief from killing mice and parrying the sour mood of my Cuban friends. Then there were the petty jealousies any form of success attracts. Losing my rank of Salutatorian made my father sensitive to school politics, and when another unfair matter occurred, he became angry. Col. Doyle asked my family to allow two top male science students to receive the school's Outstanding Science Achievement Award, and the Bausch & Lomb Science Award, instead of me. He argued that because I had won all the important exterior awards and scholarships for the past two years, these students had nothing to point at in their fields to help them get scholarships. He was especially concerned with the need for one student to impress the entrance committee at West Point. Col. Doyle, a

West Point graduate, was sponsoring him.
When the Awards Ceremony was held, my father came to observe if Doyle would really go through with it. Dad refused to sit, standing in the back of the assembly hall, his arms folded, frowning his disapproval. “An Art Award!” he huffed, when I was called to the front to receive it.

“You can see the cards are stacked against you, Judy,” he told me, when I returned to his side with the medal. “Give up your dreams. These people will always screw you over.” He was bitter because I’d given many speeches to civics groups, raising over a hundred thousand dollars for the Science Building. I’d praised the school to reporters and doctors, and with Col. Doyle, had brought in microscopes, chemicals, equipment and even black-out curtains so we could see science movies for the first time. “It’s because you are a female!” he huffed again. “If they would let females into West Point, Doyle would be waltzing you right up the aisle. Instead, it’s *him.*” When both science awards indeed went elsewhere, Dad took me by the arm and drove me home, not allowing me to attend the awards banquet.

“If you think this world is going to let you do what men do,” he said, “forget it. Look what MHS just did to you! And that D in English! Your hormones will betray you next,” he said, ominously. “That’s why there aren’t any female scientists worth a penny,” he scoffed. “That big waste of time you called ‘cancer research’ is going to get you nowhere. The world has no use for women in science.”

“I’m going to Roswell Park, Dad,” I reminded him. “Mark my words,” he replied. “Nothing will come of it. Name one famous woman scientist, and I’ll change my mind.”

“Madame Curie,” I told him. “She won the Nobel Prize.”

“She was helped by her husband,” he answered, “and then she died of radiation poisoning. Name another!” I couldn’t. Not in science. “If you think you’re any different,” Dad said, “forget it.” He chastised me for missing my own Prom. “In the end, working night and day with those germ-free mice,” he snorted, “what good did it do? You never got to wear your Prom dress. You looked like hell for your own Senior picture.” [48] That night, my father got quite drunk and came staggering into my bedroom. Seeing me reading my Yearbook, he ripped it out of my hands. “You’re never going to see this damned thing again!” he fumed, throwing it aside.

---

[48] A hostile reporter found Steve Bassett – not a friend-- who claimed 45 years later that I pee’d my pant, out of fear of having to recite in front of Key’s English class. His claim took most of the space of the reporter’s story about me. The “pee” came from the odor of spilled mouse urine on my teacher’s raincoat. One “lab tech” then mocked the idea of collecting mouse urine, displaying an abysmal ignorance about the need to detect murine metastases to the kidneys and bladder.
https://journals.sagepub.com/doi/pdf/10.1258/0023677041958945 “Experimental animal urine collection: a review”

"I'm going to keep it. And twenty years from now, when you're a nobody, I'll go through it with you and show you the bankers, the lawyers, the business owners. There won't be a woman on the list," he predicted. "We never had a son," he went on, "and all my wishes for a son meant I gave you training in electronics. But you went into biology! That's your hormones, working against you! But you won't be giving us any grandchildren either. The doctors told us you're as sterile as a mule." With that, Dad picked up my Yearbook and stomped away, leaving me in tears.

Dad felt happier when my cousin Ronnie asked if he could live with us. His parents (my Auntie Elsie and Uncle Emery), missing Florida living, had purchased a house some distance from us on the same island, but would only be staying during the winter months. Without a car, Ronnie's only transportation to junior college, where he was studying electrical engineering, would be my parents. My father welcomed him with open arms, thrilled when Ronnie said he hoped one day to become a rocket scientist. My mother was happy, too, because she had a golfing partner: neither Lynda nor I were interested in golf. Ronnie seemed to fill the void that my father felt for not having a son.

And despite the pain in his infected leg that made him drink too much, Ronnie's presence helped him cut back. My mother, too, loved Ronnie. So Lynda would not be alone. The burden I'd felt most of my life, to protect my sister from my parents when they got drunk, was now lifted.

It was almost time to leave for Roswell Park, but I still had some innocent mice left - the control animals, free of cancer. I had set aside about 50, including Romeo, who was now a crotchety old man. These mice presented no danger to anyone, but nobody would take a mouse from my cancer project! Undeterred, I brought an empty aquarium to school (it used to hold the black mollies) and loaded the mice into it, giving Romeo a kiss goodbye. Not wanting a single soul to know what I was going to do, I had a hard time carrying the heavy aquarium with all those mice in it very far. What on earth had I been thinking?

As I struggled along, I modified my plan to let the mice go at the lush, weedy banks of the Manatee River. I'd never get the mice that far! But at the end of the bridge over Ware's Creek, I spotted a stately landmark, close to a church: a magnificent banyan tree, with dozens of twisting roots where little mice could safely hide. It was the perfect solution!

I set the aquarium down, tipped it over, and let an avalanche of white mice scamper away. The next day, there was a newspaper article on the front page, saying I was leaving for Roswell Park after doing cancer research with white mice for two years. But was anybody fooled when, deeper inside the very same newspaper, it was reported that a quiet women's Church Social, being held on the parklike grounds of the church by its beautiful banyan tree, had turned into a scream-fest when dozens of white mice came running in? "They weren't even afraid of the cat we brought over, hoping to make them run away!" one lady reported. The mice were climbing up the chairs and clinging to women's legs. Yes, it was time to leave Bradenton!

==== ==== ==== ==== ====

"I'll miss you so much, Juduffski," my mother said. "I don't want you to be lonely there," she went on, "so here..." I couldn't believe my eyes. My mother handed me a big metal cage with two parakeets in it. I had given them to her for Mother's Day, and now she was returning them. With Col. Doyle waiting in his car, and Mrs. Watkins quietly sitting in the front seat, it was no time to argue, so with a big suitcase and my purse in one hand, and the cage with the parakeets in the other, I navigated toward the car with the load, when Daddy rushed forward and helped me load.

Then I said goodbye to my parents, Lynda, Ronnie and Grandpa. Col. Doyle drove us to the train station in Tampa, where we told him goodbye. I never realized we'd never meet again. As Mrs. Watkins sat with our luggage and the parakeets at the platform, I went inside and stood in line to purchase two sandwiches at the station's lunch counter, hoping Mrs. Watkins would want one of them later. A poor, elderly Negro (the term back then) was standing in line at the counter to get one, but she was ignored. As I was handed my sandwiches, the train pulled up. We all had to rush to board the train, but after Mrs. Watkins was settled in, I found the old Negro lady and gave her my sandwich. I just couldn't eat it. It was a long train ride. Mrs. Watkins seemed to get weaker every hour, and by the time we reached Penn Station, I was so concerned that I got off the train with her. "You'll miss your connection!" she objected.

When her relatives finally arrived, I offered them the parakeets, with no success. On the next train to Buffalo, despite every effort to give the parakeets away, the little critters were still with me when I arrived in town, four hours late. The welcoming party to take me to Roswell Park was long gone, so I found a cab. Fortunately, the cabbie took the parakeets and cage as a tip!

When I arrived at RPMI, an irritated Dr. Edwin Mirand accosted me in the hall and informed me that I was the last participant to arrive. I also missed the IQ test, messing up his statistics. I may have missed the IQ test, but I didn't miss the photo shoot, being one of six chosen for interviews. The newspaper article mentions the program lasting "eight weeks," but Helsa and I, who were now put of high school, were in the three-month program for college undergrads. My "YWCA" receipt for my last week at Roswell Park is marked 8/25 --one week's rent, paid.

It was photographed long ago on top of Roswell Park's blue brochure, where you can barely see the 3-month appointment for college undergrads. The $150/month stipend (about $1,400 in 2021 funds) can also be seen. The stipend's amount is repeated in several newspaper articles as well. That record, and others, would later be altered. (By whom?)

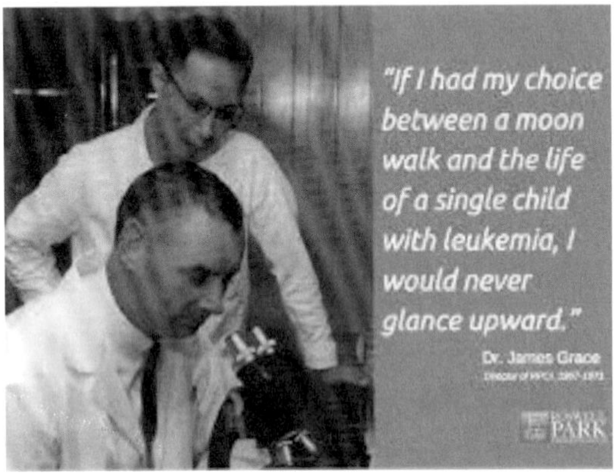

Dr. Mirand knew I would be attending his seminars and a few of his Program's training sessions, as a last-minute addition to his program. He had not chosen me – his boss had. And I'd be working primarily with his boss, Dr. Moore, and Dr. James Thomas Grace, his boss' best friend (Dr. Grace become the next Director when Dr. Moore left a few years later). Thus, many of my activities were beyond his control. I was "the outsider" and he didn't particularly like the fact that I wasn't a fulltime participant in his meticulously-designed program. I hoped we'd get along, despite our bad start. I soon met Dr. Grace, one of the kindest of men. He had lost his little boy to leukemia and was determined to conquer it. The SV-40 Monkey Virus was a concern to Dr. Grace, too: he co-authored Dr. Mirand's SV-40 monkey virus paper.[49] The big question was,: could humans get cancer from a monkey cancer virus?

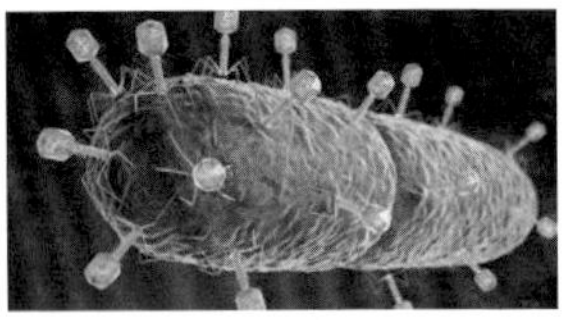

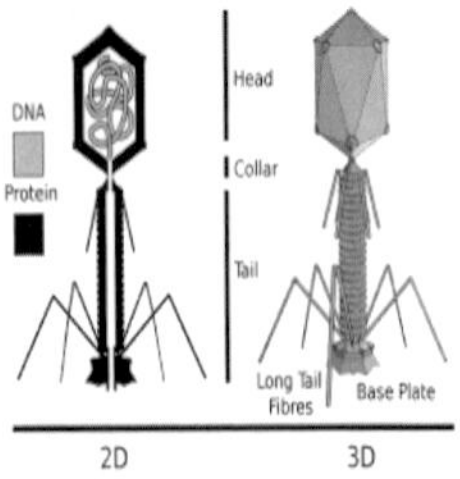

Dr. Ludwik Gross had discussed the matter at the Science Writer's seminar. The polio vaccine was grown on Rhesus monkey kidneys that turned out to be infected with countless "simian" viruses, including SV-40 (simian virus #40). There were 39 other simian viruses previously identified in the monkey kidney stew. Dr. Moore's assistants were looking into that question and much more. The Haas husband-wife team of doctors and to "Art," Dr. Moore's protégé of two years, were already wrapped up in projects. Art was studying bacteriophages. Bacteriophages ("phage" means 'to eat" in Greek) are versatile, powerful little viruses that may be the most beneficial of all to humans. They can be genetically tailored to attack almost any kind of bacteria or living cell. including cancer cells. Art was way ahead of his time. The photo shows bacteriophages dining on a bacterium. If Big Pharma had funded bacteriophage research (cheap cure?) instead of chemo (expensive treatments), I believe many types of cancer would

[49] In 1963, Dr. Mirand co-authored an important article: "Human Susceptibility to a Simian Tumor Virus." We will have more to say about simian (monkey) viruses.

have been wiped out in the 1970's.[50] The Student Program run by Dr. Mirand started the next day. Every morning, there was a general teaching for all, by world-class lectures and instructors in various fields of cancer research. There was also an excellent weekly seminar directed by Dr. Mirand. But then groups went off to learn basic techniques in various labs, while I went straight to Dr. Moore's personal lab instead.

Dr. M. A. Bender — John Alexander, Helsa Servis — William Kimber, Moira Burke — Stanley Adamson, Judith Vary

. . . Roswell scientist discusses radioactive isotopes with students

Students Start Roswell Park Work

By PAUL WIELAND

Scientific research with a high school beat began its eighth summer yesterday, brightening the ever-busy Roswell Park Memorial Institute with young people who want to be "in the know."

A group of 66 high school students and June graduates from five states and Canada started work at the cancer research institute under grants mainly supplied by the State of New York and the National Science Foundation.

But their work isn't on the high school level. Far from it.

Working closely with the institute's scientists, the students have plunged into the maze of highly - complicated research techniques being developed to fight cancer.

Officially titled the "Summer Research Participation Program," by its originator, Dr. Edwin A. Mirand, the summer study period provides outstanding science students with opportunities for original and sometimes rewarding research.

National Recognition

"Last summer we had a young lady studying here whose work in the sex determination of chickens was not only outstanding, but earned her national recognition," said Dr. Mirand, director of the program. "These young people are brilliant," he said, "and we try to give them the opportunity to display that brilliance usefully."

The teen-agers began their eight weeks yesterday with a battery of tests to determine their scientific "I-Q's," tests which will be repeated at the end of the program to ascertain the progress they have made.

Following tests, the youngsters were taken on a tour of the institute. The tour was punctuated by calculated once-overs of strange and complicated-looking pieces of scientific apparatus.

The conversation of the students was a strange mixture of the usual teen talk and an abundance of scientific words with little or no meaning to the layman.

Blond Helsa Servis, an 18-year-old June graduate from Silver City, N.M., said she would study neurosurgery techniques during her stay here. She'll attend San Jose State in San Jose, Calif., this fall.

To Study Radio Biology

Dark-haired Judith Vary, 18, from Palmetto, Fla., bubbled with the serious-sounding observation that the institute would "certainly be intellectually stimulating." She will study radio biology.

Dr. Mirand said "whatever they would study, they would study well," as he strode down the corridor to begin discussion of radioactive isotopes with a student.

In the afternoons, these students divided into small groups, to work on a project with their doctor or scientist in charge.

Some had a personal project, such as learning how to identify a certain kind of cancer. The students had 8 hours at RPMI, M-F, whereas Art and I often put in 12 hours, as well as occasional Saturdays, since we were doing some cutting-edge work with cancer. Others with similar long hours were post-grads, science instructors in training, and med school interns. This fast-track training at Roswell Park was conducted between Monday, June 5, 1961 and Saturday, Sept. 2, 1961.

---

[50]In 2000, I finally had enough recognition to dare ask various labs if they would consider bacteriophage. Not one lab was interested. Today, bacteriophage research is making great progress toward cures in many fields, including cancer.

Each group spent afternoons with their sponsoring doctor after a morning spent learning a basic skill or attending a seminar. I was not a member of any of these groups, though I attended all of Dr. Mirand's seminars, plus a few basic sessions in areas where I had no experience. One such session was on how to "harvest" and prepare tumors from humans, dogs and rabbits for tissue culture. Otherwise, I went straight to Dr. Moore's or to Dr. Grace's lab, with "radiobiology" my core work with cancer viruses. As one of only two students assigned to Dr. Moore's personal lab, red-headed Art and I did some intense research, as well. An ongoing project was testing the effect of various additives on cancer cell growth.

We tested hundreds of variations using thousands of cultures, helping to refine Dr. Moore's soon-to-be-famous RPMI 1640 formula for *in vitro* use.[51] [52]As Director, Moore came and went at will, with Dr. Haas and his wife and Art and I working on his various projects. Art and I also had personal projects. On most Saturdays, while the Program students enjoyed special outings and weekend activities, Art and I might still be working. To compensate for these six-day work-weeks, Dr. Moore often made Sundays special, taking five or six of us that he liked to his home for a nice dinner. Other times, we joined the staff for games of volleyball in the gym. The rent receipt for my room at the "Y" shows my housing was unusual, but there was nowhere else for me to go –I had, after all, been added to the list that had already been closed. At first, I liked the "Y." While Mirand's students went back and forth on a special bus, I could come earlier and leave later, since the "Y" was on a major bus line. I would have done better in the dorms, though, because the "Y" was filled with cancer patients who lived there to be close to treatments in RPMI's hospital. While living at the "Y" several residents died: there was a heart attack, a blood clot, dehydration from vomiting, an infection from surgery, and a sudden death from chemotherapy.

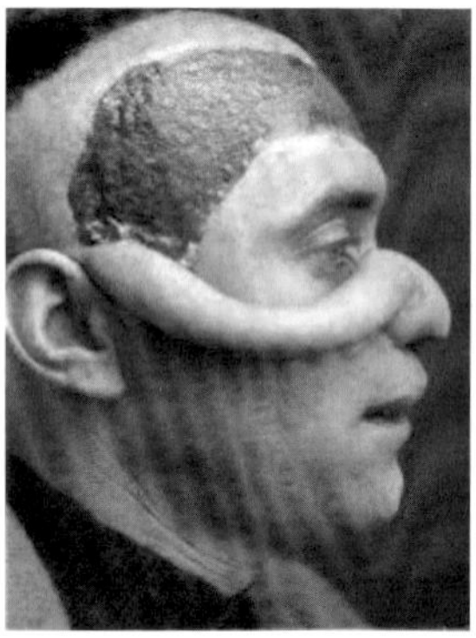

[51] In 1946, Dr. Joseph Hoffman, who had worked on the Manhattan Project, directed one of the first studies on radiation at RPMI.

[52]"During the 1960s, Roswell Park Director George Moore, MD, and his team developed a new medium to support the growth of both healthy and leukemic cells outside the body so they could be studied in the laboratory. Named RPMI 1640, for **R**oswell **P**ark **M**emorial **I**nstitute, today the medium is an important tool for studying not only cancer but also Parkinson's Disease, multiple sclerosis, chronic obstructive pulmonary disease (COPD), rheumatoid arthritis and other diseases. It is also used to support tissue transplantation for burn and trauma patients. Dr. Moore chose not to patent RPMI 1640. It is now manufactured by several companies ...and shipped to research laboratories all over the world."

Others were under observation while they grew "pedicle flaps" to restore tissues to a missing nose or missing jaw. There was a lot of interacting with the cancer patients and animals at RPMI who were suffering, only to return to the "Y" where life became even more difficult, as alone, I tried to help these patients make it through one emotional or physical crisis after another. All the pain I witnessed made me turn to God in desperate prayers. Sometimes I'd fall asleep on my knees, praying, and since the floor of that "Y" happened to be paved with ceramic tiles, my knees were objecting!

At this time, to get some relief, I began painting landscapes at night in my room, which attracted the attention of three nursing students who lived there. We became friends, along with an Italian girl, "Gianna," (Jeannette) who was there for the summer to get her English teaching certificate. Still, my personal project was exciting, and I loved my work.

I was tracking differences between irradiated cancerous tissues taken from mice and marmosets treated with *B*-mercaptoethylamine (MEA) injected under their tumors compared to those with tumors that were only irradiated. There were some encouraging results, but in the end, MEA proved too toxic to use on humans.

One Sunday, as I was jogging toward town (always running, never walking!) I paused at a façade that said 'D'Youville College." And there was Jeannette, with all three nurses! They all attended D'Youville, a Catholic girls' college specializing in health care, nursing and classical education. Some of the girls studying nursing there were planning to become nuns. Now I had a place to go to Mass, with healthy young women leading normal lives. I especially liked Jeanette. I ended up spending two weekends with her at her home near the Canadian border. Without going into details, her brother, as it turned out, was with the Mafia. As luck would have it, we had a natural liking for each other.

Is it true that all mafia guys like to cook spaghetti? This guy sure did! One weekend, we went to Niagara Falls and Crystal Beach. [53] It was touching to me that no matter how many pygmy marmosets (thumb-high primates related to monkeys) Dr. Moore had to kill, he would put each marmoset "to sleep" one at a time in a peaceful setting. He would pet them and give them a treat before etherizing them. It was evidence to me of his humanity and gentleness. Before summer's end, I also began a project studying melanogenesis. Atop that, two or three afternoons a week, I learned advanced techniques for identifying and safely handling cancer-causing viruses.

I studied and dealt with the Friend Virus, the Yaba Virus, the Coxsakie Virus, and in particular, the SV-40 Monkey Virus, in Dr. Grace's lab.

[53] This is how I later learned from Lee Oswald that he had gone to Crystal Beach, too! This helped me to eventually find the Charles Thomas family witnesses.

Dr. Moore, Dr. Grace and Dr. Mirand published many research papers together on these viruses.[54] A few of their projects that I knew about in 1961 are shown below. These titles are important because they reflect the kind of training I got and the shop talk going on. Note how many of these studies were involved with **inducing** cancers:

"Effect of chemotherapeutic agents on Friend virus induced leukemia in mice," Proc Soc Exp Biol Med. 1961 Nov; by E A MIRAND, J T GRACE Jr
"**Morphology of viruses isolated from human leukemic tissue**," Surg Forum. 1961; by J T Grace Jr, S J MILLIAN, E A MIRAND, R S METZGAR
"Induction of tumors by a virus-like agent(s) released by tissue culture," Surg Forum. 1961; by E A MIRAND, D T MOUNT, G E MOORE, J T GRACE Jr, J E SOKAL
"**Induction of leukemia in rats with Friend Virus**," Virology. 1962 Jun; E A MIRAND, J T GRACE JR.
"**Transmission of Friend virus disease from infected mothers to offspring,"** Virology. 1962 Mar; by EA MIRAND, J G HOFFMAN, J T GRACE Jr, P J TRUDEL. Some of the research was not competed for several years. One that was ongoing in 1961 wasn't published until 1965: "**Relationship of viruses to malignant disease. Prt 1: Tumor induction by SE Polyoma virus**," Surgery. 1965 Jul; by E A MIRAND,J T GRACE Jr, G E MOORE, D MOUNT. Note: every mention of induction of tumors in these published, peer-reviewed articles was associated with **a transmissible cancer virus**!

No wonder my lab was shut down! Keeping cancer cells alive in test tubes or in flasks is still a difficult task today. But with a mere pH adjustment, the formula we were working on was keeping certain cancer cells alive *in vitro* (glass test tubes, etc.) longer than any other medium on the planet. By now, Dr. Reyniers had discovered I was at RPMI and kindly called. He was fund-raising for his organization "Research, Inc." to provide medical students with germ-free mice. Wanting to help, I contacted my "Y" friends at D'Youville College, as well as Dr. Moore, about putting my paintings up for sale in a one-man show, with net profits to go to Dr. Reyniers' germ-free mouse fund-raiser. My first one-man show at D'Youville, raised enough cash to frame the remaining works of art so they would sell for a good price at the Roswell Park exhibition. [55]

On many levels, this summer would be a baptismal immersion into the tragedy of cancer. Roswell Park was a magnet for people who came too

---

[54] Edward T. Haslam found a list of their publications. These projects took one or more years to complete, to be peer-reviewed, and then to get published. A 1962 article was likely to describe work finalized in 1961 or 1960).

[55] My artwork to benefit "Research Inc." is mentioned in newspaper articles. On 8/25 I paid my last week of rent, as Sept. 1 was my last day at the "Y." I was paid $150/mo as the brochure indicates, perhaps through a fund numbered '8312.' I returned Sept. 5 to Bradenton after spending a few days with Dr. Moore.

late to be saved, who often courageously donated their last days alive as volunteers for a higher good. Thus, I saw people in the most advanced stages of the disease, fighting for their lives. I saw patients exposed to radiation, full of trust and hope, and watched them die. I saw others slip into death after being injected with chemicals they thought might save them. I saw limbs amputated and organs removed.

I saw death on the operating table.

I saw people so addicted to cigarettes that even when their cancerous tongues and jaws were removed, they still refused to quit, smoking their cigarettes through the wet, red hole that remained! A woman down the hall from me, who had part of her cancerous brain removed, had seizures two or three nights a week. I would awake hearing her scream and would rush to her room, grab a tongue depressor, and stick it between her jaws so she wouldn't bite her tongue off. Her husband had abandoned her after her operation and Roswell Park was paying her bill at the "Y."

I'd also made friends at the "Y" with a beautiful black woman, a trained opera singer. Sadly, she was battling cancer of the throat. As the summer progressed, so did her cancer, pulling her down, day by day.

She became a frail ghost of her former self, unable to speak above a whisper, yet every day, she thanked God that she was still alive.

The laboratories at Roswell Park also used many kinds of animals for their experiments. I saw their suffering in a new light. I could see the sadness in their eyes as they looked upon a world composed of metal walls, monotony and pain. I saw their fear when their human keepers approached. One day, in a "basics" lesson about dogs as lab animals, I watched five sedated dogs get 'de-barked.' A hot cauterizing iron, thrust down their throats, burnt out their vocal cords. They could no longer bark, but they could whine. The dogs were shaved for surgery, then wrapped in bandages, seeping blood, afterwards. One German shepherd had five puppies following a surgical procedure that removed her right lung. Nobody had guessed she was pregnant.

She licked her newborn puppies clean, despite the agony of her recovery without any painkillers, only to see her babies removed from the cage, one by one. The sorrow and helplessness in her eyes haunted me.

I began to question the ethics of what I'd done to all those mice in Bradenton. I reacted, too, to the death of a pygmy marmoset monkey, killed just so I could dissect it and recognize its tumors. A new part of my soul was opening as to how much pain filled the world. Then Mrs. Watkins arrived. It was good to see her, until she told me that the doctors at RPMI had found that her cancer had metastasized to both kidneys. She understood, better than most, what that meant: the certainty of a slow, gruesome death. We had a sorrowful goodbye. Georgia Watkins had encouraged and trained me in my first baby-steps toward cancer research. Even in this dark hour, her confidence in my future remained unshaken: yes, I *would* find a cure for cancer! Her life's work would not have been in vain!

Full of new resolve, I cut free from my friends and worked harder and longer. I also finished three paintings for Dr. Reyniers' fundraiser.[56] Then, the opera singer died. After an hour of tears, I no longer wished to live at the "Y" and found a small attic apartment next to D'Youville College, ten minutes by bus from RPMI. I had no idea anyone would be upset about it, but someone must have tattled on me, because Dr. Mirand and a friend went looking for me immediately, frantic with worry. Mirand acted as if he had lost a student, even though I was not his to lose! They found me in my little garret room, eating spaghetti straight from the can for dinner. Mirand, his face pale and his countenance furious, demanded my immediate return to the "Y." "Remove yourself at once from this hell-hole!" he fumed, saying other choice words.

It was an order I had to obey. I told Dr. Moore what happened, but my genial mentor only laughed and said that "Edwin" was always finding something to fidget about.[57] There was a more important thing that concerned him. It came about because Dr. Haas and his wife, who were strong Catholics, had started discussing a girl, as they worked, who had been in Dr. Moore's lab in the position I now enjoyed. "What a shame!" Dr. Haas had said, loud enough that I could hear. "What a waste!"

"What happened?" I asked. "She became a nun!" he replied.

"Is she not going to be a cancer researcher?" I asked. "Yes, she still is," Dr. Haas answered. "But now, she'll never have any children." His comment struck me like an electric shock. The words of my father reverberated through my soul: *"The doctors told us you'll never have children. You are as sterile as a mule."*

Realizing that if I married, my husband would never have a son or daughter, I believed I must have been pre-ordained to serve God by serving the sick, wounded by cancer, while proceeding with my life's work as a cancer researcher. That's when I told Dr. Moore that I wished to enroll at St. Francis College, located in my beloved Indiana. One of my student friends at Roswell Park, a brilliant Hungarian refugee, told me about the same time that she knew about St. Francis College. It was run by The Sisters of Perpetual Adoration, and some of them were trained doctors, nurses and medical missionaries. Then, one of the Catholic nurses at D'Youville told me that she knew about St. Francis, too. They had an excellent pre-med program, she said. The coincidences were

---

[56] The art sale for "Research Inc" was mentioned in a news article with various errors, by *The Bradenton Herald*. Mrs. Watkins, who was then very ill, gave the information. The 'welcome home' party of Sept. 2 was mentioned in the *Tampa Tribune, St. Petersburg Times, Sarasota Tribune* and *Bradenton Herald*.

[57] Editor Edward T. Haslam rewrote Mirand's quote, greatly improving the meaning.

adding up. Maybe God wanted me to go to this small Catholic college in my beloved Indiana. Then in the final week at RPMI, I finally heard from my mother. She forwarded a letter from "Sister Mary Veronica" at St. Francis College. The letter said I could do cancer research with small animals and even have my own lab. After a few phone calls, I learned that the scholarship they'd offered was still good. And yes, at the end of two years, I could transfer to the University of Chicago to study medicine. And everything would be paid for, if I became a nun!

Dr. Moore was not thrilled. "Dr. Diehl is coming for a visit," he told me. "He'll be a guest at our house. Some of our grad students will be there," he added. "We'll be discussing their funding for the fall. I hope you will think about coming to dinner, too, if you are free." As if 'no' was ever an option! Yes, yes, I'd be there! About this same time, I had a breakthrough while working on Dr. Moore's RPMI 1640 formula for growing cancer cells. The next day, Dr. Moore drove me to his beautiful but relatively modest home. The weather was perfect, so we ate on the screened patio that overlooked the quiet canal that had previously brought us to his home via a ride in two boats.

This scratch sheet, kept as a souvenir, shows to experienced eyes that the smallest amt shown of phenylalanine, plus .5 ml, plus the addition of fetal calf serum, would become part of RPMI's final formula

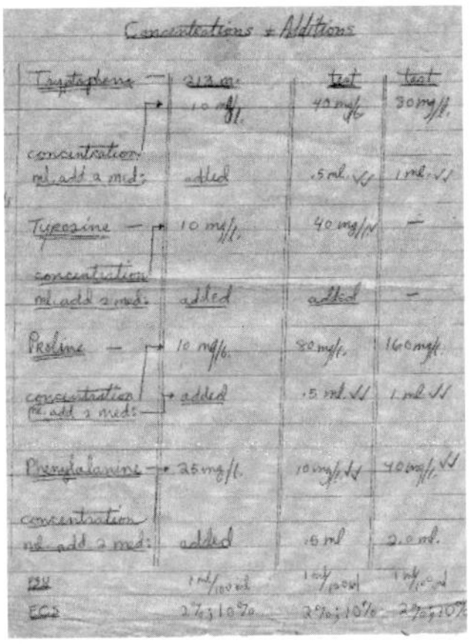

Concentrations + Additions

		test	test
Tryptophane	10 mg/l.	40 mg/l.	30 mg/l.
concentration ml. add 2 med:	added	.5 ml. ✓✓	1 ml. ✓✓
Tyrosine	10 mg/l.	40 mg/l.	–
concentration ml. add 2 med:	added	added	–
Proline	10 mg/l.	80 mg/l.	160 mg/l.
concentration ml. add 2 med:	added	.5 ml. ✓✓	1 ml. ✓✓
Phenylalanine	25 mg/l.	10 mg/l. ✓✓	40 mg/l. ✓✓
concentration ml. add 2 med:	added	.5 ml	2.0 ml.
PSK	1 ml/100 ml	1 ml/100 ml	1 ml/100 ml
FCS	2%; 10%	2%; 10%	2%; 10%

After dinner, Dr. Moore and Dr. Diehl began interviewing their grad students in the den, while I waited. When it was finally my turn, we discussed ways to fund my work if I went to

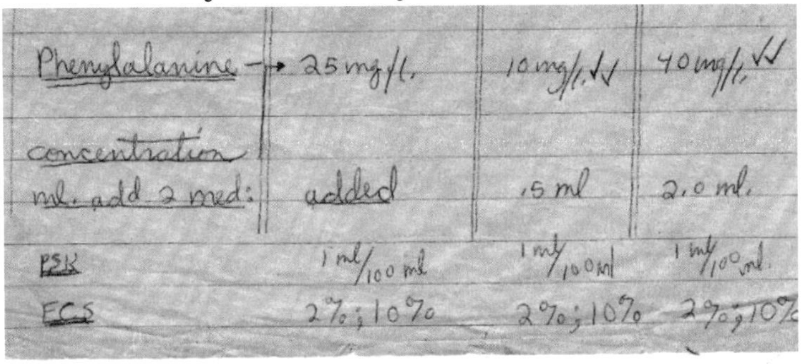

Phenylalanine	25 mg/l.	10 mg/l. ✓✓	40 mg/l. ✓✓
concentration ml. add 2 med:	added	.5 ml	2.0 ml.
PSK	1 ml/100 ml	1 ml/100 ml	1 ml/100 ml.
FCS	2%; 10%	2%; 10%	2%; 10%

"SFC." For example, both doctors had connections with Eli Lilly, which had a presence near SFC. They could arrange for grants from the NSF, the NDEA and/or the NIH to accompany me to SFC, dedicated to expanding and benefiting SFC's science program, since I wasn't a grad student who could get those funds directly. It was agreed that I'd transfer to the University of Chicago after a year. [58]Meanwhile, I was to continue my work with melanoma.

---

[58] My critics claimed that as an undergrad, I did not qualify for NSF, NDEA or NIH grants, but I was welcome at universities anyway, as I came with the promise of grants for their labs in exchange for my scholarships. Note: "The National Defense Education Act (NDEA) was ...a four-

"Dr. Ochsner himself is working with melanoma right now," Dr. Diehl explained. "We want to see what you can do with some powerful human-derived melanoma cells that we've transferred into hamsters."

"Ochsner is interested in making this melanoma more powerful," Dr. Moore added. Dumbfounded, I asked, "Why would he want to do that?"

"The key to defeating cancer is to understand what makes it tick," Dr. Diehl said soothingly. "If we learn what makes cancers more deadly, instead of what makes it weaker, we'll be forging ahead in brand-new territory."

"We want you to try the newest varieties of my medium," (the RPMI 1640 precursor) Dr. Moore chimed in. "Find out how it enhances melanogenesis in this strain of melanoma."

"I still don't understand why you chose SFC," Diehl complained. When I told them that my parents were hostile to my attending college, they believed me, for I was the only student that summer whose parents had never contacted them. However, my Catholic Hungarian relatives up north would support my choice of SFC. They would shame my parents if they objected. When I told them my Auntie Elsie was friends with Dr. Reyniers, that convinced them that a great researcher would stay in contact with me. I could go ahead and turn down Purdue University's kind offer. At Dr. Mirand's final Seminar that Friday morning, I presented a good paper on my research on the RPMI medium and received two awards, including a grant from the National Science Foundation which would be awarded not to me, but to whatever science lab I agreed to work in, in exchange for paying my college expenses, as I was an undergrad. The awards were mentioned in newspaper articles in four different cities, written by different reporters who had contacted my parents, Dr. Moore, and Georgianna Watkins. She gave them information from Dr. Diehl's secretary. It would be her last effort to help me before she died. [59] [60] I didn't arrive home until early September, where I was greeted by 50 friends and schoolmates. There was even a cake with a white mouse on it. Tony [Lopez-Fresquet] was there, too. "Mouse on the Cake" was the title of some newspaper articles. Miss Manatee County (my friend Ann Estrup) and Miss Cortez Plaza posed with me as they stuffed cake into my mouth.

---

year plan for boosting American education... the NDEA was giving out scholarships to almost any high school graduate who could present a credible case for wanting to study science at a university (Degroot 2006, p.75)
"https://tigerprints.clemson.edu/cgi/viewcontent.cgi?article=2551&context=all_dissertations As a 1961 high school grad, I was inside that four-year window.

[59] George E. Moore, Robert E. Gerner, and H. Addison Franklin registered the RPMI patent in 1966 and then released it, free, to everyone.

[60] Mrs. Watkins' last letter to me is in the Appendix, with typos and unsigned.

Sadly, I would never see most of my friends again.

Many years later, when inquiries were made about my attending *RPMI, researchers were told that I attended in 1962 (instead of 1961) as a "high school senior"(instead of a college undergrad)***!** Atop that, *all mention of my working with Dr. Grace was missing.* While the record did say I had worked in Dr. Moore's own lab, *Dr. Mirand, told researchers I had been kicked out of the program.* His lapse of memory can be forgiven, seeing he had been angry at me about the room rental, but if I'd been kicked out of the program, I never would have been sent RPMI's precious melanoma cancer cells to work with at St. Francis College, which is on record.

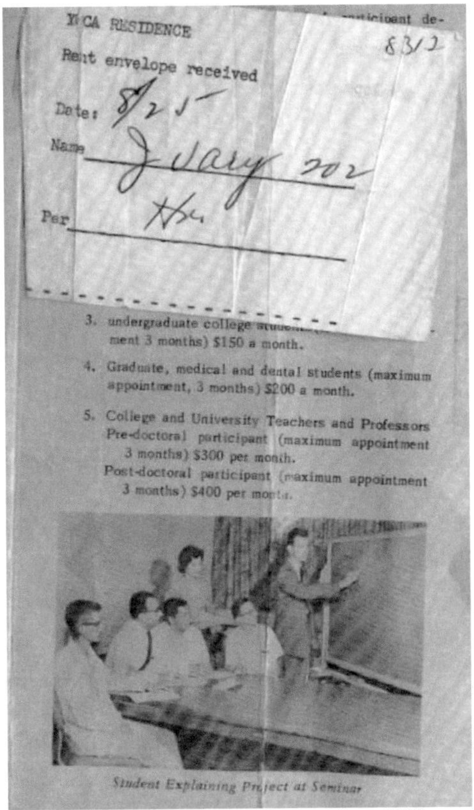

Student Explaining Project at Seminar

At St. Francis, researcher Tom Rozoff found claims that Sr. Mary Veronica never existed and that I'd never done any cancer research there.[61] But newspaper articles said The American Cancer Society was sending equipment to St. Francis to assist me in my research with melanoma cancer. Nor could I have returned to Bradenton in September to a big party in my honor.[62] Note the "YWCA" rent receipt for Aug. 25-31 for my final week at the "Y" ending Sept. 1.

Above all, consider the fact that my work at St. Francis involved doing research on live melanoma cancer cells sent to me from RPMI. I had to be in good standing with RMPI to have been sent their live cancer cells. My work with the RPMI melanoma at St. Francis was supervised by three nuns in the medical field, was formally presented, and an abstract of my findings was published. Only my father's interference stopped the paper itself from getting published. So, we have two questions to ponder: Was this corruption of the records a simple loss of information, to be expected over the years? Or did somebody not want the truth about Judy Vary, and her cancer research, to ever reach the public? One news article mentioned that I returned home "six buses late" for that surprise party, as I stopped in Tampa to give Dr. Reyniers a visit!

---

[61] Rozoff wrote that he was surprised that a nun could lie. I have his signed statement for inspection.

[62] The newspapers kept using "Dr. ***Howard*** Moore," reflecting an error in their first news story.

Mouse On The Cake

From Palmetto way comes news of **Judy Vary**, daughter of Mr. and Mrs. Donald W. Vary of Gulf to Bay estates. Judy was surprised recently at her home by 50 high school friends. She was home from Roswell Park Memorial Cancer Research Center in Buffalo, N.Y. Her time there was spent with white mice — every day, in fact. She did research work at the Center and worked under Dr. Howard Moore, the head of Roswell. They met last March when Judy was a guest writer at the National Science Writers Seminar in St. Petersburg.

The party was held a few days before the story you see here was printed in *The St. Petersburg Times*.

Saint Francis College
Fort Wayne, Indiana
June 23, 1961

Miss Judyth Vary
4402 Pompano Lane
Palmetto, Florida

Dear Miss Vary:

Thank you for your letter of June 10. We regret the delay in answering, but my absence from campus for some time has resulted in belated correspondence.

We are happy to know that you have selected Saint Francis as the college of your choice, and we are pleased to renew our original full-tuition scholarship offer of $350.00. This scholarship is renewable each year (provided that you maintain the required scholastic index), amounting to a total of $1400.00.

Since our college is comparatively small, we do not have facilities for extensive laboratory research at present. Some experimentation with white mice or other small animals will be possible. We have plans for a new science building in the near future and will begin construction of a new residence hall and a new classroom building this summer.

You may be interested in knowing that four of our science and math instructors have received National Science Foundation Grants or Fellowships within the past two years and are currently pursuing research or doctorates at Indiana University, University of Notre Dame, University of California, and the University of Louisiana at Baton Rouge. Three of the four will return to the campus as instructors in September.

You may like to know that resident students who must earn a part of their expenses may engage in part-time employment on campus. A student who works ten hours a week can defray approximately $225.00 of her expenses per year.

The college also maintains a student loan fund. Worthy students may arrange for a partial or full-expense loan. Our interest rate is four percent, and the student need not begin refunding the loan until one year after graduation.

Saint Francis College has now added "The Tuition Plan" to its student aid program. Literature explaining this convenient way of meeting college expenses will be sent to you within the next month by our Tuition Plan representative. We feel that some or all of these student aids will be of interest to you.

We are sending application forms and our catalog by ordinary mail. These items should reach you by Monday or Tuesday.

In reference to several of your questions, we do have advanced placement in languages. There are opportunities for "overloads" for students who maintain a 3.5 cumulative average. We are cognizant of originality of thought, and we feel that we are reasonably (sometimes extremely) strict.

Distance may prohibit your visiting Saint Francis College, but we do want you to know that you are most welcome any time. We wish you and your family could meet some of the faculty and students and also see the residence hall with its attractive accommodations for the girls. You will like the truly Franciscan spirit of joy and friendliness that prevails on the campus in both classroom and extra-curricular activities, uniting the students into just one big family.

We would appreciate hearing from you soon to learn about your plans. May the Holy Spirit guide you in the choice of a college suited to your needs and interests. God bless and love you always.

Sincerely in St. Francis,

Sister M. Veronica

Sister M. Veronica, OSF
Director of Admissions

SMV:sg

ALTERED RECORDS? A St. Francis official told Researcher **Tom Rozoff there was no Sister Veronica, no cancer research, no trained sisters to do such research** at St. Francis (I never claimed to be 16 years old when I attended there). But he personally had visited the campus and learned that Sister Veronica was remembered. He also knew I had proof **Sister M. Clare had supervised my cancer research** and **that I had presented a paper on cancer research, conducted at St. Francis, to The Indiana Academy of Science in 1961.** He expressed "surprise that a nun would lie to me."

Talk to your Yahoo! Friends via Windows Live Messenger. Find Out How»

Attached Message

From: Pekrul, Janice <jpekrul@sf.edu>
To: Rozoff@aol.com
Cc: Scheetz, Sr. Jo Ellen <JSCHEETZ@sf.edu>
Subject: Judyth Anne Vary Baker
Date: Fri, 4 Nov 2005 09:31:09 -0500

[Unable to display image]

Mr. Rozoff, I finally got a chance to talk with Sr. Jo Ellen this afternoon. While we do have a record of a Judyth Anne Vary having attended Saint Francis College the Fall Semester of 1961, all of the other information in the letter is inaccurate:

Sister Mary Veronica has not taught here nor been an administrator here
We did not have sisters who were doctors or research technologists at that time
We have not done cancer research
Sister JoEllen did her doctoral dissertation on the history of the school; however, she knows nothing of the situation Judyth mentions
Judyth says that she was 16 at the time. That information does not coincide with the birthdate in our records

Janice W. Pekrul
Administrative Assistant
Academic Affairs
University of Saint Francis
Fort Wayne, Indiana 46808
Reverence the unique dignity of each person

Chapter Five
A Higher Calling

On Sept. 4, 1961, I kissed my family goodbye and set off a week early to St. Francis College, anxious to meet Sister Mary Veronica, get paperwork settled and set up my lab. Live melanoma cancer cells from Roswell Park were already on the way! Sister Veronica and two other nuns showed me where we could keep mice. I'd have a private lab area with a refrigerator, incubation chamber, and necessary equipment. It was an upgrade from my high school lab, but oceans away from what I'd enjoyed at RMPI. He good news was that I'd have access to a nearby hospital for x-rays, sophisticated processes, and guidance, thanks to RPMI's connection s to Eli Lily. I signed up for a full load of pre-med courses with organic chemistry, anatomy and physiology, math and a required English course (taught by Dr. Fink – a name hard to forget!). I quickly got into a religious routine by attending Mass every day.

By this time, I knew not to gossip about my work, grants and scholarships. I was a college freshman with ties to the best cancer researchers in the country, and I had work to do for them, regarding making melanoma more deadly. It wasn't quite the topic to talk about over pizza parties and Pepsi's! I had two roommates: one was a large girl with pendulous breasts and over-sized underwear. We were not close. The other was Marilyn Ryan, an attractive girl armed with a keen brain and sharp of humor. We were enrolled in the same pre-med classes and shared the same interests. Every bit as religious as I, Marilyn revealed how she had rejected her previous liberal lifestyle to pursue a higher calling. She not only admitted that she wasn't a virgin, but at night, after our third roommate fell asleep and began to snore, Marilyn would lie on her bed and recount her romantic adventures with various boyfriends, including tantalizing bits of carnal details. I was curious and Marilyn had riveting tales to tell, laced with outrageous comments and unique descriptions. One comment I remember best: "Sex!" Marilyn said, in a stage whisper. "Yes! I loved it!" Then, with a deep sigh, she confessed, "The angels! they don't know what they've been missing!" Though I made many friends, Marilyn was dearest of all. We both joined the choir. We sang at Mass every morning. We both groaned over our comparative anatomy class.

(Run by a tyrant nun!) We got parts in the upcoming play. I worked in my lab and at the nearby hospital. RMPI's melanoma was soon doing fine, but the mice I wanted had yet to arrive, giving me time to explore SFC's fine campus.

That's when I discovered the most remarkable library I've ever known. It was located underground, in a magnificent building we called "the castle." The Bass Mansion, as it was known, held many surprises, but none so wondrous as this library, which was a maze of carved bookcases so closely guarding their treasury of great and ancient books, that only here and there could be found an easy-chair somehow stuffed between two of them, in which I'd curl up, under an antique lamp's warm light, to read. REAL reading, not as encyclopedias had taught me, but voyaging with the masters of the world's greatest literature. Dostoievsky, Cervantes, Dante, Shakespeare, Tolstoy, Faulkner, Blake, Dumas, Hugo, Pushkin, and the glories of *Paradise Lost,* were awakening my soul to their magic, their depth and their majesty!

I cursed my former habit of speed-reading everything, which had denied me the joys of rich stretches of contemplation and interior reflection, in exchange for a steely stack of ever-changing facts, figures and medical journals. The library became a refuge, a sanctuary, a font of strength, peace and learning. Here, I could practice speaking Russian, French, and Spanish in privacy, for not a soul ever seemed to venture into this silent haven. And here, I resumed my exploration of classics in Latin and Greek.

But I hadn't been sent here just to laugh at Marilyn's funny adventures, to say morning and evening prayers, and to curl up in an easy-chair and read! I had serious work to do for my doctors. My main lab was not even on campus: it was in a nearby hospital -- a brisk walk from St. Francis. Handling radiation and viruses were not so noticeable here, except for the fact that I was a minor, and had to be a Minnie Mouse, quietly working and unnoticed. The hospital was adding two new buildings and was expanding, which meant that new faces went unnoticed, as the staff almost doubled in size amid the chaos of construction. My guide was Dr. Ray W. Fuller, a young biochemist who had just arrived from Purdue U with his brand-new PhD. He was the first Director of the Biochemical Research Laboratory at the Fort Wayne State Development Center, a mental hospital where experiments with anticonvulsive and psychoactive drugs were regularly conducted without much notice.

Dr. Fuller, aware of the fragility of his new position, and hoping to please personages such as the powerful Dr. Diehl, was happy to accept shipments, chemicals and live melanoma cancer cells for Diehl's young protégé, a girl who was not allowed to directly receive them due to her status as a minor. After two years at Fort Wayne, Dr. Fuller would find a position of respect and job security at nearby Eli

Lilly, where he became the coinventor of Prozac, the famous psychoactive drug that calms the nerves of millions in our harried world, while earning billions for Lily. The goal of my experiments – to enhance melanoma cancer cell growth with the SV-40 virus –which I hoped to develop within the year--was of little interest to Dr. Fuller.

But he did inquire into my connections. I only met "Ray" a few times at the State Hospital. However, he proved incredibly useful. Some of his lab workers in Ray's sparsely-furnished oncology lab stabilized my tissue cultures when they first arrived. Currently, I was growing hamster cells transformed by human melanoma, using the same approach as in Dr. Moore's lab: testing varied concentrations of amino acids to get the fastest growth response. I was becoming an expert in enhancing cancer. In just two weeks, I revved the melanoma in those hamster cells into metabolic high gear. My reports were sent to Dr. Ochsner, who never acknowledged them directly. Instead, everything I needed came quickly. That Dr. Ochsner was also working on melanoma (as one of his many interests) did seem a coincidence. He published papers on melanoma in 1962 and 1965.[63] I was surprised, though, when a remarkable gift arrived from New York: melanoma cells with a coded ID. They came from the cancer that killed my hero, U.S. Navy Dr. Tom Dooley, who had died on Jan. 18. I'd read his wildly-popular books about his work with the poor and helpless in Laos and Southeast Asia, inspiring me to dream of serving as a medical missionary. Dr. Tom Dooley had attended Notre Dame and our family considered him a saint, admiring his commitment to serve the medically needy in Southeast Asia, even as he was fighting cancer. I kept his dying statement alive in my soul: "The cancer went no deeper than my flesh. There was no cancer in my spirit."

Only Dr. Ochnser knew about my admiration for Tom Dooley, so only he could have told Dr. Moore, who actually sent me the cells from Buffalo. It would be two more years before I'd learn from my homosexual friend David Ferrie, that Dr. Dooley was a fellow homosexual who worked for the CIA. On Friday, Oct. 6, a newspaper article appeared in *The St. Petersburg Times*:

"***<u>Word From Judy</u>* Mrs. C. R. Watkins**, *chairman Manatee Unit American Cancer Society, reports she has received a letter from Judy Vary, Manatee County's young scientist, who is continuing her work with cancer research at St. Francis College in Fort Wayne, Ind. Judy said she is "presenting a paper for the Indiana Biological Association on "melanogenesis." She is doing special research on aspects of melanoma, sometimes called "black death," which caused the death of the late Tom*

---

[63] ALTON OCHSNER, SR. AND DAVID H. HARPOLE <u>ANN SURG</u>. (1962) MAY; 155 (5): 629–636. Malignant Melanoma: Its Prognosis as Influenced by Therapy* ; ALTON OCHSNER (1965) TREATMENT OF MALIGNANT MELANOMA, POST GRADUATE MEDICINE 37:4, 452-456, DOI:

Dooley...Judy was assigned to do research on this subject, along with her studies at St. Francis, by Roswell Park Memorial Cancer Research center in Buffalo, N.Y. where she worked the past summer...The American Cancer Society has provided the equipment."

I was working on the college's telephone lines two nights a week for pin money. That, plus night-time studies with Marilyn and a few other friends, meant my late hours at the hospital off-campus were not noticed. Meanwhile, a plan began to emerge, which I believed would have the sanction of the American Cancer Society.[64] I'd join the Order of St. Francis, study to become a doctor, spend time as a medical missionary for a few years, and then plunge into a lifelong career in cancer research. Marilyn, upon learning of my distress at not being able to have children, encouraged me. "Maybe you can't have babies," she smiled, "but if you become a sister, you'll never have to worry about birth control being a sin! And you can help save babies and mommies! It's a fabulous combination." She, too, decided to follow the same path.

When we confided our plan to Sister Mary Clare, who documented my project hours at the hospital, she revealed that the Order had missionaries in Africa. The crowning statement was that after a life of service, the Sisters retired to a convent in Mishawaka, a suburb of South Bend. My home town! I could then be a Contemplative Nun and spend all my time in prayer, writing, and art. Triumphant in my new life-choice, the three of us went to the Administrator, Sister Mary Veronica.

After giving me a gentle hug, Sister put on a stern face. I was to "dispense of" my shorts and slacks! I must lower the hems of my skirts! The tight sweaters had to go! The campus had just become co-ed, she explained, so now I could help protect the chastity of the girls by setting a modest example. She even demanded that I cease to take showers! I should take baths, she said, which kept more of my body from view. On this matter, Sister checked on me nightly, as I'd protested that I was already taking showers after working on my cancer projects.

Too bad, Judy! You must make nightly tub baths a habit! Maybe becoming a nun was going to be a bit harder than I thought. My family and other friends still didn't know. Just Marilyn, my ally. Together, we would use our brains and industry to reduce the suffering in the world. About this time, an affectionate letter arrived from my mother, calling me "Juduffski." She asked me not to dissect my pet turtle, Fitzgerald (named after JFK) if it died.[65] Moved by her solicitous words, I foolishly wrote back -- on sheets of toilet paper! I did that to symbolize what I thought of the state of the world, telling her I was planning to become a Sister of St. Francis and would be entering the convent on Feb. 2, 1962, as a postulate. My friend Marilyn would be doing the same. Later, we'd

[64] Drs. Ochsner and Diehl were both on the American Cancer Society Board at this time: Ochsner as a lifetime Board member, and Diehl as ACS Vice Pres.

[65] My mother's letter is in the Appendix.

both receive more medical training, and would be headed for medical school. I said there was no need to worry about my future. After all, Dad had told me I could never have children! No husband would be put to grief. It was the best solution. Carefully stuffing the ten or so sheets of toilet paper into a fancy envelope that had “SFC” embossed in gold, I sealed the envelope and sent it off. I suppose my parents thought I lost my mind!

On Oct. 19, 1961, Sister Mary Clare and two other medically-trained nuns drove me to Indiana State College in Terre Haute for the fall session of the Indiana Academy of Science.[66] **Sister Mary Clare** “co-presented” my paper, for as a minor, I had to be “under supervision.”

BACTERIOLOGY

Chairman: Gordon Mallett, Eli Lilly

Gordon Mallett, Eli Lilly and Indiana University, was elected chairman for 1962

ABSTRACTS

Studies on the Increase *in vitro* of Mitotic Activity and Melangenesis in the RPMI HA # 5 (7113) Strain Melano. Judyth Vary and Sister M. Clare Francis, St. Francis College.—A 73rd generation un-pigmented melanoma, derived from a metastatic lesion in a human host and cultured in the Syrian hamster, was used in attempts to accelerate the proliferation of the melanoma *in vitro*, employing assays of the basic media #213 against controls of 213, Puck's, Shu, and ELH media. Several hundred variations of twelve amino acid concentrations, in correlation with fetal calf serum percentages of 2%, 5%, and 10% were tested. Although results are inconclusive at this date, indications suggest that specific concentrations of phenylalanine, alanine, and tryptophane influence from a slight to substantial extent the increase in mitotic activity of the melanoma. In some instances melanogenesis was increased to the point that some cells seemed to contain melanin in amounts noticeable under low microscopic powers. Tests with the *dopa* reaction revealed an increase in melanogenic activity in some cases.

The factors influencing accentuated mitosis and melonagenesis may provide a key in the control of this deadly cancer, since the absence or loss of such factors may reciprocally influence the proliferation and metastatic activity of this melanoma in an adverse manner. An area of future endeavor includes testing the influence of Ehrlich-derived ascites DNA; stock RNA; insulin; etc.

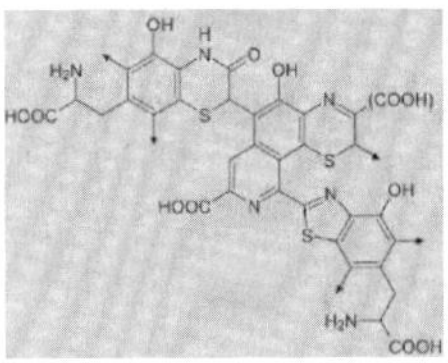

I recall returning to the chalkboard after my presentation in the lecture room, to erase an HOOC and replace it with a COOH!

[66] “The Indiana Biological Association” seems to have been an informal group at Notre Dame who got my paper accepted by the Indiana Academy of Science.

The abstract was printed in the *Proceedings of the Indiana Academy of Science*, 1961, p. 71 under Bacteriology. The Chairman was Gordon Mallet, of Eli Lilly/Indiana U. It's a small world. I had met Dr. Mallet previously on my tour of Eli Lilly at the International Science Fair in Indianapolis. A few days after my presentation, while I was working on my paper to be published by The Indiana Academy of Science, Dad called. "You're being controlled by others," he began. "You never did have the courage to be yourself. You were created by God with a body that shows you're supposed to get married. You were not created to become a nun!" He raged on: "Think! You could be the wife of a successful doctor! Maybe he could find a way to get you pregnant."

In blunt language, Dad commanded me to withdraw my application to the order of St. Francis. To that I had just one defiant answer: "No! You can't make me!" That's when he hung up on me, after which I had to go to confession. In my entire family, "talking back" was a sin.

We had been taught to respect our parents and to obey them, even if they stood before us in a drunken stupor. But I was far away, and Dad couldn't hit me. I walked back to my dorm room, feeling determined and victorious. I had stood my ground against my father's coarse interference. Flinging open the door, I saw my sweet, funny roommate sitting on the floor by her bed, motionless. Her normal sparkle was gone. She was staring at the floor. A terrible foreboding swept over me. "Marilyn, what's the matter?" I asked, my voice trembling. As I sat down next to her, my beautiful friend looked up at me with tears in her eyes.

"I have cervical cancer," she said flatly.

Her simple sentence hit me hard. I was devastated. Cancer's ugly face had burst into my life again! And this time it was striking someone young and delightful, in the prime of life; someone with great dreams and goals, someone, once again, so close to me. *Why?* Where was God in this equation? I asked her if she was still going to be a Sister. Yes, she replied. It was up to God to decide what would happen to her. She would still enter the Order on Feb. 2. Taking her hand, I told her solemnly, "I will be right with you, at your side!"

On Oct. 29, with no classes, after a Mass where I felt the Presence of God, followed by a stint in my lab, I finished a little gift for Sister Mary Veronica. It was a small portrait of a medieval lady, which I placed in an ancient oval picture frame I'd restored, which I'd found empty in the magical Castle's library. As I gave it to Sister Mary Veronica, I told her my father said I'd be wasting my life as a nun. As she put the painting, glowing in the restored frame, into the college's safe, she said, "You have made the frame valuable again. In the same way, God will use you for good, never fear." After Marilyn and I finished rehearsals that night for the upcoming play, to be performed Nov. 1 – All Saints Day-- we helped make a Halloween coffin with fake spider webs, moss, a red floodlight, and some convincing groans from a tape recorder. As everyone went to bed, I sat down at the big desk in SFC's front office to handle the college phones, studying formulas I intended to try out on a new shipment of melanoma cells sent to me from RPMI. They were infected with the SV-40 monkey virus. Grand thoughts of curing cancer were filling my thoughts. Marilyn's needs were motivating me as never before to cure cancer. Some great ideas on what to do next began lining up in my mind. Suddenly, the door opened and in walked my father.

"Daddy!" I exclaimed.

"Judy, you're coming with us!" he commanded.

"But I'm not finished with my shift!" I protested.

"I don't care about that. Let's go!" he said, grabbing my arm. Through the window, I saw my mother standing by our car with the door open. Auntie Elsie and Ronnie were sitting in the back seat. As I was propelled outside by Dad's firm grip, I cried out, "What are all of you doing here?"

"We're taking you home."

"You can't do that!" I protested. "I'm in the middle of the semester. I'm doing important research -- and I have a part in a play that opens in two days. I can't leave!"

"You are a minor, and I am your parent!" Dad said grimly. He pushed me into the car. "I have legal control over you and your whereabouts. You don't have my permission to be here," he said, slamming the car-door. "And if you don't come with us, I'll have you arrested as a runaway and returned to Florida in handcuffs."They had already been to my dorm room and grabbed clothes, but none of my paints, lab reports or precious books. Off we drove into the night, back to Florida. When I protested, my father mocked me, saying I was not the meek, humble little nun, was I, when I wanted to have my way? The others retained their silence. Finally, Auntie Elsie handed me a note from my Florida school friend Orlanda Brugnola, a young genius in art and science who had been a close friend ever since we both resigned from MENSA. *"Great One,"* she wrote. *"If you become a nun, I will never speak to you again."*[67] How many people had been told?

It wasn't until we finally arrived back in Bradenton that I realized the clothes they'd grabbed belonged to my buxom, over-weight roommate. My clothes were still in Indiana! "It doesn't matter, because you're not going anywhere," Dad announced. I was to stay in my room unless called out for meals. The telephone was removed. My sister did not dare speak to me. The next day, Sister Mary Veronica called, pleading with my father to let me finish the semester, to no avail. "All a girl needs is a high school education and a good body," Dad told her, as I, hearing him arguing with the Sister, began to cry. "Don't tell me how 'important' education is to you!" Dad went on, coming into my room. "In a few years, you'll forget all about it. Your hormones will make that decision for you." I ground my teeth with the anger I'd been taught to always repress. Where was God? I had offered my very life to Him, and now I was locked up. On a remote island with no phone. And I was being mocked for my faith. My God had failed me.

[67] Ironically, Orlanda became a noted minister. She never did speak to me again.

Look what happened to Marilyn, to Mrs. Watkins, and to my Nanitsa! My important cancer cells were dying by now. My very identity was being stripped from me. Dad had been dragged into Catholicism to stay married to my mother, but he was never a real Catholic. Now he brought everything he could find from the public library that was anti-Catholic. I learned about Pope Joan, wallowed miserably through the Spanish Inquisitions, and fought my personal demons in my lonely room. That's when I lost my faith in God, religion and a reason for life itself.

Who was I? What was I? Just the chemical outcome of an egg and a sperm, compiled by accident? Was life a mere confluence of bacteria? Dr. Harold Urey had told me his version. There was no hint of God in it.

Dr. Tom Dooley's own horrible fate suggested that none of the good we might wish to do had any particular impact on the God I thought cared personally about me. Or was 'he' powerless to relieve our miseries? Was I merely a piece of flesh, ready to be eaten? Part of a Darwinian game that meant nothing? Suicide might end my pain, but it was against the Church's teachings, drilled into me. Having my faith stripped away from me was the spiritual equivalent of rape.

Above all, the isolation got to me. I was lonely and helpless. In my despair, I stopped eating. Noticing that, my father decided I needed to be put to work, so he began taking me to his office, where I answered the phone, handled his finances and greeted the occasional visitor, with my father usually present. At home, "house rules" prevailed. I was only allowed to leave my room for meals and when my Aunt and Uncle came over. Christmas came and went: 1962 arrived. Friends who called were told I was "busy," and the calls stopped. My Auntie Elsie and Uncle Emery and Grandpa now became concerned. Couldn't I resume my education?

"Where?" Dad asked. "She turned down Purdue for St. Francis, and I won't have her going back there!" Dad then began giving me a dollar a day to eat at a nearby café instead of from a sack lunch at my desk. He would sit there and watch me eat it. Are we in control yet?

January passed. On Feb. 2, word came from Marilyn. She had entered the convent. She was now "Sister Mary Marguerite." I was not allowed to write to her. At least she did not see how much faith I had lost. But I had pledged to be at her side. Would I ever see her again? In fact, I would never see Marilyn again, nor would I learn her ultimate fate. Auntie Elsie always had a strong influence over my mother: my dear Grandpa Whiting did, too, though he was weak from his chronic cough.

As "snowbirds" my aunt and uncle lived in Florida during the cold months. Two of their three sons were college graduates. One was a chemical engineer. Ronnie, their youngest, was studying electrical engineering. Now, behind my father's back, while he was on a business trip, Auntie Elsie and Grandpa began challenging my mother to "do something" about college. I asked Mother to call Col. Doyle. When my mother refused to get involved, fearing a big fight, **Auntie Elsie** dared to contact him. Col. Doyle, hearing enough to understand the problem, said Senator Smathers might renew his promise to get me into The University of Florida and promised to speak to the busy Senator immediately. Amazingly, it worked!

If I came at once, "things could be fixed" so I might be quietly slipped inside the university's new computer system as a student who came late due to a computer enrollment error. But how to get there? I needed clothes, books, towels, a bedspread, bedding, a lamp, gym shoes, and money for supplies and meals. That's when Grandpa Whiting stepped in. My blessed grandfather took out a personal loan at the bank, picked me up in Elsie's car an took me shopping. The last stop was Sharp's Pharmacy, where I needed to pick up personal items. It had been my favorite place to meet Grandpa when he was living in his small apartment across from Sharp's Drug Store the year before: we'd get double chocolate ice cream sodas together. But today, Grandpa said he didn't want one. He stayed in the car while I went in, to shop. When I came back, I threw my arms around my Grandpa's waist with gratitude. As I did so, I heard a deep rale in his lungs. Then Grandpa took my hand and looked at me with his faded blue eyes. He reminded me that Grandma had died in 1956 of cancer and that she would have been proud of my work. Why was he saying this now? Was it because I had mentioned that Sharp's Pharmacy was located in the same building where I had given mice x-radiation just a year ago?

Or was he trying to tell me something else? Then I heard him sigh, followed by one of his coughing spasms. Grandpa had been exposed to mustard gas in WWI, and his lungs had been permanently damaged.

I was used to his emphysema's chronic cough, but this time, I heard something achingly different... the telltale wheezing sound that I had been taught to recognize at Roswell Park. My dear Grandfather had lung cancer! Must I lose him, too, to this hideous plague?

"No!" I cried, hugging him. "Please – no!"

"Don't worry," Grandpa said, "I'm tough. It's just in one lung, and I've got two of those puppies! If I end up losing the fight, just remember, I've been separated too long from your grandmother."

We met Auntie Elsie back at the shopping center. She had purchased things for my room, plus a metal trunk. Then we skipped town without saying goodbye to Lynda, who had gone innocently to school. Upon my arrival at UF, the Dean of Women, Miss Marna Brady, personally met me. "I've been given my instructions," she said, with a no-nonsense handshake. A former Major in the U.S. Marine Corps Women's Auxiliary, Brady was UF's first Dean of Women when UF went Co-Ed in 1947. By the time we met, Brady had contacted Saint Francis. The ploy that allowed me to enter UF illegally, so late, involved allowing UF's new computer to record no absences from classes. But the same computer program also assigned me grades at random to equal a 3.0 GPA, since no professors had submitted any grades. "We'll fix that problem next semester," Brady promised. "Just keep all your exam papers. And come see me if you run into any trouble with your parents." Classes were already in their 5th week, but I was determined to catch up. My heart was full of joy when I was assigned to work as an assistant in UF's new oncology research lab. They would be studying cancer-causing viruses – my field. The *Seminole Yearbook*, 1962, "To Mice and Men" describes their work: "*Laboratories in the Medical Science building...[study] various symptoms of cancer. The mice are not ordinary mice, but special ones which have been inbred so long that they have become a pure strain down to the last cell. Different families are immune to some viruses but develop others. Mice are inoculated with a fluid cancer which does not affect humans, but which do react on the mice. Reactions to different sets of mice are observed and compared.*"

In 1960, UF's med school had its first graduates, so there was a lot of flexibility and being a female didn't matter.[68] But back at home, my father was furious. Piquing his anger was an exchange we'd had before I left. I bluntly told him that if I ever got free, I was determined to lose my virginity. These were strong words for a girl raised as I was, to say to her father, but my angry statement burst from me because Dad had made me pose for some photos in a bathing suit for his water conditioning business, as a

[68] https://youtu.be/krGLeZ8z76E YouTube video of University of Florida, 1962, shows the labs I worked in at minutes 3:30 – 6:25.

"partial payment" for "room and board" in my own home.

Now, finding me gone, Dad stormed around the house, fuming over the idea of me prowling the college campus, trying to lose my virginity. In a letter he sent, he accused me of having vain, worthless dreams, of chasing a pot of gold at the end of a rainbow, as if cancer research would somehow interfere with my ability to make a decent living. After a few days, Dad worked out a plan of action to get me back. First, he cleaned out the money from my bank account that Grandpa had set up for me. Next, he called the police and reported me as a runaway. Since I was a minor, he had the power to order the police to pick me up. I had moved into Grove Hall, a seedy holdover from WWII that once had been G.I. barracks. It was the only dorm left on campus with an empty room, but I would have happily lived in a doghouse to get away from Snead Island!

Here, I made friends quickly. A good thing, too, since it was one of my new friends who told me that my Auntie Elsie was on the hall phone, and that she was crying. My distraught mother had called her, afraid to call me herself because the long-distance call would have exposed her as an accomplice. The police were on their way to arrest me!

I grabbed my books and ran to Dean Brady's office, arriving breathless, with the police only minutes behind. Dean Brady took one look at my face and, hearing that the police had entered the building, she immediately locked her office door. "That will slow them down!" she told me. Then there was the knock. *"Police! Open up!"*

"Do you have a warrant?" she bellowed through the door.

"No," they admitted.

"Well, I am not going to open the door until you do."

The cops left and Dean Brady went to work, moving a chair right in front of the door and ordering me to "sit!" as she prepared papers for my emancipation. This was a legal document that would change my legal status from minor to adult. Usually, it requires a signature from a parent, but I could "self-emancipate" if I could prove I was self-supporting. Dean Brady soon fixed that problem: through a few phone calls, she arranged for me to work in rotation between my main lab and two others -- UF's Human Nutrition Department, and UF's Animal Nutrition Department. To start, I would help tag both rat and human blood with radioactive iodine tracers. The jobs came with a stipend that would cover everything my scholarship didn't.[69] I also would have a part-time job in the Craft Shop for pin money. After a notary in the building signed and stamped the documents, we waited for the police to return with their warrant. When they did, Brady showed them the documents and argued that I could not now be detained as a minor. The police scratched their heads and went back to the judge who had issued the warrant. We had to wait several hours before a policeman returned with the news. I was now a free woman!

---

[69] Brady also found some of the grant money I'd been awarded at St. Francis College, which is why these jobs were allotted to me in the science labs.

During that long, anxious wait, Dean Brady and I learned that we had common blood through the Venables in Rensselaer County, New York, the birthplace of "Uncle Sam." She had a low shelf full of red genealogy books there in her office, on my right, next to the door, which I could see easily as I sat in the chair she'd placed against the door. I also gained an appreciation for the mentality of a Marine, male or female. Brady's self-discipline and strength of character had been developed and honed through her experiences as a Marine. Marna Brady, no ordinary woman, would remain my firm ally, and I her grateful friend. I would never have been assigned to work for three different lab directors under ordinary circumstances, but my situation was not ordinary. The professors and specialists for whom I worked understood that I had some projects of my own, and that certain grants and funds were attached to my presence there. I could "putter around" independently after finishing my assigned tasks.

Marna Venable Brady, in an earlier photo. "Brady became known for serving in the Women's Reserves of the U.S. Marine Corp during World War II, retiring as Major. Following the war, she earned her Ed.D. and became the first Dean of Women in 1948 at the University of Florida soon after the University became coeducational."[70]

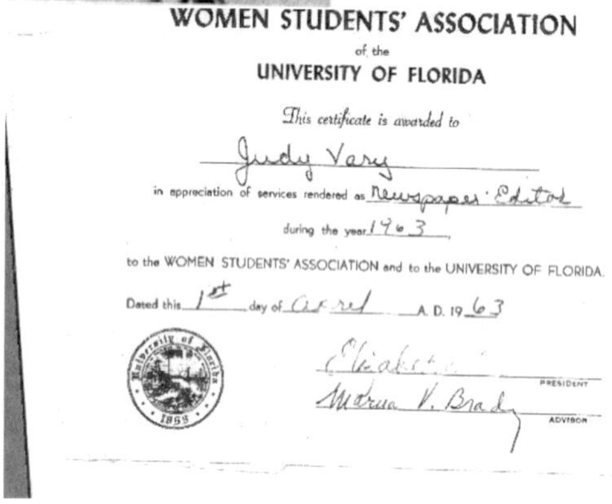

WOMEN STUDENTS' ASSOCIATION
of the
UNIVERSITY OF FLORIDA

This certificate is awarded to

Judy Vary

in appreciation of services rendered as Newspaper Editor

during the year 1963

to the WOMEN STUDENTS' ASSOCIATION and to the UNIVERSITY OF FLORIDA.

Dated this 1st day of April A.D. 1963

PRESIDENT

Marna V. Brady ADVISOR

The lab managers had no incentive to watch over my personal work, since I was an 18-year-old freshman whose reports were being sent every month "somewhere." Dr. Ochsner himself was now guiding my work, but he never sent a single personal message. Everything was a scribbled command. After a while, I was entrusted with keys to both nutrition labs and to the botany lab,[71] with the additional privilege to use radiation for my own projects.

<u>The Window of Opportunity</u> The use of radiation in research, involving human cells, is considered dangerous and was highly regulated by licenses by the Atomic Energy Commission. Various departments at UF individually petitioned for its coveted permission. UF was also in competition with the nation's other universities. Without licenses, there

---

[70] https://www.kappaalphatheta.org/heritage/notable-thetas

[71] I was allowed to keep the key to the botany lab and to use its lab facilities through 1965, as part of "the deal" that was hammered out, as will be seen.

would be no research using radiation. The result was a combination of red tape and unhealthy jockeying for special favors. By the early 1960's, UF was set to receive an avalanche of funding for scientific and medical research, but the complex AEC licensing had created a bottleneck. To solve the problem, Florida's powerful team, headed by UF's own Senator Smathers, went to work. Florida already had half of NASA's space program, which brought huge revenues and high-end employment opportunities to the state. Access to radiation research without the red tape was essential. How could America be first in science, over the USSR, weighed down by paperwork and petitions? The alternative looked attractive: the AEC would grant each Florida university its own master license. [72]

UF, for example, would have its own committee to grant sub-licenses to UF's various science departments, according to need. This special committee would be responsible for oversight, saving the AEC enormous time and trouble in the process. Of course, technically, the AEC still was in charge, with strict guidelines. Coincidentally, the Committee for the Human Use of Radioisotopes (**CHUR**) formed the same month I arrived at UF, and I became a beneficiary of the flood of new sub-licenses for "broad human use" of radiation that flowed to the labs where I worked. In this year of rapid expansion of UF's scientific research capabilities, even I obtained access to the radiation I needed for my projects, with surprisingly little oversight.

A 28-minute film was made, called "Adapting the Atom to Florida Progress – Production No. 28, 1962" that shows the use of radiation in all three of the labs in which I worked.[73] This "window of opportunity" would not last long: CHUR was shut down immediately after the Kennedy assassination for being too lenient in the granting of its sub-licenses.

But in 1962 and 1963, I had access, using radiation to track cancerous tissues and blood, available from UF's new hospital. Once I ran into my brilliant high school friends, Dave Dietrich and David Tracy, who were both studying nuclear physics, deep in the bowels of the radiation center, where I had just finished getting some of my cancerous blood samples irradiated. They recalled, years later, how surprised they were to see me there.[74]

---

[72] Legendary congressmen Claude Pepper, Robert Sikes and Wilbur Mills fought for Florida's supremacy in space and medicine. Smathers helped secure Senate support for Kennedy's proposed ban on above-ground nuclear bomb tests. Ref: Interview, Harold Brown, Dir. of Research Engineering, Department of Defense, 1963 partial test ban treaty, JFK Doc.#5, 6/26/1964, p. 38.

[73] The film has been available on YouTube as https://youtu.be/krGLeZ8z76E.

[74] In personal emails. In additional emails, an engineer who later helped refurbish and update the Nuclear Lab established the location of the small room I was allowed to use there before it was demolished.

Life was good again! And with all those smart males, who outnumbered the girls on campus...! Well, imagine the fun *that* was! I soon found myself getting plenty of attention. No more fasting and prayers for me! I was at the height of my physical strength and was trim, due to joining great bowling, volleyball and basketball teams that earned four medals. Dating, classes, lab work, teaching arts and crafts, editing "The Grove Groan," and later, the "Yuleevents" dorm papers, plus a position on Honor Council -- filled so many hours there was hardly time to sleep.

My dating life had always been good, but at UF, it was getting out of hand, so I kept asking my boyfriends – privately—to watch over me. I didn't want to be alone too late with any one boy, I stressed, because I did not want to lose my reputation. So wherever I went, at least two boys (usually more) would be with me, protecting me from each other. How long did this ploy work? Not long enough, but after escaping months of tyrannical isolation imposed by my father, and with my natural liking for the opposite sex, I was having fun, while keeping hold of my virginity on principle. Even so, there were favorites. One tall, handsome suitor was a graduate engineering student from Iran. What I knew about him may have been shallow, but it was important at the time: his father owned oil wells, and he had Arabian horses, which made him incredibly attractive to me. That's how immature I still was. Plus, he drove a red Ferrari! Strictly speaking, when I first met The Persian Prince, I liked him naturally, before I knew all of that. But it didn't hurt! I didn't select boyfriends with fancy cars on purpose, it just kept happening! He was impressed with me because once, when he went too far, I kicked the windshield right out of his expensive car. That's when he started really liking me, I suppose. But his culture intruded on any future plans, just as it had with Tony Lopez-Fresquet, because he told me I would have to put up with multiple wives, on religious principle, to please his father, to enhance his political and financial power in the Muslim world.

If this Persian Prince attracted me, so did Steve F____, fresh from Germany, who almost won my heart. I remember a day when he took me riding on his motorcycle. We drove up to a plate glass window where we could view our reflections. "Look how good we look together, my darling!" he said. "We could have blue-eyed children together." The semester ended with no victors, and I was not about to go home. That summer, when the labs were closed, I learned too late that I could have applied for an internship at the University of Miami. I vowed to make sure that in the summer of 1963, that's where I'd go, for I was attracted to the anti-Castro movement, and Miami was the Cuban capital of America. Ever since knowing Tony, I'd wanted to support the anti-Castro movement (I had lost track of Tiny and worried that he had been killed). By working as an assistant to Carlos R. in the Craft Shop, who taught me many arts and crafts skills at the Student Union, I once again was in contact with anti-Castro Cubans. Carlos, a tall, pock-marked Cuban who always wore green sunglasses, invited me to sit in the anti-Castro section at UF's home football games, where I soon learned to dislike President Kennedy for abandoning the Cuban people to communism. "It's not only Kennedy, Judy," Carlos told me. "The U.S. government can't be trusted to help anybody. Look what happened with the Hungarian revolution. It was the same Radio Free Europe, WG-Bullshit[75] and Radio Swan. They get us excited about revolution, and then when we dare to try, they go ahead and let us die."

In June, 1962, a tall, handsome math major friend who played the guitar--Bill Bernard-- enrolled in a summer course in world history. "You'd like it," he told me. "It's an anthropology course." Bill also convinced another friend to sign up. His name was Bob Baker. Over six feet tall, with dark, wavy hair, deep blue eyes and a strong, quiet personality, Bob possessed the requisite combination of brains, good looks and self-confidence that attracted me. He, too, played the guitar.

He was also lifting weights. I respected him, too, for refusing to march in the R.O,T.C. – required of all males attending UF —which made me think he was pro-peace. When I challenged him with some Russian phrases, he countered in ancient Greek. My boyfriends were all majoring in math, physics, the medical arts, or engineering, but though he was brilliant in math (which is why Bill Bernard was his friend), Bob wanted to be a writer. "I like her legs and I like her skin," he told Bill. He then entered the bevy of beaus who were making my days so happy. Because I already had another boyfriend named 'Bob,' who was a Pharmacy major, I called him 'Robert.' But my stay-a-virgin strategy --having my boyfriends guard me from each other-- didn't work once Robert joined the pack. One by one, he managed to drive them all away. One engineering major from India openly resisted Robert's intrusions. Frustrated and angry, he would walk behind us, yelling to Robert, "I KEEL you!"

My German boyfriend, impelled to send a love letter after spotting me alone with Robert at the Campus Club, complimented me as looking happy and beautiful, then added, "There is no need to fear me," having witnessed my Indian boyfriend's tirades. The last to yield was the Persian Prince, but even he finally gave up. Only Don Federman, a slightly-built Jewish intellectual on the staff of UF's *New Orange Peel*, whose passion for life and devotion to me was epic,[76] tried to prevail. Frankly, I was impressed! Robert had dominated all the others. Darwin wins again!

---

[75] Miami radio station WGBS, which broadcast the CIA's propaganda to Cubans in Florida. Can't remember Carlos' last name. Would love to hear from him.

[76] Don found a sweet girl named Carol who made him happy.

He had an extraordinarily high IQ of 186, which Exxon would eventually reward with its top research positions. The young genius would gain many patents for them, as well as for himself. But UF was not paying my tuition so I could date! I had work to do.

The great thing about Robert was his lack of curiosity about why he so often had to meet me in the basement of the Engineering Building, or why I was in the underground computer lab so many hours. My other boyfriends had pestered me with endless questions about these delicate matters. Robert's disinterest in my personal life was a relief. Robert not only never asked about my life goals or other personal questions, he also seemed to live in the present, unencumbered by worrying about the past or the future. He would meet me, carry my books, play the guitar to me in the moonlight, take me for long walks, discuss literature, and read his short stories to me. He also took me to plays and movies. The extra hours had to come from somewhere: I began coming in late, losing my Honor Council position for breaking curfew too many times. Somehow, it didn't matter, even when Robert's hands began to go where no man's hands had gone before, eroding my determination to not have sex.

Somehow, I resisted him, telling myself that, after all, Robert had never said, "I love you." As for religion, Robert was utterly neutral. Once, upon bringing him into a Catholic church, I commented that previously, I never would have dared wear Bermuda shorts inside such an august chamber. "True Majesty will not be offended," he remarked.

It wasn't long before Robert realized that the computer lab was a fascinating place. "Maybe I've made a mistake," he told me, displaying a long printout he had created to solve a math problem fresh from the computer lab. "It's too late to change my major," he added, "but thanks to you, I've decided to go into geology and computer science after I graduate next year."

I soon learned that Robert's parents had expected him to marry the daughter of a business associate, a German-looking blonde. Using an excuse ("Dad has some business in Gainesville, so why don't we meet you and your new girlfriend?"), Mr. and Mrs. Robert Allison Baker, Jr. suggested a neutral setting at a nice restaurant. At the same time, my father was seeking an opportunity to re-open channels of communication after the calamity in Dean Brady's office. Learning that a ham radio convention was being held in Gainesville, my father used it as an excuse to attempt a reconciliation. Could we meet in a neutral setting, at a nice restaurant? That's how two sets of anxious, wary parents happened to meet.

One set of parents was anti-Catholic. The other set was anti-Protestant. My father simply assumed I had gone through with my promise to lose my virginity, so he had no sweet thoughts about Robert, while Robert's mother made a low comment about 'gypsies seducing vulnerable young men.' The Bakers had arrived in a fancy 1962 Lincoln. The Varys had arrived in a fancy 1962 Chrysler Imperial. The men both wore impressive suits and smiled uncertainly at each other. Mrs. Baker frowned at my mother's long, pure gold cigarette holder: she did not smoke. Mrs. Baker had borne two sons. Mrs. Vary had borne two daughters. My mother's big diamonds trumped Mrs. Baker's shiny pearls. Her figure was better, and her hair was almost black, while Mrs. Baker's hair was silver (from an early age). They hated each other instantly. As dinner progressed, things got worse. Robert's mother played the role of a blue-blooded snob who looked down on my mother's "Hungarian refugee" family, even though she had been born dirt poor in Tyler, Texas herself and didn't know her father, as there had been a hasty divorce.

When my father tried to impress The Protestants with his connections through amateur radio to famous celebrities such as Arthur Godfrey and Walter Cronkite, Mrs. Baker rolled her eyes, which prompted my mother to start bragging about her purebred Blakeen miniature poodles,[77] to which Mr. Baker replied that his cat Felix could take on any dog and whup it. I watched the meltdown with cold resignation. [78]

My mother managed to extract an agreement from me to visit at the end of summer, knowing I wouldn't risk making our family look even worse by turning her down. In fact, her plan was to get rid of Robert if she could, in her own way, on her own turf. [79]

Soon enough, with classes over, kisses from Robert fresh on my lips, and his promise to drive down to Snead Island if I got trapped there, I was on my way. At first, things went well. Grandpa was back in the hospital 'for treatments.' "He doesn't know he has cancer," my mother told me. Little did she know! He was saying a rosary when we came. Back at my parents' house, I was pleased to see that Ronnie had moved back in. That relieved some concerns about Lynda, who now had a job at Morrison's Cafeteria. She had graduated, but just as had happened to me, there was no support for college, so she was working at a cash register and slicing lemons. But things got tense that brief weekend when my mother told me Tony Winters was coming over. The son of ferryboat Captain Joe Winters, Tony and I had become very fond of each other during a long summer we had enjoyed fishing and playing together on his dad's ferry. That's when I was thirteen and still living in St. Petersburg. Now Tony was in medical school, living in Winter Park, Florida. Even taller than Robert, he was just as attractive to me. With my heart in turmoil, at the end of the day I made my decision.

---

[77] Blakeen poodles were then the most notable of poodles. They were expensive, difficult to acquire, and were the top dog show winners among poodles. Ref: https://caninechronicle.com/current-articles/ch-snow-boy-of-fircot-and-the-miniature-poodle-revolution/

[78] A 1962 Lincoln cost $6,120. A 1962 Chrysler Imperial cost $5,589. Bakers VS Varys... "The average family car in 1962 cost $2924." REF: DangerousMinds.net

[79] "Based on... 100 years' worth of data from the Social Security Administration's (SSA) Baby Names database, the estimated population of people named MAVINEE is 0." https://www.mynamestats.com/First-Names/M/MA/MAVINEE/index.html

As we watched the sunset, I turned to him, and with the scarlet clouds and blue sky framing his handsome face, I told him, "Tony, I'm sorry. It's too late." That Sunday night I was supposed to catch the bus to return to Gainesville. Ronnie was at work and Lynda had just returned from Morrison's when my father, who had been drinking, began yelling at me. "You can marry a good Catholic who will become a doctor!" he stormed. "But no. You always insist on getting your own damned way!" When my sister tried to intervene, he slapped her so hard that I hurried her into her bedroom, Dad following close behind. I shut the door and locked it, but he unlocked it in an instant with a screwdriver.

"Forget about going to the bus station!" he shouted. Finally, after cursing us both, he left. At that time, I noticed a small but deep white scar on my sister's forehead. "How did you get that scar on your forehead?" I asked.

"Oh," she answered, "I just hit my head in the swimming pool." No way did I believe that. She just didn't want me worrying about her. The mark of the slap on Lynda's face had tuned an ugly red. Dad had gone outside to his speedboat, so now Mama knocked on the door, offering to take me to the bus station. I told her to just call a cab, but she sadly admitted that before Dad went to his boat, he had torn all the telephones out of the walls and hidden them, so we couldn't call anybody. "It's because of his leg!" my mother whispered. "He can't stand the pain anymore and he's afraid if he goes to the doctors, they'll amputate it!"[80] We sneaked out of the house in time for me to catch the last bus, with my vow never to return.

In September, 1962, Gainesville hummed with the rhythm of a new year. My friend Diane Butterfield and I won intramural medals in basketball, while Robert became a fixture at Grove Hall. The photo

shows me and Diane with our "Mystical Egyptian Tomb" display that won Grove Hall's dorm decorating contest. Robert, who was dressed as a tomb explorer, took the photo. By the Winter Trimester, 1963, Grove Hall was demolished and we all moved to the modern digs at Yulee Hall. The Fall Trimester was the first of several experimental Trimesters that UF tried out, with disastrous results due to delayed funds and grants that were semester-based. During this penniless two-week period

[80] Eventually my father's leg was amputated about ten years later.

for so many of us on grants, Don Federman shared his meagre funds with me, for I was too proud to ask Robert for money.

One of my pre-med classes required pairs of us to work on expensive embalmed cats to study their nervous systems. My friend Kathy Santi, who later became a doctor at Emery Med School, bought the cat for us with my promise to pay later, but it was still hard to manage all the other fees that popped up. That's when Don Federman, who was also in financial distress, tossed his last remaining quarter high in the air. Who would win? Tails, he ate. Heads, I would eat. The money finally came through two weeks later, but the gratitude I felt for Don's sacrifice will never be forgotten. Of course, I shared that bowl of rice with him!

Meanwhile, the Cold War started heating up again. This time, things were close to home: in October, the U.S. government told the U.N. that the Russians had moved nuclear missiles into Cuba, only 90 miles off the Florida coast. Convoys of troops and trucks and tanks, loaded to kill, came rumbling down our highways.

On October 23, the world held its breath, for a nuclear war was in the making when President Kennedy ordered a retaliatory naval blockade on Cuba. Russian ships, loaded for war, were approaching the boundary. A U2 was shot down over Cuba. Kennedy was besieged with demands to annihilate Havana and Castro with a few well-placed atom bombs. But Russia would have been forced to reply, with its own long-range missiles of mass destruction. Into this vortex of terror, Russian Premiere Nikita Khrushchev and John F. Kennedy began secretly communicating, a sleepless Bobby Kennedy at the helm. The leaders of both Superpowers were being pressured by their generals to make the first strike. The National Archive's account includes this sobering entry: *"...the first important Soviet account ...was contained in the tape-recorded memoirs of deposed Soviet leader Nikita Khrushchev ...smuggled to the West and published in 1970 ..."The account of the RFK-Dobrynin meeting in "Khrushchev Remembers," in the form of a paraphrase from memory of Dobrynin's report... claim[ed] that Robert F. Kennedy had fretted to Dobrynin that if his brother did not approve an attack on Cuba soon, the American military might overthrow him and seize power.*"[81]

We students, living so close to Cuba, knew there was a real chance that Florida could be annihilated with a few warheads. We anxiously waited for the latest announcements, crowding around radios and TV sets. As for Robert, he remained steady, calm and unconcerned. "There's nothing you can do," he reminded me, "to stop a bomb. Ignore it." After the Cuban Missile Crisis passed, I attended a few anti-Castro rallies with some friends, but Robert merely said, "The world was here yesterday, it is here today, and it will be here tomorrow."

"Your worry or mine," he declared, "will change nothing." Robert's lack of fear of the future and his unchanging calm was worlds away from the shouting, anger and hatred my Cuban friends seemed to live for.

---

[81] REF: https://nsarchive2.gwu.edu/nsa/cuba_mis_cri/moment.htm

"I stay out of everything," Robert told me, when I asked him to come sit with me and my anti-Castro friends at home football games.

I'd enjoyed all of Robert's petting and smooching, but by December, 1962, his patience was ending. I still refused to sleep with him, despite his relentless advances for nearly six months. But this was the 60's, not the 21st century, and my Catholic upbringing had deep roots. Wasn't I worth marriage to him? Robert had begun to blaze academically, exploding into straight A's in the geology and math courses he added in his 4th year. Having found his road to happiness and knowing I had led him to it, he invited me to a pizza dinner and laid out two silvery goblets. As he poured wine into the goblets he announced, "I have saved these cups, to drink from them with the woman I intend to marry."

"But can you say you love me?" I asked. When Robert said he wasn't going to say those words because I'd refused to sleep with him, and was a holdout, he stalked out, taking the goblets with him. "I'll come back when you grow up!" he growled. I let him go, figuring that if he really wanted me, he would be back. But after waiting two miserable weeks for his return, I sought advice from some of my girlfriends. They encouraged me to let him have his way. After all, by now everybody thought I was sleeping with him, I'd held out so long! So I called Robert, and simply said, "I give up." He said, "I'll be right over." I still remember that fateful evening, as would any girl. My friends Kathy, Diane,Karen and Mickey cheered me on, shouting from my open window as I ran from the dorm and rushed into Robert's open arms. He carried me away in his dusty blue Ford coupe to UF's so-called Lover's Lane. There were other cars parked here and there on this low hill covered by trees and darkness. The cars looked empty because their contents were well packed on the horizontal. After serenading me on his guitar, Robert made sure that I was transformed into a truly emancipated woman. Symbolically, our love-fest overlooked the city garbage dump.

By now, I was sure I was in love! I interpreted Robert's heavy silences as great depth of thought, when it was actually a disturbingly deep black hole. As for Robert, he saw my deepest long-term interests in cancer, medicine, ancient cultures, archaeology and survival training as mere passing fancies. As for my practicing Russian phrases on him, and my long-time fascination with Russian culture, Robert thought it a troublesome habit. To prove his point, for Valentine's Day Robert gave me Mao Zedong's "*Little Red Book*." Next, he joked, "I'll find you a copy of *The Communist Manifesto*, so you'll be well-prepared to defect to the Soviet Union. Don't tell my parents that you like the Russians," he warned. "They might think you're a communist." As a result of my new night-time excursions into forbidden biological activities, of which Robert fully approved, and despite all our precautions, I promptly fulfilled nature's most potent law: 'Life will find a way.' *I became pregnant!* "They said I couldn't have babies!" I told Robert, angry and in tears. What if my parents found out? What if Ochsner and Smathers found out? Even Robert's deep-keeled calm was shaken. Because of my

Catholic upbringing and because I personally cherished life, abortion was out of the question. Robert promptly vanished for the next few days, thinking over his options. Then the problem was solved. I suffered a miscarriage. I made it to the school's infirmary with so much blood dripping down my legs that there was no way to hide my condition. Since I was obviously not married, the staff quickly deduced that I had lost a non-immaculate conception, a big taboo back in 1963.

I collapsed into a hospital bed and did my best to rest and recover my health. A couple of days later, Robert strolled into my room. The staff could hardly believe that the fellow responsible for my condition dared show his face. The fact that he did so in such a nonchalant manner galled them even more. In contrast, my friend Don visited me with deference and empathy. His honest face was scarlet the whole time he stood at my bedside, even though he was not the responsible one.

Robert returned, ignoring the conspicuous stares and whispers. He took my limp hand and whispered to me, "I've decided I don't want to take this kind of risk again." Huh? What did he mean? Was he going to leave me again? Or have a vasectomy? I was bewildered and remained silent.

"I don't want to lose you," he said. "So, I've decided to marry you."

Still weak from the miscarriage, all I could do was stare at him blankly. Later, I started thinking about his "proposal" and realized that Robert didn't ask me to marry him. He was simply informing me of his plans. How romantic. No diamond, no flowers, no sunset and no bended knee. To receive such an offer at that time and place simply stunned me.

My stay in the infirmary was longer than I expected. I missed classes, assignments, lab work, and important interviews for a summer internship in cancer research, including a phone interview at Miami State University, which Senator Smathers had arranged. When I finally made it back to classes, there was just enough time to finish my most important work at the Human Nutrition Lab, a titration model that used blood sedimentation rates and radiation-tagged human cancer cells to obtain evidence of live cancer cells in the circulatory system. If live cancer cells could be detected in the blood, that meant the patient might be losing their fight against cancer. I had picked up the idea from Dr. George Moore, who had encouraged me to work with radioisotopes. At the end of March, 1963, UF was now firmly on a trimester schedule, but its scholarships and grants were still set up on the old system of two payouts per year. With the Craft Shop closing, I was broke. Classes were ending, but I wasn't about to go home. I finally got the courage to call Senator Smathers, embarrassed to explain why I had missed my interview. He was out of town, but I reached a sympathetic female aide, who was so friendly I told her how both Smathers and Dr. Ochsner had planned for me to interview for a summer internship at Miami U. She said she'd try to help. A few hours later, I received a phone call, but it wasn't from Smathers. It was from Dr. Ochsner! I was thrilled to hear his voice. I figured he was calling to help, but soon he had me cowering.

"What is the matter with you?" he thundered. "First you wanted to be a nun. The stupidest thing in the world!" I humbly agreed. But Ochsner wasn't finished. "The next thing I know," he went on, "after all the pains we took to rescue you from your own parents, you get pregnant and have a miscarriage!" I sadly admitted that this was so. "Judy!" Ochsner roared, *"Will you please make up your mind?"*

I said I was sorry and asked for his forgiveness. Mollified, Dr. Ochsner revealed that it was intended to steer me to New Orleans, as his star cancer specialist was interested in having me work in her lab as an intern for the summer. Would I like to come to New Orleans and work with Dr. Mary Sherman, the woman who directed the bone pathology laboratory at Ochsner Clinic? She had helped put the Clinic on the map as a respected medical center. Her brilliant articles had influenced the debate about the fundamental nature of cancer. She was famous. "She's a good, steady woman," Ochsner explained. "Just what you need to guide you." He told me that Dr Sherman had liked one of the reports I had sent about my blood sedimentation research.[82] She needed a lab assistant familiar with handling the carcinogenic SV-40 virus in fast-growing cancers. "If you should decide to work with her, after classes end, instead of going to Miami, we can arrange that," he said. "Miami has a lot of anti-Castro Cubans," he added, "but so does New Orleans. So, how do you feel about Castro?" I reeled off the litany: Castro was dreadful. He was a Communist. He tortured people. If necessary, he should be removed by force. [83]

"Good girl," Ochsner muttered. Then he sweetened the pot, making his offer irresistible. If I came and worked with Dr. Mary Sherman, I could skip the rest of my undergraduate education and enter Tulane Medical School in the Fall. Tulane accepted undergrad students only on rare occasions, he cautioned, but he stressed that he had influence there. What an offer! Next, Dr. Ochsner put the cherry on top.

He reminded me that Dr. Sherman was from the University of Chicago and they would see to it that she used her influence to get me into UC's medical school the following spring, should I still desire to go. He had me—hook, line and sinker! I gratefully accepted his offer and promised heaven and earth in return. With the air of a man covering a few minor, routine items, Ochnser added that my tuition to med school would be paid, my room and board would be covered, and I'd receive a stipend to cover other expenses. I was not to worry about expenses for my internship, either: I must fill out some papers and then could choose to live either at the YWCA in town, just as I'd done in Buffalo, New York, or

[82] Today, blood sedimentation tests can be used to help detect bone cancer.

[83] On March 28, 1963, "two Soviet-built MIG jet aircraft fired on the U.S. freighter Floridian in international waters off Cuba..." https://dolearchives.ku.edu/sites/dolearchive.drupal.ku.edu/files/files/historyday/originals/hd14_cuba_020.pdf Smathers was busy! As editor, Ed Haslam inserted Ochsner's question at this time. I can't remember exactly when Ochsner asked me about Castro.

I could stay at Brent House, on Ochsner's campus. "We will send you a one-way bus ticket," he added. "Be sure to bring all your things." Then Ochsner said, "I'll see you the second week in May!" and hung up.

I was left in shock. My classes on UF's trimester system were over, over weeks ahead of Tulane. Since I was about to get kicked out of my dorm, I was already packed. I had considered a vague plan to move in with my auntie Elsie on Kensington Rd. in South Bend, if Senator Smathers couldn't help me. Now, everything was (almost) wonderful again! Most of my friends were leaving the dorms right now. I remember running down the hall to find Mickey Rosenblatt, Diane Butterfield and Kathy Santi. Mickey was with her boyfriend, and Diane was already gone, but Kathy was still there. "Kathy!" I burst out, "Guess what? Dr. Ochsner is going to send me to Med School in the Fall!" Pretty Kathy stopped her packing to give me a hug. In the fall, she would be entering Med School at Emery University.

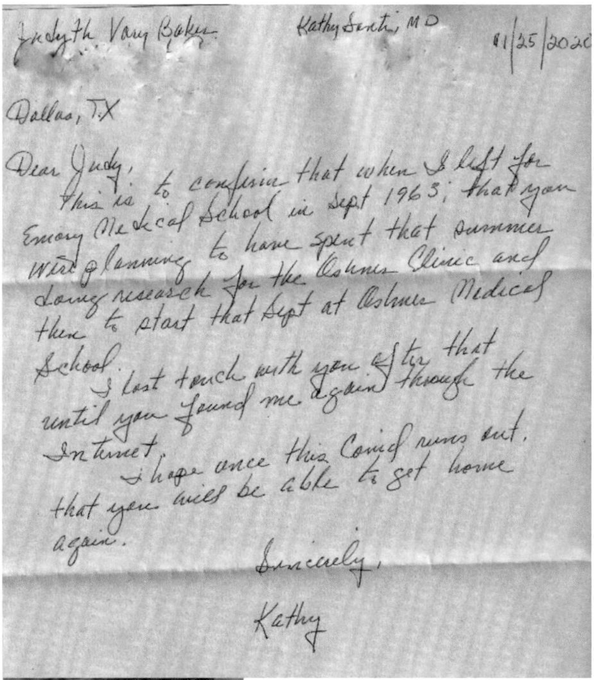
Judyth Vary Baker Kathy Santi, MD 11/25/2020
Dallas, TX

Dear Judy,
This is to confirm that when I left for Emory Medical School in Sept 1963, that you were planning to have spent that summer doing research for the Oshner Clinic and then to start that Sept at Oshner Medical School.
I lost touch with you after that until you found me again through the Internet.
I hope once this Covid runs out, that you will be able to get home again.

Sincerely,
Kathy

We would not meet again for many years, but **Dr. Kathy Santi**[84] did remember what I told her, kindly writing this note Nov.25, 2020.

But the 2nd week in May was almost a month away. Dr. Ochsner had called long distance from Washington, D.C. I didn't even know where he was. Then, I realized that I could probably lure Robert to New Orleans. After all, Louisiana's great petroleum geology schools were superior to anything in Florida at the time. We'd have a month to decide to marry or not. Maybe even go on a honeymoon, before I had to start my internship. As I considered the options, I called Robert, asking him to meet me in the University Library. There, I showed him a New Orleans newspaper full of ads from petroleum companies pleading for summer help. That got his interest.

---

[84] Dr. Kathy Santi, 2014, when we met [with joy] in New Port Richie, FL

Too shy to mention marriage, I was also afraid to tell him I intended to *stay* in New Orleans. After all, he had to return in the Fall to finish his degree.

I was afraid he wouldn't come at all if it meant months of separation in the Fall. But I did tell Robert that I was out of money and was going to go to New Orleans, where they had plenty of lab and clinic jobs, with cheap rent. "If you come," I said, "at least we can be together." Originally, Robert's parents expected him to work all summer, in exchange for paying his tuition in the fall. He had expected to visit me I in Miami, so I was thrilled when Robert replied, quietly, "I still want to marry you," adding that the drive to New Orleans would be easier. "Honey, I don't want to push you," I answered, "but you haven't mentioned any particular time for us to get married... and I can't stay any longer." I told Robert that if he didn't marry me, I couldn't get birth control pills. That's the way it was, in 1963. He would just have to use condoms, because I wasn't going to risk another traumatic visit to an infirmary! If anything could inspire Robert to marry, it was the specter of having to use condoms.

On **April 16, 1963**, two marvelous things happened: Robert finally said he

loved me! And the bus ticket to New Orleans arrived. With Robert's words of love resounding in my heart, I asked him to drive me to the bus station. "I still have to go home," he said. "But I'll convince my folks that going to Louisiana means a money-making career in geology, instead of starvation as a writer." As I got on the bus at last, I daydreamed about the wonderful time in New Orleans we'd have. We'd marry, have a great summer together, then he'd spend a semester away, finishing his degree, to reunite joyfully with me once more in The Big Easy. We'd then embark on our glittering new careers: I, the insightful cancer researcher, and he, the well-compensated geologist. Meanwhile, the same famous doctor who had quietly shepherded my career the past few years would be there in romantic New Orleans, to guide, direct and protect me with gruff, fatherly concern. His commitment was in my hand, in the form of a prepaid bus ticket. Plus, I had $42 in cash for emergencies. I had it all worked out. What could go wrong?

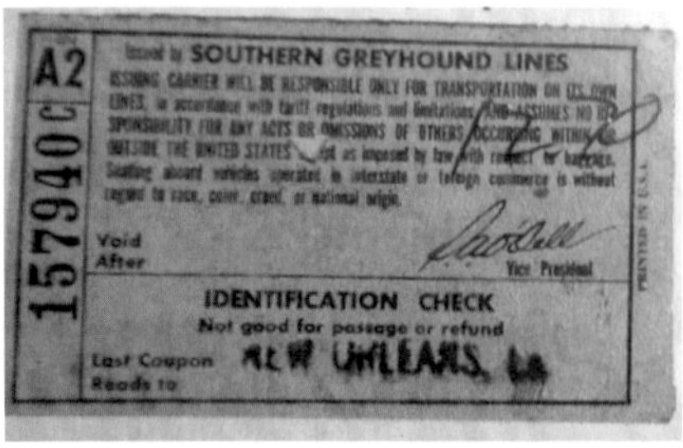

Chapter Six

New Orleans

As the bus roared down the highway to a new life, I pondered how opposites attract. Robert and I both liked writing short stories and having sex, but that's where our similarities ended. I was emotional, creative and eager to explore new horizons. Money meant little to me. Robert was steady, focused and tenacious. He seemed to always get what he went after. I guess I was just one of those things he went after. What was it about domineering men that attracted me? Perhaps their self-confidence made me feel secure. We'd marry, he'd be loyal and faithful, and would graduate and reunite with his devoted wife. We'd then embark on our glittering new careers: me, the insightful cancer researcher, and he, the well-compensated geologist.

"I still have to go home to Fort Walton Beach," he' d warned me. "My folks need me at the office. But I'll convince them that going to Louisiana means a money-making career in geoscience, instead of starvation as a writer." He then gave me a little packet of pink paper squares. "There are sixteen of them," he said. "Tear off one square every day. I'll be there before you look at the last one." On each little square were three little words, written in black ink: *'I love you!'* My heart swelled with joy: Robert really *did* love me! Tensions were still high over my being a "gypsy" who had sneakily seduced Robert from the arms of the cheating blonde beauty his parents had picked out for him, and since our parents loathed each other, we decided to elope! Robert had dropped me off early so he could attend a "beer bust" at Lake Wauberg, where hundreds of UF students were celebrating their temporary freedom. UF was now many miles away. The bus finally made Pensacola as sunset turned to darkness. Biloxi swished by in a blur of lights. There were more stops in small towns. Mississippi flew by, its pine tree forests ending suddenly at Louisiana's state line. Then the long night's darkness slowly gave way to the night-glow of New Orleans on the horizon. It was a long trip.

Then amazing buildings appeared, festooned with neon signs. Antique streetlamps illuminated the deep shadows of the sleeping city.

The bus station was bleak, almost empty. I thanked the driver for carrying my things to a couple of big lockers. I was told the YWCA was not far away, but as I picked up my suitcase and began walking down the trash-littered street, I was aware that several men were watching me, their eyes like radar. OK, time to call a cab! As I got into the cab, police sirens went off, followed by what sounded like gunfire. The cabbie told me it was just the new District Attorney, busy cleaning up the city. He called him "Big Jim." What I heard, he said, was probably one of Big Jim's raids. We reached the "Y" quickly. I was surprised to find it dilapidated inside, unlike the well-run YWCA in Buffalo. Dr. Ochsner had told me he would pay for my room, but when I inquired at the desk, my name wasn't on their list. I'd stupidly told nobody at Ochsner's that I was coming almost three weeks early, yet I was miffed that no room had been reserved for me. How naïve can you get? It was about 5:30 AM – too early to call anybody – so I rented a bed in the cheapest room available. Unlocking the door, I was surprised to see three women already inside. They looked up eagerly when I opened the door, but when they saw me, they were disappointed. "So, who are you?" one of them asked. They were anxiously awaiting a fourth roommate, who was late returning from work, and I was not her.

There were five narrow beds in the small, dingy room, but only one closet. The room was a mess. Bras and panties hung drying in an open window in full view of the street. Coffee boiled away in a battered pan sitting on a hotplate. Everything looked used and dirty, but at least the fifth bed was clean and neatly made, as if it had just been placed there. "I'm Judy Vary," I told the girls, as I began hanging my clothes in the surprisingly empty closet. "Better not hang your clothes in there," one of the girls said. "Cleaning ladies might take them." The two younger girls were attractive, but they looked tired. They had been in New Orleans only a few weeks, and both had worked that night. The third girl was heavy-set and worked days as a waitress. "If you work at night, like those two do," she let me know, "just you pay me twenty-five cents, once in awhile, and I'll watch your clothes for you. Things get took even if you sleep right on top of them, honey," she warned. I quickly gave the gentle extortionist a quarter. I didn't want to wind up with nothing decent to wear when it was time to meet my doctors!

As dawn broke, my new friends, still waiting for "Carol," began talking about their lives. The waitress said she worked at the Royal Castle out on Airline Drive, near the airport. I was familiar with Royal Castles, as we also had them in Florida. They were fast-food stops that served and breakfasts with fresh-squeezed orange juice. The waitress said they always needed help for the morning rush if I needed a quick part-time job. Thinking this dumpling could not possibly understand how the needs of "the great cancer researcher" would not include flipping hamburgers, I tried to be polite and asked her for details. My new friend said weekdays she got up before dawn, caught the Tulane bus, then rode 45 minutes to Kenner, for the privilege of serving greasy food for a dollar an hour. Minus deductions for food, lunch break, uniforms, insurance and taxes, she brought home almost seven dollars a day. I wasn't tempted. As I changed into my nightgown, one of the other girls extended yet another job opportunity. "You've sure got the boobs!" she piped. "Why don't you come work with me? We need more strippers!" I wasn't sure if the term 'boobs' meant breasts or buns, but I was sure it did not mean brains! She assured me that stripping paid lots better than slinging burgers. The idea was flattering, but when it came to nudity, I was hopelessly modest. I may have thought of myself as a free thinker, and sexually liberated, but in fact, I was a shy girl, with the lower right of my abdomen a mass of scars. Talk went on, and finally the third girl – a dark blonde with an attractive figure – started telling her tales. By far the best-looking, she said she was going to Bunny School and would soon be a Playboy Bunny, working as a cocktail waitress in the French Quarter. She showed me all the drinks she had to memorize, and where each kind of drink belonged on a tray. She had accidentally ripped her Bunny costume, which was never supposed to happen, so she had secretly brought it to the "Y" to repair it. She asked me to try it on, to inspect her work. We didn't do this in the lab! It fit perfectly. She told me they were looking for more recruits and showed me the newspaper ad. Being a Playboy Bunny was better than working as a stripper, she said, because the club had rules that protected the girls. She was told there would be no "man-handling" at the Playboy Club. I admit that this info, combined with the fact that I would wear what was basically a one-piece bathing suit that covered my scars, made the prospect a bit more attractive. The girls were still anxiously waiting for their missing friend Carol to show up. At 8:00 a.m. I went downstairs to call Ochsner Clinic.

BE A PLAYBOY CLUB BUNNY!

Pretty young girls who enjoy the glamour and excitement of night life, the sound of jazz, the world of celebrities, the atmosphere of show business, can earn GOOD MONEY working as Bunnies at the PLAYBOY CLUB.

Whether you are greeting guests at the door, snapping souvenir pictures, selling gifts or serving food and drinks, you'll meet interesting people while you are having a good time.

If you are between the ages of 18 and 24, attractive and personable, married or single, you probably qualify. No experience necessary.

That's when I learned that Dr. Ochsner was in Washington, on his way to Central America. I hadn't been expected for at least two more weeks. Even Dr. Sherman was out of town. I still had to fill out some formal application papers, which Ochsner and Sherman would sign upon their return. Until then, no funds would be released. I was advised to return home, but that was out of the question. I was truly on my own!

At first, the idea was exciting. I'd never been truly free from the scrutiny of parents, doctors and instructors. But after counting my cash, I began to panic. Upon calling my bank, I learned that Ochsner had paid for my $12.70 bus ticket from my grant funds! My account was now almost empty. I wasn't about to beg for any more money from my sick Grandpa, and my fiancé had warned me never to call. He'd promised to send money when he could, but I had no idea when.

Forget the steak dinners! I'd have to eat canned Vienna sausages, pickled pigs' feet and baked beans from the can! It was now about 8:30.

I was so tired I could have slept on a bed of nails, but just as I collapsed on my bed, Carol stumbled into the room, clutching newspapers against her naked body! Breathless and frightened, she struggled to embrace the other girls who ran to greet her. I opened my eyes in time to see her drop the newspapers in exchange for a bathrobe. This pretty girl was wearing nothing but a g-string and pasties. The night before, there was a tip-off that the police were about to raid the Sho-Bar, the club where she worked.

Being under-age and fearing arrest, Carol ran out the back when she heard sirens, snatching a raincoat as she fled. When someone yelled at her, she dropped the raincoat and grabbed a handful of newspapers to cover herself. She hid in a telephone booth until daylight, after which

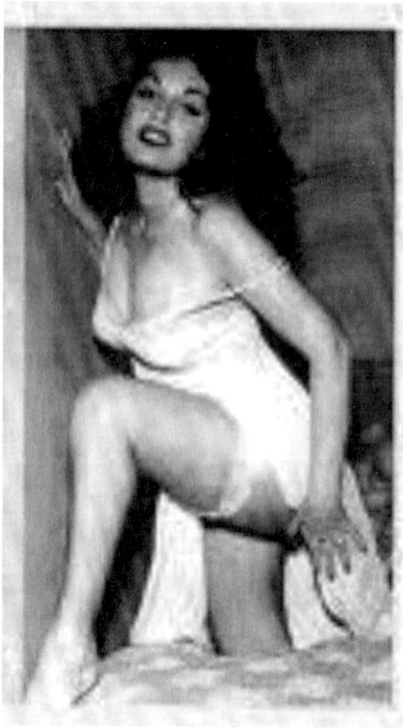

she crept from hiding place to hiding place until she reached the YWCA. Relieved, everyone agreed with the Royal Castle waitress that we needed a few hours of sleep. As for the waitress, it was Saturday, and she worked the afternoon shift on weekends. Equally exhausted, the Playboy Bunny soon followed. I should have been sleeping, too, but I couldn't resist listening to Carol, who needed a sympathetic ear. She gave me and her stripper friend, who kept dozing off, a detailed account of her adventure. I was getting a different kind of education — fast. The girls at the Club had told Carol the police were actually only interested in pestering **Jada Cuffari** (AKA Jada Conforto), the club's headline act. Jada was

Carol's mentor at the Sho-Bar on Bourbon Street, one of several clubs owned by New Orleans Mafia Don Carlos Marcello. As Carol's tale unfolded, I learned a Mafia man called Jack Ruby was in town trying to steal Jada for his nightclub in Dallas. But Jada was in love. She refused to leave her boyfriend (also named Robert) who managed the Sho-Bar, so Ruby was using his power to force Jada to Dallas. I guess "banned in New Orleans" would have been good publicity for a stripper in Dallas! As Carol explained to me, Jack Ruby and Joe Civello—the Dallas under-boss for Mafia Godfather Carlos Marcello – ran the Dallas nightclubs and would get their way.[85]Ruby was Marcello's Dallas cop-fixer. Marcello was described as a "marvelous gentleman" who "only rarely cheated on his wife." Marcello would buy a nightclub, gas station, restaurant or hotel, then "sell" it for a pittance to a "friend" who would hand over most of the profits, if he wished to keep his health. The Sho-Bar was supposed to be independent of this corrupt system, but Carol said that was a joke. True, this talk was just hearsay, but Jada had confided in her new friend, angry at being manipulated. I soaked up every word. What Jack Ruby wanted, Jack Ruby got, Carol explained. Jada and her boyfriend had been arrested two days earlier: Jada for performing "an obscene dance" and he for permitting it. Now the police had returned for an encore, but this time, everybody was on the alert, and everyone escaped. Still, Carol hoped Jada would put in a good word for her with Ruby. Maybe he would hire her away from her purgatory in New Orleans as well. The rumor was that despite his notoriously aggressive behavior, Ruby was a generous man who treated his girls well. He bought fancy clothes for them and took care of their abortions and penicillin shots. A few girls even got sent up to the big league in Las Vegas. Of course, they had to sleep with him to get ahead. Reportedly, Jack Ruby was 'bisexual.' Such was the price of success in that world. My new stripper friends, seeing I was a babe in the woods, began carefully exposing me to their brand of New Orleans – full of people who got drunk, loved music, and sometimes went to jail. They lived in a world I'd never seen, but they still had dreams of their own: to marry a man with a big house, who didn't cheat on them too much, or to become the mistress of a rich man married to a woman who did not sexually fulfill him. Both had been led into stripping by difficult circumstances.

The 16-year-old had been raped by several football players after a game and became pregnant. Her father said it was her fault for being a cheerleader and for drinking that night. After her dad paid for her abortion, he drove his daughter a hundred miles to New Orleans.

---

[85] Jack Ruby and his sister Eva ran two nightclubs: The Carousel and The Vegas Club. Ref: https://mcadams.posc.mu.edu/ruby4.htm The clubs were owned by Civello for Marcello.

There, he counted out a hundred one-dollar bills into her hands, and left her on the street. The other girl had an even sadder story, so eerily similar to mine that it sent chills down my spine: she and her fiancé had defied their parents and planned on starting a new life in New Orleans together. She came to town first while he finished up his job. Two weeks earlier, on his way to join her, he had been killed in an auto accident. He had his life savings on him in cash, but when she identified his body at the morgue, the money was missing. Desperate and broke, she had gotten herself trapped into a bad contract at a strip joint across the street from the Sho-Bar.

After a second fruitless call to Ochsner's Clinic, I gave up all hope of a quick rescue. There was no Nobel Prize winner this time to pay my way. The grant money was gone. No sympathetic Marna Brady would enroll me in part-time lab jobs. Determined to stay, The Great Cancer Researcher decided to follow her waitress friend to the Royal Castle. The waitress was being transferred to a Royal Castle downtown --a promotion that meant her long rides to Kenner were over. I signed up to fill one of the gaps she'd leave --the breakfast rush hour from 6:00 am to 8:00 am. Most of my work had been in sterile labs with precise routines, with high sensitivity to the invisible dangers of viruses and bacteria. We killed it all, using alcohol, acetone and black light. But I was given access to just one dish-cloth to wipe down counters and tables between customers! It alarmed me. I was just spreading the bacteria around.

In my mind's eye, I could see the little buggers enjoying it! When I stopped to rinse my cloth, I was admonished for wasting time. *Hurry! Hurry! Hurry!* The customers were mostly working-class males in a rush to eat and get going so they wouldn't be late for work. It seemed like they all needed attention at the same time. In my haste, I burned myself, cut myself and confused customer orders. Despite my frantic pace I was much slower than the other waitress and resigned myself to an "F" report card in waitressing. How did she manage? At the end of the two hours, I was relieved when my cranky boss said, "For some reason the customers seem to like you, so I won't fire you." Thanks. But at least, I'd earned enough to pay for another day at the "Y." When I got my first paycheck, I was surprised at how proud I was. I had enough money left to buy a nice linen dress for my wedding day, plus a hand-made, see-through black baby-doll nightie, made by a Hungarian seamstress, for my wedding night. I borrowed enough from Carol to buy a second-hand wedding band from a pawn shop, which I was told was real 14K gold (It was). She said not to pay her back: it was her present. If I dined carefully on soup and sandwiches, I'd make it to May Day, that magical date when Robert said he would come (*If* he would come!).

For the first time in memory, I had no lab work to do, no reports to write, and no classes to attend. The beauty of it all was that I was free!

Maybe I was poor, but I had been turned loose on the world, and was just ignorant enough to get into trouble! On Monday, April 22, I finally located the Central Post Office, where a letter from Robert was waiting. In this, his first letter, he instructed me to put a newspaper ad in the Personal section, using the code name "Jaryo." But why? I knew he didn't want any record of long-distance phone calls showing up on his parents' phone bill, but still, there were payphones, and it would be easy to get the phone number to the "Y" from the Information operator. Instead, I was asked to pretend to be Robert's traveling friend, Raleigh Rourke. I could send just one letter to tell him where I was, with Rourke's name on the return address part of the envelope so his parents wouldn't guess I was writing. "Just don't use any perfume," Robert counseled. "Or they'll think Raleigh is queer."

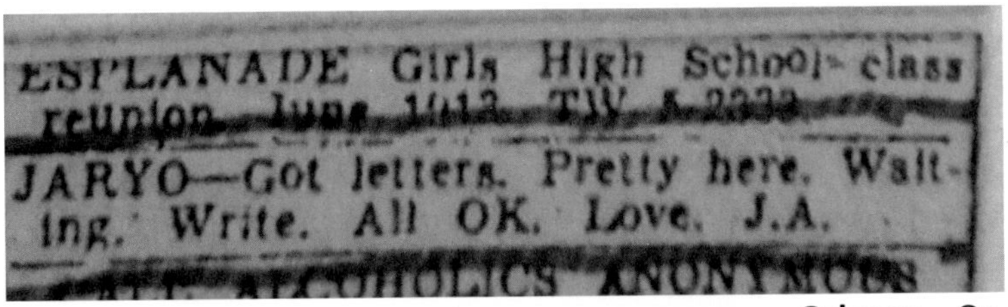
ESPLANADE Girls High School class

JARYO—Got letters. Pretty here. Waiting. Write. All OK. Love, J.A.

ALCOHOLICS ANONYMOUS

The 'JARYO' ad was placed in the Times-Picayune to show Robert I'd arrived safely in New Orleans. On the envelope of his second letter, I wrote and scratched out various words, as I had limited money. Lee Oswald would soon wonder if "JARYO" and "waiting" were code words my CIA 'handler' may have asked me to use.

The New Orleans Post Office and Civic Center.

On April 24, another letter arrived, containing a $5 bill. From a miser like him, this was some proof of love, and the letter itself was so sweet that I practically memorized it: *I've been dying to tell everyone that there's about to be someone coming into the family. Namely, judy, Judy, JUDY! I haven't told, of course, but I still think about it... I'll be so glad when these 11 days are gone. The post office will close soon, so: love, love, love, Bob xxxxxxX."* The next two days, after getting off the bus after my Royal Castle stint, I eagerly hurried to the post office, hoping for another letter, but there was nothing. Robert had promised to write every day, but so far, he had only written twice in a whole week. By now, the postal clerk recognized my anxious face. The "Jaryo" ad was published, which Robert said he would look for, to know that I was OK. When I realized his eyes would see those actual words, I bought a copy of the newspaper and began carrying around the ad section.

That way, I could look at it all the time. After all, HIS eyes had also seen that ad! I even decorated the ad with a lipstick kiss. That newspaper section took on the status of a love token, even though it was getting seriously crumpled. But even this talisman failed me when Robert didn't write. That's when fear, anger, and sorrow began to fill my thoughts. I'd been regaled the night of the 25th with a trip to the Sho-Bar, where the girls fixed my hair, and put makeup on my face. Then they taught me some of the moves they used in their acts. I saw a lot of skin, and how the girls were pawed over. Men can be very sexual beings when inside a strip club. Even fully-clothed, I received unwelcome attention. It made me feel afraid.

Then came April 26, 1963, a date that changed everything. That Friday morning, I worked again for two stressful breakfast rush hours that felt like twenty, then got on the bus. On the ride back, a skinny woman with long, white hair plunked herself down beside me. She wore a yellow flowered dress, sandals made of slices of auto tire, and a string of dried chicken feet around her neck. Her fingernails curled like long claws in different directions and she smelled like something that had died. I wanted to move away, but didn't want to hurt her feelings.

When I got off the bus, I noticed two people standing nearby on the sidewalk – a tall, thin black man talking quietly to a short, fat white woman. How nice, I thought. Colored people and white people getting along here, in the heart of Dixie. There was reason for hope!

Suddenly, the black man backed away, almost knocking me down. Then he began to run. The woman chased after him, waving a whiskey bottle above her head and screaming curses. Then she threw the bottle. It bounced off the man's head, hit a metal fence, bounced again, and exploded on the sidewalk. The shattering glass almost hit me. I was starting to experience culture shock, which I thought was only encountered while traveling in the Third World.

If only Robert were here, I thought to myself, *I would feel safe again!* Back at the "Y" I changed into a nice dress and high heels, for I planned to go sign my papers at Ochsner's Clinic. Since I easily got lost, it had taken me days to figure out how to get there by bus. But first, I would stop at the Post Office. Would today also end with no letter from Robert? I was feeling quite alone. I'd been writing the "letter from R. Rourke" for several days, including a statement that we should not even live in New Orleans itself. That was to encourage Robert to seek employment in Jefferson Parish, near Ochsner's Clinic. On the back side of the letter, which I finished today, I mentioned "nosing around the hospital." Of course, that was Ochsner's hospital. I wrote that I'd try to get a job there, as a hint. The last part of the letter also hinted that I might try waitressing "until" Robert arrived. Soon after that, I'd start my internship, which I was unwilling to mention. Now, as I stood in line at the General Delivery counter, I felt wilted. I'd been up since 5 a.m. Since I was out of my Royal Castle uniform, I was again carrying that rolled-up newspaper section, with its "Jaryo" ad emblazoned with lipstick. At the time, I was only vaguely aware that a man was standing behind me in line. Now it was my turn to speak to the postal clerk. Learning there was nothing for "Judy Vary," I made the plunge. "Is there anything you might have for a 'Mr. Rourke'?" I asked.

"Do you have any ID with you?" the clerk replied.

He was sympathetic, as he'd seen me several times before, seeking letters. I pulled out my Royal Castle pay stub. "You can call Royal Castle about who I am," I told him. "I work at the one that's headquarters for New Orleans, out at the airport." But the clerk shook his head. "No, ma'am," the postman said. "Can't do that. I'd need something saying Mr. Rourke will let you pick up his mail for him." Remembering that I had Robert's first letter in my purse, I dug it out. "How many letters come to General Delivery from Fort Walton Beach?" I asked. "And look," I said, pointing, "right here it says I should put Mr. Rourke's name on the envelope."

The clerk, seeing I also had an envelope with a return address to "R. Rourke," kindly agreed to look for something from him. As I picked up my rolled-up newspaper section again, tucking it under my arm, I got a glimpse of a clean-cut young man standing behind me. He offered a friendly smile.

Lee Oswald, USSR 1961

The clerk returned to say there was nothing for a Mr. Rourke, either. Disappointed, I sighed and bought a stamp, but as I handed the stamped letter to the clerk, the rolled-up newspaper section fell from under my arm. At once, the young man behind me picked up the newspaper, glanced at the lipstick kiss on it, and then handed it to me. Seeing no wedding ring on his left hand, I thought angrily to myself, *"I'm not married yet!"* and gave him my prettiest smile. "*Karashaw, Tovarisch!*" I told him (loosely, *Fine, Comrade,* in Russian.). Yes, I was upset enough at Robert to flirt with a cute guy. And I wasn't called "Juduffski" by my family for speaking in Spanish. On the contrary, I often used Russian phrases as an ice-breaker, expecting the other person to ask, "What language is that?" So, I was shocked when the young man leaned close to me and said, in perfect Russian, "It's not wise to speak Russian in New Orleans." I looked for the first time straight at him. "But I like to speak Russian!" I protested, also in Russian, as politely as the words allowed. As I turned to leave, the young man said, "Please! Wait!" once more in Russian. He had not yet spoken a word in English.

I just said 'OK,' in case he didn't know any English. As I waited, the young man went to the counter and enquired if there was a letter for a 'Lee H. Oswald.' Also being disappointed, he joined me. As we walked toward the bus stop, at first, he tried to indulge me by speaking only Russian, but Mr. Oswald's fluency was far more advanced than Miss Vary's, so we settled into English.

"You must be new in town" he said. "I just got into town, myself." When he offered to 'walk me home' I decided to go to Ochsner's Clinic later, absolutely fascinated by this new acquaintance. When I asked him about himself, he smiled. "I was born in New Orleans," he let me know. "I lived here as a child, but I've been away for nearly ten years. I'm staying at the YMCA right now, until my family gets into town." He said they lived in Texas. I asked where he learned to speak Russian so well and soon learned that he had lived in the USSR some thirty months. Excited, I told him about my interest in all things Russian: the literature, music, and art. "Russia is tops in countries I want to visit," I added. "My family calls me 'Juduffksi.'" After a moment, he asked if I had read Dostoievsky's *The Idiot.*

In fact, I had. I'd even written a poem about Prince Myshkin, the title character, which I proceeded to recite to my new friend. As soon as I finished, Lee translated my poem into melodious Russian. He didn't miss a line. "I notice you have no accent," he said next. Nor did he, I responded. That's when I spotted the thick wedding band on his right hand. Oops! He was married! Most likely, in Russia! My Hungarian Grandma had also worn her wedding ring on her right hand. More curious than ever, I observed him as we walked. Lee Oswald was slender, but well-built, the type of man who would never get fat. He had intense, blue-gray eyes that changed color in direct sunlight, compared to a hazel tint, when in artificial light. He had fine, wavy brown hair, as fine as my own. There was a precise way that he carried himself that hinted of a military background. As he turned to me again, I saw the neckline of a clean, white undershirt under his worn but spotless khaki shirt, which added to the military air. His posture was erect, his head held high. He took his place curbside to shield me from the traffic, like a gentleman. When my hand touched his accidentally, he moved slightly away. *What a sweetheart!* I thought, and what a nice contrast to the men I'd recently been in contact with! "So, what does the "H" in your name stand for?" I finally asked.

"Henry," he joked. "Hogan. Herkimer. Horace. Guess," he teased.

"Hoover," I replied with bluster. "That would even be worse!" he laughed. "My middle name is Harvey. I don't particularly like it. And my Russian friends called me Alek, because Lee sounds weird to them. Half the time, when I wrote it, people misread it as 'Henry,' so I started writing "H."

We walked a bit further, then he added, "I have calculated that will save me many hours during my life --avoiding writing 'Harvey.'" As we continued to walk, I began to question my shoe selection. Who invented high heels in the first place, and why would an otherwise intelligent woman wear them? Finally, we found a bench in a shaded area near the YWCA and sat down. Referring to the U.S. Marine Corps ring on his left hand, I said, "Well, you're a Marine, as well as married."

"You're so observant," Mr. Oswald replied.

"I'm terrible at remembering faces," I admitted, "and I get lost trying to find my own bathroom, but I'm good at noticing odd things other people don't."

"I won't forget *your* face," he replied, "because you look like my wife. Are you married?" he asked, looking down at my hand, which carried no ring. "Almost. In a few days. If he comes. If I still want to marry him."

"*If* he comes? *If* you still want to marry him?" he mocked.

"I love Robert," I insisted, "but if he doesn't show up, I'll survive."

"Love – unto the death!" Lee replied, with grand derision. I got his point. His directness was penetrating, his wit disarming. I wanted him to know more about me, so I told him I was in New Orleans to do cancer research. Dr. Ochsner himself had invited me, but I would be working with Dr. Mary Sherman, who ran a cancer laboratory at Ochsner's hospital. I also wanted Mr. Oswald to know that I had important contacts, just in case he wasn't as nice as he seemed. Then he surprised me again: Lee had a friend—a Dr. Ferrie –who had mentioned Dr. Sherman's name just the night before, at dinner. "She's famous," I said proudly, while calculating the mathematical odds of Lee's hearing her name only yesterday, after being out of town nearly a decade. Then Lee demonstrated some of his own powers of observation.

He had noticed the Royal Castle check stub I'd displayed at the post office and wondered why I, involved in cancer research, was working there. Fair enough, so I explained my predicament. We sat together another hour, discussing various subjects. He was well-read; we had both been impressed with Aldous Huxley's utopian nightmare in *Brave New World*, which Lee compared to George Orwell's dark view of the future in *1984*. I was surprised at his in-depth knowledge of various political issues. We delved deeper, discussing Bertrand Russell's contentious nuclear disarmament propositions, criticizing Germany for its fascism, slamming the Soviets for totalitarianism, and ranting at America's bullying of Latin America. "That leaves us nowhere to live in peace but in the most primitive parts of the world," Lee observed. He was surprised at my Socialist ideals. After all, I held a fierce anti-communist stance. We were now in his territory. Lee was the only American I'd ever met who had lived in Communist Russia, and I wanted to learn more—lots more.

It was a subject he could articulate skillfully and without prejudice, with clarity and accuracy. Just one hour of sitting on a park bench in New Orleans with a stranger had suddenly opened my eyes to a river of thought, flowing around the world. As he spoke, I got another good look at his eyes, which now were blue, reflecting the sky. *"A shame he's married,"* I thought. *Oops!* My Catholic upbringing kicked in, and guilt swelled up within me. Lee must have sensed my sudden mood shift, for he said, "My wife is in Texas because, unfortunately, we are not getting along very well right now." His sorrowful words rang true. I felt that he was simply sharing a burden, not implying that he was available for romance. Then, brightening, Lee asked if I played chess. I said I was good at the game.

He replied that he'd never met a girl before who played chess, wrote poetry, loved Russian literature, was in cancer research and also could speak some Russian. "I'd like to play you at chess sometime," he proposed. "Dr. Ferrie has a chess set we can use." Lee quickly added, "Since he's involved in cancer research himself, I think you two should meet."[86] I now understood how the name 'Dr. Sherman' had come up,and agreed. "I'll call him right away," Lee told me, standing up to leave. "Right now, I have to pick up a shirt. If you need help with anything, call the YMCA and leave a message for me." As we parted, Lee gave me a squeeze of the arm, a boyish smile, and then walked away. I just stood there daydreaming. I loved the way he talked and walked. And those color-changing eyes! His beautiful Russian... I tried not to stare at him as he walked...Then reality kicked in. *No, no, you silly! You are supposed to be in love with Robert Allison Baker, III!*

I decided to re-read Robert's two letters, to remind me who I really loved. Now calmed down, I was soon on my way to Ochsner's Clinic to fill out my internship papers. By now, I didn't want to live in Ochsner's Brent House. It was in the middle of nowhere, offered bland, expensive hospital food, with no access to New Orleans' museums, libraries, shopping, and universities.

And I'd not see any more of my new friend, Lee Oswald, so far away. That evening, Carol invited me to a new club in the French Quarter. She had become part of a new three-girl performance there, with a chance to do a solo act. As I watched from back-stage, the whole scene struck me as a strange, barbaric ritual. This beautiful woman was taking off her clothes amidst whistles, drum-beats and shouts, and it was for money. She made a lot of cash but had to give half of it to her "sponsor." It was a hard life, and it was making her brassy.

---

[86]Both Lee and I became interested in Russian culture through elderly Russians who taught us to play chess. Lee said he learned to play chess from an old Russian, Alexei, in New Orleans, as a young teen. I also learned to play chess from an aged Russian, at the Lake Maggiore Youth Center in St. Petersburg. Lee played a good game.

Next, we went to the Sho-Bar, to find her boyfriend. That night, I

thought on Mr. Oswald. How could he have gone to the USSR and been able to return with a Russian wife? And how could he care so much about literature, fine arts, and the world, having said he'd been raised poor in New Orleans?

<u>Saturday, April 23, 1963</u>

After too little sleep, at 5:30 AM I boarded the bus at Tulane and staggered into the Royal Castle to handle the familiar onslaught of men demanding quick service. I was frantically taking orders, flipping burgers, scrambling eggs and squeezing orange juice for a gallery of gulping Adams' apples. These were laborers who needed their breakfast fast before heading out for a day of exhausting work building houses or laying brick. They were basically good men who worked hard. Their voices were loud and bold. They flirted with me and called me "honey," "Babe" and "sweetie." They forgave my poor waitress skills and left tips anyway, mostly because they liked how I looked in that uniform and little apron. But the pace was frantic and for someone like me, exhausting.

Racing to keep up with the orders, I suddenly burned myself. Forcing a smile on my face anyway, I looked up to see Lee Oswald coming through the door. He had come all this way to see me! He stood in line until a seat opened at the counter. Lee was better dressed today, in dark pants, white shirt and brown tie. He looked quite handsome, sitting there with his quizzical smile and discerning eyes. He ordered a glass of orange juice, then watched me press the oranges against the electric spinner, which nicked my thumb. My thumb bleeding, I handed him the juice.

Then he said, "I'll have to drink it all, because you shed your blood making it." What an odd thing to say! But he said it in a grave tone that conveyed empathy. I couldn't imagine Robert or any of the other guys I knew to say anything so uniquely valiant. With each out-of-the-ordinary thing Lee Oswald did, he became a little more intriguing. Then he took a paperback book from his pants pocket and started reading. Though curious, I had to hurry on to other customers. When I returned to see if he wanted anything else, Lee ordered a full breakfast of eggs, bacon, coffee and toast. As I scribbled the order down, I got a chance to see the book's title: *The Prose and Poetry of Alexander Pushkin*. The founder of modern Russian literature, Pushkin was the most famous Russian author. He was killed in a duel defending the honor of his wife in 1837. I had discovered Pushkin in St. Francis College's quiet,romantic library.

I loved his poetry! Lost in daydreams, I heard my boss yell, *"Jump to it, Judy! There's customers waiting!"* As the breakfast crowd thinned out, Lee moved to a table and continued reading. That was good, because as I wiped down the tables, I could come close to him again. As I reached a table near his, I noticed Lee had turned his glass upside down, proving he had finished every drop of the orange juice. When I asked what poem he was reading, he responded by reading these lines, in a dramatic tone:
Once more a prey to doing nothing...His spirit sick with futile rage,
He sat down with the worthy purpose... Of mastering wisdom's heritage.

"It sounds better in Russian," he said simply. "I love reading, more than anything – except for making love." He said it in a voice devoid of mischief, in a way that was so natural I wasn't offended. A customer needed attention, so I slid away and tended to his needs. When the two hours were over, I clocked out, changed clothes and hurried back into the dining area. Was Lee still there? He was! Seeing that he was still immersed in Pushkin, I sat down, waiting in silence until he looked up. "I don't know how the others do it," I told him, "but I can't take much more of this job, even though I have rent with the "Y" coming up, and I have to save up for a room somewhere, for Robert and me."

Lee slowly put his book away. "Well, I contacted Dr. Ferrie," he said. "He wants you to join him for lunch today. Maybe he can help. It'll be a late lunch, because he was up all night."

"I'm grateful," I said. "My thumb can't take much more from that machine!" Lee smiled. "You mean you don't want that juice machine to take much more from your thumb!" I smiled back, as I absorbed his wry sense of humor. He added, "I'm looking for a temporary job myself. Maybe I can find a better one for you, too, until our real jobs come into play."

I knew what my 'real' job was going to be, but what 'real' job was Lee talking about? Did he also have a prearranged job? Then he said his uncle had offered him work, but he preferred not to get tangled up with Marcello's people. "Marcello!" I huffed. "Everywhere I go, I hear that name!" Lee said nothing. "Another thing I keep hearing, wherever I go, is talk about Castro," I told him. "There's as much anti-Castro sentiment here as in Florida. Maybe more." Lee's ears perked up at that. He asked me about what talk I'd heard. I told him about Tony Lopez-Fresquet and my other Cuban friends. That prompted Lee to start questioning me about Tony and his family. Unwilling to share details about Tony with somebody who had recently been to Russia, I started talking about my Hungarian family. Some of my relatives had fought in the Hungarian revolution of 1956. Lee agreed that the Hungarians felt betrayed when America ignored their pleas. He was 17 when the Soviet tanks rolled into Budapest and crushed the resistance. Lee then asked if I knew any Hungarian. He eagerly repeated some common phrases I knew, until he got it right.

Hungarian is a difficult non-European language, remotely related only to Finnish. "Now tell me about your family," I said. "That's only fair."

He did so laconically. His mother was connected to the Marcello's through her sister, his aunt Lillian, who was married to Charles Murret, his "uncle Dutz." Dutz was "bookkeeping" for certain Mob interests. In early days, Dutz had been a boxer and union enforcer on the docks. Now, years later, he was one of Marcello's most trusted handlers of income from gambling, horses, and slot machines. "I had to make a choice early on," Lee said, "whether I was going to be one of Marcello's soldiers or be another kind of soldier and join the Marine Corps, like my brother. Either the world can be an influence on you," he went on, "or you can be an influence on the world. I chose to stay out of Marcello's world. Besides," he continued, "I come from a military family." Both his brothers served, he said, as well as his father, who died before he was born. "I wanted to join the Air Force and be a pilot," he told me, "so, I joined the Civil Air Patrol. But due to this—" he tapped his left ear "—I couldn't qualify. I joined the Marines instead." Chronic infections in his left ear had damaged Lee's hearing, requiring a painful operation. In fact, he was hospitalized at the same age I was. Recalling how my long illness had influenced my religious views, I asked Lee if he was religious. He shook his head. "No. There are so many religions out there that claim they have the only God-given truth," he said, "yet they are so different from each other. So, I concluded that God must not be a good communicator. Therefore," he said, "I am not responsible." Wow. I realized that Lee was an intellectual, disguised in common clothes. Fascinated, I probed further. "Are you an atheist?" I asked. "Are you?" he shot back. I lapsed into silence, to which he remarked, "I'm nearly one. Perhaps I am a reluctant atheist. I hope there is somebody watching over things, but I doubt it. Look at the condition of the world. We seem to be on our own in this life." We stepped outside, where we discussed the God problem for nearly an hour, with a mixture of anxiety and venom. The specter of Nazi concentration camps was only eighteen years in the past, and the Nuremberg trials had painted a clear portrait of those horrible atrocities. How could God let such evil occur?

As for me, God had let me down. I had offered up my life to God, only to have my parents kidnap me from St. Francis and nearly ruin my college career. Upon hearing that I had wanted to become a nun, Lee said, "You and Dr. Ferrie have that in common. He's actually a priest who can't be ordained because he's a homosexual." Ferrie had wanted nothing more than to serve God as a priest, Lee added, but he couldn't keep his hands off teenage boys. This was bad news. I had to hide my concern. I felt better when Lee stressed that Ferrie was "reforming himself." As for the existence of God, Lee said Ferrie had strong arguments. "He almost makes you believe," he said. "He's that good." I realized I had to meet Dr. Ferrie for many reasons. Little did I know that by doing so, a Pandora's Box would be opened that could never be closed again.

CHAPTER SEVEN THE FAVOR

New Orleans Godfather Carlos Marcello in his brick office behind Town and Country Motel (photo courtesy of Trine Day)

<u>Saturday, April 23, 1963, contd.</u>

I was now interested in meeting Dr. Ferrie, who had wanted to become a priest. His being a homosexual didn't bother me: I had been friends with several guys in high school who were closet homosexuals. Lee said Dave acted very masculine – he was a fine pilot, was skilled in hand-to-hand combat, and a powerful leader. Then he said, "It's time to warn you about his appearance." Dr. Ferrie had lost almost all the hair on his body, and the little that was left on his head made him look like a clown.[87] He wore cheap wigs and put on fake eyebrows to keep dust and dander out of his eyes, which had no eyelashes – a necessity for a pilot, or someone who used microscopes, and Ferrie was both. "Ferrie is brilliant," Lee assured me. Besides being a pilot and a cancer researcher, he stressed, David W. Ferrie was also a courageous man whose anti-communist activities with Cuban guerillas, "government people," and even the Mafia[88] was well-known. I remembered Dr. Ochsner's questions about my anti-Castro feelings and guessed that Dr. Mary Sherman, who was praised was probably anti-Castro, too.

It all seemed to add up. Dr. Ferrie's mixture of aviation, medical skills and politics helped explain his relationship with government people easily enough, but I was fascinated by the idea that Ferrie also worked with the Mob. The idea that the Mafia and the U.S. government might be working together against Castro was a shock. Lee then wisely changed the subject. He said he'd found a room for me in a safe neighborhood-one that I could afford. He'd be happy to show it to me. That did it: we

---

[87] Alopecia is thought to be an autoimmune disorder, where the hair falls out, notably on the head, in a circle. Rarely, it can extend over the entire body.

[88] Lee did not use the word 'Mafia.' Instead, he used the term "Cosa Nostra' or "our thing" by which the Mafia was known to most insiders in 1963.

rode a bus together back to town. Upon arriving, Lee and I first went to the Post office, where a letter from Robert was waiting.

Inside was a $20 money order – enough to make a down-payment on a room for rent. My spirits lifted, I started to read the letter. Soon, my spirits were crashing. Robert wasn't coming on May Day after all. The one romantic element in our elopement was marrying on May Day. In the Catholic Church, a pretty little girl --chosen "Queen of the May" – bedecked in flowers, would lead a procession in the church, as the choir sang *"O Mary, we crown thee with blossoms today! Queen of the Angels, and Queen of the May!"* In my soul of souls, I thought a marriage on May Day would have pleased my Hungarian grandma. Robert's hint that he might get shipped out of town wasn't fun to read, either. I was glum, so Lee, trying to cheer me up, took me window-shopping. As we walked, my gloom faded because of an extraordinary experience we were having: every time I happened look at Lee, as we walked and talked, he was turning his head to look at me. When we finally noticed this amazing synchronicity, we started playing a game with it. On the other hand, this was New Orleans, and it didn't really matter who might be watching us. We practically gave ourselves whiplash playing this little game. Our eyes, too, constantly met in a fascinating rhythm. We slowly began to realize that somehow, we just naturally clicked. It was so easy to interact with Lee, compared to Robert. With Lee, it was smooth, natural and instinctive, whereas with Robert, I had an alert regard for him that was like doing a balancing act on a tightrope to please him. My attraction to this former Marine was growing by the hour in an uncanny way. As we paused in front of different store fronts, window-shopping, I realized that the fear factor I'd held for New Orleans was evaporating, just because I was with him. The bustle of tourists, the rumble of streetcars, the big windows full of sophisticated fashions—it all took on a new and brilliant vitality. As I gazed at the treasures on display from around the world, in one window, I saw a sign in gold lettering saying '*se habla espanol'.* That reminded me, when we sat down on a bench, to ask Lee why he was so interested in Cuba and in my friend, Tony Lopez-Fresquet. "So, what do you know about Cuba?" I ventured.

"I know a little bit," he replied.

"I wonder if you know as much about Cuba as I do," I said boldly. After all, Florida was America's Cuban capital. Lee closed his eyes, passed his hand over his forehead like a conjurer, and began rattling off the names of every city and town on the island. He began at one end of Cuba and ended at the other. His recitation was methodical and thorough. I listened, transfixed. Next, he ticked off the names of Cuba's cabinet members, politicians, celebrities and generals. When he started reciting a list of all the mountains and rivers, I was overwhelmed. "Stop!" I told him. "How do you know all of that?"

"I was ordered to memorize it," he said with a smile. "Since returning [from Russia], I've spent a lot of Saturdays with Cuban maps...

I've always loved maps, anyway, so it wasn't such an arduous task." He said he could get around in Cuba with his eyes closed, but that the Spanish he knew wasn't Cuban style. "I need to work on that," he said.

"Are you going to be involved in trying to kill Castro?" I asked. I'd heard plenty of rumors about U.S. assassination plots from my Cuban friends.

"No, I'm going there to give him a medal," he replied. "What do you think?"

I realized I was looking at a man willing to risk his life to get Castro. He had already penetrated one Communist country and was now preparing to infiltrate a second one, equally dangerous. My thoughts whirled back to Canute Michaelson, the Norwegian spy, and how his family had rejected him, for he dared not blow his cover. In his own, disarming way, Lee had proven to me that he had been specially trained concerning Cuba, and that he wasn't going there to sell bubble gum.

People have always naturally confided in me, and the attraction that Lee and I experienced was playing its magic. He could see I was thrilled to meet someone like him, with the bonus that I understood there could be issues with his family, to whom he could not reveal certain secrets.

Later, Lee told me that he had been led to believe I was more deeply involved in clandestine circles than I was, or he'd never have revealed so much, so quickly. Stopping at a payphone, Lee started making phone calls. After a half hour, he had a name and address: he had found a place through the Mafia side of his family. "Let's go look at it," he counseled. "It's right on St. Charles."

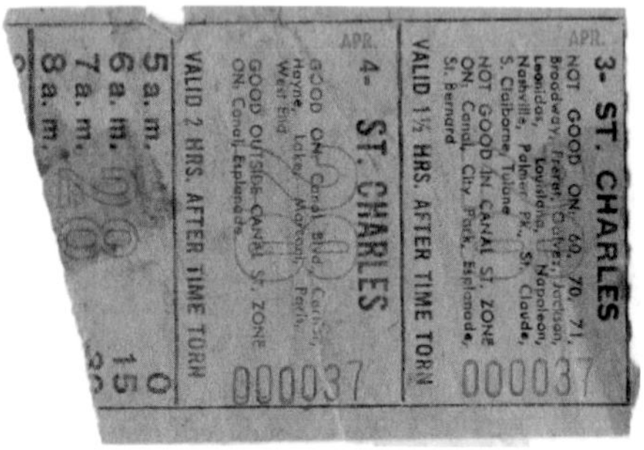

The April 28 streetcar ticket, saved because it was my first ride with Lee!

We hopped on a streetcar – my first ride! The varnished wooden seats, polished brass trim, and open windows that brought the spring air rushing across our faces made it fun. The antique cars, lovingly constructed long ago, were powered by whirring electric engines that drive their rumbling steel wheels along the dark iron tracks. They screeched when the engineer put on the brakes. As we passed different landmarks, such as Tulane University, Lee pointed them out. Then we got off the streetcar in such a nice area that I wondered how I'd be able to afford anything there. We went through a wrought iron gate to a classic white mansion with grand white columns and a generous porch.

There, a stunning door shimmered with a gorgeous cut-glass window, through which I peered as Lee rang the doorbell.

I could see a long hall, a chandelier, and a well-dressed couple seated on a red couch by some stairs. They were kissing. *How romantic!* I thought.

Then a red-haired woman wearing a low-cut, rumpled dress came plodding down the hall in her slippers and opened the door. This was Mrs. Webber, a lady well past her prime, whose grumpy-looking face expressed instant disapproval of us. "What you here for?" she wanted to know.

"This is Mrs. Baker," Lee told her. "Mr. P sent us." Mrs. Webber opened the door wider and invited us inside. "There's nothing left but the parlor," she said coldly. "You'll have to use the bathroom down the hall. But I'll let you use the fridge and stove in my kitchen." Then she looked me over more carefully, her eyes narrowing when she peered at my hand. "You aint got no ring," she stated. "Where is your ring?"

I had forgotten to put it on, but now I dug into my bottomless purse and found it. "It's so loose it falls off," I told her, and demonstrated the problem. Satisfied, Webber said, "Well, you could use more meat on your bones. You must be starving, poor thing! – You, too!" she told Lee. "Come on into my kitchen. Have a ham sandwich."

It was still pretty early in the day, and a ham sandwich seemed an unusual breakfast item, but Mrs. Webber said she was out of eggs. When she offered tea, I asked if she had any milk, just as Lee asked her the same thing. We looked at each other in surprise. "You drink milk, too?" I asked. "I love milk!" he replied.

"I don't drink or smoke. What about you?" I pursued. "I gave 'em up," he replied, "except the occasional beer, when somebody foists it on me." As these coincidences kept adding up, from then on, we started making a game of it, to see how many there were. Mrs. Webber said her parlor rented for $30 a month. I was surprised, because this was cheaper than my dorm room at the "Y." Visions of saving a little money from my upcoming stipend included new shoes, maybe some nice earrings, and books and art supplies I could buy. She took us to the entry again, where the parlor was located. There were sliding doors of mahogany that I could pull together and lock, she explained. She said there was a rosewood highboy already in the room, plus a desk and chair, and a bookcase, but no bed. "I have my mother's bed in storage," Mrs. Webber told us. "I'll have my handyman move it in right away." Thrilled with the prospect, without even looking at the room, I handed Mrs. Webber the $20 money order that Robert had sent me, promising that I'd soon have the rest when my husband came. As she took the money order, Mrs. Webber said, "I need all the money now, or it aint no deal."

"Mrs. Baker!" Lee interposed, are you going to rent the parlor sight unseen?"

"I trust your recommendation," I told him. Lee hesitated, then reached into his pants pocket and drew out an old brown wallet. "I always carry a ten -dollar bill for emergencies," he said. "This looks like one." He paid her, and off we went, to get my things from the "Y."

Lee still had plenty of change in his pocket for the streetcar, so we went to get my things. Upon arriving back at the Mansion, we found a magnificent bed had already been installed. As I gazed through the beautiful window that looked down on blooming red azaleas and dignified oaks, I told Lee I was inspired to paint the lovely scene. The bed itself was carved from mahogany and was thick with layers of silky coverlets and colorful, satin pillows. Lee pointed out the various amenities, such as the plush Oriental rug on the polished wooden floor, and the elegant wallpaper that depicted an English hunting scene.

But when Mrs. Webber handed me a generic skeleton key, I wasn't pleased. She dismissed my concerns with a shrug, saying that if I kept the sliding doors shut, nobody would know what was inside. When Lee asked how late the front door was kept unlocked, Mrs. Webber snapped, "Why do you want to know?" Turning to me, she demanded to know if I was cheating on my husband! As Lee stiffened with resentment, I told the old witch, "Mr. Oswald is a dear friend of mine, that's all. We have to meet a doctor friend for lunch and then he'll get me some groceries. He's helping me!" Mrs. Webber mumbled something under her breath about no hanky-panky being allowed in her house. "I just kicked out a girl who was sunbathing on my front porch, nekked as a jaybird," she said. "As for keys, you don't need a key to the front door. Just ring the bell, and I'll let you in."

"That's ridiculous," Lee protested. "Give her a key or give her back her money." After fumbling around, Mrs. Webber pulled a key from deep between her pendulous breasts, complaining it was the last one she had. When we went back for the rest of my things from the "Y," we set important things aside and rented a locker at the bus station to hold them. "Since your boyfriend has a car," Lee said, "he can decide if you'll stay at Webbers, or leave after you get married. Meanwhile, your stuff will be safe."

"You told her I was married and called me 'Mrs. Baker,'" I reminded him. "And I lied, too. I feel miserable." Lee frowned as he considered my comment (later, he would tell me that he had never met someone who tried never to lie!). "Juduffki," he said, "sometimes it's necessary. I hate lying, but some lies are beneficial." As we rode the streetcar back to The Mansion, Lee suddenly said, "I've had to tell lots of lies." He turned his face from me. "I had to, because the truth could have hurt somebody. I do regret one thing, though. I no longer feel bad afterwards." I pondered those words but said nothing.

Midday- Saturday, April 27, 1963 Lee mentioned that on Sunday, we could borrow his cousin's car to show me the city. Also, I could help him locate his father's grave. He recalled that the cemetery was big and crowded.[89] Lee waited made phone calls on the hall phone, I dressed.

[89] Investigators who've asked if the man who returned to the USA was the same man who defected to the USSR, should note he knew too many details.

I put on my nice brown sheath and put up my hair, so the blonde ends (from lots of swimming) made bright stripes in my hair. It looked elegant. When I emerged from the parlor, Lee told me that plans had changed a little.His Uncle Dutz needed a favor. I could come along if I liked, and he'd enjoy my company if I did, but Lee cautioned me: "It's something connected with Marcello."

"You don't have to come along," he added, "if it makes you feel uncomfortable."

It was a fair warning, but recalling that Lee said his uncle was a favorite of Marcello, it surely wouldn't be dangerous, would it? It could be an adventure! "We have to go to my uncle's first," Lee told me. "And since I'm married," he added, "it's best that you're not seen with me there, dressed up as you are. It's bad enough that they'll probably find out about my rocky marriage."

Lee added that his aunt and uncle were as dear to him as parents. They had been embarrassed and upset by the newspapers that splashed Lee's name across the country when he made his fake defection, but for them, family trumped politics, and Lee was forever 'family.' Unfortunately, the rest of his family on both sides wanted nothing more to do with him. At this time, I realized that any questions I had about Lee's so-called defection would have to wait.

After a ride on the streetcar, we transferred to a bus that took us to the Murret's house in Lakeview, just off Canal Blvd near City Park. We walked a block or two, then I waited across the street as Lee went inside. It was a cheery, peaceful neighborhood, full of kids playing and having fun throwing balls and playing tag. I could imagine Lee playing in the street with the other kids, when he lived with the Murrets.

When Lee came out of the Murrets' house, he said we'd have a long ride, and guess where to? Marcello's Town and Country Motel! It was only a few blocks from Royal Castle. Not only that, but just behind the motel was a brick building where Marcello himself reigned, a prince of all he surveyed. As we rode yet again to Royal Castle territory, I wished I'd eaten more of the ham sandwich Mrs. Webber had given me. "These are some names, addresses and phone numbers my Aunt Lil looked up," Lee said, getting my mind off my stomach as he showed me a scribbled list. "But I doubt any of them will talk to me." Lee said that even his half-brother John had heard about his defection on Armed Forces radio and no longer trusted him about anything. But I focused on the fact that people who only got accused of being "Red" could lose their jobs, whereas Lee was walking around a free man. I understood the rules of patriotism and loyalty.

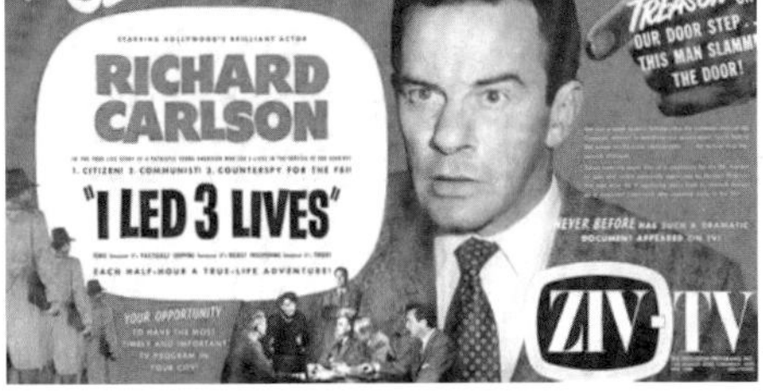

Turning to Lee, I took his hand and said, "What made you want to do it?"

"His name is Herbert Philbrick," Lee replied. He inspired me."

Philbrick was one of Lee's childhood heroes. When he had been living in New York in his early teenage years, Lee faced loneliness and neglect. He played hooky, wandered through the Bronx Zoo, and spent hours reading in the library. When his mother, who was single and working, got a TV, Lee found the TV series "**I Led Three Lives**" where the real-life hero, Herbert Philbrick, was shown as a citizen (life #1) pretending to be an active Communist set on destroying America (life #2), was reporting everything to the FBI (life #3).

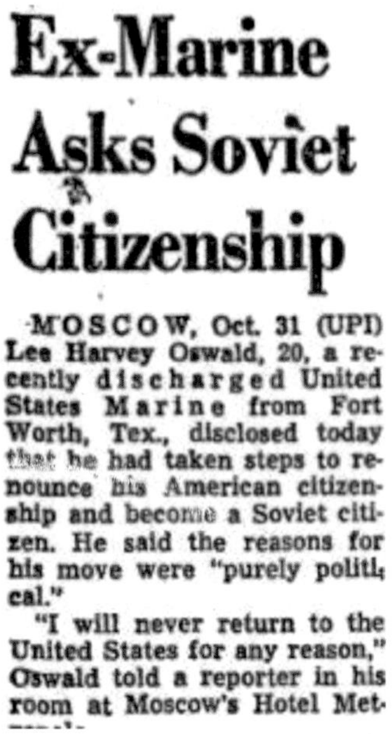

Ex-Marine Asks Soviet Citizenship

MOSCOW, Oct. 31 (UPI) Lee Harvey Oswald, 20, a recently discharged United States Marine from Fort Worth, Tex., disclosed today that he had taken steps to renounce his American citizenship and become a Soviet citizen. He said the reasons for his move were "purely political."

"I will never return to the United States for any reason," Oswald told a reporter in his room at Moscow's Hotel Met-

For a long time, just as occurred to the spy Canute Michaelson, Philbrick was forbidden to tell his family. Lee told me that one episode he saw made him kneel on the floor and cry. He was hooked. "I was determined to become a spy," he told me. "That is the secret behind my so-called 'defection.'" His simple way of saying that reflected such a deep courage that I was humbled into silence.

As we sat in the bus, Lee pointed out more landmarks, then said, "If there's time after our lunch with Dr. Ferrie, we'll visit this old aunt of mine. She might tell me where my father's grave is."

"I understand," I said. I told him what I had learned about the family rejection of double agents from my brief but important encounter with the Nazi spy, Dr. Canute Michaelson. Michaelson had described his escape from the Nazis and what would have happened to him if he didn't succeed. "Did you know Dr. Canute Michaelson became my shining hero?" I said, hoping to encourage Lee. Someday, I assured him, his reputation would be restored. Lee said nothing, but I could almost see the weight lift from him. He knew instinctively that I'd never repeat what he had been saying. Only those who have met their soul-mates could understand this confluence of trust.

We both knew that if we were making a mistake here, it would be the stupidest thing we'd done yet, if he was really dangerous, or if I were capable of betrayal. It could mean doom, but Lee's smile emboldened me. "Your aunt and uncle are being way too friendly, Lee," I dared say. "My guess is that they understand your true role." Lee then told me about his cousin, Marilyn, who was the Murret's daughter and Lee's older playmate as a child. She left New Orleans to see the world, just as Lee had, and as Lee described some of her adventures, I wondered if she, too, had been working with the CIA. Marilyn was now back, and may have had a good influence on his aunt and uncle, to help them deal with their concerns about him. We finally arrived at Town and Country.

Sure enough, I could easily see my Royal Castle, just down the street. Slowly, it dawned on me that several men were always there every morning who sat together and ate little. Who were they? The time would come when Lee would explain that they were part of RFK's surveillance team that kept watch on who came and left from Town and Country.

Mr. Michael A. Maroun

Government Deports Marcello to Guatemala

Racketeer Flown Out Of Orleans

Carlos Marcello was having to deal with Bobby Kennedy's Department of Justice, and Kennedy's agents were watching Marcello's every move, in preparation for another deportation trial. In 1961, RFK had arranged for Marcello and his lawyer, Mike Maroun, who "owned" the Town and Country Motel, to be kidnapped when Marcello came to a required parole appointment. Suddenly, RFK had him and his lawyer dumped in Guatemala, [90] where Marcello had falsely claimed he was born. But when the Guatemalan government began treating Marcello and his family, who joined him there, like royalty (helped along by a huge bribe), Marcello and Mike were kidnapped again and tossed down a snake-infested cliff in the jungles of El Salvador. They made their way to an airport after extreme hardships. There, they made secret arrangements that eventually involved David Ferrie for the final leg of their illegal return to Texas from Miami. As for Attorney General Bobby Kennedy, the powerful Godfather would never forgive or forget what Kennedy did to him. As we entered Town and Country's eerily dark and quiet lounge, Lee told me the place really hopped at night, but now, in the early afternoon, it was almost empty. I could hear the clinking of glasses being washed and a radio playing at low volume. We sat down at one of the tables and waited; when a busboy came and poured water for us, Lee asked to speak to the manager. As the busboy left, he winked at me. "I should have told you this is a pick-up joint," Lee whispered. "I'm ashamed to have brought you here. This is one of Marcello's places," he explained.

---

[90] I obtained my information through emails between me and Marcello's granddaughter Tricia, and her brother Steve, which are in my possession.

"It seems that every time I come to New Orleans, I'm asked to run errands to places like this." [91]

"But you want to please your uncle, don't you?"

"I owe him," he said firmly. "So, I have to help out sometimes." Lee explained that his father had died a couple months before he was born, leaving a pregnant mother with two young boys. There wasn't a support system to help, in the post-depression era. The entire time when he was growing up, Marguerite was desperately trying to keep a roof over their heads, except for a period when she was married a few years to Edwin A. Ekdahl, who eventually cheated on her, caused them to split, and cast them back into poverty. Lee had observed his mother hitting his step-father and throwing dishes at him. It all started when Marguerite began moving the family from place to place after his father's death. The older boys were finally farmed out to Bethlehem Orphan School.[92] With Lee at first too young, he was sent twice to live with the Murrets, who treated him as one of their own.

Lee Harvey Oswald as a child

Lee's elementary school photos. His mother neglected him, failing to get his hair cut or to feed him properly.

"My mother had a bad hand dealt to her," Lee confided, "She went through three husbands and lost everything," he said, being too proud to ask for help. Years of hardship aged her before her time and made her bitter, Lee said. He felt sorry for her, and believed his very existence was partially responsible for her misery. Marguerite Clavier Oswald made all her boys feel that way, pushing them to work when they were underage. She demanded that they help support her, not caring if they ever graduated from high school, her only concern to eventually get rid of them. [93]She urged Lee himself to join the Marines at only 16, with a faked birth certificate created by one of her Mafia lawyer friends. That effort failed: just looking at him, Lee was obviously too small and too young! Marguerite also had some of Lee's school

[91] Over time, I gradually came to understand that Lee had visited New Orleans in the Fall of 1962 when he was estranged from his wife, Marina, after a fight.

[92] https://www.ccano.org/blog/introducing-bethlehem-housing/
Bethlehem Housing ...provid[es] rapid re-housing services to stabilize families quickly to address the root causes of their homelessness." A heritage in NOLA from the 1800's.

[93] Later, Lee heard that Marguerite suffered from a thyroid problem that coarsened her features, made her gain weight, and may have accounted for her depressed feelings.

attendance records faked after they returned from New York, to make sure he didn't fail a grade when he was playing hooky back in New York. That would have embarrassed her.

"My brothers left home as soon as they could," Lee stated. "So did I. That was fine with her," he said. I began to tell Lee of my own family problems, a waiter came over. Lee shook his head 'no,' so the waiter left us. Lee then resumed his musings about Marguerite Clavier, born in 1907 into a large, poor, close-knit French Cajun family.

"After I defected," he told me, "Mother wrote letters to important people, and even pestered the FBI to find out if I was alive, which made it harder for me to stay safely in the USSR." After he was repatriated to America,[94]thanks to a State Department Loan awarded him at the US Embassy in Moscow,[95] Lee, wife Marina and baby June Lee lived briefly with Marguerite. She gave the little family bedding, towels, a tablecloth and other items, but life with her soon became impossible. "She was intrusive and manipulative!" Lee told me. "So different from my fiancé," I replied. "That's one thing I like about Robert. He doesn't stick his nose into my life at all."

"Are you sure this man loves you?" Lee asked. "I'm sure," I answered, trying to convince myself. "Even though he never says so. Well, he did say it, once!" I replied defensively.

"He never tells you he loves you?"

"He did write it," I answered, and showed him the booklet of little pink slips, each of which had 'I love you' written in blue ink. "See? He gave me these. I discard one each day. Then, he'll be here."

"That's cute," Lee said. "Where did he find pink paper?"

"His parents have a real estate business and their signs are pink and black. They use pink paper in their office." Then I took a deep breath and asked, "What else does your uncle do for Marcello?"

"I know you're curious," Lee replied, with a quick grin, "but I can't tell you. Use your imagination." A little later, Lee hushed me, for the manager, "Mr. P" was coming. He was **Nofio 'Pecora' Pecararo,** a powerful Mafia figure in New Orleans. I saw a middle-aged Italian with dark hair, with an air of importance about him.[96] He expected respect. Lee and Mr. P. talked quietly for a while, as I averted my eyes and looked down, just as Lee had instructed me to do. Since I am so short, I could see more under the table than average, so I noticed Mr. P. pass a wad of rolled-up bills under the table to Lee.

---

[94] Through the ongoing efforts of Bobby Kennedy's Department of Justice

[95] The papers, signed at the Embassy, which are publicly available, include a statement that the loan was only awarded to U.S. citizens of good standing!

[96] Onofio Pecararo, AKA 'Nofio Pecaro,' was Marcello's most important Capo. REF:https://www.archives.gov/files/research/jfk/releases/docid-32330863.pdf

The whole time, he kept talking, as if nothing transpired. Then he gave me a hard look and smiled. "Does she need a job?" he asked, surveying my body. "We could use her here."

"She's got a job," Less answered tersely, "and she's not that kind." "I meant nothing, Lee, I meant nothing," Mr. P. protested, getting up from his seat. "Tell Dutz hello for me."

"Let's go," Lee said, without bothering to look at the money, which he simply put in his pocket. "We're not going to eat anything?" I asked anxiously.

I was famished, with no concept of when we were to meet Dr. Ferrie. "I wouldn't feed my dog here," Lee growled, as he guided me outside. As we rode a bus back to the Murrets, Lee surprised me by saying more about what his Uncle Dutz did for Marcello. He "kept books" involving horse races, slot machines, betting at casinos, and so on, and if laundered money sometimes turned up as a donation to the Catholic Church, to balance an account, who was hurt?[97] Once more I waited outside while Lee delivered the money. Then Lee emerged at a quick pace, all smiles. "Dutz gave me two hundred dollars for helping him out," he announced, "so you can forget about the $10 I lent you." I told him he'd get his $10 back, with a sincere intent.

Finally finished with the favor, we headed toward the "Kopper Kitchen" eatery. Since I was still recovering from my miscarriage, my body was demanding food! With Dr. Ferrie nowhere in sight, Lee told me to go ahead and order whatever I wanted. With a chance to eat something besides canned beans, pickled pork feet and sardines, I went overboard. A burger with all the trimmings! Fries! A hot fudge sundae! A chocolate coke! I was a bit embarrassed when Lee ordered a bowl of soup and a glass of milk. What was he, a monk?

But Lee was focused on telling me about Dr. Ferrie. "He thinks he might have cancer, himself," Lee said. "Maybe that's why he's working with Dr. Sherman." Lee added that Ferrie also wondered if some of his work in the past with certain chemicals had caused his hair to fall out. "Dr. Ferrie might let you do some research of your own," he went on.

---

[97] "In 1953, Carlos purchased a group of buildings in Rossier City at 1225 Airline Highway... a motel in one bloc, a restaurant and lounge in another and his office complex in the third, it was called Town and Country Motel. This would be his base ...Two of Carlos' most trusted lieutenants, Nofio Pecora and Joe Poretto, were put in charge ...along with one of his younger brothers, Anthony. Lawyer...Mike Maroun, was Marcello's choice to oversee the operation...[It] became a meeting place for top-level gamblers, Marcello's men, crooked politicians and equally crooked cops. Frances, the wife of Pecora, acted as Carlos' secretary... in his office building, as visitors left, they were fare-welled by a message on the inside of the front door. It read: THREE CAN KEEP A SECRET IF TWO ARE DEAD." REF: http://gangstersinc.ning.com/profiles/blogs/the-story-of-new-orleans-mafia-boss-carlos-marcello-1 Marcello was also supposedly a Mason in the Etoile Polair Lodge of the French Grand Orient.[Peter Levenda Archives]

"Because suddenly, he found out he needs an assistant. He might even pay you to help keep his lab going."

"He needs an assistant?" I asked. "Very much so," Lee replied. "They've requested help." Slaving away at Royal Castle had lost its charm, while the thought of doing lab work anywhere, for anybody, was appealing. "Well, that could be me," I said, "But I'll soon be in Mary Sherman's bone lab at Ochsner's Clinic." Lee raised an eyebrow. "Maybe you're supposed to be working at both places," he said. "He's very busy, and he has to travel a lot, soon. Not only for us, but also for Marcello." The 'us" made me realize that somehow, Lee was also involved in Ferrie's cancer research. Of more concern was that omnipresent name again—Marcello! What did Marcello have to do with this? Meanwhile, Lee was observing, with some concern, how I was wolfing down my lunch. "That stuff isn't good for you," he commented. "You should watch what you put in your body."

"I know you're right... I usually do better – honest!" I insisted.

"I used to smoke and drink," Lee said, "but then I decided to respect the only body I'll ever have." Just then, **Dr. David Ferrie** arrived. He was wearing an airline captain's cap and jacket, with shabby trousers and scuffed shoes. His appearance was just as odd. Just as Lee had said, Ferrie's eyebrows were bizarre, with grease pencil dotted with bits of fuzz glued on. His movements were jumpy. His eyes bugged out – exophthalmia – betraying a thyroid problem. Orangish hair from a fake wig peeked out from under his airline cap. He could never enter a room unnoticed. Without a word, Dr. Ferrie sat down. Then he peered at me intently. He was wearing an odd, hand-made ring. It seemed to have been made from an Eastern Air Lines pin.[98] Lee introduced me as "Miss Judy Vary" and immediately, Ferrie joked about our similar-sounding names. "Vary and Ferrie!" he laughed. Despite his odd appearance, I soon forgot about it as we warmed up to each other. He asked about my medical training, to which I replied with much technical terminology. Soon, he was satisfied and turned to Lee.

"She'll do," he said. "She knows her way around a medical lab." He then offered to provide me with any equipment or supplies I might need, since I was planning to "stay awhile" in New Orleans. "I have connections," he went on. I brought up Dr. Sherman and Tulane Med school in the Fall, to which Ferrie responded that I'd still be able to help out and earn extra money on weekends. When I mentioned my magnesium project, Dr. Ferrie asked if I knew organic chemistry. "With my eyes closed," I told him. "I'm familiar with a lab in Gainesville," he said. "At times we order exotic chemicals from them. Peninsular Chem Research is the name. Your chemistry professors at UF run the place.

[98] Possibly a gift from one of his students that he had taught to fly?

When we need stuff we can't get anywhere else, Pen Chem makes it for us. I can get you a good job there if you ever need summer work between semesters." Ferrie then excused himself for a moment and went outside to his car. He soon returned with several science supply catalogs, including a Fischer Scientific. "Take these catalogs," he said. "After you see what we're doing, circle anything you want, and we'll order it." He looked around to see who might hear him, then began talking about Dr. Sherman, whom he referred to as 'Dr. Mary' to keep her last name out of the conversation. "The work Dr. Mary and I do is confidential," he told us, "since we are investigating cancer with drugs not available in the United States. We have them brought in from Mexico, if you know what I mean. So, don't talk about what we're doing at the Clinic, or anywhere else." After I promised to be careful, Dr. Ferrie said this private project was getting results faster because they did not have to do all the paperwork. However, it was all under the direction of Dr. Ochsner. What? Dr. Ochsner was involved in this? Dr. Ferrie explained that Ochsner had his own unregulated flow of funds and supplies for this private project, under his direction alone. "We're using various chemicals, with radiation, to see what happens with fast-growing cancers," he told us. "We're using it to mutate monkey viruses, too." *Mutating monkey viruses! Radiation! Fast-growing cancers!*

"That's exactly what I've been trained to handle," I commented, noting how conveniently my skill set happened to fit this project. "I was told you were," Ferrie responded. I suspected that he must have been told this information by Dr. Ochsner himself. After lunch, Dr. Ferrie drove us to the "Y" to pick up the last of my things, check out, and say goodbye to the girls. When I emerged with the few items I'd left behind, I saw Lee on a payphone, but Ferrie was gone. After Lee hung up, he told me Ferrie had gone ahead to get some provisions and that we were to meet him at his apartment. As we rode a bus to his apartment, then started to walk along a service road behind some Spanish-style houses, Lee explained that Ferrie once had a glamorous life as a pilot with Eastern Air Lines, before he got fired 'without a cause.'

He had a hard year, and then Carlos Marcello had come to the rescue. He was using David Ferrie's skills as a medical expert, paralegal, translator and pilot. Dave's need for an assistant of his own had come about because he was fighting to get his job back, which required flying to Federal Aviation Agency (FAA) meetings held in Miami at a moment's notice. We entered Ferrie's apartment through an enclosed stairway in the back (all Ferrie's friends did that). Ferrie met us at the screen door, from where we quickly entered the kitchen to the left. Ferrie, now barefoot and in casual clothes, had been cleaning up his spectacularly messy kitchen, but now he took time to show us around his apartment, which had a nice view to the street through glass doors that opened to a big screened-in porch. Ferrie's baby grand piano and his mother's old-fashioned furniture and flowered curtains adorned a living-room spilling over with a chaotic collection of material.

There were books of every kind, medical supplies, antiques, military oddities, a big shell casing, and religious statues. I accidentally found a photo of a penis when I sat down and my hand touched the edge of a Polaroid photo between two cushions. I retrieved it, only to be shocked. Ferrie's "medical explanation" about a cancer patient did not convince me. I did notice an attempt to categorize and box some of the books. Some cages were present in the dining area along the inner wall.

An old, crusty rat inhabited one cage, while the other held a few dozen white mice, lumpy with tumors. The lab, such as it was, resided on utility carts in the kitchen, with jars of various chemicals, isopropyl alcohol and acetone for clean-up. Test tubes were stacked in boxes, with more under the sink.

An untrained eye would not have noticed some of the lab items, such

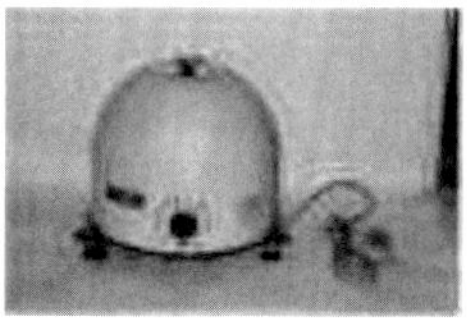

as a **table centrifuge**, an enclosed set of scales, bottles of chemicals and an autoclave (pressure cooker style) under the sink. There was also a top-of-the-line microscope, along with flasks, glass tubing, and a Bunsen burner connected to a gas valve behind the stove. Then my eye caught *The Difco Manual* – the Jan. 1, 1963 9th Edition.

So, Ferrie likely had professional level, up-to-date experience making mediums for tissue cultures. In his refrigerator, an industrial-quality Waring blender held what looked like raw hamburger meat, but I knew they were mouse tumors. Ferrie explained that mice were being bred nearby, living under standardized conditions. The mice with tumors had only been coming to his apartment for a few weeks. Before that, Dave said he hadn't been working with lab animals "for quite a while." Since all white mice look the same, the few of his friends who saw these new inhabitants of his dining room didn't know that mouse-killing and tumor extractions were ongoing, or that the white mice being constantly replaced. It looked like the same white mice to them. "It's my little secret," he said. Then Ferrie assured me that I had nothing to fear from him, because he had turned homosexual. He was only interested in young men, he assured me. I was now getting wary of Dr. Ferrie: Lee had forewarned me that Ferrie was gay, but I hadn't expected (this was 1963) such an open and frank admission. My respect for him had plummeted ever since viewing his cluttered apartment, so when he said I could call him 'Dave,' I did so. It wasn't 'Dr. Ferrie' anymore.

Even so, when he explained that Dr. Mary Sherman was coming tonight to pick up "the tumor stew" --she had just returned to town-- I was thrilled. At last, I'd get to meet the great cancer researcher! But Dave, seeing my excitement, warned me to "play it cool" when I met her. Some lesbians might be coming, he said, and any joy I might exhibit in seeing Dr. Mary could be misinterpreted. "That's just the way gossip goes in New Orleans," Dave said. "It's why I don't even deliver this stuff to her apartment, but you could. In your lab-coat, you can pass as a medical student. So nice." Dr. Mary was not a lesbian, Dave went on. She was a widow who had not had a good marriage and who had avoided another. Being single and a professional, she was careful about appearances.

When Dave generously invited us for dinner, I quickly declined, but there was no thought of going home, once this man began to treat us to a philosophical discussion. He began gently by saying that people tended to look at things two ways: either through a telescope, or through a microscope, and what they saw was colored by their own problems. They rarely saw things in correct proportion, and that influenced their judgments.

For the next several hours, Dave plowed through centuries of moral and political philosophy, reciting long classic passages from memory as he went, often quoting them in the original Old English, Latin, Greek, French, German or Italian.

When Dave articulated the thoughts of the great 17th century British philosopher, Hobbes, and his Social Contract, Lee and I met him with quotes from Hobbes' masterpiece, *Leviathan.* But when Dave juxtaposed Hobbes with his observations of Huxley, Sartre and Plato, he overwhelmed us. "The danger is over-regulating humanity," Dave finished, "and it will keep happening," he predicted, "for economic reasons. That will be just as destructive as nature's lack of any systematic regulation. The end is the same: human life becomes lonely, poor, nasty, brutish and short." Having defeated us easily, Dave moved on to his favorite topic -- religion.

He navigated us through sophisticated quotes from the Doctors of the Catholic Church, material I previously had avoided as too boring. Now I regretted that decision. When he dished up Thomas Aquinas in the form of an intellectual gourmet meal, I began taking notes. Blown away by his knowledge and logic, Lee and I had little left to challenge Dave concerning religion, when he mixed his powerful views of the universe and human nature into the brew. [99] We tried to match wits with his prodigious brain, but David Ferrie, pacing back and forth, smoking cigarettes and drinking warm beer, kept sinking our ships. Why, he snarled, were we toying with atheism? What hubris, what arrogance, to declare there was no God, when we understood so little!

---

[99] See Dave's introduction, as written, in green fountain pen Sanford ink, in Color Plates. In America, Lee also wrote with the same green ink, but then switched to ballpoint.

"It's idiotic to be an atheist!" he proclaimed. "Look at what we have learned in just a hundred years," he said. "We've now pierced the heavens with rockets and discovered DNA. What if we keep on going a million years like that? A billion? How dare we declare there is no God, when we ourselves might be considered gods by our ancient ancestors?" Dave continued to pace back and forth through an increasingly thick cloud of cigarette smoke, consuming bottle after bottle of beer, oscillating between piety and profanity. By midnight, his tone sank into confession, saying that he had tried to be a father to Lee, years earlier. Instead, he had almost destroyed the boy. "I gotta pee," he said then, and left the room.

"What was that about?" I asked Lee.

"It was the world's hardest way to become close friends," Lee said solemnly. "I'll let him tell you about it. It's going to come out, anyway, because he's drunk. It happened a long time ago and I know he feels guilty about it."

I now assumed Dave had accosted Lee when he was young, which Lee confirmed when he said, sadly, "It was the hardest fight I ever put up in my life." Alarm bells were going off, and I stiffened. "You're frightening me!" I whispered. "I want to go home—now!"

"You're safe with me," Lee said, looking straight into my eyes. I looked around to see if the windows were open. Would people hear me if I screamed? Then I looked at Lee again, and saw tears running down his face. "Don't you feel there is something wonderful developing between us?" he whispered. "Don't you know I would never let anybody hurt you?" I took a deep breath and nodded.

It was true. I might have been naïve about many things, but I'd had plenty of experience with boys telling me lies. I knew Lee wasn't lying to me; a man with tears in his eyes!

I felt a surge of concern and affection. When Dave re-entered the room, we moved to the living-room, where he sat down and began plunking a few sorrowful chords on his piano. "Go ahead and tell her about it," Lee said. Dave turned to me and began to tell his tortuous tale. It was about how Lee and some other boys in the Civil Air Patrol had enjoyed a party at a house he used to live in.

As Squadron Commander, he was their leader and mentor. Lee, being curious, had gone upstairs to where Dave kept his scientific equipment and a full-sized skeleton, unaware that the other boys had now gone home. Dave, hearing something upstairs, quickly flung open the door, entered the room, and then locked it, without thinking about how that could frighten the boy. "My intention was to make sure he didn't leave with any of my things," Dave said.

When Dave saw it was only Lee, he decided to talk to him about his fatherless condition, but Lee was sure Dave was going to assault him. He had bitter experiences in Youth House in New York, where he'd learned to fight first and ask later.

So now, he backed away, jabbed at a window with his elbow, and shattered the glass. Picking up a sharp shard, Lee dared David Ferrie to try to touch him. "He didn't believe my true intentions," Dave said. "Probably because, seeing him frightened like that, I had an erection." When Lee jabbed the glass shard toward him, Dave exploded. The combination of Lee's disrespect and his aggressive jab at him made Dave decide to teach Lee a lesson. A brutal fight ensued, but Lee kept getting back up, until a final blow to his mouth nearly knocked him out. That's when Dave realized his own condition. "I had never raped anybody in my life," he said sadly, "and it wasn't going to happen now." But then, an awful fact struck him. Lee Oswald was no ordinary kid. Right now, Lee's mother was having a date with Sam Termine, who was no ordinary man. He was, in fact, the mighty Carlos Marcello's own driver! As he saw blood running from Lee's mouth, Dave suddenly had visions of his own body cut into little bitty pieces. He helped Lee up, washed his face, and saw a cut to Lee's gum so deep that Dave had to put a stitch in it to stop the bleeding. When Lee took the needle stoically, with grim pride, Dave cursed himself for what he'd done. He told Lee that the tooth would probably be OK. But if it fell out, he was to immerse it in milk right away and go to a dentist. Then he pushed a twenty-dollar bill into Lee's jean pocket, to cover any dental fees. "I'll get you some ice cream, be right back!" he told Lee, as he dropped him off. Thank God, Marguerite wasn't home yet, but Lee had no key to get inside. As Lee sat down on the dark porch, shaking, Dave begged him not to tell. "I'm no snitch," Lee replied. "But I never want to see your ugly face again." Lee was already inside when Dave came back. "Ma just thought I'd been in another fight," Lee put in. He quit going to the nearest CAP meetings, joining a unit far from Dave's. But in the summer of 1955, he ran into Dave again.

This CAP photo, with Dave Ferrie 2nd from left and Lee Oswald far right, was seen on *Frontline* decades later.

It happened at a Civil Air Patrol two-week summer bivouac where CAP cadets learned search-and-rescue, knot typing, and survival skills. The last weekend of the bivouac, Lee was photographed at a cookout, standing as far away from David Ferrie as he possibly could. But it turned out OK. When we reached the Mansion, Lee walked me to the door and asked if I'd like to see the city with him after I got some sleep. He would also be searching for his dad's grave. I loved the idea and told him yes. But I was beginning to wonder what I was getting myself into.

Chapter Eight
The Party

Sunday, April 28, 1963

The next morning, I worked my two-hour shift at Royal Castle and returned to The Mansion on St. Charles Ave. Lee arrived midmorning and we were soon on our way to meet his elderly aunt, as planned. As we rode the streetcar, things began cheerily enough.

We even snag a duet together, appropriately about Henry the VIII and Anne Boleyn, as we would be heading to a cemetery if all went well. We transferred to a bus, after which Lee suddenly pointed to a street and said, “My cousin's visiting over there. We can use his car later today to show you around the city.”

“Why can't we use it now?” I asked. “They need it to go to Mass. But later, it will be okay.”

“Are you going to buy a car?” I continued. “On my income?” he laughed. “Cars are handy, but if I owned a car, how could I play the role of the unhappy American worker who can't get ahead? What would be my motive for wanting to go to Cuba? Most Cubans in Uncle Fidel's ‘Workers' Paradise' don't have cars.”

“Well, it could be a long time before you're sent to Cuba,” Lee put his finger to his lips. I realized I was speaking too loudly.

“Maybe a year or so,” he agreed. “But there are other reasons. For example, my driver's license. I had to stash it away,” he said.

Lee said he had been warned that the Texas Highway Patrol had tagged his driver's license as “belonging to a known Communist.”

“They could stop me for going through a red light,” he said. Then one call could give them that information. They could arrest me on some trumped-up charge. Maybe even beat me up. So there are no cars in my life for now.” When we arrived at the aunt's house, Lee hesitated, then asked me to wait outside. “She's likely to mention you, if she sees you, to the family, and my wife is still in Texas.” he said apologetically. “If she blows up at me,” he added, “at least she won't blow up at you, too.”

After half an hour, Lee finally came out. The expression on his face made it clear that things had not gone well. Soured by the news of his defection, she told him she was ashamed that he was even a member of the family, but in the end, she grudgingly gave Lee the approximate location of his father's grave.

Back in the bus, I said nothing, knowing Lee wasn't ready to talk about what happened. We returned to where Lee's cousin's car would be waiting. At least Lee had another relative who liked him! This time I stood by the car, understanding my role, while Lee went inside a nice-looking house to tell his cousin he would be taking the car, and thank you very much. [100] Soon we were on our way to the cemetery, and in this private vehicle, Lee now released his feelings about his encounter with his aunt, saying it was the price he had to pay. "That doesn't mean I have to like it," he told me. "I hope someday my children will know the truth about me."

"Your Aunt Lil and Uncle Dutz surely love you," I said, to cheer him up. That's when Lee told me that the day after Christmas, 12/26/42, Marguerite decided to take Lee away from Lil and Dutz. Lee was only three, but he could remember that he began to sob, and fought to stay, and as he did, his aunt and uncle both started to cry, too.

Lee, age two

But Marguerite took little Lee to Bethlehem House anyway, placing him in the care of his unwilling 7-yr-old brother, Robert. Their working mother visited them, paying fees to keep them there. She'd take the boys for ice cream and a movie. Lee said he was treated well at the orphanage. He had no complaints, and his brothers felt the same. They all felt better off living there. Lee stayed 13 months, records showing he was released back to Marguerite on Jan 29, 1944. Lee and his brothers were brought home. Marguerite had married a successful insurance agent, **Edwin Ekdahl**. They moved to a nice home out by Fort Worth.

---

[100] A well-used Texas driver's license for Lee was found in the records after the Kennedy assassination, but it was confiscated. See the Appendix for the affidavit by witness Aletha Frair and a list of over 30 witnesses who knew Lee (or a lookalike imposter) could drive.

Lee started attending school there, while his older brothers were sent off to a military boarding school. I knew the rest of this story by now: divorce ruined everything again, and the brief period of fatherly concern that Edwin showed to Lee ended.

Lee with one of his dogs

My heart ached for Lee: reaching over, I stroked his arm as he drove. "Don't feel sorry for me," he said stoically.[101]
Usually thrifty with words, he opened up and began sharing the problems his mother had laid on him and his brothers. Since my mother was a lioness at heart, with little compassion, my responses made Lee realize again how much we shared in common. Innocently, we started comparing his wife and my husband-to-be, insofar as they were making our present lives miserable. It seemed natural to do so. Our concerns, failing hopes and the love they failed to give, it was a relief to have someone who listened. How much was missing in my relationship with Robert! In a matter of days, Lee Oswald had learned more about me than Robert Baker had in ten months. While Lee and I agonized over issues ranging from religion to the Cold War, Robert avoided worrying about it. Lee recited poetry and loved to sing, just as I did, while Robert found my singing irritating, explaining that he was tone deaf. Unlike Robert, Lee didn't smoke or drink. I was especially unhappy that Robert had broken his promise to write every day.

By now, he had the letter that showed how terrified I was to be alone and without him in New Orleans. He had ordered me to write just ONE letter, too. "I guess he's never called, because it's too expensive," I told Lee, realizing I was making excuses for Robert's neglect. So why should I marry such a man? Lee told me that Marina, his wife, and their toddler Junie, were staying with Ruth Paine, a Quaker. Though he was worried about her because she was pregnant, he was planning to divorce after she gave birth to an American-born baby, which would allow her to live in America without getting deported. Then he'd be free.

As we exchanged our thoughts about love and marriage, being with Lee made me remember that there were lots of other good men, besides Robert, out there. Just talking to Lee was making me rethink everything. Now we entered Cypress Grove Cemetery to face our task. Cypress Grove was filled with countless rows of carved statues, crypts, monuments, and graves of every kind. They were above-ground for good reason.

---

[101] http://jfk.hood.edu/Collection/FBI%20Records/100-16601/100-16601%20Sub%20A-3/100-16601%20Sub%203A03.pdf The impression left by The Warren Commission is that Lee was kept in the Orphan's home for years. The home was actually run for children with only one parent.

Since New Orleans was built below sea-level, anything buried 'six feet under' would float right back up to the surface with any significant rain.

As we walked through the maze, I complained how I wasn't allowed to call Robert to tell him about my move, because we were eloping. "Well," Lee replied, "Marina was supposed to call me from Paine's house, but she hasn't. I've been worried sick." When I asked why he didn't call, he said, "I'm not supposed to call. **Mrs. Paine** could be listening in. The Pain is nosy," he went on. "She's keeping Marina and Junie because Marina's pregnant and I have to find a job, and a place to live."

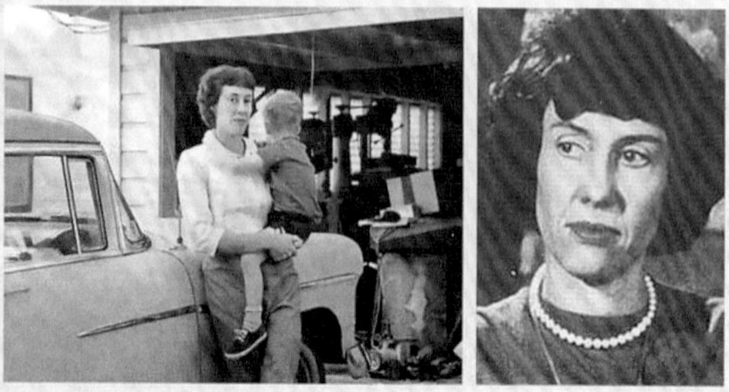

Ruth Paine

June Lee Oswald, with a kitten

"But why does it matter if she knows your concerns?" I asked. Lee hesitated, then said, "I'm supposed to be the callous creep who hit her, then left, and who's out of money." Was Lee's role-playing so deeply entangled with his personal life that he had to play such a part? "Did you say you *hit* her?" I asked, digging deeper.

Lee avoided my question. "We're really estranged," he stressed. "We're working on a permanent arrangement so I can go on with my life without worrying about her. Mrs. Paine will arrange everything this summer. She speaks Russian, and is in the middle of her own divorce."[102] But my warning lights were on. Lee had dodged the question. Was this intense young man, whom I'd only known a few days, a wife-beater? What if he was a mental case, who could suddenly harm me? Nobody even knew where I was – in a cemetery—with nobody around. As we approached a building where somebody might be inside, I gloomily sat down on a bench. One look at my face, and Lee understood.

He simply walked the rest of the way to the building without me. A few minutes later, Lee

[102] So Lee was led to believe, but the Paine divorce did not actually occur for years.

emerged with a caretaker. I watched from my bench and waited. From my view, I could see where Lee went, so after the caretaker left, I followed him to the grave.

When I saw Lee stop at a dark gravestone amidst a block of others, then lower his head, I knew he had found his dad. I waited respectfully as Lee got on his knees and placed both hands on his father's grave. He remained in this position for several silent minutes. "Well, Dad," he said as he got up, "rest in peace." [103] We returned to the car, at which time Lee said he wanted to show me the orphanage. I could hardly refuse. The orphanage was a stately structure, where many children had found refuge via the Lutheran Church.

Here, Lee turned to me and said, "You need to know more, before you judge me." He said Marina had repeatedly been unfaithful to him, and that she had said he was no good at sex in front of a roomful of her new friends in America – something she did not dare say back in Minsk, where Lee was well-known as a young Romeo. "It almost destroyed me when she cheated on me the first time," he said mournfully. "...but she did it as easily as drinking a bottle of beer." He had married her to avoid deportation, on a rebound from a busted love affair.

And she had married him in hopes that he would return to the United States.[104] It wasn't exactly a marriage made in heaven. Still, affection was in the mix, until Lee became bitter about two things: Marina's infidelity, and her insistence on acquiring all the fine things America had to offer. Hoping she would be pleased to live in America, Lee soon discovered that she wanted everything she saw advertised in the newspapers.[105] What kept them together was baby June Lee.

In the Russian way, June's middle name was that of the father.

"I thought I was past caring about people anymore," Lee said, "after what Marina had done. The problem was that Lee had grown to love Marina, and her cheating truly devastated him. Junie saved their marriage, such as it was. Her birth changed everything for him. "I was a daddy!" he said. The feelings that his daughter June awakened in Lee were intense. It no longer mattered to him that Marina's love was shallow. "She knows she's being used now, so I deserve to suffer her tongue. But think of what I have to live with!"

---

[103] Details have been added here that were left out in my book *Me & Lee*.

[104] Marina has always said, officially, that Lee fooled her, that he claimed he never intended to return to the US.

[105] Lee's friend and CIA-connected handler, George de Mohrenschildt, introduced the young couple to the Dallas area White Russians, who were anti-Communists. To buttress his fake pro-Soviet cover, Lee had to show anger and disapproval, even tearing up dresses Marina's White Russian friends gave her. He then ordered her never to see them again, claiming he was jealous that they provided her with what he could not. "I'm the one who takes care of you!" he proclaimed. But Lee was actually protecting his wife from any charges that she was a Soviet spy. Even the Warren Commission recognized that Marina had been so isolated by Lee that she knew nothing of value.

"But you said that you hit her," I said, not letting the subject rest.

"If I told you all she did," Lee replied, "you'd understand. You'd see why I lost my temper." Lee then described insults so cruel I will not repeat them here. As a result, Lee hated both what she had become and what he was becoming. He had once been a kinder, more considerate lover. While a Marine, when Lee was stationed in Japan, he had an affair with a delicate Japanese girl trained in the art of Geisha. It was a forbidden love; his next assignment forced him to abandon her. In contrast to his soft-spoken Geisha lover, he said Marina had "the tongue of a snake, and when she starts mocking me..." The way Lee said 'mocking' made me recall my Russian instructor saying, "Mere English can't crush a soul, or destroy one's self-image the way that Russian can." When Dr. Concevitch became angry or impatient with how we pronounced certain passages in Russian, I had heard some choice words myself!

When I told Lee I knew how harsh Russian words could be, he gave me a look of appreciation. Seeing signs of understanding, Lee then admitted he'd lost his temper and hit his wife, not once, but several times! Perhaps a dozen, truth be known. "I even beat her... a couple of times..." he admitted. The words fell from his mouth slowly, his head low. His voice solemn. Ashamed. I was stunned. He *is* a wife beater! I thought, in horror. I stiffened with repulsion, my mind flashing back to my father's violence, even though I knew that Dad definitely wouldn't have hit Mother if she hadn't relentlessly driven him on.

"I don't want to hear another word!" I cried. "You disgust me!"

He accepted my words in silence. What could he say? Robert may have neglected me, but he wasn't a wife-beater. Ironically, while I feared Lee for his violence, after hearing his confession, I respected him for his honesty. After a long pause, Lee humbly asked me to let him continue to show me New Orleans. Since I needed to get to David Ferrie's party later, I agreed.

I *had* to meet Dr. Sherman! And I did want to see more of the city. Lee drove us to the St Louis Cathedral, where we parked and walked. It was like plunging into the heart of Europe.

We navigated Jackson Square, admiring the paintings the artists had on display. Near the majestic Cathedral, we traversed the Cabildo buildings that held so much of the city's colorful history, then explored Pirate's Alley. After stopping for Dr. Peppers and pralines, we went window-shopping along Royal Street's antique shops and art galleries.

On Bourbon Street, Lee pointed out a restaurant where he'd swept floors and washed dishes as a teenager. "It was my first lucrative job, working for my uncle's friends," he joked, explaining that he spent the money on comic books and at pool tables. "I'm not much richer today," he quipped. "Though I do have enough change left for buses..." He smiled. "And maybe a trip to the zoo."

And here he'd spent ten dollars to put a roof over my head! Lee did have enough money for the zoo, for that's where we went next, though first we stopped where it was free, at the Seal Pool. Noticing that one of the seals had infected eyes, Lee commented that more national parks and reserves needed to be set up. "They're having to swim in their own excrement, in this little pool," he observed. His sensitivity to the needs of the seals softened me a little, so I asked him if he would beat a fawn or a deer. "Animals don't make fun of your manhood," he replied.

Lee added that there were quiet and peaceful days, mostly centered on Junie. Seeing the affection in Lee's eyes as he spoke of his daughter had its effect on me. There were children in the park playing happily, and soon we were interacting with some of them. Both Lee and I loved children.

Soon we were throwing and retrieving balls, organizing a crack-the-whip game, and judging who could do the best cartwheel. As we got back in the car, Lee said he would welcome half a dozen children if he had a loving wife, and even adopt an orphan or two on top of that. This forged a truce between us for the time being.

I needed to get some sleep before the party, so Lee dropped me off at the Mansion. He gave me a cautious kiss on my cheek, as I reminded him that Robert was coming. "You'll be able to meet my fiancé soon," I pointed out, wondering if they would get along.

Lee replied that he was headed to the Murrets for Sunday dinner, and to get some rest. As for me, the instant my head touched the pillows, I was asleep. Then into my dreams came the sound of a loud tapping on my window. It was Lee, with some groceries from a deli. I put the perishables in Mrs. Webber's refrigerator and then we sat together on the porch swing and ate oranges that Lee peeled in a special way, using only one hand to make the peel roll off in one piece! While these oranges had thin rinds, to this day, I haven't found anybody to duplicate what he did. Suddenly, Mrs. Webber came clip-clopping down the hall.

She threw open the beautiful door and stared at us with a fierce scowl. "Look at you!" she yelled at me. "You're practically naked!"

"What's your problem, woman?" Lee snapped, jumping off the swing. "She's wearing shorts. You're the one that's half-naked." He pointed at the woman's big breasts overflowing the seam of her low-cut dress. Mrs. Webber stiffened, threw her red-haired head back in scorn, and stormed off, slamming the door as she went. Lee and I looked at each other and laughed. Just then, a well-dressed couple came up the steps and went inside. Seeing them, I did feel embarrassed to be sitting on the porch in shorts. "What a harpy Webber is!" I said, getting up from the swing.

"I am used to Harpies in my life," Lee said quietly. "My mother and my wife are experts in that department." In my heart, I wished Lee had never told me that he had laid hands on Marina. As for Lee, studying my silence, he dared to say "Are you really going to go through with your marriage?

I closed my eyes, wondering what to answer, when Lee suddenly kissed me. And it was not in a brotherly way. "Oh, no!" I protested.

"I want so much to hold you in my arms!" he said in a rush, as I pushed him away (he didn't resist). "We've known each other less than three days!" I protested.

"Don't marry that man!" Lee pleaded. "If he loved you, he would have called. He would have written every day, just to keep your heart from aching. Please," he whispered. "Think! Take more time. If he treats you this way now, how will he treat you after you're married? I'm falling in love with you, Juduffki." I turned my back on him, close to tears.

"I'm going to divorce Marina," he went on. "Everybody knows that."

"Just because of you," I replied, "I might not have married Robert. But then you had to tell me you beat your wife!"

"Because I care for you!" he replied. "I didn't want to hide it from you. It would have been wrong for me to do that." As the twilight deepened, and we stood there, I fell silent. Which was more insane: to marry a man whose arrival I no longer anticipated with my former passion, or to become involved with a married wife-beater I'd just met? After more thought, I finally had a reply, reminding Lee that he had babies to care for. Then, as a wave of emotion covered me, I admitted that I cared for him, too! Shamefully, I had to admit it. But I was so shaken, all I could do was to tell Lee that I was now afraid of him.

"You could hurt me!" I told him. "My own father did it when he drank. Later, he was always sorry, but he couldn't change his ways. I wish I could believe you could change." Tears sprang to my eyes, as Lee embraced me anxiously. "Well, then," he said, "I'll prove that I can. As time goes by, you'll see. As my love grows stronger for you, so will my proof." In a voice that trembled, he added, "For as long as it takes."

"What proof are you planning?" I asked, without any real hope.

"This is my promise to you," he answered. "I will never lay a hand on Marina again. I will do this to prove how much your affection means to me." Lee's promise intrigued me. It could help protect Marina, so I planned to hold him to it. "You know, you didn't give yourself much time before falling in love," I reminded him. "How long did you know Marina before you fell in love with her?" Lee confessed that it had been mere days when he decided he liked Marina enough to marry her. They got married only six weeks later. "See?" I said, "your love is only good for six weeks. Or six months."

"There were other circumstances," Lee insisted. "I can't tell you more," he added. "I'm sorry. I am a fool."

He sat down gloomily on the swing and began to rock slowly. As he sat there, my heart simply wouldn't behave itself. As I sat down beside planned to hold him to it. "You know, you didn't give yourself much time before falling in love," I reminded him. "How long did you know Marina before you fell in love with her?" Lee confessed that it had been mere days when he decided he liked Marina enough to marry her. They got married only six weeks later. "See?" I said, "your love is only good for six weeks. Or six months."

"There were other circumstances," Lee insisted. "I can't tell you more," he added. "I'm sorry. I am a fool." He sat down gloomily on the swing and began to rock slowly. As he sat there, my heart simply wouldn't behave itself, and as I sat down beside him, I blurted out, "I've never, ever been attracted to anyone as I am to you!"

"It is the same for me." He said softly.

"I love Robert, but I never feel comfortable with him," I confessed. "It's like I always have to think about how to behave with him to make him happy. I never feel natural with him."

"But when you are with me," Lee said gently, "it's the way it should be, isn't it?"

"You know it is," I answered, my emotions raging. As I saw his eyes fill with tears, my self-control crashed. I heard myself say "This is driving me mad! Kiss me! And then—go away!" Lee took my face in his hands and gave me two slow kisses with a tenderness I had never experienced before. Then he backed away. "After you're married, I won't be able to kiss you anymore." He stood for a moment as if he were going to leave. But then he rushed forward and dropped to his knees, pressing his face against my stomach. Overcome, I asked myself, *Am I being worshipped, right here on the porch?* Then Lee got up, collected himself and his thoughts, and backed away. With his blue-gray eyes trained upon me, it seemed that he was trying to look directly into my heart. "Maybe we could be brother and sister," he concluded with a shrug.

"I never had a brother!" I replied, pondering the absurdity of his comment. Then I started to cry and stamped my foot at him. "Go away!" I commanded. "You're torturing me!"

39. Lifton wrote: Here's what I gather from the record (and if someone knows different, please email me at dlifton@compuserve.com, and please remember to citeyour source):

1. No beating at all in Russia (or it would have been picked up on the KGB tapes, and there is no hint of that).

2. A slapping incident at Robert Oswald's house, circa June 1962 3. More hitting over the summer, when they moved to Mercedes Street (in early August 1962); and more in the fall (in early November, when they moved to Elsbeth Street, and Marina left Lee, for a brief while, but then he begged her to return, and she did) 4. Some more hitting at Elsbeth (the first of the two Dallas rooming houses) 5. A terrible incident in January 1963 as described by McMillan (and which was followed by lovemaking which, per McMillan, resulted in the conception of Rachel) 6. (possibly the same as 5) Possible reported at Neely Street. Yes, not a very nice record. BUT then. . . BUT THEN. . . somewhere in the first 3 months of the 1963, it stopped. Completely stopped. And, as far as I know, there was never ever again an incidence of hitting or slapping or anything like that--during the entire 5 month New Orleans period (4/24/63 - 9/24/63), and during the last six weeks after his return from Mexico City (10/4-11/22). As I say, if anyone takes issue with this, please email me at dlifton@commpuserve.com, and provide cites... David Lifton" (Lee promised Judyth in late April that he would never hit Marina again--and he kept his word).

Read what researchers discovered about Lee's promise.

He agreed to go, but not before asking if I'd still let him take me to Dave's party. Of course I would, since I'd get lost otherwise.

When Lee returned, he brought a newspaper with him. "Look!" he said, turning the pages. "The beaches are open!"

He showed me the article. I read that several beaches "free of pollution" were now open "on a limited and controlled basis."

"That's the way they let you know that these are segregated beaches," Lee explained. African Americans ("Negroes," then) were only allowed to swim at Lincoln Beach, which Lee told me was inferior and run down. "If I asked you to swim at Lincoln Beach with the Negroes, would you go swim with me? Yes, or not?"

"Of course!" I answered. "I'm not prejudiced."

"That's my girl," Lee said, his eyes shining. "Well then, would you go swimming with me at a nudist colony?"

"Swim by yourself, Bub," I replied. "Clothing is how we protect ourselves from prying eyes." To point that out, I began telling him about a sci-fi story where sexless women all went nude, except for the elderly among them who hid their physical infirmities in black robes."

"*The Last Man,"* Lee put in. "You mean the story by Mary Shelly?" I interjected.

"No," Lee said. "I mean the one about the last real man, kept in a cage. The sexless women stared at him and his gonads, but one girl really cared. And she was the only naturally fertile woman left in the world. Am I right?"

I was amazed. "Nobody knows that story!" I exclaimed. "I read it in a Pocket Book edition that Mama had. But the last few pages were missing."

"Ah! So how much did you miss?"

"They ran away together with a mob chasing after them."

"Ah! So that's all you know!" Lee said, smiling. "Yes, they ran away, with half the planet after them."

"Tell me!" I demanded. "How did it end?"

"Hmmmm...!" Lee replied, with a Cheshire Cat smile. "Please," I begged, "how did it end? Did they become the next Adam and Eve?"

"Hmmmm!" he said, grinning. I hit his chest with a mock flurry of fists. I have never hit to hurt anyone but bullies in my life, and I'm sure Lee was amused, but he flatly refused to tell me the end of the story.

I even offered to go to bed with him. It was a hollow promise, but my proposition made it all the easier for him to laugh at me. We did not have a car now, so we used a streetcar and then a bus. And what did Lee do, then? He pulled (of all things!) an old science fiction anthology out of his jacket pocket, from which he began reading! "Oh my gosh!" I said, grabbing his arm. "Is it possible that *The Last Man* is in there, and that's why you know all about it?" But Lee only smiled and pulled the book closer to him, keeping me from seeing any pages. "Oh, come on!" I tried again. "Did they make it?"

Lee smiled and folded his arms, hiding the book completely. "I'm not going to tell you."

"Fiend!" I cried, pounding his chest again with pretend blows.

"Ah, stop!" Lee protested. "You're hurting me! You're hurting the book!" We both laughed, because this time I had scarcely touched him. Even as we got off the bus to walk the last few blocks in twilight, I was still imploring him. "At least, tell me the author's name. I've forgotten it!"

"Only if you make a promise," Lee said solemnly, "that you will never lay a hand on me again. You've hit me twice in one hour, and here you complain about me being a wife-beater! Only when I'm sure you'll keep your promise will I tell you the ending."

"Oh, no!" I answered.

"Oh, yes! Lee rejoined.

"You are a very wicked man," I declared, "because I am certain to beat you up again. And then I will never know the ending."

"Monster!" he quailed.

We walked arm-in-arm up to Dave's apartment. The upstairs porch was brightly lit, with rock n' roll music announcing the party. Competing with it were many loud voices, many in Spanish. A number of older cars were parked in the street. I saw two men sitting on one of the cars, kissing. Lee noticed them, too. "Be prepared," he said. "There will be some unusual people here."

"I'm beginning to notice."

"Dave has to cultivate a variety of contacts," Lee explained. "You can't have an information network in this city without running into some of these characters." As I tried to figure out why Dave Ferrie had to have an 'information network,' I gripped Lee's arm more tightly. "I'm glad you're with me," I said, as we walked in the darkness around to the back, where a single light feebly glowed by the door leading upstairs. To climb the stairs, we had to navigate around a pair of boys who were smoking pot and smooching. As we entered the kitchen, to soothe me, Lee said nonchalantly, "I say, to each his own. It's a human right to have sex, whatever way you wish, so long as it doesn't hurt anybody. Is that offensive to you?"

"No, no," I answered, "but my preferences are wholly traditional."

"Have you explored other options?" Lee countered. "Not interested," I assured him. "I am happy with the male variety, thank you very much."

"As for me," Lee said, "I observed that the original blueprint was successful. Men and women were built to fit together like a puzzle. But if that doesn't work for somebody, let them do whatever pleases them." He grinned. "I used to tear pictures of pretty women from comic books and catalogs and take them to bed with me," he confided. "I just never had the tendency to tear out pictures of good-looking men and fantasize about them. So, I guess I'm not gay." The apartment was hot and crowded with people. In Dave's big kitchen, the lab stuff was covered or put away, and the mouse cages were gone.

David Ferrie's big kitchen, 2003. Most of the counters and cabinets were gone.

Coolers full of beer and soft drinks were on the counter, along with sacks of potato chips and pretzels. A bowl of nuts had spilled into the sink. We each grabbed some pieces of hotdog on toothpicks and a plateful of other things, then moved to greet Dave, who stood between the dining room and living-room chain smoking. He was talking earnestly to some young white males who looked like students. The air was thick with cigarette smoke, mingled with the sweet aroma of marijuana and contraband Cuban cigars. "There you are!" Dave said, then began introducing us as "old friends." The music became louder as we said our hello's. Most of the guests were fit-looking adult males of Cuban and Mexican origin. Some had their girlfriends in tow. I managed to ask Dave where his lab animals were. "I don't want anybody messing with my mice," he said. "They've been moved for the night."

"Is Dr. Sherman here?" I asked, having no idea what she looked like. "Not yet," Dave replied. "But she'll be here before 10:00. So, enjoy yourself. And remember, I'll be taking you two home tonight." Lee and I had fun dancing to a couple of rock n' roll songs and then took time to wipe the sweat from our faces. Fortunately, a breeze began to blow in through the screened porch.

Jack Suggs Martin[106]

David Franklin Lewis

February 23, 1967 - Former investigator David Lewis following the death of David Ferrie, New Orleans

As we rested, I noticed a pair of thin, nervous-looking men dressed in black suits, with shiny shoes and slicked-down hair. Lee said David Ferrie called them 'the comedy team of Martin and Lewis,' after the singer Dean Martin and his comic sidekick, Jerry Lewis. They look like they're from the FBI," I said. "They should," Lee replied. "They work for Guy Banister." He was a big FBI hot shot, Lee said. Banister was the former FBI SAC for the entire Chicago area. "They're probably here to pick up info for Banister," Lee confided. He introduced me to the strange pair, who already knew him.

---

[106] Original name probably Jack Suggs; he is shown in the movie "JFK" getting pistol-whipped by a drunken Guy Banister. It put Martin in the hospital.

Both had wives who were not present. They were indeed opposites. Jack Martin drank, David Lewis did not. Martin was loud: Lewis was quiet. Martin flirted with the men: David flirted with me. As the night progressed, Jack Martin, who kept drinking, became more obnoxious, pushing himself on some of the gay men, while Lewis got out a chess set and asked if anyone would like to play a game.

I didn't want to, because Dr. Sherman was slated to arrive any time, so I sat in a corner and began to read from a medical text about surgical nursing, while Lee and Lewis started a chess game. It was about 10:00 and the party was in full swing when Dr. Sherman finally arrived. You couldn't miss her. She was by far the best-dressed person in the room.

She was a professional middle-aged woman with soft, attractive features, she had pulled her dark hair back into a severe French twist. She was speaking to two dark-skinned Latinos in fluent Spanish when Dave brought me over to introduce me.

"Mary, this is Miss Vary," Dave said, "She's been anxious to meet you."

"I'm sorry, but I can't talk to her now," the Doctor replied, not even looking at me. "Dr. Sherman!" I interjected. "Has Dr. Ochsner spoken to you about me?"

"I can't talk to you now!" Sherman said sharply. "Please excuse me." She then turned her back on me and resumed speaking to the two dark Latinos. As she walked them onto the screened porch, I was left alone and perplexed. My insecurities swelled. Why didn't Dr. Sherman want to talk to me? "Is she upset about something?" I asked Dave.

"Let it go," he advised. "She must have her reasons."

I felt crushed. Humiliated. "Can I go in your bedroom, and just read until she leaves?" I asked.

"I wouldn't recommend going in there," Dave cautioned. "Just go back to your corner, if you want to read. Nobody will bother you." Gloomily, I picked up the nursing book again and retreated to a corner of the dining room table full of empty beer cans. I thought about asking Lee to take me home but didn't want to interrupt the great chess game he was playing with David Lewis.

Dr. Sherman did not stay long. As she prepared to leave, she walked right past me without acknowledging my existence, opened the refrigerator door, took the blender full of tumors, and left the back way. I couldn't believe this great researcher could be so rude. After a while, Lee cleared away some beer cans and set up the chess set in front of me. "Cheer up!" he said. "I'll give you some attention. Let's play a game." Lee had walloped David Lewis, who now drifted over from time to time to watch us play. He said he was working several part-time jobs now, such as handling baggage, but was still doing some investigative work with Jack Martin for Guy Banister. "Don't tell my wife Anna," he said, "if you ever come by Thompson's to eat. She doesn't like Banister and thinks I quit." Anna was a waitress at Thompson's Restaurant on St. Charles, he explained, not far from Lee Circle. If Lee and I ever dropped by, we could count on getting a free slice of pie if we gave his wife a good tip.

When Lewis left the table, Lee began telling me about some of Martin and Lewis' other activities, such as driving vans of voters around to different poll stations so they could cast multiple votes for well-paying candidates. "That's disgusting," I told Lee. "That's New Orleans," he replied. I had heard that comment before and would hear it again. Next, I learned that Dave called Jack S. Martin, "Jackass Martin." He put up with him, Lee said, because Jackass was an artist who could create excellent fake documents when needed. To my puzzled expression, Lee only smiled. Dave overheard Lee's remark and came over to say, "Investigative work can involve some ploys. If you weren't so closely associated with Ochsner and Sherman, we wouldn't have told you anything." About an hour later, as people began to leave, Dave and Martin began yelling at each other. That didn't end well: Dave took Martin by one of his big ears and steered him down the stairs.

Then he threw him down the last few steps. As for David Lewis, he went out the front way without incident. Lee said Dave didn't make David Lewis leave in disgrace because Lewis didn't smoke or drink and was the reliable half of the comedy team of Martin and Lewis. He played the piano, liked classical music, and as was obvious, played chess. Lewis would also sometimes do a little emergency detective work for Dave. That's when I learned that 'Captain' Ferrie, the airline pilot and 'Dr.' Ferrie, Doctor of Psychology (as per a diploma in Italian that hung on his living-room wall) was also a paralegal working for G. Wray Gill, one of Carlos Marcello's top attorneys. It seemed that Marcello really did have his claws into David Ferrie.

I was feeling more and more uncomfortable. If only this were all a bad dream! When Lee left our chess game to talk to somebody Dave wanted him to meet, a half hour passed before he could get back to me. By then, it was 1 a.m. Half the people were gone. I hoped Dave would soon close down the party. The oddballs and women were gone. The dancing had stopped, but the music played on. Then suddenly, Dave started yelling again. But this time, it was that he hated President Kennedy.

"That S. O. B. Kennedy needs to keep being careless and riding in open cars, so he can get his head shot off!" he shouted. Then Dave began to describe the President in foul language over the Bay of Pigs disaster. Several Cubans standing with him chimed in with expletives in Spanish. Then they began chanting *Kill him! Kill him!* in English, followed by more curses from their drunken lips.

I looked across the room in shock and saw Lee looking steadfastly back at me. He made his way over to me, then said, "Later, Juduffki. He'll explain later." Things continued in a crazy course, including oaths to kill both JFK and Castro. Then, around 2 a.m. the police arrived and ordered Dave to shut the party down. "Jackass called them!!" Dave snarled. The music stopped, the people scurried away, and the police left. As Dave looked at the mess his guests left behind, he muttered that it would be a cold day in hell before he'd have another party. "Let them trash somebody else's place for a change!" he huffed, kicking at the debris. Seeing a chance to tell him what I thought of his party, I told him, "I object to everything you said about Kennedy!"

"You need to understand what was going on here tonight, chickadee," Dave answered. "We're trying to keep the Castro project under wraps, but Jackass Martin wants to be in on it. I don't want that drunk involved. And there are things I have to say, to be safely involved myself." Dave said he had caught Martin brow-beating Dr. Sherman, trying to get information out of her. He waited a while after she left, so Martin wouldn't connect the dots as to how important Dr. Sherman was, and then got rid of him.

"You'll be sorry you humiliated me!" Martin screamed, embellishing his threat with choice profanities. As far as Dave was concerned, their friendship was now over. "Martin is losing his mind," Dave said. "He used to be good. Then a project fell through. He said it was my fault!" Dave tossed a cigarette away. "Lewis doesn't drink, so he's okay. But whatever Lewis finds out, he has to tell Martin. He's become Martin's eyes, ears, nose and throat, because Martin can't think for himself anymore." Perhaps Dr. Mary behaved as she did because of Martin's harassment, Dave opined. Then he told me I was going to be needed in his half-baked lab whenever Dr. Mary could spare me. This was the worst news of all. I didn't want to have anything more to do with Dave, his anti-Castro Cubans, his mice, or with Lee. I had seen and heard enough. My time would be limited, I explained, adding that I'd soon to be married. "You don't seem to understand how serious this is," Dave protested. "I thought they would have prepared you better."

"Who is 'they'?" I asked. "The people we're doing this for," Dave said enigmatically. "Such as the CIA. We have to get Castro soon, or everything will be lost." It seemed impossible that 'everything' would be lost if Castro wasn't killed. And what did that have to with me? I finally told him how horrified I was to hear him say he hoped Kennedy would be shot in the head, Dave almost wilted. "I'll explain," he said, "*if* you agree to help us." But 'Dr.' David Ferrie was a blatantly suspicious character. He had been violent with Jack Martin. His friends included sexually promiscuous men who smoked illegal drugs. He possessed a foul mouth. I said I had to talk to Dr. Ochsner.

"That's fine with me," Dave replied. "After all, Ochsner's the boss." Lee rejected Dave's offer to drive us home,[107] seeing how tipsy he was, which prompted Dave to call a cab. As we waited for the cab, I told Lee that I didn't believe for a minute that Dave's project was secretly sponsored by the CIA. Lee tried to soothe me, saying, "Dave might sound like he is exaggerating, But he's not. I don't know all the details yet," he went on, "but if David W. Ferrie says it's that important, it is." I went silent. I was getting involved with a strange – maybe even violent—group of people, and I did not feel safe anymore.

---

[107] In my book *Davd Ferrie: Mafia Pilot*, Dave's access to this car, registered to "David W. Ferrie, Jr.", is fully explained.

Chapter Nine
The Target

Early Monday AM, April 29, 1963

After the disastrous party that Lee had inserted me into, I informed Lee that I was not all that impressed with *him*, either. As far as I knew, Lee could be a spy for the wrong side, right along with the so-called Dr. Ferrie. When I said Dr. Ochsner was scheduled to see me later next week, Lee frowned. "It'll be too late by then to get you in the proper position for everything," he said.

"What proper position?" I asked. "I don't even know if Dr. Sherman will accept me into her lab now."

It was about 3:30 AM when we arrived at The Mansion, and I feared that Mrs. Webber, whose schedule seemed to include staying up all night and sleeping until noon, would notice.

"There's no law against attending a party," Lee said firmly, escorting me up the steps. "You have the right to come and go as you please. But I can't leave you upset like this. What can I do?"

"I don't know," I told him. "I need proof that Dr. Ferrie isn't lying and that Dr. Sherman isn't going to dump me, and that I'm not getting into the wrong crowd." As Lee stood there, I searched for my key. As I did so, I saw the same girl sitting on the same red loveseat in the hall, just as on the first day here. But this time, she was with a different man.

I suspected that he had been with her all night, but who was I to talk? What would *she* think of *me*, talking to Lee at such an ungodly hour?

"I have an idea," Lee said then. "You need proof that Dr. Ferrie is legitimate and that we really are working on a government-sanctioned project to get Castro. You're upset because of how Dr. Sherman behaved, and you need assurances. Correct?"

"For the millionth time, yes," I said, still searching for the house key in my big black purse. "I need a keychain!"

"I have a solution to your problem. You should meet Guy Banister. He was the head of the FBI's Chicago office and can verify the legitimacy of our project. Would that male you feel better?"

"I would very much like to meet Mr. Banister," I admitted. "Then you must play a bit of a role," Lee said. "We don't want *you* seen there, so we need to disguise you as my wife. Nobody in Banister's office has seen her so far. I can fix your hair into a ponytail like Marina's.

We can take off your makeup. You can wear her clothes."

"You have her clothes?"

"A box or so," he said. "I'll look through them."

"Do you ever sleep?" I wondered aloud.

"Let me see..." Lee said, looking me over. "You're the same size, same height, same hair color, same blue eyes. And you can speak a little Russian. But you must never smile showing your teeth" As he looked me over, head to foot, he added, "You don't look exactly like her, of course, but it's close enough, since they never laid eyes on her. Can you meet me at Woolworth's on Canal Street at12:30?"

O, joy! In just two hours, I'd have to go to Royal Castle and work. Saying goodnight to Lee, I went inside, climbed into bed, and collapsed.

'Banister's Building.' The Warren Commission called it 'The Newman Building' and never interviewed Guy Banister(former FBI, deeply into Latin American intelligence work and anti-Castro activities), even though some of Lee's pamphlets were stamped 544 Camp St.—the same building. Lee spent most of 1963 in New Orleans. The 3rd floor's contents are described only in *Me & Lee,* and in this update. 544 Camp St is front, far left, with Mancuso's Coffee Shop to right. Cars are parked on the 531 Lafayette side, where Banister's office was.

After a little sleep, it was off to Royal Castle again, to handle the needs of all those guys wanting breakfast. Not long before I hung up my little apron, Lee showed up and ordered a breakfast. His visit was a surprise, since we were supposed to meet at Woolworth's on Canal St. But he had news he'd postponed, due to my anger about his treatment of Marina. On Sunday morning, his Uncle Dutz had moved Lee's things from the bus locker to his garage and invited Lee to come live with them until he found a job. "Of course, I'm pretending to be looking for a job," Lee confided, "even though one will be arranged."

The great news was that Lee had his uncle's car for the day, in exchange for another "favor" involving the amusement park that had just opened. As soon as I clocked out, we were on our way back to town. Instead of using Marina's clothes, Lee had decided that we'd go to the Salvation Army and pick out clothes that resembled what Marina would wear. To my puzzled look, Lee explained that it was better to have my own 'Marina clothes.' Then I would have them 'whenever I needed them.' *Whenever I needed them?* Would I have to pretend to be Marina for other people, too? Whoa!

But a sense of adventure had risen in me. I was being brought into Lee's clandestine world! Inside the store, Lee found an appropriate skirt and blouse. He was going for the 'peasant' look that Americans would equate with somebody from Russia. I tried the clothes: they fit fine. Back in the car, Lee brushed my hair and put it into a ponytail. He said my hair was finer in texture than Marina's, but it was the same color and length. Since this was a private detective agency, Banister's people were nosy and observant. I was to act shy and quiet, speaking no English, and just a bit of Russian. All this sneakiness like real-life theater, for I was working with an actual spy who had returned from behind the Iron Curtain. It was like a real-life Natasha and Boris from the Rocky and Bullwinkle show. But I still needed answers to my questions.

Next, we stopped at the Post Office, where a letter from Robert had arrived, as well as an official-looking envelope from Indiana, which had to be the birth certificate I'd ordered, to prove I was of marriageable age. I joyfully ripped open Robert's letter, but then I read that he'd would be coming without any money. OK then--no honeymoon. He also told me to get a job. So Robert still didn't know I was working at Royal Castle, meaning he still hadn't called the "Y" as promised last week. It only took a day for his letters to reach me, too! Anger burning in my heart, I thrust both letters into my black purse.

Lee dropped me off on Camp Street while he parked his "mafia" car away from sight. He came back soon, explaining that Banister's was just across the street from the Federal Building complex, with its courthouse, US government offices and many agencies. Inside, the air was musty from old air conditioners. The out-dated décor was like a police station from a 1930's movie. Swinging doors guarded the entrance to a file room, providing some privacy for people handling confidential files. A door marked with Banister's name was closed. Lee ignored a couple of men working at their desks and approached a middle-aged secretary, one of three women I saw in the room, who seemed to be the office boss. I had been told she was **Delphine Roberts**. She was also his mistress.

"Mr. and Mrs. Oswald are here to see Mr. Banister," Lee told her. The secretary said something friendly to me, but I kept my head down, softly replying with a few words in Russian, as Lee had directed me. "She doesn't speak English, so she really can't talk to you," Lee told her. But the secretary was curious and kept trying to talk to me anyway. This annoyed Lee, who stressed the point, saying, "I am sorry, but Mrs. Oswald *does not* speak English!" [108]I

Our wait wasn't long: Mr. Banister soon came out. He was alert and businesslike, with Authority written all over him. "So, this is Mrs. Oswald, is it?" he said, shaking my hand. Then he smiled at Lee as he ushered us inside his office. His sly smile told me that he already knew I wasn't really 'Mrs. Oswald.' Once inside, I saw even more file cabinets and piles of paper stacked everywhere, including on the floor. "I understand you needed to meet me," he said sternly. I was now standing face to face with the man who was supposed to allay my fears and instill trust. His craggy visage was framed by a square jaw and wavy gray hair. His eyes glared with a hardness that was almost arrogant. I couldn't help but notice that he was wearing a shoulder holster which held a big, fancy revolver. The man was armed and wanted those around him to know it. I managed to acknowledge his comment, as I scanned two walls covered with certificates and awards, befitting man whose career with the FBI was distinctive, and who was still an active anti-Communist. **Guy Banister** wasn't shy about pointing out the most important of his awards, making sure I knew he had been in charge of some 500 agents in the Chicago area. From early days when he witnessed Dillinger get shot, to his 'Red Raider' days, the man was a crusader intent on protecting The Land of the Free from every danger, foreign and domestic. He practically quivered with enthusiasm as he told me of his uncanny ability to find subversives, no matter how hard they tried to elude him. On Lee's cue, I told Banister why I had to meet him. I began with my concerns about David Ferrie and the Cubans yelling about killing Castro and Kennedy. He shrugged it off as necessary to expose traitors. Banister added that Ferrie was working for both him and Carlos Marcello as an undercover agent, legal advisor and medical specialist. After all, the Mafia was also anti-Castro. Shocked by his answer, I asked the big question. Was Ferrie's cancer project legitimate? Was it a secret

[108] This was **Delphine Roberts**, who was Banister's mistress as well as his top secretary. She later asserted to researcher Anthony Summers that Lee worked for Banister and that she had seen him several times. She also mentioned a "Mrs. Oswald" had visited, which Marina denied. This hurt Roberts' credibility with researchers, but she was telling the truth.

government project? Banister said it was, adding that his office was not bugged and not to worry about leaks, so long as I kept my mouth shut. He said summaries of Ferrie's work "with the doctors" were photocopied using his own Xerox machine[109] before the originals were "sent on to Georgia."

"I hear you're needed for this project," Banister assured me. Since an alliance between the Mafia and Banister looked unsavory to me, Banister told Lee to take me upstairs, gesturing toward the room above his head. To get there, we climbed what seemed to be pull-down stairs, visible behind an open wall of wooden studs to our left. Banister said the stairs would soon be concealed when the sheetrock went up and got painted and a "closet door" installed, with a key to the stairwell.

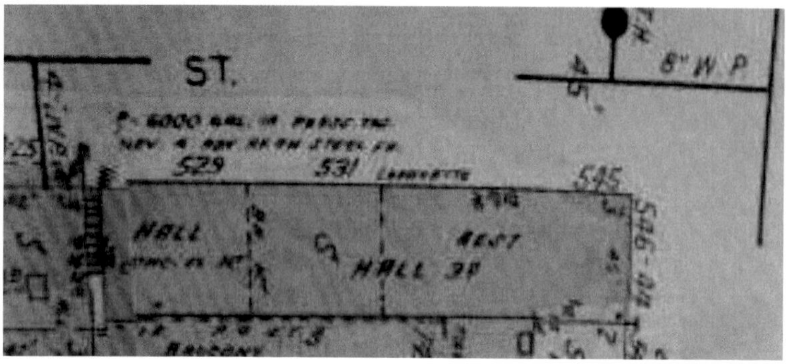

This 1940's Sanborn Fire Map shows Banister's building was brick and had a hallway connecting Banister's office (531 Lafayette) to the restaurant 546 Camp St. (shared bathroom). Anti-Oswald theorists try to say Banister had no access to the 544 Camp St. stairs and so was ignorant of Lee's use of the 544 Camp St address.

At the top, we entered a small room with even more filing cabinets. These were Banister's "high treasures"—secret files that David Ferrie and others kept updating on the corruption in the New Orleans Police Department. "Information is my business," Banister boasted.

He declared that these files were the most important ones. He showed us an example-- a damning evidence file on the Police Department's current Superintendent, muttering that "revenge was sweet." [110]

---

[109] In 1963 Xerox machines were uncommon outside hospitals, big companies and government offices. Private use was generally forbidden and official use left a paper trail, as a written record was required of what was copied. There were no such records kept at Banister's office; he also had a Telex with a list of FBI contact numbers posted next to it that Lee memorized.

[110] Anna Lewis, witness, recalled the stairs, since Banister once made her carry many files up the stairs for him when she was heavily pregnant. She had volunteered to assist her husband, David, and their friend Jack Martin, in sorting and moving Banister's secret police files upstairs in a single night. Banister insisted nobody could leave until everything was safely upstairs, but he, himself, didn't raise a finger to help. Because of Banister's lack of kindness, Anna urged her husband to find work elsewhere. She was surprised when told "researchers" said Banister had no access to the 2nd floor unless he left the building and walked all the way up and around to 544 Camp St. "Why would

And finally, in the dim-lit little room, Guy Banister told me that Lee was working with him, learning who was who and being groomed to do his part to save Cuba from Communism. Now I had a clearer picture of why David Ferrie behaved as he did in front of the militant Cubans. I also knew that a man like Banister would not have shown these files to me and Lee, except he needed our cooperation on a serious matter. After Lee and I returned to the car, I told him that part of me was still afraid. Banister was against the city police, for heaven's sake! [111]

"Let me tell you the back story," Lee offered. Banister, he said, was hired to a high position with the New Orleans police in the '50's to deal with corruption in the police force. However, Banister discovered that the evidence was being used to go after the snitches and witnesses who could testify in court against the corrupt cops. When he discovered their true intent, there was a showdown, and Banister was no longer wanted. Soon after, a depressed Banister got royally drunk – not that he hadn't been drunk before –but this time, when he had a run-in with a bartender and pulled out his gun, the police swarmed all over it. Reporters embellished it, amidst claims that the man was a dangerous drunkard. The objective was to ruin Banister by smearing his reputation so they could demote him to a nobody. That's when Banister resigned and formed **Guy Banister and Associates, Inc.**

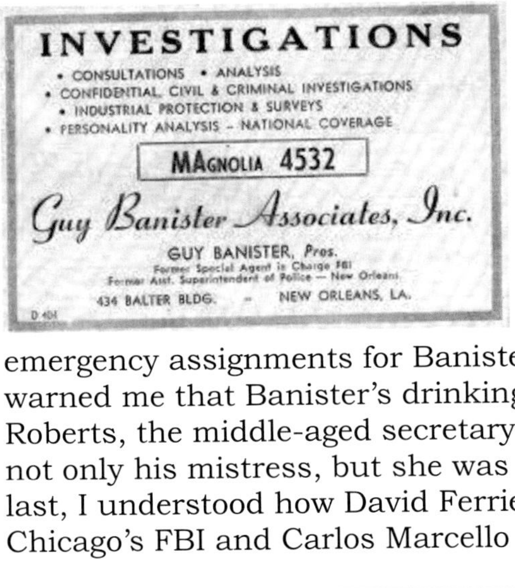

Since Marcello was interested in controlling the police, Banister was feeding him bits and pieces about the cops they both hated the most. David Ferrie was their go-between, working mostly for G. Wray Gill, one of Marcello's top attorneys, and on emergency assignments for Banister that required real brains. Lee warned me that Banister's drinking was not his only problem. Delphine Roberts, the middle-aged secretary who had spoken so kindly to me, was not only his mistress, but she was a racist who stoked his prejudice. At last, I understood how David Ferrie could work for the former head of Chicago's FBI and Carlos Marcello at the same time.

---

they think that?" Anna said to me and 3 researchers in 2000. In fact, a hallway with bathrooms linked Mancuso's and 544 Camp Street, to Banister's office. The argument was concocted to support claims that Banister never met Lee.

[111] Guy Banister had enough bona fide connections to make me believe he was involved in a secret project to kill Castro. However, this important witness wasn't interviewed, and in June, 1964, a month before Dr. Mary Sherman was murdered, Banister was found dead of a heart attack (coronary thrombosis) that his mistress and his wife refused to accept, since he also had a bullet hole in his back. Witness Anna Lewis and her husband David Lewis went at once to his office, but found it marked off as "a crime scene."

"And you finally understand that I am a good guy!" Lee concluded triumphantly. "Reluctantly—yes!" I said, laughing.

Since Lee had his uncle's car, he suggested that we could go to Pontchartrain Beach, the amusement park on the shores of Lake Pontchartrain. It had just opened for the year. It turned out that Lee had to do another "favor" for his uncle, and would have gone on, alone, to Pontchartrain Beach if I'd declined his invitation. As Lee drove, I decided to open the letter from Indiana. Yes, it was my birth certificate, but very different from the one my parents had used to enroll me in Jr. High in St. Petersburg. This one had been altered: my name was missing! It had been issued the same day that Lee met me at the Post Office:

My first concern was that I was about to get married and would need to present the certificate. I could hear the words *"do you, Female Infant Vary, solemnly swear to take this man as your lawfully..."*

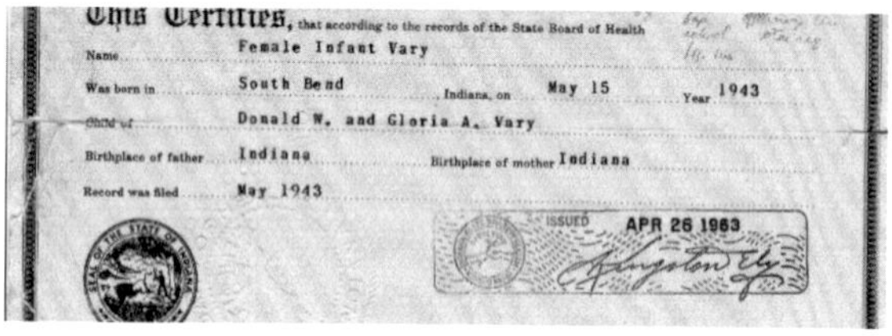
This Certifies, that according to the records of the State Board of Health
Name Female Infant Vary
Was born in South Bend, Indiana, on May 15 Year 1943
Child of Donald W. and Gloria A. Vary
Birthplace of father Indiana Birthplace of mother Indiana
Record was filed May 1943
ISSUED APR 26 1963

I wondered if it would even be accepted. I also needed to get a Social Security card for my Royal Castle job. I'd kept putting it off, waiting for the birth certificate to take to the Social Security office. "Don't worry," Lee counseled. "We'll solve that problem for you."[112] He suggested it was just a clerical error. But later, Lee told me just these kinds of things led him to thinking I was more deeply involved than I was. The birth certificate was just one in a long line of anomalies that caught Lee's attention when we first met, impressing him to the point of confiding information that otherwise he would never have divulged. Sometimes, the CIA's directive of "need to know" – where only "need to know" is given --and no more—can backfire. Lee listed the oddities: dating the son of Cuba's Finance Minister, Tony Lopez-Fresquet; my knowing the OSS spy Canute Michaelson; using a 'code name' --"Jaryo" in the 'personals' section, marked with lipstick; my writing to 'Robert A. Baker' at Eglin AFB: where Robert's parents were receiving mail while constructing housing for the military (Lee thought it was sent to FBI Agent Robert A. Baker, who was stationed in Florida). He heard me say the name "Rorke" and got a glimpse of the return address on my letter being sent to Eglin AFB to Robert A. Baker. I had written 'R. Rourke' in cursive, which to Lee's dyslexic eye looked like "A. Rourke.' Rorke's name was always being misspelled, he said, but the man behind the name was a CIA asset and friend, who had his own plane. Atop all that, I could speak Russian and knew a lot about the USSR. And finally, Lee was suspicious that I was working only two hours a day, at the awful time of 6-8 a.m., at Royal Castle, even though it took 40 minutes to reach by bus and I made less

[112] Despite my lack of ID and no proper birth certificate, Reily's got me a social security number, so Lee and I both had "Louisiana" as our social security home state.

than $2 each time for my trouble! I didn't know that JFK's brother, Atty. Gen. Robert F. Kennedy, had a team from the Dept. of Justice stationed there night and day, surveilling every car entering or leaving Carlos Marcello's Town and Country Motel. Lee suspected I was a courier, working at Royal Castle every morning so I could relay information from RFK's night-watch team back to New Orleans. So, believing I was also the person Dave Ferrie had requested, to help in his cancer research, with my specialty in exactly the proper area, and my saying I was supposed to be Dr. Sherman's intern, both Lee and Dave had been fooled, thinking I was also supposed to have a "cover job." And so, the cat was out of the bag.

#2 of two Royal Castle check stubs. The first one was for 6 hours' work (for a total of 20 full hours). Writing in pencil is Robert's, who had a strict filing system. His writing is also on the birth certificate.[113]

Period Ending	Hours	Rate	Gross Earned	F.I.C.A.	Federal Income Tax	State Income Tax	Food	Uniforms	Hospital Insurance	Advances	Total Deducted	Misc.	Net Pay
5/4/63	14	100	14.00	.53	.30		[redacted]	.30			1.13		12.87

EARNINGS — DEDUCTIONS

DETACH BEFORE DEPOSITING — ROYAL CASTLE SYSTEM, INC. – NEW ORLEANS, LOUISIANA

Lee said he would have a cover job himself, somewhere close to Banister's office, and perhaps I should opt for such an arrangement, too. He reminded me that a cover job would give me a stash of extra money, in case my marriage crashed. I didn't have time to ponder his suggestion long, because we had arrived at Pontchartrain Beach. First, we walked along the beach, but swimming in the dark, brackish lake did not look nearly as appealing as the blue-green waters of Florida's white sand beaches. The amusement park was just opening up for the day.

We reached it way ahead of the crowd. We were met by a giant clown face, blinking lights, and the usual garish scenes that all carnivals had then, but this park had even more. From a carousel with "flying horses" to a mini-golf course with a camel statue, to the most spectacular rides your imagination can dream up, it was all here! But first, Lee had to talk to some staff. I know he had to fulfill some kind of function for his uncle – in other words, for Carlos Marcello. Whatever it was he said, it was soon obvious that Lee had some pull, because we were able to persuade the crew to let us "preview" **the Zephyr**. We were the only riders on that entire roller-coaster! What a rush!

[113]It took years for me to realize that since Lee knew about RFK's team at Royal Castle, that RFK sent a Jesuit priest from Georgetown to Spring Hill to hear Lee speak, and that RFK's Dept. of Justice repeatedly intervened to expedite Lee's return to the U.S., that Bobby Kennedy had to have known Lee's true role.

Seeing how we laughed and screamed, the crew let us ride again, and it was all free. We explored the park from one end to the other, enjoying a house of mirrors where we saw ourselves as huge, or looking like string-beans. Then, as children and parents began to arrive, we joined them for cotton candy. Then Lee said it was 'time to get a real meal,' leading me to a covered pavilion where the park's personnel were eating lunch. After eating our free hamburger lunch, we strolled through the kiddie ride areas. That's when Lee quipped, "We'll have to bring our children here, too!" And I felt so close to him, as if we would be having those children together. Then Lee spotted a shooting gallery with air rifles. The proprietor was cleaning up and was not quite open for business. Knowing how to get things done in New Orleans, Lee quietly offered the man a small bribe, which was accepted. After carefully looking over the guns available, Lee chose one and started firing without hesitation. He hit every target, won a Kewpie Doll, and gave it to me. He then explained that the sights in the shooting gallery were deliberately misaligned to make people miss the target. But if you figured out the correct angle with your first shot, you could work around it and hit everything.

Lee then told me that he had been shooting since he was a child, when he hunted squirrels. But knowing he would be trained to infiltrate the Soviet Union, he deliberately made a point of scoring as poorly on his marksmanship tests as the Marines would accept That way, if the Soviets got hold of his records, they would see he wasn't a good shot and had not been sent to snipe somebody down. Later, Lee would stress to me that by no means was he an expert marksman. It wasn't 'his thing.' I would carry those words into the 21st century, to tell the world.

After a wonderful day, Lee dropped me off at the romantic Mansion. He said he had dinner plans at the Murrets and that he would meet me at Royal Castle in the morning. We kissed before parting. Even as that surge of passion hit me, I began to feel guilty. One part of me loved Robert, but I was still angry at his neglect. That's when I realized I was probably kissing Lee to strike back. With these kinds of tangled emotions, I no longer trusted my feelings. I decided to tell Robert that our marriage plans were off. That night, I was left to myself to daydream about having fun in New Orleans, with Lee at my side thoughtfully guiding me past every concern. As I approached my sliding doors to turn off the overhead light, I was shocked to see an ***eye*** at the keyhole! Mrs. Webber! That nosey old bat! I stuffed it with paper. Then I locked the sliding doors and went to sleep.

Tuesday, April 30, 1963 The next morning, Lee arrived at the Royal Castle just as I finished my shift. Whereas I thought it was so thoughtful of him to want to accompany me all the way back to town, Lee eventually told me the true reason why he came: he wanted to verify why I was there. For that purpose, Lee ordered a breakfast, but instead of eating by himself, he sat down with one of the 'regulars' to eat. Later, Lee told me that after that visit to the Royal Castle, he was satisfied as to my innocent intentions. It took me years t put two-and-two together. The 'regular' was probably a member of RFK's surveillance team, as he always arrived just when another 'regular' left. But for the life of me, I could not detect that a single word ever passed between Lee and that man. Somehow, it was communicated that I had never tried to obtain any information from RFK's surveillance team. So, in the beginning, Lee had justifiable concerns about me, just as I had concerns about him. Who was spying on who? And for what reasons? It was all because of that incredible list of coincidences that made him suspect I knew much more about the get-Castro project than he had been told. Before we left, Lee made calls on the payphone. Then, on the bus trip back to town, Lee told me he'd been talking to Dave again. I said nothing, knowing Lee would say more after we got off the bus. Soon I heard the good news: now that I'd met Guy Banister, Lee could tell me why Dr. Sherman had treated me so coldly. Apparently, Dave was right. "Dr. Mary" didn't want to talk to me at the party because there were so many homosexuals there, and she was afraid that if people saw her talking to a young female, they might conclude she was interested in me for nonscientific reasons. She had only dropped by to retrieve the tumors in the refrigerator before they got too old. Dave also confirmed that I could work on Dr. Mary's special cancer project at both her bone lab and at his place on alternate afternoons, as nobody would be in his apartment until he got home from work. All my hours at Dave's kitchen-based lab would count toward my internship—not to worry! My taking over the majority of Dave's lab work would give him the extra hours he needed to fly back and forth to Miami to get his commercial pilot's license reinstated. Guy Banister would be helping with that, Lee let me know. Plus, there were new, unexpected challenges arising in the anti-Castro movement that needed investigation. "That's why Dave asked for an assistant," Lee said. "We guessed they sent you, instead of a male, because of Dave's homosexuality."

Lee added that Dr. Ochsner would be able to meet me within the week, at which time he would personally advise me about what I was expected to accomplish. I didn't want Robert to know I would not return with him to Florida after our marriage – fearing he would call it off – but at the same time, I was supposed to be job-hunting. "Then let's register you at the A-1 Employment Agency," Lee said. "That's where I have to go today, to make it seem that my pre-arranged job was obtained through A-1. One of the interviews they'll set up will be with the company that's already been selected for me. It will all seem as if they sent me. Clever, eh?" And so I learned that the CIA often pre-arranged jobs, but hid them behind ads that employment agencies used to set up interviews. Of course, Lee let me know, he'd be hired at once, no waiting.

I had not yet decided how much to confide to Robert. I held secrets both with him, and from him. I wasn't even sure, now that Robert's coming was imminent, if I should call it all off. I'd have to see how it felt when I saw him again.

Dr. Ochsner knew nothing of my dilemma, and Lee hoped he'd never find out. As we rode the next bus, that headed uptown, Lee saw an abandoned newspaper. He scooped it up, and opened it to the horoscope section, titled "Moon Messages for You." When Lee said he read it regularly, I told him it was utter nonsense, but I did glance at its headline.

"Today's Moon rays agitate high-strung individuals," I read aloud. "Many contrasting opinions are expressed. In love-life, excitement and passion builds to a crescendo. Temper sentiment with common sense... Emotional people pull situations askew."

THE TIMES-PICAYUNE, NEW ORLEANS, LA., FRIDAY MORNING, MAY 31, 1963

MOON MESSAGES FOR YOU

Today's Rays Splendid for Research Scientist

By CULLEN MOORE

Today's Moonrays are splendid for the student, the research scientist, and all who try to discover things not apparent on the surface. Mysteries in human conduct also may be revealed.

ARIES (March 21-April 20)—Try not to irritate one who works with you (or who is connected in employment matters).

TAURUS (April 21-May 21)—Luck with those who depend on you and admire your skill. Popularity with subordinates.

GEMINI (May 22-June 21)—Some clashes in matters around

That's you!" Lee proclaimed. "I suppose so," I agreed. "After all, I'm supposed to get married tomorrow."

"He is indeed the lucky one."

"We'll need a witness, you know."

"I don't want to be there when you make your mistake," Lee said sadly, avoiding my eyes. Today is my own anniversary, when I made mine," he added, referring to his unfortunate marriage to Marina on this date in 1961. We got off the bus at Tulane University, which I had been anxious to visit. He walked me to Tulane's library, where I could explore to my heart's content while he went off with Guy Banister to do "some work" at a student meeting. The battle over integration was still front-page news in 1963, and Banister was a rabid segregationist. From his Far-Right perspective, integration was an overt act of pure Communism in America. Banister had recruited Lee to assist him in some debates with radical students, because he was too old and angry to be able to hold their attention by himself. [114] Lee was a collegiate type, who would seem to be supporting his side. It was plain to me that Lee was going to detest every moment of this 'work' – but he had no choice. When he returned, one look at his face told me it all went badly. When some of the students identified themselves as Marxists, Socialists or Far-Left, Banister

---

[114] Over the spring and summer, it became clear to me that the Horoscope section was being used by the CIA to convey certain instructions. I collected many of the most obvious ones. These horoscopes should be looked-into. See the Appendix for more examples of the 1963 Horoscopes.

manipulated them to get their names. He would be reporting them to HUAC—the House Committee on Un-American Activities. He'd also inform the FBI, and University officials, branding them as radical left-wing agitators. These students could be expelled from college as a consequence, their lives and careers ruined due to Banister's intrusion. Lee said Banister planned to set up more meetings at Loyola University and the University of New Orleans, as well as some more at Tulane – and he had to be Banister's sidekick. These students were being identified, he was told, because Banister said they were "likely to be causing riots" this summer after they got out of classes for the semester. With their names and descriptions, the police would be able to arrest them faster. Banister's "Red Raider" obsession disgusted Lee, but since these were his first assignments in New Orleans, he felt this odious task was assigned to test his obedience. "How many dirty assignments," he muttered, "do we have to do, to finally get into a position where we can have enough power to make a difference?"

"I wonder how many politicians started out with that same attitude, and got trapped in the system?" I put in. "A good point," Lee replied. He said he liked how I was catching on to the problems he faced. But there was a more appealing project ahead, Banister had promised: Lee would be involved in the creation of a training film for anti-Castro guerillas sometime this summer. After stopping for some oyster stew near Tulane, we headed for Dave's place on the Claiborne bus. As we rode, Lee explained that he had not told Marina about moving in with the Murrets, as he worried that she might try to move in with the Murrets, causing a burden for them. An apartment for them had already been selected, he said, but even that would seem to have been "found by accident." All of this fine-tuned care was employed to make everything seem to happen by mere chance. We arrived at Dave's place, which was still a mess. I noticed that the cages of mice were back. The disarray of the apartment brought back fresh memories of his raucous party. While Mr. Banister's assurances may have quelled my concerns about his patriotism, but his plans aimed against left-wing students chilled me.

He intended to get them expelled from college and placed on a "watch" list for swift arrest if they were seen in a crowd, ruining their lives. The Constitution's promise of Freedom of Speech meant nothing to him. I was glad to hear that Dave agreed with me. "Thank you for giving me another chance," Dave said contritely. "There's a hell of a lot I need to explain." But I was angry and took aim.

"I need to know more about you, too, Dave," I told him. "I don't care if you sleep with tangerines—"

"With tangerines?" Dave repeated. "With tangerines?"

"I-I only mean, that' s not what upsets me," I said, blushing. "Whether you're gay, or whatever. I don't care about that."

"If she works with you, Dave," Lee broke in, "she has to feel safe from your friends."

"I haven't worked with a murderous warrior before," I put in.

"I always worked with people who went home at night to a wife, a kid and a dog."

"I'm not a murderous warrior," Dave objected. "That's how you described yourself at the party," I reminded him. "I could hear you carrying on about how you hated Kennedy, that you hoped he rode in an open car until somebody shot him. Bragged you were going to kill Castro. Bragged about your other exploits, where people got killed." Dave pulled up some chairs to his dining room table. "I'll explain," he said, as we sat down. "And after I do, I believe you'll accept the task of taking over the lab. It will solve a lot of problems," he said, lighting a cigarette. "It's possible that your work here could benefit America." *What?* I had suddenly gone from working for Dave, to running the whole lab (such as it was). Now I was intrigued. Dave went on: "If it was known I loved the president and sang "Hail to the Chief," how many Cubans do you think would have shown up at my party? One? Two?" He drew a deep drag on his cancer stick. "I'm a private investigator, among my other talents." Then, making his deep voice even deeper, he said, "Through these blokes, I have my hand right on the nuts of the Cuban exile community, even though I haven't been part of their absurd and foolish suicide missions for quite a while."

He then told us that some new anti-Castro leaders kicked him out of 'The FRD" and "The CDC" because his homosexual activities got in the papers. "The hypocrites!" he huffed. "Those so-called homophobes didn't expel their own gay members. Just me. after all I did had done for them!" Nevertheless, Dave explained, he still held parties to attract the anti-Castroites, because they kept talking of what they'd do to JFK. "That is, if he ever dared to show his butt in Miami again," Dave finished. At this point I reminded Dave that I was a lady.

I advised him to clean up his vocabulary. "I know you're capable of speaking foully in a variety of languages," I said. "I now challenge you to express yourself in the manner of Milton, Blake, and Thomas Moore."

"Good God, girl!" Dave retorted. "Why are you such a prude?"

"Weren't you going to be a priest at one time?" Lee broke in. "In 1961, she wanted to enter a convent." Dave stared past us toward an old statue of the Virgin Mary. When he spoke again, his voice was softer. "It's all I wished," he finally said. "And in my own way, it's still all I want."

"I only wish you to be the gentleman you can be," I said. "You want me to respect you. Don't I deserve a little respect, too?"

A young David Ferrie in his seminarian robes.

"I was already known as hating Kennedy's shit concerning The Bay of Pigs," Dave replied. "I let them know I wanted to strangle that sonofabitch with my bare hands for betraying us—" With that, I got up to leave.

"Damn it!" he said. "I'm sorry!" He asked me to sit down, then started pacing the room. "At the time, I meant it. I really wanted Kennedy to die. [115]But truth is, he's my Catholic brother. My Commander-in-Chief. Most important, I now know who really betrayed us at The Bay of Pigs. It wasn't JFK." Dave said he'd been invited into several military big-wigs' secret sessions to provide them with input on any crazy Cuban plans they might consider supporting, to murder Kennedy. "I tell Marcello all their plans," he said proudly. "That puts me in tight with the Mob, and I get chances to hear their plans to try to kill Kennedy. So long as I seem to be one hundred percent on their side," he added, "I will continue to be in the know." His revelation was stunning. David Ferrie was playing a very dangerous game, involving the military and the Mob. He was an insider, gathering information that could save the president. I felt honored to be entrusted with this information by two men I had grown to admire for their courage. "What about telling the CIA?" I ventured.

Ferrie, telling me how naïve I was, said, "I trust nobody I know in the Agency. The CIA and the Mob are bed-buddies, which means no protection for the Chief. There's no telling if this talk has reached the highest levels or not," he added. "The CIA is no friend of JFK. He fired their precious Allen Dulles and wrecked Gen. Cabell's career. Then there's Gen. Walker." Dave said he was gay, which was not the problem. It was his fanatic desire for power and glory, just like LBJ. Walker and many other military officers despised 'doves" like JFK.

"The Kennedys canned him and had him strait-jacketed in a nuthouse for a while," Dave revealed. "So guess how lovey-dovey he feels toward the Chief." Dave shifted the conversation back to our project, which made Castro the target instead of Kennedy. [116]

---

[115]David Ferrie as seen, above, in his seminary robes, was expelled twice from seminaries for inappropriate behavior or beliefs. On 08/11/1961 he was arrested on morals charges after hiding a 15-yr. old runaway boy, a member of Ferrie's Civil Air Patrol, from his abusive father. There would be a second arrest, too, but in the end, all charges were dropped, partly for fear of what Ferrie might do, and partly due to loyal friends' support.

[116] Gen. Edwin Walker detested the Kennedys. He had a strong, loyal following in the army as well as among racists, white militants, the KKK, and ardent patriots. He championed anti-Civil Rights movements and supported the John Birch Society. H.L. Hunt and Clint Murchison, close friends of Dr. Alton Ochsner, supported Walker's unsuccessful race for Texas Governor in 1962. In Oxford, Mississippi, he incited a riot after an incendiary speech, comparing the Supreme Court to the Anti-Christ. On April 10, 1963, Walker was shot at, slightly wounding him, through a window. A steel jacketed bullet was recovered. It was **not** the copper-jacketed bullet the government

Dave said there was a ring of underground labs already set up, so nothing I might want would be lacking. Everything was organized through Sherman and Ochsner. Sherman was a widow with no close friends outside the research community. She traveled a lot to conventions and Latin America, so her lab was used to dealing with her frequent comings and goings.

I was useful because I wasn't a doctor yet. Who would believe that a 19-year-old college undergraduate -- and a girl at that -- would be involved in such an activity? I had a unique opportunity – a grand chance-- to be of service to my country. As I sat there and dissected what he was saying, Dave sensed my calculations. He realized that I had not yet bought in, so he tried more practical inducements. I would still get credited for my internship, since the work would be close to what I would be doing in Sherman's lab. But if I worked in his lab, rather than Sherman's, the records wouldn't need to be laundered, hundreds of control animals would not have to be killed, and importantly, the whole project would go faster. I would have the whole place to myself in the afternoons. I just needed to finish before he got home from work, because friends not privy to these matters might drop in. Time, he said, was running out. Killing Castro would focus the everyone on regaining Cuba. They would abandon their crazy dreams of wiping out Kennedy.

The project had been in existence for a year, but lately was foundering. I could save the day, since I might have some odd piece of knowledge that could help. I now had to face the fact that a bioweapon was being crafted to kill Fidel Castro. And they wanted my help. *What would Grandpa say? What would Mrs. Watkins say?* As I recalled how I'd been assigned "to make the cancer more deadly" upon finishing my appointment at Roswell Park, the stark truth sank in. The three doctors were close friends. Drs. Moore and Diehl had encouraged me to "make the cancer more deadly." They were probably supporting Dr. Ochsner. Given what I knew now, wherever I worked -- in Dave's kitchen or in Dr. Sherman's lab at Ochsner's Clinic—I would be assisting Ochsner. Dave sensed my stress. "Don't worry," he said. "Nobody will harm you if you decide not to join us. You can go on to Mary's lab, work on something else, and take it easy. But, we need you here." Dave then fumbled through his pile of newspapers and found a page published a month earlier about Ochsner's Clinic's historic big move from its Prytania location to its new campus headquarters in Jefferson Parish. A photo showed a long line of trucks moving equipment, furnishings, animals,

---

still claims was by Oswald.

Walker wrote to FBI and HSCA: "The bullet before your select committee, called the 'Walker Bullet' ...is not the bullet that was fired at me and taken out of my house by the Dallas City Police on April 10, 1963." "The bullet used and pictured on the TV by the [HSCA] is a ridiculous substitute for a bullet completely mutilated... [with] no resemblance to any unfired bullet in shape or form. I saw the hunk of lead, picked up by a policeman in my house... I inspected it carefully. There is no mistake there has been a substitution..."The HSCA ignored Walker's letter, so he complained to Attorney General Griffin Bell.

and supplies. In the confusion, a truck went missing. Pedigree mice, lab equipment, chemicals, microscopes, cages, cancer cell strains – they all somehow vanished, and Dave's kitchen was one such entity that benefited from the "loss." Wealthy Texas oilmen, Dave said, were contributing millions in visible and invisible funds to help build Ochsner's impressive new facilities. In exchange, Ochsner's medical and political cooperation with them was solid. Dr. O mirrored the Oil Barons' own views on communism, racism and taking things into one's own hands to 'save democracy.' [117] "I know you think he's God," Dave said, "but Ochsner is naïve when it comes to dealing with these slick Texas millionaires, the CIA and the Mob. They've got him wrapped up for Christmas, right where they want him. They drink together, hunt

together, play golf together, gamble together and decide what's best for the country together." Dave told us the names. Lyndon Johnson was so close to **Clint Murchison** that they said each other' names in their sleep. Former Vice Pres. Nixon was another of Ochsner's friends. Despite what the public might think of Nixon, the Powers that be knew he'd do anything to be President. Becoming President was about an imperative forged of nerve, money and connections. And organized crime was involved. "The Mob can even trump the FBI," Dave revealed, "since they know Hoover is Clyde Tolson's missus." To my astonished gasp, Dave laughed. "Also known as 'Mrs. Hoover," he said, smiling. "All the fairies know this," he said, winking. When you understand that the world you thought you knew was actually turned upside-down, it's like being on one of those crazy rides at Pontchartrain Beach. Trying to visualize it is like going through a House of Mirrors. The police, the Mafia, the government, they take your tickets and let you in for a ride, but they are running a show. Nothing is as it seems. It's just a carnival, and you are a "mark."

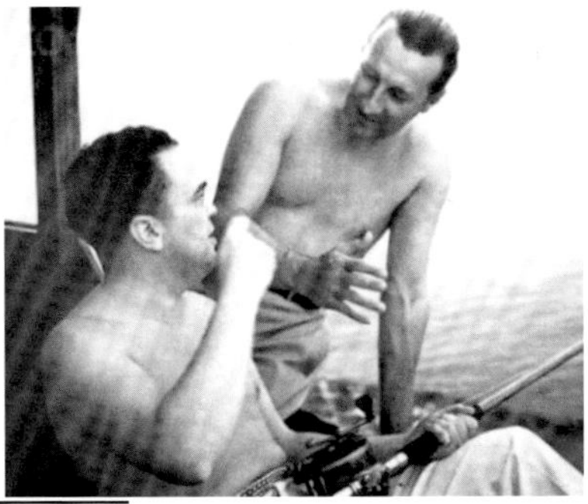

[117] Ochsner,strongly opposed to the domestic and foreign policy of President John F. Kennedy,wrote to Senator Allen Ellender: "I sincerely hope that the Civil Rights Bill can also be defeated, because if it was passed, it would certainly mean virtual dictatorship by the President and the Attorney General, a thing I am sure they both want." https://spartacus-educational.com/JFKochsner.htm

Chapter Ten
May Day

I was learning shocking truths about my country's government – a government I had been taught to trust blindly. Our national bulwark against crime – the mighty FBI –was corrupted at the very top. Even David Ferrie, a credible source, was himself a study in contradictions. He wanted me to handle his lab not only because his frequent trips to Miami to try to get his pilot's license back was interfering with the work he'd promised to conduct, but he was also getting more deeply involved with Carlos Marcello. Marcello was going to end up in Guatemala again if he lost his deportation case: being told of Dave's brilliance as a legal resource and pilot, Marcello had his main attorney, G. Wray Gil, put Dave on his defense team. Dave, trusted because of his supposed hatred for JFK and Bobby Kennedy, could get information otherwise unavailable.

He said it might help protect the Kennedy brothers. It was information he was now sharing with me and Lee. "Don't worry," he said. "I'm familiar with all the wiretapping devices, and my place is safe – so far." This was all sounding really dangerous, so I asked, "But who is going to protect us? What if Castro finds out about the project and decides to have us killed?" "This isn't the movies," Dave replied. "Castro can't kill everybody." He shifted his gaze to Lee, who had remained silent the whole time. "Lee," Dave said, "is part of our protection. He's going to help root out anybody who's pro-Castro in this town. It was one of his jobs, so don't feel guilty about it. As for the rest of it, just keep your mouth shut."

I glanced at Lee and realized that after almost three years behind The Iron Curtain, he had returned unharmed by either side. That took brains and courage. One look at that calm face gave me the assurance I needed: Lee was indeed my protector and bodyguard. By now, Lee and I had spent all of Tuesday night and the early hours of Wednesday at Dave's. As the conversation rambled from politics to philosophy to science, Lee and I explored the amazing hidden vaults of David Ferrie's brilliant mind, trapped as it was in his torrential bursts of passion that all too easily led him into sexual difficulties. By the time Lee and I got free of him, it was close to dawn. At the Mansion's doorstep, Lee kissed me goodbye.

"I won't be able to kiss you after you're married," he warned me. But I wasn't listening. As I watched him leave, with that military way he had of walking – his back straight, his feet straight ahead—I pondered the power of his kiss. But Robert would be coming soon, I reminded myself. The lady at the "Y" said he'd called and had obtained my new address. *We're going to get married!* My hormones were raging, just as my father had warned me. It seemed weeks, not days, since we'd had sex. I took the day off from Royal Castle. All I needed was a little sleep!

Then I'd bounce back, ready for Robert, our marriage, and the precious birth control pills we could not get any other way. Marriage to me was a mere piece of paper. I had a nice dress and a see-through black nightie for later. The rose on its little panty would be the only flower. The ring on my finger came from a pawn shop. But at least the birth control pills would be a pretty pink. After a few hours' sleep, I made myself ready. Hair up, decked with pearls, I donned my bone-white linen dress and put on the emerald earrings my sister had given me. As 10:00 approached – the time Robert predicted he'd arrive – I grew excited. Then I saw a dusty blue Ford pull up. It was 10:02. *Robert! My Love*! As he got out, I saw he was dressed in khaki shorts, a plaid shirt, and flip-flops. I had to laugh, thinking of our wedding picture: "The Princess and the Pauper"! But that smile! That face! I called out his name, and my man came rushing up the steps. He took me into his arms and swung me around in a circle. I relished the familiar smell of his aftershave as he kissed me. "Let's get married!" he declared, kissing me again. I was thrilled. I had almost forgotten how tall, how confident, how take-charge he was. As Robert went back to the Ford to retrieve his bags, I followed him with a due warning.

"We have a noxious old bat for a landlady!" I told him. "She thinks we're already married – so –"... Robert laughed as he lugged his typewriter, a guitar and his bags from the car and headed up the steps. In no time, everything was inside. Then we hopped into Robert's Ford and headed for the Courthouse. As he drove, I considered the little talk I'd planned about not being ready, but my head was spinning! I wondered why he hadn't dressed better for our wedding, but maybe he wasn't thinking all that straight, either! After all, how long would both of us keep our clothes on anyway, once we settled this issue and got our pills? As Robert parked his car near the Courthouse, I pointed out that we were in a 'private' parking place, but Robert shrugged it off. "We won't be in there five minutes," he told me. "We just have to pick up a marriage license and then find a Justice of the Peace." We entered the Courthouse, filled out the paperwork for the license, and handed it to the clerk, announcing we were ready to tie the knot. That's when the clerk told us there was a two-day waiting period, as per Louisiana's Napoleonic Code. "What?" Robert raged. "In a backward state like this? You're joking!" But nobody was joking. "I have only one day to marry you!" Robert declared angrily as we left the courthouse. "Right after that, I have to start working!" Now I understood the reason for his haste.

OK, no honeymoon. So what? We'd marry on Friday, then, and on Saturday and Sunday we could still celebrate. But when I told Robert I wouldn't sleep with him without a condom, until we got the pills, he dropped my hand and stomped on ahead – only to see his blue Ford being towed away! We ran after the tow truck, screaming for it to stop, but off it went, disappearing into the traffic as Robert stood there, shaking his fist and cursing.

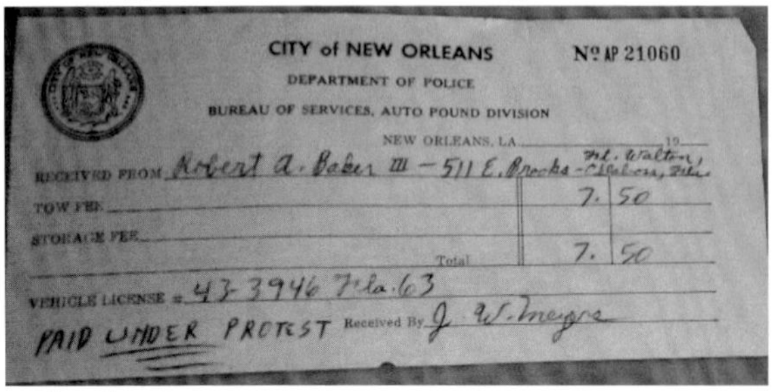

CITY of NEW ORLEANS № AP 21060
DEPARTMENT OF POLICE
BUREAU OF SERVICES, AUTO POUND DIVISION
NEW ORLEANS, LA. ______ 19__
RECEIVED FROM Robert A. Baker III – 511 E. Brooks – Ft. Walton, Fla.
TOW FEE 7.50
STORAGE FEE
Total 7.50
VEHICLE LICENSE # 43-3946 Fla. 63
PAID UNDER PROTEST Received By J. W. Meyers

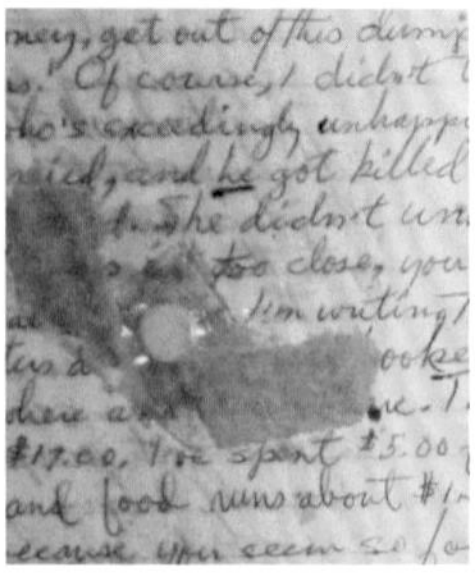

Carbon copy of the Tow Fee 05/01/1963. I also saved the first birth control pill from our marriage on 05/02/1963.

For the next hour, we walked in gloom. Finally, we reached the Auto Pound, where Robert paid the $7.50 fine-- writing "PAID UNDER PROTEST" on the receipt. "Let's go to the library," he growled to me. "We need to look up marriage rules for nearby states." There we found that only Alabama had no waiting period: Robert had found his "backward" state that didn't care who married who or when, as long as they were the same color. Robert told me it would take about four hours to reach Mobile, where we'd be sure to get things done quickly. We'd return the same night. "May Day" had turned into May 2. It had not worked out well. When I asked how it went in Fort Walton Beach," Robert's short answer was that he'd worked at his parents' office, picked up mail for them at the building site at Eglin AFB, and watched TV. The Bakers never 'caught on' that the letter I'd sent with the return address to "R. Rourke" was from a girl. Hearing that, I decided to tell Robert that I wanted to stay in New Orleans after summer was over, for Tulane Medical School. Maybe he'd change his mind about getting married, but I wanted to do the right thing. To introduce this touchy subject, I carefully asked, "Can I tell you something we need to talk about?"

"Did you find a job?" he interrupted.

"Well, yes, but—"

"I'll bet you thought I wasn't going to come!"

"I needed to hear from you more," I managed to say. I tried again. "I really need to tell you about how I feel about something—" but again, he interrupted me. "You were upset because I came a day late. Right?"

"Well, yes, but it's more than that. I'll just say this. I've made some great contacts! Life-changing! If you – if you don't want to marry me, I'll be okay, even if you go back to Florida without me."

"I said I'd show up," Robert said earnestly, stroking my cheek. "And tomorrow, you'll be legal!" I was so happy to see his shift in mood that I tried an oblique way to get the message across. Grabbing his right hand firmly, I repeated, "Seriously, I need you to hear me out. I need to tell you something more!"

"That may be so," Robert said, "but it's my turn now. As for me, there's only one thing I need," he declared, putting his arm around me. "And you're about to provide it. We'll have plenty of time to talk about other things later." He actually said he was in pain. He was so 'horny,' he said, that there was only one remedy for it – me! After all, we had all our lives ahead, just to talk. Entering the Mansion, we quietly crept into my boudoir. Robert closed the blinds, which I'd been too short to manage, and once they came down, we went to bed. However, I didn't get much sleep, with "Mr. Horny" around.

Early Morning, Thursday, May 2, 1963 Worn out after Robert's thorough exploration of my anatomy, I pondered the situation I was in. I looked down upon Robert's peaceful, sleeping face. The slight smile still lingering on his lips bespoke of his satisfaction with how things were going, but I was not so sure. How had he avoided any truly intimate conversation? We'd been apart twelve momentous days. Those twelve days promised to unleash a whole different kind of future for us.

Handicapped by what I dared to say and what I dared not say, I hadn't been able to get Robert to listen to any of it. For him, the only thing that truly mattered was Making Whoopee. What could possibly be more important? Well, marriage was. It meant safe sex, daily companionship, a chance to grow truly close to each other far from the hectic college scene. Atop that, we were living in romantic New Orleans! Sure, it was a rough place, but how could it be dangerous, with both Robert and Lee looking after me? I loved Robert. Didn't I? Look how great the sex was! Such were the thoughts swirling around in my 19-year-old brain.

By 4 am, Robert and I were on our way to Mobile. I was so sleepy that all I remember of Mobile was going through the Bankhead Tunnel and stopping at the Courthouse, where an even sleepier clerk filled out our marriage license, after a glance at my UF student card. "Old enough to go to college, old enough to get married," was the mumbled comment. I breathed a sigh of relief. The "female infant Vary" birth certificate was never needed. Then we went around the corner to 'the marrying man." The sleepy clerk was recruited as a witness, and we were married so quickly that it seemed the ceremony was over before it started. I brought out the wedding band, Robert put it on my finger, and we were pronounced 'man and wife.' Fast and cheap. I wondered if I'd have gone through all of this if Lee had not told me that he had beaten his wife. But he had. So now I was Mrs. Robert Allison Baker, III.

Afternoon, Thursday, May 2, 1963 We stopped at a fancy Italian restaurant for our wedding feast, where Robert ordered the most expensive meal, but just one, which he divided between us! "We have to be careful until my first paycheck comes in," he said, since so much money went to pay the tow fee. We ate dinner while waiting for our blood test results at providence Hospital.

Then we returned to grab the report and the prescription. [118] With our Golden Ticket, we bought our first package of pills. As we drove away from the hospital, I smiled as Robert tossed his package of condoms out the car window. Free at last!

But on the long trip back, as the sun set, Robert's mood soured. When I tried to snuggle next to him, he drew away. A frown crept over his features as he drove, staring straight ahead. What was the matter? When I started to put my arm around my new husband, he pulled away. "*Don't touch me!*" he snapped. "What's wrong?" I demanded.

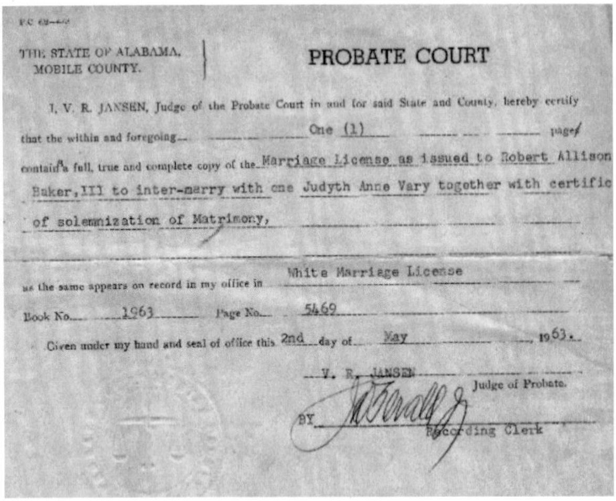

THE STATE OF ALABAMA, MOBILE COUNTY.

PROBATE COURT

I, V. R. JANSEN, Judge of the Probate Court in and for said State and County, hereby certify that the within and foregoing One (1) pages contain a full, true and complete copy of the Marriage License as issued to Robert Allison Baker, III to inter-marry with one Judyth Anne Vary together with certific of solemnization of Matrimony,

as the same appears on record in my office in White Marriage License

Book No. 1963 Page No. 5469

Given under my hand and seal of office this 2nd day of May 1963.

V. R. JANSEN Judge of Probate.

BY Recording Clerk

"My parents. They'll cut me off financially when they find out I eloped," he replied. "So you'll have to put me through school," he said. "That is, if I come back with you!" I replied, heatedly. "But if I do, my new friend, Dr. Ferrie, said I could get a job at a place called 'Pen Chem.' "I could work there part time and go to school at night."

"You'd have to work fulltime," Robert insisted. "But what about you?" I pursued. "We can get by on two part-time jobs."

"I'll be in graduate school. That means I'll have to make good grades. I can't work and do that. You'll need to support both of us."

"But what about my schooling?"

"Your schooling could wait," he concluded emphatically. I turned and stared out the window at the endless rows of tall pine trees that lined the dark highway. They looked like the bars of a prison cell. In the silence, I began to tremble. *What had I done?*

Evening -- Thursday, May 2, 1963 When we reached the Mansion, we had to park down the street because there were so many cars out front. Oddly, I'd never come home around midnight before—it was either in the afternoon or practically at dawn.

Not long after we arrived, Mrs. Webber knocked at the sliding doors. "Are you really her husband?" she asked. As I waved my hand with its loose, gold wedding ring, Robert pulled our 'White Marriage' license from his pocket and showed it to her. Then the old bag poked her bony finger at Robert and said, "Your wife is a lousy cheat! She's been runnin' around with another man, behind your back!"

---

[118] About $70 in 2021 funds went to the tow charge. The pills weren't free, either..

As my face turned red, she topped her claim with an even wilder accusation, saying I had been sunbathing naked on the front porch to attract a little business my way. Robert laughed at her and closed the door right in her face. He knew how modest I was about nudity. Turning to me, he gave me a quick kiss on the forehead. "That's for all the wicked things you might have done with other men while I was gone!" he declared. I felt a surge of guilt and decided to put off explaining about Lee Oswald for some other time.

It was our wedding night, but there were no flowers, no photos, not even a souvenir postcard of Mobile. As my husband bathed down the hall, I started thinking. Maybe we couldn't have a honeymoon, but New Orleans was filled with fun things to do, as Lee had shown me. Visions of going to Pontchartrain Beach, visiting the zoo, fishing in the Gulf of Mexico or just strolling through the French Quarter nibbling on pralines filled my thoughts. Thanks to my friends at the YWCA, I also knew what clubs could be fun. When Robert returned to our room, I told him I had to leave for work at Royal Castle in less than six hours. "I hope you'll drive me over," I said. "I'm working extra hours today, so we'll get a bigger paycheck Saturday." I gave him a smile. "Then we can go to the beach, or have fun in The French Quarter."

"Don't cash that Saturday check," he replied. "Send it to me instead."

"What?" I asked, confused. I'll explain later," my new husband said. "Right now, first things first! Open your legs, woman!" he commanded.

"But-- I have to get up soon –and I'm tired!" I told him.

Afterwards, I left the bed and stayed in the bathroom a long time. Maybe Robert would fall asleep? I had no such luck.

<u>Morning – Friday, May 3, 1963</u> The emotional and physical stress of the last few days was adding up. When the alarm went off, I was just staggering, so Robert helped me get dressed, which was a switch.

Then he drove me to work. I stumbled into Royal Castle, dazed and blanched. As for Robert, he climbed into the back seat of the Ford and went to sleep, while I lurched around inside the restaurant, trying to kill myself on the juice machine and the hot grill. It seemed every customer needed my attention at the same time, but I was a zombie, dropping things, forgetting orders, and spilling coffee. My performance was so abysmal, it didn't matter how much the Castle's customers liked me. Instead of six hours' work, at the end of the morning rush, I was told to go. Forever. And to never, ever return! I was fired. Too tired to care, I stumbled back to the car and collapsed inside.

But Robert had spent the last two hours resting up. He was ready the minute we got home to again prove he was one of the great marathon lovers of all time. I begged for mercy, but then he broke the news. "I have to get in as much lovin' as I can," he pleaded, "because our days together are going to be few and far between."

"W-what do you mean?" I managed to stammer. "I'm going to be in the Gulf of Mexico for ten or twenty days at a time." As he said those charming words, he was dressing me in the baby-doll nightie with its little red rose on the almost-panty. It was my 'honeymoon' nightie. Just seeing me in it did the trick. In no time, Robert was rarin' to go! "I'll only have two or three days off between hitches," he said, as he kissed the rose on my panty. Then he began caressing my tired body. "But now," he said, "I won't worry about you. You've got yourself a nice little hidey-hole, here, and a job to cover your expenses. You'll do fine without me, just as you said. And every time I'm back, I'll be just as horny as I am now!"

Afternoon – Friday, May 3, 1963 Robert was happy, but I was not. As he dressed, he told me, "I have to leave for Houma in three hours to sign up and get trained. By Monday night, I'll be on a quarter boat."

He'd be setting out lines of explosives for seismic depth charges. "I'm replacing a man who had both hands blown off by a charge of TNT," he told me. To my look of shock, he added, "But the pay is good. And there is free room and board as well." Hearing what could happen to him, I let Robert pounce once on his new property. Meanwhile, my brain managed to function enough to formulate one thought clearly: '*Whatever had possessed me to get married?'* I fell asleep briefly, waking just in time to see Robert packing. I was too tired to move, but my tangled thoughts were still active. It took a while, but Robert at last noticed that I wasn't speaking to him. "You're mad now," he told me. "But you'll miss me when I'm gone." When I remained silent, he said, "Finances have to come first. We have to have enough money to pay for my last semester. Now, won't you give me just a few more minutes of your sweet time, before I have to go?" Robert hadn't acted this way previously. Before our marriage, we seemed well-matched in bed. But then, classes and our schedules had intervened. This time, I heard him murmur to himself, as we made love, "Now I've *got* you*!*" and "I got my *virgin*!"

Since he was in a good mood, I finally mentioned that I needed new walking shoes for work. Ignoring my request, Robert peeled three dollars from his wallet and gave them to me, explaining this meagre amount should be adequate for bus rides and meals. As for my check, I was to send it to an address he'd give me later. "I might have car repairs to make," he explained. "I know you're mad," he went on, "so I'm not telling you exactly where I'm going. I know how stubborn you are, and I don't want you following me. You'd lose your job if you did that." [119]

---

[119] Robert would alternate between obsession with me and giving me "the silent treatment." Today he would be diagnosed as a high-functioning Aspergers and narcissist. My job was to supply his needs. In return, he would keep me. He wrote mostly on Dixie Dynamite notepads, which reminded me that he could get hurt!

That ruffled my feathers. Soon enough, I'd be getting a stipend! I'd show him! *I would get my education!* But Robert was about to leave, I had a hellion for a landlady, and I was too tired to think straight. Just then, I saw the bit of paper I'd stuck in the keyhole fall out. Mrs. Webber – *again*! I opened Robert's umbrella, laid it on a chair, and put the open umbrella up against the door. After Robert finished his final foray into my franchise, he put his Gibson guitar on the bed. "Salt air will ruin it. Same for the typewriter." He finally revealed the company's name: 'Evangeline Seismic.' "Don't worry, I'll write," he promised. He kissed me goodbye, and left.

Too tired to take off my honeymoon attire, I closed the guitar case with my foot as I lay there on the bed and fell asleep. In my dreams, I floated above the beautiful bed in this stately Victorian mansion... beneath me, New Orleans lay, misty and mysterious...

Suddenly, I woke to the sound of men yelling and a woman screaming. Police sirens pierced the night. Car-doors slammed. I could hear heavy steps going past my parlor doors and up the stairs. As shouting, crying and cursing pierced the darkness, I sat up straight in bed. *The police were raiding the Mansion!* So much for Mrs. Webbers' posturing about morality.[120] Then it dawned on me. I was living in a whorehouse! The well-dressed girl, kissing two well-dressed men... the cars parked outside that disappeared before dawn...the fact that Mrs. Webber slept every day until noon... I sat upright, realizing what I was wearing.

The see-through nightie! The almost-there panty with the red rose! It qualified me for a trip downtown if I didn't hurry up and change clothes!

In the dark, I yanked off the nightie and threw on a blouse, undies and pants. At any moment, the police might think to open the big, sliding doors! What next? Frantically, I began throwing everything I could find, in the dark, into my two suitcases. Luckily, most of my things were in the bus lockers, but there was still a lot to pack. As the police continued up and down the stairs, I stuffed the guitar case full of Robert's extra clothes, filled a box with books, and tried to plan my escape. Peering between the blinds, I saw lights flashing and a girl wearing only a feather boa and handcuffs being shoved into a vehicle.

Well-dressed men and half-naked girls with bed-sheets thrown over them were being escorted from the building by uniformed police. *Men!* The men in my life had got me into all this trouble! Lee Oswald had booked me into this whorehouse, and Robert Baker had abandoned me here! And I was here instead of with my family because of my despotic father! Thanks a lot, guys. The problem was, they weren't here, but the vice squad was. My thoughts racing, I realized I needed to find that brand-new marriage license, to prove I wasn't one of the good-time girls.

---

[120]Some say Mrs. Webber may have thought I was trying to take business from her girls.

Where was it? As I dug through the suitcases in the dark, I heard a thunderous banging on my sliding doors. Just as my hand found the certificate, the door burst open, revealing a huge, overweight policeman. Kicking aside the umbrella, he flipped on the light. “You!” he yelled, his face flushing red with excitement, as he put his hand on his gun, “What’s your name?” I froze and stared at him. “M-Mrs. Robert Allison Baker, the Third—” I managed to stammer, in a crackly voice. The policeman laughed cruelly and said that was the most ridiculous excuse for a name he’d heard all night.

“I just got married,” I said, shoving the certificate in his direction.

“So, where’s your husband?” he queried, with cop logic and in a cop voice. “H-He works offshore,” I stammered. “He just left a few hours ago." Then Mrs. Webber entered the room. I could see tears on her face. With her hands on her hips, she screeched, “*She’s one of them! She’s cheating on her husband, I tell ya*! You ought to haul her away with the others. Besides, she’s been lying around nekked as a jaybird on my front porch, trying to drum up business!”

“Shut up!” the police officer told her, with impatient contempt. “All right,” he said, turning to me. “I get it. You’re clean. But you’re going to have to leave. We’re closing this place down, so get your things together and get the hell out of here.”

“Please don’t swear at me,” I mumbled. “I’m not used to it.” The officer seemed to understand that I was a good girl after all, who didn’t belong in a paddy-wagon. He helped me move my things out to the sidewalk, where the neighbors had gathered to watch the spectacle.

Embarrassed and ashamed, I kept my head down, wondering what would become of me. I loaded everything best I could – a suitcase in each hand, the guitar case and guitar hanging around my neck, a box of books upon my arms, with the heavy typewriter on top. Within the last 24 hours, I had lost my job, my room, and my food and my husband had come and gone. I began trudging down St. Charles Ave, with no clear destination, lugging my possessions. At first, I tried to catch a streetcar, but I couldn’t manage it with all my stuff, and it was a long time between street cars so late at night. The breaks in the narrow, uneven concrete sidewalks, created by the massive roots of ancient oak trees, made me stumble. The big trees towered over me, their branches entwined with each other. Several blocks down, I realized I was going the wrong way and had to turn around. needed to go toward town, not away from it! I passed the Mansion: now everybody was gone and there was a padlock on the door. The dark street was empty. The leaves were still. Everywhere, deep shadows stretched, full of unknown dangers. I had been exposed to the rough life in New Orleans and was not interested in getting exposed to anymore. What was next for me? Did I need to get raped or robbed to complete my initiation into this strange city? Would the next bush or snarled tree release a dark figure, springing at me?

Suddenly, a cat leapt from the darkness and ran across my path with a snarl. I shrieked and fell to the sidewalk, scraping my knee. As I rolled over and sat up, digging pieces of stone and dirt out of my knee, I began to cry. Forget about "adventures in New Orleans"! I was alone, afraid, and miserable. Too tired to hold the box of books any longer, when I got up, I tried to push the box along with my foot, but the bottom soon ripped up, so I hid the box in some bushes, hoping to come back for it later. Then I remembered David Lewis – that skinny sidekick of Jackass Martin who Lee beat at chess. Lewis said his wife Anna worked at Thompson's restaurant. It was open 24 hours, farther down on St. Charles Ave, near Lee Circle. The image of a free slice of pie popped into my head. If I could just reach Thompson's! I could stay there until morning and then contact Lee. His was the only phone number I dared to call, and he sure owed me big for putting me in the Mansion.

As I struggled along, my thoughts were not holy. *Robert! You clod!* You left me, after a day and night of Whoopie! And that devil of a landlady! I made foul accusations as I slowly ground my way up St. Charles,

against everybody who got me into this position, without laying any of the blame on me. Just as I was getting ready to add God to my poop list, I looked up from my well of self-pity and saw a light, shining down from a church. And across the lit window, which glowed like gold, a figure moved. Somebody was up late, in the church! Before me, a sign read **'St. George Episcopal Church.'** Next to the church was the rectory, where the minister lived. With trepidation, I knocked on the rectory door. It finally opened to reveal a minister only as tall as myself, his wife standing behind him. He was **Father Bill Richardson**, known for his generous heart and open mind.[121] He'd been up late writing a sermon for a funeral. After inspecting me silently, Mary, his wife, gave me a

[121] "In the late 1950s and early 1960s, Father Bill Richardson stood up to parishioners who wanted to bar African-Americans. His daughter, Ann Richardson Berkey, recalled: "He stood at the door to make sure no one blocked anyone who wanted to come in and worship God. He was a small man, maybe five-three, but he wanted to make sure that anyone who wanted to come in, could come in." She also noted that he not only gave money to beggars on the street but also invited them into the rectory. "People came to the house asking for a handout, and he asked them in for dinner and maybe to stay a night or two. He believed we were all God's children." REF: https://lgbtqreligiousarchives.org/profiles/william-p-richardson

smile. She took the heavy typewriter.

As she did so, I fell to the floor and began to sob. As they learned bits and pieces of what happened, they expressed true concern. Then Mary fixed their couch with a sheet, pillow and blanket, gave me a glass of milk, and assured me that tomorrow, after I got some rest, everything would look better. The next morning, after breakfast, Father Bill asked me to listen to the funeral sermon he planned to deliver about God's providence. He was certain that God wanted me to hear it. Then it was time to call somebody to help me. Ashamed that Robert had refused to give me a contact number, I fibbed and said he had forgotten. But I did have a friend's number – that of Lee Oswald, who had found that room for rent. He'd even paid ten dollars toward the room. I asked Father Bill, as he liked to be called, to contact Lee. Lee arrived well before noon. He made a good impression on Father Bill and his wife. Would we like to have some lunch, Mary Richardson asked. [122] We accepted her offer. As we ate, Lee and I talked sensibly about religion and politics, avoiding any touchy areas that might be hard for Lee to explain, such as planning to kill a head of state. They assumed he was a college student.

Then Father Bill excused himself, saying he had to prepare for the funeral. He retired to his study, leaving Lee to make several phone calls. On his last call, an elderly widow said that she would welcome a nice, young lady whose husband was often gone, as her last two tenants were rowdy men who had done damage to the bathroom on the half of the house she rented out. Then, recognizing Lee's voice, the widow called him by name and urged him to bring me over. The address was **1032 Marengo**.

When Mary Richardson heard the address, she volunteered to drive me and Lee over, saying it was only five blocks away, in a safe and acceptable part of town. As she drove us, Lee tried to explain some of the benefits associated with moving there. "Why should I listen to you?" I told him. "This time, I'll judge for myself." Nevertheless, Lee made sure I knew that 1032 Marengo[123] wasn't far from Dr Sherman's apartment, nor far from where he intended to move. It was a one-minute walk to the Magazine St. Bus stop. That would get

[122] I didn't see their children, who may have gone on to school before I woke up.

[123] 1032 Marengo, Jan 2000, before the house was renovated; soon after, the interior was gutted and the door moved to the center.

me downtown in twenty-five minutes or less. When Mary Richardson stopped in front of a cute little house, my hopes soared. If it had a decent bed, and I could somehow afford it, hallelujah to the pastor and his wife! The moment we got out of the car, a little old lady with silver hair appeared at the front door. She immediately gave Lee a big hug, like she was welcoming a long-lost son. "Why, Lee!" she said, scolding him. "When did you come back to New Orleans, and why didn't you tell me?"

Lee told her he intended to visit often and soon, since he would be living nearby on Magazine Street.

Susie Hanover, courtesy of Vicki Rodick, her great-granddaughter.

The little old lady was Susie Hanover, whose deceased husband, William Hanover, had been a riverboat Captain. He had begun by overseeing stevedores for Carlos Marcello on the docks. Their son, Billy, was still there.

He was running an office on the docks. By now I was reconciled to the fact that nearly everybody in New Orleans seemed to be no more than two steps removed from the great Mafia Kingfish. Susie's husband had even been friends with Lee's Uncle Dutz, from the early days of working on the docks, and Lee had once given Susie a puppy. Susie's love for dogs was obvious, as at her side was a collie-type dog that I would remember as "Collie." After explaining some of these things, when Lee told Mary Richardson he would make sure that everything would work out, she excused herself, but not before inviting us to come to church Sunday. I did attend a few services.

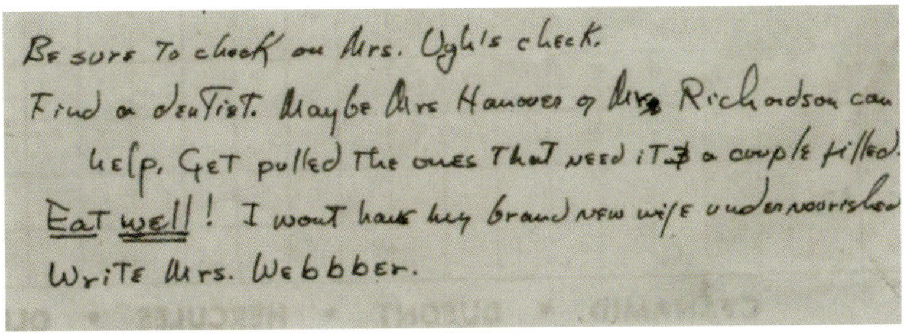

Be sure to check on Mrs. Ugh's check.
Find a dentist. Maybe Mrs Hanover or Mrs Richardson can help. Get pulled the ones that need it & a couple filled.
Eat well! I won't have my brand new wife undernourished.
Write Mrs. Webbber.

All three women—Mary Richardson, Susie Hanover and Mrs. Webber (also called 'Mrs. Ugh,'—are mentioned in this letter from Robert.

Lee apologized for my eviction, saying, "I'll get your money back!" when I told him I was now utterly broke. Meanwhile, he gave Susie twenty dollars as a down-payment, which she kindly accepted.[124] Robert named all three women –Hanover, Richardson and Webber --in one letter,

[124] Little did I know that Mary Richardson, Pastor Bill's wife, who seemed to be in excellent health, and who was the only witness that Lee had brought me to 1032 Marengo, would die of a heart attack by the end of the year.

written while on "Quarter-Boat Bob" in the Gulf of Mexico. I'd been too busy to see a dentist, and sometimes too busy to eat! He wanted me to write to Mrs. Webber to get my rent money back after the raid. He had obtained a check from her ('Mrs. Ugh') but it was no good. I loved 1032 Marengo. I had the front apartment to myself in the small, sunny cottage. There was a center room connecting to Susie's half of the house. The prior residents had trashed it, and also broke the bathtub. Therefore, I had no bathtub (it was a shared bathroom) and would have to use Susie's, which was located in the middle of her kitchen! That's how old the house was. There was a pretty bed under a window overlooking the front porch. It was covered with hand-sewn quilts, with pillowcases edged in lacy crochet. But I had no food. It had been left behind at Mrs. Ugh's. Lee, full of remorse, promised to return soon with some vittles. "I'm not going to let you go through any more hell," he vowed. "I'm going to personally take care of you!" I wondered if he meant it. But at this point, just getting some rest was all I craved. By the time I finished unpacking, Lee had returned with some groceries, but couldn't stay a minute; he had work to do. And so my saga with Lee really began.

"Ferrie's Berries": Around this time, as Lee, David Ferrie and I discussed Aldous Huxley, "soma" and psychedelic drugs, Dave obtained some "harmless' **morning glory seeds** that he called "Ferrie's berries." I was amused because he baked them (which destroyed any psychedelic properties!), and they tasted terrible, as well. To find out if the morning glory seeds were legal, Lee went to the Juvenile Division, Police, to see if they were listed (they weren't), but he was then sent to the city's chemist. After the assassination, the FBI solemnly investigated the matter, apparently to see if Lee "did drugs." David Ferrie was surprised that neither Lee nor I would drink, smoke, or "experiment."

COLOR PLATES

1. Street Car Tickets (2) Letter

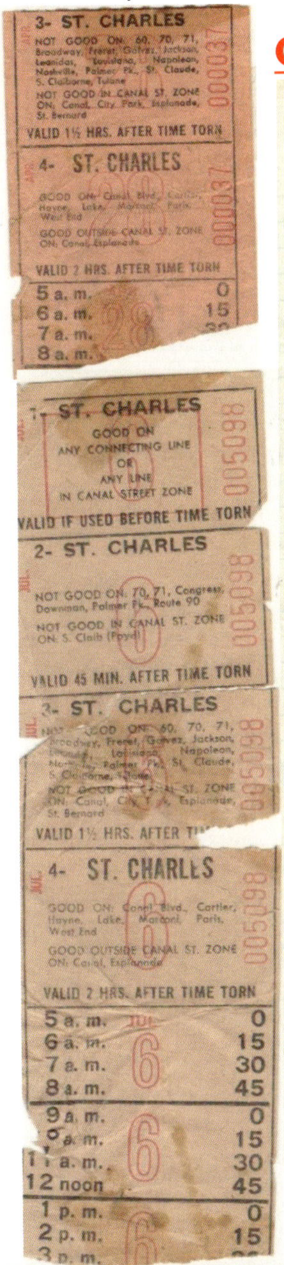

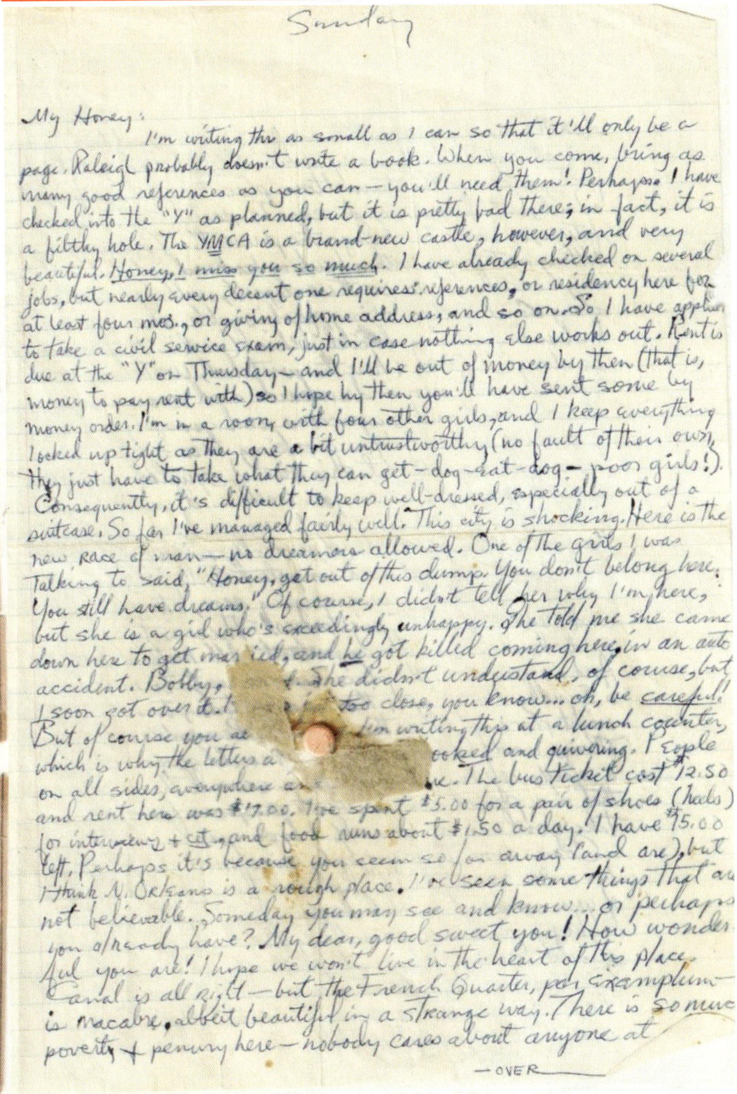

Sunday

My Honey:
I'm writing this as small as I can so that it'll only be a
page. Raleigh probably doesn't write a book. When you come, bring as
many good references as you can — you'll need them! Perhaps. I have
checked into the "Y" as planned, but it is pretty bad there; in fact, it is
a filthy hole. The YMCA is a brand-new castle, however, and very
beautiful. Honey, I miss you so much. I have already checked on several
jobs, but nearly every decent one requires references, or residency here for
at least four mos., or giving of home address, and so on. So I have applied
to take a civil service exam, just in case nothing else works out. Rent is
due at the "Y" on Thursday — and I'll be out of money by then (that is,
money to pay rent with) so I hope by then you'll have sent some by
money order. I'm in a room with four other girls, and I keep everything
locked up tight as they are a bit untrustworthy (no fault of their own,
they just have to take what they can get — dog-eat-dog — poor girls!).
Consequently, it's difficult to keep well-dressed, especially out of a
suitcase. So far I've managed fairly well. This city is shocking. Here is the
new race of man — no dreamers allowed. One of the girls I was
talking to said, "Honey, get out of this dump. You don't belong here.
You still have dreams." Of course, I didn't tell her why I'm here,
but she is a girl who's exceedingly unhappy. She told me she came
down here to get married, and he got killed coming here, in an auto
accident. Bobby, [illegible]. She didn't understand, of course, but
I soon got over it [illegible] too close, you know... oh, be careful!
But of course you a[illegible] I'm writing this at a lunch counter,
which is why the letters a[illegible] [illegible]ooked and quivering. People
on all sides, everywhere a[illegible] [illegible]e. The bus ticket cost $12.50
and rent here was $17.00. I've spent $5.00 for a pair of shoes (heels)
for interviews + etc, and food runs about $1.50 a day. I have $15.00
left. Perhaps it's because you seem so far away (and are), but
I think N. Orleans is a rough place. I've seen some things that are
not believable. Someday you may see and know... or perhaps
you already have? My dear, good sweet you! How wonderful you are! I hope we won't live in the heart of this place.
Canal is all right — but the French Quarter, per examplum —
is macabre, albeit beautiful in a strange way. There is so much
poverty + penury here — nobody cares about anyone at

— OVER

04/26/63 to RAB III /mentions "Raleigh"(Birth control pill so important, I saved it).

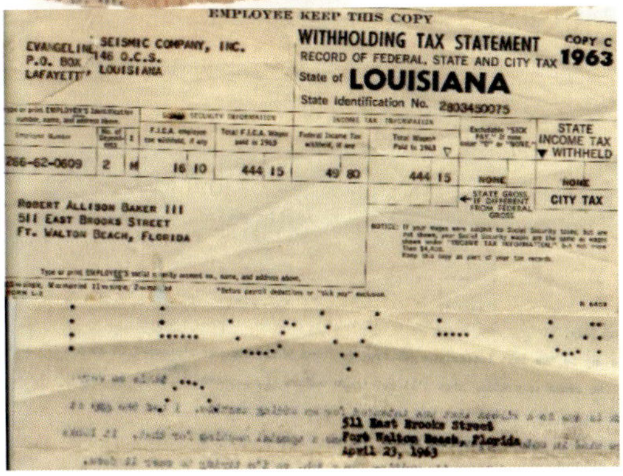

EMPLOYEE KEEP THIS COPY

EVANGELINE SEISMIC COMPANY, INC.
P.O. BOX 146 O.C.S.
LAFAYETTE, LOUISIANA

WITHHOLDING TAX STATEMENT 1963 — COPY C
RECORD OF FEDERAL, STATE AND CITY TAX
State of LOUISIANA
State Identification No. 2803450075

266-62-0609 | 2 | M | 16 10 | 444 15 | 49 80 | 444 15 | NONE | NONE

ROBERT ALLISON BAKER III
511 EAST BROOKS STREET
FT. WALTON BEACH, FLORIDA

511 East Brooks Street
Fort Walton Beach, Florida
April 23, 1963

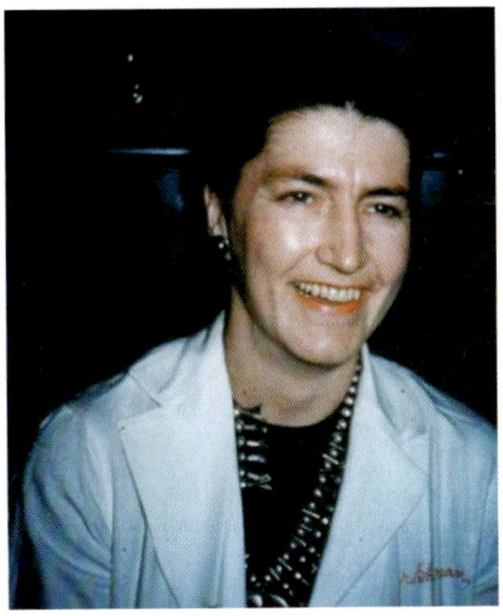

3. R.A. Baker III Documents

4. "Dr. Mary"

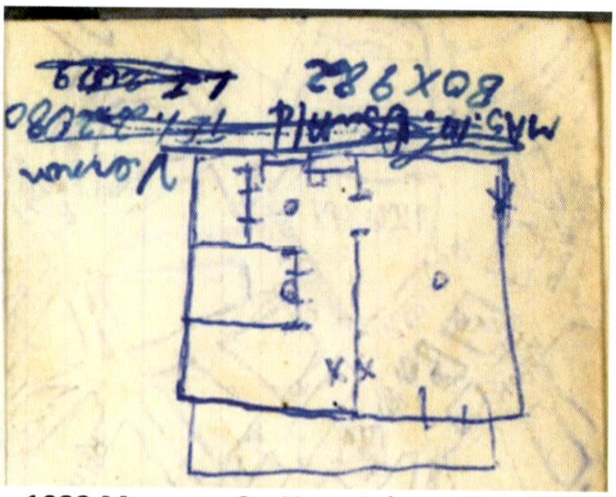

5-6.

1032 Marengo St. New Orleans. Note porch cut back by rail, and window next to door not blocked by the bed. X's were where I kept research papers, microscope. Exterior x on windowsill was where key was kept. Small circles were overhead lights (had just a bedside lamp). Door to back exit and room to Susie's apartment is marked by arrow. Drawing was compressed: drawn upside-down, Lee ran out of space.

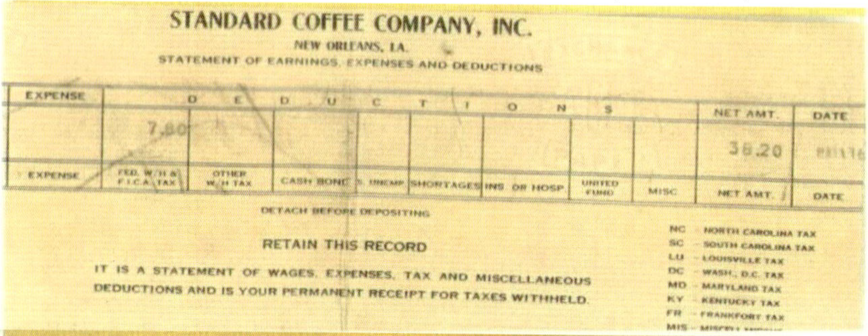

STANDARD COFFEE COMPANY, INC.
NEW ORLEANS, LA.
STATEMENT OF EARNINGS, EXPENSES AND DEDUCTIONS

EXPENSE	FED. W/H & F.I.C.A. TAX	OTHER W/H TAX	CASH BOND	UNEMP.	SHORTAGES	INS. OR HOSP.	UNITED FUND	MISC.	NET AMT.	DATE
	7.80								38.20	

DETACH BEFORE DEPOSITING

RETAIN THIS RECORD

IT IS A STATEMENT OF WAGES, EXPENSES, TAX AND MISCELLANEOUS DEDUCTIONS AND IS YOUR PERMANENT RECEIPT FOR TAXES WITHHELD.

NC - NORTH CAROLINA TAX
SC - SOUTH CAROLINA TAX
LU - LOUISVILLE TAX
DC - WASH., D.C. TAX
MD - MARYLAND TAX
KY - KENTUCKY TAX
FR - FRANKFORT TAX

7. My May 17, 1963 check stub issued by Standard. (see text to explain)

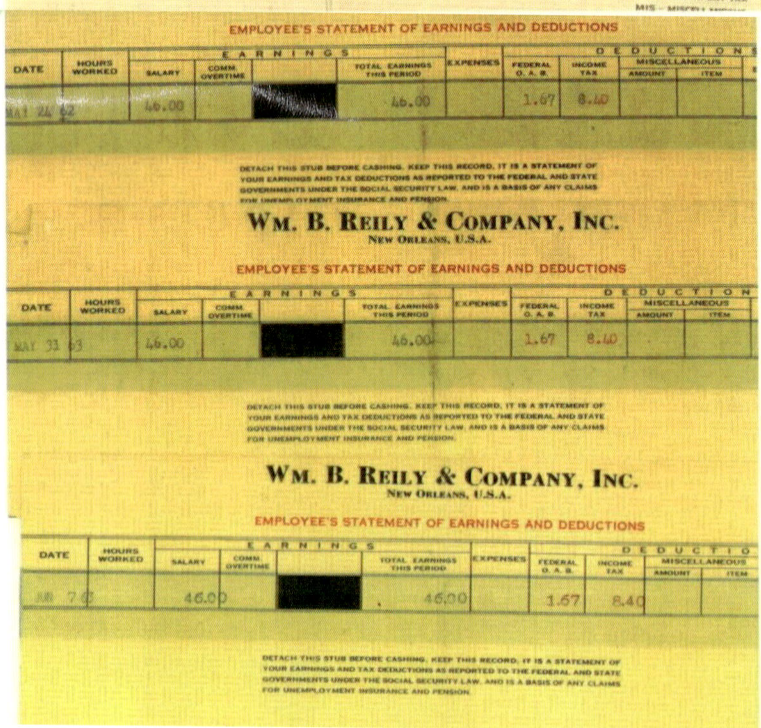

EMPLOYEE'S STATEMENT OF EARNINGS AND DEDUCTIONS

DATE	HOURS WORKED	SALARY	COMM. OVERTIME		TOTAL EARNINGS THIS PERIOD	EXPENSES	FEDERAL O. A. B.	INCOME TAX	MISCELLANEOUS AMOUNT	ITEM
MAY 24 63		46.00		[redacted]	46.00		1.67	8.40		

DETACH THIS STUB BEFORE CASHING. KEEP THIS RECORD. IT IS A STATEMENT OF YOUR EARNINGS AND TAX DEDUCTIONS AS REPORTED TO THE FEDERAL AND STATE GOVERNMENTS UNDER THE SOCIAL SECURITY LAW, AND IS A BASIS OF ANY CLAIMS FOR UNEMPLOYMENT INSURANCE AND PENSION.

WM. B. REILY & COMPANY, INC.
NEW ORLEANS, U.S.A.

EMPLOYEE'S STATEMENT OF EARNINGS AND DEDUCTIONS

DATE	HOURS WORKED	SALARY	COMM. OVERTIME		TOTAL EARNINGS THIS PERIOD	EXPENSES	FEDERAL O. A. B.	INCOME TAX	MISCELLANEOUS AMOUNT	ITEM
MAY 31 63		46.00		[redacted]	46.00		1.67	8.40		

DETACH THIS STUB BEFORE CASHING. KEEP THIS RECORD. IT IS A STATEMENT OF YOUR EARNINGS AND TAX DEDUCTIONS AS REPORTED TO THE FEDERAL AND STATE GOVERNMENTS UNDER THE SOCIAL SECURITY LAW, AND IS A BASIS OF ANY CLAIMS FOR UNEMPLOYMENT INSURANCE AND PENSION.

WM. B. REILY & COMPANY, INC.
NEW ORLEANS, U.S.A.

EMPLOYEE'S STATEMENT OF EARNINGS AND DEDUCTIONS

DATE	HOURS WORKED	SALARY	COMM. OVERTIME		TOTAL EARNINGS THIS PERIOD	EXPENSES	FEDERAL O. A. B.	INCOME TAX	MISCELLANEOUS AMOUNT	ITEM
JUN 7 63		46.00		[redacted]	46.00		1.67	8.40		

DETACH THIS STUB BEFORE CASHING. KEEP THIS RECORD. IT IS A STATEMENT OF YOUR EARNINGS AND TAX DEDUCTIONS AS REPORTED TO THE FEDERAL AND STATE GOVERNMENTS UNDER THE SOCIAL SECURITY LAW, AND IS A BASIS OF ANY CLAIMS FOR UNEMPLOYMENT INSURANCE AND PENSION.

8. May 24, May 31 and June 7 Reily check stubs

9. Most of Lee's FPCC flyers were yellow. Here is a green one.

10. David W. Ferrie

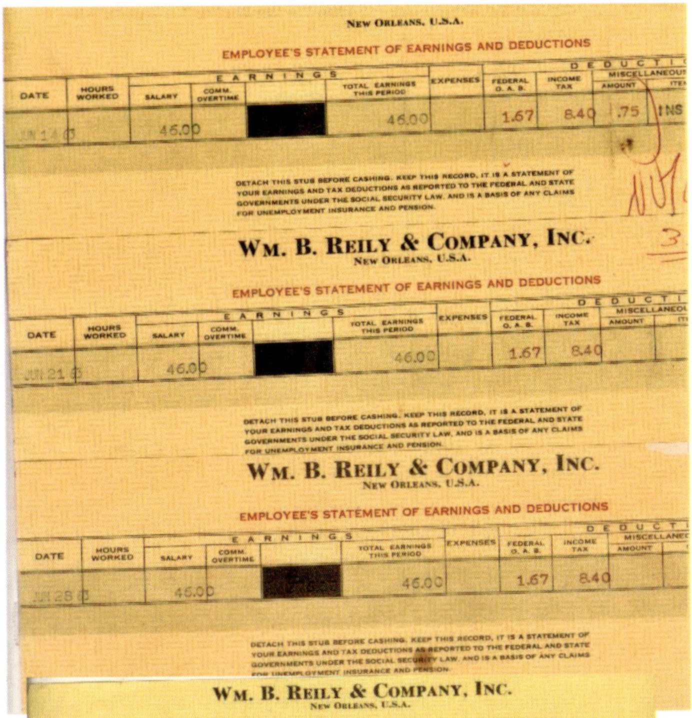

New Orleans, U.S.A.

EMPLOYEE'S STATEMENT OF EARNINGS AND DEDUCTIONS

DATE	HOURS WORKED	SALARY	COMM. OVERTIME		TOTAL EARNINGS THIS PERIOD	EXPENSES	FEDERAL O.A.B.	INCOME TAX	MISCELLANEOUS AMOUNT	ITEM
JUN 14 63		46.00		[redacted]	46.00		1.67	8.40	.75	INS
JUN 21 63		46.00		[redacted]	46.00		1.67	8.40		
JUN 28 63		46.00		[redacted]	46.00		1.67	8.40		

DETACH THIS STUB BEFORE CASHING. KEEP THIS RECORD. IT IS A STATEMENT OF YOUR EARNINGS AND TAX DEDUCTIONS AS REPORTED TO THE FEDERAL AND STATE GOVERNMENTS UNDER THE SOCIAL SECURITY LAW, AND IS A BASIS OF ANY CLAIMS FOR UNEMPLOYMENT INSURANCE AND PENSION.

WM. B. REILY & COMPANY, INC.

11. Reily paycheck stubs for June and July,1963.

368.43

.43 414.86

460.86

12. Running carbon totals.

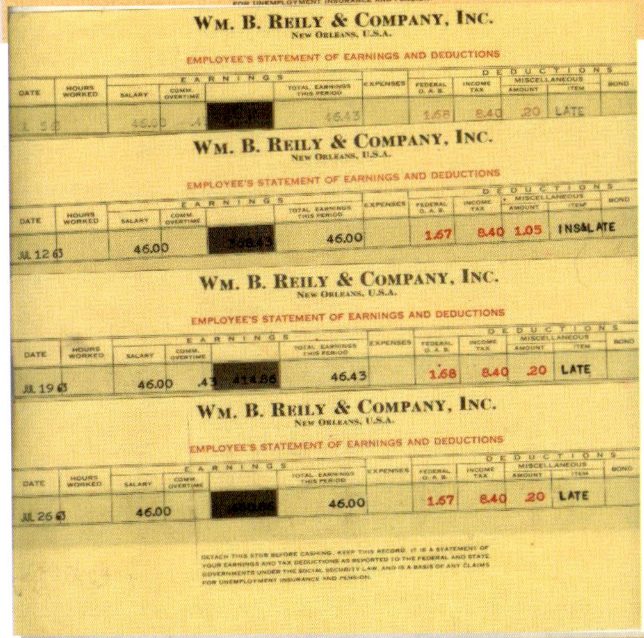

WM. B. REILY & COMPANY, INC.
New Orleans, U.S.A.

EMPLOYEE'S STATEMENT OF EARNINGS AND DEDUCTIONS

DATE	HOURS WORKED	SALARY	COMM. OVERTIME		TOTAL EARNINGS THIS PERIOD	EXPENSES	FEDERAL O.A.B.	INCOME TAX	MISCELLANEOUS AMOUNT	ITEM	BOND
JUL 5 63		46.00	.43	[redacted]	46.43		1.68	8.40	.20	LATE	
JUL 12 63		46.00		[redacted]	46.00		1.67	8.40	1.05	INS & LATE	
JUL 19 63		46.00	.43	[redacted]	46.43		1.68	8.40	.20	LATE	
JUL 26 63		46.00		[redacted]	46.00		1.67	8.40	.20	LATE	

DETACH THIS STUB BEFORE CASHING. KEEP THIS RECORD. IT IS A STATEMENT OF YOUR EARNINGS AND TAX DEDUCTIONS AS REPORTED TO THE FEDERAL AND STATE GOVERNMENTS UNDER THE SOCIAL SECURITY LAW, AND IS A BASIS OF ANY CLAIMS FOR UNEMPLOYMENT INSURANCE AND PENSION.

13. Fired Aug. 9, 1963, for having been seen with Lee Oswald, who was arrested shortly after (See text)**;** my paycheck for **July 2- Aug. 8** was suspended when I was fired "to inspect" if I had worked 40 hours, due to "late lunch absences" that Reily Vice President Monaghan covered for me. After a successful petition, Reily made a direct deposit to our bank account on Sept. 3, 1963. (See text and bank deposit record). **Aug. 9 check stub shows only one day's pay, as I was fired on the spot. Friday began a new pay week, instead of Monday.**

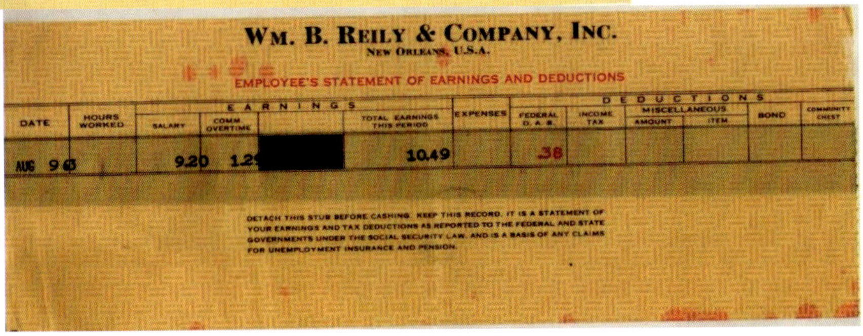

WM. B. REILY & COMPANY, INC.
New Orleans, U.S.A.

EMPLOYEE'S STATEMENT OF EARNINGS AND DEDUCTIONS

DATE	HOURS WORKED	SALARY	COMM. OVERTIME		TOTAL EARNINGS THIS PERIOD	EXPENSES	FEDERAL O.A.B.	INCOME TAX	MISCELLANEOUS AMOUNT	ITEM	BOND	COMMUNITY CHEST
AUG 9 63		9.20	1.29	[redacted]	10.49		.38					

DETACH THIS STUB BEFORE CASHING. KEEP THIS RECORD. IT IS A STATEMENT OF YOUR EARNINGS AND TAX DEDUCTIONS AS REPORTED TO THE FEDERAL AND STATE GOVERNMENTS UNDER THE SOCIAL SECURITY LAW, AND IS A BASIS OF ANY CLAIMS FOR UNEMPLOYMENT INSURANCE AND PENSION.

Friday 08/09

14-15: "Female Infant Vary" birth certificates shocked me. The first shocker was issued April 26, 1963, the same day I met Lee Oswald, ordered for ID purposes. David Ferrie, then working on Marcello's fake birth records, told me to order the birth certificate again, when Lee left Mexico City, so my order would show the record was sent to Gainesville, Florida, not to New Orleans. I now had two worthless birth certificates. In 1986, Exxon obtained my original birth certificate.

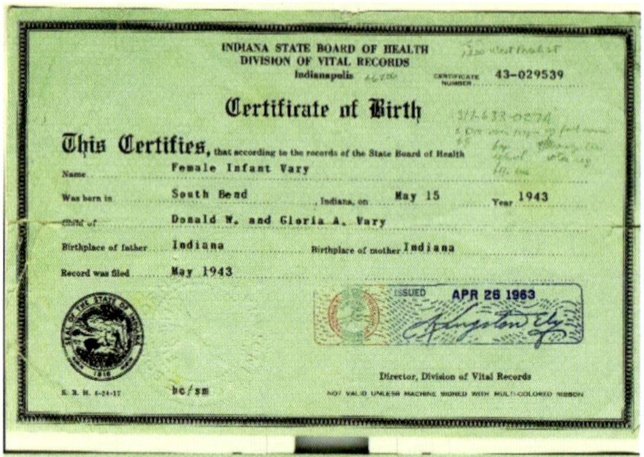
INDIANA STATE BOARD OF HEALTH
DIVISION OF VITAL RECORDS
Indianapolis
CERTIFICATE NUMBER 43-029539

Certificate of Birth

This Certifies, that according to the records of the State Board of Health

Name: Female Infant Vary
Was born in: South Bend, Indiana, on May 15 Year 1943
Child of: Donald W. and Gloria A. Vary
Birthplace of father: Indiana Birthplace of mother: Indiana
Record was filed: May 1943

ISSUED APR 26 1963

Director, Division of Vital Records

bc/sm

NOT VALID UNLESS MACHINE SIGNED WITH MULTI-COLORED RIBBON

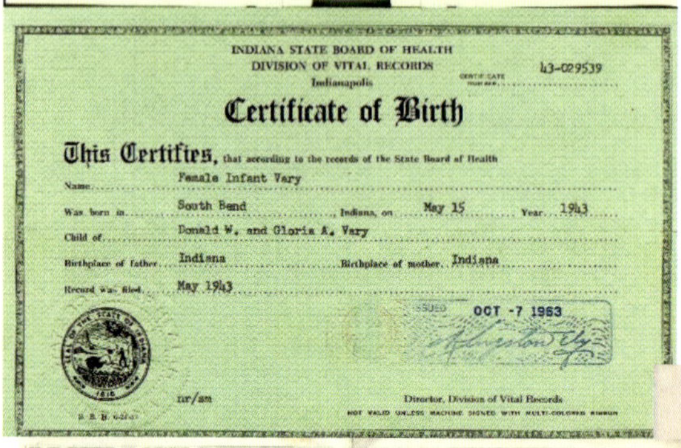
INDIANA STATE BOARD OF HEALTH
DIVISION OF VITAL RECORDS
Indianapolis
CERTIFICATE NUMBER 43-029539

Certificate of Birth

This Certifies, that according to the records of the State Board of Health

Name: Female Infant Vary
Was born in: South Bend, Indiana, on May 15 Year 1943
Child of: Donald W. and Gloria A. Vary
Birthplace of father: Indiana Birthplace of mother: Indiana
Record was filed: May 1943

ISSUED OCT -7 1963

Director, Division of Vital Records

rr/sm

NOT VALID UNLESS MACHINE SIGNED WITH MULTI-COLORED RIBBON

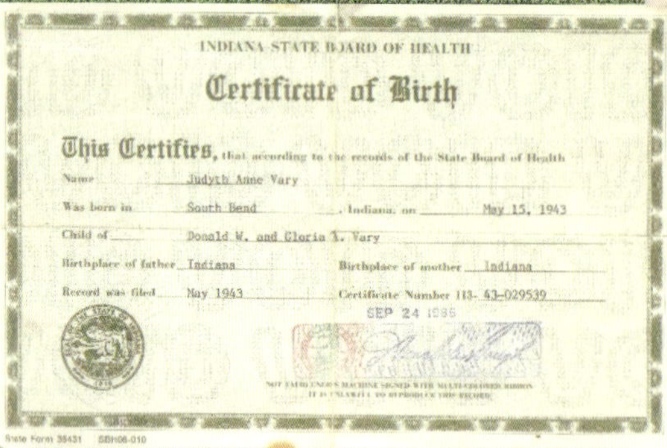
INDIANA STATE BOARD OF HEALTH

Certificate of Birth

This Certifies, that according to the records of the State Board of Health

Name: Judyth Anne Vary
Was born in: South Bend, Indiana, on May 15, 1943
Child of: Donald W. and Gloria A. Vary
Birthplace of father: Indiana Birthplace of mother: Indiana
Record was filed: May 1943 Certificate Number 113- 43-029539

SEP 24 1986

State Form 35431

<u>16. AMEX KISS</u>
<u>May 27, 1963</u>

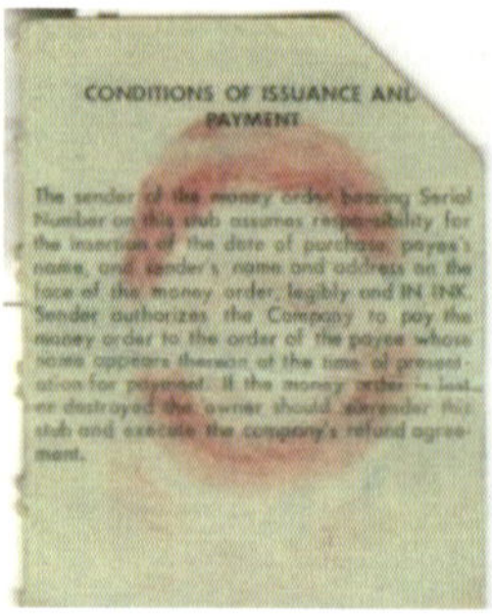

17.<u>Reily Stationary</u> (watermarked) Executive & Vice President stationary

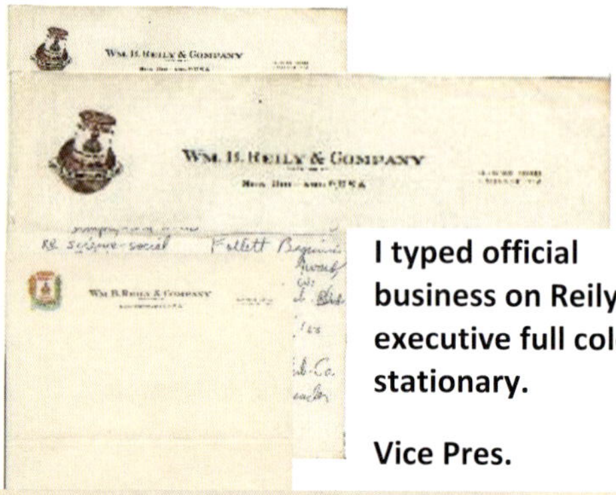

I typed official business on Reily's executive full color stationary.

Vice Pres.

Monaghan also had me use the brown "Field Correspondence" stationary for salesmen, employees and his personal business.

18. Lee Oswald Museum, Langshyttan, Sweden

19. The 'Caracas' page in color; Lee's address book.

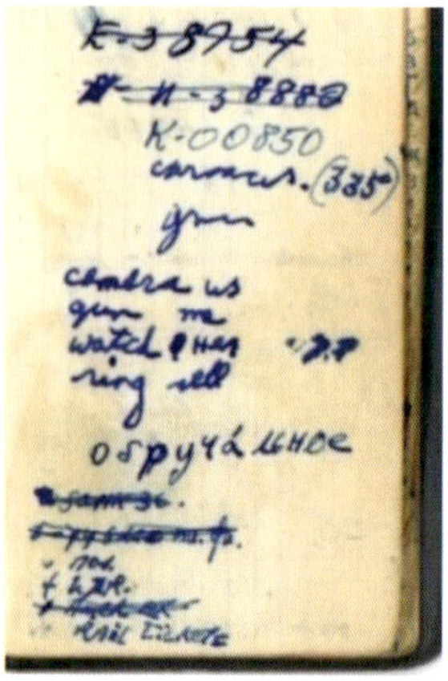

<u>19. Witnesses</u> (L to R)
Claudia Rodick
Wm. 'Mac" McCullough
Anna Lewis RIP

(all 3 were taped)

<u>Witnesses</u> (L to R)

Victoria P. Sulzer (taped)
Dr. Kathleen Santi (written)
Kelly Thomas & family
(interviewed by Dr. Williams)

Witnesses (L to R) Mary Morgan J. Ed Haslam Kris Millegan Wm 'Tosh' Plumlee
(Below, L) Witness Robert K. Tanenbaum [all on film and/or witnessed/recorded]

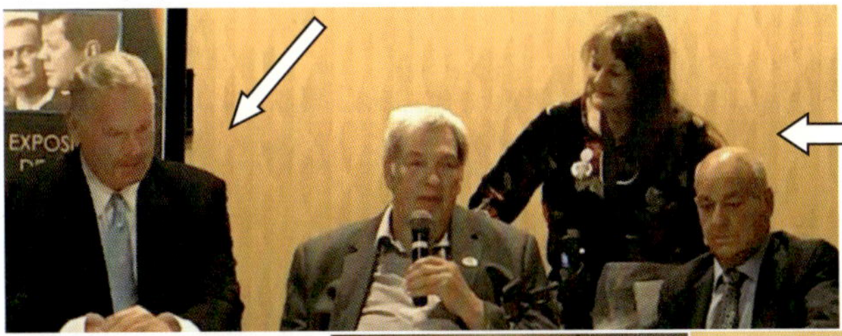

(Ctr) Robert Groden

(R) Dr. Cyril Wecht

20. Friends for the Cause

(L) Judge Jim Botelho

(Ctr) Oliver Stone

Jim Marrs RIP

Saint John Hunt Edgar Tatro Hubert Clark RIP Abraham Bolden

(L)Phil Singer
& Jesse
Ventura
Antoinette
Giancana
Gerry Hemming RIP

Dennis David
RIP
Dick Russell
Phillip
Nelson
Dr. John
deLane Williams

Dr. Jim Fetzer David Denton Dr. Howard Platzman Larry Rivera

Tom Rozoff

Beverly Oliver M. Jeffrey Holmes

Randy Benson Ole Dammegard

RFK Jr. and Peter Hymans

Don Ratliff John B. Wells Gary Fannin

Playwrights Jason Trachtenberg

Lisa Soland

Ray Hale

Director Lukas Ettlin

Poet/Attorney
Mark Mueller

(Apologies to all the many speakers, researchers and supporters whose photos were not included. Many photos were unreachable in Europe due to COVID travel restrictions. Many of you are listed in "acknowledgements.")

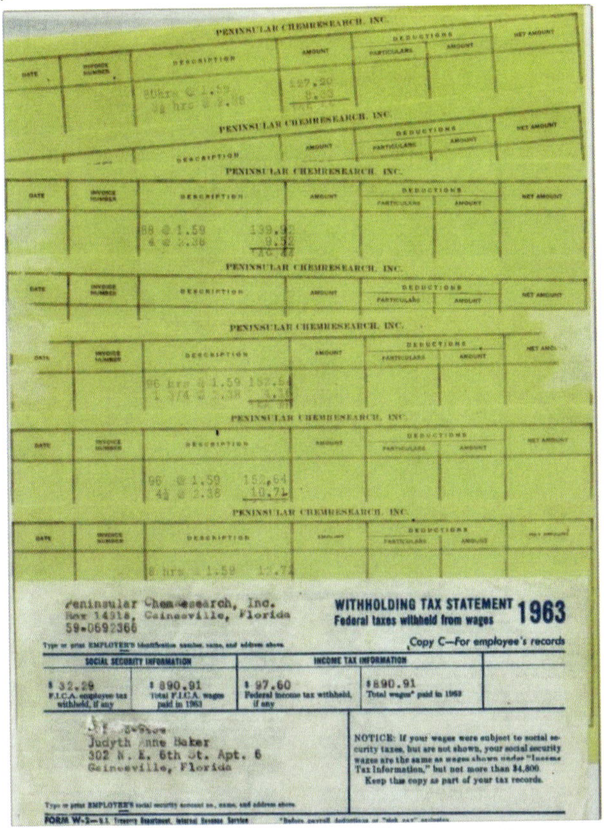
PENINSULAR CHEMRESEARCH, INC.

80hrs @ 1.59 — 127.20

88 @ 1.59 — 139.92
4 @ 2.38 — 9.52

96 hrs @ 1.59 — 152.64
1 3/4 @ 2.38

96 @ 1.59 — 152.64
4½ @ 2.38 — 10.71

8 hrs @ 1.59 — 12.72

Peninsular ChemResearch, Inc.
Box 14918, Gainesville, Florida
59-0692366

WITHHOLDING TAX STATEMENT 1963
Federal taxes withheld from wages
Copy C—For employee's records

SOCIAL SECURITY INFORMATION		INCOME TAX INFORMATION	
$ 32.28 F.I.C.A. employee tax withheld, if any	$ 890.91 Total F.I.C.A. wages paid in 1963	$ 97.60 Federal income tax withheld, if any	$890.91 Total wages* paid in 1963

Judyth Anne Baker
302 N. E. 6th St. Apt. 6
Gainesville, Florida

NOTICE: If your wages were subject to social security taxes, but are not shown, your social security wages are the same as wages shown under "Income Tax Information," but not more than $4,800.
Keep this copy as part of your tax records.

FORM W-2—U.S. Treasury Department, Internal Revenue Service

<u>21. Peninsular ChemResearch Check Stubs and W-2 Form</u>

22. 2017: Dallas. Judge Jim Botelho signs 5 albums of classical music he & Lee bought together while stationed at El Toro (Marines) and gives them to Judyth. He believed Lee was training to become a spy.

23. <u>Annually:</u> Lee Harvey Oswald's Birthday Party every Oct. 18 as an act of defiance.

24. <u>2018</u>: Oliver Stone publicly endorses Judyth's testimony at her 7th annual conference, Dallas, after an intense 3-hr interrogation session with witnesses present.

25.-This brown shirt may be the one Judyth bought for Lee. He owned two similar reddish-brown, long-sleeved shirts. (photo National Archives, 2013)

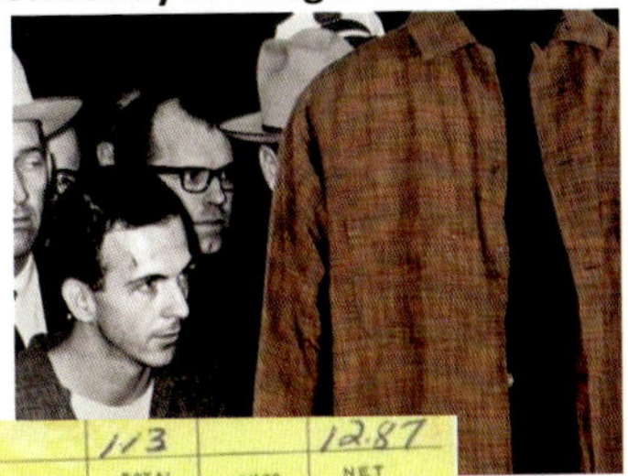

26. The Green Glass **27.** Royal Castle Check Stub.

PERIOD ENDING	HOURS	RATE	GROSS EARNED	F.I.C.A.	FEDERAL INCOME TAX	STATE INCOME TAX	FOOD	UNIFORMS	HOSPITAL INSURANCE	ADVANCES	TOTAL DEDUCTED	MISC.	NET PAY
5/4/63	14	100	14.00	.53	.30		[redacted]	.30			1.13		12.87

EARNINGS — DEDUCTIONS

DETACH BEFORE DEPOSITING — ROYAL CASTLE SYSTEM, INC. – NEW ORLEANS, LOUISIANA

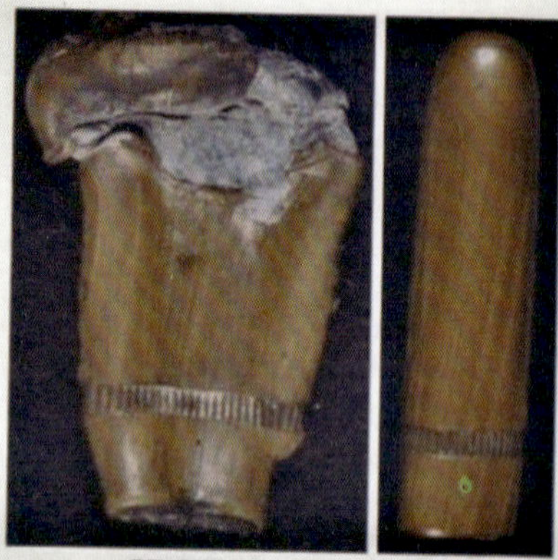

CE 573 CE 399

Bullet on right is the famous "magic bullet." The Warren Commission tried to link Lee Oswald to the Walker shooting by saying bullet on the left is the one he fired at Walker. However, the report below clearly states that the Walker bullet was steel jacketed.

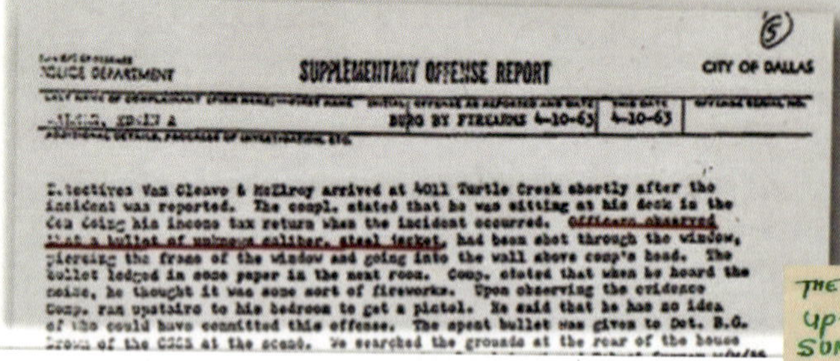

(5)

POLICE DEPARTMENT SUPPLEMENTARY OFFENSE REPORT CITY OF DALLAS

BURG BY FIREARMS 4-10-63 | 4-10-63

Detectives Van Cleave & McElroy arrived at 4011 Turtle Creek shortly after the incident was reported. The compl. stated that he was sitting at his desk in the den doing his income tax return when the incident occurred. Officers observed that a bullet of unknown caliber, steel jacket, had been shot through the window, piercing the frame of the window and going into the wall above comp's head. The bullet lodged in some paper in the next room. Comp. stated that when he heard the noise, he thought it was some sort of fireworks. Upon observing the evidence Comp. ran upstairs to his bedroom to get a pistol. He said that he has no idea of who could have committed this offense. The spent bullet was given to Det. B.G. Brown of the CSCS at the scene. We searched the grounds at the rear of the house

26. Gen. Walker himself said this copper- jacketed bullet 'CE573' was substituted for the steel-jacketed bullet shot at him. Police report shows "a bullet of unknown caliber, steel jacket, had been shot through the window."

27. Jack Ruby and his Carousel Club girls.

28. Lee's Passport application. OK'd in 24 hrs. Lee's height is 5' 11" in govt records (he was 5' 9"). 'Photographer' filled in by Young.

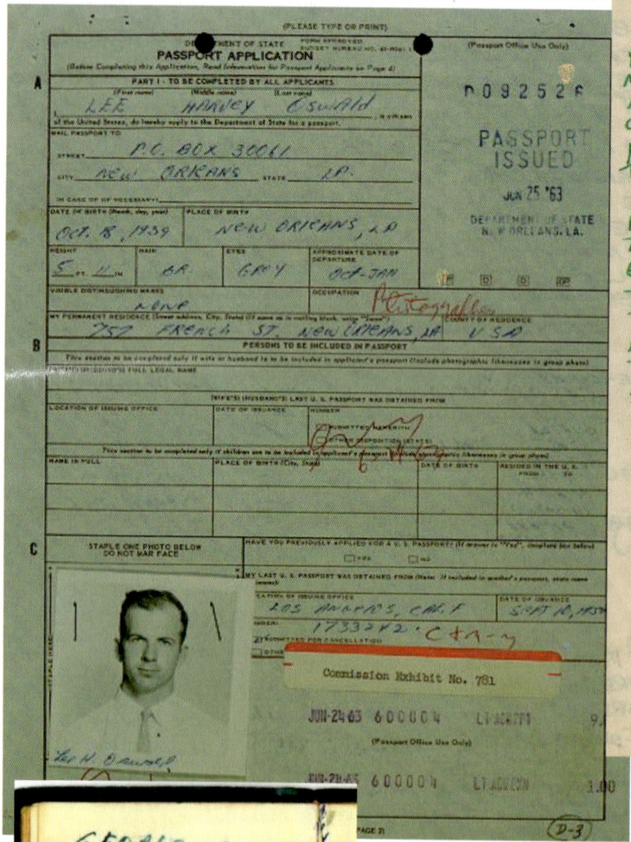

(PLEASE TYPE OR PRINT)

DEPARTMENT OF STATE

PASSPORT APPLICATION

PART I - TO BE COMPLETED BY ALL APPLICANTS

LEE HARVEY OSWALD

P.O. BOX 30061

NEW ORLEANS LA

OCT. 18, 1939 NEW ORLEANS, LA

5 11 BR. GREY OCT-JAN

NONE

Photographer

757 FRENCH ST. NEW ORLEANS, LA USA

D092526

PASSPORT ISSUED JUN 25 '63 DEPARTMENT OF STATE NEW ORLEANS, LA.

LOS ANGELES, CALIF SEPT 10, 1959

1733242 C+A-y

Commission Exhibit No. 781

JUN-24-63 600004

Lee H. Oswald

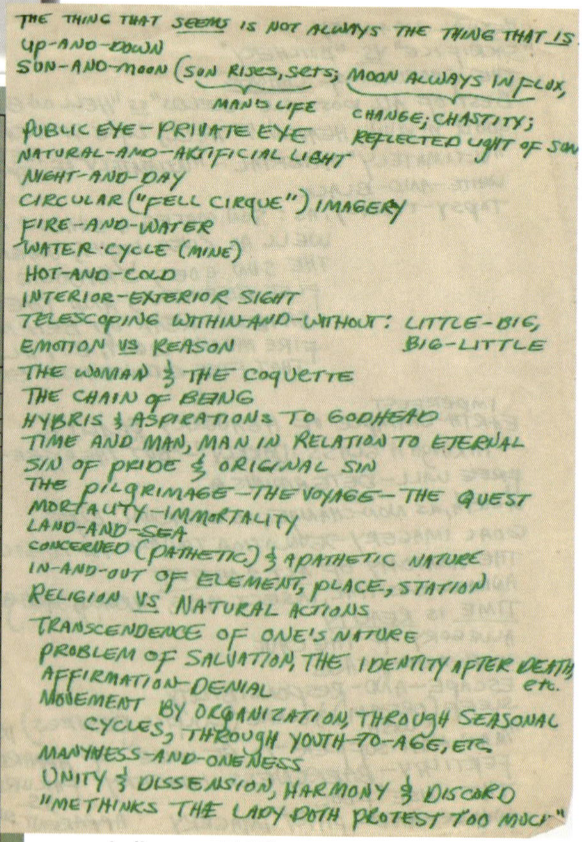

THE THING THAT SEEMS IS NOT ALWAYS THE THING THAT IS.
UP-AND-DOWN
SUN-AND-MOON (SUN RISES, SETS; MOON ALWAYS IN FLUX, CHANGE; CHASTITY;
MAN'S LIFE
PUBLIC EYE - PRIVATE EYE
REFLECTED LIGHT OF SUN
NATURAL-AND-ARTIFICIAL LIGHT
NIGHT-AND-DAY
CIRCULAR ("FELL CIRQUE") IMAGERY
FIRE-AND-WATER
WATER CYCLE (MINE)
HOT-AND-COLD
INTERIOR-EXTERIOR SIGHT
TELESCOPING WITHIN-AND-WITHOUT: LITTLE-BIG, BIG-LITTLE
EMOTION VS REASON
THE WOMAN & THE COQUETTE
THE CHAIN OF BEING
HYBRIS & ASPIRATIONS TO GODHEAD
TIME AND MAN, MAN IN RELATION TO ETERNAL
SIN OF PRIDE & ORIGINAL SIN
THE PILGRIMAGE - THE VOYAGE - THE QUEST
MORTALITY - IMMORTALITY
LAND-AND-SEA
CONCERNED (PATHETIC) & APATHETIC NATURE
IN-AND-OUT OF ELEMENT, PLACE, STATION
RELIGION VS NATURAL ACTIONS
TRANSCENDENCE OF ONE'S NATURE
PROBLEM OF SALVATION, THE IDENTITY AFTER DEATH etc.
AFFIRMATION - DENIAL
MOVEMENT BY ORGANIZATION, THROUGH SEASONAL CYCLES, THROUGH YOUTH-TO-AGE, ETC.
MANYNESS-AND-ONENESS
UNITY & DISSENSION, HARMONY & DISCORD
"METHINKS THE LADY DOTH PROTEST TOO MUCH"

GEORGE BOUHE
4740 HOMER ST
TA-72288
ANNA MELLER
5930 ½ LA VISTA
TA 8-2219
RI-74011

29. My notes from David Ferrie's 1st lecture, in green fountain pen ink. 30. Lee used the same green ink; we shared an ink bottle. Note green ink, Lee's address book. Note: FBI tore out a page.

Chapter Eleven
The Project

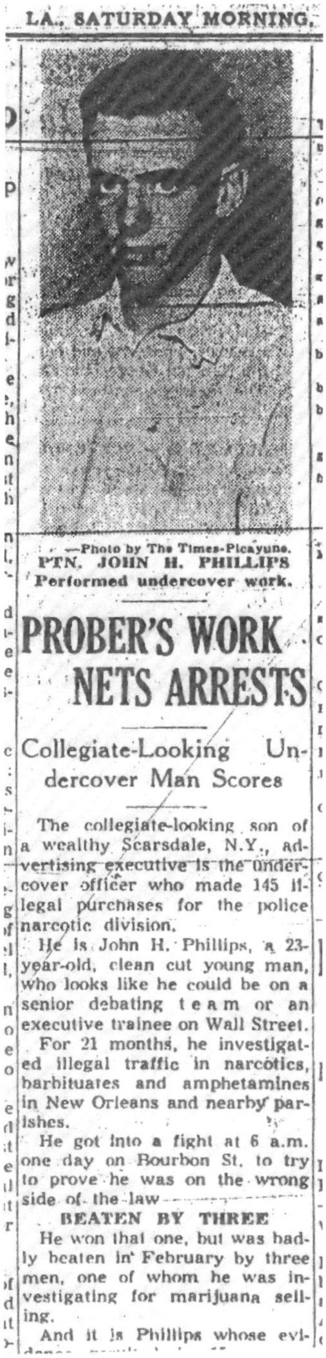

LA., SATURDAY MORNING,

—Photo by The Times-Picayune.
PTN. JOHN H. PHILLIPS
Performed undercover work.

PROBER'S WORK NETS ARRESTS

Collegiate-Looking Undercover Man Scores

The collegiate-looking son of a wealthy Scarsdale, N.Y., advertising executive is the undercover officer who made 145 illegal purchases for the police narcotic division.

He is John H. Phillips, a 23-year-old, clean cut young man, who looks like he could be on a senior debating team or an executive trainee on Wall Street.

For 21 months, he investigated illegal traffic in narcotics, barbituates and amphetamines in New Orleans and nearby parishes.

He got into a fight at 6 a.m. one day on Bourbon St. to try to prove he was on the wrong side of the law

BEATEN BY THREE

He won that one, but was badly beaten in February by three men, one of whom he was investigating for marijuana selling.

And it is Phillips whose evi-

_Guy Banister was running Lee now as an anti-communist ultra-conservative, but soon enough, he'd have to reverse that image 180 degrees and portray himself as "pro-Castro" after the city's universities closed for the summer. As Lee hunted for a good way to transform himself from one side of the equation to the other, he had come across an article in the May 4, 1963 *Times-Picayune*, as we hunted for news about the raid that got me kicked out of the mansion. "Here's how I can convince everybody that I'm really a Marxist and pro-Castro," Lee let me know. He then read the article out loud. Lee explained to me that to enter Cuba safely, if so ordered to do so, he had to prove he was pro-Castro in some open manner that wouldn't get him jailed for years or beaten to a pulp by a band of anti-Castroites. So now he read aloud the following story: *"The collegiate-looking son of a wealthy Scarsdale, New York advertising executive is the undercover officer who made 145 illegal purchases for the police narcotics division. He is* ***John H. Phillips****... a twenty-three-year old, clean-cut young man..."*

Lee broke off and smiled at me. "I'm also twenty-three," he said. "And I'm clean-cut, too!" He then resumed reading the rest of the article out loud:

"...for 21 months, he investigated illegal traffic in narcotics, barbiturates, and amphetamines in New Orleans and nearby parishes. He got into a fight at 6 a.m. one day on Bourbon St. to try to prove he was on the wrong side of the law..."

Lee chimed in his approval, insisting that this was the way for him to proceed, several months down the line. He and Banister had some deep plans. They were plotting on how to lure pro-Castroites to places where their names could be recorded and photos made. They'd attract them by handing out pro-Castro pamphlets in highly-public spots. Radio and TV contacts would be prepared to cooperate. I thought it was a good idea, too. That is, until Lee read more to me.

"Beaten by three... [Phillips] won that [fight], but was badly beaten in February by three men..." "Oh, no, Lee!" I cried, "Don't even consider it!"

"Oh, I'd make sure they would secretly be my friends, don't worry!" Lee said. "I don't want to get 'badly beaten.' Maybe just a punch in the nose. That would do." Suddenly, I realized how much I cared about the man sitting next to me. I did not want to see any harm come to him. Despite myself, I took his hand, as if that might be able to stop Lee Oswald from doing something dangerous. I never felt more 'married' to Robert than when I took Lee's hand. Though I was married to Robert, he was acting as if I were just a piece of property. He cared mostly about money and sex. I was just one-half of that equation. And he wanted me to go back to Gainesville and support him through Graduate School, my own education meaning nothing! A swell of anger rose within me. I had a right to be educated, too! Lee, watching intently, then asked a question that showed how in tune he was with my thoughts. "Did you tell him about your plans to go to Tulane Medical School?" he asked.

"No, I didn't get a chance. He cut off the conversation as soon as I mentioned the possibility of getting a job at 'Pen Chem' in Gainesville." Lee's smile had turned into a grin. "You mean, you didn't tell him anything about Ochsner?"

"No," I said. "He thinks I'm still working at Royal Castle, even though I was fired there, right under his nose." I sighed sadly. "And now he's gone, for ten days at least. He made me so mad, I stopped talking to him."

"So he's without a clue about everything that's happened?"

"Pretty much," I replied.

"That's good news," Lee responded. "So, you might consider taking a cover job with me, at Reily's?" he ventured.

"I might," I replied, with a smile. Lee had told me how his 'cover job' at Reily's would provide visible income for his family, while he would still have enough time to conduct his clandestine work.

"It looks like David Ferrie might get his wish, after all," I told him. And with that sentence, I sealed my fate. I had agreed to participate in the Ferrie-Sherman-Ochsner plan to help develop a biological weapon to kill Fidel Castro. I had bought in. The die was cast.

Sunday, May 5, 1963 Waking from a good night's sleep in my new apartment, I lay half-dreaming, musing how events of the past week had turned my life upside-down. Though Lee Oswald had led me to the Mansion and all that transpired there, he had also stepped forward and found this pleasant little cottage. And he'd paid a third of my rent. The rush of affection I felt for Lee must have been because he rescued me. The scrap of paper that represented my marriage was just a birth control pill generator. As Lee had said, when I first met him, "Love – unto the death!" did not apply to RAB, III. I got up, dressed, and visited Susie to see about how to get the mail. That's when she showed me a big loop of sausage, crowned with a medium-sized wheel of cheese and some red ribbon. Susie said it was a "housewarming gift" from "somebody in Marcello's family." Food! Hurrah! Lee arrived around 9 a.m. to escort me to David Ferrie's. He marked it on a map for me, and taught me the route. We caught the bus on Louisiana Avenue and quickly plunged into an impoverished black neighborhood. At the far end of Louisiana Avenue, at Claiborne, a branch of the road turned into Louisiana Avenue Parkway, where the ghetto-y buildings around us vanished, and the vista opened to rows of stately oak trees and nice Spanish-style houses. Opulence and squalor lived uniquely side by side in New Orleans. David Ferrie was all business today, introducing me and Lee to "The Project." I'm sure it had an official name, but none of us knew what it was called officially. In the clandestine world, 'need to know' did not include the playbook and its title.

The makeshift lab hidden in David Ferrie's kitchen was but a single spoke of a wheel in this Get-Castro effort, the culmination of a year of work conducted in a ring of labs that did not know much about each other. But they might at last figure it out, which is why Ferrie's lab existed, breaking the chain. The configuration of these labs was basically a circular process which repeated itself over and over. With each lap around the loop of laboratories, the cancer-causing viruses would become more aggressive and deadly. Many mutations occurred that led nowhere.

But due to the sheer number of runs, a dangerous biological weapon was being crafted. Originally, these viruses came from monkeys, enhanced through mutations caused by radiation. The star of the show was the SV-40 monkey virus – the same infamous carcinogenic virus that had contaminated the polio vaccines in the 1950's. But we didn't have the sophistication, in 1963, to isolate just this virus. Cross-infections between species, let along monkeys, was common. The virulent mix of carcinogenic viruses that had been created in the past year contained an unknown number of original and mutated viruses. All that mattered is that it could kill—rapidly. Since I had produced lung cancer in my germ-free mice in a mere week, no wonder Dr. Ochsner, who was running this project, brought me in. The ring included a large colony of identical white mice with red eyes, kept somewhere near David Ferrie's apartment. We called it "the mouse house." Once or twice a week, fifty or more young, live mice were selected, based on the apparent size of their tumors. They arrived in a cardboard carton and were brought upstairs through the back way. Once in Dave's kitchen, they were sacrificed, using ether. The biggest tumors were excised, measured, weighed, recorded, and their cells saved for the cancers they carried. The odor was of death itself. A fan in the window pumped the noxious odor outside.

The biggest, most aggressive tumors had a destiny. We first cut very thin slices from them and examined the slices under a microscope to identify the kind of cancer. Next, slides were made to fix, stain and preserve certain specimens so they could be examined again.

The "finest" live specimens would be macerated, strained, and teased out to obtain cancer cells to send to Dr. Sherman's laboratory. I had been well-prepared for such work at Roswell Park Institute and elsewhere. Besides being virtually untraceable, I had also memorized the formula for the world's most advanced medium in which to grow cancer cells – the precursor of what would become the famous RPMI 1640 medium.

It would best enhance and support these cancer cells' survival *in vitro.* [125] The rest of the biggest tumors were chopped up in the Waring blender and cooled down, prior to being sent to recover the deadly viruses they harbored. The high-voltage radiation source itself was a highly-secret, extremely expensive linear particle accelerator. Only a few existed at this time in the world, and one of them was in New Orleans.[126] Newborn mice, whose immune systems could not resist these powered-up cancer viruses when injected into their bloodstream, were also subjected to high-voltage radiation, to induce mutation *in vivo* as well. These mice were returned to the Mouse House, where those with the fastest-growing tumors were sent to Dave's kitchen lab, to start the whole process over again

. It was an endless loop, with Dr. Mary and others selecting the most vicious of the cancer lines for more work. Precisely what these mutated monkey viruses had become was anybody's guess. But lately, the project became bogged down because the cancers were not transferring successfully back into monkeys. And if they didn't work in monkeys, they probably wouldn't work on humans such as Fidel Castro. David Ferrie was so concerned that he might "catch" something that he had me check the back of his neck, where he had some old, healed boils, and to probe his enlarged thyroid.

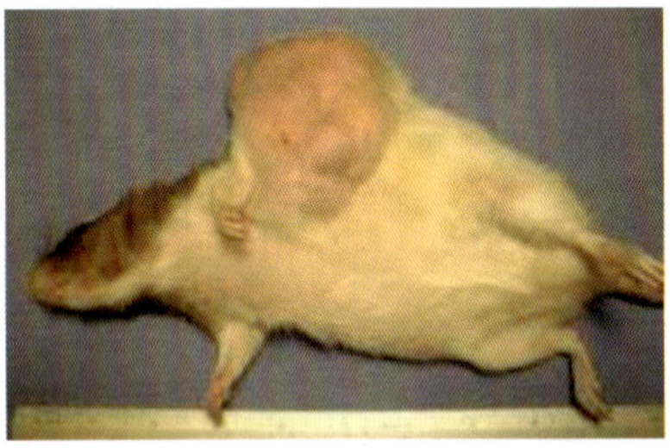

---

[125] Gibco's catalog describes the RPMI 1640 Medium as "... unique from other media because it contains the reducing agent glutathione and high concentrations of vitamins. RPMI 1640 Medium contains biotin, vitamin B_{12}, and PABA, which are not found in Eagle's Minimal Essential Medium or Dulbecco's Modified Eagle Medium. In addition, the vitamins inositol and choline are present in very high concentrations. RPMI 1640 Medium contains no proteins, lipids, or growth factors. Therefore, RPMI 1640 Medium requires supplementation, commonly with 10% Fetal Bovine Serum (FBS). RPMI 1640 Medium uses a sodium bicarbonate buffer system (2.0 g/L), and therefore requires a 5–10% CO_2 environment to maintain physiological pH."

[126] In May, 2020, **Dr. Jack Kruse** of New Orleans revealed that during his training with Dr. John Ochsner, Dr. Alton Ochsner's son, he had seen a linear particle accelerator housed deep in a basement area of Ochsner's Hospital, which surprised him because he knew how expensive they were. Its original location was at the New Orleans U.S. Public Health Center's Contagious Disease Bldg. Witness Hy McEnery, a New Orleans Marine and pastor, photographed the special heavy wiring in the building before it was razed.

He was worried that he might have cancer. His own mother, he said, had cancer.[127]

Another of my tasks was based on my speed-reading. I was assigned to read and digest cutting-edge cancer research, passing on the most promising ideas and information to Drs. Ochsner and Sherman. They would decide which, if any, of my recommendations to implement. To get me started, Dave gave me a foot-high stack of papers. More kept coming on a regular basis from dozens of sources world-wide. I wasn't surprised to see that Ochsner's friends, including Drs. Moore, Grace, and Mirand at Roswell Park, were working on related subjects, and I could guess that Dr. Ochsner's influence was likely a factor.

There were also papers from colleagues at Sloan-Kettering, Baylor, M.D. Anderson, and the University of Chicago, as well as some from the USSR, Germany and Japan. Most of these articles were reprints from recent conferences and journals, but some had not yet been published. It was exciting to be informed of the very latest efforts in cancer research.

Lee also had a part to play, which required him to learn almost every detail of what we were doing. It went beyond finding me a safe apartment, and finding a suitable cover job. Lee was also assigned to learn how to keep the cancer bioweapon alive, so he could take it into Cuba himself, or pass it on to a medical contact who knew enough to handle the bioweapon safely. Nothing could be written: every detail, every procedure, had to be memorized. But Lee had a prodigious memory. There was more involved than that: Lee would also have to get to know the anti-Castro community, in part to help test which medical contacts could be trusted to get the bioweapon to the 'right' doctors in Cuba. That might involve posing as anti-Castro, to ferret them out. Over the years, Dr. Ochsner had trained dozens of young Cuban interns to become fine surgeons. He resented Castro's cutting him out of the picture, for Castro was now sending interns that used to study with Ochsner to the USSR, for what Ochsner called "inferior training." There were plenty of Cuban doctors who resented the cut-off, too, upset that their loved ones were denied the world-class training they had enjoyed, free of charge, at Ochsner's Clinic. Many of them, living in New Orleans, could even visit their families in Cuba over long weekends. But now there were long absences in the USSR, dividing these close families. Some of these doctors were also secretly anti-Castro. To get to Castro medically, one had to know which doctors were which.

---

[127] At this time, I didn't know if Dave's parents were dead, but since he spoke of his mother's suffering from cancer, and her furniture was in his apartment, I believed she must have died fairly recently. Much later I learned Dave had "sent her back to die" according to his younger brother, Parmely. However, Dave had taken his Catholic mom on a trip to Italy. She saw the Pope, which he said thrilled her. Her trip was a cover for his CIA activities. As he was an airline pilot at the time he sent her away, Dave probably couldn't take care of her when she got worse.

Lee would also be working with Guy Banister to identify Castro's spies. With his ties to the Mafia, the CIA was just fine with that. Lee's wife and their daughter, who was just learning to walk, would soon be arriving, so Lee would always be busy night and day. I, too, had most of my evening hours devoured by the speed-reading assignment. Dave and I talked about the schedule and decided on Wednesday, Thursday and Friday afternoons, when the lab work was heaviest. Most of this work cycle was continued on weekends elsewhere, when fewer personnel were present, the weekly cycle ending every Tuesday a.m.[128]

So long as I exited Dave's apartment before he got home from work, I would not run into anybody. Mice would come and go, but since they were all white, with red eyes, nobody would dream they were different batches of mice. Dave said he dreaded having to write reports, so I volunteered to help with that, too. Why not? I had an empty bed every night. Thank God for Susie Hanover's cheery invitations to watch TV with her, and to munch on popcorn, before she fell asleep on her couch!

In fact, Lee took a nap on Dave's couch, tired out after several days of hard work, while Dave briefed me. He woke in time to hear me say I didn't have a TV or radio of my own. "So, what would you like to do today," he asked, "besides make love to me?"

"Gee, that's a hard question!" I replied. "Why would I want to do anything else? How about horseback riding? It's been a year."

"I like horses, too," Lee said. "Let's do it!" Dave told Lee where two different stables were, adding that they were expensive. "Well then, we'll only go riding an hour," Lee told him. "After that, we'll just play chess in the park." He got up and snatched a chessboard from one of Dave's cluttered shelves. "Do you have an extra set of pieces?" he asked Dave. "I have Robert's medieval chess set," I offered. Dave, who didn't want us to leave, said, "They ride the horses into the ground on weekends. Why don't you go in the middle of the week, when they won't be so tired?" Reluctantly, we sat down again. "Do you know why the Queen is the major playing piece in chess?" Dave asked. As I whirred through my brain, which had absorbed everything about chess that the *Encyclopedia Britannica* had said about chess history, before I could reply, Dave went into a long explanation about the Indian and Persian origins of the game. It was this kind of variety in Dave's kit of knowledge that fascinated us. But then, Dave stopped speaking, mid-sentence. "Wait!" he said to Lee. "Chess! That's the key. They're using chess terms in our codes. As if we're in a colossal chess game." Lee raised an eyebrow. "I have to think about that," he said. "In Russia... over there, my keys involved a queen, three cards and an opera's libretto."

---

[128]Dr. Sherman was murdered, researcher Edward T. Haslam determined, early Tuesday morning, July 21, 1964, away from her apartment, though her body was moved there to hide that fact. This would have fit our 1963 cycle for her clandestine work to be finished, then, for the week. A fresh cycle would have begun on Wednesday, with the "product" ready by Saturday for more work.

Lee said he was ordered to memorize an entire opera by Tchaikovsky, in Russian. It was *The Queen of Spades* –Пиковая дама, [*Pikovaya dama*]-- based on a short story by Pushkin. Lee liked the opera very much, but had grown indifferent after having to memorize it for contact purposes. I had never heard of it, so Lee promised to read the original Pushkin short story to me. It was in a little gray book he had, printed in the USSR. I'll never forget that little gray book with the floppy cover: Lee read to me from it on several occasions.[129] We ended up staying the rest of the day and night, spellbound by David Ferrie's vast stores of knowledge, wisdom and experience. The night had scarcely begun when Dave showed us how to fetch his two young Cuban helpers by phone. They arrived within twenty minutes, bringing in a new batch of mice. These boys were poor, and knew little English, but they were diligent and dedicated. Miguel and Carlos also helped with lab cleanup, carrying off mouse carcasses to incinerate, bringing autoclaved, sterile test tubes and flasks, and quickly cleaning up the counters and floors. Usually only one boy came, but this first time, we needed to meet both.

After caging the mice, Dave said, "Watch this demonstration of hypnosis." He gestured towards the boys: within seconds, both collapsed onto the couch in a trancelike state. Dave admitted he took advantage of them sexually when they were hypnotized but insisted that they wanted that relationship long before he ever started any hypnosis. They obviously liked Dave, but I felt uncomfortable, seeing how helpless they looked. Under hypnosis, the older boy, Carlos, went into a snoring sleep, but Miguel was ordered to stand up. He acted as if awake, but he obeyed Dave's order to steal a dollar bill from my purse right in front of me. It was the last dollar I had, so I was anxious to get it back. Dave told Miguel I couldn't see the dollar, and amazingly, the boy behaved as if this was true, denying he had taken a thing while waving the bill up and down in front of me! "He'd walk right off a fifty-story building if I told him to," Dave said. "But people resist bad suggestions unless they're really brainwashed." After the boys left, I declared that weak minds might be hypnotized like that, but not strong ones. Dave laughed, saying it was easier to hypnotize smart people, because 70% of them would agree to turn off the more rational left side of their brain...

---

[129] MARY FERRELL AND THE GRAY BOOK. In the presence of witness Debbee Reynolds (not the movie star), my sister, and others, including [at a later date] Jim Marrs [who questioned Ferrell in her retirement apartment], while we helped her pack to move from her Holland Ave. address, I mentioned the little gray book. Ferrell, astonished, strictly questioned me. She had seen the book when she and husband Buck visited Ruth Paine at New Year's some years earlier. Paine had brought forth the book, saying "the police missed this one" in their searches for Lee's possessions. I had described the little gray book of Pushkin's works exactly, down to its size and its floppy gray cover. An attempt by trolls to say I had only described a book in U of SW LA's library fell failed when that book was found to have a RED cover. Ferrell knew I had a personal connection to Lee Oswald through that book. She told Jim Marrs the same thing.

... they'd allow their right brain to take control, making hypnosis easier. Dave then asked permission to hypnotize us, with interesting results. He worked awhile with Lee but failed to get him to cooperate. Finally, in frustration, he griped, "Why don't you trust me?" Lee laughed, reminding Dave that perhaps he still had some deep inner fears of Dave, so he would always resist hypnosis from him. Besides, Lee said, he had been trained to resist all forms of hypnosis and mind control before his defection. The ONI had reacted vigorously to Korean and CIA mind control methods with its own collection of unique resistance methods. Dave countered by saying Lee's imagination was deficient, and that's why he wasn't 'going under,' but I disagreed. I had been reading a science fiction story, "Her Way" that Lee had been writing at my apartment. It clearly displayed creativity and imagination. I then offered to let Dave try to hypnotize me. "Go ahead, Captain," I told him, seating myself on a chair before him. "Have fun."

What Dave didn't know is that my sister Lynda and I had practiced hypnosis on each other during the time we used it for pain control when doing our acrobatics acts for charity. Since then, I'd learned every trick in the book to resist being hypnotized. For some minutes, Dave struggled to take me down. Once he thought I was under his control, he ordered me to do a few absurd tasks, such as to rub the top of my head. I complied, keeping a blank face. "See?" Dave told Lee. "Women's minds are more flexible, they are more receptive to suggestions, because they are more verbally oriented. Now watch this," Dave said, "and don't jump on me when I do it."

"Be nice to her!" Lee said, uneasily, when Dave brought out a large hatpin. "I only wish to demonstrate that, in this state, she can feel no pain," Dave assured him. "J—" Dave said to me gently, "I am going to stick this needle into your arm, but you will damned well not feel it. Hold out your left arm, please." Oh, brother! I extended my left arm and Dave pushed the hatpin into my flesh, as if he were giving me an injection. Having been jabbed a thousand times during my long stays in the hospital, I had learned to tolerate the pain of needles. I didn't move.

"See?" Dave said triumphantly. "Why don't they use this for childbirth? Think how this could help women... Do not move," he told me. Taking up a Polaroid camera, Dave snapped a photo of the thing in my arm.

But I'd had enough. As soon as he lowered the camera, I said, "I thought you weren't going to use 'damn' in my presence anymore!" With that, I pulled out the hat pin and rubbed the sore spot on my arm. "Damn!" Dave repeated, oblivious to the irony of his word choice. As Lee realized what I had done, he began to smile. "Why be so violent?" I complained, finding some alcohol and a wad of cotton. "You didn't even swab my arm first. I could get tetanus from that old thing." I explained that I not only had prior experience resisting hypnosis, I'd gone through weeks of round-the-clock intravenous feedings, penicillin shots, cortisone shots, blood tests and spinal taps, so I'd learned to ignore the pain of needles long ago.

"But if you'd tickled me with a feather, I wouldn't have been able to keep a straight face!" I told him.

Lee then recounted his own horrific hospital experience from his early childhood, when he endured an operation to remove part of a bone. The mastoid process is a part of the skull that juts down behind each ear. It can get painfully infected if an ear infection becomes severe. Infections in bones are extremely painful, and in the 1940's, operations to cut away the rotting part of the bone resulted in incredible, unremitting pain for days, really more than any five-year-old could be expected to handle.

Lee still could remember the agony. Such experiences stay with children and help them understand pain and suffering in ways others cannot. Perhaps that's why both Lee and I could burst into tears if we saw a person or animal in great pain. Dave was defeated. His attempts to hypnotize us had failed. Trying to regain some of his former stature, Dave said he wanted to show us something special, and brought out a black light. This was a welcome sight to me, because germicidal lamps can kill cancer viruses. Of course, Dave would have one. He invited us to follow him into his messy bathroom.[130] He closed the door, turned off the light, and switched on the ultraviolet lamp. There we saw the germs, mold, and microscopic flora and fauna thriving in Dave's dirty bathroom, all of it splashing to life in hideous swatches of fluorescent yellow and orange.

"I can get any hospital closed down," Dave crowed, "just take a black light and go in with the sanitation inspectors. They use the same bucket of dirty water over and over, and just spread the germs around." I was horrified to see rivers of dried yellow urine, flowing in, over and around the toilet, with splotches of orange bacteria covering the toilet seat. "You think this is bad?" Dave said defensively. "You should see what a public toilet seat looks like. They think Howard Hughes is nuts. Why?"

Dave paused. "It's because he takes Kleenex everywhere he goes, to handle doorknobs. Because he knows what regular light won't show you. He saw all this stuff with a black light."

We immediately resolved never to sit on David Ferrie's toilet seat again. Dave continued to expound on the benefits of ultraviolet light in the germicidal spectral zone, explaining it could kill anthrax, flu, tuberculosis and even the black mold that plagued cruise ships and houses that had flooded. "People don't know how to kill black mold," he said. In Louisiana, he added, people died from it. "But if they kill that stuff with mineral spirits or acetone," he advised, "then follow up with a germicidal lamp like this one, it won't come back. I use this lamp to kill whatever crud the mice are bringing in here," he told us.[131]"I do have my housekeeping standards, you know." Lee and I looked at each other and smiled. Heck, we never noticed any!

---

[130] I can affirm the credibility of any witness claiming he/she was often in David Ferrie's apartment in 1963, if they can describe what he kept in his bathtub.

[131] I am paraphrasing some of Dave's words for more readability here.

We returned to the dining table and Dave brought out a variety of things for us to view under the black light. He presented a fossil horse tooth, seashells, rock samples such as fluorite and uranium, and three rings. One, an aquamarine, had belonged to his mother. He also had a small ruby ring that glowed purple under the light, which prompted Lee to remark that he, too, had a ring with a ruby in it, which we later tested under the ultraviolet light to see if it was a real ruby. The third ring had an ugly mythological creature carved into it that reminded me of a griffin. "This is my **priestly ring**," Dave told us. "I use it for black magic. And satanic rituals." "Are you serious?" I asked, taking up the ring. It was heavy. "Of course not," Dave replied. "When I say a Mass – and sometimes I do – it isn't a Black Mass. I'm not a son of Satan, so I wouldn't wear that thing." But he said he had to wear it to be accepted in certain groups.

A "Griffin" ring similar to David Ferrie's.

"I love God," he went on, "but I use things like this to penetrate religious cults... with that ring on, they think I'm one of them." Dave said he knew about every religion on earth and had witnessed the rites of Voodoo and Santeria. In fact, his interest in hypnotism came from observing religious oddities like speaking in tongues (glossolalia). Saying rosaries, he added, also created a hypnotic effect, so he would gladly say a rosary with a suffering Catholic friend to help them cope. When the CIA came to Dr. Robert Heath of Tulane for mind control ideas, he sent them to Dave, since he had investigated Voodoo and zombies. Under the influence of drugs, these people became slaves without a will. "I became a consultant," he said. "At first it was about Voodoo drugs. After they went to Haiti about that, then it was about hypnosis." Dave had continued his relationship with Dr. Heath, famous for mind-controlling animals and humans with implanted electrodes in their brains. He had often provided Heath with homeless and mentally-disturbed persons nobody would miss, for experiments. The CIA even had Dave get a "doctorate in psychology" from an Italian university (diploma mill). Next, Dave brought out a large, olive-colored metal file box. At the same time, he declared that if we ever heard that he had committed suicide, not to believe it, as he was a Catholic. When I told him I felt the same way, even though I was an atheist, Lee remarked that the right to commit suicide should be an individual decision. Dave argued back that a passing mood should not dictate one's final decisions. Waiting out your depression was superior to giving in to suicide's one-way street. "I've saved people's lives by diverting their crazy impulses!" he insisted. He had forgotten all about the box.

"What's in the box?" I asked. After extracting a promise from us never to reveal its contents while he was alive, he opened it. There was his will, some letters, photographs, some postcards and booklets from England with churches on them, and under all that, a fat brown file, wrapped with a black cord knotted in front. Dave pulled out the file and opened it. From my position, it was upside-down. The pages were held at the top with fold-over spindles going through two holes. All the pages were stamped and signed. These were MK-Ultra files. With the files was a report, also stamped and signed, that Dave pointed out proudly.

266 DICK RUSSELL

He was also on the faculty at Tulane, in Heath's department, and he got his appointment at the hospital through Dr. Heath."[128]

A paper co-authored by Heath, Silva, and a few others, and published in *Comprehensive Psychiatry 1960*, was titled: "Comparative Effects of the Administration of taraxein, d-LSD, Mescaline, and Psilocybin to Human Volunteers." The introduction stated, "The patient donors are housed in a special Tulane University Research Unit at the East Louisiana State Hospital, Jackson."[129] The experiments were supported by a grant from the Commonwealth Fund, later identified as having also been a CIA front.

In 1999, the CIA released a memorandum generated more than twenty years earlier. It pertained to "Recent Discovery of Project ZR/ALERT Documents—A Study of the Use of Psychological Programming for Intelligence Purposes." Project ZR/ALERT, according to the memo, concerned "exploration and experimentation by the CI Staff of the use of hypnotism in certain operational situations." CI referred to Counterintelligence, the Agency branch run by James Angleton.

Dick Russell shows Tulane's Dr. Heath, Silva, etc. using the East LA State Hospital in Jackson for experiments on prisoners, as did Dr. Alton Ochsner.

His name was not on the report – just a coded number. [132] But it was his. Besides files on drugs used in Voodoo, a second batch of involved the hypnosis of cadets. That occurred when Dave was a Commander with the Civil Air Patrol. He did it for the CIA, he said. Dave had sent some of his most devoted cadets into such a deep state of hypnosis that they could feel no pain. He said this ability could help wounded soldiers, for example. All Medics in battlefields should know the techniques, he declared. He said his "dissertation" for his quickie doctorate covered up his important work for the CIA. "What a crock!" he snorted. "My real work was logging responses of the size of the pupil in our hypnosis experiments." He added that the size of the pupil could tell a lot about what a person was really thinking and would even indicate if they were really hypnotized. "I shouldn't have told you to close your eyes so much," Dave said to me. "I should have looked at your pupil sizes."

"Why didn't you do that, Dave?" Lee asked. Dave frowned. "I find myself avoiding looking directly into people's eyes much anymore."

---

[132]

[128] Dr. Victor Weiss: Author's telephone interview, December 13, 1994.

[129] LSD experiments: *Comprehensive Psychiatry*: Volume 1, pp. 370–76, 1960, "Comparative Effects of the Administration of taraxein, d-LSD, Mescaline, and Psilocybin to Human Volunteers" by F. Silva, M.D., R.G. Heath, M.D., et al.

[130] ZR/ALERT: CIA "Memorandum for: General Counsel, Attention: Emile L. Julian," May 17, 1978 (www.maryferrell.org/mffweb/archive/viewer/showDoc.do?docid=26123&relPageID=2).

Dick Russell Ref.

He tapped the bald crown of his head, where ony a few hairs remained, here and there (he'd removed his wig, as he did every night.). "Ever since all my hair fell out." Dave's mood suddenly changed with this admission. He abruptly closed the box and took it back to his room. Then he got himself a beer. Despite the late hour, he said he had more to tell us about mind control and the many experiments the CIA conducted on our own American citizens. "They say the program is shut down now," Dave said, "but that's not so. It just has a different name. These things never die. It's an iron-clad law that it takes more energy to stop a government program than to start one. This one's self-perpetuating." I sat down at the piano and started to play as the two men talked and drank beer. Lee had been down some mind-twisting avenues himself: he had been taught passive non-resistance based on Quaker philosophies, to resist giving out information. He had also been put through harsh, severe training to test his ability to withstand incredible pressures. He was prepared for capture and torture when he entered Russia. Visions of what Tony Lopez-Fresquet had told me came before my eyes. Lee took big risks when he 'defected. The Soviets were aware that he'd been stationed at Atsugi, home of the U-2 spy plane. The U2 was often sent over Soviet territory. The Soviets also knew of the existence of a CIA training center at Atsugi, hidden among the bunkers.

Obviously, despite his youth, they would suspect Lee of being a spy. So how did he manage to survive? Lee saved that for when we were alone. When Dave went to the bathroom, Lee showed me his beer can. "See how much I drank?" he said, smiling. "I saw how you looked at me," he went on. "You were thinking of your father. Beer doesn't taste half bad, you know. But I rarely actually drink it. As I told you, I gave the stuff up." The can was almost full. I never would have guessed! Then Lee told me how he got himself thrown into the brig by pouring beer over a Marine sergeant's head. He said the act was necessary to prove he 'hated' the Marines. Lee said he believed his odds of leaving Russia alive were 50/50. And, if he did make it out, his own CIA boss – named "Jesus"[133] – might arrest him. "He'd wonder how I'd survived," Lee said. "Maybe wonder if I became a traitor." Lee said he had therefore carefully planned everything to prove he hadn't turned. By now, Lee and I were both tired and needed to sleep, but Dave said he had one more piece of instruction to give us. David Lewis, he explained, had been recruited to help Lee in identifying potential spies sent from Cuba by Castro. We should, therefore, cultivate a social friendship with David Lewis and his wife, Anna, so Lee and David could meet without Jack Martin.

[133] James Jesus Angleton was chief of CIA Counterintelligence from 1954 to 1975. He was paranoid about possible 'moles' and traitors working for him.

"Go on some dates with them, you two," Dave told us. "Lewis doesn't know you guys are married to other people." Lewis had agreed to this and would be paid for his services. He frequently worked on a temporary basis at Trailways, but now his hours there would be expanded. He would acquire information about Cubans arriving from Mexico on Trailways buses, the cheaper of the two bus lines coming up from Laredo. "Infiltrators like to pose as just another poor refugee seeking asylum," Dave explained, "so they tend to take the cheaper bus." The real refugees brought their suitcases crammed full, but those who intended to return to Cuba often came with half-empty suitcases that they'd fill with banned American goods. "Car parts, American cigarettes, you name it," Dave said. "That's how they make money behind the blockade. These guys are mostly harmless, but some could be pro-Castro spies who don't mind doing a little smuggling on the side." David Lewis would get names from tags and tickets and provide general descriptions of Cubans he discovered with underweight luggage, something Customs was also interested in. On some mornings, Lee would be expected to meet with Customs officers and the FBI's SAC, Warren de Brueys, to relay this information, which David Lewis couldn't do directly without being tracked back to the bus station. In 2017, more extensive files were released about bar owner and FBI informant **Orestes Pena** who observed that Lee had frequent breakfast meetings with both deBrueys and Customs officers near the Customs Building. The courageous Pena endured threats from de Brueys and a beating for speaking up. "By the way," Dave told us, "Marcello will also be getting some of that information. Marcello takes care of some of these characters himself, for his good friend Santos Trafficante." He quickly added that Marcello rarely killed these people. He preferred to return them to Cuba in disgrace. One method was to have a cooperative police officer plant drugs on the suspicious Cuban, arrest him for drug possession, jail him a while, beat him up, and then deport him. As for himself, Dave had strict instructions. "If anybody asks you if I have anything to do with anti-Castro matters anymore, the answer is always 'no.' You can say I help out the FBI from time to time. That's okay. But to my boys and everyone else, I'm just a sex fiend, a drinking buddy, and a pilot. Let's keep it that way. As far as my friends know, these mice are the same white mice, day in, day out, for some nutty project of my own."

Orestes Pena

Dave said he wasn't going to have any more parties for a few months, so nobody would be dropping by. Second, his new roommate would be here a few weekends, but when college classes ended, he would "go home to mama." As for Robert, Dave said that if he ever showed up again, he was nt to know a thing. "Robert's sure to return," I said bitterly. "he'll show up because he can't go without his 'lovin' too long." In disbelief, I told them that Robert still had not written!

"I could have been dead and buried by now, or locked up in jail!" I told them. "But this time," I told them, "if he won't let me have any rest, I'm going to dump a bag of ice cubes on the hottest part of his anatomy. Maybe then he'll cool off so we can actually talk!" They both laughed.

Lee took me home shortly before dawn. Susie's collie dog barked a few times when he did, and Susie had to hush her. When I realized we had wakened her, I felt sorry and apologized. But Susie explained that she always got up early, to feed her husband before he went off to his boat. Lee and I sat at her kitchen table as she served us a breakfast of ham and eggs, biscuits and fresh-squeezed orange juice. Lee closed his eyes as he finished, leaning back and smiling happily. He was in heaven. Susie beamed. "I have nobody to cook for anymore," she said, adding that her children rarely came to her. Instead, she went to them on Sundays. She looked forward to school letting out so her great-grandchildren could come and spend time with her. She intended to teach them arts and crafts, which impelled Lee to remind her that she had taught him how to make potholders once, in a class she had taught at a church. That inspired Susie to bring out a pot-protector made from bottlecaps crocheted together. Lee and I felt so much "at home" with Susie! "I'm glad to rent to a girl," Susie said. "The last two were men, and they didn't pay me."

"If this girl doesn't pay, let me know," Lee quipped. "I'll send a hitman over."

"Very funny!" I replied. "I see you need another beating!"

"I see you're never going to find out if Adam and Eve got away!"

"Whatever in the world is that about?" Susie asked, so we told her about the science fiction story and the ending that Lee knew. By now it was dawn, and we were exhausted. "I wonder if Robert sent a letter at last," I mumbled, as Susie and Lee guided me to my bed, where I collapsed, too tired to undress. "I'm leaving now," I heard Lee tell Susie, "but I might be back. I'm going to try to intercept the mail at Mrs. Webber's place around 10:00. If he wrote, it will ease her mind."

"Why don't you just stay, Lee?" Susie suggested. "You can sleep on my couch until it's time to check the mail." [134] Lee admitted it would be good to sleep a little, and headed for Susie's couch. I was drifting off. Almost asleep, I noticed that Susie was taking off my shoes. "Can I do the dishes for you?" I offered in a dreamy voice. "Goodness, no, child," she answered. "Sleep now!"

"Do you know why we were out so late, Susie?" I asked her. Susie paused. "I learned a long time ago not to ask what my husband did to get along with people here," she finally answered. "This isn't about Carlos Marcello and his people," I told her, aware that somebody from

---

[134] Both Claudia Rodick and her older sister, Vicki Rodick Frame, remembered the pot-holder made with bottle caps. In *Me & Lee* I erroneously described them as grandchildren instead of great-grandchildren.

the Marcello's had sent the loop of sausage and the cheese.

"Lee is a very brave man... trying to help our country. He is working for our government... but because he is also connected to Marcello through his uncle Dutz, he can go places and find out things regular agents can't."

"Oh! I hope you don't get hurt!" Susie said.

"I'm not out there risking my neck like Lee is..." I mumbled. "I just do lab stuff. But I sure owe a lot to him, for finding this lovely place. And I owe a lot to you." I gave her hand a squeeze. "Thanks for letting me stay here."

"You can stay as long as you want," Susie answered. She leaned down and kissed the top of my head. "Now go to sleep, honey," she whispered. "I'll wake Lee when it's time."

Chapter Twelve
Sparky

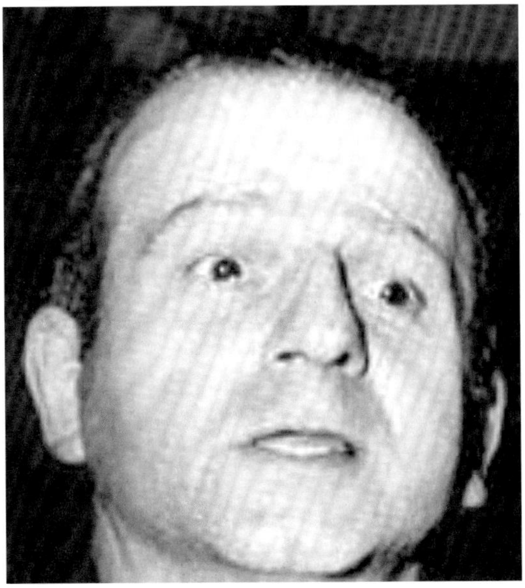

Monday, May 6, 1963

The next morning, I heard a tap-tap-tap on the window. It was becoming familiar. Lee was there, standing on the front porch with a big smile on his face, holding flower-pots full of blooming begonias. I let him in. "Good morning, Juduffki!" he said cheerily.

"I decided you needed these." He went to the small side window in my bedroom, which opened to the blank wall of the neighbor's house. "This will help brighten things up," he said, putting the plants on the windowsill. Then he stepped back to admire the pink and red blossoms. "They're beautiful, Lee." He smiled, then said, "I also brought you a radio," opening a sack and removing a little transistor radio. After he showed me which stations played which types of music, I asked him if Robert had written. "Go get ready," he said, avoiding my question. "We have to go to the employment agency." I looked at the clock. It was almost eleven. I quickly put on my red plaid dress.[135]

[135] For people who wonder how I could remember such a detail, I see the past in pictures

Lee said I looked nice, but advised that I should take some casual clothes, too, which I put into his sack. "Did you see if Robert sent a letter?" I asked again. Lee replied that there was still nothing. So much for 'love'! As we began to board the Magazine Bus, I told Lee, "I don't understand it. He wrote every day the two weeks we were separated last summer."

"He's on a boat. Maybe the mail is delayed," Lee said soothingly. "Let's go sit in the back," he added. "Why?" I asked. "See all the Negroes?" he said softly. "They are required to sit in the back of the bus. I don't want to sit up front, when they can't."[136] Lee hadn't mentioned this before, since the buses we previously used had been almost empty, but the Magazine Bus always had a lot of riders early mornings, around noon, and when the workday ended. From then on, when we rode this bus, we made a point of sitting in the rear with the Negroes. In time, people began to save us a seat. We had the privilege of making our own little statement in racially tense NOLA. I consider Lee Oswald the most devoted anti-racist I've ever known, and here he was a native son of New Orleans.

Afternoon – Monday, May 6, 1963 When Lee finally came for me, he said we would have to put off horseback riding because we'd been invited to meet some important guests at Dave's. I was wearing slacks, but Lee said I was dressed well enough and didn't need to change. We made it to the Fairgrounds before they closed and got to watch the horses exercise on the track. Then we were allowed into the stables after Lee spoke a few magic words. "Sure, we can come in here," Lee told me. "You can guess who really owns the racetracks." Yes, I could.

Lee said that as a kid, sometimes when he skipped school, he would visit these stables to pet the horses. Lee had picked up a handful of sugar cubes in the coffee lounge, which we fed to the horses. Then he showed me the grave of the legendary horse, Black Gold. He was the most famous horse from New Orleans, and his heroic story put a lump in my throat. After winning the Kentucky Derby in 1924, he was put out to stud. Proven to be infertile, he was thrown back into racing, even though badly out of shape. Even so, he fought to win so hard that even in his last race, breaking his leg in the homestretch, he kept on running on three legs before collapsing just over the finish line. He was put to sleep right there on the track and buried at the infield near the 16th post. As a horse-lover who read the story of his courage in childhood, just to stand there was a privilege. Then we headed toward Dave's.

"We practically live in this place!" I told Lee, as we again climbed the steep stairs up the back way. When I said we should have eaten something first, knowing what was in Dave's refrigerator, Lee smiled.

---

136 A new law stated that blacks (called Negroes in 1963) could not be forced to sit in the rear of buses in New Orleans, but that didn't change the reality.

"Worry not," he said. "Tonight, we get to eat in a fancy restaurant." He didn't know which one, but we were sure to like it, because the people paying the tab had expensive tastes. As we entered Dave's living room, we saw him sitting quietly in a chair, wearing priest's vestments and praying in Latin from a breviary – a black prayer book used by priests and monks. When he finished, he stood up and walked to the table to pick up the hideous griffin-like ring he had shown us the other night. As he did so, I told him, "I thought you didn't wear that ring."

"Oh, I had to wear it yesterday," he said. "And I'll be wearing it tonight for special reasons, but I took it off to say Mass. It's sacrilegious to wear it during Mass..." When I raised my eyebrows at the thought of Dave saying any kind of Mass, he told me stiffly, "I said a Mass this afternoon for my parents. They were so proud to offer a son up to God. The least I can do is pray for them." He walked slowly into his room, holding his breviary against his chest, his religious robes flowing gently as he walked. –*What a tragedy!* -- I thought. Never had I seen such a strange, sad, solitary figure.

I did not know for sure if his parents were alive or dead, but I could see how Dave was moved by his memories of them. Dave soon emerged wearing regular clothes, looking quite presentable in a dark shirt with a tie, his full wig firmly in place (not always the case). As he went about straightening up the place for the expected guests, we told him about visiting the stables and Black Gold's grave. He agreed that Black Gold was a noble animal who deserved that kind of respect. This led to a conversation about animals and pets, ending up by my telling Lee and Dave about the first dog I knew, who lived to be ten years old. We called him Sparky. He was a clever fellow who knew many tricks. He often rode on my mother's motorcycle, and he would follow me everywhere. But he had one problem: bladder control! In the middle of the night, I had the job to let Sparky out to relieve himself, and Sparky was determined to make sure I'd do just that, or he'd squat down on top of me in bed, and pee! The consequences were "Vary" wet! When I was 8 years old, I was one of the 'stars' at our Parochial School for my writing abilities, the nuns having selected me and two other little girls to read essays we'd written to a big parent-teacher audience. Seeing how bored everyone was with the first two essays the other little girls read, which were about autumn leaves and mushrooms, I decided to spice things up with a story I'd written about Sparky, instead. It ended with, "When Sparky was angry at me, he just couldn't control himself. And so, tonight in the dark, a nasty odor hit my nostrils. I could feel the hot wetness soaking into my blanket, and jumped up. *Sparky had done it again*!" There was a gasp from the audience. The nuns turned pale. My parents shrank in their seats. I will refrain from saying what my parents had to say later! Dave and Lee laughed at the story, agreeing it was a 'keeper.' Then Dave looked at his watch. Informed that "special guests" were about to arrive, I went into Dave's bathroom to check my hair.

When I returned, I could see that Lee and Dave had conspired to play some kind of joke on me. "We've decided to tell you more about one of our illustrious visitors," Lee said. "We have to!" Dave broke in. "He's got the same name as your dog, Sparky." "He's another dog who can't control himself!" Lee said, grinning. "And he knows how to train the ladies, too!" Dave rejoined.

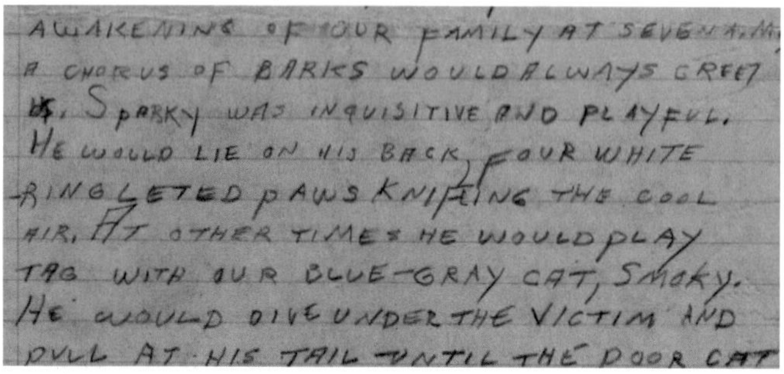
AWAKENING OF OUR FAMILY AT SEVEN A.M.
A CHORUS OF BARKS WOULD ALWAYS GREET
US. SPARKY WAS INQUISITIVE AND PLAYFUL.
HE WOULD LIE ON HIS BACK, FOUR WHITE
RINGLETED PAWS KNIFING THE COOL
AIR. AT OTHER TIMES HE WOULD PLAY
TAG WITH OUR BLUE-GRAY CAT, SMOKY.
HE WOULD DIVE UNDER THE VICTIM AND
PULL AT HIS TAIL UNTIL THE DOOR CAT

A story I wrote as a child about 'Sparky,' my dog, led to a case of mistaken identity about Jack Ruby that would last for decades.

They both broke into laughter. I had no idea what they were talking about, but at least, Dave was no longer gloomy. Dave continued his modest efforts to clean up his apartment, even bringing out a vacuum cleaner, which was a surprise. Who guessed he had one? He said Jackass Martin had demanded to know what David Lewis was up to, and accusing Dave of betraying him, after all they'd gone through together. "We didn't *go through* anything together!" Dave said. "It's all in his head. He needs to go back and get more shock treatments."

"He had shock treatments?" I asked. "Doesn't it show?" Dave snapped, putting away the vacuum. "He hasn't been *through* anything. Not like some people... as they do have ways to make you talk, without leaving a mark."

"Cattle prods," Lee said. Flashbacks to what the police did to Negro civil rights protesters came to mind, and I shuddered.

"Or 'they' put a wet suit on you," Dave said. "Tie you up, cover your eyes, ears and mouth with tape, and suspend you in a tub of warm water. The lights are off, you can't see a thing. There's no sound, no way to know you're up or down. Total sensory deprivation. Days seem to go by, even though it's only about 24 hours. Suddenly, you're lowered underwater. Water rushes in your nose. You're drowning. They pull you out and give you artificial respiration, and then you're cleaned up, dressed, and returned to your prison cell. Not a mark on you. Then they threaten you with another day in the tub, and you always talk. If you finally contract pneumonia and die, it gets listed as death by natural causes." *What horror, that human beings could do this to each other!* I felt weak and sick to my stomach. Lee said, "The Russians interrogated me. That's when I dropped out of sight. They made me stand for a couple of days. If I moved, they hit me."

"Stop it!" I burst out. I fell to the couch and started to weep. "What's the matter with people?" I stammered through my tears. "Why did they do that to you?"

"Honey, I'm sorry," Lee said, seating himself beside me and stroking my hair. He shook his head. "I didn't mean to be so graphic. It's just that people don't know what happens to political prisoners. People are no more humane today than in past centuries. They just hide it better. If it's any consolation, my personal discomfort didn't last too long," Lee said, wiping my eyes with his handkerchief. "I pretended not to know a single word of Russian. I acted so entirely stupid that the Russians finally gave up. They concluded that I was an idiot... because of all the Communist quotes I gave them, they decided I really was just a harmless kid steeped in Marxism. They even apologized for hurting me. After I promised not to say anything about it, I got a nice apartment. They knew they could trust me." [137]

"How did they know that?" I asked. "They told me I could be treated very badly upon my return to the United States," Lee said, "if I mentioned being interrogated. The Feds would want to know if I had caved in and had become a turncoat. Of course, I didn't tell. And I urge you never to speak of it."

"Well, I won't," I agreed. Dave brought in a little dish of cheese and crackers, along with some beer nuts and candy, and put it on the coffee table, which he had cleared of its medicine bottles, matches and cigarette packages. But neither Lee nor I were in the mood to eat after these sobering revelations. Instead, I leaned against him and closed my eyes. I could feel his heart beating in his chest. As we talked more about his Russian experience, Lee confided that he had learned first-hand that people are the same everywhere. It was the power structures under which the Russians and Americans had to live that made them adversaries. He felt there was hope for America, however. Before coming to New Orleans, he had been ordered to stand in the heart of Dallas with a sign around his neck proclaiming, "Viva Castro." He got away with it. True, a red Squad might have shown up and could have beaten him, or he might have been arrested and seriously maltreated. But it didn't happen.

"In Russia, had I worn a "Viva Kennedy" sign around my neck, I would have gone to prison," Lee assured me. "But of course," he went on, "the sign was just a ploy."

"Just as you're going to do again," I commented. "here in New Orleans."

"Have you ever read ***The Scarlet Pimpernel?***" Lee asked suddenly.

"Baroness Orczy's books?" I asked.

---

137 The Russians always denied any such allegations, but I believed Lee, because he never exaggerated anything and he even excused the Russians for behaving that way. It was their duty to try to break him, he said.

"Then you have!" he said, quite pleased. I assured him I loved books by Hungarians, because of my Hungarian heritage. "Sir Percival Blakeny! He fooled the French spies so brilliantly. I love Percy. An incredible man."[138]

"I was The Scarlet Pimpernel!" Lee said proudly. "And I still play 'the demmed fool,' just as Percy did."

"You've been *playing* Sir Percy?"

"Yes. I present myself as a worthless fool. If necessary, even stupid. He is my model."

"So this goes beyond job interviews? You let people think you're stupid?" I saw Lee flush. A hard knot of pride tightened in his jaw. "When I must," he said, avoiding my eyes. "... I pretended I couldn't shoot... and I also 'accidentally' shot myself in the arm to prove my incompetence."[139] Lee rolled up his sleeve, revealing a thin scar, along with a depression, in the bony part of his left elbow. I hadn't noticed it before because it was hard to see with his arm straight. "As you know, I'm actually a good shot," Lee boasted. "Shooting cardboard ducks at Pontchartrain Beach doesn't count," I countered. "I can get us some revolvers," Lee said.

"We'll go shoot at real birds, if you'd like."

"I'd love to!"

"You would?" Lee looked surprised.

"Sure," I told him, "just so long as we don't kill anything."

Lee groaned. "I knew it was too good to be true."

"If you're starving, go ahead and kill them," I said. "Otherwise, why take them out of somebody else's mouth?" Those were the right words to say to a man from Louisiana, where poor country folks hunted deer, wild pigs, ducks and alligators for their meat. Otherwise, there would only be cornbread and greens. Lee was raised in a state where squirrel and possum were often in the slow-cooked stew on the back burner.

Dave came over, asking if we wanted something to drink, but we declined. I noticed Dave was practicing some shadow-boxing moves. He was letting off tension, as we waited for his important guests to show up. "Do you know martial arts?" I asked. Dave and Lee smiled at each other. "We both do," Lee said. "So do I!" I stupidly announced.

"Oh, really?" Dave said. "Come here..." I jumped up and boldly stood before him, using one of the stances I'd been taught by one of my UF boyfriends. Though I knew enough karate for self-protection on the

---

[138] Australian blogger Greg Parker claimed that since Lee didn't mention the *movie* in the book, that when I later said Lee admired Leslie Howard, who played the main role, and that he had seen the movie while in the Marines, that I made it up. When I later saw an alias listed for Lee as "Leslie" I thought *wow! Lee used one of his hero's names*! Parker showed I was wrong, acting as if he had made a huge discovery. "Dr." Parker (who is no such thing) has diagnosed me as a "fantast" and Lee as having Aspergers. He runs an employment agency, I've been told.

[139] Lee used an advanced vocabulary. His brother Robert and others heard it. I heard it.

streets, Dave had no trouble flipping me to the floor after only a couple of feints. "I know more than you do," Dave said softly and menacingly.

"You sure do," I agreed. "No need to convince me further!" I returned to the couch with my pride hurt and my fanny sore. But I was still interested in learning more about Lee's acting the part of The Scarlet Pimpernel. He was using the role in real life. Sir Percy had composed a poem to tease the French spies, which he delivered up in his everyday disguise as a rich, useless, vain and stupid fop: *They seek him here... They seek him there...Those Frenchies seek him everywhere ... Is he in Heaven, or is he in Hell? That demmed, elusive Pimpernel?*

"Did you ever rescue anybody?" I asked. "I believe so," he replied. I didn't realize at the time that Lee understated his exploits. I didn't press for details. I should have! Instead, I focused on his role-playing. "Sir Percival Blakeney, Baronet," I mused. "Pretended he knew no French, when he was a master of the language. He concealed his powers. Nobody guessed."

"I was determined to rescue my own aristocrats from Madame Guillotine," he went on, "but so far, I haven't found many to rescue."

"Is there a book you haven't read?" I asked. "Of course!" he replied. "But just give me some time!" I then asked Lee to offer some better translations of some technical phrases I had come across in one of the Russian cancer research papers I'd been given, for Lee had learned many such terms from his Russian-speaking friends in Minsk, where he had been sent to work. His best friends were brilliant students in science, physics and technology – no dummies.

Lee with a student, Anatoly, being recorded by his friend Ernst Titovets, who became a medical Dr. with a PhD in brain chemistry

As we worked on the Russian phrases, we heard Dave, who had been bouncing out to the porch every five minutes, suddenly announce, "Hot damn! Here they come! That's Marcello's car!" I expected to see a stretch limo pulling up, but instead, I got a glimpse of an ordinary two-tone Chevy sedan as it entered Dave's driveway and disappeared behind the building. "That is the Godfather's car?" I said in disbelief. "Little Man is a wise man," Dave said. "Remember, to the Feds, he's just a poor tomato company guy. But he comes up with the goods when he needs to show off." Dave fluffed up a chair cushion. "He knows how to go all out. Chauffeur, bitches to serve drinks in the limo, the whole fucking crock of shit."

"Clean up the English, Dave," Lee said, putting his arm around me.

"Oops," said the man who, an hour earlier, had impressed me with his show of piety. Dave and Lee then hurried down the back stairs.

When they returned, there was only one man with them. He was the same height as Lee and Dave. "J—" Dave said, "I would like you to meet Mr. Sparky Rubenstein. A man who definitely reminds us of your dog."

My mother in a motorcycle outfit, with Sparky

"He's asking for a brass knuckle sandwich," Sparky said, smiling. "Happy to make your acquaintance." Standing before me was a well-built, well-dressed man whose face beamed with friendliness and self-confidence. He kissed my hand. "So, how do you like New Orleans?" he asked, in a mid-western accent that I recognized was from the Chicago area. I gave him a polite answer, then asked if he was from Chicago, and how did he like life in Louisiana. "It's been a while since I lived in Chicago," he answered, taking off his hat and setting it on the table. "You guessed that part right. But I'm from Texas now. Excuse me, I have to get something from the car." At this time, I had no idea that the man introduced to me was **Jack Ruby**! All three men would keep that little joke to themselves. As Sparky left the room, followed by Dave, I commented to Lee, "He's going bald."

"So am I," Lee replied. "I've read that the more testosterone a man has, the more chance he'll go bald," I said soothingly. "I guess you must be oozing with testosterone."

"Naturally."

"Is this guy allowed to know about the lab?" I queried.

"He brings money to help finance it," Lee said. "What happened to everybody else who was supposed to come?" I asked. Just then, Sparky returned, carrying a steel barbell with blue weights. I saw how strong he was. Behind him came Dave, puffing along with more. Sparky was carrying twice the weight but wasn't out of breath. "I can't use these things up here, Sparky," Dave protested. "It'll crack the ceiling under us if I drop it--" as he started coughing. "Let's put them on the porch, then," Sparky said, as Dave continued to cough. "You gotta stop the smoking, Dave," Sparky counseled. "You gotta pass your physical every year. How you gonna do that, smoking like you do and eating the junk you eat?"

Dave scowled. "I take vitamins," he said lamely. "Are you using the blender I gave you to make carrot juice?"

"He's using it to liquify cancerous tumors," I piped up helpfully. "The stuff in the refrigerator that looks like carrot juice and cherries is actually chopped up mouse tumors. Just a warning."

Sparky's eyes traversed my body quickly, as he smiled. "You look pretty strong yourself," he commented. "Nicely-developed arms and legs, and other stuff," he added.

"I was in an acrobatic act with my sister," I replied. "Back flips, cartwheels, hand-stands, all that stuff," I offered. "Can you show me something?" Sparky replied. I had my slacks on, so I stood on my hands and then completed a flip, landing on my feet. "That's pretty good," Sparky said. "You're in good shape."

"Thank you," I said. "It looks like you're in good shape, yourself."

"I am!" Sparky said proudly. "I can do handstands, too. I'll show you." Sparky took off his suit jacket and tossed it on the couch. Then he stood on his hands, raising his legs high into the air, with his tie hanging down. He then began walking around the room on his hands, with his feet curved over his head. There was no doubt that he was in splendid condition. Then he balanced himself on just one hand: "Dave, bet you can't do this." As he did so, the contents of his pockets cascaded out of his pants. Coins, keys, brass knuckles, business cards, an address book, and a large roll of money secured by a rubber band fell to the floor. Sparky's face turned red as he came down hard. As he sat there, Lee said, "By the way, remember that place you recommended for girls new in town?"

"What place?" Sparky asked, as he reloaded his pockets.

"Over on St. Charles, near Carrollton. The place where you said young girls and couples were always welcome."

"O God! That was a joke, Lee! You didn't take me seriously?'

"Yes, I did," Lee said, folding his arms. "And J, here, was kicked out of the place when they raided it Friday night."

"You're kidding!" Sparky laughed as he sat down on the couch next to me and Lee. "They raided it?"

"They all went downtown, except J," Lee said. "But she lost her thirty dollars for the room. Landlady refused to give it back. Same for her food."

"I'll speak to her," Sparky said, with an edge of menace to his voice. It raised goosebumps on my arms. He pulled out the roll of bills from his hip pocket, peeled off a fifty, and handed it to me. "Here, baby," he said. "That'll take care of the thirty dollars. I'm really sorry." I'd lived so many days on the edge of being completely broke that the fifty-dollar bill seemed like a reprieve from Hell. "Now I can pay Susie," I said.

"No, don't do that," Lee cautioned. "How would you explain that to Robert? You'll have to wait for a Reily paycheck or move over to Brent House at Ochsner's. Talk to Dr. O first."

"I thought you understood my jokes by now, Lee," Sparky mused. "You've known me long enough." Turning to me, Sparky said, "I've known Lee ever since he was a little boy."

When he was first sent in from Chicago, he'd gone to parties hosted by Marcello that Lee's mother, aunt and uncle had attended in both New Orleans and Dallas. He remembered Lee playing with the other children at these get-togethers, and over a period of years got to know Dutz Murret, especially when they talked about boxing. When Lee and his mother moved to Fort Worth, Lee's uncle asked Sparky to keep an eye on the boy, saying Marcello also liked him, since Lee, as a kid, had worked for Marcello's people as a gopher. "Watch over my boy, Lee," Dutz Murret had told him. "Those jobs for Marcello ..." Lee said, opening my purse and putting the fifty-dollar bill inside, "I couldn't use any of them for job references."

Sparky said he had tried to interest Lee in working for Marcello before he joined the Marines, at a time when the Godfather was expanding his influence in Dallas. Marcello now dominated Joe Civello, Sparky's business partner, who "once ran the show" in Dallas but wisely chose to "cooperate" rather than disappear in a swamp somewhere. Instead, Lee disappointed the Mob by joining the Marines, just as his older brother Robert had done. Then Dave added that he kept his promise to Lee, recommending him to the ONI for intelligence training. "I did it because he knows how to keep his mouth shut," Dave said. Concerned that Dave spoke so freely about Lee's real identity, I shot a frown in Dave's direction. "It's okay, J-," Dave said. "Sparky cares about Lee like a son. And he's a patriot, like Ochsner. The arms of the government have been wrapped around Lady Cosa Nostra in this dance for a long time, now."

"My goal was always the Marines," Lee said. "Either the world can be an influence on you, or you can be an influence on the world," he repeated. "I chose to serve my country." Dave laughed bitterly. "Are you still so naïve?" he asked. "I'm under no delusions," Lee said stoutly. "I choose to serve, anyway."

"Leave him alone!" Sparky snapped at Dave. He turned to Lee and said sincerely, "I'm glad somebody still cares about this damned country." Dave apologized, to soothe Sparky, then asked him, "How did you get that car?"

"Well, I flew in for a change," Sparky said. "Sammy met me at the airport. I can keep it for the night."

"Where is everybody else?" I asked.

"They should be here any minute," Sparky replied. Sure enough, a few minutes later, a cab dropped off three men in front of Dave's house. Sparky and Dave went down to greet them, while Lee and I watched from the porch. As the men talked, Lee began pointing out who they were. "That's Mr. Gaudet, who writes propaganda for the CIA," Lee said. "Ochsner pays him to write an anti-communist magazine that's sent Latin America...That dark one's Sergio Smith – **Sergio Arcacha Smith**. He flew in from Dallas, or maybe Houston... Used to be a big shot here with Dave in the anti-Castro movement, before they both got kicked out

Sergio Arcacha-Smith, Cuban exile

for misconduct." Even from the porch I could see that Sergio Smith looked like my father, with his mustache, hairline and face almost a copy of my dad. "Is his last name really Smith?" I asked. It was.

The third man was a heavyset Mexican Lee didn't know. [140] By now, Dave had come puffing back up the stairs to invite us to come eat with everybody. "As for you, J—" Dave warned, "act like a bimbo and they'll never suspect there's gray matter between your ears."

"O, wow!" I said, as we reached the car, that held five. "I get to sit in the Godfather's car! I get to put my little rear end down on the same upholstery that the Godfather does!"

"You little doodle-head," Lee said affectionately, "I don't think so." He was right. "Darn!" I complained, for the only place left to sit happened to be in Lee's lap. "Actually, I'm rather glad that your little rear end has nowhere else to go," Lee said, making everybody in the car laugh.

"She's an acrobat!" Sparky put in. "She knows martial arts, too!" Dave said, and everybody laughed again, as we headed to the French Quarter, with Sparky driving and Dave following on his motorcycle. When the men started talking, I knew to keep quiet and play the Dumb Broad card. Lee was silent, too, contributing nothing to their conversation. The men discussed their business as if we weren't even there. I considered how Lee was playing his Scarlet Pimpernel role: obscure, unnoticed. When we reached Antoine's on Rue St. Louis in the French Quarter, Marcello's car was recognized at once. We given the best table and instant service. Entering Antoine's was like entering a lavish movie set for *Gone with the Wind.* It was timeless and classy. Waiters in tuxedos came and went, the chandeliers blazed like diamonds on fire, and romantic music played in the background. The table, cloaked in white linen, was soon decked with red wine and an assortment of splendid hors d'oeuvres, along with Oysters Rockefeller.

Eyebrows were raised when I ordered a Roy Rogers instead of wine, so Lee, observing that, ordered the same grenadine-coke combination, which the others thought was cute. The food was fabulous, from the crab cakes, seafood gumbo, *Chair de crabs au gratin* and *Filet Toronado* (crowned with Bernaise sauce), to a bread pudding sprinkled with roasted pecans and impregnated with plump raisins in a buttery rum sauce, placed atop a cushion of luscious custard.

---

[140]"Arcacha" Smith, a Cuban exile, was the former NOLA delegate to Frenca Revolutionario, and established the Cuban Liberation Front, also being active in Miami, Tampa and Houston until 1962. He introduced David Ferrie to prominent anti-Castroites, and possibly to Guy Banister. He had an office only recently vacated at 544 Camp Street, the same address Lee stamped on some of his pro-Castro, FPCC flyers in August. In 1963, he moved to Dallas, becoming friends with extremists Gen. Edwin Walker and oilman H. L. Hunt.

At one point, Dave Ferrie mentioned that his planes were being repaired, and that one of them, his Taylorcraft, would soon be airworthy again. Then he offered Lee some free flying lessons. As the only woman at the table, the men were very polite and gracious until near the end, when they became tipsy. Then it was time to meet Clay Shaw. Marcello's car was brought to us immediately, and we took a short drive over to

1313 Dauphine, where Shaw, a close friend of Dr. Ochsner, lived. The second most important man at the International Trade Mart, he had invited everybody over for more drinks. That was a concern, because only Lee and I were now sober. After parking down the street, the six of us began walking toward Shaw's house. I was told it had a beautiful garden, but everything was hidden behind a tall wall. Shaw had overseen all the renovations himself, rescuing yet another important old building from demolition. He was famous for it. I hoped to meet Shaw, but just as we reached the big door, which a servant opened to reveal the garden, which had a big fountain, Lee pulled me back. "These men have been drinking," he warned me. "Listen to how they're talking before you decide to go in there." Lee was right. I had been too lost in the romance of strolling down an exotic street, Lee at my side, while these men were now making crude homosexual jokes and laughing as they pulled their zippers up and down.

When Lee told Dave that I should meet Mr. Shaw some other time, Sparky, who overheard it, threw Lee the keys to Marcello's car. "Have a good time!" he said. "Just come back by midnight and wait for us in the car. Besides, she'll finally get a chance to sit on the upholstery."

We decided to walk instead, and spent some time strolling through the French Quarter. We listened to music at the Old Preservation Hall and explored some of the shops still open. Finally, after enjoying chocolate cokes, we began walking back to Dauphine Street. It was now quite late. The street was dark and deserted. Not a soul could be seen. As we walked along, I thought how, if I'd been alone, I'd be frightened. Lee remarked how late it was, and that we should head for the car.

That's when a big man suddenly jumped out of the shadows. Holding a knife at Lee's throat, he snarled, "Your wallet! Hand it over!" We froze. Our assailant was a formidable blonde fellow wearing a sailor's suit. He was surely six feet tall, weighing about 250 pounds, with big, throbbing veins in his neck. He had obviously hyped himself up to do this, and Lee wasn't going to argue with him. Lee slowly reached into his back pocket.

"I want your purse, too, girlie!" the sailor said, waving his knife my way. *"Hurry up!"* Lee then moved slightly in front of me. "You don't want her purse," he said. "Shut up!" the robber snapped, as Lee slowly offered his wallet at about the sailor's belt level. As he did, a switchblade suddenly sprang out from underneath Lee's wallet, its silver blade gleaming. Furious at the sight of the blade, the sailor growled, "Throw that damned wallet on the ground, or I'll cut your face!" -- moving his knife toward Lee's head. "You may cut my face," Lee said, in slow, icy words, *"but not before I get your balls."* With that, Lee made a vicious jab at the man's crotch.

The sailor jumped back and turned, cursing Lee as he ran. Lee immediately grabbed me by the hand, and we sprinted to the car. When Lee unlocked it, we all but threw ourselves inside, Lee locking the door behind us. We sat in the stillness, out of breath, our hearts pounding from adrenalin. The dead silence in the car was calming and comforting. I even forgot it was Marcello's car. It could have been a popsicle truck. Then Lee stuck the key in the ignition and started the engine. "We should get out of here in a hurry," he said, "just in case he comes back with a friend."

"You saved us!" I told Lee, throwing my arms around him in gratitude. I took his head in my hands and began kissing him all over, grateful for what he had done. He flushed with embarrassment. Then I noticed that he was trembling from head to foot. "You're shaking!" I said, grabbing his hands, which were cold. I held them in my own warm hands.

"It's a reaction, because I was afraid," Lee said. "It will pass."

After a minute, he stopped shaking and relaxed. "You're not a coward if you feel afraid," he said. "Everyone feels afraid when confronted with danger. You are a coward only if you don't overcome your fear when necessary." And then Lee kissed me for real, in a way we realized was dangerous. We looked at each other in silence; then Lee drove me home. It was midnight. He left in silence, returning Marcello's car to Sparky.

Clay Shaw and Dr. Alton Ochsner

Chapter 13 Charity

Tuesday, May 7, 1963

This was the day we would finally meet with Dr. Ochsner. "Don't pretty up for Ochsner," Lee advised, when he came, seeing what I was wearing. "We'll be seeing him at Charity."

Charity Hospital was where the poor went to get free medical treatment. Realizing I shouldn't stand out, I changed into some very plain clothes. As I did, Lee started looking at my portfolio of drawings.

Then he found my collection of short stories. By the time I was ready, Lee had finished reading one of my science fiction stories called 'Hospital Zone,'[141]probably inspired by our upcoming trip to Charity Hospital.

"This is good," he said, adding softly, "I want to be a writer."

"I think you'd be a good one, too," I told him sincerely, having read his first draft of "Her Way," a science fiction story he had been writing. I told him Robert had wanted to become a writer, but all my science talk derailed him. Now he was out on a quarter-boat somewhere, setting out explosives for seismic tests for an oil company. "Well, you're influencing me to become a writer," Lee replied. "So now, it's even."

When Lee used Susie's phone to call Ochsner's Clinic to find out when we were to come, he learned that we might have to wait a while, as Ochsner's schedule was tight today. Therefore, I packed up the chess set and a board to take along. Ochsner's schedule was always tight.

After finishing lung, heart and other surgeries early each morning, he would make rounds with his interns-in-training, instructing them as he visited his many patients. Then he might grab a bite before driving to Charity Hospital, usually arriving by 2:30 p.m. There, he donated precious time about twice a week to help the desperately poor, offering free surgery and treatments. He invited some volunteers to his clinic, with its superior hospital facilities and world-class medical care, if they wouldn't mind being used as guinea pigs for one of his latest ideas. I was impressed with Ochsner's drive and dedication. Ochsner was a dynamo of energy.

Sometimes he spent a weekend in a Latin American country, medically treating a dictator. He also flew to Washington about every other weekend.

There, he conferred with Surgeons General in the Army and Navy. Sometimes he rode in a plane supplied by the military, to undisclosed places. En route, he'd work on one of his research papers or read medical journals. Duties in Washington (or elsewhere) finished, Ochsner would often fly back, sleeping on the plane, and go t into a morning of surgery straight from the airport, only pausing to change into his scrub suit. That same week might find him treating a dignitary in Venezuela, or at an international medical conference. Or perhaps he would take off a few days to meet oil tycoons at the Koon Kreek Klub. He was known at the Dallas Petroleum Club with Bush, Hunt, Byrd and Murchison, and would play cards or go hunting at one of their ranches. Once he was given a tugboat. Another time, it was a racetrack. The late Sid Richardson, Clint Murchison Sr. and Jr, and H. L. Hunt all gave generously to his Clinic. They also seemed to take turns giving Ochsner one or two new Cadillacs every year for his trouble.

Ochsner also co-founded INCA –The Information Council of the Americas. He was its President. *He* was also elected President of the

---

[141] "Hospital Zone," written in 1963, was published along with others of my science fiction stories in my book ***Letters to the Cyborgs***, by Trine Day.

Cordell Hull Foundation, which brought in Latino medical students to Ochsner's Hospital. Ochsner also hosted International Trade Mart events as the CEO of "IH" --International House, which later merged with Trade Marts worldwide.

P. 156-57: *Surgeon of the South,* Ochsner's official biography, mentions some of Ochsner's many anti-Kennedy contacts.

was raising money. Later, Peter Watzek, ill with a kidney ailment, hastened to New Orleans. Edgar Burns, a leading authority on the ailment, performed successful surgery. Watzek told Ochsner, "If you hadn't walked into my office, I'd probably be dead today."[16]

Ochsner had sought the advice of Samuel Zemurray, president of the United Fruit Company, in the effort to work out a deal with Touro and Tulane, and when the fund-raising drive was begun he approached another wealthy New Orleanian, Edgar B. Stern, whose wife, Edith Rosenwald, was a daughter of one of the owners of Sears, Roebuck and Company. "I was very fond of Edgar and Edith," Ochsner explained. "I went to him, and he listened and said, 'I'll give $100,000.' I told him I almost had not gone to him because Touro also was in the middle of a fund-raising campaign and I thought there may be a conflict. 'Oh, we're going to give money to Touro,' Stern said, 'and I don't mind telling you it's only $25,000.'" Ochsner was flabbergasted. "Then Edgar said the reason is that Touro is just another hospital. This is a different institution." The Sterns subsequently contributed another $100,000 to Ochsner.[17]

From the oil millionaire William G. Helis, Jr., a personal friend, Ochsner

15. Alton Ochsner, address, Ochsner Foundation Fellows, August 14, 1971.
16. AO Recollection, Benefactors.
17. Ochsner, address, Ochsner Foundation Fellows, August 14, 1971.

For several years he enjoyed dealings with a set of Texas nabobs that went beyond the everyday doctor-patient relationships. Clint W. Murchison, Sid Richardson, and Richardson's nephew, Perry R. Bass, came to the Clinic for checkups and treatment. Murchison and Richardson periodically invited Ochsner to join them in outings at their ranches or hunting and fishing preserves.

Ochsner was recommended to the Texans by David Lide, a Dallas businessman who had been a surgery patient.[19] In 1956 Murchison became ill during a stay on his island in the Bahamas, and he stopped off in New Orleans on his way home to Texas. He developed a liking for Ochsner and for A. Seldon ("Sam") Mann, the internist who was assigned to treat him. Afterward Murchison frequently sent his airplane to pick up Ochsner and Mann and take them to his ranch in Texas or the one in Mexico or to the Koon Kreek Klub, a fishing hangout for wealthy Texans. On one excursion Bass asked Ochsner and Mann to go with him to Fort Worth to see Richardson, who was ill. They persuaded Richardson to fly with them to New Orleans for treatment, and another friendship developed. Sometimes Richardson invited Ochsner to go quail hunting on his island in the Gulf of Mexico.[20]

18. AO Recollection, Friends.
19. AO Recollection, Patients.

And even though he detested President John F. Kennedy, he was in charge of Kennedy's visit in 1962 to dedicate the Dumaine Wharf in New Orleans (see Appendix). At that time, Ochsner obtained confidential medical information about JFK. Ochsner's International House was a safe venue where the CIA could contact and interview important players in international business, trade and politics. It was a hive of CIA-sponsored activities. Shaw and Ochsner had worked together for some nine years at IH.

Then they had to split when Ochsner obtained access to a LINAC—a linear particle accelerator—which may originally have been brought in to fight cancer, but which was now aimed at producing it. "The Project" began March 23, 1962, the same day as the news article on Fabry reported the break between Ochsner and Shaw. [142] Of course, The Project had an official name, but we were not privy to that information. Except for publicizing that doctors should use their talents in The Cold War, Ochsner usually projected himself as the kind, genial doctor everybody loved. On weekdays, Ochsner hardly missed a surgery. And when he could, on weekends Ochsner took his turn at night duty for emergency operations, the same as any other surgeon on his staff.

---

[142] I was able to find the news article because Lee said it had been published on Robert's birthday.

FABRY IS NAMED AS IH DIRECTOR

Takes International House Post April 1

Paul A. Fabry, Delaware public relations counsel, has been appointed executive director of International House.

Dr. Alton Ochsner, IH president, said Fabry will assume his duties April 1.

The executive director post was held for 15 years by Charles Nutter who resigned last June. Since that time Clay Shaw, managing director of International Trade Mart, has been serving as IH acting managing director.

Fabry has been associated with the E. I. duPont de Nemours Company of Wilmington since 1956 as a specialist in international public relations.

PAUL A. FABRY

From 1950 to 1951 he was connected with Radio Free Europe, heading one of its information divisions in New York and serving as editor of the monthly, News From Behind the Iron Curtain. Before returning to the United States in 1949 he was a foreign correspondent and lecturer in Istanbul, Turkey.

He has traveled widely and speaks fluently French, German and Hungarian, besides having a knowledge of Spanish, Italian and Turkish.

Dr. Ochsner said Thursday: "We are delighted to have been able to secure the services of Mr. Fabry whose background and experience will permit us to carry on the programs of our organization." He added that he is confident that the new appointee will carry out IH's various forward-looking projects.

A native of Budapest, Fabry ...

He leased his free Cadillacs to International House to benefit his Clinic, taking none of that money for himself. The Cadillacs were used to transport important trade officials and dignitaries, who were often encouraged to donate to Ochsner's Clinic as well

Concerning donations, Lee and I discussed what to do about Sparky's 'donation.' As I began to tell Lee that Robert had still not contacted me, I lost control and burst into tears. Lee soon learned that I had begun to cry myself to sleep at night. After making a few calls on Susie's phone, Lee suggested that we should go into town early on the Magazine Bus. After getting off the bus, we walked a few blocks, then stopped in front of a modest storefront.

The neighborhood was still okay, but I could see we were on the edge of an impoverished area where artists, schools, musicians and rundown buildings seemed to mingle.

The storefront said, "Rev. James Novelty Shop", with a smaller sign reading "Novelty and Religious Items." The address was 545 South Rampart. At that time, if you turned your back to the window and looked carefully, you could see Reily's main building way down on Magazine Street. The shop was known locally as "Reverend Jim's." The window displayed souvenirs, Christian religious items, Bibles and items for Mardi Gras. Rev. Jim's also had a connection to a warehouse nearby. There, grotesque and beautiful figures and animals, used on Mardi Gras floats and parades, were both housed and being manufactured. They sprayed liquid *papier mache'* over newspaper-covered armatures made of chicken wire, then smoothed over the outside with *papier mache'* paste. Shiny alligators ten feet tall, carousel horses, dragons, dinosaurs and devils filled a Wonderland that Alice would recognize. Inside the store, every kind of souvenir item was on sale.

Mardi Gras masks, jewelry, African drums, Indian headdresses, voodoo items, and amazing wigs festooned the walls, amidst pictures of The Good- Shepherd and Jesus Praying in the Garden of Gethsemane. Beyond a display of Bibles and religious tracts, and past the cash register to the right, was a table where several people were hard at work hand-lettering souvenirs with "New Orleans." This was an informal charitable effort, under an unusual industry in the Big Easy – a charitable outreach creating work for itinerary artists, musicians and job-seekers who needed a little emergency money to get by. Most of these were black musicians, but Lee was a "photographer" and I was an artist, and we had no problem fitting in.

The lady in charge was a member of Reverend James's charity and was an artist. She welcomed Lee and me and showed us around. We signed a paper saying we had financial need, read a Bible tract, and then signed a little card to carry that was our personal promise to stay sober and drug-free. Then we were seated at the table with tiny brushes and tiny little bottles of enamel paint. We started painting 'New Orleans' over and over, on maracas, ceramic alligators, and salt-and-pepper sets. But soon, Lee was told to stop. He had painted, in a very neat hand, 'Wen Orleans" on several pieces, which had to be repainted.[143] We were then sent to the *papier mache* warehouse, where we were taught how to

spray-paint some trolls and dragons, and then to give them bright red lips and scary eyes. We also painted some dwarves and carousel horses. Then, realizing we could be late for Charity Hospital, we claimed our reward. [144] Between us, we had earned five dollars and change! "I told you to trust me!" Lee said, as we emerged, blinking, into the bright sunlight.

But after a few steps, Lee popped inside a 'colored' news office nearby, saying he had to talk to somebody there, and to keep on walking toward Reily's. In a few minutes, he was back. "I have to go to Banister's right away," he told me. "You do know Banister is a raging racist, right?" Lee said he'd called the Clinic again; Ochsner was running late. I wondered who had the busier schedule—Ochsner, or Lee? We reached Banister's building, and fortunately, if anyone noticed, I was wearing the kind of plain, simple clothes that Lee's Russian wife, Marina, might have worn. If anyone came by, I was to speak Russian.

---

[143] Lee's Aunt Lillian Murret said Lee had tried to get work doing lettering at a full-time job, but he told her he failed their try-out. However, Lee was reporting his "job hunt" outcomes to his aunt so she would think, when he was hired at Reily's, that it was the result of a job hunt, not pre-arranged. It's possible that someone at that lettering business told Lee to get some experience first, at Reverend James.

[144] The shop was at the edge of a rough neighborhood near a school for black kids only.

Mainly, I should sit down and wait at the 544 Camp Street entrance. It was safe to do so.

Hardly anybody ever went upstairs there now. About a year ago, Lee said, 544 had been busy. It had been a center for anti-Castro activity, which could start up again at any time. Lee then went to Banister's office. From where I sat, I could see people coming and going from Mancuso's next door. The doors on the Camp Street side were both propped open to catch the breeze, so I could see into part of Mancuso's Coffee Shop down the hall, where I got a glimpse of David Lewis, sitting with somebody whose voice sounded like Jack Martin's. As David got up to leave, he spotted me and came over. He invited me and Lee to join him and Anna, his wife, at Thompson's Restaurant sometime soon. It wasn't far from here to Thompson's, he added. This was a pre-arranged invitation, but I sensed Jack Martin would see it as spontaneous. David said he was grateful that he had more income now, due to more hours working at the Trailways Bus Station, and so would be able to take his wife Anna on dates. Would Lee and I like to come along, to walk and talk and enjoy the French Quarter with him and Anna? I told David that sounded fine, and I would give Lee the message.

As I waited, I saw several Cubans crossing on the Lafayette side to Banister's office, followed a few minutes later by David Ferrie, who waved. "I'm late!" he shouted. "Talk to you later!" That would have 'blown' my 'cover' as the Russian-speaking 'Marina,' but luckily, nobody heard him. When Lee returned, we walked to St. Charles, boarded the streetcar and headed uptown. "Is this the way to Charity Hospital?" I asked. "No," said Lee. "Our meeting with Ochsner has been called off. He's in emergency surgery. We'll have to see him tomorrow."

We then checked the Mansion's mailbox to see if a letter from Robert was in the afternoon mail. Lee reminded me that by now, Sparky would have spoken to nasty Mrs. Webber and she wouldn't dare intercept any of his letters. Seeing my sadness, Lee said he knew exactly where to take me next—to nearby Palmer Park. It was a quiet, pleasant place with lots of benches. There we could play chess, unobserved. Besides, he said, across from the park was a nice little place called 'Lee's Coffee Shop.' I soon learned that Lee loved to take me every place he could that had the name 'Lee' in it! Lee's served a mixture of good Chinese and American food. We could get there right off the streetcar, yet it was out of the way. We would eat there half-a-dozen times. This first time, after playing a game of chess we didn't finish, we went across the street and was served by a nice lady whose young teenage son always came there after school. That young teen was "Mac" McCullough. Over the next months, we kept running into each other.

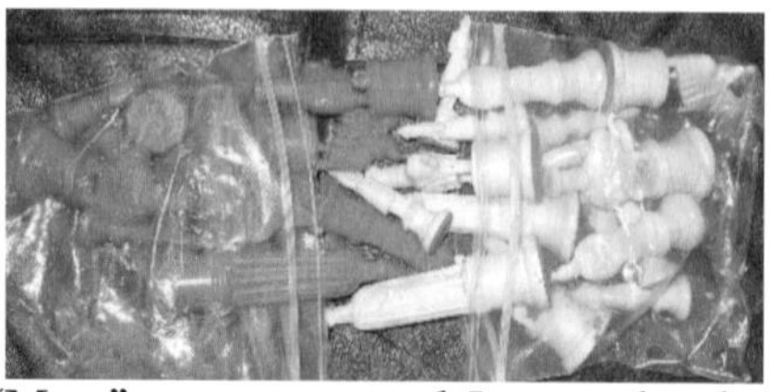

My children learned to play chess on the same set

'Mac" saw me and Lee at both Palmer Park playing chess and at Lee's

Coffee Shop, where his mom worked. Later, after school let out, "Mac" kept running into us. That's because he began singing and playing the piano as a young prodigy at nightclubs owned or run by Carlos Marcello. Mac recorded these matters on three different tapes after we met again,

many years later, in Lafayette, LA at Mel's Diner. We amazed each other when we recognized each other's faces! Mac also permitted me to publish his photograph. Mac even saw Lee being filmed on Canal Street by Hugh Ward (only a few people knew that). Mac worked for the Marcellos and the Marinos for years.

William "Mac" McCullough and I finally met again, while waiting under the eaves at Mel's Diner for a heavy rain to stop, in Lafayette, LA.

<u>Wednesday, May 8, 1963</u> I made breakfast for Susie, me and Lee this morning, serving *palascinta*--Hungarian crepes, rolled up Sopron style, filled with apricot, strawberry and raspberry preserves and topped with whipped cream, the way my grandma taught me. We ended up discussing the Hungarian Revolution. Just as I had, Lee had listened on short-wave radio to the desperate Hungarians begging for U.S. aid. It is a fact that the U.S. and CIA had encouraged the revolution, but never intended, despite their promises, to risk war by intervening. Many brave Hungarian rebels were killed for their misplaced trust in U.S. policies.

Lee had a sister-in-law who was born to Hungarian immigrants (I learned this a lot later) which may explain why he was interested in learning some of the language.

We shared the same childhood joy at reading Kate Seredy's *'The Good Master,'* – about a young, rebellious girl sent to live on a Hungarian ranch – and then began talking about other books that impressed us as children. One such book was what Lee called his 'Little Red Book – ***This Is the Christmas***. It had nothing to do with Mao's Communist book: that was just Lee's little joke. This book offered a rare Serbian folktale that introduced six-year-old Lee to racial prejudice and injustice. Briefly, it was a sad tale about a small, blind, abandoned gypsy boy.

Rescued as an infant, he was only allowed to live in a shed with the sheep. His dark skin meant he was of the detested race of Romi (*Cigani*), so he was completely ignored. He subsisted as a shepherd but was not even allowed to eat meals with anybody in the village. Nor was he allowed to attend church, when everyone dressed up and went joyously to Mass. He was left out of everything because he was *Cigani.* A 'cursed,' dark-skinned Gypsy. Shunned and alone, he could hear Midnight Mass, with its wonderful music and singing, but was not allowed in the church. Christmas was the worst of all. He wanted so much to welcome the Christ child into the world, with everyone else! In the end, as the little blind boy, broken-hearted, was once again left alone on Christmas Eve, the Christ Child personally visited him in his lonely shed, shaming the entire village and opening their eyes as to how wrong they had been.

As a young teen, Lee remembered the book and found it again in the library. At that time, Lee said he 'defaced' it by circling, marking or crossing out various passages that had angered him.[145]

Since there was still time to finish our chess game, we moved to Susie's couch to do battle, and Lee won: I had forgotten my strategy by then, but Lee had been musing over it in his head and beat me. About then, Suzi Collie began barking, which meant the postman had come. As Suzi went tearing after the postman, Susie brought me a letter. After five long days of not knowing where he was, or if he was ok, I had word from Robert. The postmark showed he sent it the day before, so it took just one day for his letter to reach me from "Pip's place"—a beer and bait house somewhere on the Louisiana coastline. Robert's letter touchingly revealed that he didn't care what my Catholic parents might think of our elopement: *"...we'll have to live with each other, not with them,"* he wrote, *"so let's tend to ourselves, our own happiness. If they wanted us, it would be different. I knew who my mother-in-law and father-in-law would be before I married you, so let me take the responsibility for it."*

This manliness on Robert's part made feelings of love surge through me, but his next words reminded me how very much I was on my own: *"I hope you haven't given up writing stories. Coarse as it may sound, take advantage of my absence. I will be back as sure as the sun will rise. Meanwhile you have a life to live without me, a secondary life, but a life not dead. There are three of us now, you, me and Us. It's too late to write anymore now. The mail leaves early in the morning. I love you, I love you, I love you. Robert."*

"I feel so guilty," I told Lee, in Susie's presence. "Is it possible to be in love with two men at the same time?" Ever since Lee had rescued us from that crazy robber-sailor and our sudden, extravagant kiss, I found

---

[145] In 2016, I located the book, which was on a bottom shelf in a neglected Christmas section of the Dallas Library. I was able to purchase the little red book for a $25 donation. It is one of my most precious treasures!

myself swimming in desire for him. For that reason, I'd not so much as touched his hand today.

A wall had come between us: we both felt it. If that wall broke down, we would not be ready for the consequences. I'd already told Susie plenty this morning about all that Lee had done for me, and about his miserable marriage and my unhappy state. She had just one piece of advice: "Follow your heart," she said. "In your heart, you already know the answers to all your questions, honey."

Lee had been looking closely at the letter and envelope, and now he told us that the letter had been dated before the call I made to Evangeline Seismic, asking them to give Robert my address. However, the address on the envelope to me was the correct one. "It would have been nice if he would have asked 'What happened? Why did you move?' or 'Are you okay?'" Lee observed.

Then Susie pointed out other peculiarities. "He didn't ask for your phone number," she huffed. "And he didn't say when he'll be back." Astonished, I went through the letter again, which began with, *'My darling Judyth'* and then described the Quarter-boat, the work routine, and then the situation with my parents. Susie was right. There was no mention of how to reach him, no request for a phone number, and not a word on when he might return. "Good Lord, girl," Susie said. "You were only married three days when he wrote this. You're supposed to be his sweetheart."

"He is adjusting himself to his new surroundings," Lee offered.

"Poppycock!" Susie said, taking back the letter. "If he had time to write the new address on the envelope, he had time to ask questions."

"He'll ask soon enough," I predicted. "Sure he will," Susie agreed. "When he wants to get back between the covers with you. As for me, I hope he stays out there all year. I don't want to meet him."

"Neither do I," said Lee. "Darn!" I told him. "And here I was going to use you to make him jealous!"

"I'm afraid I would punch him in the nose," Lee replied.

"Well, so much for you two being buddies," I said. "Scratch that one." Lee then said he had more work to do for Banister and left. I went into my room and started speed-reading through the rest of the medical journals and papers Dave Ferrie had given me. As I read, another part of my brain was working on the Robert problem. I couldn't even send a letter in reply because I didn't know if Robert picked up mail at that address or not.

Dr. Sherman still had not bothered to contact me, David W. Ferrie was definitely too strange to trust much, and Dr. Ochsner seemed oceans away, he was so busy. Susie was too elderly to burden with much, and now I knew I couldn't count on Robert. So much had happened in the five days he was gone! Throughout all these thoughts, one crimson thread stood out: Lee's steady and reliable presence, his courageous mastery of the most dreadful situations, and his obvious affection. But I'd stupidly married Robert for some pretty pink birth control pills!

Lee returned in the afternoon. At last, we were on our way to see Dr. Ochsner!

I carried a stack of medical journals and unpublished papers I'd marked up, in a big canvas bag, to show Dr. O. We took the Magazine bus, planning to transfer at Canal St. to another bus. Once again, we sat in the back with the 'Negroes,' in support of their cause. In the back corner there, a heavy-set black woman wearing a simple cotton dress sat slumped over. Her eyes were closed and she swayed from side to side as the bus lumbered along. Her arms were wrapped around a thick paper bag in her lap. We noticed a heavy odor around her. The other passengers noticed it, too, and quietly moved away from her. Then Lee nudged me with his elbow and used his eyes to point down to the woman's feet. There was blood pooling around her shoes, dripping down from her legs.

Lee, who sat just one seat from her, tapped her on the arm. She opened her eyes and gave him a weary look full of pain. I saw that her face was bathed in sweat. "Ma'am," Lee said. "We're on our way to a hospital. We would be happy to help you see a doctor there." The woman shook her head and looked away without replying. I wondered if it was because Lee was a white man, and she was embarrassed about the blood. Perhaps she was en route to a doctor herself and would soon get off the bus, so we waited as she leaned heavily again to one side, still clutching the thick paper sack. But she rode all the way to Canal St, where we had to get off through the back door. As the woman slowly forced herself to stand and shuffled toward the door, Lee placed himself behind her as she began going down the steps, leaving a trail of blood behind her. Then, as she took the last step, her blood-soaked shoes slipped and down she went, onto her hands and knees, dropping the bag as she fell. The dark bottom of the paper bag ripped open, and a small stillborn baby and placenta spilled out. Somebody screamed at the sight. Lee immediately sprang into action, hailing a cab. As I knelt down to help the woman, she desperately tried to scoop her dead baby back into the torn sack. "Billy! Billy!" she cried. Between sobs, she mumbled that her husband was a sailor who was out to sea, that her mother and daughter were both at work, and she was all alone. The doctor she called said to bring the baby and the placenta to the hospital, but she was feverish and disoriented. "We're taking you to **Charity Hospital**," I told her gently.

Blood was now splotching the sidewalk to the extent that the cab driver, when he pulled up, refused to let the woman into his taxi. But while Lee told the driver bluntly that if he did not help this woman, she could die, I dumped my pile of journals and research papers across the passenger seat and helped the woman into the cab. At this point, he had no choice. Fortunately, we hit the traffic lights the right way and soon arrived at the emergency entrance. The cabbie then jumped from the cab and raced inside. He soon brought out a wheelchair, followed by an ER medic. By then I had transferred the paper bag and the dead baby into my canvas bag, after which the cabbie and Lee maneuvered the woman into the wheelchair.

I placed the canvas bag in her lap, and the medic wheeled her inside. The crisis over, Lee and I stood there, staring blankly at each other, our emotions drained. Our hands, arms and clothes were splotched with blood; we needed to wash up before seeing Dr. Ochsner. As we entered the hospital, the medical staff took one look at us and assumed that we had been fighting! We had to calm them down and explain that we had helped the injured woman who had just come in by wheelchair. We cleaned ourselves up, best we could, in the disappointingly dirty bathrooms and then went to the registration area, saying we had come to see Dr. Alton Ochsner. As I took my seat on one of the many benches, Lee said he would have to sit elsewhere, but not to worry, as the wait would not be long. He would be called first: then, after some patients in between, I would be called. That way, it would not seem that we had come together. This pre-arranged plan was now ludicrous, since everybody noticed us when we walked in together with blood all over us! But that was the original plan, which we to follow. Only whites could sit on the benches in front.[146] Charity Hospital was founded by populist leader Gov. Huey Long, to serve the needs of the poor in New Orleans.

This 1,700-bed hospital was state-of-the-art when built. It was still functioning well in 1963. However, despite the gleam of the elegant overhead lamps and the polished wooden benches, the floor was scuffed and dirty and the overworked staff looked exhausted. Fortunately, the Sisters of Charity were providing certain essential services free of charge, or I think the system would have collapsed from corruption and underfunding. Next, Lee's number was called. He was gone about forty-five minutes. After he came out, he got a drink at the colored water fountain and then sat down at a distance from me. Fifteen minutes later, a nurse came out and asked me to follow her. She led me to a small conference room with a frosted glass window in its door. There was no name or number on the door, but when the nurse opened it, there sat Dr. Alton Ochsner, Sr., behind a nice wooden desk.

At last, we were meeting! "Won't you sit down, Miss Vary?" Dr. Ochsner asked, smiling. Distinguished, mustachioed and self-confident, power shot from this man's eyes like little electrical charges. It was like being seated before an emperor. Nobody sassed Ochsner. Nobody stood in his way. He commanded everything in a relaxed manner. "Have you caught up with the literature?" he asked. "Yes, sir," I replied.

"We're having reports flown in from both coasts, even before they're published," he told me.

---

[146] The rows of antique wooden benches were replaced with chairs sometime after this.

"Every new strain of lymphoma in the country can be in our hands within days. Breeder mice are being ordered from different sources to avoid suspicion. If you need anything, let me know."

I noticed that Dr. Ochsner avoided mentioning anything about working in Dr. Sherman's lab. "My internship...?" I queried gently.

"Of course, you're going to Tulane in the Fall," Ochsner said. "I wouldn't have asked you to come to New Orleans otherwise."

"Will I still be working with Dr. Sherman?" I asked.

"You'll see her every week," Ochsner told me. "She'll go over your reports. She'll take you into her own lab from time to time, to teach you procedures we'll want you to know by September. But you can help us if you accept an assignment at Mr. Reily's coffee company."

"How would my talents be useful at a coffee company?" I asked. "Your presence there will cut out two girls who could make problems for Mr. Monaghan," Ochsner explained. "He has to have someone there every morning, and he needs you to cover for Mr. Oswald's absences."

Ochsner then explained that Oswald had tested me and declared that I could be trusted in such a matter. Lee had his own work to do for the project. Ochsner said Lee's offer to work at Reily and to courier materials had already been accepted, but he would also be involved later in the year in another part of the same project, as well as in other matters. My position at Reily's would be salaried, at a better rate than my original stipend, so I would be able to live comfortably, but it would not be at Ochsner's Brent House. That was too far from Reily's. I would receive a week of training before taking on duties. It was important to restrict my conversations about the Project with Mr. Monaghan, my boss there. He was not privy to everything. "I want you to remember that Mr. Oswald will be there to help you," he stressed. "Mr. Oswald will have additional duties unrelated to his job at Reily's, just as you will," he said. "You can commandeer his courier services any time you need them." When I pointed out that I was not being given a choice about where I would work, Ochsner replied, "You managed, once again, to get yourself into trouble, nosing yourself into the wrong side of things." Then he gently added, "I will overlook it, however, since I didn't know your schedule had changed, and I wasn't available to direct your course."

"I also got married," I blurted out. "You'd find out soon enough..."

"Do you need birth control pills?" he asked. I was relieved that he wasn't angry. "Yes," I said simply. "As far as your husband knows, you're only a secretary at Reily's."

"I doubt he'll know where I work," I said. "He'll be out of town a lot."

"Write nothing about cancer research on any forms you fill out at Reily," Ochsner continued. "But how can I justify being hired, without any prior experience?" I asked. "I flunked my typing test at A-1."

"Make up something," he told me. "No, I won't do that," I answered stubbornly. "Damn it!" Ochsner complained. "Have you no prior office experience whatsoever?"

"Well, my dad had me running his business for him a couple of months, after he fired his accountant. I did book-keeping and answered the phone."

"Write that down," Ochsner said. "Don't mention you can't type. Do you know what creative lying is?"

"Mr. Oswald is certainly good at it. But I won't do it."

"Foolishness!" Ochsner huffed. "On the other hand, I suppose I can take everything you say and write as plain and straightforward fact, then?"

"You can be certain of it," I answered. "But to understand the project, I need to read the prior reports..." Ochsner scowled. "They're destroyed immediately after statistics are pulled," he replied. "However, Dr. Sherman keeps a log. Talk to her about that." He grabbed a notepad from the desk and began writing a prescription for birth control pills. "Take this to the hospital pharmacy," he said. It was a voucher for enough free pills to last the rest of the year. "Take vitamin C daily, and an aspirin every other day with those things," he warned me. "The high hormone doses in those pills can cause blood clots. I don't want to lose you due to a blood clot."

"All right, I'll do that, sir," I told him. "But I still don't understand why you want me in Dave Ferrie's lab. I think I could do more for the project in a real lab. The setup at Ferrie's has some problems. It's primitive."

"That's precisely why I need you in charge of Ferrie's part of the project," Ochsner said. "You know how to work under primitive conditions. Besides your capacity to work without supervision, you're the fastest reader I've ever seen, and we need some ideas. You're an unconventional thinker. I want your input. We've reached an impasse. We need your serendipity."

With that, Ochsner handed me a briefcase filled with research articles. *Oh, no! More stuff to read!* "What's the problem?" I asked. "Cross-species transfer," Ochsner said. "And, there's another problem. We can inject a mouse with a half-a-million cancer cells, but ten minutes later, the mouse has sifted all the cells out of its circulatory system. Only if we inject a mouse with over a million cells, do we get cell survival. If we injected a human with a dose of cells on the same scale, he'd have to take a pint of injections." Ochsner then dropped the magic words. *"Nobody could get away with injecting Fidel Castro with a pint of anything."* With that, Ochsner concluded our meeting, and I left.

Back in the waiting room, Lee was nowhere to be seen. Soon a nurse came over. She told me that Mr. Oswald was waiting outside the building. When I found him, Lee and I compared notes as we walked. Lee said he had been questioned closely as to his right-wing sympathies, but he knew Ochsner's extreme position, enhanced by Ochsner's training in pre-Nazi Germany and his membership in eugenics societies. Lee offered some creative lies, in admiration of Guy Banister's work ferreting out radical students who might cause civil rights unrest in the summer.

"I also told him," Lee said, "and this part is true, that I wished to mimic Herbert Philbrick's ideas about pamphleteering. I brought up Philbrick, hoping Ochsner will allow me to meet him when he comes to Reily for the INCA meeting."

"Did it work?" I asked.

"I think so," Lee replied. "I told him I could do leafleting to smoke out pro-Castroites here." Lee added that both Banister and Dave thought that would be safer after the students left for the summer." Lee also showed Ochsner the article about Phillips, who was beaten by three men, suggesting that INCA could publicize his leafleting activities to make it easier for him to get into Cuba, if nobody else could be found to transport the bioweapon. We walked in silence for a few minutes, as I contemplated the courage contained in those statements.

If Lee were to be caught inside Cuba and the bioweapon discovered, he'd be tortured and killed. Lee, sensing my concern, suggested we head to Lee Circle. "We need to turn this day around," he said. I had seen Lee Circle several times on the streetcar, but this time, we walked around the park to see it up close.[147] Lee pointed to the statue and said that he, as many others before him, had been named after Robert E. Lee. Then he pointed to an unremarkable building and explained how the city had razed a magnificent library, graced with Greek columns, at the site. It had been his favorite hangout. "They tore down a beautiful building,

constructed to last for centuries," he said angrily, "in a crooked, money-making deal." Besides historic buildings, many ancient and beautiful oak trees along St. Charles had also been ripped out, so cheap, modern structures could be built. Lee said it was because lots of bribes went into corrupt pockets. "Anything to make a crooked dollar!" he exclaimed, as we continued to walk. Lee went silent, plunged deep in his memories.[148] Then there was a shout: *"Oswald! Is that you?"* Lee looked up as a thin, young white man came loping around the Circle, carrying a Polaroid camera. "Thornley!" Lee called out. Thornley replied, "What are you doing here?" Reaching Lee, he grabbed him by the shoulders in a warm, masculine greeting. Thornley, a fellow Marine, had served with Lee at El Toro Marine Base in California. Both had wanted to become writers and see the world. Thornley said he lived nearby and invited Lee to play pool with him, but Lee declined, saying he was taking me out to eat. Suddenly, Thornley took our picture with his Polaroid, as Lee protested. When the picture scrolled out of the camera, Lee took it, watched it

---

[147]~58 years later, General Lee's statue was removed during a time of social turmoil.

[148] Lee Oswald knew details about New Orleans that an imposter could never make up.

develop, then tore it to pieces (That wasn't easy). "Hey! What did you do that for?" Thornley protested. "I just wanted to give you and your wife a picture."

"This isn't my wife," Lee said. "You're not?" Thornley asked. I shook my head. "We just found out we've been hired by the same company," Lee said, "We're celebrating. My wife won't be here for a few more days." "It's the same for her and her husband," Lee finished. "Are you sure that's all there is to it?" Thornley asked, grinning. "Tell you what," Lee said. "Go ahead, take another picture."

"I can't," Thornley told him. "That was the last one in the camera." Lee drew out a tiny camera from his shirt pocket. "Well, I have a miniature camera with me. I'll show you how to work it, and then you can take another picture of us with that. Okay?" It was a silver Minox spy camera, in a dark leather case, with a chain hanging from it. It resembled the Minox my father owned. "Very cool," Thornley said, taking it from Lee and inspecting it. "You kept it!" he said. I surmised Thornley had seen it before. "You know I like photography," Lee responded. "With this little baby, I can take pictures anywhere, and carry it in my pocket, unlike your Polaroid." Lee quickly showed Thornley how to use the camera and Thornley snapped our picture (if only I had that photo!).

Then Lee took one of Thornley. "I develop 'em myself," Lee said. "I'll bring you a print. Just tell me where you live." They talked a while longer, then Lee and I went on to Rev. Jim's, after which we ate at the *House of Lee*, a Chinese restaurant owned by Harry Lee's family. As part of Lee's wanting me to see "all things named Lee" in New Orleans, this was our next stop. Harry Lee worked part-time with David Lewis at the Trailways Bus Station, helping to support his big family. He was there that night and insisted we eat for free. Content and happy, we sang duets on the bus and streetcar all the way home, and somebody even applauded.

Chapter 14
Cover Jobs

Thursday, May 9, 1963

The day of our interviews at Reily's finally arrived. I had read research papers deep into the night, then tossed and turned, alternately day-dreaming about Lee and the feeling guilty about Robert. How could I have fallen in love with Lee Oswald only a week after my marriage?

I finally slept, only to awake to sunlight in my face. Because of the raid at the Mansion, I had neither an alarm clock nor a wristwatch, but I'd always been an early bird—except now!

I ran into Susie's kitchen and there was the clock – it was 12:30! I threw on some clothes, managed some makeup, and brushed my hair while riding in the streetcar, which the wind immediately blew in every direction. I arrived, breathless from running, at 1:15 at Walgreen's. Sure enough, Lee was waiting for me, reading a newspaper over a cup of coffee at the lunch counter. Such a late arrival would have irritated Robert, but Lee smiled as I sat down beside him, running my fingers through my hair to try to get it under control again. "You're right on time!" he said cheerily.

"How can that possibly be?" I asked. Lee said he knew I didn't have an alarm clock, so he simply added half an hour to his schedule to be on the safe side. He had interesting things to say about pretending to find his pre-arranged apartment on Magazine Street. Lee had met with an old friend of his mother's—Myrtle Evans—well before 8 am, to ask her to help find him an apartment. He knew she had nothing she could rent to him, but with her gossipy nature, she was the perfect person to take him apartment-hunting, so she could later talk about the juicy fact that she had met the 'notorious defector to the USSR' ! Lee gave Myrtle some nice tidbits to gossip about, while allowing her to drive him here and there, until it was time to 'discover' the 'for rent' sign outside the door at 4909 Magazine Street. The sign had been put out only a few hours earlier, and it would be taken down just as quickly.

Myrtle, of course, would claim all the credit for finding the apartment at 4905 Magazine St. "Now it's official," Lee said, as he held up the keys. He gave me a dollar to buy a Baby Ben alarm clock, since I'd need one for my new job, after which we headed to Rev. James' to put in an hour of work for pin money before going to the A-1 Employment Agency.[149] We were not supposed to be seen going to Reily's together for our interviews, even though we would be hired the same day. That's why Lee would go to Reily's first and then call me. Meanwhile, I'd be trying to improve my abominable typing skills.

"We'll start working at Standard Coffee tomorrow," he said. "We''ll stay there a week. You'll learn the ropes. Launder my records. Then we'll transfer over to Reily's." *What?* Launder his records? Why me, and how would I do it? I held these thoughts to myself, figuring that Lee would tell me soon enough. Standard Coffee was a small subsidiary of Reily's that distributed coffee to local offices, homes and businesses. It would grow big, later. For now, it had a small office and a garage for Reily's and Standard's delivery trucks when they needed servicing. Since Mr. Monaghan was personally in charge of Standard Coffee, the Reily brothers could always deny knowing a thing about our cover jobs.[150]

---

[149] Lee stashed unused funds in an account for Marina and his children, in case something happened to him. He spent no government-issued funds for personal pleasure, which is why he enjoyed earning a bit with me at Reverend Jim's.

[150] Australian researcher Greg Parker claims Lee Oswald (who he never met) had Aspergers. He also claimed that Standard Coffee did not exist. Forced to admit it

Upon our arrival at A-1's office, Lee asked if there were any job openings for him, but the woman said she had nothing – just the interview at Reily's. Then he asked if she could find a job opening for me. "She doesn't type fast enough to apply at Reily's," the lady told him, but she promised to make some calls elsewhere.

Lee thanked her, then asked if it would be okay if I could practice typing to get myself better qualified, while he went on to Reily. Lee also told the lady he would call me if he got the job. Otherwise, he said, he'd come back to get me. I smiled to myself about Lee's creative lying. He already knew he had the job, so this little lie was handed out to reinforce his cover story.

As I practiced typing, I pondered how our list of coincidences kept growing. First, I "accidently" met a man at the Post Office who knew a "cancer researcher" working with Dr. Sherman. That same person –Lee-- also knew Dr. Ochsner, to the extent that he had a 45-minute interview with him. My own interview with Ochsner only lasted about twenty minutes, and I considered myself to have a good relationship with my longtime mentor. Stranger and stranger! A poor kid from New Orleans, who had been out of the country for the last six years, had that kind of status with Dr. Ochsner. Both Lee and Ochsner wanted me to take the job at Reily's to help cover Lee's absences and launder his records, so Lee had to be important to Ochsner to ask me to take on such an unexpected role. Tomorrow, we would both start working at **Standard Coffee Company**, and in a week, we would transfer together to Reily's. After a half-hour, Lee called. The A-1 lady handed me the phone, standing close enough to listen. "Hello?" I said into the receiver. "You can come over now," Lee told me. "Your interview will be at four."

"Okay," I said. "Can you remind me again how to get there?" As usual, I was afraid I'd make a wrong turn and get lost, so I scribbled down the directions. But as I returned the phone, the A-1 lady said, "I know where you're going, and why. Those clerk jobs at Reily's are listed with us. If you're hired, you owe us two week's pay. You realize that, don't you?"

"You told me you had no jobs for me!" I protested. "If I do get a job there, you have nothing to do with it."

"Let me tell you something, Mrs. Baker," she snapped. "You were told to go to Reily's, using this telephone. We keep phone records of every call just for that reason. That call probably came from a Reily telephone, so we can prove you were here today. If you get the job, you'll pay, or we'll see you in court."

---

existed, he then claimed I knew a *different* Oswald who worked at Standard later that summer and that I *never* worked at Reily's, though I have only one 'Standard' paycheck stub and all the rest are Reily paycheck stubs (see Color Pages).

"Like heck I'll pay!" I answered, grabbing up my briefcase and going out the door. Unfortunately, I left the directions behind and had to go back to retrieve them. Feeling as ridiculous as Lucille Ball in *I Love Lucy*, I scooped the note off the vixen's desk and walked out again in a huff. Thanks to Lee's directions, I eventually found Reily's main building at 640 Magazine St., where I was introduced to Al Prechter, a genial older gentleman of a highly conservative bent. Mr. Prechter explained that Lee had already gone, so we would not be seen together.

He was concerned that I could only type nineteen words a minute, but I told him I had been practicing and was now up to twenty-one.[151] Mr. Prechter sighed, then had me fill out forms. I embellished my duties at my father's office, with no mention of cancer research, per Dr. Ochsner's orders. "You'll start tomorrow," he told me. "You've been hired by Standard Coffee Company, for one week. Then we'll move you over to William B. Reily Coffee Company. Please report to Personnel before 8:00 tomorrow morning, here. You'll get your timecard, you will punch in, and then proceed to 725 Magazine. You'll meet Mr. Oswald there at that time."

When I returned to the bus stop, Lee soon joined me. "I should have told you more about why we're working at Standard for a week," he said, as we waited for the bus. "Remember what I said about laundering records? You'll be purifying my past with plenty of creative lies," Lee said with a smile. "Creative lying" had become an ongoing joke. "How will I do that?" I asked. "Reily orders background checks on all new people," Lee explained. "The only time they don't is if they transfer over from Standard. Since both order background checks, it would be redundant for Reily's to order another one."

"So your background check will be ordered by Standard?" I wondered out loud. "Yes," Lee replied. "And guess who will be writing it?" he teased. Retail Credit (the company that did the background reports) could not be allowed to investigate him. Imagine what they would find! 1) Lee was in the newspapers four years ago as a defector to Russia. 2) Lee was in the local newspaper less than a year ago as a returning defector from Russia. 3) Lee had a Russian wife, and a baby born in Russia. 4) Lee had supposedly been fired from his last job.

5) Lee had an undesirable discharge from the Marines. 6) Lee hadn't been in town long enough for friends or neighbors to provide reliable information about his social habits. 7) Lee didn't even have a bank account or any credit, but we would report that he had a great credit record! I had my own background report to launder, too!

If Retail Credit had investigated me, they would have learned about my cancer research, with no qualifications as a secretary. Only key people at Reily's knew about this charade. Our records needed doctoring, but Retail Credit Co. could not be made aware of that. Lee continued to fill me in as to what was coming, as we walked toward Lafayette Park.

---

[151] Corrected from *Me & Lee*. My original shows a 9, not a 5. I typed with two fingers.

"I'll clock myself in," he explained, "but you'll be clocking me out for a full work-day, whether I'm here or not. You'll have to calculate it."

"Won't somebody notice if you're late?" I asked. "I was told that if I'm five minutes late, I'll be docked. Are you going to be immune?"

"I don't have to be on time," Lee said. "But you have to. Monaghan's phone starts ringing at eight. You're not only his credit, payroll, and shipment examiner; you're also his floor secretary in the Finance and Billing Department. I'm just doing maintenance work. Besides, if Personnel finds a problem with my card, guess who they'll take it to?"

"To me?" I said incredulously. "That's right," he confirmed.

One great advantage to Lee's job at Reily's was that he might be working on any of five floors in the office building, or he might be working in the smaller factory attached to it, where packing and shipping took place amidst noise and confusion. "It's good to have a job like that," Lee said, explaining that all the chaos would help him to be able to slip away unnoticed. "You have to be gone long enough to be missed, and then they have to hunt for you. Plus, nobody is sure when they saw you last. Since we're rich now," Lee said, referring humorously to the pittance we'd earned at Reverend Jim's,[152] "let's go do some target practice."

Since I was dressed for a job interview, and had few nice clothes, I told Lee we'd have to "target practice" some other time. Unwilling to waste time returning to my apartment, Lee steered me into a thrift store, where he got me some sneakers, a black Japanese-style shirt similar to a red one I already had, and a pair of cut-off Bermuda shorts. About that time, there was a two-for-one sale going on in an upscale store, where I bought Lee a nice brown long-sleeved shirt, plus an identical larger one for Robert. Those two shirts reflected my divided loyalties. Our next stop was Banister's building. All we had to worry about, he said, was running into one of Banister's secretaries. In case that happened, I'd have to speak Russian. Lee found the janitor, who lived in the building. He unlocked the "544 Camp Street" door for us. He then took us to the top of the stairs to the third floor, unlocking that door for us, as well. We walked into a large room that may once have been a ballroom, in some faded past when Banister's building had been a hotel. Some naked lightbulbs hung from what had once been ornate fixtures. Surely, chandeliers had once illuminated this big space, now so decrepit. The huge room was not empty. It was filled with stacks of war materiel, enough to arm dozens of guerillas. Strewn across the dusty and neglected wooden floor were piles of bedrolls and Army tents alongside crooked rows of hammers, poles, stakes, machetes, axes, and bayonets. There were canteens, blankets, bedrolls, bales of mosquito netting, and rows of wooden boxes of explosives, fuses and ammunition.

---

[152] Lee's Aunt Lillian said Lee told her he'd interviewed for 'a lettering job' advertised in the papers, but wasn't hired. It was a necessary charade. It's possible that Lee did interview there, though there is no record of it. But they may have told Lee about Rev. Jim's, for how did he come to know about day-work being available there?

More rifles were stacked against the far wall. Boxes of Sterno and Army surplus rations were heaped beside the blankets. A musty smell of mildew filled the air. The ceiling was painted a creamy green color, with splotches of brown where water leaks made it sag. Dust particles floated in a beam of light from the afternoon sun. Lee went to a table in the corner with several cardboard boxes containing smaller firearms and a clipboard. I told Lee that I needed to change into my shorts, so he should turn around to give me some privacy.

As he did, I wondered if all his espionage training had given him eyes in the back of his head. In fact, Lee busied himself with the handguns and did not turn around. After signing the paper on the clipboard, he selected a long-barreled .38 caliber Smith & Wesson revolver. The gun appeared to be in excellent condition. It had a leather holster and belt. "This is mine," he said proudly. I was close enough to the clipboard to see some scrawled signatures. One of them looked like "Nagy" or "Nagel—"[153] After writing his initials on the clipboard, Lee handed me a .22 target pistol and showed me a small .22 caliber Derringer which he also owned. "A more useless weapon never existed," he quipped. It, too, seemed to be in good condition. Lee said he kept these firearms here, and not in his home, for two reasons. "First" he said, "I'm afraid Marina might shoot me, if she got angry enough." Lee's smile informed me he wasn't really serious. Then he told me the real reason. "Junie can walk now, and I don't want her getting into my guns, and maybe hurting herself." I stress the fact that Lee said these were all the firearms that he owned. *There was no rifle.*[154] Lee put his guns into a small green canvas case and we headed for a levee on the lakefront.

There, we rigged up some beer can targets full of dirt to practice on. I witnessed what a good shot Lee was with his .38 and I did okay with the little .22. It was time for supper, so we headed to Thompson's Restaurant, where we met with David and Anna Lewis and enjoyed free slices of pie for dessert. When Anna got off her shift at 7 PM, we contributed toward their babysitting bill, giving Anna and David freedom to join us for a walk. We chose to explore the French Quarter.

As we strolled down Bourbon Street, we enjoyed the music as it flowed from the bars and clubs we passed. We moved with a crowd of tourists, hyped up by jazz trumpets and drumbeats as the sun went down.

---

[153] I reported this anomaly to the excellent researcher Dick Russell.

[154] The revolver Lee showed me that day in New Orleans was certainly not the weapon supposedly wrestled from him inside the Texas Theater in Dallas on the afternoon of November 22. Lee had shown me a revolver with a long barrel, but the one at the Texas Theater was a "snub nose." The police attempted to use that same gun to argue that Lee had killed a Dallas police office named J. D.Tippitt. The central problem with their argument was pointed out long ago by JFK researchers: the evidence abounds at the scene of Officer Tippitt's murder indicated that he was shot with a semi-automatic pistol. Those shells, marked by police, vanished. This single piece of evidence could have exonerated Lee from any involvement in Tippitt's slaying.

That brought a cool night breeze from the river. In the 400 block, we reached The 500 Club. Anna told us this was Carlos Marcello's favorite

haunt when he came to town: he had an office on the 2nd floor. He had a one-way mirror to watch for police as he conducted business. We almost went in, but it was too expensive, so we kept walking . We passed the Old Absinthe House, bought some oyster and crawfish Po Boys, and enjoyed jazz on the streets. David and Lee had been

talking about eliminating Castro, but the night was too romantic to carry that kind of talk for long.

We ended up walking behind the Café du Monde and sat down in a parklike area overlooking the Mississippi River, where we could hear the horse-drawn carriages, occupied by lovers, trotting past. Then David began to kiss his wife, so Lee and I moved to another bench to give them some space. Lee brought out his transistor radio, setting it on top of his green canvas case. Then he put his arms around me. I leaned against his chest and let the romantic spell of New Orleans take us away. That's when the radio began to play "Let It Be Me" by the Everly Brothers: *"I bless the day I found you ... I want to stay around you ... and so I beg you ... let it be me!"* Lee and I gazed over the silent waves of the Mississippi River that shimmered under the last rays of sunset. It was all so simple and natural, that we should be together.

Friday, May 10, 1963 This would be our first day at The William B. Reily Coffee Company, also known by its eponym of "William B" by its hard-working employees. I made Susie and Lee a nice breakfast.
It was a special Hungarian breakfast, since Lee would have his family with him and could come no more to our breakfast table. I got up at midnight and started cooking! At 6:45 am, Lee arrived, to the savor and aroma of home-made *kurtos kalacs* with raspberry jam, a sausage, cheese, and crusted chicken roll-up, some cold cherry soup, and hot coffee, to which I'd added vanilla and cinnamon. At 7:25 AM Lee and I caught the bus at Marengo St. and Magazine. For now, we sat apart, poingd as new hires who didn't yet know each other. When we reached Reily's, nine or ten people got off with us, all headed to Reily's. After our timecards were signed and we clocked in, we walked over to Reily's Standard Coffee office, where William I. Monaghan met us.

"Mr. M" was dressed in a good dark suit befitting a Vice-President. He wore the regulation tie and crisp starched white shirt. He stood a couple of inches taller than Lee. This no-nonsense-tolerated executive was a powerfully built middle-aged man whose well-groomed dark hair and craggy, handsome face reminded me of TV's "Highway Patrol"' star Broderick Crawford. In other words, Mr. Monaghan looked and acted every inch the FBI agent that made him such an excellent choice for Reily as officer-in-charge of security and finance. A man of few words, and usually all business, he seemed almost a clone of Guy Banister in the rigid way he thought and organized himself. He possessed a dignity of spirit, a distaste for wasting time, and a sense of self-importance that made an indelible impression. After meeting Banister and Monaghan, I no longer wondered why these agents used so many informants. They had to. From their clipped, slicked-back hair to their dark suits and spotless, shiny black shoes, they were unmistakable G-men.

Soon after we met Monaghan, Lee departed to Reily's to learn how to grease coffee machines, and Mr. Monaghan took me to the courthouse, where he showed me how to look up delinquent liquor and tobacco permits, taxes owed, bankruptcy data, and pending lawsuits, plus all the kinds of resources I'd need to help assess an account's credit-worthiness. Reily's bought coffee cans, raw coffee and tea, trucks, boxes, and many other items. They sold coffee and tea, of course, but also trucked 'outside' items, such as Blue Plate mayonnaise and soap products. Grocery chains, restaurants, and mom-and-pop food stores across the south and in the nation's big cities ordered their products. Reily's factory equipment was used to package products for other companies, as well. Getting their money from all these many consumers was forever the most important point. Reily's wouldn't send a teaspoon of coffee on credit if the business was shaky. Next, on the clerical and finance floor of the building, the most important room of all, I was shown copies of *Standard & Poor's*, the credit rating books which were kept on open shelves near Monaghan's Finance and Security desk. The financial health of Reily's customers was never taken for granted, and every one of them got checked regularly. After that, Mr. Monaghan invited me to have lunch with him in his private, glassed-in cubicle there. We ate some delicious sandwiches called muffalettas. Then I was given samples of Reily's various products, like Luzianne coffee with chickory, to sample. It was Monaghan's kind way to introduce me to the Luzianne product line that Reily sold worldwide. He wanted me to become familiar with the products Reily's salesmen offered. Salesmen and employees came and went through the arched doorway on the side of the new 5-story office building. This is where the meter for the time-cards was located, to clock in. Here, I would clock in and turn to the left and Lee would clock in and turn to the right. After lunch, Monaghan introduced me to three candidates as salesmen.

Only one would be selected to take over a lucrative route. Mr. Monaghan went over their resumes.

A "Character and Financial Report" had been generated by Retail Credit for each salesman. One was divorced. Monaghan said divorce was considered evidence of a potential problem. Another had a drunk-driving conviction. That alone was sufficient to dismiss him. "I expect you to produce a believable and unremarkable report on Mr. Oswald," Monaghan told me. Then he asked if I could take shorthand. I said "No," but I knew 'speed writing.' Monaghan scowled. "Luckily for you," he said, "I've noticed you have something going for you. "What is that, sir?" I asked. "You have good legs," he replied. "Otherwise, I'd send you back." It was hard to decipher where his humor ended and his hormones started. From that day on, I couldn't help but notice that Mr. Monaghan spent a considerable amount of time looking at my legs. Other than that, he was a gentleman. At 4:30, I clocked Lee out for the first time: it was the first and last day that Lee would be in and out on time. To clock him out, my instructions were to go to the front of the line and say, "I'm Mr. Monaghan's secretary, excuse me, please." I was then to pull Lee's time-card, check to see if he had already stamped it, and if not, I would stamp it, then return it to Lee's slot in the big yellow card- tray on the wall. Anyone more than five minutes late got docked 20 cents (unless your name was Lee Oswald). You got docked more if you were ten minutes late. Since Lee often clocked in 45 to 90 minutes late, or even later, his paycheck should have been affected, even if salaried. It wasn't. The first work-day over, Lee and I pretended we were happy, new acquaintances.

This 2000 photo shows Reily (L) attached to the factory (R).

We got off the bus at Lee's apartment, as I wanted to help Lee fix it up before Marina and Junie arrived. This was also a dry run to see how long the trip from Reily's would take, and how many employees from Reily's would be on the bus. Again, about ten Reily employees got on the bus with us, and not all of them got off before we did. That restrained us from talking a lot. Once off the bus, I mentioned the problem to Lee.

"I've thought about that," Lee said, as we entered his apartment. "We can ride down to Audubon Park, and have a nice visit. Then we can take a bus back toward town. There will be no employees on that bus, and we can sit together." It was a brilliant idea, worth the pocket change. From then on, when we didn't have to go elsewhere after work, we'd grab time together by going straight from Reily's past our apartments, all the wat to Audubon Park. There we had time to ourselves, before riding back.

Later, we sometimes waited an hour at Charlie's Bar, at 640 Carondelet, where it was safe to sit together without a Reily employee to see us. On returning home, always going all the way to Audubon Park, on the return toward town, Lee would get off first, at Upperline. Then I'd get off one stop later, at Marengo.

I liked the apartment at 4905 that Lee chose. Its high ceilings guaranteed a cooler house. It had a large living room and a pleasant, screened-in porch. A big canopy in front kept it shaded. Junie could play safely on the porch and inside the small, fenced yard, which was rich with colorful flowers, bushes, and strawberries. The living room had bare wooden floors that only needed a good mopping with oil to be shiny again. The bathroom was wallpapered, but the tub needed a good scrub.

--Photo by The Times-Picayune

Lee's apartment at 4905 Magazine St. is at the right, with a big screened-in porch (see arrow) and its own private, fenced yard. Note small mailbox (white arrow) for normal mail going to "4905," Lee's true address. Lee's subversive mail was delivered to 4907 (front R) a fake address he used to protect his family. Here Marina (L), soon to arrive from Texas, is shown with CIA asset Patricia Johnson McMillan. In her malicious biography, *Marina and Lee*, McMillan made fun of Lee's getting up in the middle of the night to spray roaches. But he did the right thing. He was protecting his family by using a less-toxic spray.

The linoleum floor was starting to curl at the base of the brand-new gas stove, so we flattened it by lifting the stove and pushing the edge of the linoleum under it. As we did so, roaches ran out. The roach droppings on the counter concerned us. When Lee said he'd be buying roach spray, I suggested a less-toxic pyrethrum product. However, that meant Lee would have to get up in the middle of the night to spray. That's when roaches would be visible, but only direct contact with the less toxic spray would kill them. Monsieur Roach was part of the price one paid to live in New Orleans. Lee said at least the double bed was clean and ready, so he would spend the night here. When I volunteered to help clean, Lee reluctantly accepted the offer. He brought out some cleaning supplies from under the sink. He knew where a broom and mop were stored in a side closet, which made me believe he had stayed here before.

While Lee mopped floors, I defrosted the refrigerator (the electric was already on). This was 4905. – The electric had not been shut off here. But Lee would later be accused of not paying the electric bill at **4907**! Indeed, Lee himself had the electricity turned on at 4907. But when he moved away at the end of September, he owed nothing, since at that time Mr. and Mrs. Eric Rogers were living at 4907, and had been, since mid-July. This is internal evidence that Lee was paying the Rogers' bills so they would take his subversive mail for him. And indeed, that's where Lee's "communist" mail went, even though Mr. Rogers swore Lee never spoke a word to him. As for Mr. Rogers, he did not get a job until after Lee moved.[155] I knew none of this at the time.

FBI duplicity: this FBI document pretends Lee lived at 4907 Magazine, to show he didn't pay a utility bill, when other FBI reports showed he lived at 4905 Magazine.

What I did know was that Lee had apartment 4905, and I was in it, helping him clean it up. I scrubbed the bathtub and bathroom sink: he scrubbed the kitchen sink and refrigerator. The kitchen fan didn't work, so Lee opened the windows and porch door to dry the place out. I saw several boxes and a couple of seabags Lee had just brought over. He removed a green and brown plaid blanket from one of the boxes. It had been used to protect some cameras, lenses, filters, and other paraphernalia useful in photography. I also saw bottles of hypo and acetic acid for developing film, carefully wrapped in brown paper. It all looked professional. Lee shook out the blanket and laid it on the bed. "It's Junie's favorite blanket," he said. "I was afraid Marina would forget it." [156] He rolled up the blanket to use as a pillow on the bed.

[redacted]

— Commission Exhibit No. 1139

FD (Rev. 3-21-61) FEDERAL BUREAU OF INVE

Date November 29, 1963

1

Mr. JOHN R. HEVRON, Assistant Secretary and Treasurer, New Orleans Public Service, Inc., 317 Baronne Street, advised that his company's records show that the electric and gas meters at the apartment rented by LEE HARVEY OSWALD, 4907 Magazine Street, were read on May 24, 1963 and a bill was rendered for $2.85 which was due on or before June 17, 1963. The records do not show the date this bill was paid or whether the payment was made by cash or check.

The electric and gas meters were read on June 25, 1963 and a bill of $7.22 was rendered and was paid in cash on July 17, 1963. The electric and gas meters were again read on July 25, 1963 and a bill for $8.54 was rendered, which bill was paid in cash on August 13, 1963.

The meters were again read on August 26, 1963 and a bill for $10.32 was rendered. This bill was not paid on or before September 17, 1963, the due date, and therefore the penalty was added to the bill, which on that date became a total of $11.36.

The meters were read again on September 25, 1963 and a bill of $11.02 was rendered, which was due to be paid on or before October 17, 1963. This bill was not paid and therefore after October 17, the penalty of $.78 was assessed, making the total amount owed to the New Orleans Public Service $23.17. Deducting the deposit of $10 which was made by OSWALD at the time he applied for electric and gas service, plus the interest earned on this deposit of $.20, the net amount owed to the Public Service was $12.97.

---

[155] All these records are in Warren Commission testimonies and exhibits and are detailed in *Me & Lee,* the first edition of this book.

[156] Lee actually paid to have the electricity turned on at 4907, where he kept a second address, which fooled many researchers. I had to show several researchers- Dr. Howard Platzman, Dr. Joseph Riehl, and Martin Shackelford, in Jan. 2000, that Lee never did live at 4907, correcting what they were told by researcher John Armstrong, who also pushes the "Harvey and Lee" false theory. The Warren Commission showed Lee's

"Well, that's all I need to spend the night here," he said. I commented that there wasn't much furniture, and the bed itself had only a sheet-covered mattress, but no pillow or bedspread. "It's only for five months," Lee said. "Then Marina goes back, to have her baby." Lee's almost complete lack of interest in Marina's comfort concerned me. "The less comfortable and more boring it is for her, the easier it will be to leave me," Lee explained. I tried to understand how someone who had treated me with such affection and gentleness could feel so hostile toward his own wife.

"No matter what she may tell others," he replied, his voice full of grief, "she knows that I know what she did." Later, I learned that Marina brought lots of pillows and bedding with her and that the Murrets supplied other missing items, including some furniture. [157]

While I wiped down the cupboards, Lee went to buy a garbage can. Seeing the label, I tried to remove it, but it ripped, leaving some of the label still on the trashcan.

"It doesn't matter," Lee said, "it's just a garbage can." He placed it outside on the curb near some others and we put some trash in it. Finally finished cleaning up, Lee and I walked toward my apartment, checking the route. Halfway to 1032 Marengo, there was a Catholic school and a playground with a large sign that said, "BINGO TONITE" in snap-on letters. This would be our meeting-place, Lee said.

---

correct address, but accused him of not paying "his" utility bill at 4907 in September, when Mr. & Mrs. Eric Rogers were living there.

157

I am a living witness that the soft, flexible blanket shown to the <u>left</u>, above, was in Lee's possession <u>before</u> Marina Oswald arrived in New Orleans, even though Ruth and Michael Paine said the blanket was used to wrap "Oswald's" rifle. Junie's blanket was not nearly so stiff as the piece of fabric, above, right) on display in the Ruth Paine House in Irving, Nov. 2020. The official photo shows Junie's blanket – soft and flexible -- easy to feel a rifle inside it—which supposedly held the rifle, with the "blanket" on display(R) at the Paine garage-museum. Even today, the truth is still being distorted.

It was a four-minute walk for both of us. As we sat on a bench near the sign, Lee suddenly said, seeing how dirty my skirt was, "Why don't you go home and change into your new shorts? Then come back with your typewriter," he added. "I'll wait for you here." I knew Lee wanted to finish his first draft of his science-fiction story, "Her Way" on the typewriter, before Marina showed up, but why should I have to drag that typewriter over to him?

"I don't want to be seen walking with you to your apartment...," Lee explained. "But if you bring the typewriter this far, I'll carry it the rest of the way to my place. I have another reason," he added. "I want to see if you can find your way back." What? Me get lost? Well, I'd show *him!* Concentrating on not getting lost, I had surprisingly little trouble finding my way back. The hardest part was carrying the typewriter.

As I approached, Lee took it, saying, "You remembered how to get back because I made you carry that thing. A mind works hard to avoid work." He was right. Seeing I was tired, Lee had me wait on the bench while he took the typewriter to his apartment.

As I waited, I noticed Lee had changed the Bingo sign to read "I Binge Not." Before long, he was back, carrying the green canvas bag. But something had upset him. "What's the matter, Lee?" I asked. "What's bothering you?"

"Well," he replied, "when I got there with the typewriter, the garbage can was gone."

"What? It wasn't out there an hour!" Lee said he should have painted his name on the can and that he knew better. But and Lee was soon cheerful again, saying we could still have some fun at Pontchartrain Beach tonight. When we arrived, at first we walked to an isolated stretch of Lakeshore Drive, near Franklin Ave. Lee said this was the back fence of the Army and Navy training centers, so there were no houses or people around. We were inside the city limits, but Lee pulled out his revolver. There were seagulls flying over the sparkling waves, as the sky turned to a crimson sunset. Then Lee spotted some mallard ducks which were paired off for spring nesting. "Quiet!" Lee cautioned. He knelt down slowly, then put a cotton wad in his right ear. "Aha!" he said, taking aim, "duck for dinner!"

"Please, Lee," I said. "Have mercy!"

"Oh, ye of little faith!" he said. "Just watch." He took aim at a drake strutting along, about a hundred feet away, and fired.

The duck flapped into the air in confusion, a couple of tail feathers falling from its rear. At the sound of the shot, all the ducks took flight, but Lee fired a second round, sending a few more feathers flying from yet another drake. Lee checked his revolver, putting bullets into the empty chambers. "I wouldn't really hurt those ducks, Juduffki," he said. "They're in love, and about to make baby ducks. I only kill when I'm hungry, and then I only kill bachelor ducks, and old maid ducks." Lee filled a row of beer cans with sand for me to shoot at from fifty feet. I hit them all, which pleased Lee very much.

When we were done, Lee quickly and carefully cleaned the guns and put them into his green bag. We then walked along the seawall toward the amusement park, until we came to an area where we could see blue crabs scuttling across the shallow, sandy bottom. Lee told me to never catch a crab wearing an 'apron,' referring to the fuzzy material on the front of a female crab, where she guards her thousands of little eggs. "That's why crabs should be checked after they are netted," he said. He hated to buy crabs caught commercially because they didn't throw back the mother crabs. That's why he planned to catch them himself, for a guilt-free family meal. Lee put his guns into a locker at the beach, and then we went on to enjoy the rides. It was now twilight, and the amusement park rides were bathed in brilliant lights. We indulged, knowing we'd soon be working hard. This time, we went on lots of rides, including the Flying Horses carousel, "The Whip" and the "Tilt-a-Whirl." But when Lee came close to the shooting gallery, the proprietor recognized him and quickly closed up. Much later, having dined on cotton candy, Coney Island hamburgers, Tiki fruit drinks, candied apples and sausage sticks [Burp!], we picked up Lee's guns again and headed home.

This photo shows adults having just as much fun as the kids on Pontchartrain Beach's "flying horses."

It was a wonderful evening, and when we got back to 1032, we did not want it to end. "If I never live another day," Lee said, "and even if I never have the exquisite pleasure of sleeping with you..." I stopped him from saying more, taking his head between my hands, and slowly kissing him, with a degree of passion I didn't know I possessed. We held each other tight, feeling our hearts pulsing against each other. Our desire was so strong, we could hardly breathe. Lee's wiry, strong arms were sheltering me. New Orleans had turned from a city of fear and loneliness to a glittering treasure chest, full of the jewels of romance. The only problem was that we felt like pirates stealing the jewels.

<u>**Very early Saturday morning, May 11, 1963**</u>, Lee tapped at my window. He said he'd be over early, but it wasn't even dawn yet. I jumped up to let him in, Suzi Collie at his side (who didn't bark even once – she loved him). Lee was cheerful and pleased. He had completed his short story! Now he had returned with the typewriter and two copies of his science fiction story, "Her Way" for me to hold onto. The top copy was white. The bottom was a carbon copy, exploiting the pink paper that came from my parents-in-laws'' real estate office. "It's finished!" Lee announced. "I worked on it all night. I used a dictionary," he added, apologetically.

"Most of the words should be spelled correctly." Seeing he was anxious for me to read it, wrapped in my robe, I read it aloud as Lee paced back and forth. It was clear that Lee had writing talent. He knew how to tie up the loose ends of a story. However, I had never read so many bizarre and alien ideas, words, and descriptions. "I can't figure out why the spaceship is trapped and can't escape the depredations of the Phoenix, if Alt and the "feely" are really from an advanced civilization," I finally said. "But otherwise, I'm impressed."

"I'll fix it," Lee said nervously. "Anything else?"

"It's a unique style all your own. And you've made up words I've never seen before."

"That's probably because I can't spell," Lee said, looking miserable. "No, no, these are really original and interesting words," I replied. "They add to the story all the way. I'm fascinated by them." Lee had read some of my poems and short stories, late at night in bed at his uncle's house.

He had expressed respect for my writing. Now it was my turn to encourage him. "Don't show it to anybody," Lee said. "But fix anything you like. By the way," he added, "you're supposed to meet Dr. Sherman for lunch at noon today, at her apartment." This was the first I had heard anything about lunch with Dr. Sherman! I set aside Lee's story, a little miffed. "Why am I the last to know these things?" I complained. "My love," Lee said, stroking my hair, "I was supposed to tell you last night, but you scrambled my brains when you kissed me." I buried my head against his chest, as he put his arms around me. I could smell Old Spice cologne on him. "I won't be able to be with you like this for days," Lee said.[158] "I'm going to hate that. But I promise to be here in eight minutes if you need help for any reason."

He took my hand, gave me a slip of paper, and closed my hand around it. "If there's an emergency, just call this number," he said. Lee had given me Mr. Garner's phone number. He was the apartment manager's husband, and drove a cab. It would not seem unusual to call him, so long as it was at a normal hour. All I had to say was I wished to reach Reily's "new janitor" and Mr. Garner would pass the message on to Lee. The word "**ja**nitor" had my first two initials, "**J A.**"

---

[158] In the book *Marina and Lee*, Priscilla McMillan Johnson denounced Lee at every turn. For example, she wrote, "The landlady [sic] was Mrs. Jesse Garner, and Lee gave her a month's rent and an application for utilities along with a $5 deposit. But then he told another of his funny, pointless lies. He said he worked for the Leon Israel Company of 300 Magazine Street. The company existed, but it was not the company that hired him." (p. 389) But Lee didn't want the 'landlady' (actually, Garner was the manager) to give Marina the address to Reily's, just in case Marina – sure to smell coffee on his clothing – might ride the bus over there and make it obvious that Lee was married to a –gasp—Russian! Then Lee would have to be fired. It has been said that Marina indeed did visit the Leon Israel Coffee Company, pushing her toddler in a stroller, seeking Lee there. So Lee's "lie" was not pointless. Before this "pointless lie, McMillan admits that Lee always told Marina exactly where he was working – except this time.

That's how Lee would know it was me. Now Lee had to hurry on to the Murrets. Ruth Paine was going to stop there first, with Marina. The Murrets would be able to see their nephew's wife and baby right away. And Lee would be full of joy to see his baby daughter again. I'd have to wait until Monday morning to see Lee again. I sighed as he left. I was now "the other woman." Even so, it was getting harder to stay faithful to Robert. I solemnly watered the four begonias sitting in my window and studied their pretty blossoms. I was writing letters to Robert, but he wasn't replying. The nights were long and lonely. What was Robert doing right now? Only God knew.

Chapter 15
Dr. Mary

Saturday, May 11, 1963

Today was the day I would finally get to talk to the famous Dr. Mary Sherman. Using Lee as the messenger, she had invited me to have lunch in her apartment at noon. Dr. Sherman lived in the Patio Apartments on St. Charles Avenue near the corner of Louisiana Ave. It was so close I could have walked there from Marengo Street, but I took the streetcar at St. Charles and got there in two minutes. Dr. Mary's apartment was at the far end of an elegant interior courtyard, up one flight of stairs. At the end of the courtyard, a small patio, lush with plants and flowers in bloom, adorned the stairway to the second floor. Looking up, I saw the **"J"** on the door of her apartment and knew at once I wouldn't have any problem remembering that. As I approached the door it opened, and Dr. Sherman, dressed in a peach-colored suit, stepped out to greet me with a gracious smile. "Judy, we've been expecting you!" she said in a warm, friendly voice.[159]

- [159] On July 21, 1964, the day The Warren Commission came to New Orleans to do volunteer interviews, Dr. Sherman was found murdered. A 2014 news article noted, "On the day after the murder, John L. Ochsner [Dr. Ochsner's son-JVB] walked into

Dr. Sherman once again had her hair done up in a French twist, but this time, in the friendliest manner, she took me by the hand and guided me into her spotless home. In the front room, lunch was already set out on a table decorated with fancy glasses and fresh flowers. Much to my surprise, there was a man sitting at the table, smoking a cigarette. It was David Ferrie.

Dr. Sherman offered me a seat and presented me with a plate of finger sandwiches. Her soothing manner was entirely different from the stern woman who had cut me off so abruptly at Dave's party. Today she was so hospitable that I soon forgot the humiliation of that earlier experience. When I addressed her as Dr. Sherman, she invited me to call her 'Dr. Mary' instead. We had fruit compote, pastries, salad, and a conversation like none I had ever heard before. Dave and Dr. Mary had

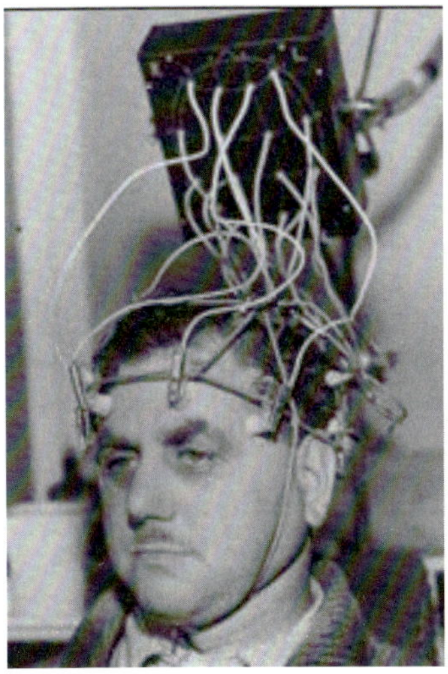

been chatting about the conquest of Mount Everest, but the conversation quickly shifted to medicine. Both Dave and Dr. Mary began describing chilling experiments on human brains being conducted at Tulane by Dr. Robert Heath. Heath's most recent exploits were described in the newspaper only yesterday. I had not seen the article to which they referred, so Dave began reading to me from the newspaper: "Listen to this, J.," he said. *"'Dr. Heath Tells New Technique. Electrical Impulses Sent Deep Into Brain [a patient]... had tiny wires implanted into precise spots in his brain. The wires were attached to a self-stimulator box, which was equipped at a push of a button to deliver a tiny, electrical impulse to the brain...'"*

Dave paused to let what he was reading sink in. "I wonder how many brains Heath went through before he had success with these two? How long did it take to find those 'precise spots' in their brains with his hot little wires?"

"Dr. Ochsner would never do such a thing," Dr. Mary said, pouring me some tea. "It sounds like science fiction," Dave said. "Who knows what kind of mind control could be exerted over a brain, twenty or thirty years from now?"

"I doubt John Q. Public will ever have a clue," Dr. Mary replied. "They certainly have no idea they are getting cancer-causing monkey viruses in their polio vaccines," she added bitterly.

Sherman's lab and told residents, "You better have a good alibi." As he recalled in an interview with documentary filmmaker Stephen Tyler, he had made the comment in jest - an example of a doctor's gallow's humor." I found his remark disturbing. Ref: https://www.nola.com/news/crime_police/article_7022729c-95bf-5fc7-b9ab-8000e1336f6a.html

Seeing my expression of shock, Dr. Mary went on to explain that she and a few others had privately protested the marketing of the SV40-contaminated polio vaccine being pushed onto the public, even as we sat here in this room --to no avail. The government continued to allow the distribution of millions of doses of the contaminated vaccine in America and abroad. She said she was assured that the new batches of the vaccine would be free of the cancerous virus, but privately she doubted it, since the huge stockpile of vaccines she knew were contaminated had not been recalled. To recall them would damage the public's confidence, she explained. I was speechless. Were they telling me that a new wave of cancer was likely to wash across the world?

THE TIMES-PICAYUNE, NEW ORLEAN

Physicians Offer Sugar Lump Toast

—Photo by The Times-Picayun

WITH CUPS LIFTED to the success of the Sabin Oral polio vaccine campaign are these three New Orleans physicians. From left are Dr. Philip H. Jones, Dr. William Rivenbark and Dr. Thomas E. Furlow Jr. Th were among volunteers handling assignmen Sunday at KO-Polio headquarters, 1000 S Charles.

While that was yet to be proven, Dr. Mary said, should we be using a hundred million people to find out? "The government is hiding these facts from the people," Dave said, "so they won't panic and refuse to take the vaccines. But is it right? Don't people have the right to be told the contaminant causes cancer in a wide variety of animals?" Dave made a snort of disgust. "Instead, they show you pictures in the papers of fashion models sipping the stuff, to make people feel it's safe." My mind raced. It was 1963. They had been distributing contaminated polio vaccines since 1955. For eight years!

Even I had received it! A blood- curdling chill came over me. Their words seared into my soul. The scale of the accusation confounded me.

The thought of a cynical bureaucracy that put its own reputation over the fate of millions of innocent people settled into me like a poison.

After Dr. Mary received threatening phone calls, she gave up public protests. Instead, she and Dr. Ochsner started working privately on ways to fix the problem. Together, they tackled the world of cancer-causing monkey viruses to see if they could figure out how to defuse them. For the past two years, they had been subjecting these monkey viruses to radiation in order to alter them into a benign form. "We're not quite sure what we have on our hands now," Dr. Mary said.

Her voice took on a tone of sadness. "Our work trying to alter the simian viruses led to the development of some rare and potent cancer strains," she said, "that seemed facilitated by their presence." I had a good idea about what she meant. It was more bad news, to my thinking. I'd brought along the research papers Dr. Ochsner had given me, having spent the last several hours frantically reading as many as I could to prepare for this lunchtime meeting. I could comprehend the unsettling revelation that an even more deadly cancer-causing virus existed now, but nothing could prepare me for what I heard next. "As you know," Dr. Mary said, "we've been working for some time on a project."

"I heard you hit a stone wall," I commented. "Dr. Ochsner told me," I said, thinking I knew where she was going with her comments. "...we may have hit upon a viable means to eliminate Fidel Castro," she said, "by what will appear to be wholly natural causes."

"No more poison pills, bazookas, or exploding cigars," Dave said. "The Beard is on to all that. Everything's been tried." Dave lit a new cigarette before his other cigarette was finished. "We worked together," he went on. "All of us. The anti-Castro people. The CIA. Cosa Nostra. The best mercenaries in the world. But he's defied the odds. Do you understand?" I nodded cautiously. "We became a machine ready to kill troublemakers who threatened American interests anywhere in the world. It was supposed to be able to wipe out Fidel," Dave said, studying his cigarette. Then he took another deep drag. "The problem is that a certain man says he will dismantle our machine if it doesn't obey him. This man is the most dangerous threat to America of all. He is soft on Communism. He refuses to go to war. He lets his baby brother go after the Mob, and errant generals. He plans to retire Hoover and wants to tax "Big Oil." He thinks he can get away with it, because he's the Commander-in-Chief."

I caught my breath, and glanced at Dr. Sherman as she began taking dishes from the table. The frown on her face told me they were deadly serious. Dave cleared his throat and coughed. "They'll execute him," Dave said, "reminding future Presidents who really controls this country ...those who rise to the top will gain everything they ever hoped for, and look the other way." Dave's hands trembled as he spoke. His nerves were as raw as his voice. "If Castro dies first, we think the man's life might be spared."

"How?" I asked, as the weight of his comments began to sink in. "If Castro dies, they'll start jockeying for power over Cuba," Dave said.

"It will divide the coalition that is forming. It may save the man's life."

"Where ... how did you get this information?" I pursued.

"You're very young," Dr. Sherman said. "But you have to trust us, just as we have to trust you. If we were really with them, you wouldn't be privy to this information. These people have the motive, the means, and the opportunity. They will seem innocent as doves. But they're deadly as vipers."

"What about Dr. Ochsner?" I asked.

"I don't know," Dr. Sherman said. "I can't tell. Perhaps..."

"He's an unknown element," Dave broke in. "But we know he's friends with the moneybags. He thinks Mary and I hate 'the man,' just as he does."

"Would he go so far as to— " I started to ask.

"I think he might aid others," Dr. Sherman said. "Perhaps without even knowing it. He functions as a go-between. His interest was to bring down Castro. He's anti-Communist to the core. But he's remarkably naïve." Dr. Sherman explained that in the past, Cuban medical students came to Ochsner's Clinic to be trained. Now Castro was sending them to Russia. Ochsner resented that. Some of those medical students realized that studying with Ochsner could have made them rich and famous, so they were bitter about Castro's denying them that chance.

Some were bitter enough to help kill Castro. Dr. Sherman's comments called to mind Tony Lopez-Fresquet's similar degree of hatred. "The clock is ticking," Dave said. "It's going to require a lot of work if we're going to succeed, where so many others have failed."

"We believe we have something," Dr. Sherman said. "But we want to see

what you make of it," soliciting my opinion and gently stroking my ego with her words. "Dr. Ochsner says you have serendipity."

"Yes," I replied. "He told me that."

"It's a rare compliment," Dr. Sherman went on. "You induced lung cancer in mice faster than had ever been done before, under miserable lab conditions." Dr. Sherman reached over and took my hand, squeezing it warmly. "That's what Ochsner likes about you. Your serendipity, he calls it. And we know you're a patriot. That's why you're here."

"This is lung cancer we're talking about," Dave said as he began smoking his third cigarette in five minutes. "Your specialty."

"That's what they wanted me to work with, ever since Roswell Park," I admitted. "You're an untraceable," Dave continued. "With no degree, nobody will suspect you, because you're working at Reily's, and you're practically a kid."

"We have only until October," Dr. Sherman said. "Maybe until the end of October," Dave amended, as he snubbed out his half-smoked cigarette.

"You can still choose not to participate," Dr. Sherman told me. "Yeah, we'll just send you over to Tulane to see **Dr. Heath**," Dave said bitterly. "A few days in his tender care, and you'll never even remember this conversation took place."

"You're not funny!" Sherman snapped at Dave, seeing my face. "Of course, nothing will happen to you, Judy! Dr. Ferrie and I are the visible ones, not you." To Dr. Mary's stern frown, Dave said, "Hell, I was joking!" "She is so young!" Dr. Sherman said reproachfully. "You frightened her."

"I'm sorry, J." he said. "What are you, nineteen?"

"I--I will be twenty, on the 15th," I said softly. Dr. Mary saw that I was trembling. She poured me a little glass of cordial and offered it to me, saying that it would relax me, but I declined it. "All I came here for was to have an internship with you, Dr. Sherman," I said, adding that I still wanted to go to Tulane Medical School in the fall. "Don't worry, you'll be there," Dr. Sherman said. "Dr. Ochsner said he'll sponsor you. That's set in stone." She paused. "We will not mention this again, at any time .... Take all the time you want to decide," she added. "If you say no, I'll just have you work in my lab at the clinic three afternoons a week. That way you can fulfill the terms of your internship, while still working at Reily's."

Dave got up and started pacing the floor. "You got onto the wrong side of this project by accident," he said. "We'd asked for more help, and you showed up, before the designee did...a matter of bad communication and timing." That was an understatement! "Ochsner always intended to have you involved," Dave said, "but it was supposed to be unwitting."

"I wish it were unwitting," I said. "You can always let me hypnotize you," Dave offered, trying to find some humor in the situation. "No, thanks," I told him. Gloom settled into the room. I noticed a large pastel painting hanging over Dr. Sherman's mantel depicting a series of dramatic scenes, such as a bull being killed with a sword, and a woman being stabbed by a Roman soldier. The painting reeked brutality and death. *"What have I gotten myself into?"* I thought to myself. "I want to think about this for awhile," I finally said. "Take your time, Judy," Dr. Sherman replied. She got up and went over to the kitchen counter, where two microscopes sat next to a rack holding some sixty test tubes, turning slowly under a light. I recognized this round rack from my work in cancer labs. The painting reeked brutality and death. *"What have I gotten myself into?"* I thought to myself. "I want to think about this for awhile," I finally said.

"Take your time, Judy," Dr. Sherman replied. She got up and went over to the kitchen counter, where two microscopes sat next to a rack holding some sixty test tubes, turning slowly under a light. I recognized this round rack from my work in cancer labs. Each test tube held a clear pink liquid in which cancer cells were growing. A motor rotated the rack, shaking the tubes slightly as they turned. Every three days or so, the fluid had to be replaced. About once a week, the cells were loosened from the glass with trypsin and transferred to new test tubes, so they wouldn't choke each other to death.

What we called "Ferrie's Wheel"

I have something to show you," Dr. Mary went on, "before you say 'Yes' or 'No.' I want you to inspect these first." She motioned me to sit down at the counter and handed me a stack of slides to view under the microscope. Each slide was carefully labeled, in sequential order. The age of the cells was indicated by hours and minutes, clearly displayed so one could see how fast the cells were growing and dividing. As I looked at several slides, what I saw was familiar. These were normal cancer cells. Then Dr. Mary gave me a second set of slides to inspect. As I began to inspect one slide--then another-- and another -- I couldn't believe my eyes.

A pancreatic cancer cell

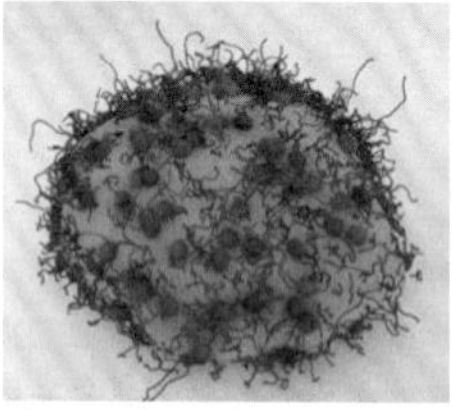

"I've never seen anything like this!" I finally said aloud, as I continued to re-check the ages of the cells at various stages and saw how rapidly they divided. "These are monsters!"

"They are, aren't they?" Dr. Mary said. It wasn't their size that got my attention. It was their aggressive growth rate. These lung cancer cells, apparently derived from pancreas cells, according to their structure, divided at a phenomenal rate. I had never seen such a fast and furious pace of division. The scientist inside me suddenly woke up: I began to get excited. "I need to see the log-books and reports. Whatever statistics you have."

"I'll get them," Dr. Sherman answered, knowing that the hook was in.

"Somebody bring me a note pad--" I said, not looking up from the microscope. "I assume you have electron microscopy studies on these things, right? Do you have photos?"

"We have them," Dr. Sherman confirmed. *Dear God!* I thought to myself, *I am looking at the deadliest cancer cells in history. Here, on somebody's kitchen counter. Who would ever believe me?*

"Well, J," Dave said, "now what?" Just then the phone rang. Dr. Sherman answered it and handed me the phone. It was Lee. He said he was at a grocery store and was in a hurry.

"They've arrived safely," he said, referring to his family. "All is well. I'm picking up groceries now. They're waiting for me in the car."

"You sound happy," I said. "I'm glad."

"Well, I am happy to see her, I can't deny it," Lee said. "So far, she's been nice to me, and my aunt and uncle already like her." I was not prepared for his next statement. "But I feel like I'll be cheating on you, if I sleep with her," he said. "I'm calling to tell you that."

"I'll have the same problem when Robert comes back in town," I said, turning my back to Dave and Dr. Mary and hoping they couldn't hear me. "How will I be able to say no to him? He's my husband. Besides, I still love him. It's just not the kind of love I have for you."

"I feel the same," Lee said.

"Just don't hit her anymore!" I reminded him. "You said it would prove..." I hesitated. "You said it would prove you love me."

"OK, just let me come over sometimes, if she riles me too much," he said. "I have to go now." With that, he hung up. "Was that Lee?" Dave asked. I nodded, then blurted out, "We're falling in love, and we're both married." Dr. Sherman turned away suddenly, her eyes laced with some inner pain. "Who do you love more, your husband, or Lee?" she asked. "I think I've already said too much," I answered. "Whatever you do," Dr. Sherman advised, "Don't stay with a man simply because you feel obliged to do so. He might turn out to be an albatross around your neck."

"She speaks from experience, J," Dave said. "Getting married was the worst mistake I ever made in my life," Dr. Sherman admitted. "It ruined my life. I hope it doesn't ruin yours."

"Probably the stupidest thing you ever did was marry Robert Baker," Dave said. His criticism did not sit well with me, nor did Dr. Mary's advice. "I wish to remind you both that I came here two weeks early...! It's easy for you to give me advice now, but where were you when I had to pay my rent? At least he came and married me," I said hotly. "And Dr. Sherman, you walked away when I tried to talk to you at the party. That hurt."

Dr. Sherman sat down on her couch, inviting me to sit with her. "I'm sorry, Judy," she said, taking my hand. "I meant to get in touch with you about that. I should have called you immediately. But I had to go out of town again, the next day. And then it slipped my mind."

"I have to divorce him!" I said, but Dave objected. "Don't divorce Robert yet," he advised. "There are advantages to having the name 'Baker.'"

"The name 'Vary' is rare," Dr. Sherman added. "People can look it up and discover your past, and your experience with cancer research. They might figure out who you are and why you are here. But nobody has heard of Judy Baker. You're protected by his name."

"Hey!" Dave said, smiling, "Dr. Ferrie, Dr. Mary, and Dr. Vary! How about that? But seriously, J," he went on, "keep your 'Vary' name as low profile as you can. Among us, you're J. Vary, but in the big, bad world out there, you're Mrs. Baker, just a secretary at Reily Coffee Company."

"It's really a fortuitous thing," he went on. "Stay married to the guy. At least until your work here is done." With that, Dr. Sherman handed me a key to her apartment and a note card with her maid's schedule on it, saying that it would be best to avoid running into her. An hour later, I was home again with Susie and her collie dog Suzi, glad to be interacting with a wholesome, normal human being. But 'normalcy' in my own life wasn't going to be possible. Not with what I knew now.

Sunday, May 12, 1963 On Sunday morning, I awoke rested and began reviewing a stack of medical reports and journals that I still had to read. As I took them from the shelf where I'd hidden them, safe under a pile of my clothes, I realized how paranoid it was to do that. On the other hand, if Robert suddenly showed up, how would I explain having so many articles and journals about cancer? Just then, Susie knocked on my door, saying she had made some breakfast for me. "I get worried about you," Susie said, setting down a little tray of toast, orange juice and scrambled eggs. I thanked her and gratefully began to nibble on the toast. That's when I told Susie that Lee had promised not to hit Marina again, but he might need a place to calm down if they had a fight.

"I suppose it would be the Christian thing to do," Susie said. "Why not make an extra key, and give it to him?" I gave Susie a hug. "You're too good to be true!" I told her. Susie explained that she and her husband had known Lee's Uncle Dutz a long time, so Lee felt like family. She then asked if I'd like to spend the day with her, starting by going to church, but I begged off. I had to spend the day reading medical reports and making notes for Dr. Ochsner.

Monday, May 13, 1963 I got nicely dressed and caught the Magazine bus, hoping to see Lee. When I spotted him sitting in the back, reading the newspaper, I quietly sat in the seat directly ahead of him, but did not turn around to talk to him. This was the "Natasha and Boris" game we would play for the next few days. When we got off at Reily's, Lee whispered, "I'll help you with the background report after lunch." He gave me a penetrating look. Then we entered Reily's to clock in. Lee walked to the right, into the production side of the Reily building, and I went back outside, heading to the Standard Coffee office across the street, where I was soon joined by Mr. Monaghan. "Time to go over to Congressman Willis' office," he said. "After that, we'll visit the Retail Credit company and go over some of their files, so when you meet with Mr. Oswald, you'll know what to do." Monaghan and I walked about a block, until we were across the street from Reily's, entering the Federal Building with its thick columns and interesting statues at the roof's pinnacles. Inside, building materials and boxes cluttered the marble halls. "They're renovating the building," Monaghan said. "The attorneys and courts are all moving to different offices. Today, you'll meet Willis' secretary. Then, whenever I send you over here, she'll know who you are." Willis' secretary had been with him for years. There was no greater patriot than Willis, she proclaimed. He was just about to take over HUAC, too – the House Committee on Unamerican Activities. She proudly showed me a stack of letters from constituents and political friends. The letters urged Willis to keep fighting Communism and to never give up the battle. I could not help noticing that some letters also condemned President Kennedy and his policies. Others attacked Kennedy for firing racist Army General Edwin Walker Another favorite topic was a call to 'Impeach Earl Warren,' the liberal Chief Justice of the Supreme Court. "He's in Washington right now," she said, "but he'll fly in next week. He goes back and forth, you know."

LA Rep. HUAC Chair Edwin Willis

"Ask Mr. Willis to call me with respect to a young man we have recently hired," Monaghan told the secretary, who wrote it down. It seemed Monaghan wanted Willis to know all about Lee. As the days passed, I would be returning to this office several times, carrying messages between the two men.[160]

After leaving Willis' office, Monaghan stopped in the hall to describe the task before us: we had to get some blank report forms from Retail Credit. These would be necessary to create Lee's bogus background report. It wouldn't be easy. Retail Credit executed tight control over anything with their logo on it as a matter of professional integrity. But Monaghan was a former FBI agent and knew some tricks of his own. We arrived at Retail Credit around 9:30 AM, at which time Monaghan introduced me to the supervisor, Mr. Henry Desmare, who gave me his card. Desmare was in charge of three or four men who were frantically working telephones and scribbling down information. Desmare hastened to say that his investigators not only spent considerable time on the phone, but they even visited character references in person. While his underlings investigated unremarkable and conventional individuals, Desmare and another supervisor handled the background investigations of important people such as executives. Those reports were more expensive and more thoroughly detailed.

Desmare treated Monaghan with great respect due to his commercial interests. The Vice President of Wm. B. Reily & Co. represented a large and important account. Monaghan wasted no time requesting access to Desmare's extensive files, saying he had the name of a candidate who could replace one who hadn't passed muster, due to a drunk driving charge. The new applicant's former boss mentioned that Retail Credit had already issued a recent report on him. Monaghan claimed that he could save Standard Coffee an employment agency fee by viewing the report. This was classic Monaghan manipulation.

---

[160] I was thus able to snatch a carbon copy of a letter to Guy Banister, which is in my evidence files, from a stack of papers that had been removed from a file cabinet, during his office move.

Mr. Desmare really had no choice: he reluctantly allowed Monaghan access to his carbon copy because he couldn't risk irritating an important client over such a small request. Desmare knew that Reily was building a big new factory for producing instant coffee and roasting beans. They would be hiring many new employees by the end of the year, and that meant lots of background reports for Retail Credit. The three of us sat down at one of the empty desks to review the carbon copy together. This was done for my sake, Monaghan explained. As the secretary he had personally selected to handle his security and financial issues, Monaghan said, I should know how to interpret what I saw. Now that Monaghan had Desmare's cooperation, Monaghan next asked him to fill out my background report, to make my hire official. Desmare asked me a few simple questions, then had one of his lackeys type up my "background report" on the spot, with Reily's VP watching him. But Monaghan wasn't finished with the manipulations.

We're going to be doing a lot of hiring soon," he reminded Desmare, "so I'd like Mrs. Baker to see some negative reports. All we have in our files are reports for people we hired, which are, of course, all positive."

Mr. Desmare had no problem with that, he said, as long as I pledged confidentiality. Once I did, he pulled out a stack of carbon copies of old reports prepared for Reily's. While Monaghan and Desmare discussed Reily's new, upcoming contract, Monaghan told me to type up copies of the negative reports, changing the names, on some of Retail Credit's blank report forms. Monaghan insisted he needed them for his secretarial training manual. Monaghan then commented that Reily would probably continue its relationship with Retail Credit, as he was pleased with the quality of its reports to date. They talked awhile, until Mr. Desmare noticed how much trouble I had typing the sample reports. "The carbon keeps getting wrinkled," I said lamely. "How in the world do you line up this onion-skin paper, so it doesn't slip?"

"You'll have to retype that more neatly later," Monaghan said, as he scooped up a few empty report forms. "I'll have her retype them at our office," he said to Desmare, as he prepared to leave. "I would prefer you didn't take any of those," Mr. Desmare objected. "They're company forms."

"I know," Monaghan said. "But we need some anonymous negative examples for our training manual. If the manual had some negative examples in it, I wouldn't have had to waste my time bringing her over here." Monaghan had pinned Desmare. He could not object further. Out we went with their precious forms in our grubby paws.

We now had what we needed to create a fake report to turn "defector Lee" into a model citizen, so he could pass Mr. Reily's muster. "You got them! I am so impressed, sir," I told Monaghan, as we headed back to Magazine Street. "Of course, I got them," he replied. "I get everything I want."

When we returned to Standard Coffee's office, Monaghan searched for a typewriter with a typeface that matched Retail Credit's typewriters.

He found one in Reily's main office and had it brought over to ours. I started to realize how careful this "former" FBI agent could be. Working with Monaghan was like working with a police sergeant. He would stand at his desk like a bird of prey, staring at the rows of women working on billing records, watching to see if anyone shrank from their duties for the slightest moment. Monaghan knew I would only be at Reily's temporarily, so he didn't bother to give me a real desk. He told me I could sit at his desk when he wasn't there, but when he was, I had to move over to a little extension desk that adjoined his. I called this my "half-desk." As a consolation prize, Monaghan gave me a nice nameplate to display on his fine, dark-walnut desk when he wasn't there. As the summer progressed, Monaghan was gone more and more often. I was not privy to what he was doing during these absences, and sometimes the workload was very heavy. I came to realize that his employment at Reily's was as much of an arrangement as mine. Monaghan was the first non-family Vice President that Wm. B. Reily Coffee Company had ever had. That was probably no accident.

Lee walked in just as Monaghan was leaving, and in a few minutes, we were out the door to have lunch together. I told Lee about my morning, and he told me about his. "It sounds like you're going to be busy," I said.

"Today, yes," Lee told me. "And tomorrow afternoon I have to go to Baton Rouge on business. You'll have to clock me out at five o'clock."

"But I get off work at 4:30," I protested. "Do I have to wait until 5:00 to clock you out?"

"Most mornings I'm going to be coming in about 8:30," Lee said, "because I usually have a meeting somewhere else first. I could even show up later than 8:30." I gloomily realized I would have to be at work from 8:00 A.M. until however long it took Lee to accrue his eight hours. If Lee were to be clocked out at five every day, I'd be putting in 2 ½ extra hours a week. Lee explained there were advantages to this arrangement. "You'll be at Dave's, and at Dr. Sherman's apartment two or three afternoons a week," he reminded me. "Sometimes I'll help you there. You'll be out of Reily's at least ten hours a week."

I disagreed. "You forget that the real rat race, or should I say, 'mouse race,' will be going on at Dave's," I reminded him. "And then I'll have a lot of work to do at night back at my place. Writing reports. Reading papers..."

"That reminds me," Lee said, taking out his address book. "I need to sketch a layout of your apartment." He found a page with room for the sketch and turned his address book upside-down. "That makes it a bit harder for others to recognize," he said, as he drew the layout. "I always assume this book might be read at any time by someone else."

Finishing the sketch, Lee said, "All right, here's your porch, the door and the living room. There's the window that's not blocked by your bed. Here's the big bathroom with no bathtub yet, and here's where the hotplate and counter is, where you still don't have a kitchen." Lee had drawn an indentation there.

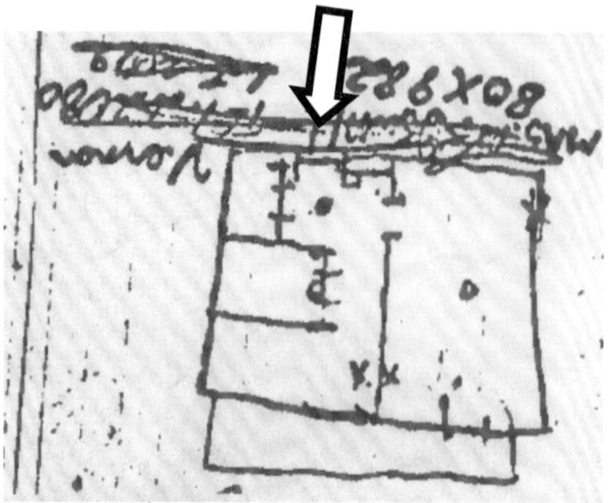

My apt. at 1032 Marengo, from Jan. 2000, before it was gutted and altered, and the sketch in Lee's address book. The cross-lines at the top of his sketch stand for the rest of the house, with a door, (see arrow) usually kept closed, to Susie Hanover's apt. by passing through a small room that also gave access to the driveway. Note the doorway and cut-off of porch due to railing. Photo shows house in bad shape in Jan. 2000. Four witnesses with me saw that the interior still matched Lee's sketch (closets added).[161]

Lee added lines showing the back entry and a step that led through a short, empty room (a central apartment) into Susie's kitchen. "Now, where will you be hiding your lab papers and notes?" he asked. I understood. If Robert ever saw those materials, he might wonder about them. "Susie said I can give you a key," I told him. "I think you would need one, to get at my stuff in an emergency." We decided that the key would be placed on a high ledge near the utility box, close to the back door linking both apartments. An 'X" can be seen sketched on the right outside wall, where a key was to be kept. I could store my microscope box on a high shelf in the living room. That's where the first of two interior x's are shown in the sketch. I kept the papers I worked on every night on a book-case in the bedroom, under my folded clothes. "If anything happens to you, we will need to remove things right away," Lee said. "We don't want Robert seeing any of this." If anything happened to me? My thoughts raced from 'emergency' to – well, something worse that could happen. Lee put X's on all three places. "I remember some overhead

[161] Witnesses: Martin Shackelford, Dr. Joseph Riehl, Dr. Howard Platzman. Photos taken. Susie's great-granddaughters claim the house was no longer in the family in 2000). Before the house was filmed for The History Channel, in 2003, it had been gutted. The door was moved to the center, no longer matching Lee's sketch. Nigel Turner and I were told "a doctor from London" renovated the house. The person we interviewed there claimed to be Susie Hanover's granddaughter. We no longer believe that, since other relatives said the house had long passed from family hands.

lights," he commented. As I pointed them out, he drew some little circles. I asked why he wanted to know. "It could save time at night," Lee said. "Those lights have wall switches." And so the sketch was finished and I finally got the courage to ask about Marina. "She was nice to me," Lee said simply. "We're trying to get along. Ruth Paine is already being a pain, though." (After that, Lee always called Ruth Forbes Paine "The Pain."). Lee said he believed Ruth wanted Marina to divorce him. "She acts like a lesbian," he said. "But maybe I'm reading too much into it."

"How did she get involved with Marina?" I asked. "She was selected to babysit Marina and Junie for me," he replied. "But she's not to be trusted, or her corrupt friends." Lee said that he had been fooled about her, because she pretended to be a peace-loving Quaker. One of his ONI trainers had been a Quaker, whom Lee had idolized. Yet her husband was helping to design helicopters for war. Our discussion then returned to Marina, who was already trying to make him buy her a washing machine.

"But Lee," I protested, "You are living like a Spartan, posing as a person unable to thrive in this country, and later, you're planning to pose as a friend to Castro, in an anti-Castro town. Did Marina agree to that kind of life?"

"She was happy enough in Russia with a tiny apartment to ourselves, contented with just a few things." Lee said. "But now she wants everything. A car, a house, nice furniture. She will have it, or else," he said. "I can't provide her those things and still look like a financial failure." Lee reminded me that we'd talked about this before. "I never cared about any of that in the first place," he said. "...We are completely incompatible. How much money you have doesn't equal your degree of happiness."

"I know," I answered. "But what are you going to do?"

"The Pain is going to stay in town until Tuesday," Lee said. "After she leaves, I'll try to make Marina more comfortable. I'll get her little things, to make her happier," he said. "But not any big stuff. If only she'll be patient! Otherwise," he said, with sudden heat, "back to Russia with her! Let her see if anybody there will give her a better life than I did!"

Seeing it was time to change the subject, I told Lee I still had no letter from Robert. "My birthday is Wednesday," I added. "I'll no longer be a teenager! But I think he's forgotten."

"Well, I'll make sure you won't be forgotten, but I can't help you celebrate on Wednesday," Lee said. "I'll have to be with my wife. It will be only the second night without Ruth. I need to spend time with Marina, because she thought I forgot our wedding anniversary. It couldn't be helped." As Lee said that, he leaned over and gave me a tender kiss. "No sadness about your birthday now, Juduffki!" he said. "You'll soon see what I'm arranging for us. We're going to have our own chance for happiness. You don't care if it turns out to be a Spartan life, do you?"

"My dear Scarlet Pimpernel," I said, "If we can be together, let it be in Antarctica, for all I care." We finished our lunch and returned to work.

At Standard's office, we sat down to look over what I'd typed on Lee's fake background report. "I used 757 French Street, your aunt and uncle's address, as your residence." I told him. "That's just fine," Lee said. "Nobody will care." He looked over the form and began to smile. "Hmm! We can have some fun with this!" he said. "Let's make Lee H. Oswald into a successful capitalist pig. Happy. Content. Perfect and prospering, with a loving wife and child."
"OK," I said. "Here goes!"

Wednesday, May 15, 1963 It was my 20th birthday. I was no longer a teenager! Would Robert remember? On the bus, Lee was in a glum mood. He confided that he'd done everything this morning. "I changed the baby, made coffee, fed the baby. I fixed my own lunch, washed out a diaper and, as usual, Marina wouldn't get out of bed."

"She's pregnant. Maybe she didn't feel well."

"She was okay," Lee asserted. "But Junie was crying, because I had to leave. Marina just stayed in bed and let her cry!" He said he placed Junie next to Marina, but Junie kept begging him to stay. "Your baby missed you when you went to New Orleans," I commented. "Make sure Marina goes to bed really early," I suggested. "Then she'll wake up earlier."

"Fat chance of that," he answered. Then I shoved a letter into Lee's hands. "Look at my birthday present from A-1," I whispered, so bus riders couldn't hear. Inside was a demand for most of my first paycheck. "It isn't fair!" I said. "Susie needs her rent money on time next month, but now, I won't have enough. We've been eating breakfast there every day, too. And her electric bill is due."

"Well," Lee said, "I can handle this. Since I can't be with you tonight to help you celebrate, at least I can go to A-1, and talk to them."

"Oh, thank you!" I put my hand on Lee's, and he slid a little closer to me. Our eyes met, then we looked away. We still had to pretend that we were just getting acquainted. At Standard, I finished the phony background report on Lee, dated it May 16, and placed the original in the manila folder marked with Lee's name. The manila folder would follow Lee from Standard to Reily's when he transferred over on Thursday. Then I worked on improving my typing speed and learning protocol and procedures from the vice president's secretary's manual. It was tedious, and lunchtime couldn't come soon enough. But when I met Lee over by Martin's grocery, Lee made life more interesting with some good news. "I found out that Banister's secretaries never doubted you were Marina," he told me. "Especially after you mumbled some Russian. So let's practice it some more. Even though Marina's in town now, we can find ways to be together and do things, because you can still pose as her. She's not really showing yet, and I keep her home, for her own good." To my puzzled look, he said, "Nobody can accuse her of being a spy if she never goes more than a few blocks from home. I've done that with her for almost a year now."

Turning the subject away from poor Marina, I asked if he'd found a chance to deal with A-1. Yes, he had. "First I went to the state employment agency," Lee said. "I pretended I still didn't have a job, so they gave me an appointment card. Then I went over to A-1 and showed them the card. That made them think I was still job hunting, that I didn't like working at Reily's. Then our friend, 'Miss-Ogynist,' found a new photo job for me to check out. It had just come up. If I went right away, maybe I could get it. I almost thought about responding," Lee said, smiling. "I have to clean out the roasters Friday, and I hear it's not as much fun as photography."

"Not nearly so much," I agreed.

"After she gave me the referral," he said, "I showed her your letter, and told her I was upset. How dare she agree that I could make a call to you, then charge you a week's wages!"

"Did she get mad?" [162]

"Yes, but I told her this would be the last time me or my friends would darken A-1's door, if she didn't at least cut your fee in half." Lee handed me an envelope. "Look at this." opened it and saw a bill for 35% of the original amount. "You did it, my *darlink*!" I said, with a fake Russian accent. "She wrote out new terms," Lee said. "Just one payment, then it's over. And it won't be due until after you're paid, on the 24th." That evening, Lee and I rode the Magazine Bus all the way to Audubon Park, where Lee let off steam about his marital problems. He told me Ruth Paine hadn't been gone an hour before he and Marina had an argument over how to discipline Junie. Their toddler was getting into everything.

---

[162] My letter may have come via Western Union. I no longer recall, but researcher Greg Parker insists Lee was sent a telegram through Western Union from A-1 Employment because "he had not supplied A-I with a phone number [so] A-1 sent a Western Union Telegram on May 13 to advise him that they had arranged a job interview on May 15." What's silly about this is that the document on exhibit in Vol. XXIII, CE 1951, p. 753, shows **Lee gave A-1 the Murret's phone number (HU-84236)**, so "no phone number" was not why A-1 sent the telegram May 13.

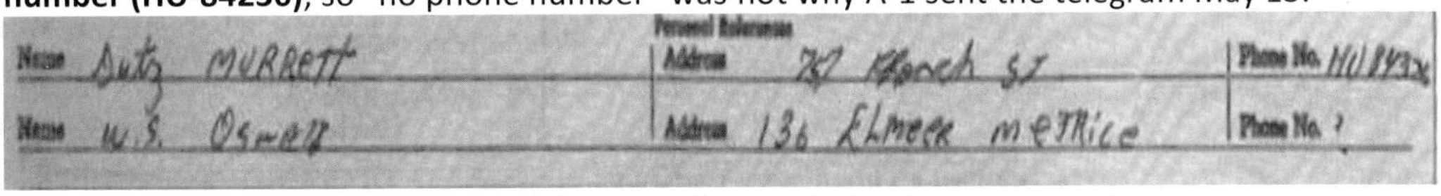
Name MURRETT | Address | Phone No.
Name | Address | Phone No. ?

The truth is on p. 2 (the contract) in C.E. 1951,p. 754, where the contract says **payment is due the first month of employment.** Lee was sent a collection notice, just like me, but by telegram**, because he'd moved**. The delivery person would be directed to the new address and Lee would get his notice of payment due. I received one in the mail, or maybe by telegram, too. On May 9, Lee told A-1 that he had already made an appointment himself to be interviewed by Reily that same day. But since Lee took his typing test (25 wpm result), and the Reily ad was posted at A-1, they insisted on being paid a fee because he went from their office straight to Reily's. I went straight from A-1, too, without a written appointment, was also hired, and was also dunned for the bill. My check to A-1 Employment shows that they required a fee from me, too, even though I had no appointment set up by them—just as they did to Lee.

Lee and I both believed that children could be disciplined without violence, while Marina slapped Junie to correct her. "The first thing I said when she slapped Junie was, 'I hope you go back to Russia!'" Lee admitted. "Change your pattern," I said. "It's pure habit. Instead of yelling at her, do something else. Walk out, if you have to. Choose to change."

As we rambled through the park together, enjoying the spring flowers, Lee felt his spirits rising. By the time we got on the bus again, he was planning to take his wife to the zoo. "I'll take her crabbing too," he said. "I'll get her away from the baby for a day. Maybe she'll have fun, if we go by ourselves." It sounded good to me. We kissed quickly, just before Lee got off the bus. As he did, the driver gave me a wink.[163]He knew! I got off at Marengo, and walked slowly toward my apartment.

I entered on the driveway side to say hello to Susie and Suzi Collie. After having some dumplings and milk, I finally checked the mailbox. Yes! There was a letter! It read: *"My Darling Judy: This is the back of a seismic record & the pen I'm writing with is the one I use to number seismic bumps with... Breakfast is 5-5:30 and supper is 4-4:30 P.M., or maybe an hour or 2 hours later. After that, there's just time to shower & relax enough to sleep. I haven't figured out how the workday can be so long & so short at the same time. Today the boss has gone ashore, so I get a chance to write. The French they speak around here is terrible..."*

I found Susie and proudly read my love letter to her. But Susie again observed that Robert didn't ask how I was. He didn't ask why I had moved to a new place. Nor did he tell me when he might be back. The letter continued: *"The work is really rough. It amounts to 6 hrs/day if I go out on the boat and 4 hrs/day if I stay here. The rest of it is eat, sleep & read. (There's an extra 3 hrs on the boat because it takes that long to get out & back). Then again, the first day I started work, the boat to take us to the quarter boat broke down, and the work day was noon 'til 8:00."*

So at last, he had written! As expected, he had forgotten my birthday. And Susie was right: there was nothing romantic about the letter. In fact, it could have been written to a man, except for the first and last words. Robert's influence in my life was shrinking, but coveting Lee's attention wasn't fair to Marina. She, too, was a stranger in a strange land. She, too, needed Lee's love and care. Many men who have an affair return to their wives after their fling. There was no safe haven for me. Robert didn't mention getting my letter, so I was afraid to send another one. Susie then went to the deli, returning with a slice of carrot cake with a little candle on top. As I blew out the candle, I realized I was a fool to ignore my parents' advice and elope, only to find myself alone.

Thursday, May 16, 1963 Back at work, before our transfer from Standard Coffee to Reily Coffee, I handed Lee's bogus background report

---

[163] Later, we learned that the bus driver was having an affair, too!

to Monaghan, who then took me to Reily's. I had learned who the salesmen were, saw their client lists, and accessed maps to trace their sales routes. Now, I was shown around in Packing and Shipping, in case I had to stop a shipment, or maybe add something to a shipment that would save a trip. Saving money was the key to Reily's success. As we went through the plant, I felt the pressure and heat of this factory workplace filled with machinery and hard-working employees.

Some were Cuban girls with kerchiefs tied over their hair so it wouldn't get caught in the machinery. Supervisors hovered around them, working as hard as their underlings. The thumping of rollers and motors filled my ears as the packing lines and conveyor belts moved rows of coffee cans and boxes of tea along. There was no air conditioning, and though it was only May, it was already uncomfortably warm. Each floor was full of machinery, sacks of products and stacks of supplies. Coffee dust floated everywhere. I saw Lee moving through this haze of dust, adjusting a belt here, squirting some oil there. "Mr. Oswald!" Monaghan called out, raising his voice over the noise of the machines. "Please come over here!"

Lee went over and stood before Monaghan as if he were a soldier. His hands were dirty, and there was sweat on his face. "Yes, sir?" he said.

"I've been advised that you have satisfactorily passed your training sessions," Monaghan told Lee, making sure his main supervisor, Emmet Barbe, heard everything. "Tomorrow morning, you'll clock in and go to the Standard offices, prior to your permanent transfer to Reily's. Mrs. Baker, here, will personally carry your Standard files over to Reily's, and will adjust your time-card and records to reflect that transfer, so your paycheck can be issued tomorrow without any delays."

"Thank you, Mr. Monaghan," Lee said. "Congratulations!" Mr. Barbe chimed in. Lee then excused himself, and left the area to go to another floor, while I was introduced to the supervisors in charge of the packing and shipping areas. They needed to know who I was. Then there was more training at Monaghan's desk. I learned how to use a Dictaphone, and then reproduced two business letters. Monaghan reviewed the letters, which took me almost an hour to type. "God help us, if you had a dozen letters to type," he groaned. "You'd be here until midnight. I hope the doctor's project will be finished before I lose patience with you." Miffed, I told Monaghan that no secretary could handle the research and lab work I had agreed to conduct.

Around noon, Dave Ferrie called and told me to make a dry run to his apartment, to calculate the time it took to get there and back. I would have to return by 5:00, to handle Lee's clock-outs. Since Lee hadn't been on the bus this morning, I was worried I'd have to wait longer than usual. In fact, Lee had barely missed the bus and Mr. Garner drove him to town in his cab without charge, so he clocked in only a few minutes later than usual. At lunchtime, I tried the test run. It took less than half an hour to reach Dave's apartment via streetcar and bus.

I noticed there were more mice now. From the logs, I knew Dave would be slaughtering this batch tonight. As I went over Dave's surprisingly well-organized logs, I recognized where we were in the cell-culture cycle and cooked up a new batch of medium, acutely aware that I was using the last of the fetal calf serum. Lee called just as I finished refreshing the cultures. "Just wanted to see if everything's okay," he said. "Is there anything you need?"

"We need fetal calf serum right away," I answered. Lee asked me to spell it, and I did so. "I'm making a list and checking it twice," he said. "Okay," I replied. I made copies of the new log entries. Now I had to head to Dr. Mary's! It took only ten minutes to get there from Dave's, because I caught a bus right away. *Okay*, I thought: *that's the deadline bus. I have to hit that one right!* At Dr. Mary's, as I arrived, I saw the gardener and stopped to chat with him. I showed him my key and told him I was interning with Dr. Mary and would be coming by a few times a week. I was surprised when the gardener said Dr. Sherman had already told him all about it. After setting up test tubes and duplicating records, I caught a bus back to Reily's. I had missed lunch, so I was starving. At the Crescent City Garage next door, I spotted a vending machine.

It held a single row of cookies, peanuts and cheese crackers. I bought a packet of Lorna Doone Cookies (my favorites), then returned to Reily to clock Lee out. At five o'clock, I waited at the bus stop, hoping Lee would show up and ride home with me, but he didn't, and I boarded the bus for home alone.

I arrived tired and sad. I was missing Lee horribly.

The house was empty. Susie had gone to visit her children. Even Suzi Collie was gone. Robert was in the Gulf. Lee was with Marina. I was with nobody. I missed my sister, my Grandpa, and even my parents. I ached to see my UF friends again! Miserable and hungry, I crawled into bed and crashed.

Chapter 16
The Office

Friday, May 17, 1963

When my new alarm clock went off. I got up, got dressed and headed for the Magazine bus, hoping Lee would be on it. He wasn't. Disappointed again! I thought about how important Lee had become to me in such a short time. Working at Reily's, and Marina's arrival, had made it harder for us to meet. I arrived, clocked in, and walked over to Standard Coffee's office, hoping to find Lee there, but he wasn't. Then, about 9:15, Lee arrived. When we saw each other, it was like magic: we couldn't stay in the office pretending neutrality, so we retreated to a private area where we held each other tight. "I've missed you so much!" I managed to say. "Hush, Juduffki!" he answered, kissing me again and again. I rested my head against his chest, listening to his heart race. Finally, I said, "I hope you've kept your promise about Marina, because I can't go on, if you ..."

"I'm keeping my promise!" he answered. "I'm not going to break it. She's okay."

"I have begun to dream about you," I said. "I know. We meet each other in our dreams." His statement startled me, because my dreams of Lee last night had been so vivid I felt it was a real meeting of our spirits. Could it be that somehow our subconscious minds had really reached out to each other? Lee slipped a tiny, crystalline plastic heart into my hand. "I made this for you on a lathe they have in the machine shop," he said. "When you look at it, remember, you can see right through it. My love for you, I want it to be transparent, hiding nothing." I saw that Lee's thumb had a bandage and mentioned it "Oh, I over-polished my thumb a bit, when I was polishing your heart," Lee said with charm. He got another kiss. Then I told him we could enjoy an extra-long lunch break together every Friday, because on Mondays and Tuesdays weekend order problems and emergencies always piled up, leaving no time for lunch. This meant we could have that long lunch today! Then I reminded Lee that Robert said he was returning Sunday and would stay until Tuesday morning. "If he asks what I'm doing, I will tell him everything," I warned Lee. "Even about us. If things in our marriage don't improve, I'll divorce him."

"On the other hand," Lee said, "as long as you are a newlywed, it would seem improbable that you and I might be having an affair. Have you thought about that?" I disagreed. "We're not sleeping together, Lee," I "We're not cheating on them," I declared. "Yes, we are," Lee said.

"Just as it says in the Bible, we're committing adultery in our hearts. The only difference is that we haven't committed it in bed ... yet."

"But I can't lie to him."

"You don't have to lie," Lee said. "You already said, 'if he asks'... If he doesn't ask, he doesn't deserve to know."

"If he finds out about you, he'll be very angry and hurt."

"Tell him we didn't mean it to happen. You were kicked out of your room, all alone. He didn't concern himself with you, or call."

"I think he'll walk out on me if I do that."

"Well, I won't abandon you, if he does. Besides, would you really notice any significant change in your life if he walked out? He wouldn't hit you, would he?"

"No, he'd just leave."

"Well, then," Lee said, "Leave it in his hands. If he asks, tell him the truth. If he doesn't ask, he doesn't deserve to know."

"I could hardly stand it this morning on the bus without you."

"I'm still having problems getting away from Junie. I'll make it up to you."

Lee took a look at my big, self-winding Benrus wristwatch which my father had given me off his own wrist as we said goodbye on my departure to St. Francis, saying I needed an accurate watch for my experiments. I had found it in the boxes I'd kept in the bus station until I moved them over to 1032. "Nice watch," Lee said. "I have a Benrus, too, but I can't stand wearing the thing anymore, unless I really need it. Speaking of time, it's time to transfer my records over to Reily's."

We found Monaghan, who put our personnel files in his briefcase and walked us over to Reily's for our official transfer. At Reily's, Lee was introduced to the Personnel director's secretary in the presence of clerks and secretaries in our huge office room, none of whom paused in their labors. Monaghan told her that I, too, would officially transfer over from Standard today. That's when I learned that as a "B" in the alphabet, my check had already been cut by Standard, and my check stub would be pink, but Lee Oswald, at "O" in the alphabet, still hadn't had his check cut. Instead, it would be cut on a yellow Reily paycheck stub. I was not to worry that my check stub said 'Standard" instead of "Reily," she explained. My next check would be a yellow one! And so it was.[164]Our files were accepted without further inspection. Thus Reily's, famed for its strident anti-communism, postures of patriotism and strict hiring practices, hired a notorious defector, a disgraced Marine, a known pro-Castro sympathizer and a purported Communist. When we rode the bus late that afternoon down to Audubon Park, we again sat in the back, even though several white people looked at us with hate in their eyes.

---

[164]Not all of Lee's check stubs have been published, but we have his timecards and other files showing his first day of work was the same as mine—May 10, 1963 (see Appendix and Color Pages).

This was the first time I'd experienced such looks, but Lee had been putting up with it for a long time. That evening, we discussed segregation and the racial situation in New Orleans.

Lee supported equal education for blacks, and he loved black children. He was also fond of the jazz heritage in New Orleans. Lee, who despised "hate groups," did not hide his feelings about them.

I naturally agreed with him. "I am willing to fight for racial equality, and would die fighting for it, if necessary," he said, loud enough for the Negroes sitting with us to hear. "I do not care a whit about money, power, or if we'd ever have a car or a nickel in our lives, Lee," I told him. "People, and their rights, have to come first."

"You and my friend George are the same," Lee said, referring to George de Mohrenschildt. "He told me I needed to get back to the survival stage, to get in touch with the important things of life again. I agreed. I told George I wanted to go walking through the jungles, just as he had done with his wife. But how can I? Marina is not that kind of woman... But you would walk through the jungles with me, wouldn't you?" he asked, as he stroked my
hair with his bandaged thumb.

"I would like nothing better, Lee," I responded, as if in a dream.

Lee said he had a birthday surprise for me, which I'd get next week after Friday's late lunch at Thompson's restaurant with the Lewises. The bus had now reached Upperline, and Lee got off: he had told Marina he would be coming home early so they could get groceries, so she was waiting at the bus stop, wearing pedal pushers. There was a scarf tied around her head. She was holding their daughter June by the hand. When Junie saw her father, she raised her little arms for him to pick her up.[165] Once home, I showed Susie my un-cashed paycheck. "You'll soon get your rent money!" I told her. "Robert said we'll have a bank account by Monday."

I was grateful that Susie was so patient about the rent, but couldn't bring myself to eat any of her food that night, because her refrigerator was almost empty. I'd had a good lunch at Thompson's with Lee, and that would do for today. Susie went to watch TV and I plunged into my stack of medical research reports, but soon fell asleep over them.... The next thing I knew, Suzi Collie was whining at the door. I woke up and yawned. It was 8:00 PM., and dark. I got up and looked out the front porch window. On the sidewalk in front of the house, I could see Lee pacing back and forth. He must have seen me sleeping and didn't want to wake me up. I ran up the hall, around to the living-room, and opened the front door. He quickly entered but didn't say a word. We went all the way around to my bedroom, where Lee sat down in the only chair.

---

[165] I have removed an incident where it looked like Marina had not acted correctly with Lee, because I did not hear the conversation, being on the bus, and I may have misinterpreted what I saw.

I sat on my bed with Suzi Collie beside me. "What a surprise!" I said. "What happened?"

"I'm here," he said, "because we had a fight."

"Did you...?"

"No. There was yelling, sorry to say, but that's all. I took your advice. I walked out." Lee had my sympathetic ear, so he poured out his story. "She burned the potatoes!" he said. "When I complained, she said it was all I deserved. So I told her, 'Go back to Russia to your boyfriends, and see if they'll put up with you.' Then she said she'd rather have sex with a German shepherd than have me touch her again."

"Oh, that was harsh!" I said. "I'm sorry. But think about it...The woman burned the potatoes. You complained. She insulted you, and once more, you told her to go back to Russia. Isn't that a big punishment for burning potatoes, Lee?" He stood up, walked over to the fireplace mantel, and stared at the alarm clock. "I peeled the demmed potatoes for her!" he said, defensively.

"What would you do if I burned your potatoes?" I asked.

"You're a good cook, you wouldn't."

"You made her feel worthless by telling her to go back to Russia for the umpteenth time, so she attacked your manhood. Also, for the umpteenth time."

"It's true," Lee mused. "That's what's been happening."

"You know why she does it, so let it be," I said. "Every time she attacks your manhood, remind yourself she's pregnant with your second child. You're a Darwinian success, Lee! I can assure you, you're a handsome man. I can hardly keep my hands off you!" I folded my arms and kept gripping them, as if I were having a real struggle controlling my hands. That made him laugh. The transformation in Lee as we spoke together was remarkable. He began to relax and returned to his chair. "I've had no desire for material things," Lee said. "And I've observed you are the same. I wish to live above the demands of the rat race and the gray flannel suit. I want peace. But I let her get to me."

"I know how gentle you can be when you interact with dogs and children," I said. "But then, they're no threat to your pride and feelings. The task is to dare to love somebody who is capable of hurting you and trusting that they won't step over that invisible line."

"It's too late for Marina and me," Lee said. "She doesn't just step over the invisible line. She has built her house on the other side of it."

"But I am not Marina," I told him. "We're building on something else here. I feel it. Trust. Faith. I feel betrayed by Robert, so it helps me understand how Marina hurts you. But I have to forgive him. If I don't, it will eat me alive. And you have to forgive her, too."

"Forgiveness!" Lee muttered. "We're not kids anymore!"

"It's the key," I repeated. "Forgiveness can take the place of what you felt when you first loved her. Forgiveness refuses to hit back."

"I didn't hit her," he said proudly. "I succeeded in controlling myself."

"Did you ever hit your Japanese lover?" I asked. "You say you loved her. It concerns me, because you abandoned her."

After a long pause, Lee shook his head. "I don't know what happened to her," he admitted. "I was so young. I thought I would get back to her someday. But it was impossible." Lee flushed, as if ashamed. Then he covered his face with both hands, in silence. I suddenly saw a tear fall from between his fingers, so I got up and put my arms around him.

"I loved her!" he said, getting himself under control. "They made me leave her!" I hugged him, as he wiped his eyes. "She was so good to me. And I let her go."

"Did you ever hit her?" I asked. "No, no," he answered. "I did not know it was possible for me to hit a woman, until I had to live with Marina."

"You *had* to live with Marina?"

"Yes, yes, I had to. I can't say any more than that." Suzi Collie came over to him. She put her head in Lee's lap. He absently petted her. "It's true," he said. "She hurt me to the core. At one time, I was fearless in love."

"If you were fearless once, you can be that way again." My words were making an impact. Suddenly, Lee stood up, went down the hall and through the 'bedroom passage' and into Susie's kitchen, calling Susie's name. Susie was either hard of hearing, or she was asleep, because he knocked at her door and called her name again. "Susie! We're going to go out for a while. We'll be getting some beignets. (Pronounced ben-yays) Can I bring some back for you?"

"Oh, I'd love some!" Susie replied. I happily began brushing my hair out and put on some lipstick. Then Lee came back, and with his finger, slowly and gently wiped away the lipstick. "Your lips are perfect the way they are," he said. "Remember, I had a surprise for your birthday? Well, it turns out that tonight is just as good as next week. Come on, Juduffki. I want to woo you." *Oh, dear*, I thought to myself, *I wonder what he has in store for me?* But as Lee guided me out the door, it was my turn to relax. Lee was my comforter and my protector, after all! Under the night sky we went walking toward St. Charles Avenue, where we boarded a streetcar and traveled to the French Quarter, stopping for a meal of oysters, shrimp jambalaya and crabs. It was delicious. "They say the world's food gets worse the further you get from here," Lee said as we walked to Jackson Square. "Here, here!" Lee called out, stopping a horse-drawn carriage.[166] "No, it's so expensive!" I protested, but Lee insisted.

[166] **I recalled a horse-drawn carriage.** Some people disputed my memory, claiming it was mule-drawn. Perhaps this helps: "**Royal Carriages** in New Orleans, Louisiana began in 1941, **using a mixture of both mules and horses for the first 30-years.** In the 1970's, Mr. Jimmy Lauga visited The Reese Brothers at their farm in Gallatin, Tennessee. Mr.

The carriage started up, with its gentle rocking motion. The clip-clop of the hooves and the jingle of the bells on the horse's collar was soothing, and the driver was kind to the animal. We passed fountains, bright-lit shops, fancy restaurants. We heard music come and go as we passed night clubs.

Lee put his arm around me and laid his head against mine. We leaned back to watch the wrought-iron balconies and the sky above. The stars were mingled with low clouds that gently rolled across the sky. "Happy birthday, my love!" Lee said. As our idyllic tour of the French Quarter came to an end, our carriage returned us to Jackson Square. Next was the Café Du Monde, one of the world's famous coffee shops, where Lee ordered their silky smooth *café au lait* and beignets for us. Two sacks of beignets were to go: one for Susie, and one for my breakfast. Arm in arm, we headed back to 1032 Marengo.

There, we sat on the porch steps, silently enjoying each other's company. It was now midnight. That's when Lee drew a small white box from his pocket and handed it to me. "It's your present," he said. "I got it for you on your birthday." I opened the box. Inside was a necklace made of faceted black beads, carved from real jet. They glittered in the streetlamp. "It's exquisite, Lee!" I exclaimed. "They are like the jet buttons in Kate Seredy's book, *The Good Master,*" Lee said. He said he wanted me to never forget my Hungarian heritage. "Then you really read the book?"

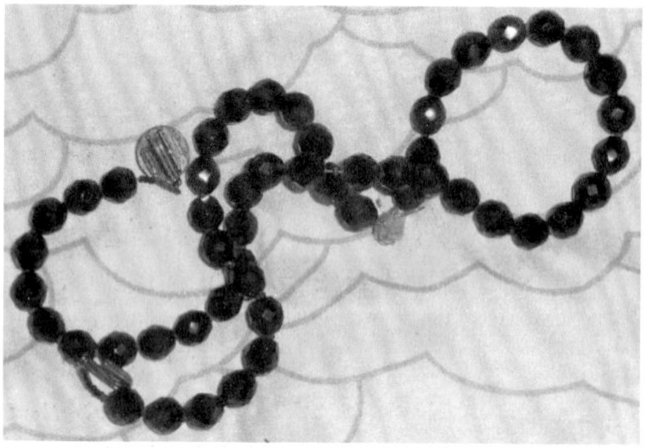

"Of course!" Lee said as he took up the necklace and fastened it around my neck. "How did you forget that?" In fact, somehow I had, perhaps because Lee had been scrambling my brains at that time as much as he said I was scrambling his! The necklace was heavy, and the jet beads glistened. "They suit your Hungarian skin," he said. "You and I have the same spirit!" he said emphatically, placing his hands on my shoulders. It had nothing to do with how different our ancestors were, he insisted. This, he said, was deeper. "That's why we've been dreaming of each other," he declared. "Yes," I said, "We are going mad with love for each other."

"But I *know* you," Lee went on. "If we were living under repression in Hungary, we'd both be freedom fighters. We'd be the ones to pull down the statues. Throw Molotov cocktails at the machine guns. That's why I want you to have this necklace." Lee was right. I'd fight for freedom.

Lauga was more than impressed with the quality and care of these extremely large Belgium draft mules. He soon replaced his entire herd with mules instead of horses, and it's been that way ever since!" https://www.neworleanscarriages.com/about-us/news/french-quarter-carriage-mules

Lee and I were the same. Meanwhile, in America, we would do our part to try to achieve equality for all. [167]

Sunday, May 19, 1963 It was late Sunday afternoon, and Robert's return from offshore was imminent. About two weeks earlier, Lee and I had gone to the library and found the telephone number for Evangeline Seismic, and I'd called the company, asking them to give Robert my new address. His letter reaching me at 1032 proved he had it. Now I was ready to tell him all about the raid. I felt it was time for him to know a lot more, too. My life had changed drastically during the seventeen days he'd been gone. Hoping to please him before talking about any bad news, I dressed to the nines for him, with upswept hair, pearls and makeup. It was a beautiful spring evening in New Orleans. I thought about the opportunities the evening held. We could go out for supper and enjoy the city's wonderful cuisine, walk around the French Quarter together, and have some real conversations that our separation had denied us. If things worked out, I would tell him everything. Confide in him. Set things straight. We could renew our relationship in total honesty and see where we'd go from there...

Then Robert knocked at the door! I rushed to open it, and one look at him was all it took. I melted and forgave all. He looked so handsome, dressed in his khaki pants and shirt from his ROTC days. His dark hair had grown long and curly. He threw his arms around me, and I could smell the salty sweat of the sea on him. "Oh, you kid!" he laughed. I had come to accept that this was his way of saying, "I love you."

He released me long enough to throw Suzi Collie out the front door. She landed with a yelp, and a pang went through my heart. That was no way to treat my innocent friend! Nevertheless, as he closed the door and locked it, I shyly put my arms out toward him and he led me to the couch, where he pulled my shoes and nylons off, throwing them across the room. I protested. "Shhhhh!" he said, kissing me. "You always want to talk. We'll talk later. Right now, there's only one thing that matters. You — and me!" He laughed, believing I was embarrassed because it was still daytime, so he carried me to the bedroom and lowered the blinds. He was amused by my modesty and found my resistance entertaining. "Come on, 'switch-heart,'" he said. "I need my lovin' — and so do you." His physical needs rolled over my emotional needs once again. There was no quiet dinner, no stroll through Jackson Square, no heart-to-heart conversation, and not much sleep... In the morning I gathered myself together. I had to head for work. Meanwhile, Robert slept in a state of exhausted bliss.

---

[167] Lee's friend in Dallas, George de Mohrenschildt, wrote in his book about Lee, called I Am a Patsy!: *"Kennedy's efforts to alleviate and to end segregation were also admired by Lee, who was sincerely and profoundly committed to a complete integration of Blacks ...."*

<u>Monday, May 20, 1963</u> As I waited for the bus, I was anxious to find out how things had gone for Lee with Marina. When I got on the bus, I saw Lee sitting in the back. This was our second week of riding the bus to work together, so everyone saw us get off at Reily's each day.

We felt it was now safe to sit next to each other, as if we were co-workers who had become friends. As I sat down next to Lee, he asked if I'd had a chance to talk to Robert.

"I never had a chance to tell him a thing," I said. "He finally fell asleep. And he's still asleep!"

"Marina's still asleep, too," Lee said, in a down voice, adding that he had played with their baby June longer than usual last night to tire her out so her mother could sleep in. It worked.

A small victory, and he was able to leave today without June screaming for him to stay. I thought about him and Marina, and wondered how they had gotten along. Frankly, I was wondering if they had sex. I told Lee that Susie had suggested we introduce Robert to Marina and let nature take its course. I thought it was an extremely clever idea, but Lee just sat quietly, without responding. I had hoped for at least a smile.

"As for sex," I whispered, to make sure he was listening, "I'm exhausted. The man should have a harem!"

"He sounds like a formidable lover," Lee said flatly. "I doubt I could compete."

"There's more to love than what happens in bed!" I blurted out before realizing that I was talking a bit too loudly. "I just hope I can get a decent night's sleep," I added, returning to a whisper. Lee reminded me about my plan to dump a bag of ice cubes on Robert's privates to cool him off. I laughed and told him I had the bag of ice but had forgotten about getting it out. I thanked him for reminding me. Mondays were always hectic at Reily's, when an avalanche of trouble always landed on Monaghan's desk. There would be dozens of items demanding immediate attention: inquiries from billing clerks, new customers whose credit needed checking, unfair parking tickets to dispute for delivery trucks, plus unusual and sometimes illegible hand-written orders. Was there enough product for a certain big order? What about an order for a discontinued product? Here was a poor credit risk, asking for a new start. Could we ship a certain product to Germany? Store X had received the wrong item and wanted a salesman to pick it up and give them the correct item… a product came damaged… products had been stolen and the payment for them would thus be delayed… All of these had to be dealt with on top of my normal workload as Monaghan's floor secretary. This included handling both his financial documents and his field correspondence, as well as approving (or rejecting) the Finance-Character Background Reports for new Reily employees. Some of the salesmen's questions could be answered on the phone, but the finance-related letters had to be typed and often needed research into files and records. I also handled queries arising from unusual or lost timecards, expense advances for salesmen and paycheck disputes.

On Tuesday, we'd get more of the same. Then the pace slowed way down, so I could leave Reily's at noon to do lab work the rest of the week. That Monday, Lee finished at 5:00. As we boarded the bus, he asked me to ride with him all the way to Audubon Park, even though I'd told him I was dead tired and just wanted to go home. "But we have to train them not to expect us until 6 or 6:30," Lee countered. "Otherwise, we'll lose this time together." He was right, of course. We spent half an hour at Audubon. Park, saw the seals, and then headed back. When I got home, Robert informed me his goal for the next day was to open a bank account. Then he said it was time for us to go straight to bed, even though I was very hungry. "Relax!" he told me. "I got us some sandwiches!" He began to softly strum his guitar, knowing its soothing effect. I closed my eyes and let exhaustion spread over me. As I rested, Robert told me that he had already eaten his sandwich. My sandwich had been waiting for an hour, he said, a bit testily. So where in hell had I been? Weren't working hours from 8 to 5? I said I was salaried and usually had to work late. That wasn't a good start to try to tell him 'everything' that was going on. I thanked him for getting the sandwich, telling him that I'd never even had time to eat my lunch. Robert actually checked my purse to make sure my little bag of cheese and apple slices was still there. It was, so he moved on to the next topic: was the Mansion really a whorehouse?

I assured him that it was and told him how Mary and Bill Richardson helped me, avoiding mention of Lee. But Robert's mind was already focused on the next issue: he complained that by my receiving a salary, I would not get extra money for overtime. It paid more money than Royal Castle, I reminded him. Then, as I ate, Robert got out the bank papers for me to sign. He had already filled in my name as *Judyth A. Baker.* But Dave Ferrie had told me to use "Mrs. Robert A. Baker, III" to keep the paper trail more obscure. The problem showed up on the first check I wrote. The bank wrote "*Judyth A. Baker*" on the back to identify 'Mrs. Robert A. Baker, III.' Despite their complaints, I continued to sign my checks "Mrs. R. A. Baker, III."

The bank didn't like it, but they finally accepted it. After the bank papers were signed, I asked, "Can we go out tonight? Maybe just walk around the neighborhood together? I know where we can get some delicious ice cream."

"I'm all for it, when we have more time," Robert said. "Besides, it's expensive to go out." Then he complained that the apartment cost twice as much as the room I'd formerly rented for only $30.00. "But that was a whorehouse, Robert!" I protested.

"We still don't have a private bathtub," he replied.

"I've calculated our budget again," he went on. "You can see for yourself how much more expensive it is now. And if the car breaks down, we're up a creek." We'd have to live on my paycheck alone, he said, and put everything he made straight into the bank, just to make sure we'd be okay. He had cashed a personal check from our new account, where my first paycheck landed, for $25 when he was at the bank. He put $10 into my purse, keeping $15 for himself. "This should cover your meals, transportation and all other needs," he said, until he returned again (whenever that would be). I asked him why he needed so much money out on the quarter-boat, with free room and board. He explained that there was no bank nearby, so he had to have emergency money. Over the weeks, Robert would have plenty of "emergencies," as it turned out (Susie thought he was gambling). Next, Robert told me he needed breakfast at 5:00 AM.

He'd be leaving for work in Houma at 6:00. He was only staying overnight! And so, he cajoled me into yet another round of whoopie. Much as I liked sex, this was overkill! After it was over, I got up and looked at him lying there, looking so cute and harmless, wondering when I could lie down again in safety. Then I heard him mumble, "Who knows how long it'll be, before I'm back?"

"You did ask how long your next hitch will be, didn't you?"

"Oh," he said, yawning, "I forgot. It just didn't pop into my head."

To my silence, he added, "By the way, babe, I'm thirsty. How about fixing me some iced tea? By then, I think I'll have another surprise waiting for you!"

Another surprise? I slowly turned and went into Susie's darkened kitchen, where I slowly mixed two glasses of Luzianne instant iced tea. Maybe he'd fall asleep. But just in case, I got the bag of ice out of the freezer... After he had his iced tea, Robert was indeed ready for more excitement the moment I got in bed. So, at the right time, I grabbed the bag of ice and emptied it on his "love machine." His response was immediate: "Hey! *What the hell!*"

"I needed your attention tonight!" I replied. "You have been gone so long! But since the attention I can get from you is of one kind only, I'm informing you that you've had enough lovin' for tonight, and I'm going to get some sleep!" I laid down with my back to him and smiled, wondering what Susie had heard in the other end of the house.
She wasn't *that* hard of hearing!

Tuesday, May 21, 1963 The next morning, Robert was preparing for another stint on the Gulf. He lugged a seabag in from his car, full of dirty clothes.

He told me to do his laundry and buy some spray starch for his shirts, so when I ironed them, they would be crisp and nice. He was too grouchy to even say 'please.' He did try to motivate me, however, by saying that the other men on the quarter-boat envied the fact that he had his own little "wifey-poo" to do his laundry and iron his shirts for him. Feeling refreshed and confident after a few hours of good, sound sleep, I could hardly hide my laughter. "That wasn't funny! I hope you grow up!" Robert growled.

"You need to grow up, too, and quit holding grudges," I replied.

"If you ever do that to me again, I'll never forgive you!"

"Fine. Besides, you should be called 'Rat' instead of Robert."

"And why in hell would you do that?" he said, seeing that I was flying the flag of open rebellion. "Thanks for asking — at last!" I said, hurt feelings bringing tears to my eyes. "First of all, we've been married three weeks, but you only wrote twice!" I wiped my tears angrily away from my eyes. "I was forced to move in the middle of the night, and — thank God! — found shelter at a rector's house! You never bothered to ask about what happened, or how I got this apartment, or how I got my job."

"I'm sure 'God' had nothing to do with it," he answered, as he picked up his car keys. "Don't you want to know how I managed to move here, with so little money?"

"Well," he replied, "I assumed the rector at the church helped you."

"Wouldn't you like to know more?"

"Do you know what time it is?" he answered. "It'll have to wait. I have to leave."

"You never once asked in your letters how I was! You didn't call!" I started crying again. "And now you can't even tell me when you're coming home again! Plus --you forgot my birthday!"

"Damn!" he said. "I'm sorry! When was your birthday?"

"Wednesday. A week ago." Robert frowned.

"Well, you have a right to call me 'Rat,'" he said apologetically. "I need to be more thoughtful." As he stood in the doorway, ready to leave, he then insisted that I go see Mrs. Webber and make her refund the rent money. After depositing several kisses on my tear-streaked face, he left. I was so upset that I didn't realize he took the house key with him, until it was too late. When I saw I couldn't lock the door, I went to Susie, who was always up early. She reminded me of the extra key on the ledge outside, but we were both too short to reach it. Finally, we pulled a metal stepladder out from under the house and retrieved the key. Then I headed sadly to work. As I got on the bus, I saw Lee in his usual spot in the back. Only then did I realize how little I had been able to tell Robert. When I told Lee that Robert had taken my key, he said he would get another copy made for me later in the day (And he did.).

With the early-week crunch over, I betook myself to Dave's lab and from there went to Mary Sherman's apartment on Wednesday, Thursday and Friday to continue our work on the Project. I saw neither Dave nor Dr. Mary all three days, though Dr. Mary did leave update notes for me.

On Friday afternoon, as per instructions from Dr. Mary, I wrapped the refrigerated specimens in a sterile glass jar insulated by newspapers and put it in a car parked in a narrow alley next to Eli Lilly, on my way back to Reily's. That was usually Lee's job, but because he was so busy this week, I did it.

View at 640 Magazine St. in front of Reily's, Jan. 3, 2000. Dark building at end of block was Eli Lilly's warehouse and former manufacturing unit. The dark wall of the alley can be seen inset at Eli Lilly. Today, the space exists as a semi-closed area. Stone building to right is the Federal Bldg (CIA,FBI,courts,etc): Rep.Edwin Willis' office (HUAC) was at the top floor on this corner. As Chair of HUAC since May, 1963, Willis and the CIA kept track of all defectors.

Once the Product was dropped off, a driver got into the car and drove away. What happened next? Was the Product subjected to another round of radiation, presumably at the U.S. Public Health Service Hospital? I wasn't told. My evening hours were often spent catching up on work I could do at home for Reily's, along with the usual speed-reading assignments.

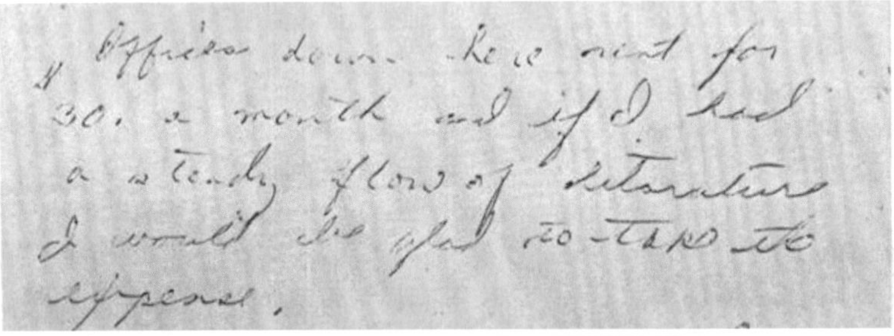

Offices down here rent for 30. a month and if I had a steady flow of literature I would be glad to take the expense.

<u>Monday, May 27, 1963</u>

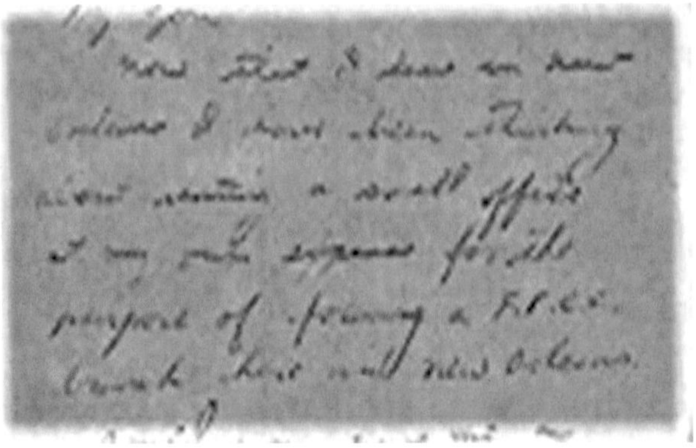

Now that I live in New Orleans I have been thinking about renting a small office at my own expense for the purpose of forming a F.P.C.C. branch here in New Orleans.

Blowup of portion of pg. 2 of Lee's letter to FPCC Chairman Vincent T. Lee, says "offices down here rent for $30. a month..." Excerpt of p. 1 shows Lee will be "renting a small office at my own expense for the purpose of forming a F.P.C.C. branch in New Orleans...." The letter was written May 26. I bought the $30 money order May 27 for his $30 office. Lee paid me back May 28.

Around lunchtime, Lee suddenly showed up. He had obtained permission from "Mr. M" for me to leave Reily's for two hours. The first time Lee had pulled such a stunt, he told Monaghan we had to go see "a film about clandestine matters." The film was, in fact, James Bond's *Dr. No*, which we had wanted to see together! I had no idea what Lee had up his sleeve this time, because it was not a Friday, when things were more relaxed at Reily's. It was a Monday, the busiest day of the week. Once we were outside, Lee explained that he needed me to buy a money order for him.

"You now have a bank account," he said. "So, I'd like you to take out $30 and buy me an American Express money order. Don't worry. I'll pay you back right away." To my question, why, he replied, "I have to rent an office for the FPCC, and I don't want a clerk remembering my face.... As long as you don't put your name on the thing, and you're never photographed with me, you'll be safe."

My anti-Castro friends had told me that the FPCC (Fair Play for Cuba Committee) was a pro-Castro organization, so I pelted Lee with questions about his rationale. "It's a ploy," Lee explained, as we walked. "We're out to ruin the FPCC. They're not on the list of subversive organizations-- yet. But HUAC and the CIA wants to put them there." Lee explained that by joining their organization and then overtly acting like a Communist pro-Castro supporter, he'd give HUAC another reason to ban the organization as subversive. "To do it right, I need to rent an office," he said, "though we'll never hold a meeting there,"

"Why rent an office at all, then?" I asked him. "It's needed to get it started," he answered. It made him look like somebody who ought to be given a charter. A money order receipt number would 'prove' to FPCC headquarters that a donation paid the rent, showing support, even though Lee didn't intend to have it open more than a month. Both the janitor and Sam Newman (the owner of Banister's building) knew Lee was Banister's man, so there was no long-term lease to sign.

"The only problem," I replied, "is my A-1 check. I have to pay them $17.44 today." Lee's face clouded over. He had forgotten about that, and my bank account was perilously low. We calculated that a $30 money order would put me in the hole if Robert wrote any checks I didn't know about. Lee then asked if I had money in my purse.

"Lee Oswald, you're a genius!" I answered. There was indeed money, and many other things, in my purse! I'd been stashing nickels and dimes in there for weeks. And I still had $14 left over from Sparky's $50. Robert had just given me $10 for lunches and bus rides. As I hunted, I pulled out tissues, various lipsticks, a hairbrush, a plastic horse and fifteen mouse pins, much to Lee's amusement. By the time I finished my search, I even found some money left from Reverend Jim's. All totaled, I located $31.00 in bills and change, and gave it to Lee. He took the money, counted it, and said it was enough. Then he handed it back to me. I would have to go into the American Express office alone.

"Just don't write anything on it," he reminded me. "You don't want to have to explain who 'Sam Newman' is to Robert," he advised. Lee then told me that he would pay me back after he got his unemployment check from Texas in the morning. My straight-arrow Catholic upbringing sprang to the fore. "But you're working. Isn't it dishonest to get unemployment checks when you're working?"

"Was it honest for my boss to tell people I was fired at my last job, when I did good work there six days a week?" Lee asked. "It was all part of the plan."

"But how did you get the State of Texas to ...?" Lee smiled and put his finger against my lips. "I... can't... tell.... you..." he said slowly, letting each word fall with its own weight in four beats. "But I can guarantee that the money isn't coming from Uncle Fidel." I gave up trying to follow the players, techniques, and motives in Lee's complex covert world, and bought the American Express money order. In return he bought us hamburgers and Dr. Peppers, which we ate before I returned to Reily's.

<u>Tuesday, May 28, 1963</u> The next day, as I toiled away at Monaghan's desk, Lee arrived, bringing me a banana, $33 in cash, an envelope from my bank, and a deposit slip for me to sign. "You need to put $30 in the bank right away," he said. "You're skating too close to the edge."

"But how will I explain it to Robert?" I asked. "Easy!" Lee said. "Just tell him you cleaned out your purse!" He was right, that's all I needed to say. Robert would never object to my depositing every red cent I had!

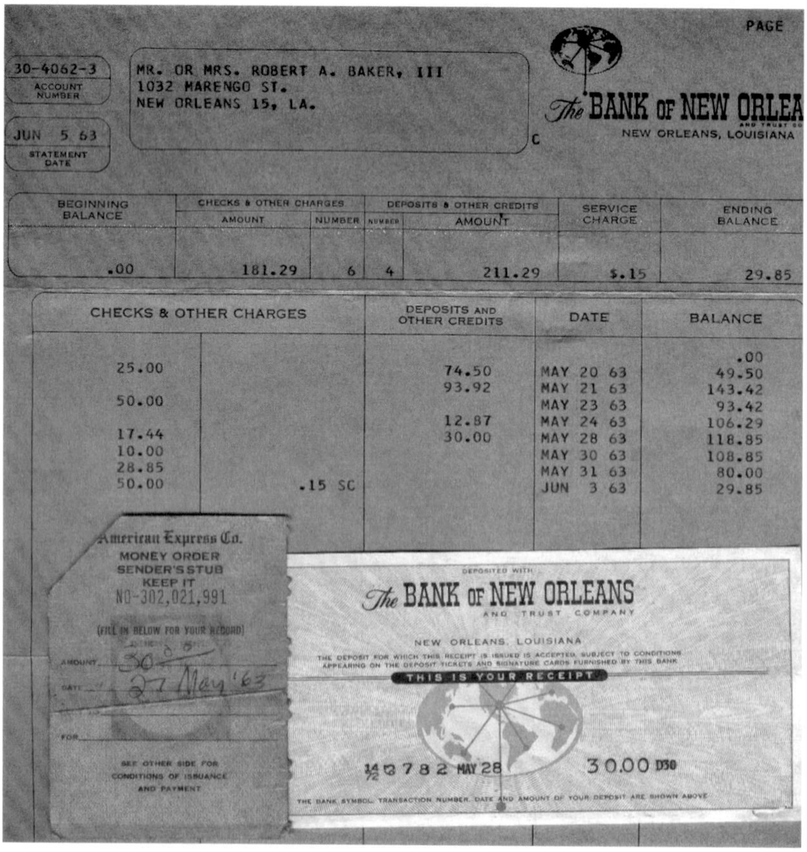

PAGE

30-4062-3 ACCOUNT NUMBER

MR. OR MRS. ROBERT A. BAKER, III
1032 MARENGO ST.
NEW ORLEANS 15, LA.

JUN 5 63 STATEMENT DATE

The BANK OF NEW ORLEA[NS] AND TRUST CO
NEW ORLEANS, LOUISIANA

BEGINNING BALANCE	CHECKS & OTHER CHARGES AMOUNT	NUMBER	DEPOSITS & OTHER CREDITS NUMBER	AMOUNT	SERVICE CHARGE	ENDING BALANCE
.00	181.29	6	4	211.29	$.15	29.85

CHECKS & OTHER CHARGES		DEPOSITS AND OTHER CREDITS	DATE	BALANCE
				.00
25.00		74.50	MAY 20 63	49.50
		93.92	MAY 21 63	143.42
50.00			MAY 23 63	93.42
		12.87	MAY 24 63	106.29
17.44		30.00	MAY 28 63	118.85
10.00			MAY 30 63	108.85
28.85			MAY 31 63	80.00
50.00	.15 SC		JUN 3 63	29.85

American Express Co.
MONEY ORDER
SENDER'S STUB
KEEP IT
NO-302,021,991
(FILL IN BELOW FOR YOUR RECORD)
AMOUNT 30.00
DATE 27 May '63
FOR
SEE OTHER SIDE FOR CONDITIONS OF ISSUANCE AND PAYMENT

DEPOSITED WITH
The BANK OF NEW ORLEANS AND TRUST COMPANY
NEW ORLEANS, LOUISIANA
THE DEPOSIT FOR WHICH THIS RECEIPT IS ISSUED IS ACCEPTED SUBJECT TO CONDITIONS APPEARING ON THE DEPOSIT TICKETS AND SIGNATURE CARDS FURNISHED BY THIS BANK
THIS IS YOUR RECEIPT
14 3 7 8 2 MAY 28 30.00 D30
THE BANK SYMBOL, TRANSACTION NUMBER, DATE AND AMOUNT OF YOUR DEPOSIT ARE SHOWN ABOVE

Lee's $30 Office Payment, re letter May 26

$30 AMEX, May 27

$30 deposit slip, May 28

$30 Deposit on Bank Statement May 28.

End balance, $29.85.

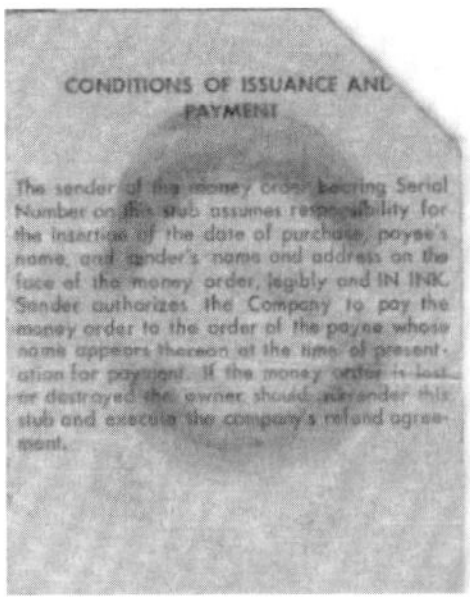
CONDITIONS OF ISSUANCE AND PAYMENT

The sender of the money order bearing Serial Number on this stub assumes responsibility for the insertion of the date of purchase, payee's name, and sender's name and address on the face of the money order, legibly and IN INK. Sender authorizes the Company to pay the money order to the order of the payee whose name appears thereon at the time of presentation for payment. If the money order is lost or destroyed the owner should surrender this stub and execute the company's refund agreement.

I deposited the money during the lunch break, which turned out to be vital, because the balance on the next statement was $29.85, thanks to Robert's unbudgeted expenditures. I kept the American Express receipt in a safe place, just in case Lee ever needed it, but because Lee had handled it, I kissed it!

I was clocking out at five, then working another hour or more at my desk, waiting for Lee's clock-out time to roll around. This staying late every night was noticed by the clerks, helping to cover the fact that I was absent Wednesday through Friday from 11:30 to 4:30. Since I worked through lunch on Mondays and Tuesdays, too, the impression was that I worked a full 40-hour week. That day, I had assumed that Lee would clock out at 6:30, as he had been doing recently. But he surprised me. He had clocked in an hour early, so we could leave an hour earlier. He said this was my reward for helping out with the money order. He then handed me a library card and asked me to pick out books for us to read together. Lee and I rode the bus up Magazine Street to Audubon Park an hour ahead of schedule, because Lee had clocked out early. Just as the bus stopped in front of Lee's apartment, we saw Kerry Thornley sprint up to the porch, open the screen door and enter without knocking, as if he owned the place. To Lee, the situation was self-evident: Thornley was fooling around with his wife! That was unlikely, I thought, but Lee exploded in jealousy and started to get off the bus to confront Thornley, so I grabbed him. Think!" I whispered. "You now know something about Thornley that he doesn't know you know.

That can give you an advantage." Lee remained seated, but he was fuming with anger. You could see it in his eyes. The bus started up again, but I was afraid Lee would get off at the next stop. I only had a few blocks to talk sense into him. "If you go in there with blood in your eye, you'll upset your little girl, and somebody may call the police," I whispered. "Do you want the police coming to 4905? Will your family be safe during your pro-Castro stunts, if the police know you live at 4905?" Lee frowned, squeezed his hands together, and calmed himself. "I'll get to the bottom of this," he said. "Please stay with me," I said. "That way, you'll be coming home at the expected time. If he is still there, maybe he has nothing to hide."

Thanks to research by Edward T. Haslam, we now know that "The Mouse House" was at 3225 LA Ave Pkwy, some two blocks from Dave's apartment, across the street. No wonder we got our mice so quickly! In 2003, I was able to show Nigel Turner, for the History Channel documentary "The Love Affair" the incinerator used to burn mouse carcasses, which was still in the back yard at that time.

Lee later told me that things were not as they seemed. He and Thornley had a truce. It was now the end of May, and the Project's weekly cycle of slaughter-harvest-irradiate- and-reinject mice was fully operational. On Wednesdays we sacrificed the mice, harvested the tumors, weighed them and prepared their tissues to process on Thursday. The mouse carcasses were then picked up by the Cuban boys from the **"Mouse House"** for disposal. On Thursday, the remnants were minced, and cultures created.

<u>The Cultivation Process</u>: The cancerous cells were started in a Roswell Park 1640- type solution + 10% Fetal Calf Serum (FCS). The recovered cells would be centrifuged in the little tabletop centrifuge, the pellets then placed in fresh medium plus FCS, The cells would now start to attach to the glass of the test tubes, where, bathed in RPMI medium, they began to grow. We also used plastic stackable mini- flasks for cultures, insulated at 37° C. The cultures would be examined on Friday for cell density and morphology. Cell cultures only remained with Dave or Dr. Mary one to two days. Back-ups were kept longer in case any cultures got contaminated. A pH indicator (Phenol Red) was added to tell us when waste product build-up in the test tubes required a fresh medium, as it turned from bright pink to yellow as wastes made it more acidic. When Lee was not available, I left the Product, insulated in a package, in the afore-mentioned car parked next to Eli Lilly's.

On a few occasions, I even went directly to Ochsner's Clinic to pick up hard-to-get materials such as neonatal umbilical cord serum and ascites fluid. A few times I had to go to Hugh Evans' lab on Camp Street to get chemicals that we needed. Through it all, I was becoming overworked. My typical day started before 6:00 AM and ended around midnight. The final task of my nightly routine was to hide the lab reports and research papers, in the unlikely event that Robert showed up unannounced.

There were a few meetings with Dr. Sherman at her apartment, at which time she taught me to recognize different kinds of cancer and new staining techniques. I only met Dr. Sherman a few times on a social basis, as a friend, because under lab conditions, she was a strict and rigid boss. An occasional night at Dave Ferrie's also entered my schedule for several weeks. Because we were all working hard, we felt abused when Ochsner demanded more from us. He had called me at Reily's several times to ask for ideas. His calls were not considered unusual, since Reily was INCA, Ochsner was INCA's President, and I was Monaghan's secretary 'just 'taking a call.' I offered Ochsner several ideas that were implemented. One recommendation was to try the transfer from mice to monkeys again, but this time, to expose the monkeys to radiation beforehand to suppress their immune systems. Ochsner liked the idea and noted that they had concentrated their radiation efforts on tissue cultures, not living hosts. I was surprised they had not adopted this approach earlier, since I had used this method to develop rapid cancer in mice in 1961. But it would not be long before I would regret ever reminding Ochsner on "how to make the cancer more deadly."

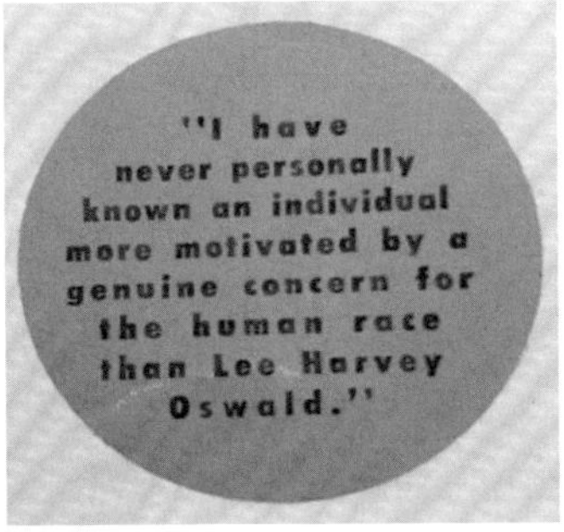
"I have
never personally
known an individual
more motivated by a
genuine concern for
the human race
than Lee Harvey
Oswald."

Quote: attributed to Kerry Thornley

Chapter 17
The 500 Club

David W. Ferrie

Friday, May 31, 1963

Today, Lee and I were told to meet Dave Ferrie at Charity Hospital at noon. At least, this time we did not have to wait. As soon as we registered (using only our initials as advised), we were sent to the same room in which we had met with Dr. Ochsner. This time Dave was waiting for us, seated in the same chair that Ochsner had used and conjuring up an air of importance. I wondered why we were meeting him in Charity Hospital instead of at his house. Perhaps he had just finished meeting with Ochsner? Whatever the reason, Dave gave us fresh medical reports, which had been flown in from New York,[1] and then informed us that Ochsner had approved our proposed transfer of cancer from mice to monkeys. "It's an expensive step," he told us. "But time is running out. We have maybe a month to succeed," he said, smoking his cancer stick as he spoke. Since we would soon kill a large number of very expensive monkeys in the process, replacements were being ordered from Africa. They were slated to arrive at the primate lab before researchers on other projects, beginning in the autumn, would wonder what happened to their monkeys. "Here's my updated schedule," Dave informed us. It was getting full. It included flying to Toronto for Dr. Sherman. Then, Dave told us that an important arms shipment was expected from Venezuela.

[1] Including reports from Dr. Chester Southam, who injected live cancer cells into 22 unwitting elderly patients at the Jewish Chronic Disease Hospital in Brooklyn, which will be discussed later.

Our meeting at the hospital, he said, was to provide some extra security. Certain persons had been invited for an important meeting to be held openly in downtown New Orleans. "The most secret of matters are discussed under circumstances that seem the most harmless and ordinary," he told us. "So come when you're called, and don't ask any questions." When I asked what the meeting would be about, Dave replied, "The crux of the matter is simple. The shipment has to get through. If it's confiscated, people will be murdered in retribution. It will come in one of three sister ships. We'll know which one, when it's time. We must protect this shipment," Dave explained. "The problem is, some of the stevedores and dock workers are spies. Some are pro-Castro, some are FBI informants, but they're all stool pigeons. They will talk to the highest bidder, or go to the FBI." Dave made a derisive snort. "Hoover loves to see JFK get blamed every time he orchestrates another crackdown on an anti-Castro project."

"Marcello will cooperate in this because he backs the anti-Castroites here," Lee explained to me.

"One reason you're being told about this," Dave said to me, "is because Ochsner wants to mine your brain for some ideas about the rifle shipment. He thinks you're creative, even though we all know how stupid you are."

"Very funny," I told him.

"I've already talked to Marcello," Dave added. "We might not be able to disable all the spies, so we also have to figure out how to protect the shipment from being recognized." Now I understood. "What will the cargo look like?" I asked.

"Well," Dave said, "The rifles will probably be packed in unmarked crates, or maybe in barrels."

"Not good," I replied, intrigued by the problem. "Part of protecting something from discovery is to make it look like something else entirely." I suggested using crates marked as furniture, which would actually have rifles slipped in with an unassembled table, or with two nested chairs. After removing the rifles, the tables could be assembled — or the nested chairs placed side-by-side — to fill the crates, and nothing would seem amiss. "Good idea," Dave said. "I'll get our friend Shaw to help us out with this one," referring to Clay Shaw. "He can tell us if we can get stuff like that boxed and shipped in from Caracas."

As an Executive Director at the International Trade Mart, Clay Shaw was at the center of the international trade community in New Orleans. Shaw's longtime mentors, Ted Brent and Lloyd Cobb, had deep connections to both Ochsner and the CIA. Connections between Dr. Ochsner and Ted Brent were so strong that Brent left the fortune he had amassed during his lifetime to Ochsner's Clinic upon his death.

The hotel on the campus of Ochsner Clinic was named Brent House, in his honor. The CIA's presence in New Orleans was as blatant as it was logical. Shaw and his business associates who traveled abroad cooperated with the CIA's information gathering as a patriotic duty. They would fill out reports for the CIA on people they met and matters they observed. Some of them spent far more time gathering information than others, and the line between a mere "domestic contact" and a spy could get fuzzy.

Shaw had a long history of cooperating with Dr. Ochsner's anti-Castro efforts. His friendship with Dave Ferrie was based on their mutual interest in the homosexual scene in New Orleans. Dave said Shaw was a devoted patriot and CIA asset. International House was the Trade Mart's formal link to Dr. Ochsner and that Shaw and Ochsner had run International House together for years, with secret deals created through dinners, meetings and private sessions at "IH." Ochsner certainly got around. Naturally, a spy and informant ring thrived there. Dave abruptly closed the meeting: he had to give a flying lesson to a young Cuban. Leaving Charity Hospital, Lee and I headed to Dave's, on Louisiana Avenue Parkway, to finish the week's lab work. I also began to teach Lee the necessary procedures to follow to keep cell cultures alive. After that, we returned to Reily's, where I picked up my paycheck and punched out. Since Lee had clocked in quite late that morning, I would have had to wait two more hours to clock him out, so he suggested that we get something to eat and then come back to clock him out. OK, fine! "Don't worry," Lee said. "I have a key to Reily's, and we can get back in."

Lee cashed his paycheck at Martin's Grocery-Restaurant, but we went on to Thompson's, where Anna Lewis cheered us up with her down-to-earth jokes. Her husband David was there, too, so after a snack, the four of us walked to the **Preservation Hall** to enjoy some New Orleans jazz.

It was all going so fine, when suddenly, we remembered that Lee hadn't been punched out yet! Hurrying back to Reily's, Lee unlocked the door, and in we went. But it was terribly late: Lee was clocked out at 7:32 P.M.

"Luckily for you," I told Lee, "I am the one who will have to resolve your late clock-out when Payroll starts screaming about it next Thursday."

"What are you going to tell them?" Lee asked.

"I'll say I was working late. You called and said you forgot to clock out."

"That will work," he confirmed. "Another lie!" I said wistfully. "I hate having to lie all the time."

"Think about what Dave told us today," Lee said. "We're shipping rifles in secret, and if the secret is discovered, people will die. Sometimes there's no choice. A lie can sometimes save a life." Despite how late it was, I stopped and bought some needed groceries, knowing I was going to be too busy on Saturday because Dr. Mary had invited me to tour the Crippled Children's Hospital with her. Then – a shock! The moment I got off the Magazine bus, I spotted Robert's blue Ford sitting in the driveway! I was so glad that I had groceries to help explain my lateness. It was now far too late to tell him about anything I was involved with, outside of work at Reily's. But I doubted he'd even ask. I quickly stuffed the research papers I had with me between some colorful brochures from the Crippled Children's Hospital, and entered the apartment quietly, the groceries in my arms. Robert's blue and white denim duffel-bag with its red initials 'RAB III' was sitting just inside the door, filled with dirty clothes.

Had Robert returned so soon to get his laundry done? I could see him lying asleep in the bed. His army boots and ROTC pants were on the floor. I tiptoed quietly through the connecting room into Susie's kitchen, where she was humming to herself as she bent over the oven. I entered just as she removed a fragrant, bubbling apple pie from the oven. Usually, Susie was in bed this time of night. But tonight, she'd been inspired to bake. "Have some tea, my dear!" she said, adding, "You do know who is in your bedroom tonight, don't you?"

"I think he's asleep," I told her. "Have a piece of pie," Susie said. "While you still have a chance!" We both laughed. After putting away the groceries, and eating a slice of Susie's delicious pie, I returned to Robert, who immediately woke, as if triggered by some insatiable urge... but then, I knew all about that insatiable urge, and kept my distance. Craving some answers about what was going on, I was determined to trade accessibility for information. So, I began to negotiate. "How long will the next hitch be?" I demanded. "I have no idea!" he answered. "They keep changing the schedule on me."

"How come they know the schedule at the office over in Lafayette?"

"Weather happens," he said. "Problems come up. You're mad over nothing."

"You need to write and to call! I'm your wife! I need to know you care!" I almost blurted out that I was struggling hard not to sleep with another man and that I needed love in ways other than sexual, which Lee was providing, but I came to my senses in time.

"Do you realize you never say 'I love you'?" I said, starting to cry. "I tell you I love you, but you never say it back. I have feelings!"

"I might be gone twenty-one days, next time out," Robert replied. "They're trying to finish early. That's why I came home for a day. And you're wasting all the time we could have together by fighting! So how do you feel about that?" We stopped talking again as Robert, in a huff, decided to check my expenditures. I saw that as a punishment now. He broke the silence by observing that I had lost weight and told me to be careful to eat enough. About as soon as those words of concern were out of his mouth, he reminded me not to buy anything frivolous, such as dresses, fancy food, or any more shoes. His spate of advice finished, Robert picked up his guitar and began playing a song on his guitar. Now he was purring like a lazy lion. Laying the guitar aside, he turned on the radio Lee had given me and found some relaxing music. Then came kisses. My body responded, betraying me again, but this time, a part of me held back.

When "love" was over, Robert brought out some sandwiches he had purchased from the deli. Susie knocked on our door then, and offered us some of her apple pie, which we enjoyed. While Susie went off to bed, I knew that my night was probably just getting started.

"Did you get any of my letters?" I asked. He said he had, then asked me if I had washed and ironed the clothes he'd left behind.

My sadness deepened as I began ironing his shirts on our end table, for I still had no ironing board and had put off ironing, too tired from my long hours to tackle Robert's clothes. I'd washed his shirts, though: they were clean. I'd used Susie's beat-up old washing machine out on the patio. It had a hand wringer on top to squeeze out the water. As Robert watched me iron, I felt like a pit stop in his routine, without considering that I was doing nothing to make things better between us. "We've been married almost a month," I told him, moody, still in a snit. "And there are no photos of us together."

"Why did I come?" he replied. "I might as well go back right away." I couldn't believe it -- Robert decided, just like that, to leave! He took the shirts I'd ironed out to his car. When he came back, he said his parents would take photos in Fort Walton Beach, and we'd see them soon. "Things don't seem to be going anywhere here tonight," he added, "so I'll just go. I'll call you Sunday." Then he was gone. Once again, he took the house key with him. He'd gotten his sex, and that's all that mattered. I put away the iron, then went into the bathroom to wash. That's when I saw that Robert left his shaving brush and lather cup behind. In my black mood, I thanked the God I no longer believed in that Robert had stayed only a few hours. Then I fell asleep.

Saturday, June 1, 1963 Early the next morning, feeling guilty, I baked some brownies and packed them with Robert's shaving equipment in a little box with a note that read, "Look for mold before eating!" I mailed the package at the post office, using his address at "Pip's Place," then continued to the Crippled Children's Hospital to meet Dr. Mary._She took me around to see the patients. There were children in iron lungs, in traction and others with bone pain so extreme I had to leave their bedside to get control of my emotions. Some were still recuperating from surgeries which Dr. Sherman had performed. As she handed out little stuffed animals and candy suckers laced with aspirin, **Dr. Mary** explained that several of the children in the polio ward had actually been crippled by the faulty polio vaccine. This was another reason Dr. Sherman was discreetly engaged in polio vaccine research, and why she was so interested in the cancer-causing virus that had contaminated the polio vaccines. Dr. Ochsner's horrific experience with the flawed polio vaccine that had killed his grandson in days and had crippled his granddaughter put these two colleagues on the same page. Both were aware that SV40 and other contaminants were still present in millions of doses of the new, "safer" vaccine; both doctors realized its potential to cause an epidemic of cancer in the future. But for professional and political reasons, they had remained silent as the pro-polio vaccine propaganda machine continued to churn out fresh ad campaigns. As the political landscape changed, Dr. Mary lived with knowledge that she knew she could never speak about. Not if she wished to stay employed. Our government was withholding the truth about the safety of the new polio vaccine, even as she operated on the legs of children that the vaccine was crippling. Because I had been raised to trust my government, the shock to my young, patriotic soul was devastating.

Tuesday, June 4, 1963 Lee had a meeting with David Ferrie at Banister's, so he once again clocked in late. There, strategies were discussed to protect the upcoming arms shipment. When the meeting broke up Dave gave Lee his own personal card to access Tulane's medical library so I could access materials related to our cancer work without having to travel up to Ochsner's medical library. Lee told me to go to Tulane's medical library right_after work and have the librarian call Dr. Ochsner's office right away, to verify that my name was added to

Ferrie's card. "Ochsner said you could use Dave's card until you're issued your own in the fall," Lee said. "That eliminates a paper trail." Mr. Monaghan agreed to clock me out early so Lee could take me to Tulane's medical library before it closed. At the library, we sat at a research table while the librarian called Ochsner's office. He was worried about Marina. She had fainted during a walk. He dreaded the idea of taking her to Charity Hospital, where he had already been seen memorably with me, due to our bloody incident with the poor colored woman, so he had cared for her assiduously all weekend, keeping her in bed as much as possible. In the middle of this humane concern for the health of his pregnant wife, he said, "I now tell her every day that she should go back to Russia."

"But Lee," I protested, "I thought you were going to stop doing that to her. And here she's been fainting!"

"I know," he replied. "It looks mean. But I need her to think she has a choice between being happy without me in Texas or being happy without me in the Soviet Union. I've already started processing things with the Russian Embassy." Lee meant that he knew Marina would never return to the USSR. She would always choose Texas and the friends and support she had there. Of course, if she really wanted to return to the USSR, he couldn't stop her. "So, I keep telling her to go back to Russia," Lee explained, "but I would refuse to divorce her if she did, which helps develop my pro-Castro image." I caught on. "Because, if you say you'll send her back to Russia without divorcing her, it means you still love Russia and Cuba. Is that it?" "Precisely," Lee replied. "If it's known I want her and my baby to go back, that proves I prefer Mother Russia as the place to raise my children. That looks good for my Cuban credentials."

"But in actuality, she'll choose Texas, won't she?"

"Yes. And that will be good, because I can readily pop in and see my babies if they're in Texas. Here, there's nobody to help but Marcello, and my aunt and uncle, especially if I end up in jail, or in prison over this."

"Jail? Prison?" I asked, taking his hand. "Could it come to that?"

"Anything can happen with the New Orleans police," Lee said. "Somebody might draw a gun on me. An incident could happen. They could plant a gun on me, or drugs, or try to send me up the river. Because I'll be acting like Fidel's best friend. That means danger for my family, if they stay."

There was so much Lee did not dare tell Marina. Lee said, "The Pain" (Ruth) was planning a long vacation, which would delay Marina's return to Texas. That was okay, he added, because he wanted to be with Junie as much as possible before his more dangerous work started. I was then called to the desk. The librarian said Ochsner's Clinic OK'd the card.

I would be issued a temporary pass for the summer. When I used it, I should show the original card. In fact, after a few times, the Tulane librarians recognized me and never asked about Dave's card, which remained in my purse. I eventually forgot it was there. That was a mistake.

When we returned to Reily's, Lee spent an hour oiling the roasting machinery. Then I clocked him out. By now it was both dark and hot in the closed-up factory area. Lee came out covered with sweat, heading to the bathroom on the first floor by the canteen to wash up. At his locker, he changed his shirt. We got on the bus, which was almost empty, and Lee, exhausted, rested his head in my lap. When I got home, I found Susie in the dark, crying. "What's the matter, Susie?" I asked. By now, she meant a lot to me. "Pope John has died!" she said mournfully. "It was stomach cancer!"

I was thunderstruck. So many people were dying of cancer! I thought of my grandpa: full of worry, I decided to risk calling him. He told me he was in remission, and not to worry. He also promised he wouldn't tell my parents where I was. The Pope's death reminded me that instead of striving to cure cancer, I was creating a bioweapon from cancerous materials! How could such a once-devout young Catholic girl stray so far from her path? I was disgusted with myself. Sick to my stomach, I collapsed among the pillows and wept. For the first time, I feared that I might never again be involved in curing cancer. How could things have gone so wrong, so quickly?

June 5, 1963 — Wednesday The two hardest days at Reily's were finished for the week. Today, the hard work was at David Ferrie's. Dr. Ochsner wanted us to speed up the project, so he had doubled the number of mice we had to kill.

Instead of fifty, I had to slaughter one hundred weanling mice, eviscerate them, then salvage and weigh the largest tumors. Lee had business elsewhere, so I was on my own. It was disgusting work, and it took longer than usual to clean up. I returned late to Reily's. There, Lee met me with a book under his arm: *The Huey Long Murder Case*, by Hermann Deutsch. Lee was interested in the case because Dr. Ochsner had personally known the accused assassin, Dr. Carl Weiss. But did Weiss deserve all the shame and blame he had received? Lee had decided to visit a few bars to see if some of the old-timers remembered details about the murder. He eventually learned from "the old-timers" that Weiss was shot at least fifty times, rather than the thirty-two reported. They said bullets removed from Huey Long didn't match Weiss' smaller caliber revolver. Two decades after the assassination they were describing Weiss as a decent man, a good doctor. That's when I learned what the word 'patsy' meant. Lee said Weiss was "probably a patsy," – a slang term for an innocent man forced to take the blame for a guilty one.

Thursday, June 6, 1963 I clocked out at five, then returned to Mr. M's desk. There had been so much to do at Dave's that I'd left a note telling him I had to return to finish. Then the phone rang. It was Dave.

"No lab work for you tonight, bright eyes!" he said. "I've taken care of it for you. And guess why?"

"Because you're a kind, sweet, wonderful, sensitive man," I said. "No, seriously, why are you being so good to me?"

"Call Susie Hanover and make sure your hubby's not in town," Dave answered, "because if he's not, you're going out!"

"I am?"

"Indeed you are. Remember that Sparky fellow who walked around my place on his hands?"

"How could I forget?"

"He's going to foot the bill for all of us, including you, me, Lee, and the Lewises -- over at The 500 Club. But we have to be there by 7:00."

"What about Marina?" "That's Lee's problem," Dave said. "Not ours. He has to attend. Marcello's going to be there." By the time I met Lee at Thompson's Restaurant, I was nicely dressed. Lee was wearing a white shirt and tie. He had just finished talking to Marina on the phone. He was still concerned about her fainting. I asked him if he knew how her day went. "Oh, she's feeling all right, so far," Lee replied. "But I'll just stay an hour or two. I told her I had to work late. But I promised to bring her a treat." Lee asked Anna to wrap up two slices of pecan pie for him to take home. He gave me the pie slices to carry in my semi-bottomless purse. When Anna got off fifteen minutes early and went to freshen up, I asked Lee how he had been able to change into such a nice shirt without going home.

That's when I learned that Lee kept a nice shirt in his locker at Reily', for special meetings. As soon as David arrived, away we went to 441 Bourbon Street. *The 500 Club*! I couldn't wait to get inside! We arrived at seven o'clock, as instructed. Sparky came to our table right away, giving us special attention and chatting with us. He sat with us until Carlos Marcello arrived.

He was accompanied by several large, muscular companions, a couple of attorneys, and a couple of his brothers. Others kept arriving, who Sparky needed to see. Next, a tall silver-haired gentleman entered with another man, who was flanked by a woman covered with jewels. They sat down with the Marcello group, but were hard to see because of the way the tables were lined up. Lee leaned over to me and began identifying the important people with Marcello. “The one who just came in, that’s Clay Shaw, the managing director of the Trade Mart,” Lee whispered. “He’s the one building the new trade center and can get things set up in Caracas. We can trust him for that.”

“Do you know anybody else over there?” I asked. “Yes. That’s a railroad guy with him,” Lee said. “And next to him is another railroad guy, too. Over there, on the other side of Shaw, is a guy from Terry Smith Stevedoring. I think that’s his wife with him...” After a minute, another person came in, younger than the others. “That’s Hugh Ward,” Lee told me. “He’s a pilot, and Banister’s partner. Dave and I have worked with him. Next to him, I don’t know. I think he’s a bodyguard. The other guys are Marcello’s brothers, Sammy and Pete. And Mr. Gill and another attorney, they are sitting at the table with Dave, behind Marcello.”

“Why are they meeting here, at a night club?” I asked.

“I suppose, because Marcello wants it this way.”

“But why are we here?”

“Because, sometime tonight, they’ll get around to talking about the Venezuelan shipment.” As we waited for our food, I took a sheet of note paper from my purse. It was full of notes on one side from a Dave Ferrie lecture, but I’d also jotted down some of Lee’s remarks about married life in Russia. I began to sketch a small black horse, and a little later, impressed by some dancing girls that came out to perform, I began to draw one of them.

That’s when Sparky noticed I was drawing something and came over to investigate. After viewing my sketch, he returned with a poster and turned it over, blank side up. “Can you draw me a black stallion?” he asked.

Impressed by Lee’s story of the famous horse Black Gold, and his remarkable history, I began to draw at once.

As I worked on it, the waiters would stop by to look. Sparky checked on my progress at one point, then sent a waiter to bring the drawing over to Marcello's table when I was finished. Soon, I was asked to draw a cat, then a dog, and so on. That kept me busy.

Sparky delivered each drawing to the person who requested it. It has been suggested that this activity stopped me from sketching the faces of any of the attendees who were there that night. Meanwhile, the club filled up with people and smoke. At our table, Lee, David Lewis and I had Dr. Peppers, while Anna had a beer. Everybody else was drinking fancy alcoholic drinks. The music got louder as plates of food came and went. Marcello made a point of smiling at Anna Lewis several times. Anna finally told us that Marcello had "always liked" her.

Finally, Sparky signaled Lee to go over to Marcello's table. I saw him sit down next to Clay Shaw. Though I could not hear the conversation with so much loud music playing, I could see that there was quite a bit of talk. Later, Lee told me they discussed how to handle the security aspects of the Venezuelan arms shipment, which would soon be on its way. Meanwhile, the music was exciting, the food was rich, and the stage show was titillating for the guys, but then Lee said he didn't want to leave Marina alone any longer, so we had to leave. We said goodnight to David and Anna. Then, as we stepped outside, we found ourselves escorted to a Cadillac. We were driven home in style. I was dropped off first. It was about ten o'clock when the Caddie reached my apartment. I handed Lee the pecan pie slices to take home to Marina at the last moment, then watched him get whisked away.

This was a pivotal event for Lee and me, for we never again had to pay for anything at any Marcello-connected restaurant in the French Quarter. That included free entry and meals at the 500 Club. In hindsight, this should have triggered concern. Lee was being compensated "on the arm" by the Mafia boss himself. But at what ultimate cost? At the time, nothing was normal in this strange, new world. If the CIA and the FBI were in with the Mob, I certainly couldn't stop them; and if it meant that Lee and I could eat for free in nice restaurants, so be it.

I still treasure the black Japanese blouse Lee bought me.

Friday, June 7, 1963 On Friday, I clocked Lee out at 5:30 and we finally got to spend some private time with each other. We had so much to talk about! As we strolled along the shops at Canal, Lee spotted a black Japanese-style blouse, bought it, and had me put it on in the dressing room. This was the second Japanese style blouse that Lee bought for me. Then, as we sipped sodas at Walgreen's, Lee had me practice some Japanese phrases he had learned while stationed in Japan.

Back on the bus, Lee put my hair into as ponytail, like Marina. Then we went to **Mother's**, a restaurant close to Reily's, where I spoke Russian and impersonated Marina as we stood in line. It was practice. Everybody there thought I was Mr. Oswald's Russian wife, who had no English.

Lee ordered two Po' Boys — one for me and one for Marina, to take home. Then we got on the bus.

On the way home, Lee revealed he would be busy during the afternoons next week. He would not be able to ride home with me on the bus. We would not be able to have our private time together in the park, but he would see me on the bus in the mornings, and "in his dreams." So, I focused on the Project, reading research papers and writing reports. I also met with Dr. Mary, who was no fun when she was teaching. She sternly reviewed my work and taught me a few new lab procedures. A one-page letter from Robert arrived. Yes, he had gotten the brownies, and he enclosed his paycheck to deposit in our account. The letter was sent from Pip's Place in Hopedale. Dr. Mary helped me find it on a map. It was a hamlet with a couple of docks and a gas station located on a bayou in the remote marshes of southeast Louisiana. Boats refueled and picked up people and supplies there. A few days later, another letter from Robert arrived. Wow! Two in one week! This one was seven pages long. Maybe it was the brownies! Robert said bad weather was delaying their seismic readings. He could be gone another twenty days. It was this letter where Robert, perhaps realizing that it might be almost three weeks before he'd see me again, released his emotions and wrote beautifully of our relationship, and that he didn't care what our families thought. It melted my heart, and I wrote a love sonnet to him. Robert ended his letter with advice about money and a directive to eat more. But it was Lee who brought me bread and milk twice a week and who also made sure I ate well, and for free, in Marcello's restaurants.

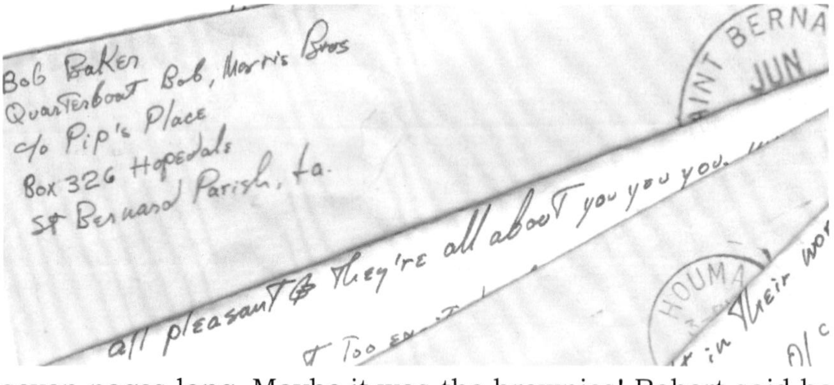

<u>Monday, June 10, 1963</u> On the morning bus, Lee told me that Marina was still not feeling well. He was frustrated that he was told they hadn't been in New Orleans long enough to get free prenatal care at Charity Hospital. If he took her to a private clinic, he would have a problem. How could he explain where a "poor working man" could afford that much money? Ochsner had assured Lee not to worry when the time came, but it focused Lee's attention on how little health care was available to the poor. He consoled himself that Ruth Paine had arranged for Marina to deliver her baby at a clinic in Grand Prairie, Texas, which was an excellent facility. And he reminded himself that the birth of Junie had been easy and quick. Still, Marina wasn't feeling well and should have been seen by a doctor.

"Nobody should be denied medical care," he said. "It's a basic human right! Just as the right to own a house. The people in this country are serfs and slaves," he went on, heatedly. "If they don't pay taxes on the house they think they own, they can be evicted. So who really owns their house? The government! They might as well live in Russia. And hell, if they get sick and are new in town, they can drop dead. Nobody cares. We're living in a world as barbaric as ancient Rome!" About this time, Lee created a fake health card, so he'd have vaccination 'proof' — necessary for travel to backward countries. His vaccinations were up-to-date, thanks to Dr. Ochsner, but he couldn't put that name on his health card. Instead, he used the fake name "Dr. **A.J.** Hideel." There was that name again! I'd seen it on the third floor at Banister's, and a variation on a fake FPCC membership card Lee carried. "Hidell," Lee told me, was a 'project name' used on fake ID's to access certain funds. Further, he said he was not the only person using "Hidell."[169]

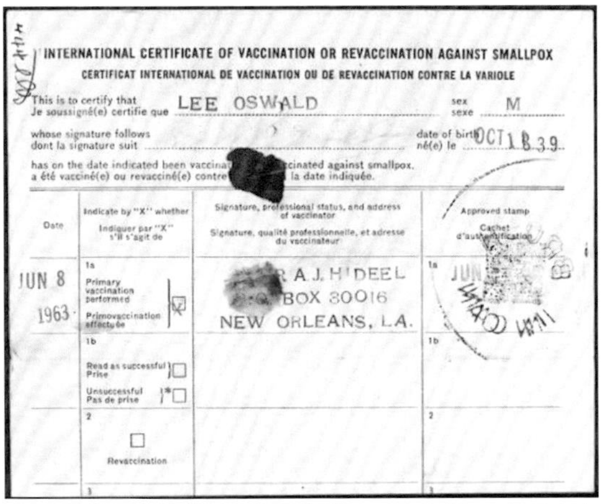
INTERNATIONAL CERTIFICATE OF VACCINATION OR REVACCINATION AGAINST SMALLPOX
CERTIFICAT INTERNATIONAL DE VACCINATION OU DE REVACCINATION CONTRE LA VARIOLE

This is to certify that / Je soussigné(e) certifie que LEE OSWALD sex / sexe M

whose signature follows / dont la signature suit date of birth / né(e) le OCT 18 39

has on the date indicated been vaccinat[redacted]cinated against smallpox.
a été vacciné(e) ou revacciné(e) contre[redacted] la date indiquée.

Date	Indicate by "X" whether / Indiquer par "X" s'il s'agit de	Signature, professional status, and address of vaccinator / Signature, qualité professionnelle, et adresse du vaccinateur	Approved stamp / Cachet d'authentification
JUN 8 1963	1a Primary vaccination performed / Primovaccination effectuée ☒	R A.J. HIDEEL BOX 30016 NEW ORLEANS, LA.	1a JUN
	1b Read as successful / Prise ☐ Unsuccessful / Pas de prise ☐		1b
	2 ☐ Revaccination		2
	3		3

In June 1963, racial tensions were like flaring wildfires all across the South. The integration of the school systems and the universities was a major battle ground in this struggle. Segregationists, such as the White Citizens Council, somehow equated integration with Communism. Some argued that segregation was part of the natural order of things. Lions and tigers should not mate. Birds of a feather flock together.

[169] There has been speculation that Lee used the card as a key to enter the USPHS LINAC building. I don't know. Lee never told me.

Dr. Martin Luther King and the NAACP staged protests, calling for equal access to all public institutions and public places as a fundament legal right. Both sides claimed the moral high ground. We had the Cold War to deal with, and racial turmoil from within. The outcome of the struggle was still uncertain. In New Orleans the struggle had been going on for years, with the local segregationists led by the White Citizens Council of Greater New Orleans, with 25,000 members.
Violence erupted at civil rights marches in Birmingham and Selma, Alabama. Footage of white police beating black protesters and carrying them off to jail filled the TV evening news and the news specials in movie theaters. While the courts ordered integration of school systems and universities, the new laws were met with stiff resistance. Alabama's Governor George Wallace and Dallas' General Edwin Walker incited riots on college campuses with their speeches. The Klu Klux Klan (KKK) burned crosses to intimidate black leaders. Black churches were burned and bombed. When NAACP leader Medgar Evers was murdered in Jackson, Mississippi, Lee and I decided to sit in the front of the bus for a while. The situation was so volatile that President Kennedy called out the National Guard to enforce integration at the University of Alabama, and Lee applauded his courage for doing so. Though I'd been prejudiced against JFK by my anti-Castro friends, Lee was making me a believer.

By the end of the week, relief came for Lee when Marina said she was feeling better. She also had visitors. Ruth Paine had written to ask the Kloepfers, who were fellow Quakers in New Orleans, to check on Marina and June. Mrs. Kloepfer just happened to be married to Tulane professor Henry Warner Kloepfer, a genetics and radiation expert who just happened to be working with the Project.[170] Later, the Kloepfers would just happen to move from Pine Street to Louisiana Avenue Parkway, close to David Ferrie and almost on top of "The Mouse House." Kloepfer might have been involved with our mice.

Friday, June 14, 1963 Lee was finally able to join me for our evening rendezvous at Audubon Park. He told me that he had ordered both *The Militant* and *The Daily Worker* to be delivered to his "faux address" at 4907 Magazine Street to bolster his leftist image. When I admitted that I didn't know the difference between the two publications, Lee was surprised. "With all you know about Russian culture and literature!"
"I read Dostoievsky, Gogol, and Tolstoy, not Marx, Engels, and Lenin,"

[170] In 1990, Ruth Ann, the Kloepfer's daughter, claimed Lee made a pass at her; her mother denied it (re personal email from Hugh Murray, 10/06/13). Marina was unaware that Dr. Kloepfer, a geneticist at Tulane, was involved in the Project. Dr. Kloepfer's name, address and phone numbers were in Lee's address book as a separate entry from his wife's.

I countered. "I can't have a decent conversation with you about what I'm doing," Lee put in, "until you get some basic understanding of Communism. And that starts with understanding the difference between Marxist and Marxist-Leninist philosophies." He put his arm around me and drew me close. "You do know the difference between the KKK and the ACLU, I presume?"

"That's easy. One has its initials all the same, and the other has its initials all different," I said, facetiously. "But seriously, I don't know the difference between a Marxist and a Marxist-Leninist."

"Do you care about the difference?" he inquired. "I do now, Lee," I replied. "Castro betrayed Marxism," Lee said. "He's a Marxist-Leninist."

"So, which one will you be posing as? A Marxist, or a Leninist?"

"I'll let you decide," Lee said, "after I give you some stuff to read. By the way, I'm going to be handing out pro-Castro flyers Sunday next to the aircraft carrier USS Wasp. The sailors on the Wasp will be coming back after a night on the town. I'll try to give them flyers, too. We'll see who takes one. Those are the ones we'll be interested in. Of course, I hope they don't knock my teeth out." Lee made a little laugh.

"Oh, stop!" I cried. "Why must you take on such risks? Haven't we had enough problems with sailors?" I reached out to him and kissed him.

"Ah, my little mouse," he replied, kissing me back, "I'll be all right. There will be someone with a camera taking photos, and others to support me."

"Why don't you do it on Saturday, when there will be a lot of people there?"

"Why, then I might really get hurt," Lee replied. "The docks are crowded on Saturdays. No, it's best on Sunday. We've been spreading rumors that a pro-Castro nut is going to be hanging around the Wasp on Sunday. Now, who would be interested in that?" "Precisely," Lee said. "Sir Percy Blakeney, at your service, putting on yet another disguise..." Lee made a mock bow. Then he sighed. "I've had to go to a lot of taverns, strip joints and bars these last few days. It was tiresome getting picked on, just because I ordered milk."

"Milk?" I said. "What do you mean, milk?"

"Oh, I order milk, or lemonade, and you should see them carry on about it," Lee said. "I get a kick out of it. I got the idea from Hopalong Cassidy."

"I remember," I said "Good ol' Hoppy. What was the name of his horse?"

"Topper," Lee said. "So anyway, they're saying to themselves, 'what is it with this guy who orders milk?' And they're saying, 'What does he mean, some pro-Castro nut is gonna be at the Dumaine Wharf this Sunday?'" Lee smiled. "Our local patriots will be upset. They'll try to stop me...

Maybe they'll call the police. Little do they know we'll be looking to see who doesn't feel that way... like the stevedore who stands and watches, and then takes a flyer. Or the one who decides to talk to me, and then takes a flyer."

Hopalong Cassidy and his horse, Topper. Cassidy was a good guy dressed in a villain's black clothes, who ordered milk in saloons, which sometimes led to a fight when he was picked on for it.

"And then?" I asked. Lee shrugged. "They'll fire the suspicious ones. They'll follow the others." As he drew me close to him, he said, "You smell so fragrant."

"I've been working in a coffee company," I told him.

"I've been in so many gay bars the last couple of weeks," Lee said, "I've almost forgotten I'm straight. Surely you can help out a poor fellow, who's almost lost his way...?"

"Do you need more girl kisses?"

"Many, many more." After I straightened him out a little, we talked about the Venezuelan project. "This is fascinating to me," I said. "So you believe you'll catch the pro-Castro stevedores this way?"

"There's no telling if we'll get them all on Sunday," he said. "But there's more we'll be doing between now and when the shipment arrives. In particular, we've taken up your idea about disguising the cargo."

"Did you follow through on that?"

"You'll see." I was excited to hear they had adopted my idea, although I didn't think I would ever be able to put "rifle smuggling" on my resumé.

<u>Saturday, June 15, 1963</u> Lee came a little before noon with his daughter Junie. He said Marina wasn't letting him near her, so he wanted another kiss to remind him what grown-up girls were like. He handed me a little blue bottle of "Evening in Paris" perfume, which I'd told him I wore in grade school. I was charmed, and Lee got his kiss.

<u>Sunday, June 16, 1963</u> Sunday was USS WASP Day. I was worried sick for Lee's safety. The thought of Lee being mauled by a bunch of drunken sailors was more than I could bear. Finally, Dave Ferrie called Susie to say the event was over and that Lee was okay. Lee later told me that his activity was reported to the Port police, and to the FBI, who downplayed it. The FBI did not interview Lee about his adventure. I found that remarkable. That Lee could hand out pro-Communist literature to U.S. Navy personnel – an outrageous act, at the height of the Cold War—without a glance from the FBI-- was a dead giveaway that Lee and the FBI were already well aware of each other's roles.

Considerations

1. The CIA was close to its New Orleans business contacts. A Congressmen from New Orleans prepared the CIA's budget for Congressional approval. Former CIA Deputy Dir. Gen. Charles Cabell, who Kennedy fired after the Bay of Pigs debacle (his CIA brother, Earle, was Mayor of Dallas when JFK died there in November) came to NOLA in 1963 to talk to the trade community about political developments in Cuba and Latin America.

2. In the book *Marina and Lee*, McMillan wrote: "Sometimes he went a whole day without speaking, and then spent the next day making it up to her. He would take her and Junie to the park, do the laundry, and mop the floor. He would even hang up the wash, while Marina leaned out the window and shouted directions, and Junie waved at her "Papa." He often told Marina how much he had missed her... But Marina was anxious. She was afraid that Lee was nice to her because he would soon be getting rid of her."(p. 402)

3. New Orleans District Attorney Jim Garrison asked why Lee leafletted the U.S.S. WASP in mid-June, when his FPCC wasn't public until August. Quote:"...in New Orleans, in the summer of 1963, Lee Harvey Oswald was engaged in bizarre activities which made it appear ostensibly that he was connected with a Cuban organization, although... there was no such organization." Upon request of the commanding officer of the Wasp, Officer Girod Ray of the Harbor Police... [told] him... to stop passing out leaflets and leave the wharf area."

Chapter 18
The Passport

Monday, June 17, 1963

I headed to work as usual, but this was one of those days when Lee did not wish us to be seen together going to Reily's. Since he had been leafleting at the Dumaine Street wharf, he could have some anti-Castroites recognize him today. He also said he was sunburned. About 2:00 P.M., when I was away from my desk stopping a shipment, Lee left a banana and a book for me. When I returned, I was hungry and ate the banana gratefully, but when I saw the title of the book, it alarmed me.

"*What We Must Know About Communism*" could be a touchy subject in a place like Reily's. I slipped it under the desk beside my purse. In 1963, any book about Communism in this part of the world was better left

unseen. Lee had checked the book out from the Napoleon Branch library. Lee rode with me on the bus that evening. "You don't know enough about Communism," he told me. "We can't have a decent conversation about politics until you read it." But there was something else on Lee's mind; something that was troubling him. When we got to Audubon Park, we fed the ducks with Lee's lunch sandwich, which he had been too upset to eat.

"We need to talk," he said. My warning lights flashed on. I could feel his tension as we sat down at a picnic table, but I said nothing. Finally, Lee took my hand, and I heard that tiny 'clink' of his wedding band hitting mine. I instantly felt guilty, so I told Lee I was feeling bad about it. "It reminds me that I'm married," I said. "And I'm having problems with that."

"I'm having problems in the same department," Lee said. Lee had finally told Kerry Thornley to leave town; but that same night Marina resisted his advances, saying she preferred a former lover named Anatoly, who was one of Lee's best friends in Minsk. Angrily, Lee had sex with Marina anyway. "I didn't hurt her. I wasn't mean, but I didn't respect her," he said. "Now I'm sorry."

I was moved that Lee confessed his sins concerning Marina with such frankness. But I was disappointed at this new revelation. "So you have kept your promise not to beat her. But it's okay to force yourself on her! That doesn't count?"

"She keeps talking about other men!" Lee said, miserably. "It makes me furious. I was afraid to tell you. Will you be afraid of me, now?"

"Of course, it scares me, Lee," I said. "You acted like a cave man. As for Marina, she's five months pregnant. She's carrying your baby, isn't she?"

"Of this, I am certain," he answered. "It's not Thornley's baby, or Anatoly's baby," I said. "So, let her talk."

"I'm disgusted with myself," he said. "At one time, I was serene. I did not let anything get to me...." Lee closed his eyes. "Now, if she says something, at once, we play the old game. I tell her to shut up. She tells me I'm not a real man."

"But you said that-- before you married Marina-- you had always been gentle with women. Did you lie to me about that?"

"No, no," he assured me.

"Remember, then, when we make love for the first time," I said softly, "that I'm the woman you'll marry after Marina. A different woman."

"Women always think they can change a man," Lee answered, "but usually, they can't..." He looked at me with his blue-gray eyes and said sincerely, "It's the man who decides to change. Well, I can decide to be the man I want to be. And I'll do it. For you."

Lee's challenge was to do no harm, to make a safe haven for June, and to forgive Marina. His reward would be my respect, increasing trust, and growing love. As he struggled to meet these goals, I saw Lee grow before my eyes that spring and summer. Though I could speak wisely to Lee, when it came to forgiving Robert for his neglectful ways, I wasn't so resourceful. Meanwhile, as the get-Castro project evolved, it began to consume much of our free time. On June 19, we heard that monkeys had been ordered from Africa, set to arrive by the end of August.[171]It took weeks to get live monkeys shipped in. If we killed as many as we planned to kill, researchers and med students arriving in the fall to work on their simian projects would wonder what happened to all the monkeys. Classes and new projects began in September, so the monkeys had to arrive before the end of August. They did, as this obscure newspaper article reveals.

Tulane Monkeys Arriving Today

Some 8,000 pounds of liv[e] monkeys will arrive at 7:4[0] a. m. Sunday at New Orlean[s] International Airport on [a] chartered flight from Portland Ore.

.. Ken McKinsey of United Ai[r] lines said the animals, "at lea[st] a couple of hundred of them," will be used by the Tulane Un[i]versity Medical School primat[e] center in Covington.

This article appeared in the *Times-Picayune* on Sunday, August 25, 1963, on an inner page. No fanfare was wanted. With expected arrival at 7:40 a.m., by the time anyone read the paper, the monkeys would be out of sight. There were 8,000 pounds of them.

<u>Friday, June 21, 1963</u> On Friday afternoon there was extra work to do in Dave's lab, so I was there later than usual. Dave arrived while I was still there, and told me I could go with him to the airport, if I finished my reports in time. When I asked him why, and he only said, "It's a surprise." As Dave helped me clean up my work-space and I put the files in order, Miguel came and took away the mouse carcasses. Then Dave drove me to Dr. Sherman's apartment, where I took the reports up to apartment "J". When I returned to Dave's car, he was under the hood, cursing. It was just a stuck carburetor, but Dave grumbled that he deserved a better vehicle for all the work he was doing for everybody. We reached Lakefront Airport just before sunset.

---

[171]Tulane's National Primate Research Center was founded in 1962, perhaps the best source for research monkeys in the world. Our project destroyed most of Tulane's monkeys that summer, so "a couple of hundred" replacements arrived August 25,[th]as described in the newspaper article above.

After Dave parked his car and helped me out politely, he went to a shed and got a clipboard. Then we crossed the tarmac to some hangars, where I saw several small planes. The plane of interest was silver, with a long stripe down its side. It had an oversized cargo-release door, and an extra fuel tank. Someone was inside the plane, curled up on the seat, sleeping. It was Lee. Then two men arrived. One looked like a Cuban. The other introduced himself as 'Mr. Lambert,' but it was Clay Shaw. I remembered him from the 500 Club, but kept mum. I was beginning to get the hang of things. Dave was going to fly these men to Toronto and back. Lee got up, stretched, then jumped down from the plane and shook hands with the two men. As he walked over to me, Dave pointed to us and said to Lambert, "Those two are in love, you know." I blushed, Lee coughed, and Lambert laughed. "There's no need to feel embarrassed," he said. "After all, love's what makes the world go 'round."

"In their case," said Dave, "it's going 'round and 'round!"

We thanked Dave for letting us have some time together, then watched watched the plane as it taxied for the take-off. Suddenly, it screeched to a halt, and Dave came running toward us. "Lee, can you do me a big favor?" he asked. "Will you come along and help me fly this thing? You'll be back by tomorrow afternoon," he promised. "I'm dead tired," he added. "I'm afraid I'll fall asleep at the controls."

Dave said Lee could sleep in the plane after reaching Toronto, so he'd be alert for the trip back. With a shrug, Lee agreed. Dave handed me some money for a cab. Alone and envious, I watched the plane take off, then went to the airport office, called a cab and went home. Such sudden demands on Lee's time and energy occurred all summer. How Lee managed to stay so cool and collected was beyond me.

A little after midnight, Suzi Collie began to bark. I woke to hear the front door open, and then Robert shushed the dog. Wait--*the journals, the logbook*! I jumped out of bed and hid them in the 'X' spot, under my folded clothes, as quickly as I could. Even so, hearing his voice sent a thrill through me. I was so entirely mixed-up. He was a hunk, and he was *my* hunk! Into the bedroom he walked, wearing his big, heavy army boots and tight blue jeans. For once I was rested, my hair damp from a bath. I held out my arms, and he came into them.

Once Robert was finished 'getting into port,' he informed me of his plans. We were going to Ft. Walton Beach – now! It was time to tell his family our news! He promised we'd get back in time for me to put in a full day's work at Reily's. I found myself hustled into the car with only enough time to scribble a note to Susie, who was gone for the weekend and had expected me to take care of the Suzi Collie. She had never left her dog behind before, and here, I was leaving! Robert said, "It's only two days. The dog won't die." But I loved Suzi Collie.

I knew the neighborhood kids would watch her tomorrow, but what if something happened to her tonight in the dark? She had gone under the house, detesting Robert, and would not come out. Sullen and grumpy, I sat in silence in the blue Ford as Robert drove. "There's a chance the folks will be very angry," he warned me. *There's a chance that I will be very angry, too*, I thought to myself. Robert hadn't given a hint that we were going to spend the weekend in Florida until he told me we had to leave! Nor did he ask if I had any plans or obligations. He just hurried me into the car. I barely had a chance to dress.

I hoped Lee would come over after he returned from Toronto, [172] would see the note on Susie's screen door, and feed Suzi. I prayed she wouldn't get run over by a car. To my continued silence, Robert muttered, "Don't say I never take you anywhere." The trip was tense and silent: Robert was worried about being disinherited, and I was feeling guilty about being in love with Lee. Once more, I didn't try to open his eyes. I didn't want to get dumped on the side of the road.

When we arrived in Fort Walton Beach the next morning, Robert parked the Ford on the side of his parents' big real estate office and vanished inside. I waited anxiously in the car. I gazed at the pink and black signs, the well-trimmed hedges and the red brick wall against which the car was parked. Beyond the parking lot rows of identical palm trees stood shimmering in heat waves. It all looked so peaceful, but how would the Bakers react to the news?

Finally, Robert appeared with his parents and I got out of the car; Robert A. Baker, Jr., ruddy-faced and white-haired, reached me first and offered his hand — and gave me a check for $700 (worth ten times that in today's funds). It was our wedding gift! Robert immediately pocketed it. Mrs. RAB Jr. said hello, then added that I wasn't wearing any nylons, but opined that my skin was "tan enough" that I didn't need them, though *ladies* here *did* wear nylons. We would have to go shopping for nylons and "other appropriate clothing" before I could meet her friends, who were "all ladies." Determined to dress me "sensibly," Mrs. Baker took me downtown at once. There, she purchased a black dress — "suitable for work" — plus two "leisure sun-dresses to go with your swarthy skin," that were "nicer than wearing those shorts all the time." She topped her choices with a hideous flannel nightgown.

[172] This was one of several times I know Lee made an overnight trip by plane. Technically, he had been home this evening, but then he walked out, and didn't show up until late the following afternoon. Those who say Marina's word should be trusted — that Lee was 'always' home "right after work" — must remember that Lee's clock-outs varied between 4:30 and 7:30. And Lee clocked out many times at 6:30! It took up to a half hour to catch a bus and go straight home, as well. If they fought, he had no set hour for returning at night.

I didn't know such nightgowns existed in Florida! Oh, there were also two bras. She insisted on personally fitting them, which embarrassed me.

She commented, as she adjusted them, that she was surprised at my rather oversized breasts. It only dawned on me later that she was wondering if I was pregnant. Meanwhile, as Robert was having fun with his brother and old school friends, I faced a gauntlet of prim matrons interested in whether my belly was distended (Did he have to marry her?). When I returned, still wearing my own clothes, the promised photos were taken.

My body language speaks for itself: I have my arm around Mrs. Baker and am leaning toward my new mother-in-law in preference to Robert, who holds my hand (but I am not holding his).

The whole weekend was surreal. Robert, as always, kept me up half the night, then spent most of Sunday napping, watching football, playing Monopoly and drinking beer, while I was hustled all over the place.

First, it was the Country Club, after a formal brunch at the Yacht Club. There, I was challenged to play bridge (a game I did not know), with some more of her friends. This was followed by an interesting visit to Eglin Air Force base and a tour of Hurlburt Arms, one of Mr. Baker's construction projects. Next came a tour of Choctawhatchee High School.

Then came a dinner with Mrs. Baker's former colleagues, for she had taught "business" at the high school. Mrs. Baker herself had quit teaching to help Mr. Baker run their real estate office, turning it into a whopping success. It was about 8 PM when we returned, where Robert was waiting by his blue Ford. It was time to go back to New Orleans.

We reached New Orleans in the deep dark of Monday morning, at which time Robert said he had only a few hours left before going back out to the Gulf. I knew what that meant! I have to admit that he was a talented invader, as he plundered my ravaged coasts.

Monday, June 24, 1963 At 7 a.m., Robert finally let me get dressed for work. There had been no sleep, except what I'd managed to grab on the trip back. As I stood staring into the mirror at the dark circles under my eyes, I noticed that my hands were shaking. I was wearing the new black dress, my black high heels and had my big, black purse. It was now summer, but I was dressed for a funeral. Seeing how tired I was, Robert drove me to work. It was the first and only time he came near Reily's. As I sat down at Mr. M's desk, I was in a daze, hardly able to focus my eyes. Then the mail boy dumped the dreaded Monday avalanche of letters and problems on my desk. There was so much of it that some of it fell on the floor. I wondered how I would make it through the day.

At about the end of lunch, Lee slipped in with some hot, black coffee. I was still working, though the big room was almost empty; everybody else was eating lunch. "I called Susie," he said. "It seems you haven't had any sleep."

"Oh, Lee!" I said, "I'm afraid I'm going to get sick. I'm so tired!"

"I can't stand here long. It will attract attention."

"I love him, but he never notices if I'm tired--" Lee frowned, then said, "I can't ride home with you tonight. Can you make it okay, without me?"

"I know you'd be there if you could," I told him, staring at the pile of Reily credit problems, requests and demands. One of the head clerks, Annette, suddenly came over to help me open the letters. When I looked up, Lee was gone. I normally did not drink coffee, but the caffeine helped me make it to 4:30. Afraid I'd fall asleep before clocking Lee out, at 5:15 I went to the canteen and walked around and around to stay awake. At exactly 5:30, I stamped Lee's timecard. At 5:45, I got on the bus, but I kept standing, afraid I'd pass out and miss my stop, holding unsteadily to the pole as the bus lurched along. Because the driver knew I was a regular, he called out "Marengo!" when we reached my street.

I made it the two blocks, opened the front door, went down the hall around the corner -- and gasped with amazement! There was the bed, carefully made, the pretty quilts turned down. A box of chocolates rested on the pillow. There were balloons tied to the bedposts, with a sign suspended between them on yarn.

"Welcome back!" was written on it, in colored crayon. There were roses on the little table that I used as a desk and to iron clothes. Rose petals dotted the floor. Lee was there, standing by the head of the bed. "Go get undressed," he said, smiling. "I'll wait." *Oh, no.* I thought to myself. *He wants to make love, today, of all days?* We hadn't yet slept together and I wished I had more strength.

As I undressed, Lee talked quietly to Susie in the kitchen. I pointedly put on my horrible new Granny nightgown, crawled under the covers, and having eaten so little all day, opened the box of chocolates. "You can come in now!" I called, ready for the exhausting efforts ahead. In came Susie, Suzi Collie, and Lee. Susie kissed me on the cheek, Collie whined hello, and Lee sat at the foot of my bed. Then Susie left, discreetly taking the dog with her and closing the door. Lee moved from the bed and knelt by the bookshelves; he had brought in a portable record player. He turned on the record player, picked up the needle, and gently set it down. It was the Everly Brothers, singing our song.

"...Each time we meet, love...I find complete love...Without your sweet love...What would life be?....So never leave me lonely...Tell me you love me only... And that you'll always... let it be me."

"You were gone all weekend," Lee said, quietly. "I missed you!"

"Come here, Lee," I said to him. "I give up. I can't say no to you."

"I don't want you to say, 'I give up,'" Lee replied. But I saw that he was taking off his clothes. "I already knew you wouldn't say no to me." He got into bed with me and began stroking my body. "I love you, Juduffki," he said. "But I'm not here to take you. I'm here to show you that I will never unite with you, unless you want me."

"But I do want you, Lee!" I told him. "I want you more, all the time."

"Shhhhh..." he said. He took off my nightgown with great care, folding it and placing it at the foot of the bed. Now our bodies rested close together, naked in the bed. I waited, as he began to rock me gently. Then, as he held me in his arms, I fell asleep. It was dark when he woke me. "I have to go home now," he said. "In case you are wondering, not a thing happened that would have embarrassed you. Only, your whole body knows you are cherished. You won't get sick now." He got out of bed and bent over and kissed me. Then he dressed in the darkness. "Good night, Lady Blakeney," he said. "Until tomorrow." He closed my bedroom door and let himself out through the back way. I could hear his footsteps going down the back steps. I was so hyper that I even heard the key land on its place high on the windowsill. I reached for the alarm clock, to wind it.

It was already wound, and the alarm set. *Oh, my sweetheart!* I said to myself. *You've won... You've won!*

Though I slept all night, I was still exhausted the next morning, so Lee asked me to see a doctor. But there wasn't time in my schedule for it, so I dragged myself to work again. At about 10:00 AM., Monaghan told me I had accrued a day of sick leave and might as well use it. He said to take the rest of the day off and see a doctor. A taxi showed up, compliments of Dr. Mary, which carried me to Charity Hospital. The doctor did a blood test and said I was suffering from anemia. I felt so stupid, because I used to do my own blood tests and knew I was a borderline case. He gave me a B-12 shot, ordered me to eat more red meat, and advised I should take iron. Lee was waiting for me when I left the hospital. When I told him I had anemia, he said, "Maybe that's what's the matter with Marina. I'll have to bring more meat home." As we got into the taxi, he added, "Would you feel up to meeting somebody? He's a friend of mine. Dr. Mary says we can keep the taxi for a while, so don't worry." We rode to the Customs House, where I waited in the cab about ten minutes, while Lee went inside.

When he returned, he was accompanied by a gentleman with silvery hair. Lee helped me out of the taxi and introduced me. "This is J," he said. "She knows all about this, so I wanted her to shake your hand." Turning to me, Lee said, "I would like you to meet Arthur Young, who expedited my passport for me." As we shook hands, I was startled to see tattoos on the fingers of this distinguished-looking gentleman. Mr. Young, smiling, said that he had "hurried the process along" before anyone looked too closely into Lee's past. He had also "hurried along" several other passport applications at the same time, so Lee's would not stand out.

Had Young not stepped in, Lee would have had to rely on a fake one. It was always better to have the real thing, Mr. Young opined. It turned out that the taxi was not just for me: Mr. Young had to return at once to Miami, and he needed the taxi to get to the airport. As he helped me back into the taxi, I noticed again Young's unusual finger tattoos. While he spoke Spanish to the Latino taxi driver, to us he spoke English, with what I felt was a German accent. When I asked Young if he was an American citizen, he said he was that and more, because he was married to a Native American, a Chitimacha Indian. The Chitimacha Indians only live in a limited part of Louisiana, and there aren't very many of them. This, plus Charles Thomas' tattooed fingers, was an important second clue that helped me locate Charles Thomas' family some 37 years later.

Lee and Mr. Young were obviously friends, and as we headed to my apartment, the two men talked briefly about when they first met more than a decade earlier, while Young was a Customs official at the border between Canada and the U.S. at Niagara Falls. Lee had been playing hooky from school and had hitch-hiked all the way from the Bronx, itching to cross the border so he could say he'd been off American soil.

Lee was not yet thirteen, and Young, impressed with the boy's zest for adventure, permitted the young truant to cross over for the day, with one rule: he must return by dark. Then, he wouldn't tell, and would send him back to New York on a bus.

Young did ask for Lee's name, address and a phone number where his mother could be reached in case he didn't return, but Lee was afraid he'd call the authorities. Young promised he would not do that, reminding Lee that he was "the authorities," in charge of the border station. Lee gave him the information, crossed the border, and went on to the Crystal Beach amusement park. And yes, he returned by dusk.

Later, Young contacted Lee in New York and they ate lunch together. At that time, Lee confided his dream to become a spy to his new friend. Impressed, Young gave Lee the name of a fellow Customs agent in New York who might mentor him. But not long after, Lee was arrested for truancy and sent to Youth House, where he was brutalized. Young's friend intervened to get Lee out. Soon after that, Young moved to Florida. Now they had met again, with great pleasure. Young and his wife still lived in Miami, but he was semi-retired, occasionally working with Customs on a clandestine basis. He may have been operating a clock and jewelry store by then.

Captions and scan are by Thomas' grand-daughter, Kelly Thomas.

Lee said he was affiliated with the CIA's anti-Castro movement and had many Cuban and Mafia friends who were working together against Castro. I was able to speak with "Young" for nearly half an hour before I was let off at my apartment. By then, I realized that Arthur Young was not his real name. His real name was "Thomas," though Lee did not say if that was his first name, or his last, and I – not being as alert as usual-- did not think to ask. [173] Arthur Young' was the pseudonym Thomas used when he approved and signed passports in New Orleans on June 25, 1963, including Lee Oswald's --which included Lee's written intention to visit the USSR—which he approved in only 24 hours.

Kelly Thomas Cousins H. –Thomas' grand-daughter. Charles Thomas, Jr., Kelly's dad. Family photo on the page above is of Charles Thomas, Miami, 1954. (Caption written by Kelly) Note tattooed fingers.

'

"He's a good guy, like me," Lee later assured me. Lee's passport application was submitted on June 24th, at the height of the Cold War. Nevertheless, Lee boldly indicated that he planned to visit communist Poland and the USSR! That's not all he did. He wrote his marriage date to Marina as **April 31,** though no such day exists. That's so typical of Lee, and his sense of humor!

I WAS NEVER MARRIED
I WAS LAST MARRIED ON APRIL 31 1961
MARINA PRUSSAKOVA
WHO WAS BORN AT ARXANGELS, USSR
JULY 17, 1941
WHO IS A U.S. CITIZEN
WHO IS NOT A U.S. CITIZEN
MARRIAGE NOT TERMINATED
MARRIAGE TERMINATED BY DEATH DIVORCE ON

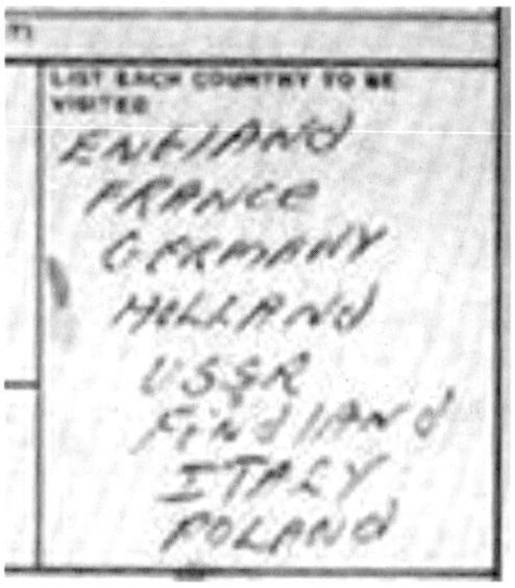

LIST EACH COUNTRY TO BE VISITED
ENGLAND
FRANCE
GERMANY
HOLLAND
USSR
FINLAND
ITALY
POLAND

When I told Kelly Thomas that Lee had known her grandfather, who was a U.S. Customs officer at the border between Canada and the US, and that he let Lee take the bus to Crystal Beach, she was amazed because she knew of a photo in the family's albums that showed her grandfather carrying luggage at the US-Canadian border, with a bus arriving from Crystal Beach!

[173] An anonymous person wrote and said Thomas' accent was Welsh, not German, and that he had also been married previously, but left me no way to verify this.

The photo, below, shows **U. S.** Customs officer Charles Thomas, AKA Arthur Young, at the Canadian-US border. The Crystal Beach bus is at right.

US/Canada Border

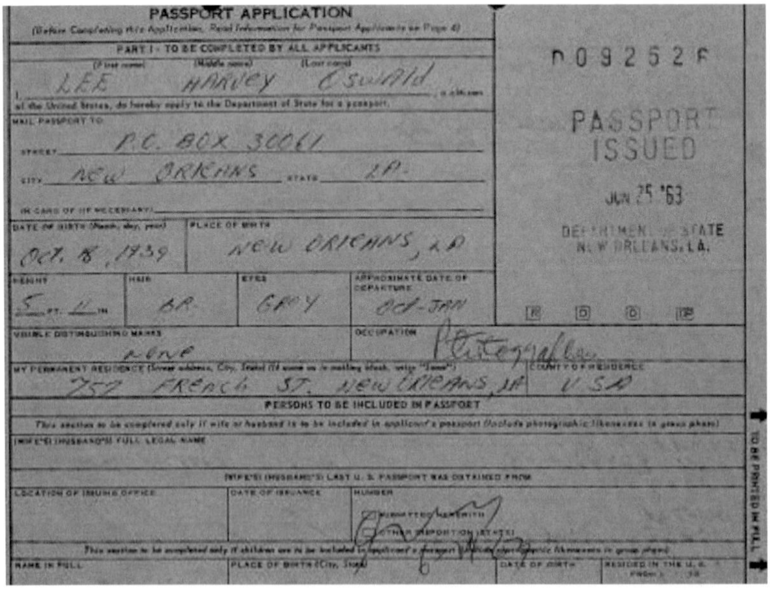

PASSPORT APPLICATION

(Before Completing this Application, Read Information for Passport Applicants on Page 4)

PART I - TO BE COMPLETED BY ALL APPLICANTS

(First name) LEE (Middle name) HARVEY (Last name) OSWALD

I, ..., a citizen of the United States, do hereby apply to the Department of State for a passport.

MAIL PASSPORT TO

STREET P.O. BOX 30061

CITY NEW ORLEANS STATE LA.

IN CARE OF (IF NECESSARY)

DATE OF BIRTH (Month, day, year): Oct. 18, 1939 | PLACE OF BIRTH: NEW ORLEANS, LA

HEIGHT: 5 FT. 11 IN. | HAIR: BR. | EYES: GRY | APPROXIMATE DATE OF DEPARTURE: Oct-JAN

VISIBLE DISTINGUISHING MARKS: NONE | OCCUPATION:

MY PERMANENT RESIDENCE (Street address, City, State): 757 FRENCH ST. NEW ORLEANS, LA | COUNTRY OF RESIDENCE: USA

PERSONS TO BE INCLUDED IN PASSPORT

This section to be completed only if wife or husband is to be included in applicant's passport (Include photographic likenesses in group photo)

(WIFE'S) (HUSBAND'S) FULL LEGAL NAME

(WIFE'S) (HUSBAND'S) LAST U. S. PASSPORT WAS OBTAINED FROM

LOCATION OF ISSUING OFFICE | DATE OF ISSUANCE | NUMBER

SUBMITTED HEREWITH / OTHER REPORTION (STATE)

This section to be completed only if children are to be included in applicant's passport

NAME IN FULL | PLACE OF BIRTH (City, State) | DATE OF BIRTH | RESIDED IN THE U.S. FROM

D09252F

PASSPORT ISSUED

JUN 25 '63

DEPARTMENT OF STATE NEW ORLEANS, LA.

TO BE PRINTED IN FULL

Special Treatment for "Defector" Lee Harvey Oswald's Passport [174]

Lee also put his height as 5' 11" instead of 5' 9" (he did that consistently for official and government records)._Lee also left "occupation" on his application form blank. The passport application is included in the

[174] As I didn't ask Lee if "Thomas" was a first or last name, I hunted at first for Arthur Thomas or Thomas Young. Realizing that fellow grad student, Kelly Thomas, was on a Chitimacha Indian scholarship, I hoped to find the elusive "Thomas" at last – and I did.

color pages, where the word 'photographer ' was not filled in. Instead, Thomas' (Young's) red ink pen filled it in._Later, Lee said jokingly if he had put his name down as Santa Claus, it still would have been approved.[175]

June 26, 1963 Dr. Ochsner was speeding up our research by increasing the number of mice to be processed to two hundred per week-- a weary burden. Ferrie hoped I would feel well enough to handle the mice, but Lee objected, saying I was sick and needed to rest. He volunteered to do the dirty work in my place. "You stay put at Reily's!" he commanded. "I'll do the mice, and Dave will pick you up for the technical part later." On this day, Lee anesthetized and killed 200 infant mice suffering from huge cancerous lumps. [176]The mice were sliced open from stem to stern, and the biggest tumors cut out. The smell was noxious. At the end of the day, I arrived at Dave's later than usual, and found Lee looking green. When we were finished inspecting the tumors, Dave said he would start the new cultures the next day at the Prytania lab because his boyfriend was coming over for a day or two.

Thursday, June 27, 1963 I ate a minute-steak for breakfast and felt my energy returning. Monaghan was pleased that I put in a full day's work. I even managed to type a few letters at a decent speed. Then, just as I was about to clock him out, Lee phoned. "No more 6:30 clock-outs," he said. "You're working too late." He asked me to meet him at the 500 Club. "I have a special reason for taking you there today," he added. At the club, where we ordered dinner, Lee told me the arms shipment from Venezuela was supposed to arrive the next day. We'd then know if the efforts to trap pro-Castroites and keep the FBI's informants off-track had paid off. But I could see that more than tomorrow's challenges weighed on Lee's shoulders. "Lee, what's the matter?" I asked.

Lee avoided my question. He had not eaten much because his appetite was still off, because of the mice. Still, there was something else...

---

[175] Lee's application hints that Marina and he would split. For example, Lee did not give Marina's name as the one to contact "in event of death or accident." Instead, he named his Aunt Lillian Murret. For his 'permanent' address, Lee gave his aunt's 757 French St. address, for the arrangement between Marina and Lee was not permanent.

[176] **BOB OWENS' WITNESS STATEMENT**: The transition from mice to monkeys was occurring. **Dr. Bob Owens** (Slidell, LA) wrote in 12/20/2010 that **his father managed Tulane University Delta Regional Primate Center.** "The radiation center was built at a substantial cost...with...a blockhouse...with 9 foot thick concrete and lead shielding... **the site was completely abandoned ...coincide(ing) with the death of Dr. Mary Sherman**. I, too was a math and science whiz kid who later was accepted to LSU Med School after only 2 years of undergraduate study."

I could sense it. "Please eat, my sweetheart," I urged him. Then, his words hit me between the eyes. "Don't call me sweetheart!" he said, not looking at me. "We have to talk. Now." In his eyes, I saw a look of despair. I took his hand, but felt him stiffen. "After calling you," he said slowly, "I began to think about things...Where you and I are going," he blurted out. "I love little Junie," he said softly. "I know I will also love the baby to come, and how much they both will need me."

Lee sighed deeply. Life was precious, he said. Killing so many innocent animals had made him think about how helpless his own children were. I couldn't speak. I sensed the guilt he was feeling. "I have to make a final decision, but I don't want to hurt you," he said, avoiding my eyes. "If you can say those words to me, Lee, then you've already made your decision." I pulled my hand away.

"I could lose Junie forever, if I'm not careful," he said. "I've thought about this. I don't think I can handle that." Tears stood in his eyes, and he got up abruptly. "I'll be right back," he said. "I have to go to the toilet." I watched him walk away, thinking to what an extreme I'd brought him to. Now he felt forced to make a choice between his family and me! I realized that Lee's affections ran deep, or he simply would have slowly withdrawn from our relationship. He always said he'd be transparent. I thought of the little plastic heart Lee had given me. How he must dread losing contact with Junie, and their unborn child! Lee and Marina were getting along better now: perhaps their marriage would succeed. Perhaps I was now the element that was causing Lee distress.

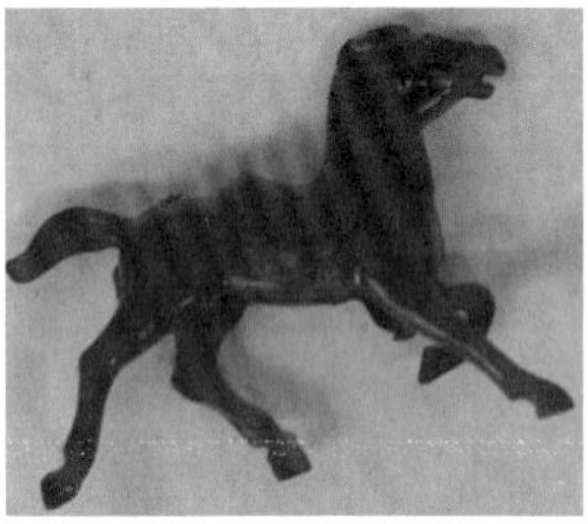

I began to cry, then grabbed a napkin, found a pen, and wrote:

I have no right to interfere with the hope you have for a happy life with your family. Forgive me for bringing you this grief. Do what is right. Love, J.

I took my little plastic horse out of my purse that I had carried with me since I was five years old in the hospital. I wrapped the important napkin around it and laid it on the table in front of Lee's dish. I hurried from the club and went home, where I fell into bed, tossing and turning under the covers, sleepless and heartsick.I never learned what happened on the evening of June 27. Lee never spoke of it to me, but according to McMillan, one of Marina's CIA-sponsored biographers, "*Lee was sitting in the dark... staring down at the floor. Marina put her arms around him, stroked his head, and could feel him shaking with sobs. "Why are you crying?" she asked. Then, "Cry away. It'll be better that way." Marina held him for about a quarter of an hour and he told her between sobs that he was lost. He didn't know what he ought to do. Then he said suddenly, "Would you like me to come to Russia, too?"*"

Friday, June 28, 1963 I almost didn't go to work, such was my misery. But I knew I would have to cover for Lee because the Venezuelan shipment was coming in. That was more important than my feelings, or even his. Lee was not on the bus that morning. Personnel, upset when he went missing, lodged a complaint. Monaghan and I had to concoct an excuse for him. We said Lee had been sent over to Reily's new instant coffee plant, which was under construction, to do emergency work as an oiler for a crane operator there. Mr. Prechter was forced to promise, however, that he'd find a replacement for Lee.

COFFEE PLANT WILL BE BUILT

Luzianne Production to Be Consolidated

A new $1¼ million roasting and ground coffee plant will be erected in New Orleans by William B. Reily and Co. Inc.

Construction will begin this fall on the new plant adjacent to the firm's present instant coffee facility on the Chef Menteur hwy. at Jourdan Rd.

Occupying part of an 11-acre site, the masonry building will contain 75,000 square feet of space. It will be ready for use in 1964.

The plant will replace the firm's present ground coffee facility at 640 Magazine St. Managerial offices will remain on Magazine St.

John C. Clark will serve as vice-president in charge of operations at the new plant, which will consolidate all of Reily's Luzianne brand ground and instant coffee processing in one location in New Orleans.

Other plants in Baltimore, Charleston and Los Angeles will continue to serve those areas.

Architects for the new plant are Curtis and Davis of New Orleans.

In announcing the new facility, William B. Reily Jr., president of the New Orleans-based firm, said, "This ultra-modern building will double the present ground coffee output of Luzianne and will enable our company to maintain its expanding position in the

Coffee Plant to Be

THIS IS DRAWING of the new Luzia[n] ground coffee plant after expansion of present instant coffee section at Chef M[en]teur hwy. and Jourdan rd. The broken l[ine] indicates the separation between the old

Shot Is Fired

PECOS, Tex. (AP) — Pranksters or terrorists fired a bullet into the rambling residence of convicted swindler Billie Sol Estes on Friday night and the family prepared to flee Saturday.

The shooting was the third incident in a week around the residence.

planted a Klux Klan sy on Estes' pulled loose tric sign on ing, "Home

Newsmen culated in P firmation th sell his hom

Prechter met with Monaghan in his glassed-in cubicle, which blocked out typewriter noise for his private conversations and phone calls, discussing the problem. Before long, Monaghan came out of his cubicle, with Prechter in tow. He glanced at a fistful of "maintenance man" job applications Prechter held, then handed them to me.

"I don't care what he's doing for God and Country," Prechter told Monaghan. "I can't make up any more excuses for him."

He said that every time he turned around, Lee was missing. He was either sitting over at the garage next door, reading, or "had just arrived "from some damned errand you people have sent him on." If he got one more complaint from the production people in the back, it was "Goodbye" Lee. Nobody at Reily believed Lee was just hiding in a corner somewhere.[177] He had been gone too often and for too long.

---

177 "…ready for use in 1964…"with construction to begin in the fall, the 11-acre site was being prepared with bulldozers and cranes. It was our last, desperate excuse for why Lee had gone missing today.

At 4:30, I clocked myself out and returned to my desk to catch up with the last of the usual credit problems. At 5:30, I clocked Lee out. As I handled his timecard, I noticed that he had clocked in after 9:00 a.m. That was the first time in three weeks. Had last night been as rough for Lee as it had been for me? He obviously had a slow start this morning. I knew the arms shipment from Venezuela was scheduled for today. Romance or not, I was worried and wanted to know what happened.

Did my smuggling disguise work? Was Lee safe? I stood at the bus stop, worrying myself almost to tears, when suddenly, Dave Ferrie drove

up and honked to get my attention. I got into the back seat of his car, since a thin, good-looking young man was seated beside him. Dave introduced me: his name was **Layton Martens**. Then Dave drove us to the Trade Mart's warehouses on the river. "Hot damn!" Dave said, weaving in and out of traffic with immense skill. "We did so damned good today!" He was so excited he repeated his last sentence in all the languages he knew. I asked where Lee was, and Dave laughed. "You'll find out," he said. "It's okay, I understand," I said gloomily.

"Just wanted you to see what we did," Dave said. "It was pure genius." (Referring to my idea to hide the rifles in furniture crates.) Then Dave and Layton started discussing how they would mark some of the weapons to make them seem to have come in from Cuba. Dave, realizing I had no perspective on what they were talking about, then clarified things: the donors were rich, anonymous oilmen who could purchase weapons anywhere, anytime, to further their causes, and if that meant planting weapons with falsified markings on them to make Castro or any other "Commie bastards" look bad, all the better. They were also financing training camps to enhance the chances of a Cuban getting Castro killed, as well as to remove any other leaders in Latin America viewed as threats to their personal desires.

"They want their Cuba back," Dave said. He turned his head and gave me a smile, continuing to steer like a race car driver through the traffic. "We'll use this method again, for the next shipment."

Delta Steamships mainly carried coffee and cargo, with luxury cruise cabins for passengers.

"It seems to me that too many people are in the know on this," I said, uncomfortably. "I don't think that will work."

"So, who's going to talk, J?" Dave said. "Me, or Lee? Will Marcello? We all have too much to lose. That includes you. You're getting a ride today because Lee is up to his eyeballs in bananas at this very moment. And it's your fault," he said, once again reaching for humor.

"How could bananas be my fault?" I asked Dave. He laughed again.

"We took your advice and were very creative. We took the furniture idea all the way. It made a really good disguise for the shipment," he said. "So yeah, it's your fault." Dave pulled over to the curb and let "Layton Martens" out of the car. It was the only time I ever saw the man. Dave continued to the warehouse where the Delta ship's cargo had been taken. He parked as close as he could get. Then we got out of the car and walked the rest of the way. As we walked, Dave told me to hold tight to my purse. Laborers, sailors, longshoremen and stevedores had

finished their work for the day and were now leaving. Dave said the docks were the battlefield of every port city. The unions ruled and headed the fight to stop the Communists from taking over. I was surprised. "There are Communists out here?" I asked. "There's everything out here," Dave said. "Organized crime, labor unions, stockholders, Communists, Castroites, anti-Castroites, drug dealers…." He waved his hand over the panorama of cranes, tractors, dollies, forklifts, trucks and elevators. The "sister ship" handling this arms shipment was one of three Delta ships that made regular trips – including to a port close to Caracas in Venezuela. [178]

A Delta ship's coffee cargo unloading

The three Delta ships had elegant quarters and special activities for passengers, but their primary income came from cargo, not passengers. Their cargo was mostly coffee, but bananas, textiles, furniture, leather products, bottled drinks, pottery, cacao and exotic fruits were also shipped. [179] This Delta ship's cargo had just been unloaded, stacked high in boxes, barrels and bales.

---

[178] Ref: https://www.cruiselinehistory.com/2018-may-delta/

[179] Martens was young teen who was an avid anti-Castro activist. He was a gifted musician and one of David Ferrie's best friends. We planned to meet in March, 2000, after Martens was no longer involved with Mardi Gras. But he died that same month.

New Orleans was one of America's major ports, Dave reminded me, with its docks controlled by the Mob. Lee's uncle Dutz got his start there. The unions kept things going 'the right way.' We now entered one of the Trade Mart warehouses. Dave said it was Mr. Shaw who had been so instrumental in helping rain to fall on Castro's parade, but Reily was involved, too. Reily Coffee used Delta ships for some major coffee bean imports, and the Trade Mart's warehouses were always available for "anything else" Reily wanted to import. Inside one storage section, some fifty boxes of furniture were being re-sealed and stacked. They were marked in Spanish. Their labels indicated they contained hardwood chairs or tables, suitable for dining. Dave encouraged me to inspect one of the unsealed boxes. It contained chairs. I saw two chairs, side-by-side. A thick felt pad protected them. I saw nothing out of the ordinary. "What am I looking at?" I asked.

"Where the rifles were," Dave said, smiling. Dave explained that hundreds of rifles had been shipped in the furniture boxes. In this case, originally packed four chairs to a box, two chairs had been removed to make room for rifles. The two remaining chairs were nested together. After the rifles were removed, one of the two chairs was placed beside the other, using up twice the space. Then the carton was resealed. My smuggling idea had worked.

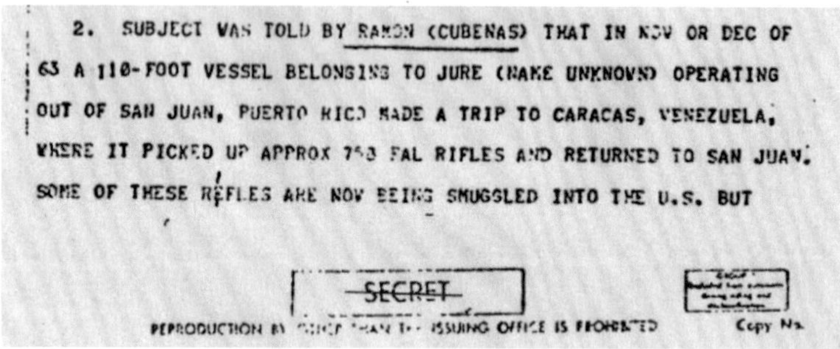
2. SUBJECT WAS TOLD BY RAMON (CUBENAS) THAT IN NOV OR DEC OF 63 A 110-FOOT VESSEL BELONGING TO JURE (NAME UNKNOWN) OPERATING OUT OF SAN JUAN, PUERTO RICO MADE A TRIP TO CARACAS, VENEZUELA, WHERE IT PICKED UP APPROX 750 FAL RIFLES AND RETURNED TO SAN JUAN. SOME OF THESE RIFLES ARE NOW BEING SMUGGLED INTO THE U.S. BUT

SECRET

REPRODUCTION BY OTHER THAN THE ISSUING OFFICE IS PROHIBITED Copy No.

This document, released in 2017, describes ~750 rifles smuggled in from Caracas to San Juan, a Delta port of call, which then were sent to anti-Castro Cubans in Miami in Nov/Dec. 1963, supporting my 1999 report of this similar shipment in June, 1963, which I made public in 2009. Quote: "On a southbound voyage, San Juan in Puerto Rico was usually the first stop" for the three Delta sister ships. [180]**Additional records about smuggled gun stashes found on Cuban beaches, etc. were also released.**

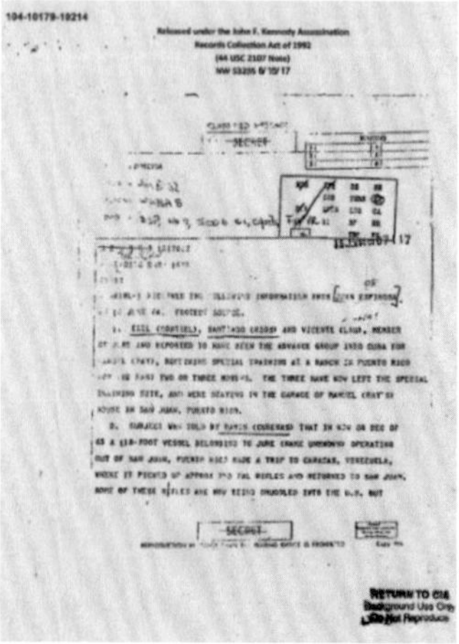
SECRET

RETURN TO CIA
Background Use Only
Do Not Reproduce

[180] Ref: https://www.cruiselinehistory.com/2018-may-delta/

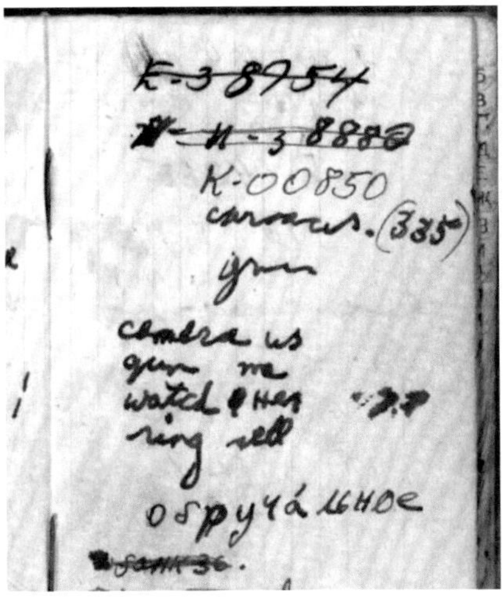

This section from p. 14 of Lee's address book shows the word '<u>caracas</u>' with a coded number of some kind. Under that is the word 'guns' and under that, Lee wrote 4 items in a row; (a)'camera us' (take photos?) (b) 'gun me' – Lee may have been asked to protect the shipment with a gun (c) '<u>watch her</u>': -Lee and I had a crisis at this time. Did he worry that I might expose the operation? Is this why Dave picked me up, to make sure I was under control? Finally, (d) 'ring sell' which may have meant selling rifles.

But why did Dave talk about Lee being involved with bananas? I soon learned that most of the rifles removed from the cartons were stacked in the bottom of big crates with bunches of bananas placed on top. The crates were then loaded into trucks, along with some regular fruit crates, and hauled away, supposedly to "Cuban markets." But what to do with the bananas left behind? There were heaps of them. But Lee had apparently worked out a plan. He and a few others were selling the bananas dirt cheap to the big ships along the docks. They gave away what they couldn't sell quickly (see Appendix for a file on this). That night, Lee called at about ten pm from a pay phone near his house. "Just to let you know," he said, "we're not going to run out of bananas for lunch any time soon." His voice was soft and gentle. He said he had called to see if I was OK. "I'm as well as can be expected," I told him. "I have only one thing to say. Yes, your little girl and unborn baby have to come first. They are hostages of fortune. But please!" I said, sobbing, "Don't come over anymore! I can't bear the pain!" When Lee protested, I answered, "No, Lee! This has to end. Now! I only want you to remember one thing. If you ever feel like hitting Marina again, remind yourself that I fell in love with a great man. To me, you'll always be my shining hero." When I was finished, there was only silence. He had hung up. Distracted by my roaring emotions, I could not work on my lab reports, nor could I sleep.

<u>Saturday, June 29, 1963</u> In the morning, a letter from Robert came. With all my heart I had tried to look at things from his viewpoint, but right now, I wanted no part of men. He had written, *"June, a Thursday. Ma Chere Judy, Lovey-dovey, don't write me anymore! Monday at latest I should. be off...."*

I calculated: Robert would probably be home by July 3rd, then. That made sense because the 4th was a national holiday. At the end, aware he had failed me once again, he signed his letter "Rat."

Robert rarely mentioned national events. His letters reflected little outside his immediate radius. Locked into his own mini-universe, I know he did the best he could to share it with me. Years later, my oldest son would dub his father "Mr. Spock"—the ever-logical, almost emotionless alien genius from Vulcan in *Star Trek*.

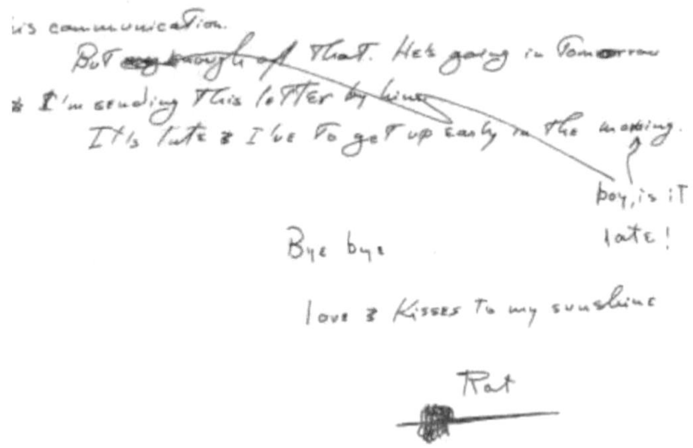
its communication.
But enough of that. He's going in tomorrow
* I'm sending this letter by line
It's late & I've to get up early in the morning.
boy, is it late!
Bye bye
love & kisses to my sunshine
Rat

I'd married a man who wrote, *"...the lowest form of life in the state of Louisiana is, of course, the Nigger."* He meant it as a joke, but there was no humor in what was happening at Birmingham, in Jackson, Mississippi, or in the bombed black Baptist churches. I had given my affection and love to two men. Lee was withdrawing from my life, but the man who married me had never quite entered it. I lay on my bed, and pounded my pillow. Desiring something — anything — to reduce the misery, I turned on the radio. Little Peggy March's song was playing. It just made everything worse: *I love him! I love him! I love him! And where he goes I'll follow, I'll follow, I'll follow!... I will follow you...*

But Robert hadn't wanted me to follow him. As for Lee... I stared over at the begonias I'd placed nearer to the bed, just because they reminded me of *him*. I looked upon the roses, still fresh in their containers. I would have to throw them out before Robert returned. Tears sprang to my eyes. I fell into a dreamless sleep, to waken a few hours later when I heard that familiar tapping at my window. I sure knew who that was! "Go away!" I yelled, a pillow over my head. The tapping continued. I threw the pillow at the window. Suzi Collie was whining. I could hear Lee's voice. "Now, Collie, I saw you chasing Mr. Cat up the tree. You know you shouldn't. Now I shall have to get him down." Lee had an endearing habit of calling animals he did not know "Mr. Cat" or "Mr. Dog" or "Mr. Squirrel." It was our little joke. It had started when I began calling Monaghan "Mr. M." Curious, I betook myself to the window, to see what was going on, peeking through the crocheted curtains. Lee took Suzi Collie around the back and put her in the house on Susie's side. Now he was carrying the stepladder.

I watched him go across the street and lean it against a tree. After a few minutes, he brought down a squalling tomcat, and let it go.

He was coming back with the ladder, so I hurried back to the bed. I just wanted him to go away! There it was again, the tapping!

"Please, Juduffki..." I heard him say.

"Go back to your family!" I shouted. "Don't do this to me! You're killing me!" I began to cry again. There had been so many tears lately. He was carrying the ladder again: I could hear him put it back under the house. Then I remembered. *He has a key*! I got under the bed, taking the pillow with me. In he came: I could see his scuffed shoes as he stood there, from my position underneath the bed on that cool wooden floor. There were dust bunnies all around me. Yuck! I held my breath, keeping as quiet as I could. Then he said, "If you wish to persist, and stay under the bed, may I hand you a quilt?"

"No, Lee!" I whispered. "I can't take the pain of seeing you. I know you belong to her. Go home." He slowly knelt down, and peered at me.

"Well," he said, "I planned to go down on my knees to you today, anyway. I just didn't think you'd be way down here when I did it."

I told him not to tease me like that. He said it would be quite a while before he could straighten everything out, but in the end, he believed he could. Then he whispered, looking into my eyes as I lay curled up under the bed: "Please, Juduffki. Let it be me in your life... *I bless the day I found you...*!" He was quoting from our song, '*Let It Be Me...* I could not reply. Tears were again rolling down my cheeks. When I wiped them away, a dust bunny clung to my nose. I knew I looked ridiculous.

"Judyth, my love," he said, "Will you marry me?" I lost my breath.

"It's you I love and want," he said. "I tried with all my might to send you out of my heart. I even told Marina I would go back to Russia with her. But I can't do it. I'll find a way to see my babies, if I can't get custody of them." He reached down. "I want you to take my hand," he said. I didn't move. "I'll wait, then," he said, "if you want to stay under the bed. I know I hurt you." When I still didn't speak, he added, sadly, "I just want you to say something besides 'go away'! Anything."

From the depths of my soul, all the love I felt began to pour from my heart. Lee was back! Lee was asking me to marry him! So I told him what he meant to me. "Lee," I said with adoration, "you are still my shining hero." I saw his face change, the anxiety fall away, the pain in his eyes change to happiness. I let him help me out from under the bed. We smiled shyly at each other as I dusted myself off.

"I only want to hear you say 'yes,'" he persisted. "Say you'll marry me, as soon as we can get Robert and Marina out of the picture. Then I'll go home, if you wish." I looked into his eyes. "Ask me again," I said.

"I'm perfectly aware that Baker never asked you to marry him," Lee replied. "So I will ask you a hundred times, if only you will say yes just once. Will you?"

"Ask me again." He knelt down.

"Please give me the inimitable pleasure," he said, "of your hand in marriage." [181] He took off his wedding band and laid it on the floor. "The day will come," he said, "when I will come to you, without this wedding ring." I told him I would consent, but that it was all so sudden. I felt overwhelmed. "I'm not finished trying to overwhelm you," he said. "I've dreamed to show you my love, as I dreamed from the start," he said. "But only if you are ready."

"Come ...!" I said, sitting down on the bed and starting to unbutton my blouse. "No — I want a fresh bed for us!" he insisted. "Besides, you still haven't said yes. So — will you marry me?"

"Ninety-eight to go!" I said, smiling. "Put on your nice brown dress," he said. As I dressed, and then hunted for my purse, he went out to talk to Susie. I was surprised to see him return with car keys to the car that was always sitting in the driveway. "I'm going to go kiss that woman!" I told Lee. "How easily you are kissing everybody but me!" he said, for I had not even touched him yet. I started to put my hair up, but he shook his head. He took the pins out of my hair. "I want it long and free," he said. I put on the emerald earrings my sister had given me on my sixteenth birthday, then Lee guided me to the car. We went to the Roosevelt Hotel. There, Lee brought in the best the hotel had to offer — a glorious feast, with music and flowers. He even had a record player brought in, and once again, put on the Everly Brothers' song, "Let It Be Me." He kept asking me to marry him, over and over. He asked me in the car. He asked me standing on a chair, standing on one foot, and standing on his head. He asked me ninety-nine times, and I counted every one. We counted the last few together. Then he picked me up in his arms, like he was carrying me across a threshold, and placed me on the beautiful hotel bed. As his body hovered lovingly over mine, and our lips met, we melted into each other's embrace.

How tenderly, how slowly, we loved! "Will you marry me, my beloved?" he asked, for the hundredth time.

As I exploded with a joy I didn't know could exist, I told the man I would love forever, *Yes*!

[181] Yes, Lee used the word ***inimitable.*** I stress, again, that he had a remarkably good vocabulary.

Considerations: "The car in the driveway" issue: I assumed Susie Hanover drove because a car was in her driveway, but when she went out, somebody always picked her up. As Sunday was my only "day of rest," Susie was usually gone when I got up. The car may have been kept in running condition or even used while I was at work. It probably belonged to a teacher next door who had recently died. When Vicki Rodick and I corresponded in 2021, I told her my memory is in 'pictures.' They never included seeing Susie drive, so it isn't mentioned in *Me & Lee* (prior edition of this book). Perhaps the car was parked in Susie's driveway to make room for the new tenant's car. In late August, everything belonging to the deceased teacher was in a yard sale after a search for relatives came up empty. We were told her car had been sold to pay rent due. The garage sale and the car sale incident are mentioned in the prior edition of this book. I was very upset at tis time and didn't notice that the car was gone. Since the landlord did not live next door, perhaps Susie had the keys so she could move the car if needed.

Chapter 19
The Garage

Next door to Reily's was the Crescent City Garage. Though privately owned, the FBI, CIA, Secret Service and other government agencies parked their vehicles there, since it was directly across the street from the Federal Building and courthouse, convenient to the various government offices clustered around Lafayette Park. What few knew was that its location was very important to Lee Oswald.

First, Lee frequently needed to slip out of Reily's for his various covert activities, in a way unnoticed by the staff. But the windows of the Reily offices looked out onto Camp Street, Capedeville Street and Magazine Street, so their staff could easily observe pedestrians on these sidewalks. It was simply not possible for Lee to slip out, unseen, from the front doors. The back was quite different. In the back, Reily's coffee and tea products were loaded onto trucks for delivery from a dock at the rear of the factory. Here, next to two big doors, trucks came and went all day, backing up to the loading docks and blocking the view of the alley. When Lee needed to leave quietly, he would go through the Crescent City Garage, having slipped out through Reily's loading docks.

Reily's loading docks, where trucks backed up to be packed.

Lee Oswald used the Crescent City Garage to leave Reily's unseen. The real reason Lee Oswald read "gun magazines" at the Crescent City Garage was to befriend manager Adrian Alba, so he could pass through the garage to go unnoticed to Banister's. [182]

Lee would typically stroll through the garage and then leave through the front entrance onto Magazine Street, unseen by anyone at Reily's. The nearest cross street was Lafayette, where Guy Banister's office entrance was located. To facilitate this route. Lee cultivated a friendship with **Adrian Alba,** one of the owners of the garage, so his presence would not seem unusual. To this end, Lee spent some extra time at the garage reading magazines there, and sometimes eating lunch there on Mondays or Tuesdays, when we couldn't eat lunch together. Lee talked with Adrian about the man's favorite subjects — hunting and guns. Another benefit of this garage was that Lee was able to communicate easily with members of the local intelligence community, since they parked their cars there, including delivering and receiving intelligence information.

Alba, 2006

---

[182]https://www.archives.gov/files/research/jfk/releases/docid-32176315.pdf De Brueys always denied being connected to Lee Oswald, but the testimony of Orest Pena established the connection. Further, de Brueys denied being transferred to Dallas , which occurred, we now know through new documents released in 2017, on Oct. 25, 1963, less than three weeks after Lee returned to Dallas from Mexico City, for "a temporary assignment." That assignment was over, it seems, after the Kennedy assassination and Lee's death, since de Brueys was transferred back to New Orleans at that time.

On "First Fridays" (a payday), Lee's visits with Adrian might be in the afternoons, since he had to wait for his CIA pay to show up. Lee may have received his pay envelope from a passing Agency car (Alba saw Lee receive a large envelope, which he hid in his shirt, when a car drove up, which he recognized as a government car).

During the month of June 1963, Lee ran his faux Fair Play for Cuba Committee out of the office he rented in Guy Banister's building. He had received an authentic FPCC membership card, which he duplicated. He also stamped pamphlets and flyers with his fake organization's address, which changed from time to time when necessary. If Lee had to be absent from Reily's, it was likely that he had last been seen at the Crescent City Garage. Usually, Lee went to Banister's. I know RFK wanted to go around the FBI and support anti-Castro groups on the sly, which is why he worked with rebel supporters like Guy Banister, and why Banister tolerated working with RFK, whom he despised. This is only one reason why I believe Bobby Kennedy knew who Lee really was.

Our Plans to Escape: Our First Ideas By late June, Lee was at a watershed in his personal life. We were falling deeply in love, but Lee struggled with his inner turmoil each night, oscillating between the poles of love and loyalty. Here's the background: Trying to preserve their family, he initially chose **Marina and June**.

Now he was doubting that he would ever return to the USSR again. She had been delighted when Lee wrote to the Soviet Embassy (in Russian) requesting their entrance visas. Then, when Lee changed his mind completely, he was ready to leave Marina for good. We planned to divorce our current mates and go live somewhere remote, like Mexico. That's why Lee wrote to the Soviet Embassy again (this time in English, so the FBI, which read all of Lee's mail, could read it easily). This time, Lee asked that Marina's visa was to be rushed through, but his own was to be considered *separately*. That way, he could send Marina back, if she wished, while making it seem that later he might also return. Marina understood this change of plans as a change of heart. She wrote to Ruth Paine, saying Lee didn't love her anymore. She didn't understand why Lee refused to divorce her now, but he had a good reason. If he did, Marina could have been deported before her baby was born. If their baby was born in the USA, Marina would not get deported. It was that simple. Lee's earliest idea was that I would pose as his wife until we could get quickie divorces in Mexico, since we had read that the actress Jayne Mansfield had done so.

But now, looking back on all our plans, we realized that our biggest challenge was to escape the arms of the octopus. Caught up in plots and plans that we now hated, we just wanted to start a new life, free and without guilt. To prepare Marina for his planned disappearance, Lee also told Marina that he had a "burning desire" to live in Cuba. Marina even told the Warren Commission that Lee said he might even hijack a plane to get there, but Lee never mentioned any such thing to me. However, Lee did study every plane route available to Mexico City and to Havana. Marina saw him lay maps out, as he plotted how best to manage our disappearing act. When she saw all those maps, Marina was sure Lee was sincere about flying –somehow—to Cuba.

As for Marina, when Lee disappeared, she would think he disappeared behind Cuba's "iron curtain." But Lee always planned to re-establish contact after a safe waiting period. He was determined to see his babies again. Meanwhile, Lee and I held the belief that the CIA would use us as informants in Mexico, that we'd go to college, and then proceed with our lives under our fake names, with passports to match.

As we talked about where we would live and how we would earn a living, Lee said his friend, George de Mohrenschildt, was in charge of Lee's stowed-away money. He would help us, making sure that a large sum would be given to Marina and the children after we disappeared. Some of it was Company pay, accrued while Lee was a spy in the USSR. **George de Mohrenschildt**-- one of Lee's immediate handlers-- was a sophisticated Soviet-born petroleum geologist of bona fide Russian aristocracy, displaced by war and revolution. He still claimed the title of Baron. His brother Dimitri became important in D.C. and George was in The Social Register ("The *Social Register* is a semi-annual publication in the United States that indexes the members of American high society. "). George was now in Haiti, representing the interests of Dallas oil magnate Clint Murchison, among others, which caused Lee some concern, since Murchison was one of Dr. Ochsner's closest friends.

George de Mohrenschildt, with his two Manchester toy terriers who disliked outsiders, but were very fond of Lee. George had dated Jackie Kennedy's mother: Jackie called him "Uncle George."

It meant we'd have to consider how Ochsner felt about this, though the CIA would have." the last word. In Lee's eyes, George was a romantic character. His recent trek with his wife through Mexico and Central America fueled Lee's desire to follow in his footsteps. One Thursday, as Lee and I read "survival books" at the Napoleon Branch Library, I was surprised at how much Lee knew about survival in the wild. He was equally surprised at how much I knew. Anybody who knows me, to this very day, also knows I'd gladly take on such an adventure! As for Lee, he said, "You're the woman of my dreams!" --simply because I loved what he loved.

Wednesday, July 3, 1963 Our cover jobs at Reily's conveniently obscured our activities at Dave's primitive lab. Today's job was to process 200 mouse pups at one go—a huge task. Thankfully, Dave and Lee had conspired to save me, again, from the nastiest part of the work. To do so, Lee left Reily's well ahead of me. But when I arrived, I discovered they were trying to solve a bottleneck: the pups were being suffocated in a standard Bell jar, with ether-soaked cotton wads, but it could handle only 5-10 pups at a time. When I told Dave to buy some big glass cake covers, in a little more than an hour, he returned with the cake covers and the problem was solved. Sealed around their rims with petroleum jelly, they became large, efficient gas chambers. But the act of slaughtering, then slicing open these helpless mice literally made Lee ill. Dave nor I had no stomach for it, either. We all felt like vomiting.

The Fourth of July was the next day; Robert had said that he would be coming home. I had no idea when, so we worked as fast as we could.

On the 4th, some poor soul would have to handle all these tumors, but it wouldn't be us. But what if Robert got to Marengo Street before me? Lee suggested I should stop on the way home for groceries, as the stores would be closed on the Fourth, and I could use that as an excuse for my late arrival. Monaghan, faced with our lab problem, obligingly clocked us both out so we would not have to return to Reily's. Finally finished, I headed home, arriving with an armload of groceries at about 7:30. I was relieved to see that there was no blue Ford in the driveway. I still had time to hide everything, and to bathe! I took a full bath in the tub in the kitchen and tried to wash off the cancer odor. I was sure Lee was doing the same. We both took evening baths, rather than morning showers, to remove any noxious odors that we felt was clinging to us, no matter how much we scrubbed up (this may have been psychological).

When Robert finally arrived, he brought his usual load of dirty laundry, and his usual big appetite for "lovin'." I had given up hoping for the slightest gift, or so much as a walk in the park. It just wasn't what he did. What he wanted always came first, I realized glumly. Even so, I tried to please him, partly out of shame. Feeling like the latest edition of low-life, I was astonished that Mother Nature was absolutely no help in resisting. Robert had been my first lover and I responded, though my heart belonged to Lee.

<u>**Thursday, July 4, 1963**</u> I got up to make breakfast (of course Robert slept in!). As I was cooking, Dave called Susie to let me know the tissue cultures had been delivered to the Prytania Street lab, where an unlucky tech would be spending his or her Fourth of July holiday dealing with "The Problem." Dave was more talkative than usual. He went on to say that he had to go back to Miami next week to deal with his Eastern Air Lines troubles. Mouse slaughters were to be halted until July 12th. By then, we should have the results of Ochsner's experiments on the marmoset monkeys, which had already been inoculated. Before his Miami trip, Dave said he was going to fly to Illinois. An ancient but primitive branch of the Catholic church had accepted his seminary credentials. He proudly said that he hoped to get ordained at last.

"Good luck, Dave," I said as he hung up, wondering to myself why it would be so important for such a brilliant man to be ordained by a conspicuously bogus church.[183] As Robert enjoyed his French toast, strawberries, and scrambled eggs, I asked if we could go somewhere.

"I have to leave tomorrow, while you're at work," he protested. "That only gives us twenty- two hours together. Besides, I'm too horny to do anything else," he added. Robert had obtained a piggybank from a bank, to hold our pennies and nickels. He said that when it filled up, we could go out to eat. I was also urged to put all my nickels and pennies into "the pig." After spending all morning making sure Robert wasn't "horny" anymore, Robert finally conceded that he needed a break. I'd earned a trip to the French Quarter—hurrah! I put on makeup, braided my hair, and put in my brown contact lenses to match my brown dress. By 2:00 PM, we were in the French Quarter at last![184] As we strolled through the historic streets enjoying the sights, Robert navigated us to Pat O'Brien's, eager to sample one of their famous Hurricanes, the rum drink for which O'Brien's was famous.

---

[183] In my book *David Ferrie: Mafia Pilot*, and in books by Peter Levenda and Dick Russell, strange churches and "wandering bishops" are associated with JFK's assassination. They were often CIA informants. They were often homosexuals. For these reasons, David Ferrie may have had more than a religious interest in these groups.

[184] We rode the streetcar up to Saint Charles the first time so Robert could try to get our rent money back from Mrs. Webber. As I waited outside, I could hear them arguing. Then Robert appeared, holding a check aloft in victory. "She gave it all back!" he announced proudly. "No, she gave you a check," I amended, figuring that Mrs. Webber had given him a bum check just to get him out of the house. I couldn't believe he fell for it. We boarded the streetcar and stopped at the bank on the way home to deposit the check. Robert instructed me to call in the morning to see if the check was good. (It wasn't).

Entering through an ancient brick tunnel, we soon found ourselves in a lush tropical paradise. The moment we found a table, a waiter appeared, and Robert promptly ordered two Hurricanes before I had a chance to say a word. I reminded him that I didn't drink, but Robert didn't believe me. So, when the Hurricanes arrived, and I rejected the drink, he bit the bullet and drank both of them. "If I buy you something," he said then, "we'll blow our budget. You're the one who made that choice, so you'll have to live with it." After leaving O'Brien's, we found a hole-in-the-wall that served delicious chicken gumbo and rice. I don't remember what Robert had.

Then we took the streetcar home. That was the first and last of the French Quarter I saw with Robert. Since Lee and I went there so frequently, only because my hair was up and I was wearing my brown contact lenses and speaking English, did I feel it was safe. When we got home, it was getting dark. We sat reading for a while, when Robert, who was reading *The Rise and Fall of the Third Reich*, set it aside. "Arf, lover!" he said, grabbing up his keys. "Let's go watch the fireworks!" *Fabulous!*

We jumped in his car, but soon ended up stuck in a massive traffic jam on top of the Mississippi River bridge. Robert sat there, quietly cursing, ordering those cars to *move*! When they didn't, he became angry. "Why did I listen to you?" he griped. "We should have stayed home!" But Robert seemed to miss the point. We were perched on the 400-foot-high Mississippi River Bridge -- probably the best view of the fireworks— which were exploding over the river! That's probably why the traffic wasn't moving. Everyone was enjoying the fireworks, except Robert, who wanted to get across the bridge. For the first time, I felt sorry for my genius husband and his linear mind.

Friday, July 5, 1963 Robert was gone again, pleased with nice, ironed shirts and another good breakfast. I looked forward to a long Friday lunch with Lee, after hard work at Monaghan's desk. We first went to Banister's building. Lee's Fair Play for Cuba Committee "office" was now closed, but Lee still had his 2nd floor keys, since his dark room up there was now complete. Pro-Castro posters and flyers decorated its windowless walls.[185] Noting my interest in the posters, Lee said, "I took the rest of them home, to impress anybody who might show up there, just to show how much I love my Uncle Fidel."

We didn't stay long, soon heading to the Prytania Street lab, where I picked up the Project's log books which Dave had dropped off.

---

[185] Antony Summers interviewed Delphine Roberts, Banister's secretary who mentioned knowing about Lee's presence "upstairs."

I also inspected the cell cultures and gave them to Lee to courier to the U. S. Public Health Service lab for Dr. Mary.

I remember all these details because it was such a relief not to have to slaughter any more mice for now. The July 4th holiday meant less mail than usual, too. That gave me time to type some letters for Mr. M. But it was hard to concentrate, for Lee and I had planned a romantic tryst this afternoon. After clocking out, I went downstairs and sat in the canteen, waiting restlessly until I could clock Lee out. Then I returned to the big room. There I paced, waiting for Lee to return. Finally, the last Reily employee was gone, but the lights still blazed. Then Lee came up by the company's main elevator, which was a surprise, and took me in his arms. "Well, we're the last ones in here," he said. "As Maintenance Man, it's my duty to shut off the lights." Lee turned off the main light switch and, in the semi-darkness, we realized how amazingly quiet and peaceful it was in a room so clangorous and noisy during the day that earplugs would have been welcome. Struck by the silence, we had a novel idea. "Are you willing, Mrs. Oswald?" Lee asked me.

We sneaked into Mr. Monaghan's cubicle, and there, we embraced. Then, the idea of defiance arose within us. Defiance of *them.*

We would make love in Their Cave of Power! Lee said he had learned a lot from the geisha he'd loved in Japan, as they made love on a flat mattress, not a bed. And he would show me...his hands began to touch me ever so lightly, drawing me into a tide of passion. My mind and body was caught up, entranced, as Lee's slow love swept tenderly over me. "I thought I had lost these powers," Lee whispered, "but you have brought them back. I have at last returned to that kind of giving."

I felt myself transported to an exotic, timeless dimension, even as I loved the smell of the coffee and oil on him. His legs were as hard as steel. His thoughts were one with mine. Our hipbones smoothed us together as if we were literally one. Lee was right: man and woman was a puzzle that, when put properly together, was for us the most natural thing in the world. We melded perfectly, as if born to it.

But finally, it was time to come to our senses. As we left Monaghan's cubicle and made ourselves presentable, we began talking about the future. Lee mentioned that Mr. Barbe had to stop pretending that he didn't know where Lee was. "My time here is obviously drawing to a close," Lee told me. "I suppose after you leave, you'll be doing the leafleting again?" I said, in a voice that failed to hide my fear for his safety. Lee avoided answering, as he so often did, taking some keys from his pocket.

"Here, I have a surprise for you!" he said showing me the keys. "It's in Alba's garage. And it's ours, for the next few hours."

We then went out the back to the garage next door. Lee unlocked the door to the garage with one of the keys. As we entered, I noticed the heat. It had to be over a hundred degrees in there.

"Wow, it's hot in here," I observed. "Well, in a few minutes we'll be out riding, enjoying the breeze," Lee said, as he led me to a shiny red van. We got in the van, but the engine wouldn't start. Lee got out to look under the hood. There he discovered a problem with the van's solenoid. "It's shot, I can't fix it," he said, wiping the sweat from his forehead. We looked at each other. Once again, we were utterly, entirely alone. And the van had pull-curtains. "I've got an idea," Lee said...

After undergoing our own form of purgatory in the red-hot red van that had so cruelly tempted us, we staggered from the garage drenched in sweat, feeling like utter fools. As we stumbled toward the French Quarter, looking forward to gulping down as much fluid as we needed to recover, Lee (who never complained) complained. "Me and my bright ideas!" he said gloomily. "And all because I haven't got two pence to rub together!"

"It's all right, sweetheart," I told him. "Who would have guessed that red vans could be a source of medieval torture?"

"You don't deserve this," he said. "Neither do I. We have a hell of a lot left to do this summer, and we need a safe place to be together."

"There's 1032," I reminded him.

"I can't," he replied. "The sheets there are still warm from Robert. The very thought makes me jealous." I understood how he felt. Robert had confessed that he enjoyed making love to me in the blue Ford as a sort of revenge, for it once belonged to the girlfriend who'd ditched him. "That's two good reasons, never to make love to you in a car again," Lee said. "Well," I answered as we walked, "we still have public rest rooms, university listening rooms, the place behind the Seal Pool at Audubon Park, and —" Lee burst out laughing. "You silly little Minnie Mouse!" he said affectionately, "and how about that plane? It's got a bench seat."

"Don't think so. Dave has flown it up to Illinois. I guess we're sunk."

"You just wait," Lee said. "By this time tomorrow, I'll have an answer to this." Despite our rumpled clothes and our hair still in sweaty strands, we walked into The Acme Oyster Bar on Bourbon Street, gulped down tall glasses of iced tea, and then devoured two plates of oysters. I posed as Lee's wife, speaking only Russian. Then we caught the Magazine Bus home. Now alone in my little apartment, I noticed a letter addressed to me on the side table. Robert had opened it before he left. It was from Robert's mother. It contained an invitation to a ladies-only bridal shower, to be held on July 20th, at The Coronado Hotel in Fort Walton Beach. A note accompanied the card, expressing regret that only her own female friends were invited. She felt she would not be able to get along with my mother.

Mrs. Robert Baker, Jr. would also feel awkward inviting my sister without inviting my mother, and she did not know any of my friends. She hoped I would understand. I certainly did. *"I am really looking forward to this!"* I thought, inspecting the engraved invitation. Would Robert be back in time? Probably. After all, the invitation was engraved and Robert would want "the loot" as he called it.

Saturday, July 6, 1963 Lee went to Customs for a business meeting, then spent the rest of the day with his wife and daughter. Susie and Suzi Collie were still gone. I hated being alone, but I busied myself, washing clothes by hand in the bathtub. Then I hung them out to dry. If Lee had been there, I would have used the wringer washing machine in the patio, but it was too hard to wring out the clothes without his help. I ironed some things, then started reading medical reports about dying monkeys. O, joy!

Then Susie and Suzi Collie came back, with 9-year-old Claudia, her great-granddaughter, who was going to spend the night. School was out, and Claudia would be visiting more often now. At this time, her 16-year-old sister Vickie had begun driving, while Claudia still liked being with her great-grandma all day. In November, 2020, Claudia told our 8th annual JFK Dallas conference, in person and on Zoom, that she saw Lee at my apartment so many times she thought he lived there.

Claudia Rodick, New Orleans, 2017
Susie Hanover (1st row 3rd from R) with her big family.

Claudia remembered Lee playing with her and the neighborhood children, and how Lee helped Susie and me wring out our wet clothes on Susie's old wringer washing machine. She remembered Lee offering to help her mow, and how once, he intervened to stop a dull-witted young man, a neighbor, from making the wrong kind of approaches to her.

. **Sunday, July 7, 1963** Lee had asked me to meet him in front of the Fur Shop on Canal Street. When I arrived, Lee steered me across the busy street into the French Quarter. "I have a surprise for you!" he said. "Uh-oh!" I replied. "I've heard those words before. Not the van again!" "Not by any means!" said he, leading me straight into the handsome lobby of the Monteleone Hotel, an elegant and famous site in New Orleans. We were already registered as "Mr. and Mrs. Robert E. Lee."

(After some rethinking, we never did that again.). As we walked through those hallowed halls toward our room, Lee said softly, "Tennessee Williams... Sherwood Anderson... William Faulkner... They all lived here. Masterpieces were written here." [186] Our room was, in fact, a grand suite that included a color TV set, a record player and a stack of records. A basket of fruit and flowers graced an antique table, accompanied by a simple white card. "Look at the card." Lee said, as he opened the drapes to reveal the lush courtyard below.

"*Best wishes to the young lovers,*" I read aloud. "*May you enjoy this music as much as I have.*" It was signed "CLS."[187]

"Who is CLS?" I asked. "That is Clay LaVerne Shaw," Lee explained.

"But how--?"

"He felt sorry for us," Lee said, kissing me. "I had to see him Saturday morning at his office. We had business to discuss about using the Trade Mart as a future site for my pro-Castro demonstration. He'd just been updated by Dave about the cancer project and was pleased by my involvement in it."

"Is that the tall gray fellow from The 500 Club?" I queried.

"Yes, the same. He's working night and day right now, trying to lease offices in the new Trade Mart building, but he took time to meet with me," Lee said. Shaw represented important anti-Castro interests. "When he asked about you and me, I described some of our recent adventures. After he finished laughing, he told me to meet him in a few hours at a rather remote location. He was going to get some money from his safe. In return, all he requested from me was an FPCC flyer, to keep as a souvenir." Lee showed me the money.

---

[186] Lee did not have a name choice the first time: our "sponsor" had pre-paid for this first hotel and selected the names we were to use.

[187] Shaw had written plays and appreciated literature. It is logical that he would have chosen The Monteleone for us. Also, the young owner, Billy Monteleone, was himself an active anti-Castro Cuban.

Shaw had given him a thousand dollars, in hundred-dollar bills. [188] "He volunteered to make reservations for us." Lee continued, saying he turned that idea down. "I will only have to call to make arrangements... We'll use different names and different hotels," he added.

"We're playing Boris and Natasha again?" I asked.

"Well, not quite," Lee said. "But he hoped this would be enough to keep us out of the closets in Reily's offices. And out of the INCA van for a while." Lee said Shaw, a longtime friend of both Ochsner and Dave, had stronger connections to the CIA than simple involvements with the Trade Mart.

He'd been useful to generals in the military. He was fiercely anti-Castro and had cooperated with Lee's Wasp project and various clandestine rifle shipments. But Lee also suspected that Shaw was a member of the get-Kennedy coalition. His most important friends hated JFK. He believed Dave was one of those anti-Kennedy patriots who agreed with him. Therefore, Lee considered Shaw a wildcard. So why was he being so generous about our hotel bills? It made Lee suspicious, but these thoughts melted away as we relaxed and turned our attention to each other. That led to an experience with Lee that I would never forget. As previously mentioned, I have two large scars on the right side of my abdomen from my childhood operations. My body was sleek and strong, but marred. Embarrassed by my scars, I closed the curtains and darkened the room, but Lee protested and reopened them. "Ah, but I want to see you. All of you!"

"No, you don't," I replied, closing the curtains again. "I have a big scar."

Lee opened the curtains once more. "You're not going to hide under the covers," Lee said. "What's more beautiful than a young woman, standing in the sunlight?"

"While I believe you are among the most remarkable and handsome of men," I replied, "I am not so blessed among women. I have a major flaw."

"Judy," he said tenderly, "I need to see this scar that concerns you so much. "

"You've already felt it," I said, blushing, as Lee began to undress me.

"I myself once had a dangerous scar," he told me. "It could have been

[188] Several years later, a witness in the Garrison trial said that he had seen Shaw and Lee together at the seawall on Lake Pontchartrain, while the witness, Vernon Bundy, was doing drugs. If Bundy's testimony was accurate, this may have when Lee and Shaw met. Bundy, who was black, an addict, and a vulnerable convict, was portrayed as "not credible" by Shaw's attorneys, who noted that there were no corroborating witnesses.

used to trace me wherever I went, so I had it hidden by a very simple procedure." [189] Lee had discarded all my clothing by now, and I had finished removing most of his. There I stood, in full view of the window's light, the large, thick scar on the right side of my belly displayed for Lee's scrutiny. He walked around me, looking critically at every part of me. He laid his hands on my hips and rotated me.

"My God, you're beautiful!" he said.

"You say that to all the women you conquer," I replied, smiling shyly.

"No, no," he answered. "It's true. But I need to look a little longer."

"I think you're taking advantage of me," I complained.

"I hope so. But first, I must find this scar that concerns you so much," he said, continuing to inspect me. "I can't understand it," he concluded. "You puzzle me." I felt his finger-tips trace my body, always with a single point of attention that communicated his affection. "Hmmm!" he said, with an enigmatic smile. "Hmmmmm!" he said again, stepping back, and looking me over again. Then, he shook his head. "What scar?" he asked. I understood, and fell into his arms...

<u>**Monday, July 8, 1963**</u> Mondays were always busy, so I worked without a break. Lee knew the drill by this point and avoided me. However, I got a glimpse of him in the back, near the shipping lines, working with some female Cuban exiles. I had a glimpse of Lee with the Cuban girls that is especially vivid, as they clustered around him, enjoying his attention. I saw his charms in action. A few girls, over the weeks, had been hired by Reily, based on David Lewis' suspicions. Lee eventually managed to test them to see which ones knew Russian. After work, we rode the bus past our apartments. By then, all the Reily personnel were off the bus and we sat together. Lee said he got a letter from his cousin, Eugene Murret, who was studying to be a priest. Gene invited him to give a lecture on his experiences in Russia at the Seminary at **Spring Hill College**, in Mobile, Alabama. There were important reasons why Lee decided to go. Lee suspected his cousin was manipulated to invite him.

[189] As for Lee's scar, while hospitalized in Minsk, Belarus, USSR, to have his adenoids removed (his tonsils had already been removed when he was a child) Lee had a slight operation done on the affected ear—his left ear—by a doctor with CIA connections. The doctor tucked the skin showing Lee's mastoidectomy scar under his ear. This took several days to heal and is the real reason why Lee stayed in the hospital so long for his very minor adenoid operation.

Dave had confided Lee's true identity to a Jesuit priest with connections to Bobby Kennedy. That Jesuit priest, who was close to the Kennedy family, would be coming in from Georgetown. Lee's 70-minute lecture would be held on Saturday, July 27. Some 50 seminary students in senior college, plus some graduates and several college professors, would be attending.

The day-long seminar would focus on the issues of Communism and Marxism. Lee would be speaking in the evening session on his experiences living in the USSR. The lecture would be followed by rounds of questions from the audience. Because the invitation had come from his son, Uncle Dutz was quite supportive of Lee's part, offering to drive everybody who could fit into the car all the way. He also reserved rooms at a nice motel. Lee said there was far more preparation behind this invitation than met the eye, behind the scenes._When I asked why the Jesuits would be interested in Marxism, Lee explained the Jesuits' predicament. The Order was traditionally conservative, but the younger generation of missionaries, working in places like Nicaragua, were preaching 'Liberation Theology.'

The theory supported Castro's Marxist-Leninist ideals. "What would Jesus do?" included getting rid of right-wing oligarchs who had close ties to the US. But these same right-wingers were also fanatically anti-Communist, and loyal Catholics. On the other hand, Castro's revolution in Cuba became both pro-Communist and anti-Catholic. That put the Jesuits in an awkward position. Where should their loyalties lie?

Should they promote or resist Marxism in Central and South America? Lee asked me to help him prepare his lecture. Even Marina would enjoy this trip, he said. A Russian-speaking Seminarian would be showing her around (women couldn't attend the lectures). Marina was planning to bring some Russian music along for the Russian-speaking Jesuit priest.

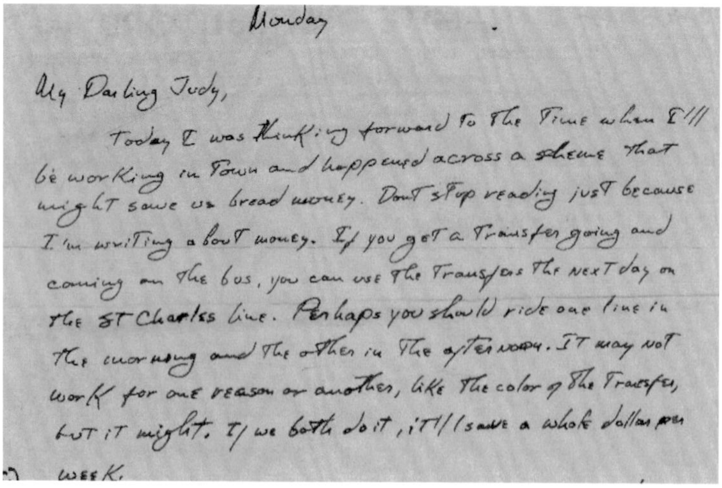

Monday

My Darling Judy,

Today I was thinking forward to the time when I'll be working in Town and happened across a scheme that might save us bread money. Don't stop reading just because I'm writing about money. If you get a Transfer going and coming on the bus, you can use the Transfers the next day on the St Charles line. Perhaps you should ride one line in the morning and the other in the afternoon. It may not work for one reason or another, like the color of the Transfer, but it might. If we both do it, it'll save a whole dollar per week.

At home, I found another letter from Robert in the mailbox. He wrote "Don't stop reading" just because he was writing about money, but I had to laugh when he described a scheme to cheat the transit system out of five cents a day!

"My Darling Judy, Today I was thinking forward to the time when I'll be working in town and happened across a scheme that might save us some bread money. Don't stop reading just because I'm writing about money. If you get a transfer going and coming on the bus, you can use the transfers the next day on the St. Charles line. Perhaps you should ride one line in the morning and the other in the afternoon. It may not work for one reason or another, like the color of the transfer, but it might. If we both do it, it'll save a whole dollar a week."

Robert's letter about how to try to cheat the transit system showed how little he knew about my working life or the New Orleans transit system.

The Magazine bus went straight to-and-from Reily's every day. Mere steps, and I was inside. No transfer needed. If I used the streetcar instead, I'd have to walk a total of a quarter of a mile each way, instead of a couple of blocks. Robert didn't even know what kind of work I did there. Just for fun, Susie Hanover, Lee and I had made a pact: if Robert *ever* asked me "What did you do today?"—*I'd tell him!* Let the chips fall where they may! But if he didn't, I was not going to volunteer a thing. He never did ask. [190] Robert also counseled me about finding a dentist. He wanted my mouth to be in top condition. He wondered if Susie or Mrs. Richardson could help. I was surprised that he had remembered Mrs. Richardson's name. I had only seen her at church a few Sundays, since that day she drove Lee and me from St. George's to Susie's house, and I had only mentioned her to Robert on one occasion, when he saw me write her a thank-you note, using Reily's full-color stationery. [191]

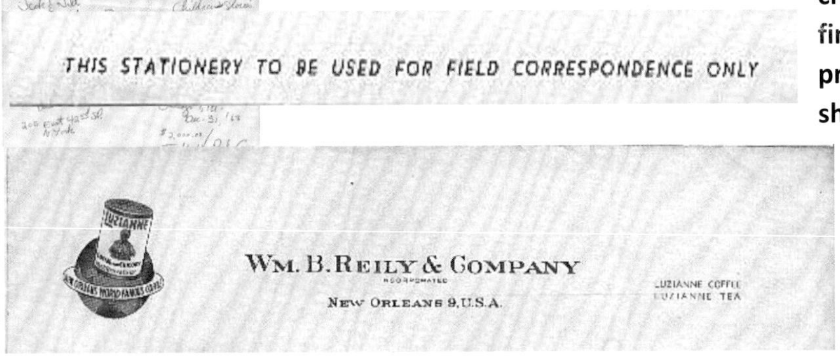

I used Vice-Pres. Monaghan's "field correspondence" stationery to write to grocery route salesmen and companies where Monaghan had concerns about security, credit, bills, finance problems and shipments. It was printed in black and red-brown.

(You can see the important executive stationary in color, in the color page section).

[191] Dave Ferrie had laughed about Robert's scheme to cheat the transit system, giving me a wooden nickel so I'd always "have some change" that Robert couldn't stash away. The nickel is shown in the color section.

Since I'd scribbled personal notes on this sheet, I took it home as a souvenir.it is water-marked. I also used Reily's fancier executive stationery for important official correspondence for the Vice President. See the color photo section of this book.

Wednesday, July 10, 1963 I received an important call at Reily's from a Dr. Bowers, who told me Dr. Ochsner had asked him to relay some good news. The call was important to me because it proved that other doctors were also involved with the project, not just lab techs. Dr. Bowers said that cells isolated from two of the lymphoma strains from the mice had produced dramatic results in the marmoset monkeys.

They suffered from not one but two variations of a galloping cancer. We had broken through the barrier between mouse and monkey with a virulent pancreatic cancer strain. Now we could move on to specific types of lung cancers, which was the goal. We would still need to keep some mouse cancers going in case problems occurred transitioning from marmosets to African Green monkeys. This was the only time I heard from a doctor other than Ochsner or Sherman.

By **Friday, July 12, 1963**, Dave was back in town and it was time to resume the unpleasant task of slaughtering mice. Dr. Ochsner had decided to have us process 400 mice (gulp!). We considered this cruelty. The argument was that "it would finish the run."

This was such a daunting task that Lee came to work a half-hour early to get an earlier start at Dave's. For the first time in five weeks, he clocked out at 5 PM, so we could finish faster. For the rest of the week, Lee tried to get to Reily's in time for a 5:00 pm clock-out, but with his heavy schedule, he was late an hour, mid-week. It couldn't be helped, but this time, Personnel had a hissy-fit. It was the beginning of the end of Lee's time at Reily.

On the 12th, by the time I got there, Lee had been killing cancerous mice by the armload, then cutting tumors out of their bodies. It was the height of summer, and the fans couldn't drive out the stench of 400 young, sick mice fast enough. Then Dr. Mary arrived to help us again. She was hard and stern, grimly working, wordless. Later, as Dave drove us home, he told us he had to go back to Miami again, and that Marcello's court case that Bobby Kennedy kept pushing was heating up. He would have to fly to Guatemala, most likely. My thoughts racing, I wondered if Dave had established a personal contact with Bobby Kennedy. He had been dropping so much information lately about him. What if Marcello learned of Dave's true loyalties? But soon enough, my thoughts returned to coping with our disgusting evening.

"I've been so busy I didn't even have time to eat," Dave said. "Not that I want anything after this."

"I knew better than to eat lunch," Lee said. "I would have puked."

"I didn't eat before coming, either," I said.

"What a jolly bunch we are!" Dave said. When Dave drove us up to my place, which we simply called "1032" I didn't want to get out because Lee was looking sick. "You'll be home in a couple of minutes now, sport," Dave said to Lee, who had to put his head out the window to get some fresh air. "Those baby mice," Dave went on, "were the saddest, most tormented little creatures I have ever seen." He shook his head. "To think they fought so hard for their lousy little shreds of life, only to be gassed to death."

"Stop!" I snapped. "Sadist! If you keep it up, I'm going to be in the same state as Lee. And to think we're trying to give Castro the same thing. It's just plain evil, Dave." The pure horror of it had finally hit me, but Dave's grin turned to a scowl. "Get this straight, chickadee!" he snapped. "This is about Kennedy, not Castro!"

Grimly driving, he said bitterly, "Kennedy is surrounded by his enemies. He can do nothing right in their eyes. And he's gonna' die, unless we can stop it." Dave threw his cigarette out the car window at the red light, and lit another one. "Listen," he went on, "You'd better know what your boy Lee, here, is up against. And me, too. We're risking our lives to get this stuff to Cuba. Yes, we're saying we want to help them take out JFK, and they believe us. If that son-of-a-bitch Castro is eliminated, we might save more than Kennedy. We might save the whole god-damned country from becoming a fascist nation."

"Well put," Lee said. "Excuse me, while I puke." I later helped Lee out of the car in front of his apartment, despite the risk of being seen (I was wearing a white lab coat.), as Lee was sick from vomiting. Then Dave drove me home, where I took a long bath, trying to wash the sickly smell of cancer off my body, which could have been a psychological impression. That night, about midnight, Lee came over, pale and grief-stricken. He looked so sick and dehydrated that I got him a glass of water. "She told me I was a dirty beast," he said, sitting miserably on the floor. "And it's true! I stink! I couldn't get clean if I sat in the tub all night. When I closed my eyes, all I could see was cancer."

"I understand," I told him. "Not even Castro deserves to die like that."

"Is there any way you can sabotage it?" he asked.

"No. But I'm ashamed. I feel like telling them to go on without me."

"You can't," Lee said. "Something could happen to you."

"I'm not going to work with murderers," I protested. His eyes narrowed into a steely gaze. "All right, I said, "I withdraw that statement."

"We're stuck," Lee observed. "Besides, you must weigh the life of the one against the life of the other." I understood him to mean Kennedy versus Castro. "If we do that, then we're playing God," I said.

"I'm now going to confide in you," Lee said, as he drank the water. "...I've done that with no one. I tell you this: They really are planning to assassinate Kennedy. In Florida, or in a stadium up north, or in Texas.

They'll show what happens to somebody who doesn't play their game." He put his arms around me, as if somehow, he could shield me from all of it. "Dave was right. If Kennedy dies, a new system of government will take over. It will exist to generate profit, mostly by waging wars that will not result in clear victories. It's the old Orwellian idea. Today, we're at war with Oceania... We've always been at war with Oceania! Tomorrow, we're at war with East Asia...We've always been at war with East Asia."

"We can still vote and choose our leaders." I replied.

"If you're black, try to vote in the South!" Lee said heatedly. "And who will you vote for if JFK dies?" he went on. "Your choices will be Lyndon Johnson, Barry Goldwater, or George Wallace. Good God." I said nothing. The gloom settled in. "You know," Lee said, getting up, "as I've said, JFK is slow to wage war. That's a man worth taking risks for."

Lee glanced at my alarm clock. "Someday, I'll have to conform to society and wear a watch again, like everybody else," he said. "It's my last holdout against western slavery."

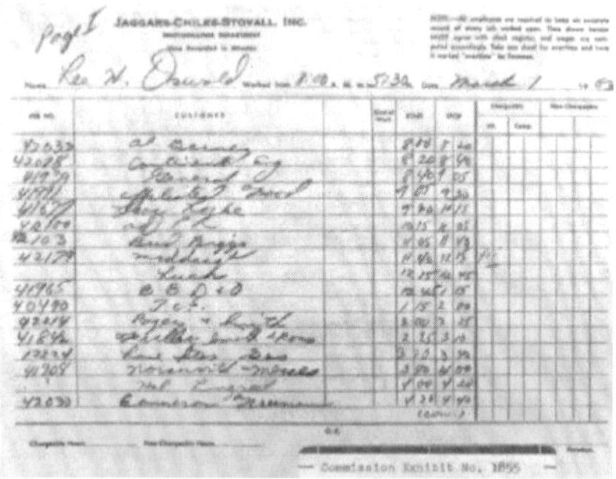
JAGGARS-CHILES-STOVALL, INC.

Lee H. Oswald

Commission Exhibit No. 1855

Lee had to account for every minute at Jaggars-Chiles-Stovall on weekdays. He also worked off-clock on Saturdays, when Lee said he worked on classified maps on Cuba for the CIA.

Lee had stopped wearing a watch the day he quit working for Jaggars-Chiles-Stovall, back in Texas. That was April Fool's Day, 1963. He said he had to log in everything he was doing, minute by minute, for months. He loved his work because he had access to clandestine maps and photos on Saturdays, when he worked alone. But logging in every moment of his life five days out of seven got old. Straightening his shirt, Lee got up, then pulled a comb through his fine, wavy hair. "Time to go back and face some more of her music," he said. Maybe I deserve what she calls me. By the way," he went on, "I didn't hit her."

"I'm proud of you. Remember that!"

"Well, she's going to be mad tomorrow, too." To my inquiring look, he said, "I'll be gone all day Sunday, working on the training film. I'll be out with paramilitary. And next weekend, it will be the same."

"But when will we be together again?" I asked. "Robert's job is about to terminate."

"So is mine," Lee said. "And after that, you'll have to leave Reily's, too."

"But it's too soon! I need a paycheck to keep Robert satisfied!"

"You were just there to cover for me. Monaghan can't wait to get a real secretary again," Lee replied frankly. "Still, they should pay you enough so you'll make it to September."

"I hope so," I said. "Maybe we'll be in Mexico by then."

"Look at the bright side," Lee said. "I'll be fired. So will you. We'll go to Reverend James' again. And we'll have twice the time to spend together. You'll see. Kiss me! I have to go back." Our jobs were ending, but our most dangerous days were just beginning. When Lee, now worried about his family's safety, told Guy Banister that his family needed more protection, Mr. and Mrs. Eric Rogers were moved into 4907 Magazine to keep an eye on things. The place had been empty for two years, but in mid-July, that changed. Mr. Rogers also took Lee's communist and Russian mail, no questions asked. After all, his rent and his utilities were being paid for out of Lee's CIA subsidy.

Wednesday, July 17, 1963 At Reily's, a complaint rolled in at 8:30 from Mr. Clark, the main Production Manager. It was Lee's turn (there were three maintenance men) to oil the three coffee machines, but nobody could find him. When Lee finally clocked in an hour later, Mr. Clark yelled at Lee, grabbed his logbook, and sent it to Monaghan, where it landed with a thud on my desk. It was full of fake entries. All I could do was to look at it helplessly. At about noon, Personnel instructed us to find a replacement for Lee at once. Monaghan and I could no longer keep rejecting new applicants for Lee's job. We had one ploy left: recommending a man whose background check was incomplete, so he could not be hired at once. It was all we could do. Lee's cover job at Reily's had to end soon anyway, because he had to go public with pro-Castro activities detrimental to Reily's anti-Communist image. Later, when Lee went missing again, I located him at Dave's; Ochsner had insisted that a final batch of mice was to be processed at once!

Lee finally told me why he'd clocked in so late: he had spent some important extra time with his family. I couldn't write any of that in Lee's logbook. After clocking out Lee at 6:00 p.m., I hurried to Dave's apartment, where I found Lee and Dr. Mary working hard in Dave's kitchen lab. But the level of laboratory precautions had suddenly increased dramatically. Both Lee and Dr. Mary were wearing surgical masks, hats, plastic aprons and surgical gloves. Dr. Mary's hands were thrust into the portholes of a portable germ-free "clean bench" with an air-pumped filter to prevent airborne contaminants from floating around the kitchen and into our lungs. Dr. Mary noticed me staring at the equipment. "The marmosets are dying," she told me somberly. "All of them, including the control group."

The implications were immense. The bioweapon had migrated from one group of monkeys to another caged group nearby, presenting the terrifying possibility that our mutated cancer could be contagious.

The keepers swore it had been transmitted through the air. If so, we needed to exercise extra caution. Of course, all kinds of monkeys got polyoma cancer from the SV40 monkey virus, but it seemed to stay latent in humans who got the contaminated vaccines. "We'll have years before it shows up," I had heard Dr. Ochsner say. "By then, we'll have cured cancer." But we had been roasting these cancer viruses with radiation, enhancing them, and we no longer knew exactly what we had. Today's cancer victims may be suffering from it. Most Americans probably carry the SV40 Monkey Virus (and possibly related viruses) in their bodies. Studies are now being conducted, decades late, on what cancer-causing monkey viruses we carry and if they are contagious. But in 1963, our present concern was, *What if this mutated virus gets loose?* I'd had my lab shut down for that very reason.

A simple glove box, used for safer sterile work.

For the next hour I worked with microscopes, noting that Lee and Dr. Mary had formed a friendship (She had initially been wary of him.). Then Dave showed up. As my eyes were tired, Dr. Mary took over the microscopes and I came over and kissed Lee's perspiring forehead. "You shouldn't touch me," he said, through his face mask. I could see a book in Lee's pocket through his clear plastic apron. "I see you brought along *Profiles in Courage*," I said to Lee, hoping he was finished with it, and I could borrow it from him.

"I'm trying to get my hands on everything I can about 'The Chief' [JFK]," Lee answered. "I'll read it tonight. I will also pretend I can't hear Marina when she starts yelling at me for being late again." When Lee said 'Marina,' an image of her flashed in my mind. I could almost see her, pregnant and alone, sitting in their apartment, little Junie at her side. I thought about how neglected a woman can feel, and how Robert had forgotten my birthday. Then, it hit me! "Oh, Lee!" I exclaimed. "Didn't you tell me that today was Marina's birthday?" Dave heard my question and whistled like an in-bound missile. "The ding-dong bells are gonna' ring all over your poor head tonight, boy!" he teased, as Lee pushed his chair back, pulled his hands from the glove-box, and started peeling off his apron, and lab cap. "I need a clean t-shirt!" he said urgently. "This one stinks!" He stood up and hurried past me, going toward the hall to the bathroom to scrub up. Dave headed for his bedroom and went down on his hands and knees to search through a heap of clothes on the floor.

"Here, Oswald!" he yelled, holding up a white T-shirt. "Mary!" he said then, "Throw me your car keys!" Dave tossed Lee the clean T-shirt, caught the keys, and started down the back stairs with Lee behind him. "I'll be right back!" Dave yelled. "Your book!" I called out to Lee, seeing it on the floor. "You take it!" he called back. "*Go, go, go!*" Dr. Mary called out, from behind her surgical mask. For the next two hours, Dr. Mary and I continued working as Dave, who returned quickly, kept things sterile. We managed to finish before midnight. Then Dr. Mary drove me to 1032. "Try and eat something to keep your strength up," she advised me. "Let's hope this is the end of it." After drinking a glass of milk, I took *Profiles in Courage* to bed and slept with it, because Lee had given it to me. [192]

Thursday, July 18, 1963 Even today, after four concussions, my memory is still superior. In 2003, I fled overseas to live in exile, protected by friends and researchers, to avoid Concussion Number Five. I can still see much of the past in pictures and recall words in important conversations. It is a gift. But don't ask me to remember where I put my purse! I woke up tired and yawning, soon becoming irritated because I couldn't find my purse. I missed the bus because of it and punched in late. When Lee came in person to my desk to resolve his own late clock-in problems, I was concerned. He had obviously been sent to me because Thursday was when Reily and Standard checks were printed up. This had to be another "40 hours made" problem again. My initial "J" ended up on the majority of Lee's timecards, justifying his full pay for the week as the final authority. But this time, Lee himself had to show up to defend himself, while holding a written reprimand in his hand from Mr. Clark's Production notepad. He had first been sent to Personnel, who then sent him to me. Of course, I approved Lee's timecard one more time. I wrote "Made 40" (hours) on it, well knowing Personnel was sick of Lee's many late clock-ins and absences. For example, Lee had clocked in only once at 8:00, the original time he was supposed to show up, in nearly eleven weeks. We switched him over to a "late shift" which his clock-outs rarely matched, because Lee had to show up at Mancuso's near Banister's office almost every morning to get Banister's agenda passed on to him for the day. The official excuse was that he had to come in late because his wife was not well, which was true part of the time. "This is my fault," I told him, knowing that killing hundreds of mice on odd afternoons was never in his job description. "No," Lee said kindly. "I had a choice."

---

[192] Marina was upset: Lee got home too late to take her out to celebrate her birthday. Lee took her to a nearby pharmacy that was still open. I think he bought her some face powder, a coke, and some candy. Later, he bought her some caviar, a luxury she loved.

Monaghan and I knew Personnel was closing in on Lee, so we sent them a memo saying we would have a replacement by next Friday, in hopes of

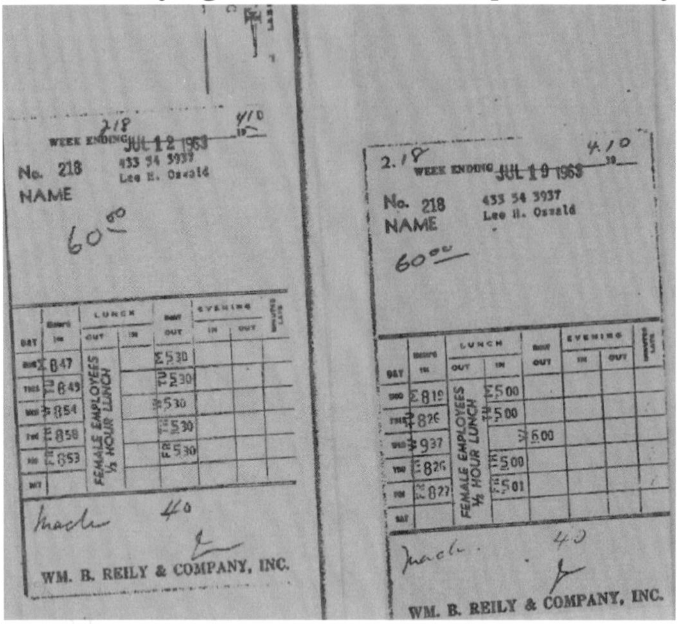

delaying the lynching. Personnel fired back a memo saying that they would take somebody straight from the Birmingham Jail, if that's all we could find.

My "J"s and "Made 40" approved Lee's time-cards despite his disappearances. See appendix.

Lee was hounded so much that he was unable to take any breaks, even for lunch. He practically had to ask permission to go to the toilet. He had been scheduled to pick up something from an agent at Alba's garage but could not get away long enough to do so. Worst of all, the factory's Production Manager, Mr. Clark[193] came to my desk. He had never done so before. Lee hadn't worked on a shipping and packing line this week, so why did I say he did?

To justify 'made 40' hours, I had lied. To cover the lie, I said that I'd mixed up Lee's hours with those of another Oswald also working in the factory (though I wasn't even sure if the other Oswald was still working there!). As the lie spilled out of my mouth, I hated myself as I went on to explain that since I hardly ever saw any of his factory workers, except those who loaded the trucks, I didn't know which Oswald was which. Reminding me with a sneer that the two men had different employee numbers, he stomped away. I was glad Mr. Monaghan was not present. When five o'clock finally came, it was a relief. As had become our recent habit, Lee and I met at Charlie's Restaurant and Bar. Thankfully, we had always avoided being seen together at Reily's, and today, that was especially important. Charlie's was on 640 Carondelet, a straight walk

---

[193] I had forgotten Clark's name over the years, as I only spoke to Clark a few times, for we worked in different buildings. A critic said "nobody" in the **factory** remembered me, hardly a surprise, since I spent 99% of the time in the office building and was there only three months over 50 years ago. Even so, my clerk, who became Annette **Carr**, wrote that she remembered me. Her recent email and photo are shown later in this book.

from Reily's. It was a good place to meet because I couldn't get lost. There we had Dr. Peppers and discussed Lee's fate next Thursday. I would have to resign soon after that.

Little did we realize that some of our meetings were being noticed by an unusual man.

A 'mute' saw me and Lee at Charlie's Bar. This is a portion of a memo that surfaced in 2013 (It may have been released earlier). Deaf and mute, he relied on lip-reading and assumed I was a librarian. Lee and I planned meetings at various libraries such as at Tulane (random days), Napoleon Branch(Thursdays) or the City Library (random days).

for a draft beer. While in this bar on one occasion, he met a deaf mute he had known from Monroe, Louisiana. At this time Mr. Myers bought this man a meal and began to communicate with him. The mute was probably a seaman at this time. The mute conversed with Mr. Myers by writing on napkins found in the bar and restaurant. The mute told of seeing OSWALD in the place on many occasions. He also recalled having seen OSWALD in there with a girl from the Louisiana State Library. On one occasion the mute was in the bar and restaurant when OSWALD was in there with other people and they were discussing the assassination of the President. The mute read their lips and rememberd what they said. He wrote this down on the napkins and gave them to Mr. Myers. Mr. Myers went to the FBI but was given no real encouragement. Mr. Myers stated that he kept these napkins for approximately 1½ years but finally destroyed them. This man is definitely not a crank, and holds a very responsible position with probably the second largest manufacturers representative firm in the country. He does not know the mute's name but does know he came from Monroe, Louisiana, and feels that Charlie might know who the mute was and where he might be contacted.

Determined to turn our day around (Marina was too angry to tolerate Lee at home anyway), Lee called the Monteleone from the payphone and reserved a room for us. As we walked to The Monteleone, I learned that Lee's immediate supervisor, Mr. Branyon, had pounced on him, too. Since Mr. Barbe was nearby, Barbe had to show displeasure as well, skewering Lee for putting false entries into his logbook. That's how the logbook got into our hands. But Reily was just a job problem; The Monteleone gave us a different world, where we could comfort each other and be ourselves. Soon enough, we were joking and being silly. We ended up, after great fun in bed, simply resting together.

Then Lee called room service. I ordered a nice dinner, but Lee ordered only soup and milk, even though he'd missed lunch. "How can I eat well," he explained, "when Marina's eating leftovers? I'm no saint," he went on, "but I've been thinking. I've harmed her. I made her pregnant again. Somehow, she must now stand up... have the courage and self-confidence to live without me. After I had beaten her black and blue! And then ... I forgot her birthday!" He sighed. "I don't deserve anything better than soup." Remembering that Lee had told me that it all started when she would hit or kick him, then dare him to be a man and hit her back, I told him, "You've changed...you've become a better man. You have to forgive yourself."

After we ate, as Lee placed our tray outside the door and came back to the bed, I observed how utterly glorious he looked. He had been exercising, and was in perfect condition. For a while, he was very quiet. "I'm listening," I told him. "Just talk to me."

"Perhaps the man I wanted to be is dead," he said, finally. "Just a memory I can no longer revive."

"That man exists," I replied. "He's a man with much to give." I reminded him that all this time, he'd kept his word. Once, she'd even slapped him, and he had let her. "Then I will succeed," he said finally. "Let Marina rave on. I'll bear it, because I have you. It won't be too much longer. She's ready to leave."

"Maybe she'll find happiness in her next marriage."

"Just stay by my side. If you do, I know I can be strong." Lee was quoting from his current favorite popular song, "Exodus," from the movie of the same name. As before, we had a record player, and after we listened to "The King and I," Lee put on the Everly Brothers album again. As it played, Lee whispered beautiful thoughts in my ears, of where we could live, far from Reily and Robert and Marina, in Mexico. Dr. Mary had said she'd help us to get into Mexican universities. I'd become a doctor, he would be a sociologist or anthropologist, who'd understand and help my patients. We would teach, have a hacienda, write our science fiction stories, raise some animals and our own food, have a couple of horses, and throw in lots of kids.

Our hearts pounding with love and emotion, as twilight turned to darkness, and love songs poured out from the record player, we made love again.

I had never experienced such joy as Lee gave me, and I shook from head to foot and started to cry. "What's happening to me, Lee?" I sobbed. "I don't understand!"

Somewhere within, we were striking a mutual chord, powerful, deep and sad. We hung suspended between the present, and eternity.

"We'll die someday!" I finally whispered. "We've been looking at it, at death, for days in the lab. All we have turns to dust, or to words on a page."

"I know!" he answered simply. We were breathing together, our hearts beating at the same pace, in the same rhythm. It was uncanny. I could feel a wave of electricity travel between us. With Robert, as virile as he was, the skin was always between us. With Lee, somehow, it seemed that we were meeting past the skin, soul to soul. I can't explain it better than that. It only happened with Lee, and I never experienced it again. We were truly one, and we knew it. We held each other, whispering about what we had discovered and lamenting the moments as they passed.

We had been given a great gift, one so subtle and elusive that it scared us to think that we might have missed it. It might have slipped through our fingers unnoticed. "What if I hadn't spoken Russian to you in the post office?" I asked. "What if we had never met?" The enormity of these few words filled the room.

"No, sweet," he said. "I think we would have found each other even if the very universe was folding itself away."

As we sat in the back of the empty bus, returning home, I was in such a wonderful mood that I dared ask Lee if this meant he would now truly confide in me about his clandestine adventures. "If I won't tell you," said Lee, "then God Himself is not allowed to know."

"All right," I said. "What agency do you really work for, and who is your most important handler?"

"You little spy!" he said, smiling. "Here's the answer: I'm loaned to the CIA from the ONI, and must sometimes help the FBI, but who my main handler is, not even God knows the answer to that. Certainly, I don't. I call him 'Mr. B."

"As for me," I told him, "I'm just a pair of hands belonging to Ochsner."

"They don't belong to Ochsner anymore," Lee said. "They're mine now."

When I asked him if I had a 'handler,' Lee said, smiling, "Of course you do. It's me." He said I was a lucky woman. "I shall be your protector," he said. "I won't let any of them hurt you."

"Them?" I asked. "Why would any of 'them' want to hurt me?" I asked. "I'm on the 'good' side."

"If you're no longer useful to them, you could be thrown out, unless you're well-educated," Lee replied. "You're safer than I am," he added. "Officially, you are supposedly an unwitting asset. A good position to be in." Then Lee snapped his fingers, saying that, in a heartbeat, I could become his very own Marina Oswald. "Once she's back in Russia, who's to say that you are not her? You even have the same bad teeth. If we pulled just one tooth, your dental records would match."

"Her tooth, or my tooth?" I asked, anxiously. He said that would come later, so not to worry. But I should not obey Robert's orders to go to the dentist. I told Lee he seemed to know a lot about changing identities.

"I should," he said, "It happened to me."

"So, do you know your own name?"

"By the grace of God," he said, "I do. But nobody would believe I was me, if they went through my records." The advantage, he said, was that he could appear and disappear. Fake records had been created for him so that he could seemed to have lived in two different places at once, over a period of years, making tracing the true whereabouts of the real Lee H. Oswald difficult. Today we are now familiar with witness protection programs, involving fake records and ID's.

In the 1960's, apparently that's also how the CIA sometimes chose to protect some of their secret agents. "As you know, I have a bunch of funny records, too," I put in. "I could even start a second personality."

"The only second personality I want you to start is a baby for us someday," he said. "That is, if you want to." [194]
I told him I would have a dozen babies, if he'd help change the diapers. Lee told me he washed Junie's diapers regularly. But if we lived in a place like Samoa, nobody would have to wash any diapers. We could rinse off our babies in the ocean waves.

Lee, ironing diapers.

As usual, we got off at Audubon Park. As we waited for the next bus, Lee asked if there was anything more he should know about the Project. "Well, you should know about the etiology of the cancer," I told him. "I've never discussed it with you."

"Etiology? What's that mean?" he asked, ever curious to learn new words. "Etiology means origins," I told him. "This is no ordinary cancer, as you know. It's probably contagious," I went on. That startled Lee, since Dr. Mary and I had not really discussed this point explicitly in front of him. I told Lee that the monkey virus, now altered by radiation, had moved spontaneously from the deliberately infected marmoset monkeys to the control animals, without direct contact. With it came the cancer. All the marmoset monkeys were now dying. That's why there were suddenly all these extra precautions.

"Remind me again, never to eat or drink anything over at Dave's," Lee said somberly. "But humans are not monkeys," I reminded him. "It could be quite different for us. At Roswell Park, I think I saw a way to cure cancer, with **bacteriophage**. Maybe we can go that direction next. We should be studying bacteriophage. These are viruses that attack bacteria." I was passionate about bacteriophage and wanted Lee to know why. "Say you have a staph infection," I went on. "They could genetically alter a bacteriophage to target the staph. Even if the staph became resistant to the usual antibiotics, if they injected the altered bacteriophage into you, it would not only kill the staph, it would stay in your system, forever, ready to attack the staph again if it ever showed

[194] There was no "Lee" and "Harvey" per se, as two different men, though records and files might show "them" in two different places concurrently. Such records and files were created for various reasons; others came from tipsters, as in any murder case.

up. Bacteria can't build up resistance to them, as they do to penicillin."

"Would it work for typhoid, or cholera?" Lee asked.

"Sure, just alter it for the specific bacterial infection," I replied. "Now, if a bacteriophage could be engineered not to touch any cells in your body but cancerous ones, it could eat common cancers like meatloaf, leaving a bag of pus behind. [195] But I don't think the cancer treatment industry would like that. They'd lose a lot of money. Of course, you'd have to update the bacteriophage from time to time."

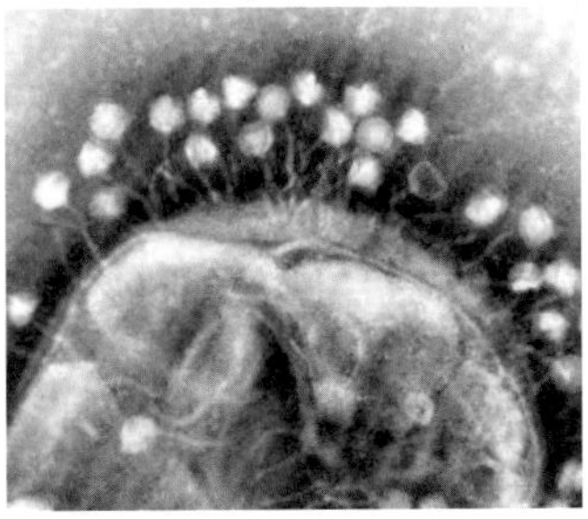

Bacteriophage attacking staph

"Bacteriophage..." Lee repeated the word. "We've created a galloping cancer," I said. "But bacteriophage could take it out. But only the Russians are going down that road right now. We're developing a bioweapon to eliminate a head of state, but what if we do get Castro? Will they then throw it out?"

"It could be used as a weapon of mass destruction," Lee replied.

"Yes," I agreed. "Think how Hitler would have loved this, to use against the Jews in those camps. They could say a plague went through."

"Or to eliminate blacks in Africa," Lee said, with a cold tone in his voice. That's when I realized it had my fingerprints all over it. I almost wished I'd never been born. How had my dream to cure cancer gone so wrong?

[195] Even in 1963, we had seen some resistance develop against against penicillin and were seeking new antibiotic candidates.

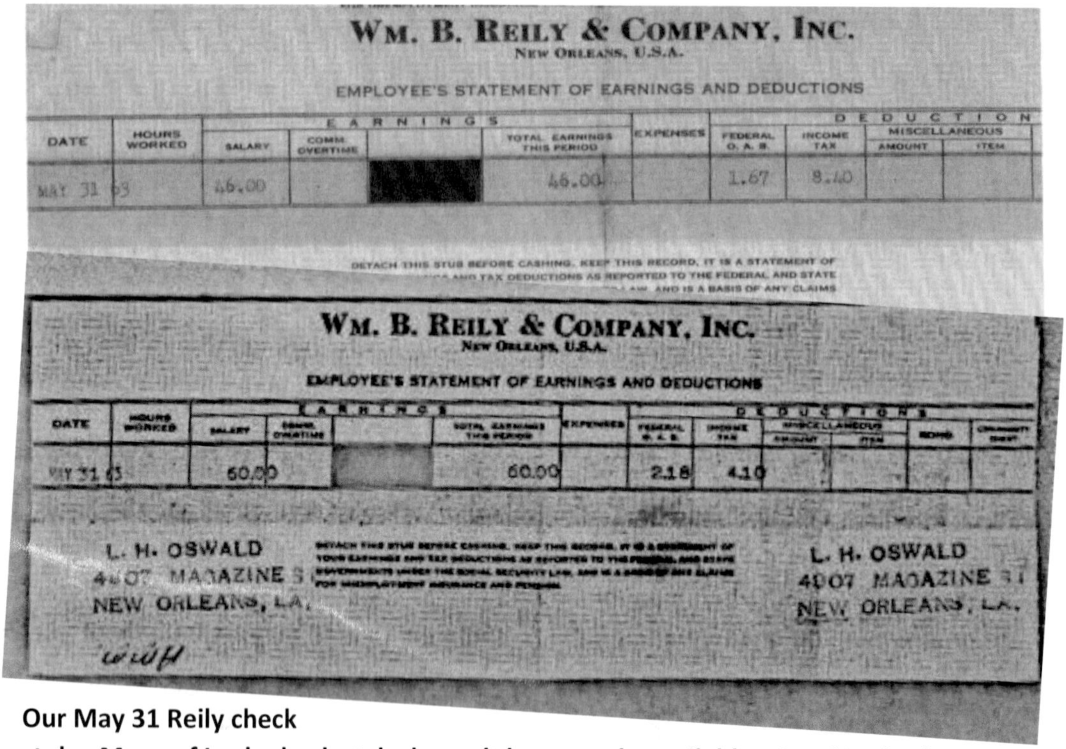

Wm. B. Reily & Company, Inc.
New Orleans, U.S.A.
EMPLOYEE'S STATEMENT OF EARNINGS AND DEDUCTIONS

DATE	HOURS WORKED	SALARY	COMM OVERTIME		TOTAL EARNINGS THIS PERIOD	EXPENSES	FEDERAL O. A. B.	INCOME TAX	MISCELLANEOUS AMOUNT	ITEM
MAY 31 63		46.00		[redacted]	46.00		1.67	8.40		

DETACH THIS STUB BEFORE CASHING. KEEP THIS RECORD. IT IS A STATEMENT OF ... AND TAX DEDUCTIONS AS REPORTED TO THE FEDERAL AND STATE ... AND IS A BASIS OF ANY CLAIMS

Wm. B. Reily & Company, Inc.
New Orleans, U.S.A.
EMPLOYEE'S STATEMENT OF EARNINGS AND DEDUCTIONS

DATE	HOURS WORKED	SALARY	COMM OVERTIME		TOTAL EARNINGS THIS PERIOD	EXPENSES	FEDERAL O. A. B.	INCOME TAX	MISCELLANEOUS AMOUNT	ITEM	BOND	COMMUNITY CHEST
MAY 31 63		60.00			60.00		2.18	4.10				

L. H. OSWALD
4907 MAGAZINE ST
NEW ORLEANS, LA.

L. H. OSWALD
4907 MAGAZINE ST
NEW ORLEANS, LA.

Our May 31 Reily check stubs. Many of Lee's check stubs haven't been made available—just his checks.

Chapter 20
Tightrope

<u>July 19, 1963 Friday</u>

For the first time since the very first day we began working at Reily, Lee was on the Magazine Street bus with me in time to arrive at Reily's before 8:00 A.M. He knew a supervisor would be waiting to see if he was late. As the bus worked its way down Magazine Street, we discussed the upcoming weekend. I told him Robert had called last night and said to get ready for another trip to Fort Walton. There would be a bridal shower that his mother was hosting.

Lee also would be tied up for the weekend. He planned on spending all day Sunday working on the training film, presumably at the camp across the lake, but he also wanted to take Marina and Junie to the Pontchartrain Beach amusement park to give them a break from the monotony of Magazine Street. When I clocked in shortly before 8:00 AM Lee was immediately needed to run an errand to Eli Lilly's for the Project, involving refrigerated products.

So despite his effort to be on time, Lee clocked in late again and got chewed out. I didn't dare clock in for him because Lee's card was flagged. For the rest of the day, Lee's supervisors were all over him. He couldn't get away for our usual long Friday lunch, but we did manage to meet briefly at the front entrance to Alba's garage, where the vending machine with Lorna Doone cookies was located. We dined on the cookies, then hurried back to Reily's. With things so tense for Lee at the office, I didn't dare go to the lab that day. It was not a typical Friday, and tension was everywhere.

At about 3:30, I had to stop a big tea order which was about to be shipped to a poor credit risk. Knowing that the trucks had to be loaded by 4:00, I hurried to the shipping and packing area with a stop-order slip. There I saw Lee on the production line, loading extra-size boxes of Luzianne tea onto a belt. They were going to be sealed. Lee had been set to work at a task where he couldn't drop out of sight for even a minute.[196] As I approached the noisy production line, I noticed a chute-like machine dropping green glasses into the tea cartons. It must have been a special promotion of some kind, because it was a short run. There weren't many glasses left to pack. They were deep green, with clear crystal bases — perfect for iced tea. I stared longingly at them, but I'd have to buy a carton to get one. As the glasses dropped into the boxes, I managed to tell Lee, as I passed him, that "They're beautiful! I wish I could afford one."

My comment had an impact on the man who loved me that I would soon regret. Mr. Clark, who was close enough to hear me, said that if I wanted a glass, I needed to buy a carton of tea at the order counter.

I went to the counter to see if I could arrange to buy a carton, but since I had no cash, the girl at the counter wouldn't let me pay in installments. Disappointed, I returned to Monaghan's desk, where I soon found another credit risk for the same truckload. This was highly unusual. A new salesman was selling to high-risk clients. Of course, I had to return to the factory and walk through it to the loading docks. When Lee saw me, and that Clark was gone, he followed me a moment, then slipped me a small note he'd written. It was a fake receipt.

---

[196] Co-worker Mike Kettenring told colleagues that he worked "side by side' next to Lee Harvey Oswald on the production line at Wm. B. Reily Co. (Luzianne Coffee) in 1963. Mike later worked as a news reporter for WDSU- TV, the station owned by INCA's Edgar Stern that sent the crew to film Lee's leafleting. Kettenring later managed three TV stations, and eventually became a Catholic Priest after his wife died. source: http://www.neworleansradiotheatre.org/wdsupersonnellist.html An anti-Oswald newsgroup later reported (conveniently after Kettenring's death) that Kettenring denied working with Oswald.

"I want you to take a carton of tea!" he told me. "You can use this, if you have to. I know you'll eventually pay for it."

I tried to give it back, but Clark had assigned a new supervisor to keep watch on Lee, and when he saw Lee refusing to take the note, he came over, inspected the note, then threw it to the floor. "So you thought you could fool that guy!" he told me. "You might be Monaghan's secretary, but in here you have to follow the rules like everybody else!" Turning to Lee, he gave him a shove. "What are you looking at?" he yelled. "Get back to work!" As he did so, I reached down, snatched the fake receipt from the floor, and hid it. Though outraged by the reprimand I received from the supervisor that had become Lee's temporary foreman, I was in no position to protest his abuse of Lee.

Upset that Lee had been shoved, I followed him back to the packing line and said, "It's okay, I can do without." But the self-important super was watching. Rushing over, he snarled, "Why are you still here? Is there anything else you need, besides a free glass?" At that, Lee's eyes narrowed with anger. "For what she gets paid here," he snapped, "she deserves a damned glass!" Then he snatched one from a carton moving along the conveyor belt and pressed it into my hands. I was stunned. I stood frozen, holding the glass. Before anyone could react, the carton was taped shut automatically. Just then, Mr. Clark returned. Hearing that Lee had "caused trouble" he came toward Lee with his hands in fists. My coveting of a simple glass had triggered a disaster!

"But I bought that carton of tea!" I said desperately, telling a bald-faced lie. "I just forgot to bring my receipt! The man just tried to help me out, before all of the cartons got packed!" "If you weren't the boss's secretary," the supervisor said, "they'd have your hide for this!"

As Clark tried to figure out what had happened, one of the Cuban girls called out, "You better leave, senorita!" I took her advice. As I did, I heard the machines shutting down and could hear somebody cursing. "What in the hell got into his god-damned, stupid head?" somebody shouted. "He's ruined the run!"

Nobody knew which box was missing its green glass, but the trucks had to leave soon, so they started up the belt again to finish the run. Realizing I had to do something to cover up the mess, I hurried to my desk, my heart tight. Hiding the glass, I borrowed $2.00 from one clerk and a dollar from another, promising to pay them back on Monday. Then I went to the mail boy (who I knew liked me) and asked him to help me out. I gave him the $3.00 and asked him to go buy a carton of tea from the special run, before they all got packed up, and to tell the clerk that it was a present for somebody. When he brought me the tea carton and gave me the receipt, I gave him a quarter. I quickly removed the green glass packed inside, replacing it with the glass Lee had given me. I then hid the carton under Mr. Monaghan's desk. Then I slipped into the

bathroom and hid the extra glass in the garbage can. As I returned to my desk, Monaghan burst into the room, his face furrowed with a frown. He marched into his cubicle.
He made a phone call, then headed upstairs to the president's office. Trouble! Then one of the Cuban girls from the packing area came to me pretending to ask my help with a hard-to-read label, but she was really there to tell me that the young man who could speak Russian was going to be fired.

At about 4:15, the female supervisor, who was a nice lady, demanded to be shown the glass. I showed her the carton and my receipt, so she allowed me to keep the glass. I hoped that would be the end of it, but in a few minutes, Mr. Barbe and a man in a dark suit came to Monaghan's cubicle. After a few minutes, Barbe and the stranger left, and Monaghan came to me.

"You purchased that carton of tea, didn't you?" he asked. Wordlessly, unable to speak another lie, I showed Mr. M. the carton and receipt. To my pleading eyes, Monaghan shook his head. "There's nothing I can do," he said. "Your boy is sunk."

One of the Reily brothers now appeared — I don't know which one — It was such a rare event to see a Reily brother on our floor that every toiling clerk actually paused a moment before plunging into yet harder efforts to look busy. Monaghan sighed as they went to his cubicle. Suddenly, Mr. Barbe brought Lee into the cubicle and Monaghan left, seating himself in his big brown chair at his desk, with me at his side. From our chairs, we could see and hear everything.

Barbe now loudly commenced to list Lee's many company crimes to Reily, as Lee stood at attention like a Marine in his dirty, sweat-soaked shirt. We watched helplessly and silently as Lee took several unfair accusations as calmly as he'd taken the shove from the fake, self-important "foreman." Both Reily and Barbe knew who Lee was, but they put on a show of humiliating him anyway.

And it was my fault! And all for a green glass! Tears welled in my eyes, and guilt washed over me. I swore to myself that I would never again express any desire to Lee without thinking twice. Mr. Reily's senior secretary, an elderly lady who never spoke to me, came to the cubicle with Lee's personnel file, and Barbe handed Lee a pink slip. Since Lee didn't have a bank account, his last paycheck would be mailed to him.

Lee stood stoically, never speaking. Told to leave at once, Lee glanced at me and Mr. M. and shrugged. Then he marched out of Wm. B. Reily Coffee Company for the last time, looking straight ahead. I clocked him out. It was 4:30 P.M. Then Mr. Monaghan called me into his cubicle.

I figured I would be fired next and braced myself. [197]

"Frankly," said he, "I wish we could get rid of you today, too, but that would look suspicious." Then he explained that a 'scene' had been made about Lee's many sins so that Mr. Reily's attention would be diverted from anything that might have included the green glass and me. In addition, Mr. M. said Ochsner wanted me to stay another month because I was "doing a good job in the labs."

Relieved that my job was not in jeopardy for the moment, I turned my thoughts to the event ahead. At the upcoming bridal shower in Fort Walton Beach, I'd once again be presented to the prominent women Mrs. Baker knew, who were married to successful gentlemen ensconced in designer homes on private, green golf courses with private, blue Gulf views. Lee's weekend would be very different. He would be helping to make a training film for anti-Castro insurgents, which was officially an illegal activity. He'd be working with guns, bayonets, jeeps, explosives and angry young men full of hate. Now it was time to go home and get ready for Fort Walton Beach. Ugh!

Lee was fired after eleven weeks and one day of employment at Wm. B. Reily Coffee Company. But he was really an undercover agent, whose job at Reily's was a cover job, as was mine. In Lee's case, the discrepancies between his real job and his cover job were blatant.

For example, Lee was always late for work, and yet he was never docked for being late like I, or others at Reily, were. He was also allowed to work erratic hours. He was frequently missing and unable to be located by other employees.

My job looked more real than his, in that I was expected to be on time every morning, to catch Monaghan's early phone calls and to clock both me and Lee out at the end of each day. I had a constant workload and was essentially chained to my desk all day on Mondays and Tuesdays, and for half a day the rest of the week. But my real task was in the cancer lab, and Monaghan knew it. When I punched Lee's timecards to cover his absences, I did it with Monaghan's knowledge and consent

Lee's timecards were so squirrely that they had been frequently sent to Monaghan, as VP, to review (see Appendix). Monaghan would hand them to me to resolve. I would write "made 40" on them, indicating that Lee

[197] Lee didn't tell Marina he had lost his job for two weeks, to give us more time together. Marina originally told the Warren Commission that Lee worked at Reily's until the end of August (WC Vol. 1, p. 20) — six additional weeks.

had worked a forty-hour week, and then sign the disputed cards with my initial "J" to approve them. The ones I didn't sign with a "J" had no 'absent from the job' complaints to resolve. I also had to resolve an occasional dispute regarding other timecards from other employees. That happened once in a blue moon.

Monaghan and I largely succeeded in protecting Lee from the suspicions of the other employees and supervisors. Lee was forced to leave only one week earlier than originally planned. He was then ready for the next phase of his assignment. The larger question how much Mr. Reily himself knew about what was going on in Monaghan's office. We do know that he was patriotic and strongly anti-Communist. We know he was involved in INCA with Dr. Alton Ochsner. But was he aware that Lee and I were helping Ochsner develop a biological weapon? I can't say. Gerry Patrick Hemming, a CIA operative, went on record concerning William B. Reily. He told me to my face, years later, that the Reily company cooperated with the CIA, United Fruit and Standard Fruit, to keep coffee products as cheap as possible. This meant supporting governments that made lucrative deals with exploitive plantations.

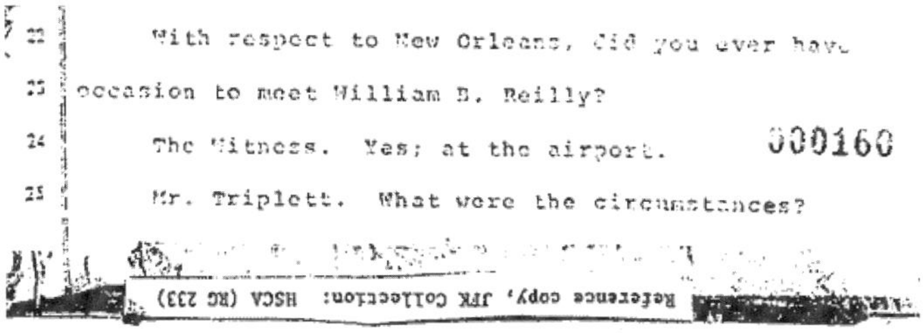
With respect to New Orleans, did you ever have occasion to meet William B. Reilly?

The Witness. Yes; at the airport. 000160

Mr. Triplett. What were the circumstances?

Reference copy, JFK Collection: HSCA (RG 233)

CIA asset Gerry Hemming mentioned meeting Wm. B. Reily (the Garrison investigation) deposition. He also stated that William B. Reily had been with the CIA "for years."

Whatever happened upstairs, when the moment of severance finally came, it was made unpleasant. By 5:00 I clocked out and went outside to catch the bus back to 1032 Marengo, where happily, Lee intercepted me. We walked from Reily's towards Charlie's Bar, so we could talk privately. I was so upset. "I'm the reason you got fired," I confessed to Lee with remorse. "I had to be fired sometime next week anyway," he replied, "because I have to go to Mobile and talk at Spring Hill about Communism. Reily's couldn't have let me do that while I was on their payroll. Now I'll have more time to be with you."

After chatting at Charlie's, we headed home on the late bus, where I sat with the big carton of tea on my lap, feeling the weight of the precious treasure – the green glass - inside. Lee got the driver to slow the bus down as we neared Marengo Street, so we could see if Robert's car was in the driveway. All seemed well, so we got off. We wanted to hide the green glass before Robert arrived!

Lee carried the tea, just in case Robert happened to come while we were still walking. I said, rather sadly, "They'll all be speculating if I'm pregnant at my bridal shower."

"Why don't you put a pillow in there, and really shock everybody?" Lee joked.

"Lee," I said, "I know you're used to leading three lives, or thirty. But I'd rather tell the truth. Today, for example..."

"Ah," he said, "You're still not used to it, like I am ... false trails, fake records, fake names. It meant nothing to me to create one more fake document." As we reached the house, we saw that the car in Susie's driveway was gone.[198] Stunned, we realized that Robert's car could have been parked deeper into the driveway, and we might have been caught! We'd have to remember that possibility. "I'm going to give this tea to Susie," I told Lee, "before Robert sees it."

"But see how complicated things can get?" Lee commented, smiling. "How are you going to account for the $3.00 you spent?" It was true. Robert watched what I spent to the nickel. "You might have to lie," Lee pursued, smiling. "The little complications of life."

"We should try for higher ethical standards, Lee." I countered.

"Until then," he teased, "you're going to need this." He handed me three dollars to pay back my girlfriends at Reily. "But he'll see my paycheck. He'll know the $3.00 was from somewhere else."

"You can say you got $3.00 cash from selling a drawing."

"But I didn't! Oh, Lee, I hate all this deceit! I must divorce him!"

"Not yet," he said. "You first have to go to the party in Florida, and prove you're not pregnant."

"How am I going to deal with this? I don't love him anymore."

"Yes, you do," Lee said. "You still 'love' him, just like I still 'love' her."

"But I don't want to sleep with him anymore!"

"Shhh! Don't tell me that, I won't be able to bear it." We entered Susie's kitchen, where I asked Susie if I could hide the $3.00 in her sugar bowl, where she kept her extra change. She, too, was getting ready to leave for the weekend, and was taking Suzi Collie with her. After kissing her goodbye, we went into my bedroom, where I carried the tea. There, I removed the green glass from the tea carton so Lee could see how rich and deep its color was in natural light. Lee noticed his fake receipt inside the glass, so I told him I'd rescued it from the floor to avoid more trouble for him. "Fast thinking, Juduffki!" he said, giving me a little kiss to reward me. Then, suddenly, we ran out of time. We saw Robert's blue Ford, turning into the driveway! He'd be inside in a minute! Unwilling to risk being seen going down the hall and leaving

---

[198] Since Susie was still home, I should have realized that the car didn't belong to her, but I never thought about it.

through the front door, Lee pulled the bed aside and exited through the front bedroom window. I closed it behind him, pushed the bed back into place, and then ran to Susie's kitchen with the green glass, which I hid high in her china cupboard. Then, hearing Robert open the door that allowed entry either into Susie's apartment or ours, I called out, "Bob! Is that you?"

In response, Robert burst into Susie's kitchen, smiling and full of energy. His curly hair that I loved had grown out even more.

Never much for words, he dropped his blue and white duffle bag, with its red-embroidered "R.A. B III" on Susie's kitchen floor and kicked the door shut. He was a big, confident man, with a one-track mind. As I melted in his arms, I began to understand what Lee had said about different kinds of love. I gave up trying to compare the two men and accepted that I lived in two different worlds. I was Mrs. R. A. Baker III, the wife of a math genius. But I was also Juduffki, beloved of Lee H. Oswald, a former spy, CIA operative, and FBI informant.

Robert soon spotted the box of tea in the bedroom. Upset, he demanded to know why I'd wasted money on such a ridiculous amount of tea. Changing my excuse—that I'd bought it for Susie--I told him I had bought it for his mother, as a "Thank you" present, for arranging such a nice bridal shower. Once again, I felt miserable at being forced to lie.

A few hours later, as Robert drove us to Fort Walton Beach, his mood still soured over the tea, we argued about money. Tired of his criticism, I complained about the sad state of our relationship, to which he responded, "Tell my mother about it. Maybe she'll call off the shower." When we finally arrived at his parents, it was after midnight.

The Bakers' beautiful home overlooked a bay that sparkled under the stars. His parents had waited up for us with the light on, and kindly met us at the door. They were dressed in white silk Japanese bathrobes that matched their silver hair. As we entered, suddenly a big black cat pounced on my leg and grabbed my ankle, digging its claws into my leg.

Dropping the box of tea, I tried to pull it off, but its claws had become enmeshed in the nylon stocking I'd put on to "be a lady." Clawing my leg wildly, the cat fought to get loose and bit me again. "Help!" I shouted.

"Stop it, Felix!" yelled Robert's father, quickly grabbing the cat. "Bad boy!" He opened a sliding glass door and threw the cat into the bushes. This was the cat that Mr. Baker had once bragged 'could whup' my mother's poodles. No doubt he could. The cat was grizzled, with torn ears, having had many battles with other tomcats. I looked down at my ankle and said, "It's bleeding." "If you go into the bathroom, my dear," said Mrs. Baker, with abstract calm, "you'll find a nice, clean washcloth, and I'll bring you a band-aid."

I went into the guest bath, washed the blood off my leg, and inspected the damage: two purple punctures in my heel, and a pair of deep, four-inch-long scratches on my leg. I took a washcloth to the scratches but knew it wasn't enough. A cat bite can easily get infected. Mrs. Baker returned with a single band-aid. "Do you have any antibiotic ointment?" I asked hopefully. "I don't think you'll need ointment for that," she said. "He does it to me all the time."

"If he does that to you all the time, I'm surprised you can walk."

"You seem to have very thin skin," she said coldly, then turned and left. I felt very small and unwelcome in their plush home.

This photo of the "Playground Shower" at the Coronado "honoring the recent bride" hit the local newspapers July 21, 1963.

Saturday, July 20, 1963

Robert had taken our bags into the bedroom, so he hadn't witnessed Felix the Cat's attack. After telling me he didn't know where there was any antibiotic in the house, he had no more interest in my sore foot; after all, it was pretty far from his favorite part of my body.

After a nice breakfast, Mrs. Baker took me to the hairdresser, and then to buy "a proper dress." I knew she meant well, but I felt like a doll she had decided to play with. The event was held at the Coronado Banquet Hall, with a country club luncheon. following. I was the lone "young thing" amongst a gaggle of women with dyed hair and double chins, dripping with diamonds and jewelry. We wound up with the predictable cache of gifts — Pyrex dishes, designer cookware, stainless flatware, an electronic knife, a toaster.

There was also an electric blanket, a griddle, linens, silver serving trays, and a ceramic seashell bowl. There was so much "loot," as Robert called it, that it took two trips in the little Ford to get it all safely back to his parents' house. Robert made a list as he inventoried his treasure, saying he would leave most of it there until we moved to Gainesville. I said nothing, sitting on the bed and nursing my foot, which was getting swollen and hot. But it was time to hurry to a fancy restaurant for a steak dinner! On the way, Robert handed me a Trailways bus ticket. He informed me I would be returning to New Orleans in the morning. *What?* It would get me back in time for work at Reily's on Monday, he told me. Meanwhile, he had decided to stay for a week or two. First, they'd pay him to help out in their office again, since their secretary was on vacation. Second, they would drive him to UF to register for the fall, and pay all his fees. "Pretty cool, huh?" he said.

Another photo taken 07/20/63

"But why must I leave tomorrow morning?" I asked. "Dad wants to try out his new yacht," Robert replied. "It's going to be an all-day affair. I checked the schedule, and we wouldn't be back in time for the last bus. Obviously, I won't be driving you back. But you need to show up at Reily's."

"But what about your job on the Quarter-boat?"

"Oh, that," Robert said calmly. "It's over. I forgot to tell you. I'll look for a new job when I get back to New Orleans." He said it nonchalantly, as if finding a job in New Orleans would be as easy as buying a newspaper.

Mrs. R. A. Baker, Jr. 1969

<u>Sunday, July 21, 1963</u>

Early next morning, Robert made sure he got one more round of lovin' in, and then, as soon as I dressed, he drove me to the bus station. We rode in silence. I was tired, grumpy and sleepy from Robert's endless sexual demands. As we reached the bus station, he gave me some silver-plated trays to carry back with me. As he waved goodbye and drove off, I realized I was quite hungry, but he had sent me off without breakfast. Only after boarding the bus did I realize that I would also miss lunch, for I was also without any money. I was broke! I almost thought about selling a silver tray, just to be able to eat.

At 3:00 P.M., I arrived in downtown New Orleans tired, hungry, and with my foot throbbing from the cat bite. I dragged my bags and the silver trays Robert had asked me to carry back to the nearest bench, then sat down and looked at my foot again. The cat scratches and the bite on the back of my heel were both hot and sore, clearly infected. Not good. Then I dug through my purse, seeking some bus fare, but all I could find were some pennies. Not enough for a bus ride. As I considered my situation, I ran across a collection of photos of friends and family.

I hadn't looked at them for a while, so I went through them, wondering where everyone was. That's when I realized that I had no photos of Robert and me together, let alone of me and Lee. Well, I couldn't put it off any longer: what were my options for getting home? Hitchhike? Crawl? Hop on one foot? It was only about two miles to my house, so I could walk it, If I could remember how to get there!

I tried to hype myself up: *Come on, Judy! You can do it!* As I prepared to stand up, I realized that somebody was hovering behind me. Then I felt a tap on my shoulder. I turned around and saw David Lewis grinning, with Lee beside him!

"Need a ride?" Lee asked.

"How... ?" I managed to ask.

"David spotted you getting off the bus, and called me," Lee said as he swung my suitcases up off the bench. "He wanted it to be a surprise!"

I had no idea David Lewis would be working there on a Sunday! As for Lee, he explained that he had spent the morning at the training camp shooting film, and then had gone to process the film in his second-floor dark-room in Banister's building. About the same time, David called Banister's office, where David Ferrie was waiting for Lee to finish processing the film, to see if he knew where Lee was. Dave had advised David to keep an eye on me, but not to say a word — unless I got up to leave — until Lee got there.

I gave David Lewis a grateful hug, then followed Lee to an old car that I had seen before -- an unusual car called a Kaiser-Frazier, which was discontinued in 1951. It was a roomy, surprisingly luxurious dark green 4-door sedan. I was the same car that I had seen parked in the alley space near the Eli Lilly office several times. Lee had been given access to the car to get to the darkroom with the precious film."You might want me to take you straight home," Lee said, "if you're too tired. But if you come along with me, you'll get to see Carlos Marcello's plantation. And there's food," he added. "Lots of it."

I said, "Let's go!"

After we crossed the river, Lee stopped to get me a Dr. Pepper, as he heard my stomach growling! Then we followed the long road out of town. The landscape was wild and desolate. Green water pooled between towering cypress trees and Spanish moss hung from ancient oaks, adding to the mystery. This was Churchill Farms property where, it was said, the Godfather dissolved the bodies of his enemies in tubs of lye, before sliding them into the silent waters of these alligator-infested swamps.

When we arrived, we could see that Churchill Farms was a real working farm, with a barn and tractors, a farmhouse and several outbuildings. Today, dozens of cars were parked willy-nilly in a large unpaved area in front of the barn. Women and children were busy enjoying a broad feast laid out across several picnic tables, while men of all ages paid their respects at the nearby farmhouse.

Some men stood in clusters outside the buildings. First, Lee went in the farmhouse, while I stayed in the car and watched the children play. As they played hide-and-seek in the tall grass beside the barn, I remembered what "Sparky" had told me about seeing Lee at Mafia parties when Lee was just a little boy.

Now I understood what he meant. When Lee returned, he moved my luggage over to Dave's car and brought back paper plates loaded with boiled crawfish, potatoes, corn, hush puppies, okra and watermelon. As I ate of this seemingly limitless and delicious gallery of food, I considered the irony Robert's decision to send me back to New Orleans by myself was a grave tactical error on his part, for it turned out to be a blessing, giving me and Lee extra time together. On the way back to New Orleans, Lee, Dave and I shared our very different adventures of the day.

At home, I was finally able to care for my sore foot, but it was going to take a while to heal. As for Marina, Lee didn't tell her that he'd been fired,[199] so his days were open as she sat at home, thinking her husband was working. Lee continued to avoid taking Marina anywhere except to the nearby grocery and the library on Napoleon Avenue. She declined to go to the movies with him, because they were all in English, she told The Warren Commission. I know he would have happily taken her, but instead, it was Lee and I who saw "To Kill a Mockingbird" and some other films. From time to time, until the end of July, when Marina began showing too much with her pregnancy, I posed as Lee's wife (and I felt I was!).

<u>Monday, July 22, 1963</u> Lee called me at Reily's, asking me to meet him at 5:00, via a cab that took me straight to the Roosevelt Hotel. After Lee paid the cabbie, we had a delicious meal, then danced to music in The Blue Room, where a quartet was practicing for an upcoming event.

After Lee, who had waited in the Lobby, paid the cabbie, we had a delicious meal, then danced to music in *The Blue Room*, where a quartet was practicing for an upcoming event. Then we headed upstairs to our elegant room. Seeking adventure, after Lee and I had read about it at the Tulane Library, Lee had obtained a copy of the *Kama Sutra*.

[199] Marina wrote to Ruth Paine that Lee didn't tell her he had lost his job for more than two weeks.

That ancient Hindu book about sexual techniques was so intriguing! So now we eagerly assayed to try some of those fabled, if strange, positions. It turned out that the drawings did not necessarily represent modern human anatomy, and at one point, we broke a chair. As Lee put it, "The guy from India said it would be fun."

"In the book it looked like it would be fun," I said, as I lay on the floor, a bit bruised. Back in bed and recovering from our mishap, Lee said

that he had been even busier since his dismissal from Reily's. Besides the training film and his normal load of intelligence errands, Lee asked if I could help him prepare his lecture, which was only five days away. Of course, I agreed. He wrote it by hand.

Tuesday, July 23, 1963 The result of our international sex experiments at the Roosevelt were quite evident on Tuesday, when Lee and I met at Thompson's Restaurant, right after work. "As much as I love you," I told him. "I'd rather not go anywhere a bed!" Lee laughed. "That's good news," he said. "I can hardly walk. The worst part was, when I got home, Marina wanted to make love!" I had to laugh myself, knowing what feats Lee had performed at the hotel. "I can't imagine how you were able to

rally one more time," I said teasing him. "It helps because she's cute, all puffed up like that," he replied. "I have to go to Banister's Building," he said. "Let's go!" As we began walking down Lafayette, Lee pointed out a tall man striding confidently along, well ahead of us. "That's **Gerry Patrick Hemming**," he said. "He's the guy running 'Interpen.' He's a big shot, also works with Alpha 66." I was impressed, since my anti-Castro friends in Florida had told me about Alpha 66 and this man "Patrick." Now I could see him with my own eyes! As he turned the corner, I got a glimpse of his handsome face and piercing countenance.

He had dark, curly hair and a powerful body, but what struck me was his height. "How tall is he, anyway?" I asked. "Six foot seven?"[200]

"In army boots, maybe," Lee said.

"He doesn't look like a ruthless killer."

"Who told you Gerry was a ruthless killer?" Lee said. "You called Dave that, too." When I told him Hemming had a reputation with my anti-Castro friends in Gainesville, Lee said, "Don't get me wrong. He's had to do things, but he's no psycho. Not that I want you to fall for his charming ways," he added. "He's out here for the training camp, but you might have to talk to him sometime."

"Why would I have to do that?"

"I've been pointing out people you should know," Lee went on, "because things can happen. Situations can come up." Lee then told me several things that I could tell Gerry, to prove that Lee put trust in me. "Gerry has a soft place in his heart for women," Lee said. "He'd protect you, if you needed it."[201] By now, Lee and I had reached 1032 Marengo. There, after he typed out the last two pages of his science fiction story, "Her Way," he brought out his cherished gray-cover book of poetry and short stories by Pushkin. It was all in Russian. He translated for me in bed, where we lay together with our clothes off. Susie was out getting a new battery for a hearing aid, so we had some privacy.[202] Wrapped in a light cocoon of sheets pulled up to our chins, the fan in the window rotating back and forth to cool our faces, Lee read to me from his gray book in fluent, melodious Russian for some time. Then Susie suddenly knocked on our door. We looked at each other and shrugged.

"Come on in, Susie!" I called out. "Just close your eyes!"

"Oh, my goodness!" she said, seeing us wrapped up like that. "Ain't you two the lovebirds, now?"

---

[200] I later began a novel with Gerry Hemming as its model, called "Six Foot Seven." Some pages have survived. Photo shows Gerry teaching anti-Castroites parachuting.

[201] Before I flew to Gerry in Fayetteville, NC, I talked to him by phone, as Dr. Howard Platzman recorded our conversation (and also participated). Gerry and I then became friends. I told him more details about "the secrets" that proved I had known Lee Oswald. They had been closer friends than he ever admitted to the outside world. Without going into detail, the three secrets involved El Monte, California, his plane's location in Marathon, Florida, and his recruitment of Karl Smith (later known as Karl Faber-Smith), an engineer who taught him superior ways to use explosives. After that, Gerry gave me his Interpen list of contacts and began to secretly cc me when he sent email messages to his Interpen group, which emails I own. After I shared Lee's secrets with Gerry, admitted that indeed, he'd been in New Orleans in the summer of 1963.

[202] Susie hardly needed a hearing aid, but that summer she tried one out. Her family doesn't remember her ever using one.

"We're just reading poetry together," Lee said. "Oh, dear!" Susie said. "I see! But, what about Robert? When is the Rat due back?"

"He stayed behind in Florida to work for his parents," I answered, "so they'll pay his tuition at college." Then I told her about Robert sending me back to New Orleans by myself with no food or money.

"Just more nails in his coffin," Susie commented. "Well, "Gunsmoke" is going to start, so I'll be going..." Lee suddenly sat up. "It's already 7:30?" he asked. "Oh, you have fifteen minutes," Susie replied calmly. "I've got to get home!" Lee said, shooing Susie and Suzi Collie out. He then got up to dress. "I'm working on the film again tomorrow," he said, buttoning his shirt. "After that, I have to go out of town. After that, Spring Hill. Dutz is paying for our trip," he said, putting on his shoes. "Marina can finally get to see the Gulf and eat fresh seafood." After a kiss, he added, "Stay where you are, and rest. I'll call tomorrow. If you need anything, let me know. I'll get it for you." As he left, I thought about the green glass, and then about Robert, who had sent me back to New Orleans with so many needs. Lee was so different. He would always try to make me happy if he could.

Wednesday, July 24, 1963 It was time for more cancer work. It had rained last night, and the steamy heat of a New_Orleans summer day hit me as I left Reily's air-conditioned offices to catch the St. Charles streetcar uptown to Dr. Mary's apartment. There I picked up our medical reports and reviewed them on the streetcar on the way to Charity Hospital, where I was to meet Dr. Ochsner. I had to wait in the lobby until he found time for me, so I continued to re-read the articles. When I finally entered Ochsner's meeting room, he greeted me warmly. I had never seen him so genial. This meeting was necessary because it was time to test the Project's biological weapon on larger primates. It had worked on the Marmosets, so it was time to try it on African greens. They were closer to humans but considerably more expensive. The next steps involved precise work at the monkey labs. New people would do that. After much technical talk, Ochsner suddenly said, "By the way, your boy Oswald is going to be a movie star."

"I know he's working on a film," I said cautiously, not knowing how much Ochsner was privy to. "I don't mean out there," Ochsner said, suggesting that he knew about the filming at the training camp. "I mean here in New Orleans, on TV. Do you have a TV set?" I told him that I did not. He said they had them in Tulane's dorms, where I'd soon be living, forgetting I was now married. "But go over to Lee's house when we put it on the air," he suggested. "Watch it with his wife. I assume you're friends with her by now." I pondered his comment, but didn't answer. It made me wonder again how much he really knew about Lee's life, or mine. "They don't have a TV set, either," I said. "They're too poor."

"He gets enough money!" Ochsner said stiffly. "Though I am aware he's frugal."

"Sir," I said proudly, "he doesn't spend a dollar of the Project's money on anything extra for himself. He's a patriot of the first order."

"Well, he's all of that," Ochsner agreed. "I don't deny it. I've taken the trouble to look into his records. And I'm thinking about better ways to use his talents."

"He wants to go to college, sir," I said. "Can you help him?"

"Young lady, we want him to stay put for a while, where he's most useful." He was clearly talking about continuing to use Lee as a low-level operative, showing me that Ochsner was in a position of great power.

"So, sir, who am I really working for?" I asked Ochsner bluntly. He shook his head in dismay and said that I was asking a lot of questions today, as if talking to the wall. Then, he turned to me and said: "You're working for the foes of Communism." After a short pause, he smiled grimly and added, "I'm not ashamed to say that I would spill every drop of blood I have for my country. And I have known that you feel the same way." Ochsner then glanced at his watch and cut me off with a wave of his hand. He indicated that I was to take a stack of new material with me. "Read these for us," he said, "and give us your input as soon as possible. The final step will be with our human volunteer."

"Have you already found one?" I queried. "You would be surprised," Dr. Ochsner replied, standing up and leading me to the door. "There are many unsung heroes who have bravely stepped forward to accomplish the impossible." Then he added, a little sadly. "There are risks that must be taken for great causes."

"Am I doing all right, sir?" I asked meekly. "It feels strange, not preparing for Tulane yet. I mean, all I've looked at for months now are cancer cells."

"Only two months, and you'll be marching through the doors of Tulane Medical School," Ochsner said confidently. "Are you using Mr. Ferrie's medical library pass?"

"Yes, about once a week."

"Good. Go twice a week, and study there. After you leave Reily's, go every day."

"What will I do for money when Reily's ends?" I asked. "If you have a problem," he replied, "ask Mary. She'll give you enough to tide you over," he said tersely. I wondered if my way was going to be paid through laundered funds. Dr. Ochsner, finished with our meeting, smoothly slipped back into his charming professional manner. "It's been good to see you again," he said, adding that I was to make my reports quickly. The new materials had been rushed to us, flown in from New York at great expense, just for me to read and distill for everyone. Once outside again, I hobbled to Canal Street on my sore foot.

I had meant to ask Dr. Ochsner for antibiotics, but forgot to do so in his overwhelming presence. At last, I spotted the Magazine bus, got aboard, and headed home. It was now quite dark, and when I got on the bus it was a driver who didn't know me. But surely, I could recognize my stop, even without Lee. Right? *Wrong!* We passed it before I realized, so I rode all the way to Audubon Park, where I caught a bus going back. Though I asked the driver to call out "Marengo" for me, he forgot. By the time I recognized where I was, I ended getting off far beyond my stop. As I walked on my sore foot, my shoe, too tight for my swollen foot, was tearing open the sore on my heel. The sidewalk was so littered with broken glass and trash I couldn't go barefoot. I, once so proud because the great Dr. Ochsner had craved my opinions, had to face the cold truth: on the streets, always losing my way, I was a danger to myself! By the time I reached 1032, humbled completely, my left foot was bloody.

Two little boys greeted me at the porch, asking where Lee was. He had often played ball with them and given them piggyback rides. I had played with them, too, but this evening, pain ruled all, and I waved them off. But I did grab the mail, which included a postcard saying "Greetings from New Orleans." Since it was dark, I limped inside to sit down and read it. That's when I got a shock. *The card was from Robert!* It had been mailed yesterday at 8:00 P.M. --from New Orleans! It read, *'I'll be back through in a couple of days."* What? I was hurt, angry and confused. Robert was supposed to be working in his parents' real estate office. He had failed to call to see if I'd arrived safely — I was used to that — but the postcard said he'd returned and was going away somewhere for a few days! Upset, I showed the card to Susie.

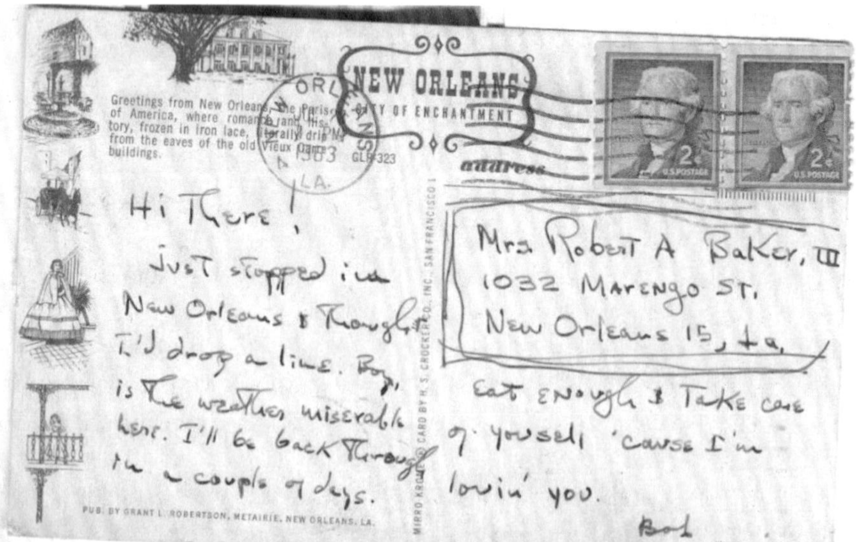

"Call his parents," she advised. "Maybe they know where he is." So I did, only to be shocked again when Robert answered the phone.

He'd just mailed a letter to me, he said, apologizing for not calling. "By the way, just because I'm earning money again, that doesn't mean you can just go and buy those white shoes," he warned me. I had wanted new white shoes to wear with the new pink dress Mrs. Baker had bought for me, but Robert saw no reason to be so picky. But now I needed new walking shoes! My sore foot had to have them! But first-- what was the post card all about? "It would have been decent of you to call," I said bitterly. "But at least, I got a postcard from you! Mailed from here — postmarked yesterday."

Robert coughed, then said, "Oh—that! I was out partying with the guys for a few days, after they shut down our jobs. We happened to be having a little fun in New Orleans," he went on, "so I wrote you a card. The guys said it would be stupid to mail it, so I threw it away, even though that wasted some stamps. I guess somebody found it and mailed it."

"So when the job stopped, you went off and partied!" I shot back. "That's where all the money has been going!" In my mind's eye, I was listing all the $50 checks Robert had been writing. "But for us, there's never any time, never any money!"

"I wasn't driving!" he said defensively. "And was I supposed to sit out there in the marsh all summer, and not have a break? Be reasonable — I know you're capable of it."

"And I am capable of buying new shoes, without your permission!"

"You just want to fight, don't you?" he snapped. "If you hadn't bought that ton of tea we didn't need, you'd have enough money for new shoes."

"You know I have a hurt foot. I need new shoes, that won't hurt my feet, and I'm getting them!" I ended up slamming the phone down, and in tears started telling Susie what had happened. Then the phone rang.

"It's him!" Susie said. "Don't answer it!" But I did. It was indeed Robert. "Don't you ever hang up on me again!" he growled. Having had quite enough, I did just that.

Thursday, July 25th One of Reily's salesmen had gone missing. He was a reliable man, so Monaghan asked me to find him. I looked at his route, made phone calls, and checked his old expense reports to see where he stayed when he was in that area. Finally, I located him at The Saint Francis Motel. He was quite ill, so one of the Reily brothers upstairs immediately sent a doctor. My sleuthing pleased Mr. Monaghan, but I was now late for the lab work at Dave's apartment. Monaghan agreed to clock me out so I wouldn't have to run back from Dave's at 4:30. Leaving Reily's, I headed for Dave's kitchen to work with the last marmoset tumors. By dark, Dave, Lee and a Latino had entered the living room to edit film from the training camp that Lee had processed the day before. I quietly stayed in the kitchen and continued working. For all the Latino knew, I was just doing dishes.

David Sanchez Morales, aka 'El Indio,' worked for the CIA under the cover of Army employment. He... rose to become Chief of Operations at the CIA's large JMWAVE facility in Miami... [where] he oversaw operations undertaken against the regime of Fidel Castro in Cuba. Morales was involved in other covert operations of the CIA, reportedly including plots to assassinate Fidel Castro, training intelligence teams supporting the Bay of Pigs invasion of Cuba, the CIA's secret war in Laos and its controversial Operation Phoenix in Vietnam, and the hunting down of Che Guevara in Bolivia. After Morales' retirement in 1975 he returned to his native Arizona, and supposedly died of a heart attack in 1978 [before the HSCA could get him to testify]. HSCA investigator Gaeton Fonzi traced Morales to Wilcox, Arizona shortly after... and talked to his lifelong friend Ruben Carbajal and a business associate of Morales' named Bob Walton. Walton told Fonzi of an evening, after many drinks, when Morales went into a tirade about Kennedy and ...finished this conversation by saying "Well, we took care of that son of a bitch, didn't we?" Carbajal...corroborated it. ...Howard Hunt [said Morales] was a participant in the JFK assassination. Carbajal described the long line of cars and men in dark glasses who paid their respects at the funeral... Morales operated under deep cover for such a high-level officer." https://www.maryferrell.org/pages/David_Morales_We_Took_Care_of_That_SOB.htm

After a while, Dave closed the blinds and started running the film, to new sections of film were being spliced. Several times that night, Lee called to me, saying, "Look, J — there I am!"

That's I went into the living room to see that part of the film. The first clip I saw showed Lee sitting in a room with a cement floor, demonstrating how to clean and care for firearms. Another scene showed Cubans firing rifles in a maiden-cane field with Lee walking behind them, wearing a baseball cap. When each segment was over, I went back to my lab work and they went back to editing.

From time to time, I stuck my head into the living room where I saw other film clips, some with Lee in them. The Latino man never said a word to me, but I noticed he had a scar up over one eyebrow.

David Morales, CIA

Years later, I finally saw a photo showing the scar clearly – it had not been so obvious in other photos I'd seen. I am convinced Lee's companion was David Morales, a CIA legend.

Before Lee left with the Latino, he came into the kitchen.

"I'm heading to the airport," he told me. "Have to collect some materials for the Project from another city." He said he'd barely make it back in time to join his family for travel to the Seminar at Spring Hill the next day. He hugged me goodbye, promising to call when he could. Dave went with them, and I was left alone. When I finished, I hobbled to the bus stop and headed home in the dark. Somehow, I didn't miss my stop!

Friday, July 26, 1963 Just before lunch, Lee called long distance. He was still somewhere out of town. I told him I could hardly walk, and this time it wasn't because of Hindu gymnastics. My foot was still infected, and (blush!) getting lost recently had made it worse. "Gee, I didn't notice!" Lee said. "We were so busy with the film."

"I even phoned Robert," I added, "and got the courage to tell him I was going to cash a check for new shoes. When he dared me to, I hung up on him."

"Good for you!" Lee replied. "It's about time you spoke up for yourself. Did you get your shoes?"

"My foot's too sore to walk on — even if I had the time, which I don't."

"I can't help you personally," Lee said. "And tomorrow, we're going to Mobile. But you need shoes now, so I'll send a cab to Reily's at 4:30. Go downtown," he added. "Make the cab wait. Buy your shoes, then get some bread and milk before you go home." His comment about bread and milk touched me, since Lee had a habit of bringing Susie and me bread and milk all the time.

I protested that the cab would be expensive, but Lee replied that it was "Lambert's" money (his word for Clay Shaw when we spoke on the phone), so it was okay. Lee then said, "I'm in public, but imagine what I wish I could say." With that, he hung up. I now understand where Lee went that July 26. I know he sometimes used his CIA money to pay for plane fuel, and I assume he used a plane, since he showed up at Oak Ridge, TN that day. Marina would complain to a Jesuit acolyte at Spring Hill that Lee was "gone all the time." This time, he was at Oak Ridge. Lee apparently had to obtain supplies for the Project.! A record was found showing an entry in Lee's handwriting at the Oak Ridge Museum of Atomic Energy's Visitors Register on July 26. He wrote: 'Lee H. Oswald USSR Dallas Rd Dallas Texas.' He probably used the visitor's log to show he had arrived and was ready for contact. In his own humorous way, he left us a little souvenir

To me, writing 'USSR' is just the kind of outrageous humor we've seen with his passport application that said he married his wife on April 31, 1961. He probably was picking up something radioactive, such as tracers. If so, they would be used to trace the uptake, survival and death rate of injected cancer cells. Or, Lee might have been asked to courier a container full of radioactive materials for use with the LINAC, back to New Orleans

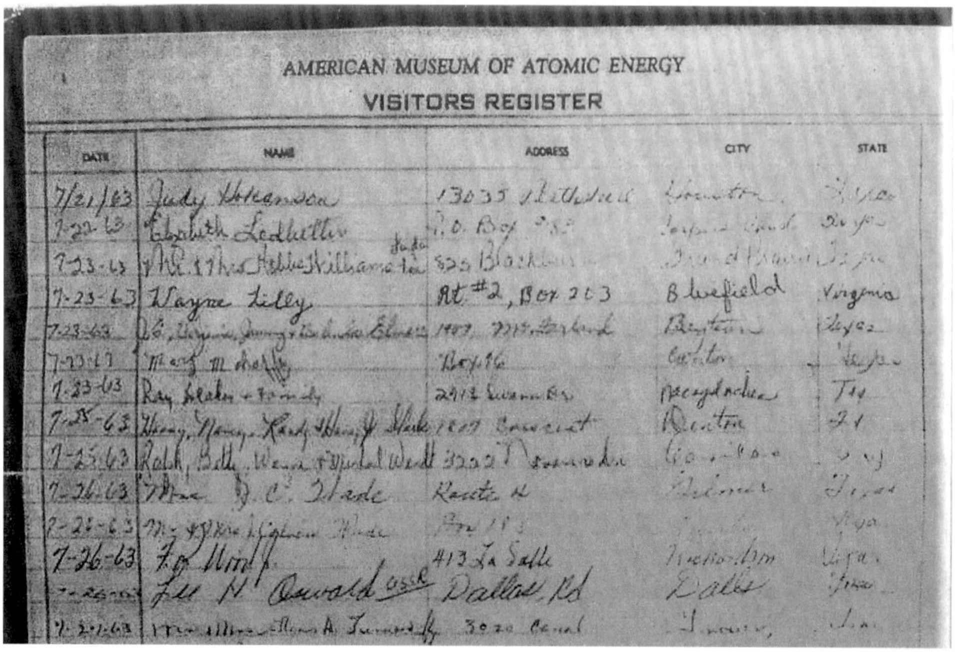

AMERICAN MUSEUM OF ATOMIC ENERGY

VISITORS REGISTER

DATE	NAME	ADDRESS	CITY	STATE
7/21/63	Judy [illegible]	13035 [illegible]	[illegible]	[illegible]
7-22-63	Elizabeth Ledbetter	P.O. Box [illegible]	[illegible]	[illegible]
7-23-63	[illegible]	[illegible]	[illegible]	[illegible]
7-23-63	Wayne Lilly	Rt. #2, Box 203	Bluefield	Virginia
7-23-63	[illegible]	[illegible]	[illegible]	[illegible]
7-23-63	[illegible]	Box 16	[illegible]	[illegible]
7-23-63	Ray [illegible] + family	[illegible]	Nacogdoches	Tex
7-25-63	[illegible]	[illegible]	[illegible]	[illegible]
7-25-63	[illegible]	[illegible]	[illegible]	[illegible]
7-26-63	Mrs. D. C. Wade	Route 2	[illegible]	[illegible]
7-26-63	[illegible]	[illegible]	[illegible]	[illegible]
7-26-63	[illegible]	413 La Salle	[illegible]	[illegible]
[illegible]	Lee H Oswald USSR	Dallas, Rd	Dallas	[illegible]
7-27-63	[illegible]	3020 Canal	[illegible]	[illegible]

"[On]the 50th anniversary of the JFK assassination…**Gerald Boyd**, former manager of the Department of Energy's Oak Ridge office, …said he'd been given a copy of the [above] document… when he was still manager of DOE's Oak Ridge office…The museum registration sheet …suggest[s] Oswald was in the presence of a number of other people from Texas. The old museum,…was owned by the Atomic Energy Commission and situated on the Oak Ridge Turnpike…."
http://knoxblogs.com/atomiccity/2013/11/22/lee-harvey-oswald-oak-ridge/

Meanwhile, Lee's uncle was arranging to take him, his family and assorted relatives to Mobile for Lee's presentation at Spring Hill Seminary, where some 90 graduate students studying for the priesthood, plus professors and guests, would hear Lee's 70-minute speech – a speech which anti-Oswald biographer McMillan said lasted only half an hour, and which the Warren Commission's attorneys called a speech given to "boys."

.

Saturday, July 27, 1963 The Jesuit scholasticate, Robert J. Fitzpatrick, took Marina for a walk around the campus. *"Fitzpatrick spoke Russian and it fell to him to keep company with Marina, who spoke almost no*

English...He told F.B.I. agents later that the follow-up letter he wrote (in Russian) on August 8 was never answered... Strolling the Spring Hill grounds, ***Marina told Fitzpatrick that Oswald "kept her completely away from other people."*** *As to their homelife in New Orleans, the F.B.I. interview with Fitzpatrick reports that "[Fitzpatrick] said she told him* ***Oswald is away from home a great deal and she did not know of any of his associates or any of his activities."***

While Lee would be giving his talk at Spring Hill, I was expecting Robert to return from Fort Walton Beach. Then I got an urgent phone call from Dave, who said he needed help to keep some tissue cultures alive. He couldn't get back in time to handle them himself. I unhappily headed to Dave's apartment, knowing I must be careful because one of Dave's boyfriends might show up at any time. Fortunately, none did. When I finished refreshing the tissue cultures, I called Dr. Mary, who, hearing of my sore foot, eventually came and picked me up for a working lunch. She looked tired and was not particularly friendly. We talked about the Project, the dying marmoset monkeys and the upcoming injections of the African green monkeys, but Lee's trip to Spring Hill wasn't discussed. She was all business, no small talk. She may not have known why Lee was unavailable. After lunch, I went back to 1032, a friendly Susie Hanover, and a load laundry. I waited for Robert's return, but he never showed up, so I decided to get some sleep, while I could!

Sunday, July 28, 1963 Late Sunday afternoon, Robert finally returned from Fort Walton a day late, not having bothered to call. Trying to make up for his 'Rat' activities, and our fight, Robert took me to the Pontchartrain Beach amusement park, but we didn't go on a single ride, when he saw how much they cost. We had ice cream and sausages on a stick, then came home again. It was the last time Robert took me anywhere in New Orleans.

On **Monday, July 29, 1963** I quietly got out of bed, leaving Robert safely asleep. When I got to work, I told Mr. M that my husband was underfoot and needed a job to keep him out of my hair. Monaghan said he could set him up as a commission salesman for Standard Coffee. That would keep him out of the house, pounding the streets. It wasn't much money, but it would be easy duty. All Robert had to do was fill out an application. Robert took the job, and I thought all would be well... but that's another story! I was puzzled when Lee called my desk before noon and asked if I could meet him for lunch at Katzenjammer's. It was a dingy bar that Reily employees avoided. Lee knew how busy Mondays were for me, so it had to be important. On the phone,I sensed an edge to Lee's voice that I hadn't heard before. Something was up.

When I told Mr. Monaghan the lunch meeting was important, with a resigned sigh, he said that he would cover for me. When I arrived at Katzenjammer's, smoke hung in the still air of the dark room and a baseball game was playing on the television set at the bar. Lee greeted me in Russian and called me "Marina" loud enough for others to hear, then quietly explained that Banister frequently had lunch here with his girlfriend.

I would pose as Marina, just in case they came in. Our food was waiting on the table: Lee said he had ordered it early to save time. After asking about my foot, he began reporting on his adventures over the weekend at the Jesuit seminar. The Jesuits[203] were concerned about problems emerging in Nicaragua, where their missionaries were preaching Liberation Theology. A movement called "the Sandinistas" was taking up arms against Somoza's repressive pro-US government. An insurrection was in the air, and the Jesuits were in the middle of it. I knew that the Somoza family was one of Ochsner's important contacts in Central America. It was obvious what side he would be on.

Alton Ochsner with Antonio Samoza, 1967

Lee then said that Bobby Kennedy's Jesuit priest from Georgetown had asked Lee questions about the training film.[204] This same priest cautioned Lee that there were spies at the conference seeking information about Jesuit activities in Latin America. Lee found himself walking a tightrope: both the CIA and the Mafia had asked Lee to advise the Jesuits not to support the Sandinista insurrection, while Dr. Ochsner and Banister both wanted Lee to report any comments the Jesuits might make. By nature, Lee was on the side of the Sandinistas, as were most of the Jesuits, so he was, de-facto, one of the "spies" attending the conference. I was pleased that Lee trusted me this much. He was revealing the dimensions of the dangers he was now facing.

After Lee told me about Spring Hill, he suddenly said he wanted to spend more time with little Junie, even though he didn't expect her to remember him after he split with Marina. With that sad prediction, he

---

[203] Later, I'd learn that The Warren Commission called these college graduates 'boys' and the media spread around that Lee spoke for only twenty minutes. But I had worked with Lee on his speech. It was an hour long. Lee said he had over twenty minutes of questions afterwards. There were other presentations that day, as well.

[204] This might be how the film ended up at Georgetown U, as reported by the HSCA's own Robert Tanenbaum, who along with me, also saw the film.

sighed and sank into silence. What was troubling him so? He hadn't even touched his food. I took his hand, hoping he would talk to me. "Why such sadness when you spoke about seeing Junie?" I asked. "I have concerns," he said enigmatically. "Especially for us. I have romantic dreams for us, but I see what is developing..." He paused mid-sentence, turning his eyes from me. Then he said firmly, and with finality, "I'm sorry, but despite my promises, I have to keep some things from you. For your own safety."

"Before you say anything more," I told him, "Ask yourself why you would hide anything from me now? What am I to you? Another Marina? Or just a Portia to Brutus?" I was referring to Shakespeare's play about the assassination of Julius Caesar, which Lee and I had recently discussed, sensitive as we were about the growing dangers to President Kennedy. Brutus put off confiding to his wife about his plan to help kill Caesar, and she ends up killing herself because he didn't trust her.

Lee withdrew his hand from mine coldly. He suddenly stood up and glared at me with an anger I had not seen in him before. Then he kicked the chair and walked out. My emotions roared. I was filled with a torrent of inner pain that I had never felt before. "*Oh, Lee!*" I screamed inside. I bit into my lower lip to distract myself, so I would not follow him. This was not the time to act on impulse. I was determined to wait it out at the table, gnawing on my lip to control the turbulence raging inside me. Why had he withdrawn his trust? Why would he not tell me about the dangers he faced? I bit into my lip even harder. Did he think I would betray him? *I would die first!* Then I tasted blood in my mouth. I didn't care. I was in so much emotional pain, I scarcely noticed.

Suddenly, Lee came back. He quietly slipped into the chair and finally looked at me. Seeing the blood draining out of my mouth startled him. "What have you done to yourself?" he asked, taking up a napkin. Carefully, he started blotting the blood off my chin. "God, Judy, it's still bleeding!" Lee said, wetting the blood-spotted napkin in his glass of ice water. I turned my face away from him, rejecting his help. He dropped the napkin, then held his head in his hands, looking down at the table. I heard him hiss through his teeth as he shook his head, his fingers pressed hard against his temples as if in a vise. He was in as much emotional pain as I was, but I wasn't doing this to hurt him. My heart suddenly wrenched me to action, and I reached up and grabbed his wrist. He tried to pull away, but I didn't let him. I sought his eyes with mine. When I found them, I saw that they were still filled with anger. "So, you think I would *talk!*"

"Damn all the women in my life!" he said with quiet venom. "I can't make a scene here, they'll notice. I wish I had never learned to love. It's ripping me apart." He put some ice cubes into the napkin and gave it to me to nurse my lip.

As I held the icy napkin against my lip, I wondered if I'd have to get a stitch. "Lucky you didn't have a dagger," he said. "I would've had to take you to the emergency room. God, Judy! All right. I give up."

"No," I mumbled through the napkin, "I don't want you to give up. I'm not trying to win anything. But, I am not your harlot," I concluded, not knowing how he would respond. A long moment of silence passed.

"All right. All right," he said, grasping my point. Another silent minute labored by, as I pressed the napkin against my bleeding mouth. "I will hide nothing from you. I can't," he said. "But I warn you, you won't like it."

"Let me hold your hand, and then tell me," I said, thinking that I had some inner strength to share with him that would counterbalance what he was about to say. He looked at me with empty eyes and said, "I think they're going to kill me." A chill ran down my spine.

He said that his efforts to advance in the Company were being stymied, probably because it was too risky to fully trust a returned fake defector. "And the more you know," he said, "the more dangerous it will be for you. Past a certain point, I might not be able to protect you. You might even need to denounce me to protect yourself."

"Would they actually risk sending you into Cuba?" I asked.

"Probably not. Not now," he said.

"Because of the lab project?"

"Of course. I know too much. It's not your fault," Lee emphasized. "I was supposed to spy on the project for the CIA, just to keep everybody honest. And then, all the other little things they've had me do, such as these pro-Castro stunts... as if they still want me to prepare to enter Cuba!" Lee laughed bitterly. "What a joke! Both sides would prefer to see me dead first."

"But why?" I pleaded.

"Because I'm not important enough for either side to take a chance on, knowing what I know. If I can't find a way to avoid being expendable soon, it's over. Now that's the truth. They'll kill me, just to get rid of me."

I think Lee told me again that his former handler was called "Jesus." Lee may have called him "Jesus," but I knew the man was evil. "He said the only way he could trust me, is if I had come home in a coffin."

After he let his words sink in, Lee revealed more, in words that came slowly and with a sense of finality, as if what he was telling me meant he would not live very much longer. He explained that, with Dave Ferrie's help, he'd penetrated to the heart of some groups in New Orleans who were serious about killing Kennedy. Through these contacts, he had discovered an elite circle of even more powerful men, many from Texas, composed of politicians, oil magnates, and the military, including CIA officers. Their fanatical patriotism was mixed with monetary ambition and a lust for power.

From their perspective, the country was being held hostage by a President who refused to bring Communism to its knees. Nor could they reap the lucrative benefits of war that America's power-brokers, such as Lyndon Johnson and others in our government wanted. To them all, Lee Oswald was a pawn to use or to discard as they saw fit. Realizing his fate was in their hands, Lee had weighed his options. They weren't good.

"They want to kill the Chief," Lee stressed. "And as the only "insider" with a publicly provable motive to kill him — since I'll look like Castro's agent with all they want me to do — they could set me up so easily. I can see it coming."

I put my arms around Lee, trying to comfort him. "I've seen their faces," he went on. "I know names. I know who's behind a lot of it. I know about the big group in Texas. But I could prove nothing. I'm snuffed, any way you look at it. So here is where my end begins." A shiver vibrated through his body as he buried his face against my hair.

"Can you become indispensable to them?" I asked.

"I'm thinking, I'm thinking!" he answered.

"I'm afraid," I confessed. "Are you?"

"Sure, I'm afraid!" he whispered. "And if I played the Cowardly Lion, and left now, I might survive to tell the tale. But I can't. If I do, Dave will be suspected of bringing in a spy. They might kill him for that. And maybe they'd still find me. As for Dr. Mary, she's been sticking her neck out too far. They might kill her, too. What I need to figure out is how to keep you safe. You, and Junie and Marina." He looked at me with anguish and said regretfully, "I got you into this. I never meant to."

"I asked for it. But I don't want to lose you!"

"You can't lose me, Juduffki," he said. "As long as I'm alive, I'm yours."

Better off dead, to both sides! What could be done? The power of these people was enormous. With all these terrors rolling through my mind, I had to get up and walk back into the world of Wm. B. Reily Coffee Company, leaving Lee sitting there by himself at Katzenjammer's, staring at my blood on the table. I arrived back at Reily's, still horrified at Lee's revelations. My mind in over-drive, I tried to concentrate on my work, but it was difficult. As I waited to clock out, I sat at my des, and wrote Lee a letter, ending with:

Together, today, we live forever. I won't forget! And I love you forever, dearest beloved, no matter what! I finally understood what it meant to love someone forever, even if death was in our future. Then I got on the bus and went back to 1032 Marengo Street, where Robert was waiting for his dinner.

<u>The Letter</u> The letter I wrote, below, was copied online. The_inserted comment was made by critics to try to discredit me.

In actuality, the comment reveals the prejudice of the critic, for *nobody normally writes "name for recipient" on the right-hand side of a letter.*

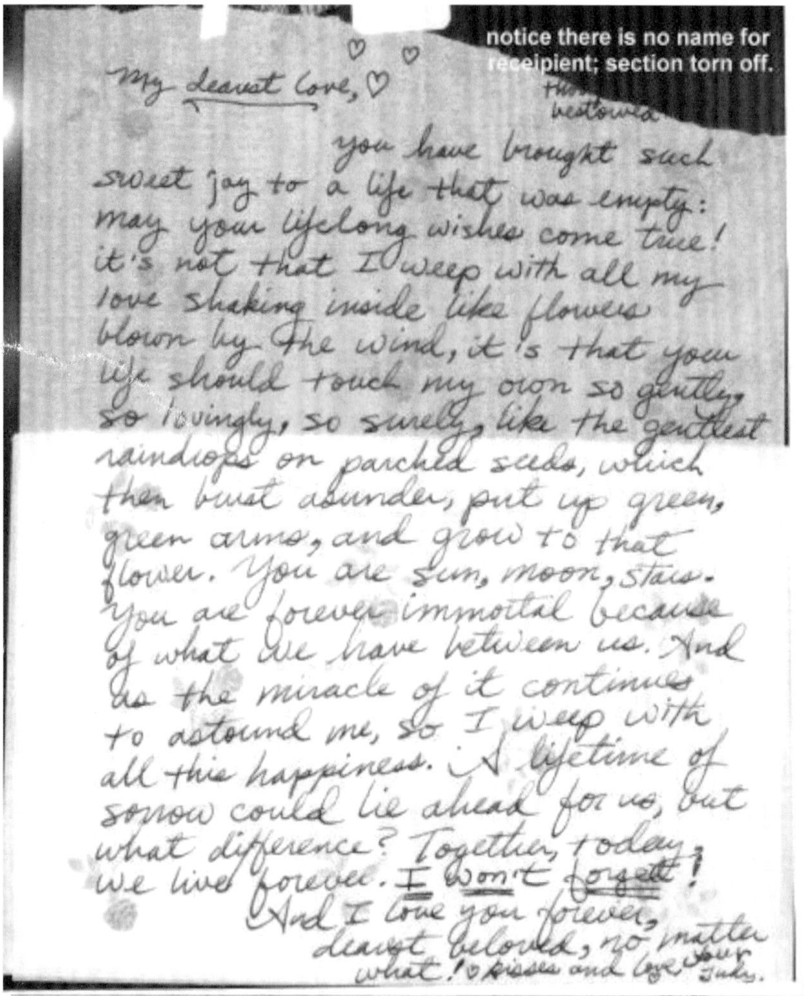

My dearest Love,

thee bestowed

you have brought such sweet joy to a life that was empty: may your lifelong wishes come true! it's not that I weep with all my love shaking inside like flowers blown by the wind, it's that your life should touch my own so gently, so lovingly, so surely, like the gentlest raindrops on parched seeds, which then burst asunder, put up green, green arms, and grow to that flower. You are sun, moon, stars. You are forever immortal because of what we have between us. And as the miracle of it continues to astound me, so I weep with all this happiness. A lifetime of sorrow could lie ahead for us, but what difference? Together, today, we live forever. I won't forget! And I love you forever, dearest beloved, no matter what! kisses and love your Judy.

Magnified, some writing still remains that can be seen to be part of a quotation, possibly: "Upon thee are my thoughts and love bestowed."

.

This was not a letter to "the Rat."

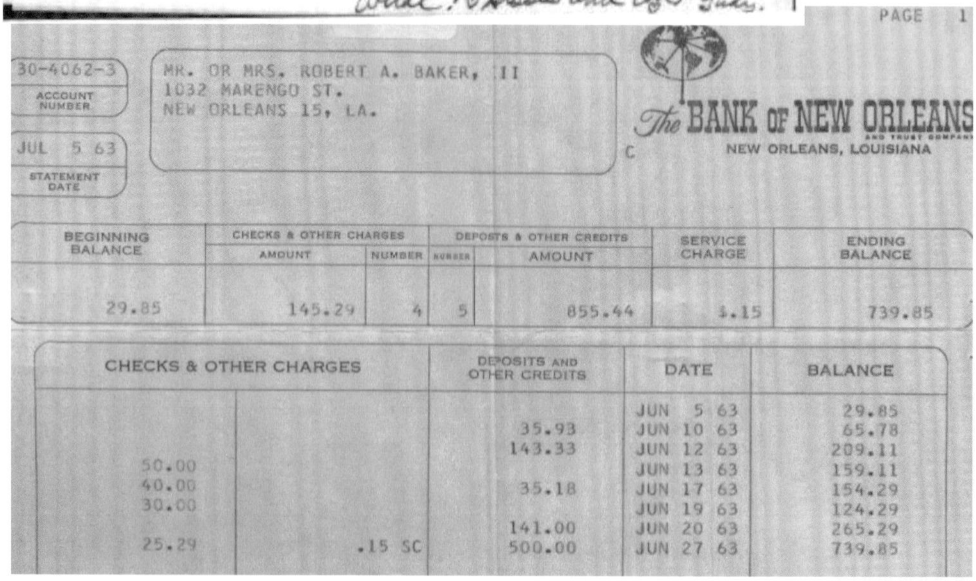

PAGE 1

30-4062-3 ACCOUNT NUMBER

MR. OR MRS. ROBERT A. BAKER, III
1032 MARENGO ST.
NEW ORLEANS 15, LA.

JUL 5 63 STATEMENT DATE

The BANK OF NEW ORLEANS AND TRUST COMPANY
NEW ORLEANS, LOUISIANA

C

BEGINNING BALANCE	CHECKS & OTHER CHARGES AMOUNT	NUMBER	DEPOSITS & OTHER CREDITS NUMBER	AMOUNT	SERVICE CHARGE	ENDING BALANCE
29.85	145.29	4	5	855.44	$.15	739.85

CHECKS & OTHER CHARGES		DEPOSITS AND OTHER CREDITS	DATE	BALANCE
			JUN 5 63	29.85
		35.93	JUN 10 63	65.78
		143.33	JUN 12 63	209.11
50.00			JUN 13 63	159.11
40.00		35.18	JUN 17 63	154.29
30.00			JUN 19 63	124.29
		141.00	JUN 20 63	265.29
25.29	.15 SC	500.00	JUN 27 63	739.85

Considerations

1. Robert and Money **REFER TO THE ABOVE BANK STATEMENT:** I kept one of the Standard Coffee pay-slips Robert got for a week of work, during which he sold nothing whatsoever. His pay was only $3.25! On the other hand, Susie Hanover told me he hardly ever 'went to work' before noon.

When I checked our bank balance by phone, I was shocked. I told Susie and Lee that Robert must have spent $120 in the past three weeks, on God knows what. That's when Susie and Lee urged me to open the bank statement and learn the truth. Though Robert continued to spend freely, he would no longer let me write checks without permission, because I'd "overspent" $3.00 on the tea. When we received $700 from Robert's parents, he put $500 into this bank account and sent $200 to my bank account in Florida (it would soon be a joint account). Our $60 rent and electric bill was due at the end of the month and doesn't show here. What does show is Robert's checks for **$50, $40** and **$30 (for what?).** The **$25.29** was what I spent on groceries. Robert spent **$120.00** – over $1000 in today's funds. His room and board were provided by Evangeline Seismic. Robert said we'd have to live off my paycheck, but meanwhile was spending almost half of what he earned on unknown activities. Susie speculated that he was gambling, since he mentioned crew members playing poker and gambling.

2. The Bridal Shower Newspaper Article Robert's July 24th letter mentioned he wouldn't be home until at least Friday, the 26th. He actually arrived late Sunday, the 28th. He enclosed the July 20, 1963 newspaper article from the coffee social with the comment, "the mistakes made by the paper are mistakes given them by my mother." The newspaper article said both Robert and I were English majors, which wasn't true.

Chapter 21
Fired!

Monday, July 29, 1963

When I reached 1032 Marengo, about 6:00 p.m., Robert was sitting at his typewriter thinking. As I entered, food was on his mind. "I couldn't find any of our stuff in the refrigerator," he began. "It all seemed to belong to Mrs. Hanover. Are you always eating out? No wonder we've run short of money."

"I buy groceries on Mondays," I said. "That's why the fridge is empty."

"Here, I brought you something, honey," I added. "Red beans and rice. It's traditional on Mondays in New Orleans." I handed him the small grocery sack that held the lunch my friend Annette had given me. He ignored my gift and asked if I'd deposited my paycheck today.

He added that he had not found a deposit receipt, and pointing out that this meant I hadn't deposited it on Friday. I suddenly realized that Robert had been going through my things. His comment about the refrigerator made me consider how the combination of his calculating mind, his need for control, his obsession with money and his idle presence, meant I had to be more careful about the little details in my life. Before Robert moved in, I'd had many free meals, thanks to both Lee and Dr. Mary, but I couldn't tell Robert about that. The Project was now both secret and dangerous. Robert had to be kept in the dark for everyone's safety. So, I told Robert that, yes, I deposited my paycheck, and had kept none of it for myself, which was a fact. Then, he noticed that I was wearing comfortable new shoes. "So, how did you manage to buy *those*?" he demanded.

"I borrowed money from work," I told him quickly, as I felt the cut in my mouth bleeding again. "I'm getting a raise. It'll cover it. I hurt my mouth. Can't talk anymore!" When Lee's reluctance to confide in me had driven me to prove he could trust me, I didn't know my cut would bleed so long. At any rate, Robert's scowl vanished. He got up from his typewriter and came to me. "Gee, I should have noticed!" he said. "What happened?" His voice carried a mixture of concern and curiosity. I avoided the details and switched subjects, saying I could not even kiss.

"Well," he answered, bending down and kissing me in the small of my back, "As long as your other end is still okay!" in his most adorable voice. Old one-trick Robert! Then he handed me five dollars and said: "Hope you don't mind going to the store by yourself to get groceries. I want to finish this short story." I would have laughed if I could. "Be sure to spend it wisely," he instructed me, as he began typing again.

As I picked up my purse, I compared Robert's concern about carefully spending five dollars, to Lee's fear of being terminated by professional killers.[205] Robert's world seemed so microscopic. As I opened the kitchen door to leave, Robert called out, "Be sure and get Skippy peanut butter!"

As I closed the door, I juxtaposed the priorities of the two men in my life: One was worried about saving himself and his loved ones from death, and the other wanted a particular brand of peanut butter. At least Robert's problem would be easy to solve.

<u>Tuesday, July 30, 1963</u> When I got on the bus, I was happy to see Lee waiting for me in the back, and I sat down next to him. The swelling in my lip had increased overnight and was really sore, so I brought a cup of

---

[205] Years later I learned that at a critical time in Robert's young life, his parents lost everything and temporarily had to move in with his grandparents. It was humiliating and stressful for them, and it left Robert terrified about being financially helpless.

ice to chew on. Lee said he was concerned about the swelling. Then we had the following exchange:
Me: "Gave up on the cut staying shut, so I sewed a couple stitches in."
Lee: "Ouch! I know how that hurt. He should have taken you to a doctor." **Me:** "I used a lot of Oragel. He didn't know. He was writing a short story. I didn't want to interrupt." **Lee:** "So you wouldn't interrupt me if I sat there, writing a short story?" **Me:** "Kiss you, maybe. You'll be a good writer." **Lee:** "Even with my execrable spelling?" **Me:** (pleased he could pronounce so many difficult words he couldn't spell!)[206] "That's only dyslexia. I just found out about it, in a journal." **Lee:** "What's dyslexia?" **Me:** "The brain sees letters upside down or backwards. It has nothing to do with your writing talent. Some famous writers have had the same problems." **Lee:** "Really? They punished me for it. It's why I hated school." **Me:** "Well, dyslexia is a new discovery... Boys have it more than girls. Especially smart boys. It's a brain wiring problem. *[pause—sore mouth!]* For example, Col. Doyle is brilliant, yet he can't smell a thing! Does that mean he's stupid? *[pause]* No, of course not. It's bad wiring! Well, you're not stupid. You just have to work around it. How you conquered Russian, with its weird letters, I don't know."
Lee: "I just kept trying."

Lee was obviously relieved by my explanation of his problem. Lee then told me he and Dave had been advised that an FBI raid on the training camp was imminent. He was trying to stay away, so he wouldn't get arrested and be exposed as a militant anti-Castroite. But being absent too much might seem suspicious to the others, so Dave was going to spread some plausible excuses. I was starting to see the daily dangers that an undercover agent in Lee's world might face.

At Reily's, an unusually high pile of credit problems arose, requiring a lot of phone calls to make with slurred speech because of my sore mouth. After about an hour, Mr. Monaghan showed up and started teasing me about my swollen lip. Then, in a voice loud enough for others to hear, he said I must have it examined. Once he was sure everyone within earshot thought I was going to the doctor, Monaghan pulled me aside and whispered, "Go to Ferrie's apartment!" In fact, Dave had spent the night near the training camp and again needed intervention at the lab. Monaghan said he would cover my workload at Reily's. Another blasted emergency! He even muttered something about being sorry he had ever met Dr. Ochsner.

At about 9:30, as I entered Dave's apartment, I heard a strange sound, and froze. Someone was in the house. The sound had come from Dave's bedroom, where the door was partially open.

---

[206] Lee's vocabulary was surprisingly extensive. He constantly worked on improving it.

I tiptoed down the hall and looked inside. There, I saw a young man sprawled on Dave's bed amidst a jumble of sheets, magazines, newspapers, clothes and pillows.

He was snoring. I figured it was probably Dave's new lover, who was spending more and more time there. My larger concern was that he might wake up at any moment and find me there. I could not be discovered in Dave's apartment. It might blow everything, so I quietly gathered up what I needed and left. I'd have to do the work at Dr. Mary's apartment. As I rode the Louisiana Avenue bus to her apartment, I felt my frustrations percolating. My time to work on the Project was being whittled away on all fronts. I could no longer read and write reports at home because Robert was literally underfoot. Meanwhile, I was stretched to the limit, working at two demanding jobs and trying to deal with the needs of two very different lovers. And now I was not even able to work at Dave's, because his young lover was sleeping in his bed!

As soon as I arrived at Dr. Mary's, I wrote her a note to vent my frustrations, then turned my attention to our tissue cultures. There was so much to do that I wondered whether I would finish in time to get back to Reily's and make my token appearance there. But then Lee arrived, carrying a blue duffle bag. He had made a token appearance of his own at the training camp early that morning, staying a few hours. That made it appear that he was unaware of the raid to come. Now he cleaned himself up in Mary's bathroom and put on a fresh shirt. Soon, Dr. Mary arrived, too. She'd spent the morning performing surgery at the Crippled Children's Hospital. She brought welcome antibiotics for my mouth, at Lee's request, and I took them at once. Seeing how much work was still needed, Dr. Mary and Lee pitched in. By noon, we were caught up, except for some microscope work. "I'll wait for her, so she won't have to go home by herself," Lee said to Mary. He then asked me, "Are you feeling better?" My mouth was still so sore that I was reluctant to speak, but I fluttered my eyelashes at him. Dr. Mary, who was in a rare good humor,[207] caught my gesture. "There's only one life!" she declared. "You two go on," she said. "I'll finish up." It was nice to see her break out of her professional shell.

Dr. Mary Sherman. She kept things professional.

[207] Dr. Sherman was a tough bird in the lab and was usually not particularly friendly, being overworked herself with these additional hours of intensive labor. Her attitude when we met outside lab work was entirely different. That's when I felt we were real friends.

To get time with Lee was worth a call to Reily's, where I took the one sick day I had left. We took a taxi from Dr. Mary's apartment and headed to The Roosevelt Hotel. In its gilded chambers, we relished another wonderful afternoon of love, far from the care-filled world.
Aware of our uncertain future, Lee's tenderness drained all the tension from me, even without kissing my wounded mouth. Once again, we reviewed our plans. How could we meet safely in Mexico? Or should we go on to a friend Lee knew in the Cayman Islands? We couldn't escape together: that would be noticed. We decided to learn Spanish. After enjoying some extravagant pastries and cold milk, we relaxed together, made love, and pretended we hadn't a care in the world. At the end of it all, Lee took me by taxi to our local Piggly Wiggly grocery. And why? *So I wouldn't get lost!* Lee taught me the way to and from The Wiggly. I had to avoid Winn-Dixie now, because Lee had brought Junie with him to my place so many times, she would surely call out to me now, if she saw me at Winn-Dixie when Junie was there with Marina. Piggly-Wiggly would have to be my grocery store from now on, but Lee promised to bring me bread and milk, from time to time, to save me a trip or two.

Wednesday, July 31, 1963 I was at work next morning, as usual, when Lee called and said the FBI had raided the training camp across the lake. And yes, he was safe! I had just finished typing a letter for Mr. M. As I handed it to him, I mentioned the raid. "I already know," Monaghan said. "Mr. Reily told me." Then, looking at my letter, he added, "It won't be long now before I have a real secretary again. We're going to try out a new girl in your spot this afternoon." Despite Ochsner's wanting me to stay with Reily another month, Personnel disagreed and had immediately ordered an ad in the *Times-Picayune* to get rid of me the moment Lee was fired. It appeared July 20, and I saved a copy of it as a souvenir. "You know, I'll miss those rich timbres of yours on the Dictaphone," I told him. "What I do for my country!" he replied.

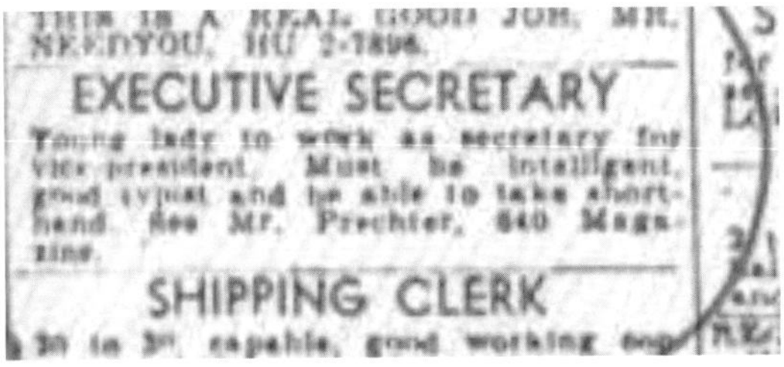
EXECUTIVE SECRETARY

Young lady to work as secretary for vice president. Must be intelligent, good typist and be able to take shorthand. See Mr. Prechter, 840 Magazine.

SHIPPING CLERK

The July 20 ad: "Young lady to work as secretary for vice president. Must be intelligent, good typist and be able to take shorthand…"

Monaghan muttered, "You need to go back to your lab today," he said, "after you show her what's in your desk. Then I'll work with her." By now, we'd tried out a couple of girls. but they hadn't met Mr. M's needs, so a new ad, mentioning good pay had been ordered.

An attractive woman appeared who seemed bright, was a good typist, took shorthand and had mature phone skills — a real secretary! [208] And he wouldn't have to cover for her! She didn't have a sore, swollen mouth slurring her speech, either. Unfortunately for him, it turned out that she was divorced (she hadn't mentioned it on her application, and her background report was in the process.) Monaghan would have to try again. Even so, Monaghan declared that my last day at Reily's would have to be August 16th. By then, he surely would have a replacement. With so much to do now in the Project, I was being stretched thin. As always, I worked through lunch so the staff would see me at my desk when they returned from their lunch break. I looked oh-so-dedicated to my job!

Then I headed to Dave's to work on the Project. Lee was already there when I arrived.I was now training Lee on how to keep the bioweapon alive outside the lab so it could be transported to Cuba from Mexico City. Lee would pass on the same instructions to the medical tech who was to pick it up. Everything was oral: nothing was to be written down.

Several hours later, I returned to Reily's to clock out, then headed to Tulane University, where Lee and I met again. We wanted to figure out

how to get quickie divorces in Mexico. We also discussed thoroughly, for the first time, where we might go and how we would live after Mexico City. Luckily, Tulane's Latin American Library had plenty of answers.[209] Of special interest to us was a poster there, announcing an upcoming exhibit about an excavation now being conducted on the Islet of Cancun by Tulane archaeologist, **Wyllys Andrews**. Lee recognized the unusual name and said he was connected to the CIA. That got us interested in the entire area. Andrews and his son were presently living on a little coconut plantation on Cancun. They would be returning to Tulane by the end of August. It was safe, remote, and all mapped out, with its own airstrip on the beach, so we could meet there! On an old map, we saw that Cancun was also called "Kankun" – meaning "Basket of Snakes." This was only 1963, so there was no city there.

---

[208] I was paid near-minimum wage for my cover job, which Personnel forgot to upgrade, so a new ad mentioning GOOD pay was placed, to attract a truly competent secretary.

[209] "The **Latin American Library** Special Collections at Tulane University is one of foremost archives and rare books libraries dedicated to Latin America and the Caribbean in the world. The collections are topically wide-ranging but have special strengths in the following areas: Mesoamerican anthropology, archaeology, and history..."REF: https://libguides.tulane.edu/special_collections_LAL

However, Lee said we would end up staying in a "fine hotel." I thought it was a joke at the time. Even so, nothing was set in stone. In the end, our plans would change drastically from this tentative, initial plan. Still, our whole lives were ahead of us. Lee was only 23. I was 20. We had dreams.

We wanted world peace and equality among all people. We believed in the essential goodness of people. We were willing to sacrifice a lot.

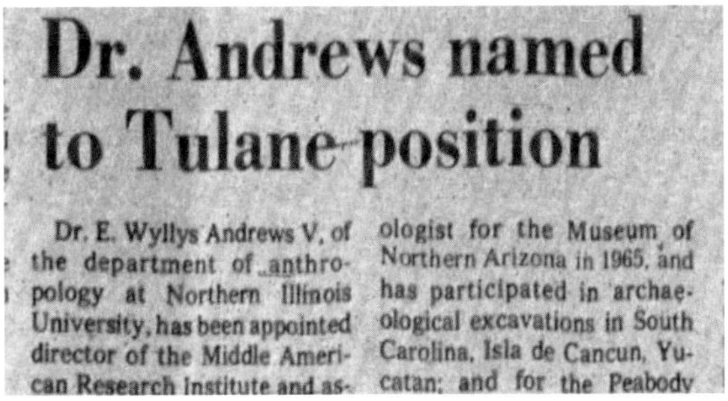

Dr. Andrews named to Tulane position

Dr. E. Wyllys Andrews V, of the department of anthropology at Northern Illinois University, has been appointed director of the Middle American Research Institute and as- ologist for the Museum of Northern Arizona in 1965, and has participated in archaeological excavations in South Carolina, Isla de Cancun, Yucatan; and for the Peabody

In 1975, Wyllys Andrews became Director of Tulane's Middle American Research Institute. "After his death in 1971, Andrew's son, E. Wyllys Andrews V, served as director of the Middle American Research Institute at Tulane, from 1975 until 2009 and continued as an emeritus professor."[210]

Perhaps we could become a husband-wife team. I'd be a doctor. He would be a social worker and an anthropologist. We'd write science fiction and get it published together. We'd work among the deprived people in the Yucatan, or in Central America, and explore ancient ruins. We'd follow Kennedy's Peace Corps ideals and perhaps explore the whole world that way. But the reality was, for the present, we had to remain committed to our missions. Even so, we continued perusing Tulane's wonderful Latin American collection, full of ideas about our future, with some intriguing books stirring our interest. One was about the ancient Maya, with old photos of a primitive village in the Yucatan, not far from Chichen-Itza, which we already wished to explore. Now, Lee asked me, again, "Would you really go to a place like that with me? We could live in that little village awhile."

"Nothing would thrill me more!" I told him, excited at the prospect.

"I need to get in better shape," Lee told me. "I did get some workouts at the training camp," he added, "but I need to do more. Marina doesn't like the outdoors, so that's made it harder."

"You're already in perfect condition," I told him. "Your legs are like steel. I've had problems myself, getting the right kind of exercise."

"What about hunting?" he asked.

"For survival, sure," I told him. "I had a boyfriend who hunted."

"So you would be able to cook, in the rough?"

---

210 https://www.ebay.com/itm/ARCHEOLOGIST-E-W-ANDREWS-SIGNED-POSTCARD-1956-MERIDA-YUCATAN-MAYAN-MEXICO-/154082247328

"Be it snake, gator, deer or frog, I can do it," I told him. "I can render fat from white grubs to grease a skillet, if the meat is too lean. Then there are cat-tails. As for ant eggs — "

"I get the picture," Lee said. "How did you learn all that?"

"It started in Girl Scouts. We had a 'survival' camp-out. I cooked a hamburger meal for our troop on a stove made from a big can. 'Twas a great success, until they learned the hamburger was made of worms."

"So, you wouldn't find a walking tour of Mexico a life-threatening experience?" Lee's eyes were shining with hope. "I'd go today! Right now, if I could!" I told him.

"God, I thank you!" Lee said, his eyes looking up at the ceiling. "You've sent me the woman of my dreams!" We started to kiss, which wasn't a good idea with my mouth as it was, but then a librarian came around the corner. "Does Robert like camping?" Lee asked. "Did he take you places like that?" I tried not to laugh. "He took me spelunking, scuba diving, rock hunting... But since he'd just had a case of mono, he said he was too tired. He basically watched. Once, when I went through a challenging crawlway with a few spelunkers, he just walked to the other end to see if we made it out alive. Actually," I confessed, "Robert only pretended to like any of it." To Lee's further questions, I finally admitted, "He said, 'As for the guitar, I learned it to impress you. Same for everything else. And now that I've got you, I have to go on to the rest of my list.'"

"Good God!" Lee said. "That's amazing."

"He also said, if he hadn't done those things, I wouldn't have married him. So he did them. Then he said, 'But now we have to give up frivolities, because the real world runs on money. You'll be grateful when we're rich.'"

"Well," Lee said, "...a wench on his knee will spend it when he's old."

Lee then asked about fishing, which he loved. I waxed eloquent, for I'd been fishing ever since I was three, with parents, uncles, cousins and grandfathers, beginning with Nickerbocker Lake with sunfish, and ending with Tarpon and Marlin fishing in Tampa Bay. "We'd be able to get fat on fish, along the rivers," Lee commented. "We'd need a good knife or two, and camping equipment," I put in. On we talked, about our college educations, our future, and the world's problems.

The Mayaland Hotel lobby. Built in 1939, the hotel is next to Chichen-Itza, visible beyond the archway. Mayaland is indeed "a fine hotel." Lee had said we'd end up in "a fine hotel." I thought he was joking.

We returned to Tulane's Latin American Library a few more times. A new book, *The Lost World of Quintana Roo*, intrigued us. Lee said there was a CIA presence in Merida.He had been asking around. Merida also had a university. Lee never indicated that we would actually move to Merida, but it was a well-known city in the Yucatan, and we hoped to marry there. [211]

.

Thursday, August 1, 1963 I trained my replacement in the morning, then left Reily's after lunch hour to meet Lee at Mancuso's restaurant. Lee was already there, drinking coffee with David Lewis and Jack Martin, but I sat at a table as far away as I could, pretending to read a paper, since Dave did not want me to speak to Jackass Martin. When the two investigators left, I joined Lee, who noted disapprovingly that David Lewis had started smoking.

As we walked out, Lee pointed to a well-dressed Cuban kid hurrying toward Banister's office. This was Carlos Quiroga. Because Quiroga's father was locked up in one of Castro's prisons and his mother still lived in Cuba, Lee didn't trust him. With the kind of family pressure that could be put on him, he could be forced to spy for Castro, even though he proclaimed that he hated the man. It hadn't been easy to get Lee to talk about his work, but those barriers were coming down. So now, I dared ask Lee to tell me more about the raid, reminding him that Dave would probably tell me a lot anyway. Slowly, as we walked toward the French Quarter, Lee described what happened. Only the munitions storage area had been raided. Lee joked that the FBI told the media that the U-Haul and nearby house was a "training camp." A handful of Cuban wannabe rebels and a couple of rightwing gringos living in the house near the U-Haul were arrested. The FBI confiscated arms, ammo, and explosives. Meanwhile, the true camp, with its dozens of MRR rebels from Miami, and its jeeps, huts and film crew, was ignored. But the raid discouraged and angered the recruits there. The FBI could go after them next. Instead of finishing their training and getting shipped to Guatemala to prepare for an invasion of their homeland, most of them now wanted to return to Miami and CIA protection. Outwardly, Guy Banister displayed anger over the FBI raid, but the big anger was in the hearts of the anti-Castro Cubans, who saw the raids as a cruel betrayal.

---

[211] When Lee applied for his Mexican visa in September, William Gaudet, a CIA asset who wrote The Latin American Report (office was in The Trade Mart) had the number just before Lee's. He said he never saw Lee, but coincidentally, when Lee set off for Mexico City, he flew to Merida, where we planned to get quickie divorces and marry. In the 1964 Polk Directory for New Orleans, after years in The Big Easy, Gaudet indicated that he had [wisely] moved to Mississippi!

Instead of JFK helping them retake their homeland, as he had promised in Miami after the Bay of Pigs, the President was doing nothing. It stoked their hatred. There was serious talk that "somebody needed to shoot that bastard."

But how did the FBI find their stash of explosives and ammo? Who gave them its location? Lee finally told me that he did. He had been instructed to give the FBI "a map." Lee explained the game inside the game. Giving the map to the FBI proved Lee was a trusted FBI informant to the local Bureau. That would provide him some FBI protection in case a problem with the corrupt police developed, if Lee got arrested in his upcoming FPCC demonstrations. "Arrested?" I asked.

"Remember the news article about the fake drug dealer?" Lee reminded me. He said he had to get 'in trouble' to buff up his pro-Castro image. He would soon be passing out Fair Play for Cuba flyers and defending Castro's Cuba on radio and TV. It was all being set up now. That would make it safer for him to courier the bioweapon to Mexico City without suspicion. But such a blatant display of loyalty to "Uncle Fidel" would shock and infuriate the rebels who had worked with him at the training camp. The FBI was currently fixing that problem by warning the MMR's supporters that yes, they should "Get their butts back to Miami." Most of the MRR (CDC) recruits had to be gone before Lee went public.[212]

To bolster his image of innocence, Lee offered his Marine-based expertise to the local anti-Castroites while the MRR rebels were still in town. That made him look good as an anti-Castro warrior.[213]

Then, after the rebels left, and it was safer, he'd put on his show as pro-Castro. Carlos Bringuier –who knew the truth—would make a scene to generate the desired publicity. Bringuier would pretend to be outraged at Lee's earlier offer to "help" when he saw Lee on the streets handing out pro-Castro literature. The argument would go like this: the same fellow who had offered to help the Cuban patriots in their fight against Castro was now promoting Castro! *How dare he? Outrageous*! It would be the excuse needed to make a scene that would get mentioned in the papers. I reviewed how Lee's ploy was patterned after the

---

[212] How many spies did Castro have out there? On Jan. 31, 1980, the Rev. Manuel Espinoza released the names of 92 of Castro's spies, many of them undetected since the beginning, which were listed by *The Miami News.*

[213] Lee's offer to "help" was to make him look innocent while the MMR rebels were still in town. After the MMR's were gone, Lee could then portray himself as "pro-Castro," which would label his offer to "help" anti-Castroites as nothing but an attempt to infiltrate the training camp and expose anti-Castro activities to the FBI. That would gave "anti-Castro" Carlos Bringuier an excuse to attack Lee on Canal Street as a "traitor." From what Lee told me, Bringuier knew Lee only pretended to be pro-Castro.

newspaper article back in May that he had shown me, where a 23-year-old "clean-cut" "collegiate type" got himself and several bad guys arrested, after which the drug dealers thought the 'good guy' was 'one of them.' Lee planned to do the same. "It's a problem, Juduffki," Lee went on. "I have to run my 'demonstration soon. It can't be put off — even though it's practically on top of the raid." If Lee got arrested, he did not dare carry enough money to post bail. That would make him look too prosperous. Instead, he had set aside money with Marina to cover the problem so he wouldn't spend the night in jail as a "Commie," at the mercy of the police.

Lee would ask his uncle to pick up the money from Marina to post bail. He said the anti-Castroites in on the ploy would yell at him, shove him and stomp on his flyers, but it was all a sham. He would even wear a sandwich board as a kind of shield. There was no real danger.[214] If, however, angry anti-Castroites not privy to the charade joined in, he could find himself in the hospital instead of jail. That's why David Ferrie would be putting on an anti-Castro demonstration of his own, farther down Canal St. Even so, there was a chance of danger. "Can't you get it put off until it's safer?" I asked.

"I tried," Lee said. "Originally, they wanted me to do it this week, while Garrison was still out of town, to look like a protest against the raid on the camp. They didn't seem to care that every Cuban in town would want to beat me up."

"So, you got the date changed?"

"I got it delayed until the 9th," he said. To protect Lee, the FBI's Warren deBrueys promised to find somebody else to blame for the raid. The problem was that Banister wanted Lee to take the blame, as that would provide more evidence to support Lee's new pro-Castro image.

Fortunately for Lee, a real pro-Castro spy had indeed infiltrated the training camp. His name was Fernando Fernandez. He was picked up near the scene of the raid, then let go. Banister's informants were now helping Lee spread the word that Fernandez was the traitor. Currently, Dave Ferrie was still out of town, but Jack Martin and David Lewis had just been told Lee's "official story" which went like this:

1. Fernandez, pretending to be anti-Castro, asked Lee to give him a map on how to get to the munitions cache. **2.** After the raid, Lee would say that he now realized Fernando was a traitor who gave the map to the FBI. **3**. Banister would support the tale by sending his people everywhere to warn the Cubans about Fernandez. **4**. Fernandez would try to say that Lee gave the map to the FBI, to get him off the hook. But Fernandez was in for a surprise.

---

[214] NOLA Lt. Francis Martello told the Warren Commission he thought the incident was staged.

The FBI had possession of a letter he'd tried to mail to a high Cuban official, incriminating himself as pro-Castro. The FBI planned to use the letter to expose Fernandez to the entire anti-Castro world. Lee explained that pro-Castro spies were a dime a dozen, so it was no great loss for the FBI to expose Fernandez. It was preferable to Fernandez' attempt to label Lee as an FBI informant, which could have ruined Lee's campaign to appear pro-Castro. "We'll send out threats," Lee said. "Enough to scare him back to Miami. Once he's there, we'll say he left New Orleans because everybody found out he was with the FBI." Poor Fernando's days as Castro's spy would be over.

By now, we had reached the Acme Oyster Bar on Bourbon Street, just as the lunch crowd started to filter in, and we savored the blast of air conditioning. My mouth was still sore, but oyster stew is nice and soft!

We ate quietly and conversed in simple Russian. It would be the second-last time I could pose as Marina. She was so obviously pregnant now. Lee spoke to me tenderly about his wife's pregnancy, knowing I wouldn't be jealous. "She is carrying my son," he said firmly. "I'll call him David."

"And if it's a girl?"

"Junie will have a little sister!"

"Named David?" We laughed. Then, a waiter came to our table. "The boss wants to see you over at La Louisianne," he said. Without a word, Lee got up and went next door. When he returned, I sensed the change in his mood. "I have to go out to the Town and Country Motel," he said. "Again. Marcello's people need me to run an errand. I'll meet you at Dave's after that." It was another "favor," as they call it, but I started to see that our free meals weren't so free, after all. "I don't mind doing it," Lee said. "While I'm out there, I'll talk to Marcello's people about this Fernandez character, that he's in hiding. They'll help us flush him out, so we can finger him."

The end of the story was good for Lee: once Fernandez learned he was a target, he fled New Orleans, arriving in Miami August 8, where newspaper reporters, anti-Castroites and the authorities were waiting for "the spy who had infiltrated the training camp." This "blame game" protected Lee from suspicion just in time. When Lee hit the streets of New Orleans the next day, with his pro-Castro literature, in faraway Miami the buzz amongst the anti-Castro crowd wiped out any and all talk of Lee Oswald. It was all about Fernandez:

"A spy was found in camp in August, driven to Miami and questioned by Laureano Batista . . . CDP tried to turn the spy over to FBI, but Bureau had no jurisdiction ...Fowler points out there were two camps -- one CDP where the spy, Fernando Fernandez, was caught; another run by ultra conservatives . . .

Turns out CDP camp didn't break up when the spy was caught (claim they knew he was there all the time and kept him for protection against other infiltrators)…" (The CDP was a branch of the MRR). Until the news broke, I didn't know how things would go. Would Fernandez get disgraced in time? To calm me a little, Lee told me the name of the ringleader who would "attack" him at the upcoming "protest" – Dr. Carlos Bringuier. "Bringuier will play the 'let's pretend' game," Lee said. "He knows who I really am, of course. But he can never tell." [215] I knew who Bringuier was. He wrote blazing letters to the local newspapers demanding stronger anti-Castro actions in U.S. foreign policy. Lee said the CIA considered Bringuier an asset. He had a stack of anti-Castro picket signs in his secondhand store on Canal Street, ready to wave in front of the cameras whenever big-shot politicians came to town. Though young, Bringuier was experienced in street demonstrations-- the perfect actor to create an aura of outrage-- so Lee had recruited him to lead the fake attack. Maybe Lee told me his name because we'd stopped at a Cuban second-hand store to buy fresh clothes after the bloody incident at Charity Hospital. Maybe it was Carlos' store.

On **Sunday, August 4, 1963** I met Lee in the Catholic playground located about halfway between our apartments, where Lee was writing a letter to the FPCC as he sat on a bench beside me. As I played with Junie on my lap (perhaps that's why the letter is written a bit sloppily), Lee wrote to the FPCC's leader, Vincent T. Lee. He predicted that "*Through the efforts of some exile gusanos* [anti-Castro 'worms'] *a street demonstration was attacked and we were officially cautioned by police.*

---

[215]REF: Richard Billings' *New Orleans Journal*: http://www.jfk-online.com/billings2.html Bringuier became a traitor who pretended the ploy never existed. He even sold Lee's Marine Manual--which was important to Lee and had been only loaned to Bringuier -- rather than return it to Marina Oswald, its rightful possessor. Bringuier tried to implicate Lee by telling the Warren Commission that Lee was a pro-Castro infiltrator: " (viz p 33 of transcript of testimony by BRINGUIER. Also, the Cuban"spy" FERNANDO FERNANDEZ "then in New Orleans, Louisiana, by letter to CARLOS LECHUGA, former Cuban Ambassador to Mexico, warned him to be alert for the period prior to August 8 (1963), and, according to BRINGUIER, it was on August 5 (1963) that Oswald attempted to infiltrate BRINGUIER's anti-CASTRO organization at New Orleans." Note **Silvia Duran**, Cuban Consulate secretary, who had an affair with **Lechuga**, would later interact with Lee in Mexico City. REF: http://jfk.hood.edu/Collection/OINO%20Appendix/Pages%20661-665.pdf However, if Fernando Fernandez is warning Castro's ambassador about Lee Oswald's infiltration attempt, that means Oswald was NOT working for Castro. The letter had been intercepted by a training camp member Fernandez had trusted, who, suspicious, opened it and learned that Fernandez expected something bad to happen before August 8 (probably the raid).

This incident robbed me of what support I had leaving me alone. Nevertheless thousands of circulars were distributed..." (But Lee only distributed about 200 flyers!) This letter, predicting the long-planned attack, was written *five days before Lee's demonstration.* Lee would ask me how to spell a certain word, here and there, as I played with little Junie.

This improved the letter's spelling considerably. Later, researchers would wonder at Lee's vastly improved spelling! [216] Lee brought Junie with him. I later mailed the letter.[217] **On Monday, August 5**, I had to cover for Dave again at his apartment. I was told he had flown to Miami. But when I arrived, I heard a strange sound... *Uh-oh!* Thinking it was Dave's lover in the bedroom, I tiptoed past the closed door, when suddenly, I heard Dave groaning. At first, I thought somebody was beating him, and in anger, I grabbed a frying pan, preparing to defend him! But no—it was Dave! He was groaning as he whipped himself with an electric cord. Tremendously embarrassed, at first Dave slammed the door and hid from me. My sudden appearance had been a shock. But after a while, Dave allowed me to give some attention to the literal stripes he'd laid on his own back. He was tormenting himself because he'd tried to force a teen to sign a letter he needed to help clear him of immorality charges by Eastern Air Lines. But he'd molested that teen, too, and now was full of remorse.

The rope with its thumbtacks, that he had knotted tight around his waist, was medieval torture. It broke my heart to see him like that. Dave confessed that he had been going through a period of penance, trying to stop his habit of sleeping with teenaged boys. Tears in my eyes, I confessed to him that at one point, I had also gone through some similar penitential ordeals, when I had decided to offer my life up to God, to become a nun. It had been my deepest secret. Then I told him how bitter I'd become when my father abducted me.

---

[216] Circumstantial evidence that I helped Lee with his FPCC letters: https://jfk.boards.net/.../erasing-past-protect-fairytale... (QUOTE)"Until the authorship of the letters to FPCC is settled,I think it reasonable to suppose that Oswald did not compose them, at least not without help. If the FBI did not employ Oswald or work with him, then who wrote the letters he addressed to the Fair Play for Cuba Committee in New York? Oswald alone certainly didn't. Whoever wrote the letters to New York was coherent, commanded a good vocabulary, rarely misspelled a word, and punctuated decently.==that happened to be me (Judyth Vary Baker)==see Appendix (Harold Feldman, OSWALD and the FBI, *The Nation*, January 1964

[217] Later, I would worry about fingerprints that might be on the letter. I wrote to Lord Bertrand Russell about it: as author, I will gladly explain all details as to what happened, which have been garbled by Joan Mellen, to any researcher with honorable intentions.

Now, I no longer—as he knew—believed that God existed. Dave responded that even a 'creature' like he was, could be forgiven because God is love and He knows our hearts. He declared that God would not let me die an atheist. This incident created a bond between us. As we talked, and I attended to his injuries, Dave told me I had now become his friend for life, and that he would stick his neck out for me in times of trouble. He then left on his Harley. He had to hurry back to Miami, where his FAA hearing (to get his job back with Eastern Air Lines) was going into a second session. I don't know if he got there in time for his own hearing.

Friday, August 9, 1963 Lee's staged pro-Castro drama would occur today in the heart of the Central Business District, in the 700 block of Canal Street. On my way to work, Lee gave me a stack of the flyers.

He wanted to save about 300 back from destruction at the hands of Carlos Bringuier or the police. Since I always had "long lunches" on Friday, I was the ideal person to deliver them to attorney Dean Andrews, who planned to view the demonstration at his office door. Lee said a second demonstration was already in the plans. Now, I have a penchant for perfection, and when I saw that some of the flyers had margins too high at the top, I decided to fix them.

FPCC flyers were printed mostly on yellow paper, but other colors were also used. Some needed trimming. Most were destroyed. Note location on flyer to the left was covered with tape. However, it may never have been stamped. Note flyer on the right has a thinner top margin, which is why I say I might have trimmed it.

The mail room empty at lunch time, I trimmed the worst of the flyers, using Reily's paper-cutter. I threw the trimmings and a couple of crumpled-up flyers into the trash can. When I returned to Mr. M's desk, our newest candidate for secretary was waiting for more training. After showing her what we could expect with Monday's avalanche of problems, there was time for just a coffee break before we continued. Since the secretary had missed lunch (and so did I), when her training session was finished, Monaghan invited her out to eat and I took off for Canal Street, carrying the flyers with me in a sack. I reached Canal Street at maybe 3:00 PM. I soon spotted Lee, who was wearing a short-sleeved white shirt, a brown tie, and slacks.

He also wore a protective "sandwich board" which had leaflets and flyers attached. A half-dozen men stood there glaring at him. As I approached Lee, I said softly, "I'm so worried for you, honey." "Well," he replied cheerfully, straightening his placard, "I'm going to be all right. Dave's back in town, just a few blocks away, and Carlos will be here any minute, so don't worry." He handed me a flyer: I pretended to be

interested in it and began walking away. I knew better than to be seen with Lee more than a moment, so I continued down Canal a couple blocks, looking for Dave. Then, afraid I'd miss Andrews, I turned back. Lee was now quite busy handing out flyers. As I walked past him, Lee indicated that it was time to give my flyers to **Dean Andrews**, who had now stepped out of his office nearby. I had briefly met Andrews previously when Lee pretended to be checking on his protest about his undesirable discharge from the Marines.[218] Andrews was Carlos Marcello's most recognizable attorney. His presence was unforgettable. He was overweight in th cutest way, with a face round as a doughnut. He always wore office clothes and dark sunglasses. I was told he had lots of kids and was a good musician. I spotted him less than a block away.[219] As I approached Andrews, I could see that his shirt was soaked with sweat and he appeared ready to have a stroke. With a friendly smile, he said that he just had to see "the fireworks." I handed him the flyers, saying they were from Lee. He flattened them and put them in his briefcase. "Gonna watch?" he asked. "No," I said nervously.

"You're his girlfriend, right?" Dean stated it as if it were a fact. I told him I was married, and so was Lee. "That makes no difference in this town," Dean replied, laughing. At that moment, Carlos Bringuier and two of his friends made their entrance and immediately began heckling Lee and pushing him around. Lee was remaining calm under the hot sun and at first pretended to ignore them.

---

[218] Lee had already made his protests. The true reason for his two visits to Andrews was to establish Andrews as "Lee's attorney" in case of future need. On Nov. 22, 1963, Andrews was indeed contacted in his hospital bed and asked to function as Lee's attorney, by the mysterious "Clem Bertrand" who was probably Clay Shaw, according to New Orleans D.A. Jim Garrison. The contact was made, I believe, as a token to assuage the concerns of Lee's Uncle Charles "Dutz" Murret, that his friend Carlos Marcello would "do what he could" to help.

[219] Dean Andrews' office was at 921 Canal.

Then, what had been a disorganized group of bystanders suddenly moved in to surround Lee.

He gave me a quick glance that meant "get out of here," as the men engulfed him. Among them was the dark Latino I'd seen at Dave's apartment, who had helped Dave and Lee with the training film. Was he there for Lee's protection, or was this physically powerful man now enraged, because Lee was handing out pro-Castro flyers? Being so short, I couldn't see what was happening now, but I realized Lee would worry about my safety if I stayed, so I began walking away as fast as I could.

I heard some Cubans shouting terrible curses in Spanish at Lee, with voices full of hate and scorn. Suddenly, I spotted a policeman and waved urgently at him. I told him there was a commotion on Canal Street, that a crowd had gathered, and people were screaming at each other. I was worried that somebody might get hurt. The policeman headed to Canal Street, and I hurried back to Reily's. It was all I could do. As I entered 640 Magazine St., I realized I had been working in Dave's lab all week, and this was the first time in weeks that I had even been in Reily's before 5 PM.

As I exited the elevator and walked down the aisle, the big room hummed with the clickety-clack of billing clerks working with electric typewriters and adding machines. It sounded like business as usual, until the typing slowly stopped and the murmuring began. Then I saw Mr. Monaghan sitting at his desk with Mr. Prechter at his side. Both men were silently staring into the big work room as I approached.

Monaghan and Prechter together! That was a bad combination! My instincts immediately went on alert. As I walked toward Monaghan, I saw the look on his face and realized who was in trouble. It was me.

As I reached Monaghan's desk, he simply said, "You were seen with him," in a deep, vibrating voice that hissed with anger. Then he held up a crumpled yellow "Hands Off Cuba" flyer: "And you left this in the wastebasket. What in hell were you thinking?" Monaghan stood and motioned for me to follow him into the dreaded glass cubicle. Mr. Prechter followed us in, carrying my personnel file. He closed the door. "I'm asking you to sign this statement which says you have decided to resign," Monaghan said. "They're cutting you a check right now."

"And you're going to be docked for taking all those long lunches," Prechter chimed in spitefully. "You were only supposed to do that on Fridays. Where have you been spending Reily's time?"

"We'll talk about that later, Al," Monaghan said to Prechter. "She's not leaving town or anything. Go get her check."[220]

---

[220] Monaghan had been told that the project was now at its most important point, which is why I had to be absent so much.

Prechter walked back to his secretary's desk, which was close to us, but farther up in the big room. Then I turned to Monaghan and said, "I'm sorry. I didn't think anybody would notice."

"Judy," Monaghan moaned, "I have trouble equating your famous IQ with the fact that you actually spoke to Oswald in front of some thirty or forty people. And you were seen."

"It was way past lunch hour," I protested. "I didn't think anybody from Reily would see me."

"Well, the new secretary and I were out that way, and the little snitch saw you," Monaghan said, removing my things from his desk and placing them on top of the half-desk. Then he ran both hands across his neatly combed dark hair to collect his thoughts. "For your information," he continued, "Mr. Oswald was arrested a few minutes ago. They'll find out he used to work here. Everyone will be talking about it. I have to get rid of you before anyone who saw you with Oswald links you to Reily. I have no choice." Then in a soft voice, he said "I have to admit, I'm going to miss you, lousy typist though you are."

Stunned, I prepared to leave, taking comfort in the fact that the girl I had been training was not there to witness my humiliation.

Mr. Prechter soon returned and handed me a check. It was for only $10.49. *What*? "Where's my pay for the week?" I asked. *"What have you done to my paycheck?"*

"Please keep your voice down," Mr. Prechter said condescendingly. Then he told me that I'd been gone all afternoon on Tuesday, Wednesday and Thursday, so my "long lunches" would need to be evaluated. For now, my paycheck had been held back. This check was cut for today's work only. The "overtime" reflected the $1.29 "raise" in pay that Lee had arranged. If the matter were resolved in my favor, an adjusted amount would be directly deposited in my account.[221]

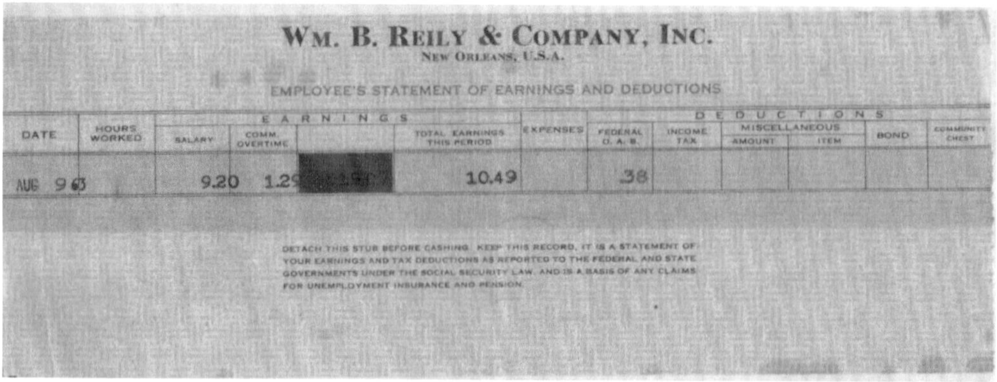

WM. B. REILY & COMPANY, INC.
NEW ORLEANS, U.S.A.

EMPLOYEE'S STATEMENT OF EARNINGS AND DEDUCTIONS

DATE	HOURS WORKED	EARNINGS SALARY	COMM. OVERTIME		TOTAL EARNINGS THIS PERIOD	EXPENSES	DEDUCTIONS FEDERAL O. A. B.	INCOME TAX	MISCELLANEOUS AMOUNT	MISCELLANEOUS ITEM	BOND	COMMUNITY CHEST
AUG 9 63		9.20	1.29	[redacted]	10.49		.38					

DETACH THIS STUB BEFORE CASHING. KEEP THIS RECORD. IT IS A STATEMENT OF YOUR EARNINGS AND TAX DEDUCTIONS AS REPORTED TO THE FEDERAL AND STATE GOVERNMENTS UNDER THE SOCIAL SECURITY LAW, AND IS A BASIS OF ANY CLAIMS FOR UNEMPLOYMENT INSURANCE AND PENSION.

221 My "raise" was in the form of "overtime" ($1.29- see check stub), unusual for a salaried position. I would have had $53.95/wk instead of the prior $46.00/wk.

Monaghan listened silently, as I tried to hold back tears of outrage. "What about my husband?" I blurted out. "What am I supposed to tell him?" Visions of Robert exploding in anger played in my head. What could I do? I could not ask Lee for money. He was in jail. Robert would soon learn that I didn't get the usual paycheck. If he knew I was fired, he would want to leave ASAP for Florida, to avoid paying Susie August's rent. It was due. If I refused to go back with him, he would demand to know why. Tenacious as he was, he could cause real problems for everyone, including himself. My mood changed from grief to fury. This was madness! As I turned to leave with my box, the head clerk of her row, Annette, slipped me a photo of herself with her fiancé.

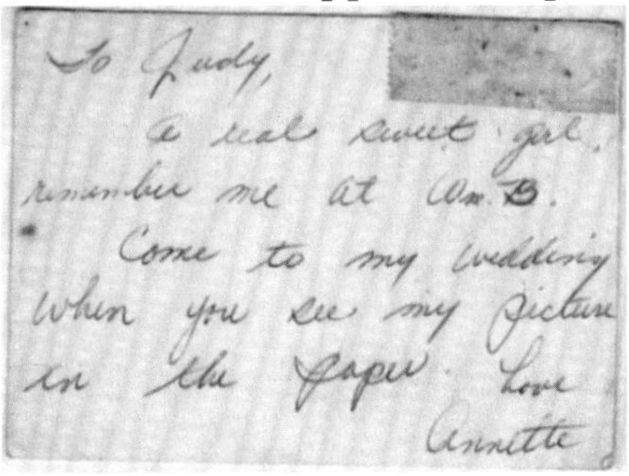
To Judy,
a real sweet girl,
remember me at Wm. B.
Come to my wedding
when you see my picture
in the paper. Love
Annette

I headed back to 1032 Marengo, determined to say nothing to Robert about losing my job. I knew that I could walk right in with my box of items from work with the photo of my clerk on top of the heap, but Robert wouldn't notice. His inability to notice much of anything around him became classic when he discovered Lee's Old Spice aftershave lotion sitting on the windowsill in the bathroom. He assumed it had been there before I moved in, and that he'd simply not noticed it before. He didn't even ask where it went, when I gave it back to Lee. Annette, whom I sometimes called "Anita" (little Annette) did get married as she had said, and became Annette Carr. We have corresponded. She acknowledged I worked for Mr. Monaghan as his secretary. I didn't remember the name of her immediate boss. Annette, long and happily married, with children and grandchildren, still lives in the New Orleans area. [222]

---

[222] **May 6, 2017:** from an Email from Annette Carr—"To answer some of your questions, I'm still married and will be celebrating another anniversary on June 20th. (53 years)**[1964].** We have 2 children, a daughter ...with 2 grandsons and a son ...with 3 children which include a set of twins that will be graduating from high school in May... My immediate boss was not Mr. Monaghan, do you remember who my boss was? He sat in the back of our area against the wall we had a small group of 3 girls working together one of them actually stood in my wedding. I really don't remember much about Reilly. I quit shortly after you left and went to work for an insurance company..." Annette has asked to stay out of the spotlight.

Saturday, August 10, 1963 I awoke on Saturday, knowing Lee was probably still in jail and had spent the night in the hands of the Commie-hating New Orleans police. I was sick with a worry that I could not share with my husband. I knew Lee was OK going to jail, if that meant it would get into the newspapers.

In case that happened. Lee did not want his pregnant, Russian-speaking wife going to the police station to bail out "the Communist." The police might be unkind to her. Therefore, he had counted on the Murrets to deliver the bail money. But on the morning of the demonstration, when Lee went to talk to Dutz about picking up the bail mone, in the event he got arrested, he learned (possibly from cousin Marilyn, who had been visiting that summer) that Dutz was out of town at a Catholic retreat. As for his Aunt Lil, Lee learned that she was in the hospital recovering from an eye operation. Despite his tight schedule, Lee immediately went to the hospital to visit her, but did not tell her of his plans, not wishing to worry her. Now, after spending the night in jail, Lee phoned his cousin Joyce Murret and asked her to pick up the bail money. He didn't want to stay in jail until Monday. But she refused to comply and hung up on him, even though she'd been on Mobile trip with him and Marina, and they had enjoyed each other's company. Only then did Lee realize what deep shame his arrest had caused his family. Finally, at midday, Carlos Marcello sent an attorney, Emile Bruneau, a "business partner" of Lee's uncle Dutz, to post bail. Lee hoped that such an obvious link to the Mafia would go unnoticed. By-and-large, it didn't.

What was I doing that weekend? Very little. I ironed Robert's clothes, worried about Lee, and fretted. As for Robert, he read and read -- and took me to bed. Between these events, I managed to peruse Susie's newspapers, listen to the radio and watch the local TV with Susie, for news of Lee. I even got Robert to go with me for a walk, so I could steer him by Lee's apartment, hoping I might get a glimpse of Lee there, to no avail. I called Dave Ferrie's apartment, but there was no answer. I called Dr. Mary, but she didn't answer, either. Robert finally noticed my fidgety state and concluded that I had PMS. I was glad he had a diagnosis that would explain my behavior.

Then, late Saturday afternoon, Lee called Susie to say that he was okay! Susie came to our door and summoned me to her living-room, where she quietly handed me the phone, as Robert continued to read another book about Hitler in the bedroom. Lee said he hadn't had a minute of privacy until now to call. He also said that he heard my job at Reily's was on the rocks, but I should not tell Robert. On Monday morning, I should leave at the normal hour, but should wait at a breakfast counter until Rev. James' Novelty Shop opened. "You'll only work at Reverend Jim's one or two hours a day," Lee said, "then we'll head to Dave's for the Project. Between the Reverend's charity and me, you'll bring home enough money to make ends meet, and you'll be able to account for your absences. You won't get lost, will you?"

After I told him I wouldn't, Lee added, "I have to go to court Monday, to pay my fine, and then do other stuff, but I'll see you Tuesday morning!" I was amazed at how cheerful Lee sounded, given that he had spent the night in jail and was about to appear in court. He didn't say so, but I knew he had to deal with his family's needs. Ironically, the loss of my job at Reily's freed me up for more hours at Dave's lab, plus more time with Lee. Robert's total lack of curiosity about my absences was a great help. He didn't even know where Rev. Jim's was for nearly two weeks, and that was only when I asked him to drop me off on his way to his job pounding the streets for Standard Coffee, when it was raining. I'd been so grateful to Mr. Monaghan, who ran Standard, for getting Robert this job. Sadly, it turned out that Robert preferred lying around our apartment, reading and writing short stories, to knocking on doors in New Orleans for Standard Coffee in the August heat, which Susie was quite happy to point out to me. Robert was paid all of $3.25 a week to sell coffee to new customers, with sales on commission. But after two weeks, they had to fire him. The reason was simple. He didn't acquire a single new customer on the route Standard gave him to develop. But was Robert worried? Nope. I made enough money to keep us afloat, while Robert enjoyed staying home, "vacationing." After all, he had a "cute little wifey-poo" who did his laundry, all the housework, worked to pay the bills, cooked him meals, and provided him with all his sexual needs. Little did he know that the young man who sometimes came over to help Susie and me with her recalcitrant wringer washing machine, and who played outside with Susie's great grandchildren, was Lee Harvey Oswald, who gave what he could to make my life better.

Monday, August 12, 1963 I left "for work" as usual, this time taking the St. Charles streetcar to Dr. Mary's apartment. She had called just after Susie returned from church on Sunday, asking if I had a few hours to spare. I expected to be involved in some intricate new laboratory procedure at her apartment. Maybe I'd be able to corner her about my internship for September, necessary to get the promised stipend. I even brought the application form for the internship with me, so she could sign it. But when I entered Dr. Sherman's apartment, I saw about a hundred mice, in cages by the front door. They had been in Dr. Mary's apartment nearly two weeks. Despite every measure, the place was now starting to reek. I had been in her apartment recently, but had not seen the mice, kept secluded in her small second bedroom, which she had converted into an office. They were backups, ready to inoculate in case significant problems arose with the marmosets. But no problem had emerged, and the African greens were now developing cancers as hoped.

Normally, Dr. Mary would have paid the maintenance man something to help her, but moving so many mice would have raised questions. We lined the back seat of her car with newspapers to protect the upholstery and started loading up the cages. As we worked, Dr. Mary said she would be taking them to the new building on Ochsner's campus, built specifically for lab animals. .[223]

She had delayed moving them earlier because such a sudden influx of mice, without their documents, might have been noticed. But now, with new projects for the Fall soon to begin, with many mice for experiments already overflowing the shelves, a few more cages would not be noticed.

As Dr. Mary drove, I told her I would miss reading her books at her apartment, but looked forward to medical school in the fall. I hoped she would still allow me to work under her tutelage in the bone lab. "Don't worry, I want you," Dr. Sherman told me. "And I've got a grant, so I can afford you." When we arrived at Dave's apartment, I gave her my completed application. Then I went inside alone to retrieve the last of the monkey tissue cultures. From now on, I would be working with human blood samples, focusing on perfecting my innovative cancer test for humans, in anticipation of using it on the volunteer. As she placed the test monkey tissue cultures into a safe container, I asked Dr. Mary to drop me off at the Tulane Medical School library. I didn't want anybody to know about Rev. James. I could walk there from the medical library without getting lost. Then, as I was about to exit her car, this good woman turned to me, smiled graciously, and took my hand. She was not the stern teacher now, but was speaking as a friend. "I know you've been worried about Lee," she said. "And I have an idea that some divorces are about to occur. Will that interfere with your plans with us?"

"I don't think so," I said as politely as I could, not knowing how much she really knew. Then I told her, "Lee said that he would try to get his people to send him to college." Lee was, in fact, spreading this myth, for which he no longer had any hope, to mask our secret plans. "If you end up in Mexico," Dr. Mary said, showing she knew more than I had expected, "I have ways myself to get you both into a university there. I hope it all works out for you," she said, with a gentle smile. Then she drove away.

As I waved goodbye, I gauged her curious question about our plans,

---

[223] I had spent plenty of time in Dr. Mary's bedroom, reading her books on her bed. She was a Book-of-the-Month Club member. I read *Annapurna, Kon Tiki*, and *The Twelfth Physician* there, from a shelf that was part of her bed's backboard. Dr. Mary also belonged to The Audubon Society. She had a large Audubon stamp collection and gave me some stamps, including a brown pelican she wanted me to paint. I still own them.

and her pregnant comment about hoping everything would 'work out.' After checking out some journals I needed from the medical library, I went to Rev. James's. I wasn't afraid of the neighborhood, just afraid I'd get lost! Once inside the cluttered shop, I was welcomed back by the lady in charge, who recognized me. Soon, I joined the others (this time, some black musicians between gigs), painting "New Orleans" on ceramic Gators and Mardi Gras masks. It never bothered me that this charity outreach (not a business) inside the store was run by colored people. I was not always the only white person there, either, but I enjoyed making an anti-segregation statement, and that was recognized by those at Rev. Jim's. At the same time, Lee was making his own anti-segregation statement by sitting with "colored people" on their side of the courtroom, waiting for the judge to fine him.

Tuesday, August 13, 1963 I returned to Tulane's medical library, this time researching ways to tag cancer cells with radioactive markers. Then I returned to Rev. Jim's. At about 1:00 P.M., Lee arrived. I could scarcely restrain myself from running into his arms! The lady in charge remembered Lee as the one who painted words backwards and moved us over to the warehouse again. This time the warehouse was hot. The big, poorly-lit storage building was filled with sculptures of gnomes, dragons and other mythological objects. We were instructed to re-paint some papier-mâche horses for a carousel that had been created for a Mardi Gras float. Then she left. Realizing that we were utterly alone, with some paint cans, Lee and I fell into each other's arms for a long, deep embrace. It was the first time I had seen him since August 9. When we finished our affectionate kisses, Lee opened some doors to let air in, and we started painting. As we worked, Lee told me about all that had happened to him. On Friday night, the three Cubans posted bond and went home. Lee was then interrogated by the police. They pinched his face and ears, and struck him, but Lee stayed cool. He endured the mistreatment without complaint and simply answered their questions. When Lee finally got served the usual jail food, he saw they'd scooped up some dirt and dead roaches, and sprinkled it on top. Lee responded by saying, "Ah, Roach à la mode!"

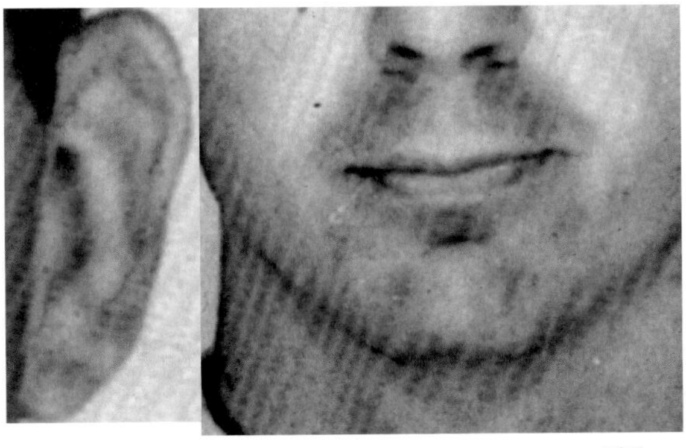

Anti-Oswald theorists said these marks were caused by 'acne.' But earlier photos show no such pattern. When Lee was filmed for TV, the pinch marks could not be seen due to less detail on TV film.

"Oh, Lee!" I said, "they were horrible to you!" Lee simply replied that they were reacting to who they thought he was --a Communist. How could he get mad at them? This steady, stoic attitude, combined with dark humor, had its effect on both the inmates and the police. The inmates with him in jail respected him and the police complied with Lee's request to speak to the FBI. Though it was Saturday, when the FBI ran a skeleton crew, an agent showed up.

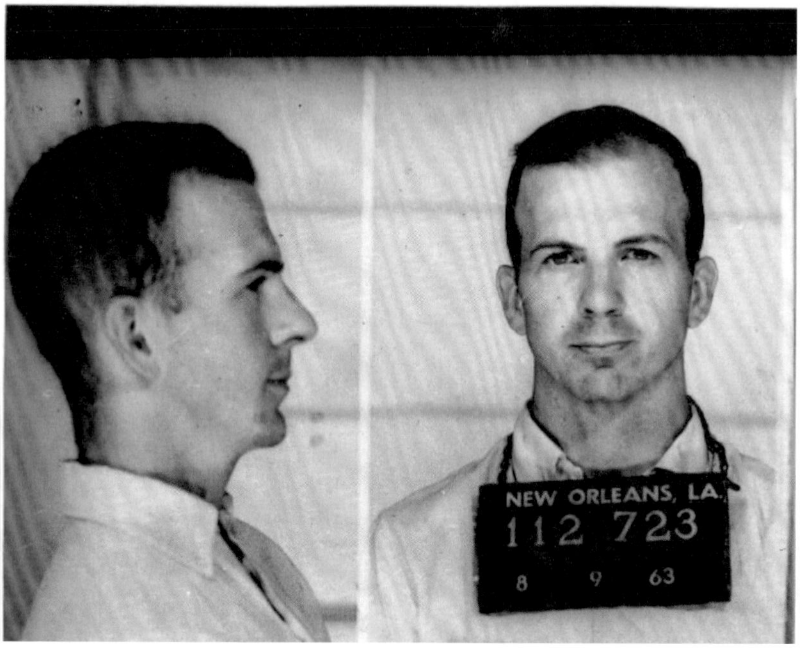

Lee's mug shot shows the marks of his abuse on his chin and ears, as well as his sideburns, which Lee let grow out while he was at the training camp.

Lee said **John Quigley**, a 27-yr-FBI veteran agent, took a long report and would give Warren de Brueys, Lee's FBI handler in New Orleans, an accurate account. A little later, a Marcello lawyer, Emile Bruneau, showed up to post bail. Then Lee was released.

Months later, New Orleans police Lt. Francis Martello, with just that brief day's exposure to the real Lee Oswald, who took so much abuse from the police without any display of anger, told the Warren Commission what he thought about Lee, as reported in the *NEW ORLEANS ITEM* on March 30, 1964:

"Oswald's image Peaceful,

Gentle" by NEIL SANDERS..."*...Lee Harvey Oswald told a New Orleans policeman in August,1963, that Russia does not have true communism — that there are "fat, stinking politicians over there, just like we have over here." Oswald had been jailed on Aug. 9, 1963, as a result of an altercation with an anti-Communist Cuban leader, Carlos Bringuier. He was interviewed while in custody by Lt. Francis Martello of the New Orleans Police Department.*

Above photo: Lee (L), Bringuier in sunglasses. Aug. 9 Canal St. demonstration.

Martello is now a major. Oswald gave the impression that he "seemed to favor President John F. Kennedy more than he did Russian Premier Nikita S. Khrushchev," Martello 'recalled. The officer observed that ***Oswald had "remained absolutely peaceful and gentle" in the face of provocation by the anti-Red Cubans during the disturbance...***"

Martello also told The Warren Commission (quote): *"Well, as far as being capable of an act,* ***I guess everybody is capable of an act, but as far as ever dreaming or thinking that Oswald would do what it is alleged that he has done, I would bet my head on a chopping block that he wouldn't do it.***"

Much later, Lee also told me of his decision to sit with the blacks on their side of the courtroom, while he waited to pay his fine. "They're my black brothers and sisters," he said, "I wanted them to know we were equals." But something more important occurred on Sunday night—an incident that brought tears to my eyes, as Lee related what had happened. That Sunday night (August 11), Lee's uncle Dutz made a surprise visit to Lee's apartment on Magazine Street. In front of Marina, Dutz expressed his keen disappointment that Lee had been arrested. Then he pointed to Fidel Castro's photo pinned to the wall and told him how disgusting that was. He ordered Lee to straighten out his life, get a job, and start taking care of his family. Lee said hearing such criticism from his uncle was a heavy blow.

"It almost felt physical," he said. "I had grown up in tough neighborhoods. All around me, kids got in trouble, got arrested. But I stayed clean. It was a point of honor. But now —"

Tears welled up in Lee's eyes as he spoke. Miserable from the tongue-lashing he'd received, Lee then walked with his uncle out to his car, leaving Marina and Junie inside. There, they continued to talk. After some minutes, Lee managed to say that "things are not as they seem." That's when Dutz turned to him, placed his hands on Lee's shoulders, and said,

"I know, son." Lee was stunned, so he asked him, "Do you understand what I am really all about?" Dutz replied, "Do you know how long Marcello and I have been friends? He told me, son." Dutz put his arms around Lee and hugged him.

"As for your wife," he said, "I don't know what she knows." He said he didn't trust her,[224] then added, "I felt if you trusted me enough — sometime, somehow — you would confide in me, and you finally did. So, I'm telling you, son — and don't forget it — I've known since you arrived in town what you're about. And I'm proud of you." [225]

Lee then told me, "He is the father I never had." I knew Lee himself did not trust Marina, but only in 2020 did I learn that Marina wrote to the Soviet Embassy on July 2, 1962, to an important KGB officer.

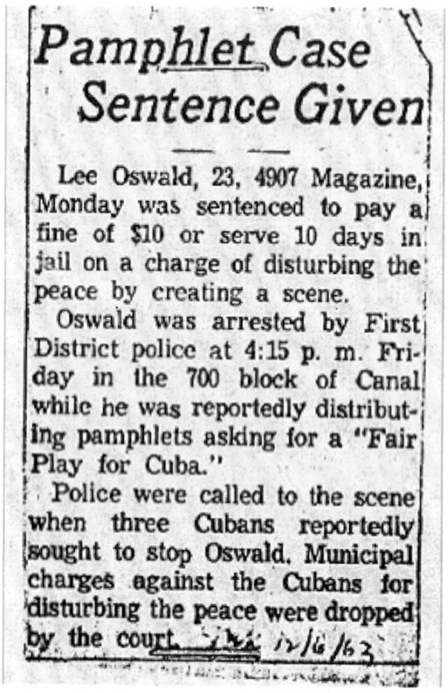

Pamphlet Case Sentence Given

Lee Oswald, 23, 4907 Magazine, Monday was sentenced to pay a fine of $10 or serve 10 days in jail on a charge of disturbing the peace by creating a scene.

Oswald was arrested by First District police at 4:15 p. m. Friday in the 700 block of Canal while he was reportedly distributing pamphlets asking for a "Fair Play for Cuba."

Police were called to the scene when three Cubans reportedly sought to stop Oswald. Municipal charges against the Cubans for disturbing the peace were dropped by the court.

She wrote that she wished to return to the Soviet Union. She hadn't been in America a month! The letter was intercepted by the FBI. [226]

After Lee told me about his Uncle Dutz knowing that, as Lee put it, he "was a good guy," he showed me a newspaper clipping. His plan had worked. He had gotten some press coverage. The media had started the task of turning Lee into a pro-Castro sympathizer. He'd already been filmed for the news reel cameras by Ochsner-friendly WDSU-TV and he was filmed again at court, but Jim Garrison had just returned from his annual stint with the National Guard, so a lot

[224]REF: http://jfk.hood.edu/Collection/Weisberg%20Subject%20Index%20Files/T%20Disk/Times-Picayune/Item%2029.pdf

[225] Unlike Dutz, Carlos Bringuier would put Lee in the worst light. Bringuier told The Warren Commission:" ... in the court you have two sides, one for the white people and one for the colored people, and ...he sat directly among them in the middle, and that made me to be angry too, because I saw that he was trying to win the colored people for his side... That is one of the things that made me to think that he was a really smart guy and not a nut." He called it a mere propaganda trick, but Lee's friend, George de Mohrenschildt revealed Lee's true intentions: "Lee was indeed all wrapped up in his work, books, his ideas on equality of all people, especially of all races; it was strange indeed for a boy from New Orleans and a Texas poor white family, purely Anglo, to be so profoundly anti- racist. "Segregation in any form, racial, social or economic, is one of the most repulsive facts of American life", he often told me. **"I would be willing any time to fight these fascistic segregationists — and to die for my black brothers."**

[226]"...in July 2, 1962, the FBI intercepted a letter from Marina Oswald to **Vitaly A Gerasimov** at the Soviet Embassy, Washington, DC., requesting permission to return to the USSR. "The FBI found it significant that Marina chose Gerasimov,...[as] as he was a top KGB case officer, in addition to a consular officer." (*The Secret History of the CIA*, p. 283, 257-258) quoted by Richard I. McManus, 2019, **Some Unpopular History of the United States** *The Lyndon Johnson Years* - Nov. 1963 to Dec. 1968

of footage wasn't aired. If Garrison saw too much of Lee, a long jail sentence instead of a fine could be the result, since Garrison was looking for an anti-communist poster child to draw some media attention to himself. That was part of the New Orleans political scene. [227] After a two-week absence from the news, Garrison would have pounced on the chance to please his constituents by targeting Lee Oswald. But Banister, Leander Perez,[228] and other segregationists wanted to make sure Garrison would go after civil rights leaders instead. Therefore, the newspaper article about Lee had to be more discrete, instead of the front-page news that was the original goal.[229] The next demonstration would have to be a quicker one, too, to make it safer for Lee. Clay Shaw's boss, Jesse Core, was now involved. He would make sure WDSU's TV cameras would come quickly to cover the action at the Trade Mart, where there was less foot traffic. I also volunteered to call yet another TV station. I hoped Lee could get on more than one channel before he had to stop the demonstration. As Dr. Ochsner had told me in our last meeting, "Your boy Oswald is going to be a movie star." Lee soon got his flyers back: Dean Andrews handed them over to whoever was in charge of Carlos Quiroga. Quiroga would later lie to Jim Garrison's team, saying he came to Lee's 4905 Magazine Street address with only a few flyers, as an excuse to spy on Lee, when he'd been given a substantial batch to deliver. Lee stamp a new address on less than half of them at that time. He'd first used 544 Camp St-- Banister's building address – then changed it to 4907 Magazine St, after which he used his post office address. Beginning with the USS Wasp leafletting back in May, each change of address uncovered new suspects.

---

[227]Researcher Ed Haslam wrote: "Concerning Alton Ochsner's and Ed Butler's INCA, **Ochsner** told the New Orleans States Item: "We must spread the warning of the creeping sickness of communism faster to Latin Americas, and to our own people, or Central and South America will be exposed to the same sickness as Cuba." (16th April, 1963)... Edgar and Edith Stern, owners of **WDSU** radio and TV, were INCA members."

[228] "Corrupt democratic politician ***Leander Perez*** Sr., a staunch segregationist, served as a district judge, district attorney, and president of the Plaquemines Parish..." REF: https://64parishes.org/entry/leander-perez

[229] In 1998, researcher Jerry Shinley wrote of Garrison's early October 1963 raid on the offices of the Southern Conference Educational Fund, Inc. (SCEF), "active in fostering civil rights for Negroes in Louisiana and other states of the South...Early in October 1963 appellant[s]...were arrested by Louisiana state and local police and charged with violations of the two statutes. Their offices were raided and their files and records seized." Shinley wrote: "Garrison 's participation in this raid raises many questions. One of them is why was that commie Lee Harvey Oswald immune to prosecution under Louisiana's Ant-Subversion laws. My suspicion is that the Louisiana authorities knew that the laws where[sic] legally questionable and wanted to save them for the SCEF raid." In fact, that's exactly what avid racist Guy Banister would have wanted.

A suspect usually tried to attend a meeting or lecture, when no such activity was ever held. Others wrote down the information, then threw the flyer away. These responses were being watched by the FBI, Customs and Banister's people. [230] But Lee saw a dark side to it all.

Lee realized his reputation in New Orleans was being systematically destroyed. Yes, Dutz knew his little secret, but who else? How could he and his family live safely in New Orleans after this? Was anybody planning a future for him? In the days ahead, as Lee prepared for Mexico City, where he was to deliver the bioweapon for transport into Cuba, he was also preparing to never return to a life in New Orleans or Dallas. But we were also in love, and since both of us no longer had a "cover job," we had time to make substantial plans. Meanwhile, Lee was scheduled to put on a final demonstration. The surprise was that the CIA and FBI were cooperating. Both agencies wanted to catch pro-Castro agents. Even Customs was involved. What concerned Lee was that he had too many masters, none of whom seemed interested in his future. He had now become too visible to be used in any clandestine operations. When these assignments were over, of what use would Lee be to any of them? Lee was not stupid. He had no real connections to any pro-Castro people. He realized that when they said he was not going to be sent to college, which was the original plan, that his true worth was zero to them. As Lee explained it, he was being used by two agencies –the CIA and the FBI --to create the impression that he was "a commie" and both agencies could plausibly deny any link to him. What would happen to him next? He could see the handwriting on the wall.

Lee Oswald at the WDSU TV studio.

[230] Quiroga's short visit to the Oswald residence, which he described later to the FBI as being an act of spying, was noticed by Mrs. Jesse Garner, who testified that Quiroga carried a **stack** of flyers, not just the few he claimed. I had entrusted Andrews with about 300 unstamped flyers.

Chapter 22
On the Air

Wednesday, August 14, 1963

The day started out solemnly at Rev. Jim's, where Lee met me. We had a lot on our minds. For one thing, we had to figure out how to camouflage the bioweapon for transportation to Mexico City and Cuba in a way that would not be noticed. We spoke to Dave from a pay phone, and he told us to expect a trip out of town, to test the weapon on a human subject. The "volunteer" would be a prisoner from Angola Penitentiary, but he would be transferred to the state mental hospital in Jackson, Louisiana where we could perform our tests in secret.

Then Lee went to Banister's office, where he picked up some unpublished medical articles for me. He also needed to retrieve the flyers that I had given Dean Andrews for safe keeping.

Most of the others had been ruined or confiscated. Andrews was not about to be seen handing Lee a stack of pro-Castro flyers for his upcoming Trade Mart demonstration, so Carlos Quiroga was sent to Lee's apartment with the flyers. This was the same nattily-dressed Cuban kid that Lee had told me not to trust. Later, Quiroga would tell Jim Garrison that he came to Lee's apartment holding just a single flyer But here is what Mrs. Jesse Garner, Lee's apartment manager, told the Warren Commission:

Mrs. GARNER - ...that Cuban or Spanish looking guy one time rang my bell in the late afternoon, kind of short, very dark black curly hair, and he had a stack of these same pamphlets in his hand...<snip> **Mr. LIEBELER** - How many pamphlets did this man have in his hand? **Mrs. GARNER** - I don't know. You know how thin those things are, and he had a stack about that high. **Mr. LIEBELER** - About 5 inches or 6 inches, maybe?... **Mrs. GARNER** - Yes.

One of the men who owned the property where the munitions dump was raided said he drove Quiroga to Lee's apartment with the flyers (Quiroga later denied that, too). Quiroga said he first went to 4907, the address on the flyer, and was then directed to 4905 (by Mr. Rogers). Lee then spent some time probing Quiroga, testing his loyalties.

"I told him I hated Cubans," Lee said. "I said this to a native Cuban, and the kid still stood there and said he was interested in joining the FPCC. So I don't trust him, and neither should you."

We headed deep into the French Quarter to the Royal Orleans Hotel, anxious to be alone. Being together and taking away all the strain of our troubles was what mattered. After some silly fun and teasing each other, we enjoyed a late lunch, after which I sang some of my grandfather Whiting's World War I ditties. I'm sure one of them was "Mademoiselle from Armentieres," after which Lee sang some raucous songs he'd learned in the Marines. Leaving the Royal Orleans, we headed to Jackson Square, walking hand-in hand through the historic streets. It was late afternoon and the heat had dissipated. But on Royal Street, the sign for WDSU-TV studios brought the real world on top of us again with this reminder of Lee's upcoming event at the International Trade Mart on Friday. It was to be televised by WDSU. Lee wanted no more arrests, so everything had to be timed just right: the TV cameras would film Lee and a couple of helpers with him. That way, Lee would not be the only person to target. Lee would hand out his "Hands Off Cuba" flyers, then would leave before any police might arrive. As for me, I intended to make a second anonymous call to WDSU-TV to report the "disturbance." WDSU had already agreed to send the film crews; they just needed a phone call or two to pretend they had received a real tip. Lee remembered my offer to call WWL-TV and said to tell them the same thing. Lee didn't think WWL would actually send a crew because they were not part of the deal, but if they did, it would add credibility to his event. As we walked, we discussed aspects of the upcoming trip to Jackson. Lee would go, too, to practice transporting the bioweapon in preparation for the trip to Mexico City and to hear all the instructions Dave Ferrie would deliver to the techs at the hospital. Clay Shaw would drive Dave and him up to Jackson, bringing money with him. They would deliver the Product, and the volunteer would be injected. Within 72 hours, Lee would have to drive me back to Jackson, to see if the bioweapon worked. There was a lot of stress on my part, as I was calibrating the proper radiation load for the cancer cells and was barely ready, with the range of statistics. By the end of this week, I would gain

confidence in the test, which I first developed at UF, and was now standardizing.

Carlos Marcello

As we continued our stroll, the St. Louis Cathedral came into view — a magnificent building rich with mystery, ghosts and legends. We were walking under its portico, admiring the colonnades, not noticing the people passing us. Lee was carrying some drawings I'd offered for sale at Reverend Jim's (they bought one), and I was carrying copies of research papers from Banister's office. We then passed a group of men, but I had eyes only for Lee. That was a mistake. A tall man (a bit taller than Lee) broke from the group and grabbed Lee's sleeve.

"Hey, Oswald!" he demanded. "What's going on?" He was a florid-faced man, impressive in his expensive, pin-striped suit. He oozed brutal power and authority — and he was upset. The group had stopped and turned, then began staring at us. Carlos Marcello was in their midst. The Godfather! "So, Frank," Lee said, "what's the problem?"

"The problem is your girlfriend, Oswald." Frank then addressed me. "We all want to know, young lady, why you ignored Mr. Marcello, and didn't say a word, or acknowledge him in any way, when he tipped his hat to you."

"He isn't wearing a hat!" I managed to blurt out. I hadn't noticed that Marcello had tipped his non-existent hat at me. "Don't smart-mouth me!" Frank snapped. "What's the matter with you? Why didn't you show Mr. Marcello some respect?"

"I-I didn't see him!" I stuttered, truly terrified.

"You didn't see him? How could you miss him?"

"I don't know, but I did. I was just looking at Mr. Oswald, sir. Please give Mr. Marcello my apologies — as fast as you can! I'm very sorry. I'm awful at recognizing people!"

"She wouldn't recognize me, if she didn't see me every day," Lee put in. "Seriously. She also can't remember where she lives, half the time. For eleven weeks, we rode the bus together, but when I quit riding with her, she didn't know where to get off, and got lost," said Lee, appealing to Frank's sense of humor. "She's an absent-minded professor."

As Frank began to grin, Lee added, "She's good in science and art, but she doesn't notice a thing around her."

"It's true!" I chimed in. "I got lost in my own high school..." Frank smiled and returned to Marcello and his men. He began talking to them, adding some dramatic gestures. A minute later, the six or seven men, including Marcello, exploded with laughter. A couple of them laughed so hard they bent over.

I wished I could crawl into a hole, but Lee was laughing, too. "It's okay, honey," he said. "Better they laugh, than stay sore at you."

Then Frank walked back to us. "Miss," he said, "I've just learned that you have a reputation for not being able to find your way out of a paper bag. Mr. Marcello extends to you his own apology for upsetting you and wants you to know you don't have to worry. Somebody like you is never going to be any problem for us." Frank grinned. "The next time Mr. Marcello passes you on the street, he says he will forgive you if you don't notice him. But how in the hell you can be that blind, deaf and dumb is a mystery to me."

Friday, August 16, 1963 In the morning, when I left 1032 Marengo Street, Robert was still asleep in bed, but this time he had a decent excuse. His new job was selling Colliers Encyclopedias, and his training sessions required him to work from 2:00 P.M. to 11:00 P.M. Robert laid out the long, colorful brochure on the floor that he would show a customer. It was about four feet long, showing how big and impressive the set was. The appointments were made by knocking on doors, then returning in the evenings to give the sales pitch. That could last a while. Then the same night, he had return to the sales office for more training. Robert's schedule was now incredibly convenient. I wondered if he had been guided into taking this job, as had been the case with his stint with Standard Coffee. I had my own "art job," of course, so we weren't seeing much of each other. That morning, I headed for Dr. Mary's apartment, where I looked forward to meeting Lee.

It had been one week since Lee's August 9th arrest on Canal Street and, today, the next scene was to be acted out at the Trade Mart. The camera crew from WDSU-TV was scheduled to film Lee handing out his pro-Castro flyers in front of the **International Trade Mart,** 124 Camp Street, where Clay Shaw worked as General Manager. 6 WDSU-TV was owned by Edgar Sterns, a strident anti-Communist, and founding member of INCA. All of this was planned by Guy Banister and ultimately arranged by Dr. Ochsner. The plan was set.

As usual, any Cuban keeping one of the flyers would be filmed and followed. Lee arrived at Dr. Mary's apartment about 10:00 A.M. I had wanted to help, but after what happened the last time, Lee was afraid I would be photographed and identified. So I decided to play "Natasha" for "Boris" and dress up as a Cuban girl. I put in my specially tinted brown contact lenses. In Dr. Mary's bathroom, I put on too much make-up and curled my hair like Latinas did back then. I donned one of the two sundresses Mrs. Baker had purchased for me and wore my black high-heel shoes to complete the cha-cha look. Lee was amused by my efforts and thought I could be a "good extra" in the scene to attract attention, but he wanted me to disappear when the TV cameras arrived so I would not get captured on film. All went well: Lee handed out flyers, assisted by Charles Steele, an FBI informant, with Rafaelo Cruz, an anti-Castro Cuban from out-of-town that locals wouldn't recognize, to protect Lee. Both were reliable men, Lee told me, who could be trusted. Because I was concerned for Lee's safety, Lee steered me past Rafaolo so I could get a good look at his face. After my humiliation at not being able to recognize Carlos Marcello, this was as much a joke as it was serious.

Rafaolo, Lee had explained to me, would watch Lee's back more than he'd be handing out flyers, though he'd be holding some. He was a fervent anti-Castro activist, and he would protect Lee, he said, "like the guardian angel Rafael." I told Lee that Rafael was more than a guardian angel – he was a very powerful archangel. As Lee walked me past his "archangel" I made a point of trying to remember his face! I was not going to mess up, this time! Later, I'd see "Rafaolo" again, as he crossed Lafayette Park. When Lee pointed him out, he said, "Look! There's my archangel!" After viewing Rafaolo, I turned around and began speaking to several Cuban girls, hoping to help attract a crowd, for there wasn't much foot traffic. After a few minutes spent talking about America's poor treatment of Cuba, I saw some TV cameramen approaching. I knew they were for TV because of the bulky TV cameras hanging on their necks.

Before I got a good look at them, on cue I disappeared, heading to Thompson's Restaurant to wait for Lee. Thompson's had a great view of who was coming and going, no matter what size the windows were. While I sat there, enjoying a slice of the cafeteria's pecan pie, suddenly, David Lewis arrived. Anna, his wife, wasn't working today, so I was surprised to see him. He had a message for me: Lee wanted me to leave right away. Carlos Quiroga was coming, and Lee didn't want Quiroga taking to me, a fake "Latina. [231]" I left Thompson's at once and headed home. As soon as the WDSU cameramen got their story, Lee shut down the leafleting operation and also left the scene before any police might show up. Later, Quiroga would testify that a Latino official spotted him sitting at "Thompson's cafeteria" and that's when he was handed a flyer. Told that "somebody" was handing out these flyers at the Trade Mart, Quiroga said he called the police! When the police came, he said Lee was already gone. It was hard to believe Quiroga, because handing out flyers on the streets was such a common occurrence. Generally, the police wouldn't respond.

Years later, when asked by *The National Enquirer* and researchers if the Cuban man I saw in photographs "handing out" flyers with Lee was Rafael Cruz, the father of Sen. Ted Cruz, then a candidate for President of the United States, I affirmed that I thought it was the same man. His sharply sloping shoulders, protruding ears, square chin and unusual features, such as the extra distance between his nose and mouth, his short stature, and the expected pattern of his receding hairline argued that he was likely the same man. He should not be ashamed, for he was a trusted FBI informant, just as was Charles Steele, the other individual assisting Lee in a scam supported by the FBI.

As soon as they filmed him, the WDSU TV crewmen invited Lee to come to their studio on Royal Street. Edith Stern and her husband, Lee said, owned the station, were INCA members and were good friends of Dr. Ochsner, so that's how Lee got his interview. Lee's FPCC leafletting adventure was to be televised on the 6:00 news, and of course, Lee wanted his family to see it. Ever since his Uncle Dutz had secretly told him that he knew what Lee "was all about," Lee had felt more comfortable interacting with them. But when Lee asked Marina to come with him to the Murret's house to watch the TV segment, she refused to go. She was still frightened and upset about Dutz' scolding of Lee and no longer felt as welcome.

After pleading with her awhile, Lee realized it was now too late to go to the Murrets. There was even a danger that he would not see the broadcast himself.

---

[231] Carlos Quiroga would later be subjected to a polygraph by Jim Garrison's office, where he failed numerous questions. Quiroga either lied about when he went to 4905 to deliver the flyers, or Lee had enough saved back still at home.

Thinking Robert might be at my apartment (it was only Robert's second night learning his salesman spiel at Collier's') Lee first went to a store on Magazine Street that had a TV, but they were closing, so he ran to Susie's apartment. Seeing Robert's car was not in the driveway, he burst in, breathless, only moments before the news came on. Susie and I were late, too — we'd barely seated ourselves in front of the TV when Lee ran in. I just had time to tell him that Robert would not be home for hours when the news started. So we sat together, with little Claudia Rodick, her great-grandchild, who spent that weekend with her "Gram," to watch Lee's first TV appearance. I wish it had been his last.

To R: Elderly Rafael Cruz vs 1963 earlier Rafael w/less-receded hair-line, Rafael 1963; 2006. Above photo: note sloping shoulders. X is Lee. Note Cruz' square chin, protruding ears, and distinctive nose. Cruz went unidentified until the 21st century. Rafael was shorter than Lee, who stood at 5' 9". Ted Cruz, Rafael's son, is also 5' 9" tall. Top Photo: Ted is taller than his father. Rafael's Selective service ID says he was six feet tall! Just as Lee, whose official records showed him at 5' 11" instead of 5' 9", Rafael Cruz' Selective Service card,

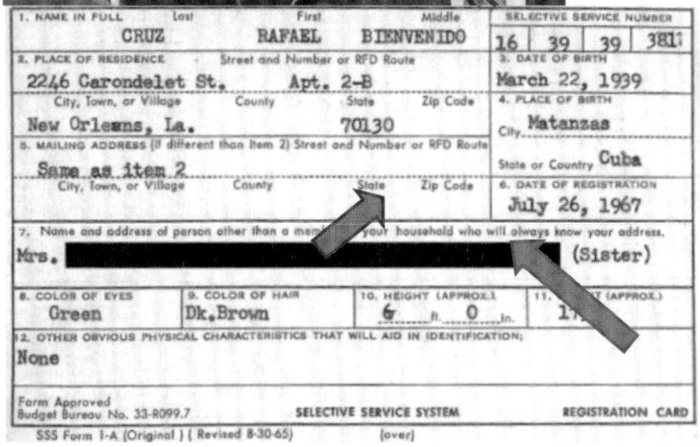

1. NAME IN FULL Last First Middle
CRUZ RAFAEL BIENVENIDO
SELECTIVE SERVICE NUMBER
16 | 39 | 39 | 381
2. PLACE OF RESIDENCE Street and Number or RFD Route
2246 Carondelet St. Apt. 2-B
City, Town, or Village County State Zip Code
New Orleans, La. 70130
3. DATE OF BIRTH
March 22, 1939
4. PLACE OF BIRTH
City Matanzas
State or Country Cuba
5. MAILING ADDRESS (If different than Item 2) Street and Number or RFD Route
Same as item 2
City, Town, or Village County State Zip Code
6. DATE OF REGISTRATION
July 26, 1967
7. Name and address of person other than a mem[ber of] your household who will always know your address.
Mrs. [redacted] (Sister)
8. COLOR OF EYES Green
9. COLOR OF HAIR Dk. Brown
10. HEIGHT (APPROX.) 6 ft. 0 in.
11. [WEIGH]T (APPROX.) 1[..]
12. OTHER OBVIOUS PHYSICAL CHARACTERISTICS THAT WILL AID IN IDENTIFICATION:
None
Form Approved Budget Bureau No. 33-R099.7 SELECTIVE SERVICE SYSTEM REGISTRATION CARD
SSS Form 1-A (Original) (Revised 8-30-65) (over)

issued in New Orleans in 1967, shows his height at 6 feet instead of 5' 7." Ted Cruz, top R, is 5' 9".

Saturday, August 17, 1963

WDSU's **Bill Stuckey's** radio show was called "Latin Listening Post." The program "kept an ear open" for news about Latin America. Told to contact Lee after his leafleting at the Trade Mart, Stuckey visited Lee at his home.

There he invited Lee to be a guest on his show. Unbeknownst to Stuckey, me or Lee, Dr. Ochsner was arranging for Lee's past as a Soviet defector to be exposed there. Of course, such a move, exposing Lee like that, would "prove" that WDSU had done its homework. The FPCC at this time was so heavily infiltrated with FBI informants that probably 10% of its members were FBI spies! INCA's Ed Butler went to HUAC Chairman Edwin Willis to obtain Lee's record as a defector. Even then, though it took Lee by surprise at the debate, we initially thought Ochsner was doing Lee a favor. With Lee declaring himself a Marxist, as a former defector, the broadcast of the "debate" by INCA as a "Truth Tape" was sent to some 300 Latin American stations. Supposedly, Lee would then be safer to fulfill his task in Mexico City. But what about later? And what about HUAC, who tracked all defectors? HUAC's chief was now Rep. Edwin Willis, right next to Reily's! I had visited Willis' office several times for Monaghan. His office literally overlooked Reily's. Willis could see Lee Oswald coming and going from Reily's every day. He had the files on every defector. He knew Lee's location, where he worked, and what he was doing, but until now, he had been silent, never informing the FBI of any of that. Now, he had to. We didn't understand the depth of Ochsner's treachery at the time. Certainly, I did not, until Nov. 22, 1963, the day President John F. Kennedy was assassinated. *That same day*, INCA had thousands of Lee's" "debate" records, ready to sell!

Dr. Ochsner himself attended the debate. His photo is on the back cover. Of the three photos shown, Ochsner's stands out. "Impression by..." means Ochsner was responsible for getting the record printed. Ochsner is described as "the only listener who knew of Oswald's defection before the debate." We can hear Ochsner's voice on the record. He was there. But there is another recording that is important. Since I'd nearly missed his short TV appearance, Lee told me that before this "debate" with Carlos Bringuier, Ed Butler, and Bill Stuckey, etc. at WDSU's studio, he had a very short radio interview.

Impression by . . .

Dr. Alton Ochsner, world famed surgeon and President of both the Alton Ochsner Medical Foundation and the Information Council of the Americas (INCA), who was perhaps the only listener who knew of Oswald's defection before the debate.

WDSU's Bill Stuckey had recorded it. Lee told us when it would be on the radio. What happened is that Lee devised a fun way to "test" me. I had wanted to prove I heard his broadcast, so Lee prepared: "a special word" to say. WDSU taped an intelligent but cautious half-hour discussion about Lee's views on U.S. policies towards Cuba, of which some five minutes were aired. Of course, I listened for that "special word" and fortuitously, it was captured in that five-minute segment. Lee's special word was "New Or-leens" — pronounced the "Yankee way" instead of "Naw-lins", "Norlins," or "New Orlins." Lee had corrected my Yankee pronunciation several times. Some have tried to say that the 'real' Lee Oswald did not return to America —that his place was taken by a clever Soviet imposter who did not know how to properly pronounce "New Orleans." The issue was also raised that the FBI's J. Edgar Hoover told Lee's worried mother that "somebody else" might be using Lee's birth certificate in the USSR. In fact, the FBI was no expert on the CIA's fake defector program. They knew even less about Lee Oswald's fake defection, which was a CIA and Dept. of Justice matter.[232] Lee was impersonated numerous times during and after his trip to Mexico City, efforts to frame him came into play. Lee was aware of some rumors about imposters, but at the time believed they were to help mask his trip to Mexico City, giving him more protection. But the "debate" of note was the one scheduled next. Both Carlos and Lee were running organizations that held no meetings, sponsored no lectures and had no member list.

---

[232] **Lee As Defector** Lee told me his mother's greed played a role. Told by the AG's office that she had been complicit in helping Lee get his 'dependency' discharge, when she was actually well, Marguerite herself could get in trouble—and that finally shut her up. Lee never used a birth certificate in the USSR. He used his USMC-issued US Passport and ID. Hoover simply tried to get the persistent Marguerite Oswald off his back. Faked records created by the CIA to protect Lee while he was in the USSR, to help cover his tracks, are used to promote John Armstrong's theory that "two Oswalds" existed from childhood, named "Harvey and Lee." Lee's brothers complicated matters by giving different addresses and histories than their mother, but they were not dating Mafia figures, as was Marguerite. She had lots to hide from the FBI and CIA. Just because she lied or "forgot" a detail doesn't mean there were "two" Marguerites. After the Kennedy assassination, every tipster who claimed to have seen Lee Oswald somewhere—anywhere-- if it fit Armstrong's 'Harvey and Lee Oswald' theory, it was used. He claimed Lee was born a Hungarian refugee, and spoke fluent Russian from childhood, based on a single anonymous phone call! I am a living witness that Lee worked hard to perfect his Russian. I'm supported in this by Lee's Russian friend, Ernst Titovets, who also knew how hard Lee worked to learn Russian.

(Sounds like "front" to me...). Despite his poor English, Carlos was a passionate speaker and would diligently question Lee. Ed Butler, INCA's co-founder and Director, was a professional anti-Communist who would soon get a cushy job at Tulane as a highly-paid publicist. Ochsner and Butler backed up Bill Stuckey by adding the experienced WDSU reporter, Bill Slatter, as moderator. That was a lot of talent stacked up against 23-year-old Lee Oswald, with his GRE from the Marines.

Wednesday, August 21, 1963 When Lee appeared on the WDSU Radio program called "Conversation Carte Blanche," it was four against one. Dr. Ochsner was also there, too, sitting on the sidelines in the studio.

Ochsner wanted to make sure there were no slip-ups. Lee handled himself well. The big surprise was when INCA's Ed Butler produced a newspaper article and accused Lee of defecting to the Soviet Union. During the tense exchange, Lee pointed out that a defector would not have been allowed to return to the United States, as he obviously had. Lee also mentioned that he had been protected by the U.S. government—quickly retracting that statement when he realized the implications. The final sentences of the "debate" are shown below. They were altered by CIA asset John McAdams, showing that even the slightest details that might get the CIA or government in trouble are subject to censorship. However, we have the recording of the debate on thousands of records, where we clearly hear Lee's actual words. McAdams had this version on the Internet as of June 2021: [near the end of the 'debate]

STUCKEY: *Mr. Oswald ...I'm curious to know just how you supported yourself during the three years that you lived in the Soviet Union. Did you have a government subsidy?* **OSWALD**: Well. As I er, well -- I will answer that question directly then as you will not rest until you get your answer. I worked in Russia. **I was *not* under the protection of the --** that is to say **I was *not* under protection of the American government,** but as I was at all times considered an American citizen I did not lose my American citizenship.

Here's what it says on the recording.: **OSWALD**: Well. As I er, well -- I will answer that question directly then as you will not rest until you get your answer. I worked in Russia. **I *was under* the protection of the --** that is to say **I *was not under* the protection of the American government,** but as I was at all times considered an American citizen I did not lose my American citizenship."

After the show, [233] Stuckey took Lee to Comeaux's Bar, a favorite hang-out for the New Orleans media, and bought him a beer.

---

[233] Skilled investigator James K. Olmstead has revealed many details about Lee's defection, how he was given a "fraudulent" discharge, with passport irregularities and special permissions to expedite his passport, apparently to place Lee in the USSR at a

The final week of August was busy for me and Lee. After discussing everything that had occurred, we agreed that Lee's documented pro-Castro views and activities could be used to frame him in the murder of President Kennedy, which many in the right-wing cabal seemed to be planning. To get perspective, talk of killing JFK was now everywhere, among those with whom Lee was associating. It was getting hard to ignore. The specters of bioweapons, spies, lies, betrayals and talk of assassination started to have an effect on both of us. Was Lee really being 'protected'? With so much publicity, how could Lee ever be used in a different role by the CIA or the FBI, after publicly playing the role of a pro-Castro Marxist? He was now disposable. Dispensable.

One evening, we discussed it. When Lee had brought up the problem to his handler, he had been told that he should now be "as quiet as possible" so all interest in him would die down. Soon, Lee would be doing nothing, so far as the outside world was concerned, except sitting on his screened porch and reading, which he did nearly the entire month of September.

Then, if all went well, he'd courier the Product to Mexico City, then we'd meet, escape the madness, and vanish. If The Product didn't kill the volunteer, Lee had put in a request to be reassigned to Mexico City, or nearby, since he already had so much training about Cuba, Mexico and Latin America in general. Either way, Mexico looked to be our next destination. Meanwhile, I inquired more about Lee's sore face. That is when I learned of Lee's passive resistance techniques. He said that he had learned the skill from the Quakers, and from reading Gandhi. The marks on his chin and ears were still present, but he dismissed all that: "They were defending their country," he said. "I don't hold it against them." That's how our discussion began. "When I was eleven," Lee said, "I venerated comic book heroes. I vowed to stand against evil. I slipped along the way a lot, but I still have that dream."

"When I was fifteen," I responded, "I felt the same, about fighting evil. So I wanted to be a saint." "Well," Lee replied, "good for you. As for me, I haven't had much success 'fighting evil' so far. Instead, I've had to fight the evil I've found in myself, as you well know."

"But you're winning the battle," I said earnestly. "Yes!" he answered, proudly. "I am. I'll be 'demmed' if I'll help give the world another Hitler. (He meant, rather unkindly, LBJ). I prefer to play it as the Scarlet Pimpernel, or maybe Zorro. Wearing my mask."

"But Zorro was a Don. And Lord Blakeney was a baronet — "

"Oh, I have a little money," Lee said modestly. "My friend George is in charge of it."

---

specific time. He explains Lee's specialized training and why it was so easy to frame him. REF: "The early 'out' of Oswald "
http://www.paulseaton.com/jfk/newsgroup/ng2.htm .

"I hate money!" I told him. "I, as well," Lee agreed. "I despise those who live off the labor of the poor. It's one reason I chose to do menial work. I was graviting – gravitating-- too quickly to a life of ease."

"But you hated working at Reily's." I told him. "God, yes! The heat, the noise, the lack of respect." [234]

"By the end of the century, they say the average American worker will only have to be on the job thirty hours a week."

"I hope so," Lee said. "If we keep men like Kennedy in office, who don't owe their souls to cartels and corporations. Maybe he will keep us from blowing ourselves to hell."

Lee had been trying to make me care about President Kennedy as much as he did. He brought up JFK's July 26 speech on a treaty with Moscow to ban nuclear tests in air, water, and in space. The speech had infuriated ultra-conservatives who thought JFK was displaying weakness in the face of Communism. But Lee praised the President for his foresight. The media has downplayed how brave Kennedy was. But I won't forget. As for Lee and me, we wanted to abandon the rat race and "gray flannel suits."

"We'll leave their money and corruption behind," Lee said. "We'll be like Lord and Lady Blakeney. We'll play the old part, like in the movie. And I will make sure you'll be safe."

"And what if they kill you?" I asked. "We're forewarned," he said. "That's a mighty good advantage." He had adopted the light, devil-may-care voice and manner of the Scarlet Pimpernel, but both of us knew we were in deep trouble. We walked along more slowly now, wrapped in silence, heading toward Audubon Park, holding hands, aware of our wedding rings that touched and made the tiny clinking sound that meant we were still linked to others. But soon, we would leave our rings behind!

There were other troubles: Dave had held two parties, when he'd promised not to have any more until September. I kept my own little secret about Dave's penance: I knew Dave was holding these parties to bring in older males, determined to never touch an underaged teenager again. Since that was a raw point with Lee, I felt it best to not bring it up. Dave's parties meant putting away the breakables, and of course, now all the mice were gone, never to return. I told Lee that I wondered where the mice had been kept. "The two Cuban kids know," Lee replied.

[234] I remember Lee correcting himself about this word.

"Why couldn't we just work over there, instead of having to go through all of this hassle at Dave's?" I asked. "Dave doesn't want you to see the others," Lee said, with a sharp look. Lee had pinpointed the problem. Who was really in charge of the Project? Then there was the Product. Dr. Mary had mentioned that some cultures might be stored in liquid nitrogen as back-ups. In that state, they could be kept dormant, but alive, at minus 200 degrees C. in essence, immortalizing those deadly cancer cells. They could be used any time in the future. The thought gave me chills.

Our goal was simple. Kill Castro with this bioweapon, and free Cuba, saving a good president from the cusp of extinction. But how naïve was that? Who would willingly give up this bioweapon, once it was available? It would be there, waiting to be activated, whenever needed.

I confided these fears to Lee. "There's nothing you can do about it, Juduffki," Lee said patiently. "It's not your fault, either. Who can you complain to?"

Lee was right. I couldn't even prove there had been a lab at Dave's, even though I now went to his apartment almost daily. Most of my work was now focused on developing my radioactive blood test.

I had created it to track live cancer cells in the body, and was now perfecting the titration method. The deadly cancer cells, with their radioactive component, would be injected into a volunteer (or maybe several) brought in from Angola prison to participate in "cancer research." It would take place at Jackson's mental hospital. Prisoners – "volunteers" -- were routinely used in secret research projects there by Drs. Ochsner, Heath, Silva and others. Their deeds have become known, spearheaded by Bill Davy in his book *Let Justice be Done.*

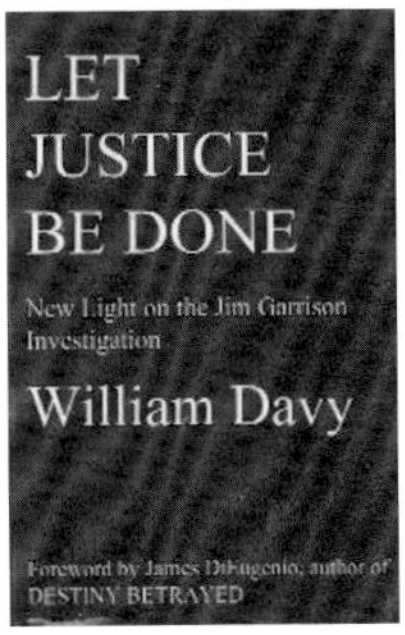

His book was released only a few weeks after I spoke to researchers for the first time of prisoners being used for experiments at Jackson. There have been statements from victims, such as from William Livesay, a Louisiana realtor who recounted how prisoners – he had been one -- were known to volunteer for transfers to Jackson for medical experiments. Livesay brought forth verified information for researchers. He was a New Orleans area resident incarcerated in Angola in 1963 after assaulting a patron at the Gas Light Lounge. Livesay kindly provided this statement:

"...I was in New Orleans Parish Prison for nearly a year awaiting trial in 1962, then sent to Angola from 1963-5... While at Angola several others & I volunteered for medical experiments to be held at Jackson. There were 8 or 10 in my group to board the bus to the hospital. The only 2 names I remember are Dan Robertson & a guy with the last name of Mayes.

After we were there for 4-5 days, Mayes walked out of the ward one night after seeing one of the hospital orderlies come in from outside & forgetting to lock the door. The next morning the bus came & took us all back to Angola. I remember we were given some pills every morning but I have no idea what the experiment was about. I learned later that half of us were given medicine & the other half were given placebos.

Several years later I went to New Orleans at the request of Dan Robertson to testify on his *behalf in a lawsuit he had brought against the State (or possibly the hospital) to show that the pills he took during that brief stay had caused him mental problems. I remember the doctor from Jackson testifying also about the experiment. If I can help further please let me know. Sincerely, Bill Livesay "*

Livesay wrote a second letter later, reemphasizing his participation in the medical experiment at Jackson as a prisoner from Angola.

Since then, more information about similar experiments at Jackson and elsewhere have been posted on the Internet.

Still, we had worked in secret and most records were destroyed, even as we worked. With my concerns about the bioweapon's disposal growing, I wanted to see something to prove this bioweapon would be destroyed after its use. That it would not be held in deep freeze. But what would happen to me, if I raised objections? And if I did, how could I prove a thing?

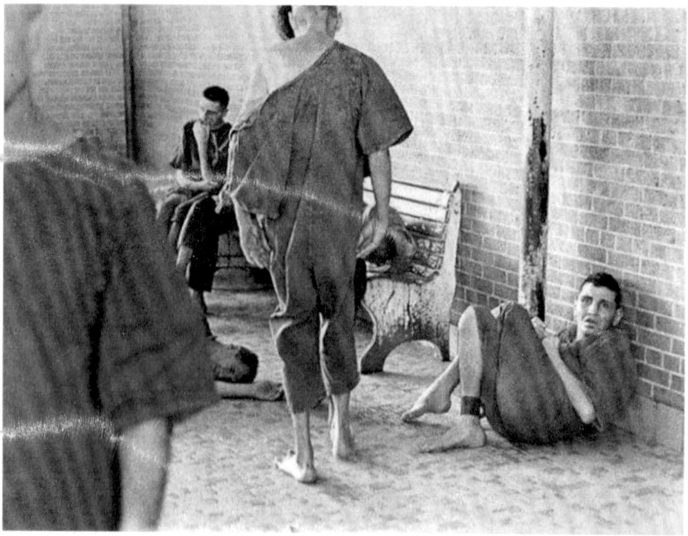

Patients in East Louisiana State Mental Hospital, 15 February 1963 (Richard Avedon).[235] **Nobody cared about these inmates being used for experiments.** [236]

[235] https://medium.com/@jakepagano/giving-soul-richard-avedon-khalik-allah-and-the-touch-of-the-photograph-e4a0d79d0aae

[236] Only when Edward T. Haslam began investigating, years later, why "The Mouse House" stank so badly, and looked into how Dr. Mary Sherman was brutally murdered, would the clues and evidence mount up, due to his thorough and diligent efforts, culminating with his harsh, but fair investigation of me. Later, Haslam would edit *Me & Lee*, correcting many typos and sternly deleting boring details.

Dr. Mary couldn't defend me without losing her position. Ever since David Ferrie had given me the wooden nickel, stamped with methylene iodide, one of the most powerful cancer-causing agents on earth, I realized how easily cancer could be given to almost anybody, simply by spraying something like methylene iodide on food. But that could be traced. Into what hands could our untraceable bioweapon fall? I knew Dr. Mary's ethical standards were high, and I was determined to share my suspicions. But I knew the answer: the project had taken too long

and had cost too much to simply throw it away afterwards. Not when these expensive cancer cells -- and the deadly viruses with them-- could live virtually forever if kept in deep freeze. I talked to Lee about it more than once, even though there was little that either of us could do concerning the decisions made by Ochsner and those influencing him. "Maybe I could talk to Dr. Diehl," I told Lee, after more discussion. After all, Dr. Diehl had been fond of me, and I knew I could talk to him in private. I found his card in my big black purse.

But Lee pointed out that Diehl, the Senior Vice President for Research for the American Cancer Society, and Dr. Alton J. Ochsner, the Society's former President, had been pals for years. Their mutual friend, "Wild Bill" Donovan (who died of lung cancer despite Ochsner's efforts) had been a leading ACS official, too. Donovan however, was the head of the OSS and the founding father of the CIA. With all that baggage, Diehl would probably do nothing. Lee said we should wait until Dave came back from Miami again before trying to tackle this new problem.

Before his trip, Dave helped draw anti-Castroites away from Lee on August 9th, by holding an anti-Castro demonstration a few blocks further up Canal street. Before that, he'd spent time in bars and nightclubs with Lee, helping to spread rumors of Fernando Fernandez infiltrating the anti-Castro camp. "As I said, I had to hang around bars..." Lee said. "Think of my sufferings!" he went on. "Instead of playing chess, reading a good book, or making love to you, I had to encourage grown men to drink until they vomited... Come on, let's have some fun before going home!" Lee said cheerily. "It won't take long. It's one of my favorite places," he added, putting his arm around me.

"It's close, a place that made me happy when times were tough." By now, we had arrived at a tall, grassy embankment in Audubon Park that I'd seen before. "I've been exercising," he said, as we gazed at the hill. "Bet I can keep up with you all the way up this thing!" After hiding my purse in some bushes, up the hill we went.

Lee was ahead all the way. As we stood panting at the top, I remarked that it wasn't fair: his legs were longer, and he did not have a pair of breasts weighing him down. Lee said, on the contrary, he was weighed down by all that equipment between his legs! Exploding with laughter, we kissed.

Monkey Hill

Monkey Hill was built for all the kids of New Orleans, Lee said, especially those who had never left the state and had no idea what a free-standing hill looked like. I remember I was wearing my tight olive-green skirt, and actually believed Lee when he said any grass stains, if I rolled down the hill with him, would not show. Wrong! But Robert didn't notice my stained skirt. Still fascinated with Hitler, he was busy re-reading *The Rise and Fall of the Third Reich.* "Mr. Rat has been home again all day," Susie said, anxious for me. "He ate the last of my pie. When is he going to get a real job?"

"He's trying to sell encyclopedias at night now," I told her.

"He's had to memorize spiels. He's going around with some salesmen tonight, as they give their sales talks. He won't be getting home until 11:00 PM for a while, after tonight." When Robert got home, at about 9 pm, I finally told him my job at Reily's was over. "I couldn't promise that I would stay after the summer was over, so they made me resign," I told him. *Lies again!* --I so hated doing that -- but they worked.

After learning that I had immediately landed a "job" at Rev. Jame's, Robert calmed down. I wonder what he would have thought if he saw that Rev. James' shop, which was on the edge of a tough neighborhood and was run by blacks! I faithfully handed over the "earnings," which largely came from Clay Shaw's stash to us. Once he had the cash in his hands, Robert told me how his job was going. "I came home early today," he commented, lighting up a cigarette. "Because I had no luck. I can't seem to close deals. My boss had to move in and close. If I can't learn how to sell, we'll go to Florida, and move in with my folks until school starts. You'll have to deal with my mother, that's all."

"We don't have to leave early," I objected, staring at his cancer stick. I was unwilling to tell him I did not intend to go with him. He'd broken his promise not to smoke in front of me.

It would not be hard to leave Robert behind, when the time came to meet Lee Oswald in Mexico City.

Chapter 23
Clinton and Jackson

Wednesday, August 28, 1963

This was the day that Rev. Dr. Martin Luther King, Jr. delivered his "I Have a Dream" speech in front of the Lincoln Memorial in Washington, DC to a live audience of 200,000, and a television audience of millions. Hope swept across the land. It was a monumental date in American history, and a true watershed on the social landscape. Lee and I watched the news together at Susie's, as Dr. King quoted from the Declaration of Independence: "That all men are created equal." To the black population, it was an inspirational moment that gave them strength and confidence to challenge the racist structure that had denied them their voting rights and so much more. To the white supremacists, it was a call-to-arms. Few places in the country felt the weight of this dramatic collision of perspectives more than rural Louisiana. There, organizations like the Ku Klux Klan secretly controlled the voting apparatus, and illiterate blacks still toiled in the fields. Violence was in the air, and this is where Clay Shaw, David Ferrie, and Lee Oswald were headed next.

As the final days of August arrived, most of the Project's goals had been reached. A deadly galloping cancer had been dramatically enhanced and successfully transferred from mice to marmosets, and then to rhesus and African green monkeys, progressively working up the evolutionary scale toward humans. The final step was to test the bioweapon on a human. He was supposedly "a volunteer" from Angola Penitentiary, an infamous prison located near the banks of the Mississippi River, north of Baton Rouge. The test itself would be conducted about 30 miles from Angola at the East Louisiana State Mental Hospital in Jackson, Louisiana.

The hospital was about 120 miles northwest of New Orleans, just below the Mississippi state line. Everything had been carefully planned.

Thursday, August 29, 1963 was expected to be just a typical summer day in a small Southern town. Lee and Dave had been trained to conduct the test. They had been drilled on how to teach the clinicians to keep the bioweapon alive, and how to use it. Of course, they had no idea it was a deadly cancer. The components of the bioweapon were made ready for travel. Alibis were in place, with plausible deniability for key people. A reliable, air-conditioned vehicle was provided for the safe transportation of the team and the bioweapon. The car was a big black Cadillac — an automobile that oozed importance.

In Clinton, they would wait for a call from the small town's only payphone that was available outside a building. When the vehicles escorting the prisoner called, the team would intercept and slide into position behind the two State vehicles, creating the impression of an official convoy. In this way, the arrival of the test team would not be challenged. For this last step, timing and coordination were critical.

As for the bioweapon, I had personally trained Lee and Dave on how to handle its set-up and use at its new destination. With this trip under his belt, Lee would know how to convey the instructions to preserve and use the bioweapon to the medical contact in Mexico City. Not a single written word would be on paper. I did not accompany them on this trip, so what I report here is what both Lee and Dave told me.

Thursday, August 29, 1963 Early Thursday morning, Lee, Dave Ferrie, and Clay Shaw acquired the black Cadillac, which was registered to the International Trade Mart. The bioweapon had been placed inside two special Dewar jars. To an outsider, they looked like common lunch thermoses. A couple of sandwiches had been tucked in with them, inside an ordinary-looking lunch sack which Lee would carry. Shaw was at the wheel because he could legally drive the Cadillac. He was also necessary to "grease the skids" with a financial contribution to select officials at the hospital.

After crossing Lake Pontchartrain, the Cadillac stopped briefly in Hammond, Louisiana (Shaw's home town) where he checked on his ailing father and called his secretary, providing an alibi, should it be needed, to account for Shaw's rare absence from New Orleans.

From Hammond, Shaw drove north to Clinton, Louisiana, where they picked up a fourth passenger, an orderly who worked in the mental hospital in nearby Jackson. The orderly knew the layout and location of the various buildings, for Jackson had a large compound.

Discussions about Kennedy, Johnson and Castro stopped when the orderly entered the car, and an uneasy silence prevailed. Clay Shaw then drove the foursome to the courthouse in Clinton. There they were to wait for word of the convoy's departure from Angola penitentiary. Once there, Shaw again called his secretary, saying that he was at someone's office. He gave her a phone number where he could be reached, promising to call her back when he was leaving. But this "office" was actually a pay phone near the courthouse in Clinton, Louisiana, where they began waiting, in the black Cadillac, for the phone call from Angola.

Secrecy was an important factor in this operation. Clinton had been selected as the staging area because unlike the smaller town of Jackson, where it would have been difficult for a black Cadillac to park and wait without being noticed, Clinton had a courthouse. It would not seem unusual for an official-looking vehicle (such as the Cadillac) to be parked nearby. When the trip was planned, Clinton seemed an excellent choice. The hospital was approximately halfway between the towns of Jackson and Clinton, so the distance was perfect for Shaw to rendezvous with the convoy. The presence of a known hospital employee in the black Cadillac, as well as Shaw's impressive business-like appearance, would add to the patina of legitimacy. Once inside the hospital's gates, the orderly would direct the Lee and Dave to the proper outbuilding on the hospital's campus, where the test was to take place. Their plan looked good on paper, but there was a hitch: Thursday, August 29, 1963 was no "ordinary day" in Clinton, Louisiana. Just the day before, Dr. Martin Luther King, Jr. had delivered his historic "I Have a Dream" speech in Washington, D.C. His words ricocheted through the national media. Dr. King was the talk of the town. He was either a brave hero or a disgusting villain. Hoping to leverage the momentum created by Dr. King's impassioned speech, the Congress of Racial Equality (CORE) -mostly run by college students -- held a voter registration drive in Clinton. Clinton was a KKK-controlled bastion of White Supremacy that routinely denied blacks their right to vote. Emboldened by the massive outpouring of support in Washington and the presence of CORE, the local blacks gathered peacefully, to register. The sun was hot and the delays were long, but it was no worse than a day spent picking cotton or digging potatoes.[237]

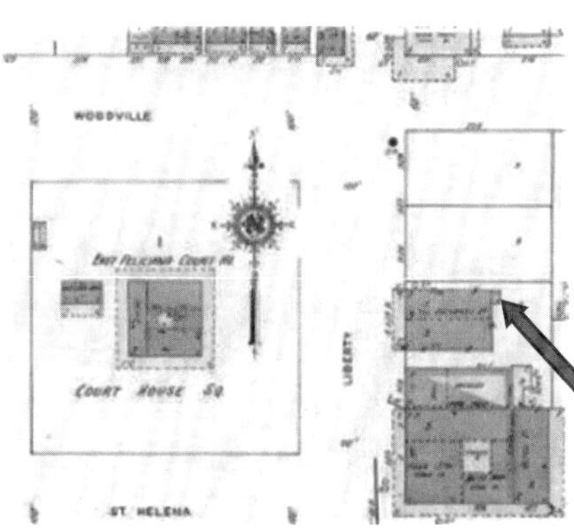

The telephone exchange (curb pay-phone <u>Sanborn Fire Map, 1940</u>

---

[237] The Congress of Racial Equality (CORE) workers were mostly student volunteers still on summer break who would be returning to their classrooms in just a few days. This helps pinpoint the voter registration drive at the end of August. After CORE left, these

Conservative whites ruled this town. People were wary, and tensions were high on both sides. Local white folks watched with scorn as blacks eager to register stood in a line that barely moved.[238] The local Registrar of Voters was stalling, trying to wait them out. Meanwhile, police officials worried about the possibility of violence erupting in the tense atmosphere. The FBI and various troublemakers could show up at any time. Into this scene came a black Cadillac, full of strangers. Naturally, the car attracted a lot of stares, but the men inside the car, committed to waiting for the phone call, could not leave.[239] The pay-phone booth was in front of the building where the Telephone Exchange was located (it was on the 2nd floor). After a while, Lee and the Aide got out of the car, and David Ferrie moved into the front seat.

1963: lined up to register to vote in Clinton, LA[240]

Lee got out of the Caddie because it was becoming an "object of interest" but he had to stay close to the car, in case the pay phone rang. While standing there, Lee said he encountered an angry young black woman on "Liberty Street" who had just been denied her right to register to vote. Lee thought it ironic that she spoke to him as they stood on a street named "Liberty. She said she had been in line even before the office opened. When she got her chance at last, she produced proof of residency and was then asked to read a section of the U.S. Constitution. When she did, she was told she had "failed" her literacy test. She had earned her A.A. degree in Business from Tuskegee Institute. Hearing this tale of injustice angered Lee. He returned to the car and made a bet with Shaw, Dave and the orderly that, because he

---

newly registered African-American citizens, and even members of their families, of all ages, were thrown in jail.

[238] One researcher said only six black voters were able to register that day. The aide was identified as Estus Morgan, a local.

[239] Those who claim Lee was brought there only to try to register to vote have to deal with why did Shaw and Ferrie wait, enduring the gaze of the curious for hours, when they could have dropped Lee off and waited in a coffee house, or at least could have moved the car and parked a few blocks out of sight. But they couldn't move: they were waiting for an important phone call.

[240]From Pinterest: joeinct.tumblr.com

was white, he'd be able to register to vote without a glance at his credentials, even though he didn't live in Feliciana Parish. Dave, Shaw and the Aide bet a dollar each against him, and Lee got in line to try to register. The Aide got in line with him to "keep him honest." These two men were noticed as almost the only whites in line.

At one point, somebody who knew the Aide saw him and stopped by to talk. That's when Lee heard about a job opening at the Jackson Hospital. It would fit in nicely for an excuse to be there. Two long hours wore on, but the pay phone still did not ring. The delay "terribly angered Shaw," Dave told me, but there was nothing that could be done. The Cadillac was essentially trapped in this amazing scenario.[241]Sometime after noon, Lee finally reached the head of the line and the Registrar of Voters, Henry Palmer. Lee -- polite and friendly -- took out his wallet, flashed his ID, and asked if he could register to vote. Palmer was willing, and invited Lee to sign the register. [242] After Lee signed, he said he had done so in hopes of getting a job at the hospital. Palmer told him he might want to speak to a "Mr. Morgan." He was a security guard there. He joked that Morgan "had the key" to getting a job there. Lee said he was glad to know that, and now that he was a real, bona-fide resident of East Feliciana Parish, he would make him a visit!

Realizing that Lee was flaunting the fact that he was not a resident, Palmer, who would be the area's Grand Cyclops of the KKK in 1964, demanded to see Lee's ID again. As Lee displayed his ID (which indicated that he lived in Orleans Parish), Lee put in that surely having a voter's registration card in East Feliciana Parish would improve his chances to get a job, correct? Angry that he had been taken in, Palmer quickly erased Lee's ink signature as best he could and told Lee to leave the area, saying "Forget about a job there, you belong in a mental hospital!" Lee told me, later, "I did get registered, but it was only for two minutes." Even though his name was erased. Lee added that he collected his $3 bet. "Well, you were registered longer than the colored girl," I replied.

The town's town marshal, John Manchester, also a KKK member, eventually approached the Cadillac. After all, it looked suspicious to have it just sitting there, with people inside, for so long. Manchester asked the driver to identify himself.

---

[241]The Warren Commission and FBI claimed Lee's whereabouts were unknown during this time. The Clinton Incident, as it is called, was discovered and documented in the late 1960s during Garrison's Investigation and again in the 1970s during the HSCA Investigation. Some related documents were kept secret until the 1990s.

Records from Jim Garrison's trial of Clay Shaw show that Clay Shaw identified himself as from the International Trade Mart. Soon after Lee returned to the car, the pay phone rang: Shaw answered. The prison convoy was on its way. They had to leave at once in order to join it before the convoy came into view of the hospital's manned security gate. All went as planned. The vehicles entered as a unit, without a problem.

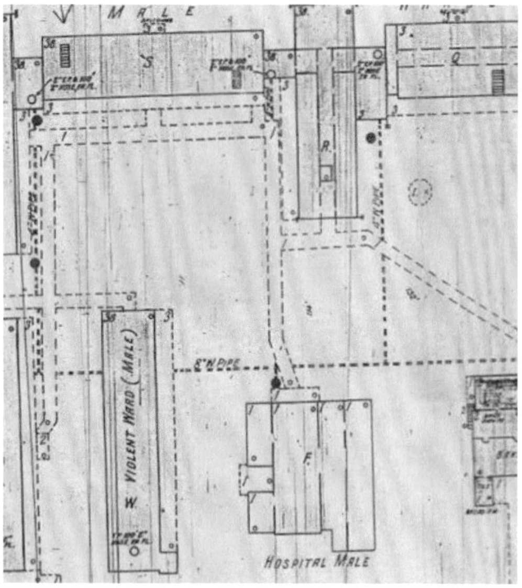

Once inside the gates, Shaw parked the Cadillac and entered the main building to take care of "the money part." Meanwhile, the Aide guided Lee and Dave behind the main building to the Men's Hospital and Clinic (on this old map, "Hospital Male,"). It was a smaller structure well behind the massive administration building with its impressive white-columned façade (at the top in this diagram).

The Bioweapon, Its Set-Up and the Follow-Up Test

At the Male Hospital and Clinic, Dave and Lee met the medical and technical personnel who would oversee the experiment and would conduct any additional ones later.[243]

Lee carried the bioweapon in his "lunch sack," with the sandwiches, even though it was now well after lunchtime. That made the lunch sack as an object to be remembered by a nurse working there, rather than as an ordinary accessory. The thermos bottles had clear glass liners on which the cancer cells had been grown. The liners were, in essence, giant test tubes, easily pulled from the thermos bottles. A rich "soup" was freshly poured every few days into these glass liners, to feed the cancer cells adhering to the glass walls. In order to use the bioweapon, the cancer cells were subjected to a trypsin bath to "unglue" them from the sides of the thermos bottles. The loose cells then became part of the "soup" itself (the "medium."). These floating cancer cells could then be easily concentrated, with gentle centrifuging, into test tubes. They could then be injected into the test subject. More injections from the same batch would follow, if the first injection "took." The second thermos provided a backup batch, in case the first batch got contaminated. Both sets of the bioweapon could be kept alive for weeks with proper care.

[243] Ochsner had to know how many prisoners were being tested.

Dave taught the clinicians how to keep the cells alive, which wasn't difficult, because they were already familiar with cell cultures and knew how to prepare the sterile medium. They were given the RPMI recipe I had tweaked, of course.

Lee observed everything. It was his duty to memorize everything. He would orally pass on the information to the medical contact in Mexico City, who would be picking up the bioweapon. Nothing was in writing.

The contact was considered utterly reliable and would destroy the bioweapon after it had been used on Castro. The cells, in fact, could not be kept alive without being preserved in deep-freeze before they had gone through a certain number of reproductive cycles. Ochsner had assured me that Castro's medical team hadn't developed the skills at this point, to properly preserve the bioweapon. In contrast, he said, the USA had the technology: M.D. Anderson had such a set-up. That remark would haunt me to the present day. We hoped the same ploy – a "lunch thermos" – would safely transport the virulent cancer cells. The cells were invisible. The growth-medium bathing them looked (and even tasted like) weak chicken broth. In fact, you could even pour out some of the medium and drink it to "prove" it was "broth" as stomach acids would kill the cancer (we assumed!). We believed these cells had to be injected into the bloodstream, rather than into a muscle.

[129] LSD experiments: *Comprehensive Psychiatry*: Volume 1, pp. 370–76, 1960, "Comparative Effects of the Administration of taraxein, d-LSD, Mescaline, and Psilocybin to Human Volunteers" by F. Silva, M.D., R.G. Heath, M.D., et al.

A paper co-authored by Heath, Silva, and a few others, and published in *Comprehensive Psychiatry 1960*, was titled: "Comparative Effects of the Administration of taraxein, d-LSD, Mescaline, and Psilocybin to Human Volunteers." The introduction stated, "The patient donors are housed in a special Tulane University Research Unit at the East Louisiana State Hospital, Jackson."[129] The experiments were supported by a grant from the Commonwealth Fund, later identified as having also been a CIA front.

Investigator Dick Russell revealed LSD experiments reported at Jackson in 1960

We based this on data which led to tests at Brooklyn's Jewish Chronic Disease Hospital, by an immunologist, Dr. Chester Southam. Thanks to Southam's experiment, we knew the injection route had to be through the bloodstream.

Dr. Chester Southam and His Cancer Injection Experiment

Southam, a good friend of all three of "my " doctors, received funding from The American Cancer Society and the NIH to inject HeLa cancer cells into elderly Jews.

All the patients were ill and senile, with compromised immune systems. These elderly Jews had no idea the injections could possibly kill them. Southam was assisted by JCDH's Dr. Emmanuel Mandel. The tests proved that even these patients' weak, compromised immune systems could fight off cancer cells injected into the muscle. Besides Southam's work, a regional radiologist also had assisted in expediting the success of the experiment with The Product.

LA. X-RAY GROUP MEETING NEARS

Technicians Plan Talks, Beauty Contest

Aug. 29, 1963 "X-ray Group Meeting Nears" (*Times-Picayune*

The "volunteer" Lee saw was prepared for the experience psychologically. He knew he would get x-rays and receive a shot.

He didn't know the x-rays he got that day were set at such a high dosage level that soon he would feel sick. He didn't know that the injection he would receive next was full of live cancer cells that his now-damaged immune system would not be able to conquer. He didn't know that due to fears of contagion, he would suffer in isolation, with no visitors or social contacts. He didn't know that he was expected to die.

The State Radiology Committee was packed with Ochsner's own close colleagues and friends.[244] Dave gave the injection and Lcc obscrvcd the site. The prisoner Lee saw was promised a "good report" for "cooperating." The volunteer perhaps congratulated himself that some x-rays and shots would save him from labor on a chain gang. After Dave finished injecting the prisoner, he asked Lee to leave, as Lee also had to set up an excuse as to why he might be seen again, within 72 hours. "Applying for a job" would provide a good excuse, so Lee asked the nurse at the Clinic's desk how to find the Personnel office. Lee didn't enter the campus through the usual route – the main entrance-- where a sign to that office was easy seen in the main building.

Dr. Frank Silva, the Director, would later claim that someone who "may or may not have been Oswald" had asked him if he needed to register to vote to get a job there. Silva told him yes, it was necessary, later explaining to an investigator that he was upgrading staff and the requirement to read and write was important.[245] Silva also reported that the person he encountered in the hall was talking to other people and bragging that he was going to kill Castro. If true, this was just the kind of stunt Lee would have pulled to make people remember that he had been there seeking a job *and should not be hired.* His outrageous behavior would guarantee that he would not have to worry about getting the job. Not every seeming anomaly in Lee's behavior was proof of an

---

[244] The roster was filled with Ochsner and Tulane radiologists. I own the documents.

[245] According to Oswald-did-it theorist Patricia Lambert, who interviewed Silva.

"imposter." Lee did fill out an application, which one of the clerks there recalled seeing.[246] She told her information to Garrison investigator Andrew "Moo Moo" Sciambra, who interviewed Reeves Morgan, an important employee at the hospital who Lee had visited Saturday evening, and his daughter, Mary. Sciambra's report said, "*At that time ALINE WOODSIDE, who works in the Personnel Department at the hospital, told Mr. Morgan she saw OSWALD's application in the Personnel files at the hospital but that she does not know what ever became of it.*" The report was signed by Reeves Morgan.

Lee would return within 72 hours with me. His excuse for his return was that he wanted to find out about his job status. Since that was a Saturday, when the Personnel Office was closed, Lee would look like a fool. That was part of his role-playing. Our Saturday visit was vital: these virulent cancer cells had been tagged with radiation, but each time the cells divided, the radiation signal would be virtually cut in half. If radiation could still be detected between 36 and 72 hours, that meant the victim's immune system had been unable to kill the invading cancer cells. My test, and a sensitive Geiger counter, would determine that. I now believe that Dave injected up to five more prisoners, based on the number and labeling of blood samples involved. Afterwards, Shaw drove Lee and Dave home. When Lee told me how healthy the prisoner looked, I went on the alert. Dr. Ochsner himself had told me that the prisoner -- terminally ill -- had "volunteered" to be injected with this deadly cancer, knowing his days were numbered. To properly do the blood test, I still had to know what kind of cancer the volunteer had, so I could distinguish between "his" cancer and "our" cancer.

So, I asked Dave, as soon as he returned, to advise me as to what cancer the prisoner had. "Oh, don't worry about that," Dave said matter-of-factly. "He doesn't have cancer. He's a Cuban who is about the same age and weight as Castro, and he's healthy."

I felt a chill sweep through my body. My heart turned over. This revelation was sickening. We would be giving cancer to a healthy human with the intention of killing him.

This was not medicine. This was murder. It was wrong, morally, ethically, and legally. They had gone too far.

---

[246] The statements about Lee's (1) asking for the location of the Personnel Office, (2) his carrying a lunch sack, (3) his application for a job, and (4) the application's 'loss', are in the Grand Jury and Trial of Clay Shaw transcripts. Numerous witnesses testified as to Lee's presence there. Lee had even claimed he was living with Dr. Silva! Silva's statement that he "could not be sure" this person was Lee Oswald borders on the absurd, since others at the hospital and elsewhere in Clinton and Jackson recognized him. But then, Silva knew about the experiments and had much to lose.

Friday, August 30, 1963 We all have heard the spiels about "What do you stand for?" Would you have pulled the lever in the German gas chambers if the Führer told you to, like Adolf Eichmann did? Would you have killed Hitler, if you had the chance? These are defining moments. Who are we? What should we do?_ I was the girl who hated cancer because it killed her grandmother. I was the girl who dreamed of finding a cure to free humanity from this curse. I was the one who sang in church and prayed on both knees to ask God for his help in this noble task. I had thrown myself into the heart of this beast with all my conviction. I had suffered the solemn pain and exquisite sadness of watching those poor people (and animals) die at Roswell Park. I knew what this weapon would do in terms I cannot describe here. But now, I was involved in what could only be called pre-meditated murder. The question was remarkably clear to me: Was I a murderer? No, I was not.

And I was not ready to become one. Not for Dr. Ochsner. Not for Old Glory. Not to get my medical school education.

What they were doing was wrong. It was evil. They had lost their moral compass. I wrote a note of protest to Ochsner, my former hero. Yes, he had told me not to write down anything about the Project. There was to be no paper trail: I realized that if the note got into the wrong hands, the entire temple would collapse on us. But my righteous indignation was fired up and in high gear. Under the great Dr. Ochsner's direction, we were violating the Hippocratic Oath. We were going to kill a man --with cancer-- as a practice exercise, just to see if the Product would work, to then use it on Fidel Castro. I protested this corruption of the spirit. But that wasn't all. I had finally read the news from the 1963 Science Writer's Seminar, the same one I'd crashed in 1960. That's when I learned that in April, 1963, my friend and mentor, Dr. George Moore --Dr. Ochsner's friend— had stood side-by-side with the notorious Dr. Southam at the Sixth Annual Science Writers' Seminar to declare that *"doctors should be allowed to shelve the requirement that they receive the 'informed consent' of their subjects before proceeding with an experiment..." What?* I had to re-read the words. *No!* Not Dr. Moore, too!

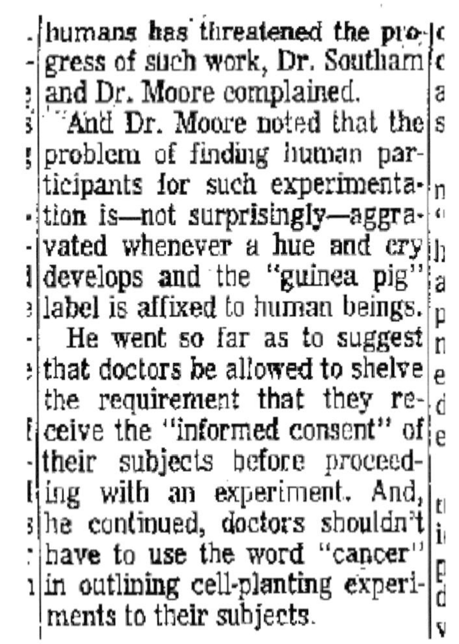
humans has threatened the progress of such work, Dr. Southam and Dr. Moore complained.

"And Dr. Moore noted that the problem of finding human participants for such experimentation is—not surprisingly—aggravated whenever a hue and cry develops and the "guinea pig" label is affixed to human beings.

He went so far as to suggest that doctors be allowed to shelve the requirement that they receive the "informed consent" of their subjects before proceeding with an experiment. And, he continued, doctors shouldn't have to use the word "cancer" in outlining cell-planting experiments to their subjects.

Experiment Fears

Cancer Battle Imperiled

By CHARLES PETERSON
Review City Editor

PALM BEACH SHORES, Fla. —Fears that doctors may accidentally give healthy people cancer while looking for ways to stamp it out are damaging the fight to control the disease.

A prominent cancer researcher who branded such fears unrealistic and uninformed leveled the charge here yesterday as he addressed the sixth annual science writers seminar of the American Cancer Society.

Dr. George Moore, director of the Roswell Park Memorial Institute in Buffalo, N. Y., pleaded for more understanding by press and public alike of the need for —and the precautions used—in experiments on human beings.

ABANDON QUEST

If it's not forthcoming, Dr. Moore suggested, doctors probing, for example, the possibilities of an effective cancer vaccine might abandon their quest rather than risk being propelled into public debates—or into defenses against malpractice.

And if this happens, he hinted, humans has threatened the progress of such work, Dr. Southam and Dr. Moore complained.

And Dr. Moore noted that the problem of finding human participants for such experimentation is—not surprisingly—aggravated whenever a hue and cry develops and the "guinea pig" label is affixed to human beings.

He went so far as to suggest that doctors be allowed to shelve the requirement that they receive the "informed consent" of their subjects before proceeding with an experiment. And, he continued, doctors shouldn't have to use the word "cancer" in outlining cell-planting experiments to their subjects.

ISN'T POSSIBLE

Truly "informed" consent just isn't possible "unless you confine your experimental work to Ph.D.s in biology," Dr. Moore said.

And besides, the more times the word "cancer" is used, the harder it is to find participants for the tests.

cer patients who received live cancer cell injections were unable to fight off the cells in the same period of time.

Besides tending to confirm the notion that there are natural "defense mechanisms" which help ward off cancer, Dr. Southam's figures suggested another possibility—that such infections might give a clue to the presence of cancer in persons who don't suspect they have the disease.

If these "defense mechanisms" do exist and can be identified, "it would mean the possibility of utilizing such host defenses in the treatment or prevention of cancer as is being done so effectively with infectious diseases," Dr. Southam said.

Then the cancer war could perhaps shift from one of improving techniques for treating established cases to ways of arming the human body to fight off cancer before it can take its lethal foothold.

Dr. Moore endorsed Dr. Ochsner's and Dr. Southam's live cancer experiments on their unwitting patients! Southam may have still been conducting his experiments on his captive Jewish patients when this news article was written. Our team had been given the details months ago. My note to Dr. Ochsner simply stated: *"Injecting disease-causing materials into an unwitting subject who does not have a disease is unethical*."

I signed it with my initials, J.A., and hand-delivered it to Dr. Ochsner's desk at his Clinic. His regular secretary-nurse was on vacation. Instead, an older, gruff secretary was covering for her. Dr. Ochsner, she said, was in surgery. When she asked if the matter was "urgent," I said it was. She said she would read it to Dr. Ochsner over the phone when he called in for his urgent messages. But as I turned to leave, in an agony, I heard her read the note aloud to Ochsner over the Intercom! My heart sank. I should have told the nurse that the note was "personal."

I left on the run, and because I was frightened, headed at once for Dr. Mary's apartment. As soon as I arrived, which took some time by bus, Dave Ferrie called. Dr. Ochsner had contacted him and was frantically trying to locate me. He was furious! After Dave talked to me about ten minutes to calm me down, mainly by telling me about the Clinton trip, he finished by saying, "He's your enemy now, J. He told me that you and Lee are expendable." Then he said, "Dr. O. even exceeded my own prowess in profanity. He's looking for you even as we speak. Good luck, J." Then he hung up. I was thunder-struck.

Before I could recover from Dave's call, the phone rang again. It was Dr. Ochsner. He began by telling me that I could forget about Tulane Medical School. I protested that he had promised, and his word was supposed to be his bond.

"I'll set something up for you in Florida with Smathers again," Ochsner said with an air of accommodation. "He still likes you. As for me, I've lost interest in you. And if you think I'm upset about your piece of paper," he added, "if you talk about this to anybody, you will regret every damned word you ever said. *Have I made myself perfectly clear*?"

Then he coldly reminded me that I had to go to Jackson tomorrow to perform my unique cancer diagnosis blood tests. This was not a request; it was an order. No one else could do the work, and it had to be done tomorrow. Intimidated, I promised to go. Then he became abusive again. "There was to be no paper trail!" he roared. "What in the name of God made you decide to write a letter?"

"Sir, it wasn't a letter. It was j..."

"There was to be NO paper trail!" he bellowed again. Dr. Ochsner told me that Lee and I must be separated. He also said that if something bad happened to me, it would not be his fault! He was absolving himself from any guilt in advance. Anything I suffered from now on had resulted from my own actions. The word that Dave had used was "expendable."

I now understood that my life was being threatened, but only after Ochsner hung up did I realize that his phone call had just wrecked my entire life, as if I'd been nothing but a three-minute egg he'd decided to boil. I sat down on the sofa with my head in my hands and cried. The phone rang again. It was Dr. Mary. She said that she had heard about Ochsner's wrath over my letter and had called him, saying that I should have been informed that the prisoner was a convicted murderer, as well as a certifiable mental case. "I'm so sorry," she told me. "He's made a mountain out of a molehill." This was a hint that Dr. Mary was still on my side, which was some comfort. I hoped she would still give me good references to a medical school in Latin America, which was one of the plans Lee and I had considered. The only positive note she had to offer was that Dr. Ochsner had agreed to a civil, calm exit interview. Little did I know that I would never hear Dr. Mary's voice again.

I wish I had told her how much she meant to me. Soon after our conversation, Lee called, telling me to take a cab ASAP and meet him at the Fontainebleau Hotel. Dr. Mary would pay for it. I hurried out: the cab came quickly. Lee and I reached the Fontainebleau at about the same time. As soon as we met, Lee broke the bad news. In a few hours, Dave was to drive me to Charity Hospital to face Dr. Ochsner for the "civil" exit interview. It would be a late meeting, because Dave was still in court with Carlos Marcello, and Ochsner had to talk to some other people first. While we waited for Dave, Lee and I ate dinner in the lounge of the Fontainebleau. Young William 'Mac' McCullough, whose mother worked at Lee's Coffee Shop, and who himself was associated with Marcello's people, recognized us. He crooned some love songs our way with his velvety voice, as he played the piano. Lee and I held hands, our eyes closed... The lounge's early patrons had filled the room by the time

Dave showed up and joined us at our table. He had the car instead of his motorcycle. He had been told to take me to Ochsner. Lee then said he had to go home –there was no choice-- but he would walk over to Susie's later that evening. Then came the dreaded ride to Charity Hospital for Ochsner's dismissal meeting. As I got out of the car, Dave said, "Don't worry. I'll wait for you." I entered Charity Hospital feeling very small and very alone. Soon, I was escorted to a large, silent conference room, where for several minutes I was left by myself to meditate. Ochsner's tirades were famous. They were so horrendous that his students were known to have fainted onto the floor.

He was coming — in all his fury. What did my pitiful stab at "morality" mean to the great Ochsner? Nothing! Nevertheless, he could hang me, if he liked. I'd never back down on this. Nor, I determined, would I cower before him. When Dr. Ochsner entered the room, the look on his face was hard and unforgiving. Without a word, he handed me some important blood work code sheets, with which to make my reports. Then, rising to his feet, he exploded. It was unlike anything I had ever encountered. He ground his teeth, his eyes bugged out, and spit came flying from his mouth in his fury. I felt that he was throwing me, my heart, and my soul into the gutter.

Then, he suddenly sat down and regained his composure. "When you finish your assignment at Jackson," he said, with a voice of hatred, "Give us the results. And consider your work for us over."

After his fuse burned a little further, he stood up again, and with clenched teeth said, "Consider yourself lucky you're walking out of here with your teeth still in your head. Now-- *get out!"* He struck at me as I turned, but I avoided the blow. I now know there was a witness to this encounter just beyond the door, who had overheard everything.

The violent side of Ochsner Dr. John Ochsner, his son, mentioned severe beatings his father administered to him and his brothers, even once breaking a belt on him during a thrashing. Ira Harkey, Ochsner's official biographer, said that today, the severity of Ochsner's beatings would be called child abuse.

An Undocumented Mafia Witness This witness is now dead, and is presented as mere hearsay, but it is worth describing. In Nov. 2020 ,the son of a New Orleans Mafia member told me why the Mafia didn't kill me. Claudia Rodick, Susie Hanover's great granddaughter who located the witness, was also on the phone line. The man's father and an associate had been assigned to follow me for a few days to protect me, at the end of August 1963. Why? Because Carlos Marcello feared for my safety! One of Marcello's own had heard Ochsner screaming at me, even through the door, and had seen "the motion of his arm, as if he was trying to strike you," as a shadow through the frosted glass of the door's window. He said Marcello had --"a favorite" incarcerated at Angola Prison. He was among a batch of "volunteers" brought to Jackson to be injected "in some kind of cancer project." But my objections had stopped the rest of the prisoners from receiving the injections. Marcello, advised of the immediate illness of those who had been injected, felt my action may have saved his friend's life. For the next few days, the New Orleans Mafia member said he and a friend had been assigned to watch over me, until Ochsner calmed down. What's hilarious is the problem they had once, while following me. They thought I'd "caught on" that I was being followed, and was trying to ditch them, when actually, I was simply lost, trying to figure out how to get home. By placing a street barrier in front of a turn I'd already navigated, they managed to steer clueless me in the right direction toward home. As the informant told me this, he burst into laughter, saying how everybody in the Mafia knew I always got lost.

I know that later, when Dave Ferrie told me that I was being watched by Florida Godfather Santos Trafficante — a fact that terrified me.

But what if Santos had been asked to protect me, so long as I remained a quiet little mouse.? [247] Not knowing any of this, demoralized and

[247] Claudia and the man's son, who didn't want his name revealed, called from "Ben's Burgers" in Metairie, near the airport, New Orleans area.

shell-shocked though I was, I refused to cry in front of Ochsner.
I walked out without a tear on my face. As Lee had marched stoically out of Reily, so I steeled myself to march out of Charity Hospital.
Outside, Dave was waiting anxiously. It was the sight of those fake eyebrows and concerned eyes, that made me burst into tears. Dave put an arm around me and said: "I'm sorry, J. He's done with you, isn't he?" It was the only time Dave ever touched me kindly, in all that time. It must have been the priest in him. Dave walked me to his car and I got inside, slumping down in the seat as he tried to start the engine. It did not cooperate.

"Damn it!" he said. "The starter in this thing is driving me nuts." Then Dave's mood shifted, and he said a prayer aloud about the engine.
On his next try, the engine started. Dave shot me a sharp glance. "See?" he said. "God exists."

"Oh, shut up!" I told him. "You're full of fear and trembling," he said. "*Quo vadis*? What now?"

"I'm about to get my head cut off, just like St. Paul," I answered. "My future in medicine is finished, at least in the United States." I had refused to duplicate the sins of the Nazis. But my world had collapsed. And what would happen to Lee?

"You did the right thing to let him know your opinion," Dave said. "A shame you wrote it on paper, though. They hate records that remind them of their mischief. That's why they invented all those terms like Need to Know, Eyes Only, and Plausible Denial."

One of the last photos of David Ferrie, 1967.

When we reached my apartment, Dave got out and walked me to the door. When I went inside to wash my face, Dave took that moment to talk to Susie. Then Lee arrived, and we sat with Susie on lawn chairs in the back of the house. We talked for a while, then Dave began telling Lee about his car problems, and the two men walked toward his car and talked a bit, while looking under the hood. When they returned, we began discussing my fate. Lee looked at Dave and said, "Now you can have parties on weekends again." Dave gave us both a hard, sad look. He pulled his cap further down over his face. "It won't be the same without you guys," he said. Then he returned to his car. He drove off with flare, screeching his tires and honking his horn. We waved goodbye. At the time, I didn't realize I'd never see my eccentric friend again.

Lee handed me my purse and said, "You left it in the car. You must be very upset." I took my purse and clutched it, as our tears fell again. Susie brought us lemonade, then left us to ourselves in the humid night. So, what was good, and what was evil? Evil didn't care about destroying lives. As we talked, Lee took out his *Pocket Aristotle.*

He had been underlining various passages, even numbering them. Aristotle was the first writer to talk about ethics, and "the highest good." David Ferrie had ordered the book for Lee after they had a debate about women's rights. He had flown to New York to pick up some unpublished research papers, and at that time, picked up the book hot off the pres. To get Lee to read it, Dave had challenged Lee to find anything about "women" in Aristotle's writings. Dave claimed that women didn't count in Aristotle's world. Lee took up the challenge.

As Lee spoke about ethics, kindness, and morality, I began to see what riches Lee exhibited, in his fierce struggle to rise above the turmoil, wickedness, and pettiness all around him. He had matured since I met him, right before my eyes. Did he sense, somehow, how short his time was now? There was a youthful majesty about him, a spirit fit for a young philosopher king who cherishes his freedom and wants happiness for humanity. All nations bring forth a few, consumed by a lust for power and fortune, who force their rule on others, he said. Such persons may be remembered for their infamy, but the greatest rulers were known by the good they did for their people. At the height of these musings, Lee put the Aristotle book in my lap, took my hand, and looked sadly into my eyes. "My wife!" he said to me. "Tell me I'm your husband."

"You're my beloved husband!" I replied. Lee leaned over and rested his head against my breast, and I stroked his hair. After a few minutes, he said, "I'm tempted to tell you the end of that science fiction story, where Adam and Eve are fleeing for their lives."

"Tell me!" I urged him.

"Not yet," he said, smiling and sitting up. He brought out a large envelope, which he had been carrying inside his shirt. "When we meet in Mexico," he said, "then I'll tell you how the story ends." Shyly, he handed the envelope to me, his eyes cast down. "Open it," he said. "I want to see your face. Then I have to go." I opened the unmarked envelope, which was unsealed. Inside were twenty brand-new $20 bills. $400 in all. (almost $4,000 in 2021 funds). "It's for you," Lee said. "Money so you can reach me, wherever I am. Money to go to school. In Florida, next semester, if we have to wait that long." I tried to resist the gift, but he told me I had to take it. I must have the means to come to him when it was safe. He also added, bitterly, that Dr. Ochsner should have given me money to help keep my cover more secure. "And besides," he said, "you might need new shoes!"

After embracing him, as we both tried to laugh, I asked, "How am I going to account for this? It's too much to risk hiding it. "You'll have to find a way," he said. "I need my wife by my side down there." The envelope fell into my lap, as we held each other in silence. Then, in the deepening night, Lee sighed, got up and walked away, not looking back. Unable to bear it, I followed him wistfully as he headed out to the sidewalk. As I stood there, I noticed a yard sale next door. I had long needed an ironing board, and spotted one on the porch, where a lady sat. But first, I saw a scarf I liked, in the back of a car that was parked at the curb. It was the landlord's car (he did not live on the premises). He was selling his own items from his open trunk. When I spotted a brand-new hunting knife, still in its box, I recalled that we could use something like that in the Yucatan. But for now, I only dared buy the ironing board, still wondering how I would explain the $400 windfall to Robert. After lugging it inside, I had an idea. I crumpled and ironed the bills so they wouldn't look so new, then put them back in the envelope and shoved it all under the ironing board cover. I made sure I was ironing something when Robert returned home at about 11:30 P.M. As I ironed, I contrived to have the envelope fall to the floor, and called out, "Bob! Look at this!"

Then I opened the envelope and showed Robert the money, which was warm from the iron. I told him that I had just bought the ironing board from the yard sale next door, and the money had fallen out of it.

"Then this doesn't belong to you," Robert declared with finality. "We'll have to give it back." Morality from the Miser! Despite the shock, I was proud of him. As much as he craved money, he wouldn't take it, if it didn't belong to him. We could have used some of that morality on The Project. Still, I dreaded the coming of morning. I knew Lee had sacrificed to pull together that much money.

Early next morning, as soon as the yard sale opened, we went over to check it out. We learned that half the items, including the ironing board, had belonged to a retired teacher who had died. She had never married and had no known relatives. The landlord had waited quite a while to see if anybody would claim her belongings, but nobody did. Finally, he was selling her things to collect overdue rent. I asked if the sale had made enough to cover everything. Yes, it had. They'd even made plenty extra, by selling her car. Robert and I looked at each other, shrugged, and we left, with the $400 still in my purse. He went back to bed, and I finished up ironing the clothes. Dr. Ochsner's verbal hellfire had demoralized me. With my medical career on the rocks, I was in mourning. But at least I still had our money. I would have the funds to reach Lee. In Mexico, in the Cayman Islands, or on the moon.

Once Robert was asleep, I returned to the yard sale and bought the black and gold Imperial hunting knife for Lee that I'd spotted, and a collection of silk scarves, all of which I stuffed into my purse.

On **Saturday, August 31, 1963,** a final, important trip was necessary for The Project. Lee had to return to Jackson to pick up blood test results. Blood tests on the "volunteer" were needed to see if the cancer had established itself in his system. For that, Lee had obtained a car.

As Lee and I waited for Robert to leave, I think we played with little Claudia and a couple of other little kids who were there. 'Gram' as Claudia called her great-grandmother, liked to teach the children arts and crafts, especially on the weekends, and Lee was helping her. When Robert finally left, he said he might come back early-- we'd be cutting it close. We said goodbye to Susie and the kids, then walked to an old, dark green Kaiser-Frazer, a semi-luxury 1951 model. It was the same car Lee used to drive me from the bus station to Churchill Farms for Marcello's gathering. I still thought of it as the "Eli Lilly car" because I had seen it parked near their building so often. As I climbed in, I noticed a big basket in the back seat area. Lee said Anna Lewis was pregnant again (she would end up having ten children!), and the basket was a bassinet that David Lewis had bought for their next baby. David had put it in this car to protect it from his toddler, who wanted to play in it.

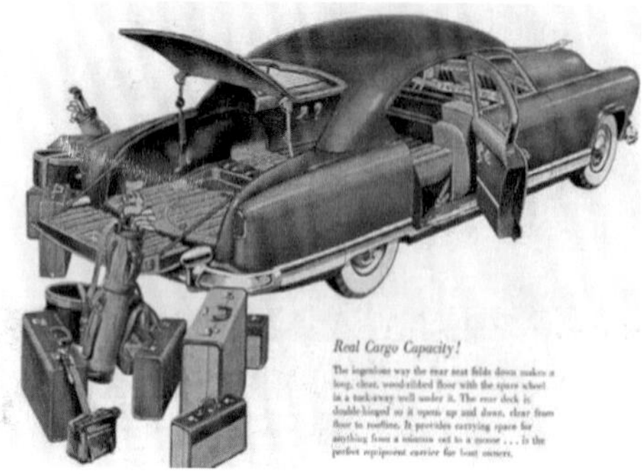

The bassinet had plenty of room to hold my papers and the materials we had to bring back to New Orleans after the blood tests Lee said he had five gallons of extra gas, oil and transmission fluid in the trunk, plus five gallons of water. We were ready for anything. As we drove off, Lee said he was mailing off some red-herring letters to obscure his intent to live in Mexico with me. One was to the Communist Party and stated his intent to move to Baltimore. Lee apparently mailed the letter too late for a postmark of Aug. 31.

He had already written other letters saying he planned to move to Philadelphia, Houston, and so on, avoiding all mention of his actual intention to go to Mexico City. These letters were sent out to keep everybody guessing as to his actual location at this critical time; Lee's mail, of course, was also being regularly opened by the FBI. His business for the CIA was none of their business, Lee said.

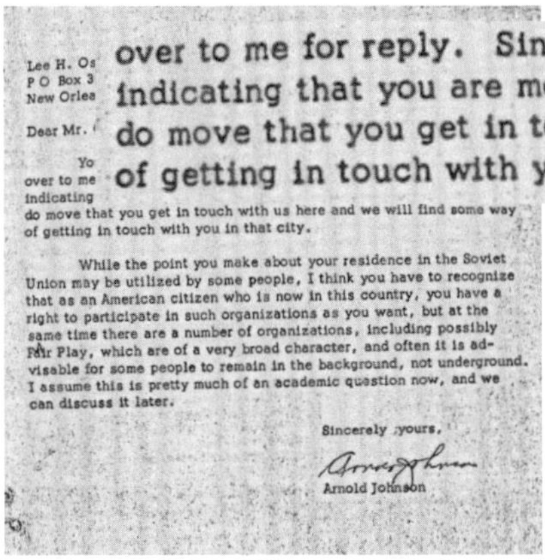
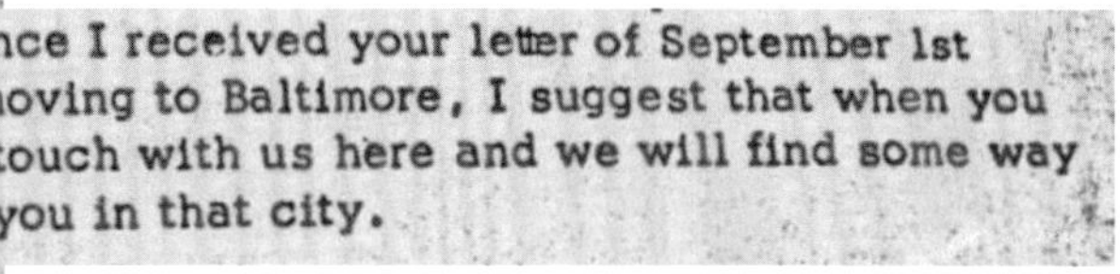

over to me for reply. Since I received your letter of September 1st indicating that you are moving to Baltimore, I suggest that when you do move that you get in touch with us here and we will find some way of getting in touch with you in that city.

Lee H. Os
P O Box 3
New Orlea

Dear Mr.

Yo
over to me
indicating
do move that you get in touch with us here and we will find some way of getting in touch with you in that city.

While the point you make about your residence in the Soviet Union may be utilized by some people, I think you have to recognize that as an American citizen who is now in this country, you have a right to participate in such organizations as you want, but at the same time there are a number of organizations, including possibly Fair Play, which are of a very broad character, and often it is advisable for some people to remain in the background, not underground. I assume this is pretty much of an academic question now, and we can discuss it later.

Sincerely yours,

Arnold Johnson

Lee also said we would stop to pick up a back-up set of cancer cells on our way to Jackson. It was some kind of test of the drop-off method to be used in Mexico City.

Once we reached the highway, Lee sped up, as he filled me in about what happened in Clinton and at the Jackson mental hospital two days before. I was able to fill in the blanks that Dave Ferrie had left out when we had talked so briefly during the Ochsner disaster. When they got

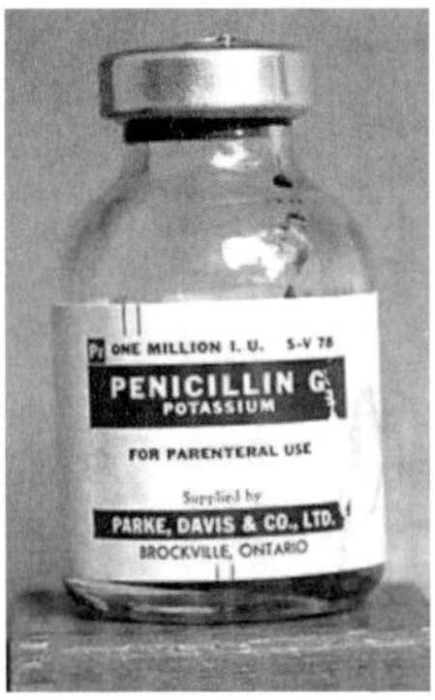

inside the compound, Lee said, the Aide escorted him and Dave behind the main building into the Men's Clinic, while Clay Shaw went into the main building with "funds." The plan to kill Castro depended on the fact that Castro got regular vaccinations, check-ups and x-rays to make sure he was clear of tuberculosis – at that time a plague in Cuba-- as well as to make sure he was still free of tropical diseases, parasites and infections from his previous jungle life. In 1960-1961, Cuba lost half its doctors. They fled to the West. About 200 were leaving the island every year, unhappy with Castro's truly amazing revamping of the health care system that displeased so many of his medical professionals, who no longer grew wealthy on urban clients. Castro forced medical students to work in rural areas as part of their training, which many of them deeply resented. But I admired Castro for doing that. His people were finally getting the medical care previously denied them. There were reports and statistics to back this up. I reviewed how Castro would be killed with the bioweapon. Castro, x-rayed regularly to check for TB and lung cancer, would get a dose strong enough to compromise his immune system. He had dedicated doctors, but

there were technicians and radiologists who could rig an x-ray machine. He'd feel terrible: he would likely develop a dry cough, a sore mouth, diarrhea and a fever. Bloodwork would reveal a reaction like an infection, for which he would be prescribed antibiotics. Shots of Penicillin would be recommended to deal with the 'infection', which a tech could easily contaminate with the deadly cancer cocktail.

How clever! How horrible! So, the Product was probably going to be pumped into a bottle of penicillin, such as could be found in every doctor's clinic, or he'd be vaccinated for tetanus, giving him more of the cancer cells. "For parenteral use" meant "brought into the body through some way other than the digestive tract, as by subcutaneous or intravenous injection." Reactions to the foreign material would bring on more fever, with more x-rays to check for 'pneumonia.
Plus, more 'penicillin' or similar contaminated shots. Only one shot had to reach a vein. Then the cancer would get its chance if the X-rays had been used, for this was a galloping cancer. Castro's chances, if it worked in humans as it did in monkeys, were zero.[248] By the time the cancer was diagnosed, it would be too late. It had killed the African green monkeys in mere weeks. Castro's death by cancer would be ascribed to "natural causes"—via his careless and constant use of cigars. While at Jackson, Lee said that after the cancer cells were removed from their glass container, he observed the volunteer being x-rayed and then injected. After that, Dave asked him to leave. But why? What did they not want him to see? Were there more "volunteers" to work with, besides the one he had seen? Perhaps this was why the convoy was so late. Maybe it took longer to get organized because more than one prisoner was involved. Based on the size of the transfer vehicle in the convoy, more prisoners could have been brought in.

Knowing that it would upset me, perhaps Dave didn't want this information passed back to me through Lee. But Lee had expected Dave, who knew the layout of the entire hospital[249], to take him to the Personnel office, where he planned to fill out a job application. That would fit well with his statements to Clinton's Registrar of Voters. Lee wanted people to remember his interest in a job, not his presence at the clinic. Without Dave, Lee had to ask the clinic receptionist for directions to the personnel office.[250]

The application also provided an excuse for Lee's return, when he had to drive me there. That's how I came to learn of the ploy. Once we were settled in the car, we had to drive pretty fast. Lee took a more direct route to Jackson this time, avoiding going through Clinton again, where he might be recognized as the man who rode in a fancy black Cadillac. As he drove, I told Lee what had happened concerning the $400.

---

[248] https://elischolar.library.yale.edu/cgi/viewcontent.cgi?article=2863&context=ymtdl

[249] Dave said he had rescued several teenagers who had acted "crazy"—usually due to drugs -- from long-term imprisonment at Jackson. Certainly, Dave knew the layout of the hospital.

[250] Mrs. Bobby Dedon testified in the Clay Shaw trial, as a receptionist at Jackson, that Lee Harvey Oswald, whom she identified by a photo, asked her where to go to apply for a job. It had to be after 1:00 pm by now, but she said she was ready to eat lunch, and recalled his lunch sack. She was discredited because she couldn't remember if Lee had a beard, but Lee's application was found in the Personnel office files (though it disappeared soon after the assassination).

He replied, "You're worth more than $400 to me," he said. Then, he told me more. "I once left somebody behind that I loved. They beat her, because she pined for me. Never again."

I said nothing and waited for Lee to open up a little more. But he didn't. Finally, he added, "When it is time for you to come to me, just don't let me down." He gave me a quick glance, smiled, and added, "I hope you won't get lost."

"I won't get lost!" I assured him. He smiled again.

"It was my whole month's pay, you know...hold onto it." I was stunned. We went on in silence for some time. I let him muse. Then he said softly, "Never again..." as if speaking to himself. When enough time passed, I said, "But without the money, how will you —?"

"I've been careful," he broke in, knowing I'd bring this up. "There will be just enough for everything. Besides, after I reach Mexico City, I'll have all the money I'll need. If I need it." He stated this firmly. "My friend Alex has agreed to fly you out of Florida and over to Mexico, but if that doesn't work, you can still take a commercial flight to Mexico from Tampa. I'll be there to meet you, if there's a breath of life in me."

I wish he hadn't said it that way. As we reached the outskirts of town, we stopped at a gas station. The attendant filled the tank to the brim, washed all the windows squeaky-clean, checked the oil, and made sure the tires had the proper pressure. While that was going on, Lee went inside the gas station. When he came out, he was carrying a paper bag and two Dr. Peppers. In the bag was a thermos containing the cancerous bioweapon. The thermos had been delivered to the gas station, along with a small cooler full of ice, for preserving the blood samples we'd bring back.

Dewar Thermoses showing the glass liners

Since our car had no air conditioning, we needed the ice. The timing was perfect: I was impressed. On we went, crossing beautiful blue Lake Pontchartrain, and then heading west to Baton Rouge. From there, we headed north, driving through open country, with lots of clouds overhead to keep us cool. Lee also developed an idea to hide the true reason for his second trip to the Jackson hospital in less than 72 hours. In small towns, strangers and their cars get noticed.

Lee planned to ask people in Jackson about "how to get a job at the hospital" -- even though he'd *already* filled out an employment application two days earlier. He had a reason: mixing up the timeline.

If any witnesses from Jackson and Clinton were asked about seeing "Lee Oswald," the only reason they knew for Lee to be in the area, was job-hunting. That took "biological weapons" far from the table.

The witnesses would also argue about having seen Lee Oswald connected to different cars "at the same time." In Clinton, witnesses would remember two or three or four men in a Cadillac. In Jackson, witnesses recalled an old, dark green car, with a woman in it. Both sets of witnesses would say Lee Oswald was linked to the car they saw.

This would cause confusion, with two stories in conflict with each other. It was a CIA-inspired classic. For decades, researchers have tried to figure out what you, reading this, can discern: that there were *two trips, not one.* It was a long drive, so to calm ourselves, I took Lee's *Pocket Aristotle* from my purse and began reading to him about ethics, righteousness, the characteristics of both great and petty men. Then--finally – when I read something about 'women' Lee said, "Whoa!" He stopped the car. He took the book from me, and with a stub pencil I found for him, he underlined some words and then made a note in the margin, writing 'feelings about women.' "I don't want to forget where it's at," he said. "Dave told me Aristotle hardly ever wrote anything about women," Lee added. "He told me Aristotle believed women were inferior, but that's not what it says here—"

"All I want is to accomplish something good and beautiful, instead of this!" I cried out, as he started driving again. "You were boxed in," Lee said. "I've been there, too. This is the last of it."

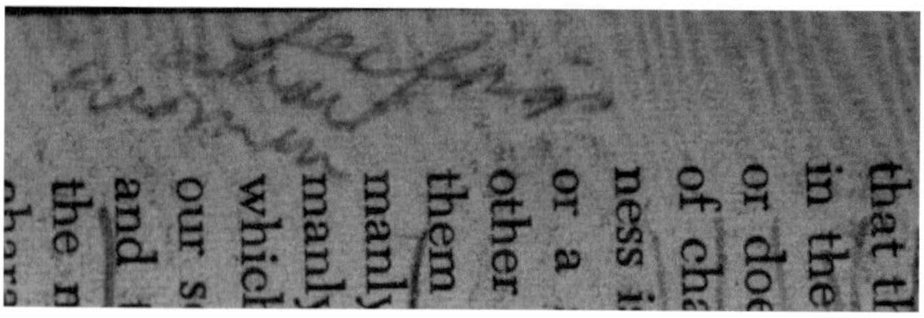

"It's got to be," I agreed. I continued to read aloud from Aristotle as Lee drove on. [251] [252]As we approached Jackson, the car overheated, so Lee said we would stop soon to let the engine cool down. Upon entering Jackson, we looked for a sign to tell us where the hospital was, but did not find one. Lee decided to stop at the local barber shop. "Town barbers know everything," Lee explained. "I'll ask for a haircut. I can tell my little story here, too, about looking for a job." Though it was late August, the weather was cooler than normal[253] and the sky was overcast with clouds, making it possible for me to stay in the car. When Lee came out about 20 minutes later, I looked at his hair and wondered if the barber had even cut it. The barber, Lea McGeHee later testified at Clay Shaw's trial. By doing so, he

---

[251] Lee had already underlined parts of the book and written a little more in the margins.

[252] My children knew about this book for years. My son James once asked me about the writing in it. Robert stamped it with "R.A. Baker" as he did to all our books 1963-1973.

[253] Weather records show it was ½ to 1 degree cooler than the average August. That may seem small, but there was also less rain; the low humidity made it seem cooler.

helped establish the date of our trip to Jackson and how Lee was dressed "to get a job," as seen in the following statements (author's emphasis):

> **A:** Well, **the last part of August** we had some relatively cool nights, which was unusual for August, and we commented on that several times in the barber shop. If I had to say it, I would say **the last of August. <snip>**
> **Q:** Now let's see if you can be a little more accurate on your description of this automobile that you saw this man get out of. **A:** Yes, sir. **Q:** Was it a large automobile or a small one? **A:** If I had to say what it was, it was a -- **it resembled a Kaiser or a Frazer** or an Old Nash. **<snip> Q:** Now, did you give Oswald a haircut on this occasion? Is that correct? **A: Yes,** sir. **Q:** Do you remember how he was dressed? **A:** He had on a sport shirt and slacks. **Q:** Did he have shoes on or not? **A:** I am sure he did.
> **Q:** Would you say he was neatly dressed? **A: Very neatly dressed. Q:** Very neatly dressed? **A:** Clean shaven. **Q:** I see. now, Mr. McGehee, by your voluntarily adding the words **"very neatly dressed," would I be correct in assuming that his neatness actually impressed you? A: Yes. That is the reason I referred him for the job."**

The barber told Lee the correct road to the hospital, as well as how to reach an influential friend -- Mr. Reeves Morgan. (Mr. Palmer, the Registrar, later claimed that he gave Lee the name of Reeves Morgan, but that's not what Lee told me.) When Lee started up the car again, he said that we were still on time. Upon reaching the mental hospital's main gate, Lee saw the Aide who had been with him at Clinton waiting for us. The timing of our arrival had been planned to coincide with the hospital's shift change, when lots of cars were coming and going through the gates. We were taken behind the huge white main building, where we were in a large semi-paved area. There, we took a rough service elevator to the second story, into a fancy area of the hospital. Only important persons were kept in this upscale area of the building, sometimes to dry out from an alcoholic binge. Obviously, our prisoner was being given special treatment.

Once Lee knew where I was going to be, he went on to the personnel office to provide an excuse for his presence at the hospital. Meanwhile, I asked a male nurse seated at a little table if I could interview the "client." I was curtly told that he was in isolation and that nobody was allowed to see him. This angered me, but like it or not, I had work to do. In the clinic area everything was already laid out for me. I checked the blood-work and data while using a centrifuge to spin down the freshly-drawn blood samples to soft, dark pellets sitting in their plasma. I also inspected slides and blood counts prepared for me. An additional task was to look for particular cancer cells. Some were found — a sign that the bioweapon worked. The original cancer cells had been tagged with a radioactive tracer.

If radiation was detected in the pellets, the volunteer was surely doomed. There was trace in the preliminary scan, so it seemed everything was a 'go.' I had agreed to do this disgusting work because if the cancer "took" I could say no more prisoners were needed. If it failed, I planned to recommend dropping the whole idea. My goal was to stop the testing of any more prisoners, period. My work complete, I packed it all into the cooler for transport, with fresh ice. Then I insisted on observing the prisoner's current condition. I wanted to see if this patient was the same person Lee had watched get inoculated. I had prepared myself to look and remember the face I saw, as was my weak spot. I was so persistent that the nurse reluctantly took me to the door of the prisoner's room.

I was not to be allowed inside, but I could view the patient through a small window. The room was barred, but basically clean. Several storage boxes sat on the floor on the left-hand side of the room. Some flowers sat on a stand next to the metal bed. *What a nice touch*, I thought, *for somebody you're killing.* The patient was tied to the bed, thrashing around in an obvious fever. I knew the intravenous fluids he was getting would do him no good. It was very sad. Sorry for the part I had played in his sufferings, I had to force myself to look pleased with the prisoner's poor status. Told that "a gentleman" was waiting for me downstairs, I was allowed to descend the stairs and leave the front way. We had spent some forty-five minutes at the hospital.

Back in the car, Lee and I compared notes. When I described the patient I saw to him, Lee pointed out that his hairline and nose was different from the patient he had seen injected. Between Lee's comments and the blood samples, I had to believe that more than one "volunteer" had been injected. As Lee drove, suddenly we could hear a hissing sound from under the hood. A leak! Lee pulled over to inspect the engine. Sure enough, a pinhole leak at the connector end of one of the radiator hoses needed attention. I retrieved a rubber tourniquet from the cooler. Lee said that would help, but we still needed something to hold it in place, so I stripped off my nylon stockings and handed them over. Lee smiled and took out his handkerchief, placing it over the rubber tourniquet and tying both into place with my nylons. It worked well enough for us to continue. It was now twilight. A strong, cool breeze came up and some raindrops started falling. But it wasn't enough: the engine was still overly hot. "I had planned to stop soon anyway," Lee said. Lee then turned into a long, curved driveway. "We were going to stop here, anyway," he said. "We have to let the car cool down." We parked under a big tree, near a nice white house with a big front porch. This was the home of Reeves Morgan, who had "prestige at the hospital."

The Morgan home was painted a dark color by the time photos of it became public.

Reeves Morgan outside the house where Lee Harvey Oswald visited him in 1963

<u>**Ignored Witnesses:**</u> In 2014, as **Mary Morgan Jenkins** drove me and publisher Kris Millegan to her childhood home, she asked me many questions, such as the kind of driveway (curved), how and where the car was parked, the car's color, the color of the house (then white, with no known public photos in the 60's), etc. As she parked in the driveway at the now dark-brown house, Mary asked if I recalled anything on the porch. I recalled a large, reddish object. Mary said that was their big, rusty freezer. She had come out to the porch to get something from it. She said her brother Van was easily led, for author Joan Mellen said Van, up in a tree, saw a black Cadillac pick up Lee, an event never mentioned in the original records. Mary is on record, just as the barber, telling Sciambra she saw an old car with a woman sitting in it. Mary also said Van was too old to be climbing trees. Mellen, who has a one-day Jackson - Clinton theory, knows I say I'm the woman they saw, but refused to interview me, though I asked her as we sat together six hours, signing books (I ruin her theory). As for <u>**Mary, she said Mellen never interviewed her, either**</u>!

"I'll be right back," Lee told me. He went up the porch steps, called out a friendly "Hello!" and walked right in. But this may have just been the hospitality that Louisiana prides itself on. I recalled that Kerry Thornley had done the same thing at Lee's porch.

As the sun set, I worked on my charts and then checked blood samples. Unable to see anymore as darkness set in, I looked up and saw a teenage girl standing on the porch. This was Reeves Morgan's daughter, Mary. Since it was almost dark, I didn't think she could see me. But she did. She later told Garrison investigator Andrew Sciambra that she saw a woman sitting in Lee's car.

Mary Morgan Jenkins with my book *David Ferrie: Mafia Pilot*, 2014. She recalled the old car – even its color-- and I satisfactorily answered her questions.

Lee was inside talking about half an hour to Mary's dad, after which he came out, put water in the radiator, and we drove off. Conscious of Robert's pending return, and this being our third delay, we were now in a hurry. Lee drove us back to New Orleans on the dark and narrow roads as fast as was safe, keeping a careful eye on the temperature gauge.

We were miserable over the fact that my work was now finished, and we would be forced to separate. So much had gone sour. I would never go to Tulane Medical School. Ochsner had demanded that I return to Florida. He had decreed that Lee and I were "expendable" and that after this necessary trip, that I must never contact anyone in the Project again. He made it plain that I would be eternally sorry if I ever breathed his name again. I would have to leave at once, though Lee still had work to do for the Project. With such obstacles to face, Lee and I talked a long time about what we would have to overcome to have a life together as husband and wife. Lee was told to break off contact with me immediately after this trip. The orders came straight from Dr. Ochsner. They were passed to Lee by Dr. Mary. But he and Dave had already figured out how to circumvent some of Ochsner's instructions. Lee said Dave could set us up with a safe phone line, (one of the Mafia bookie lines), but for a while we should "break clean" so everyone would think it was over between me and Lee. We had acquired powerful and dangerous enemies, so we had to be careful. On his side of things, Lee said that he already made it plain to Marina that he would soon leave, never to return.

"I told her she had a hundred people in Dallas to take care of her," he said. "She'd be happy there; or she could live with me, and never be happy. Lee said his divorce from Marina was inevitable, even if we'd never met. He wanted to do it while the kids were young. Why should they have a lot of bad memories about their Dad and Mom arguing all the time? There were tears in his eyes as he drove and told me these things. Lee was currently getting along well with Marina, but it was a strain. He understood the weight of his decision, and how it would affect his children. How often would he see them? Would he ever see them again? Even though we had been ordered to break up, we were determined to spend as much time as possible together, tomorrow, at our favorite hotel, the Roosevelt.

It was about 11:00 pm when we returned to 1032, relieved that Robert's car was not there. Since we expected him home any minute, Lee parked his car down the block. But as Suzi Collie came running down the street to greet us, wagging her tail, a car rushed past us and struck her! Suzi Collie yelped in pain and flipped over! We rushed to our canine friend to check her over, anxiously searching for broken bones and signs of internal bleeding, like pale gums, under the streetlight.

Except for a bruised shoulder, she appeared to be all right. After we carried Suzi Collie to the front porch, Lee had to leave. He still had to drop off the reports and blood samples, then had to hurry to buy a round trip bus ticket before midnight. The purchase date had to be as far as possible from the prisoner's death date. This ticket could become the first leg *en route* to Mexico City. At this time, Lee had no idea that he would ever be ordered back to Dallas, so it was a round trip with New Orleans as the city of choice. The round trip purchase was needed to make it seem that Lee never stayed in Mexico. That was part of the original set of plans, before he was betrayed in Mexico City. Lee also had to return the car. I had been carrying Lee's *Pocket Aristotle* when Suzi Collie got hit by the car, and now, finding the book on the ground, I picked it up and slowly walked home.

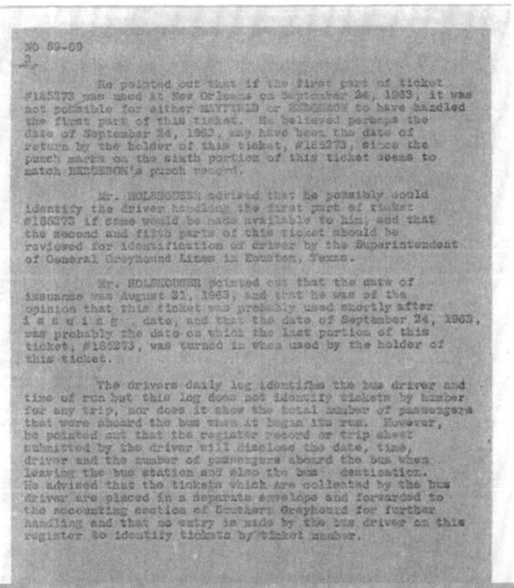

NO 89-69
2

He pointed out that if the first part of ticket #185273 was used at New Orleans on September 24, 1963, it was not possible for either [illegible] or [illegible] to have handled the first part of this ticket. He believed perhaps the date of September 24, 1963, may have been the date of return by the holder of this ticket, #185273, since the punch marks on the sixth portion of this ticket seems to match BERGERON's punch record.

Mr. HOLSHOUSER advised that he possibly could identify the driver handling the first part of ticket #185273 if same would be made available to him, and that the second and fifth parts of this ticket should be reviewed for identification of driver by the Superintendent of General Greyhound Lines in Houston, Texas.

Mr. HOLSHOUSER pointed out that the date of issuance was August 31, 1963, and that he was of the opinion that this ticket was probably used shortly after i s s u i n g date, and that the date of September 24, 1963, was probably the date on which the last portion of this ticket, #185273, was turned in when used by the holder of this ticket.

The drivers daily log identifies the bus driver and time of run but this log does not identify tickets by number for any trip, nor does it show the total number of passengers that were aboard the bus when it began its run. However, he pointed out that the register record or trip sheet submitted by the driver will disclose the date, time, driver and the number of passengers aboard the bus when leaving the bus station and also the bus destination. He advised that the tickets which are collected by the bus driver are placed in a separate envelope and forwarded to the accounting section of Southern Greyhound for further handling and that no entry is made by the bus driver on this register to identify tickets by ticket number.

This part of the FBI report shown describes a Greyhound bus ticket purchased Aug. 31, 1963. Lee was the purchaser, late that night. Eric Rogers saw Lee leave his 4905 Magazine St. apartment on Sept. 24. Records claiming Lee took a Continental Trailways bus between Houston and Laredo should be considered a fabrication, as the agent who claimed Lee bought that ticket, also around midnight, in Houston, in late September described Lee wearing clothing and shoes he didn't own. The timing for that ticket was too close to the prisoner's death.

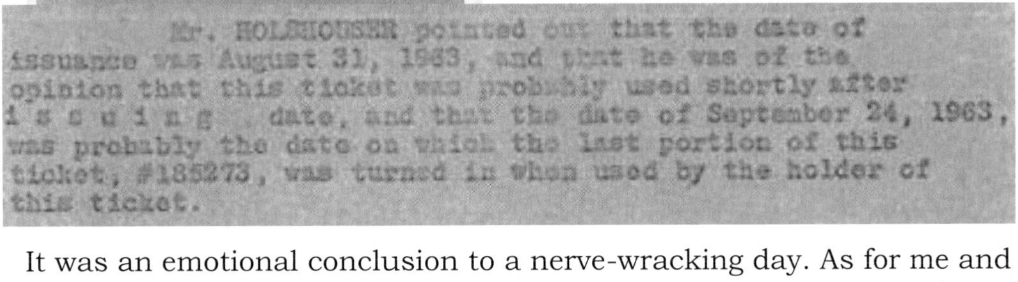

Mr. HOLSHOUSER pointed out that the date of issuance was August 31, 1963, and that he was of the opinion that this ticket was probably used shortly after i s s u i n g date, and that the date of September 24, 1963, was probably the date on which the last portion of this ticket, #185273, was turned in when used by the holder of this ticket.

It was an emotional conclusion to a nerve-wracking day. As for me and Lee, we had just one day left before our separation. Worn to numbness, I took a birdie-bath and went to bed. I'm not sure when Robert got home, but he was wonderfully late. When he did make it home, he woke me up, as always eager for *l'amour.* But around 2:30 the next day, the man who loved all of me was in my arms. We met in the lobby of the glorious Roosevelt Hotel and spent almost the whole day and most of the evening together in our suite. We pretended that time stood still. I delighted Lee by dancing for him, wrapped in my new collection of silk scarves, first to music from *Lawrence of Arabia.*

And then, I danced to *Bolero*, teasing him to the brink. Though we loved to talk, we spent several hours doing everything we could think of to express our pleasure and delight in each other without words. I wore the black necklace he gave me, and little else. There was joy, laughter, and love on many levels, with a keen longing to make time stand still. I gave Lee his black and gold Imperial hunting knife, in anticipation of our meeting in Mexico. Lee gave back the love letter that I had written to him, asking me to keep it for him. He said he could not keep it with his things and felt it was too precious to destroy. He also asked me to keep the nice Vesuvio brown tie his uncle Dutz had given him, so he could wear it at our marriage ceremony.

To grow so close to another person, young, strong and clean as we were, with the uncanny electric sparks that flew between us, the way we kept catching each other's glance at the same moment, the way we relaxed with total trust: I now know this is a rare and precious gift. At one point, we stood together on the balcony overlooking New Orleans, which had been transformed from a place of darkness, uncertainty and violence, into an incredibly romantic city filled with life, energy, light, and music.

All because I got to see it through the eyes of someone who wanted me to see all of it. As our time together drew to an end, we grew solemn, knowing that a long period of separation was about to begin. It was painful to think about. As our last moments together approached, we held each other as if our hearts would break. Finally, and sadly, we had our last streetcar ride together, and then we kissed goodbye at Marengo Street. Robert was not home yet, so I called Dave on Susie's phone and asked him to tell Dr. Mary we expected to leave in the morning. I didn't know that Dr. Mary had already left for London, where she would spend almost a month out of the country. She was distancing herself from The Project. My heart was heavy. When I hung up the phone, I realized that my dream of finding a cure for cancer was dead. My great reward for trying to do what was right was that Lee and I were now in great danger.

The Burglary of Dr. Mary Sherman's Apartment, the Night of Aug. 31, 1963 That same night, at about the time Lee and I returned to New Orleans on Aug. 31, someone broke into Mary Sherman's apartment.[254]

A neighbor at the Patio Apartments called Dr. Mary's friend, **Dr. Carolyn Talley**, about the burglary, and Dr. Talley called Mary, who was in London, who said that she would file a police report when she returned to New Orleans. This is why the police report is dated 9-27-63, though the time and date of the burglary was listed as 11:00 pm on 8-31-63, almost exactly the same time Lee and I returned from Jackson. The police report showed the value of the stolen property: $35 in currency, $350 in jewelry, $350 in furs, and $1,760 miscellaneous, totaling $2,495. *$1,760, just in miscellaneous*! $1,760 in 1963 dollars would be worth over $17,000 in 2021. [255] What was so valuable in Mary Sherman's apartment that was not money, jewelry or furs? We don't have the itemized list of stolen property attached to the report-- but I told Edward T. Haslam, who asked my opinion, that medical equipment from the Project, such as an oil immersion microscope, a centrifuge, the safe box with its attached rubber gloves and venting system, and what we called Ferrie's Wheel, for rotating and shaking the test tubes, were contenders. Importantly, *the research phase of the Project was officially over that same day.* A convenient burglary occurred the day Mary left town, distancing her from the theft and enabling her to quietly file an insurance claim to recover her losses when she returned.

Chapter 24
Separation

Monday, September 2, 1963

At dawn, Robert got up and started to pack the car. He was anxious to leave, but we had to wait for the bank to open so he could withdraw all of our money. Then, during his pre-trip safety check, Robert discovered a problem with the car and took it to a garage, hoping we still might be able to leave that day. But the repair didn't happen because it was Labor Day. Robert said the bank was closed, too, so we'd have to wait a day.

---

[254] This information was obtained through the research of Edward T. Haslam.

[255] A researcher told me in 2021 that The Patio Apartments were owned by Carlos Marcello. We couldn't find official records, but in 2020 became private condos.

Then Robert's parents called when we didn't show up in Ft. Walton as planned.They said I could earn $150 if I drew an architectural rendering of their new apartment buildings at Eglin Air Force Base for the newspapers before we had to be in Gainesville on the 6th. Meanwhile, forbidden to speak to each other, and concerned that Susie's telephone might be bugged, Lee and I did not dare communicate.

Tuesday, September 3, 1963 Once again, we prepared to leave. I hugged Susie goodbye for the last time. The bank would open at 9:00 A.M., so at 8:45, we left 1032 Marengo Street forever. All that time, my heart was aching. If only I could see _him_ – just one more time—and

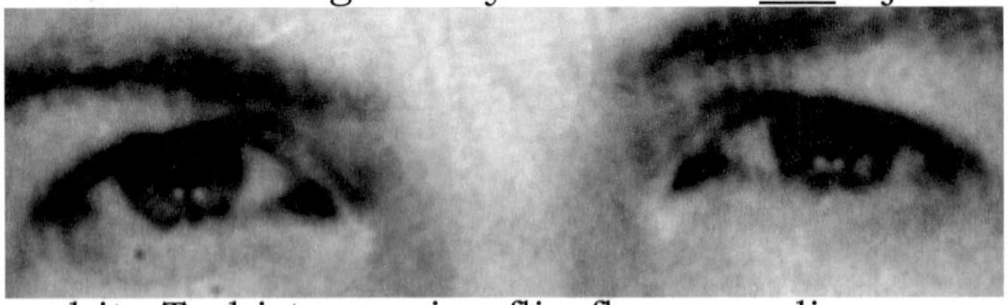

then, I did.

As Robert braked to turn onto Magazine Street, I saw a tanned young man, dressed in a white T-shirt, wearing flip-flops, reading a newspaper. As the car turned, he looked up from the newspaper, and looked directly into my eyes — *Lee!* It was the last time we saw each other.

By 9:15, we withdrew our money, including the Reily settlement money for a week's work at $46.20 that was finally deposited. Robert transferred the balance to our Florida bank, and then we were on our way to Fort Walton Beach. When I started to sing, Robert turned on the radio. He told me he didn't like my singing, which increased my sadness. The trip was otherwise peaceful.

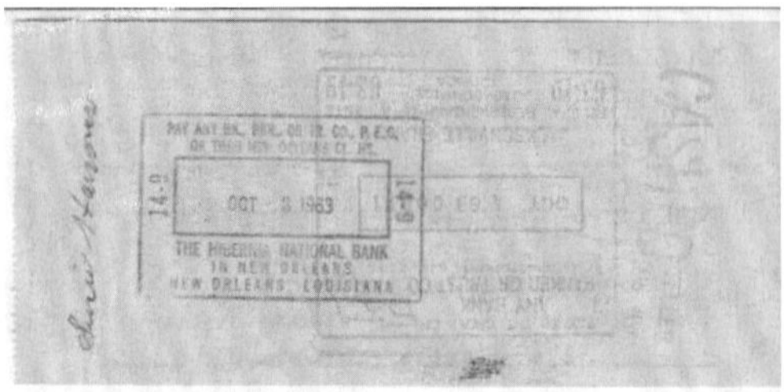

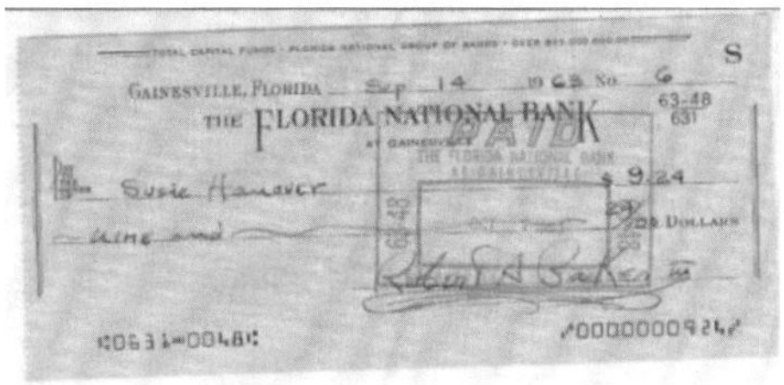

GAINESVILLE, FLORIDA Sep 14 1963 No. 6

63-48 / 631

THE FLORIDA NATIONAL BANK AT GAINESVILLE

PAID

Susie Hanover $ 9.24

nine and 24/00 DOLLARS

Robert A Baker III

⑆0631⑉0048⑆ ⑈0000000924⑈

The only bill we hadn't paid was our share of Susie Hanover's electric bill, which hadn't yet arrived. On Sept. 14, Robert wrote a check to Susie. She endorsed it on Oct. 3, 1963. After that, I never heard from her again. In 2020, I finally learned that Susie had moved in

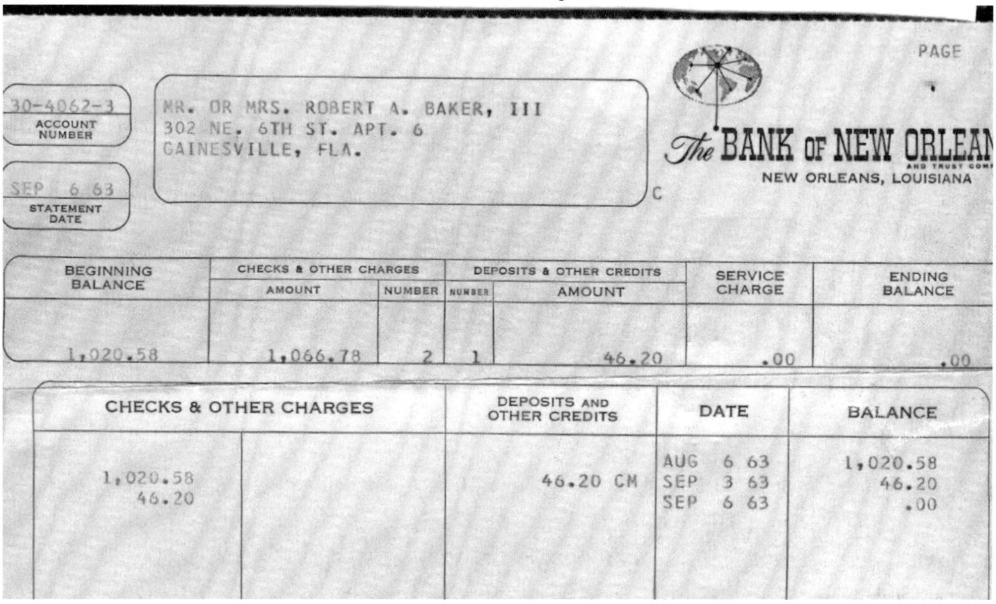

The BANK OF NEW ORLEANS AND TRUST COMPANY
NEW ORLEANS, LOUISIANA

PAGE

30-4062-3 ACCOUNT NUMBER

MR. OR MRS. ROBERT A. BAKER, III
302 NE. 6TH ST. APT. 6
GAINESVILLE, FLA.

SEP 6 63 STATEMENT DATE

BEGINNING BALANCE	CHECKS & OTHER CHARGES AMOUNT	CHECKS & OTHER CHARGES NUMBER	DEPOSITS & OTHER CREDITS NUMBER	DEPOSITS & OTHER CREDITS AMOUNT	SERVICE CHARGE	ENDING BALANCE
1,020.58	1,066.78	2	1	46.20	.00	.00

CHECKS & OTHER CHARGES		DEPOSITS AND OTHER CREDITS	DATE	BALANCE
			AUG 6 63	1,020.58
1,020.58		46.20 CM	SEP 3 63	46.20
46.20			SEP 6 63	.00

with Claudia's parents, taking Suzi Collie with her. Later, she went to live with another of her children, and then to a nursing home. Her family remained loving and caring.

The $46.20 Reily settlement payment for a week's work came in on Sept. 3, at which time Robert, satisfied, said we could now leave New Orleans.
We lived on cash I earned and that Lee gave me between Aug. 6 and Sept. 3. The Sept. 14 check (#6 on our Florida account) for our share of the electric bill was $9. Because I loved Susie, and it had her signature, I kept the check.

At Fort Walton Beach, I drew a 3-D rendering of Bob Baker, Jr's **"Hurlburt Arms"** housing project (see photo), which ended up in a big newspaper ad. I was paid $150, which was way too much. We ate at the Yacht Club, too. We also enjoyed a trip into the Gulf on Bob Baker Jr's yacht. We met Nonnie, Robert's grandmother. She was a delightful lady, white-haired and bent over with osteoporosis. We liked each other at once.

Then, on the 6th, we left for Gainesville, heading for the cottage Robert's mother selected for us.

Our 302 NE 6th St. cottage, 2018 (photo: Google maps)

September 6, 1963 We arrived in Gainesville after sunset and found a key under the mat on the front porch. Then we opened the door to our "furnished" cottage. It was as primitive as could be, but I was way too tired to care. The furniture was a double bed, a Formica-topped table, a wooden chair and an aluminum fold-up chair. At least the mattress was clean. The tiny cottage was on a dirt road between two buildings at 302 NE 6th St., zip 32601. It is still in existence and the names of the tenants were online in 2019. It was just west of UF, but too far to walk. Mrs. Baker had told us it was "cute" —and it did have a charming little porch, draped with passion-flower vines. But the kitchen was the size of a closet, with a leaky gas oven where roaches raised their families. Our little palace was well stocked with a sink, a refrigerator, some wooden crates, some planks of wood, and a bunch of bricks, from which we fashioned a desk and bookshelf. The bathroom is best left undescribed.

Near our mildewed haven, on the left as viewed from the porch, was a row of new red brick apartments, where I made new friends. Ron Ziegler and his pretty wife, Karen, lived in one of them, and were newlyweds too. They bought a 'forest painting' from me, and sometimes I would visit them, watch TV, and play cards with them. One of their parents owned a furniture store, so they had comfortable furnishings. I was too embarrassed to invite Karen over to our place.

EVANGELINE SEISMIC COMPANY, INC.
P.O. BOX 146 O.C.S.
LAFAYETTE, LOUISIANA

WITHHOLDING TAX STATEMENT COPY C
RECORD OF FEDERAL, STATE AND CITY TAX 1963
State of LOUISIANA
State Identification No. 2803450075

Type or print EMPLOYER'S Identification number, name, and address above.

Employee Number	No. of Dependents	‡	F.I.C.A. employee tax withheld, if any	Total F.I.C.A. Wages paid in 1963	Federal Income Tax withheld, if any	Total Wages* Paid in 1963	Excludable "SICK PAY." If none enter "0" or "NONE."	STATE INCOME TAX WITHHELD
266-62-0609	2	M	16 10	444 15	49 80	444 15	NONE	NONE

SOCIAL SECURITY INFORMATION — INCOME TAX INFORMATION

← STATE GROSS, IF DIFFERENT FROM FEDERAL GROSS

CITY TAX

ROBERT ALLISON BAKER III
511 EAST BROOKS STREET
FT. WALTON BEACH, FLORIDA

NOTICE: If your wages were subject to Social Security taxes, but are not shown, your Social Security wages are the same as wages shown under "INCOME TAX INFORMATION," but not more

Our "legal" address was Robert's home address for tax purposes, as even Robert wanted to move ASAP from "Roach Cottage." We moved to "FlaVet" married housing --an old barracks building refurbished for poor married couples—in 1964.

Prior to our goodbyes in New Orleans, Lee had taught me a phone call scheme he called a "call wheel" so he, Dave and I would know how and when to call each other using rotating call-times and phone numbers. For security reasons, we would call Lee by the name of 'Hector' on the phone. I was 'Minnie Mouse' --one of Lee's pet names for me. For now, Lee could not call from New Orleans safely, so he sent messages through Dave, who was an expert at detecting bugs and phone taps. Dave had some contacts in Gainesville and one of them left a phone number for "J" at the Craft Shop in UF's Student Union, where I used to work. Dave told me Lee was confident that even I could find the Craft Shop again, since I had worked there for an entire year. At this time, my friend Don Federman was now an editor of *The New Orange Peel* --UF's witty student magazine — asked me to do some illustration work for the magazine. After Robert dropped me off on campus on his way to class, I stopped by the Craft Shop and got my old job back. The Craft Shop had a private phone that would become one of the numbers Lee could call on the Mafia racing line.

When Dave called the next time, he updated me on the civil rights unrest in New Orleans, which was making Guy Banister foam at the mouth. Finally, Dave told me, "Hector was in Dallas." Lee had gone to Dallas briefly to prepare for his trip to Mexico City. That's when I learned of Lee's momentous meeting with the CIA's David Atlee Phillips, the propaganda master the CIA relocated to Mexico City. Only, at the time, we didn't know that was his name. He had arrived in Dallas around noon, having been flown in. Then Lee proceeded to the prestigious Southland Life Building downtown, where he met his handler, "Mr. B." Lee called him that because recently, Lee said he called himself 'Benton.' But before that, he'd said his name was 'Benson.' Currently, "Mr. B" wanted Lee to know that he was to plan on going to Mexico City before the end of the month. He would be given funds to fly there (not quite what happened). Then, just as "Mr. B" gave Lee a confidential code word and phone number for contact purposes, a Cuban rebel came walking down the hallway toward them. This man was **Antonio Veciana**, head of the CIA-directed Alpha 66. In his own words, he was "trained to kill." When the Cuban addressed "Mr. B" as "Senor Bishop," that's when Lee realized that only the letter "B" had been consistent in "Mr. B's" name. Lee had been told that he'd not only meet his handler, but also a

contact who would make sure the bioweapon got into Cuba. He assumed the Latino was that man. This would prove to be a falsehood.

Veciana was well-known. He and his men had tried to assassinate Castro more than once. Only because Veciana arrived early did he happen to see Lee with "Bishop." A young teenage couple noticed this meeting. One of the two, Wynne Johnson, in 2016 told me of seeing Lee Oswald, the CIA's David Atlee Phillips, and Antonio Veciana together in the Southland Life Insurance Building's lobby when he was a teen. [256] Later, Wynne presented what he remembered to various conferences, and finally, to Veciana himself, who vaguely recalled seeing Wynne's girlfriend in the hall where Veciana stood with Lee Oswald and David Phillips. Shortly before he died, Veciana admitted to Marie Fonzi, the widow of the HSCA's Gaeton Fonzi, that the man he'd identified to Fonzi as "Maurice Bishop" was indeed David Atlee Phillips. Veciana later spoke out about it publicly, just prior to his death.[257].

But now, all Lee knew was that his handler --the man he met at the Southland Building -- had given him three different names beginning with the letter "B" and was not to be trusted. Later, when we were able to talk again by phone, Lee said that "Bishop" knew so much about the trip to Mexico City that it was now clear that the CIA had control of the bioweapon, despite what Ochsner Clinic or Alton Ochsner may have believed. Maybe the CIA had always been in control.

"Mr. Bishop did not even introduce me to Veciana," Lee said. But he knew who he was. Lee had come across Veciana's photos, thanks to his contacts with Customs. It was an eyes-only encounter, after which the meeting abruptly ended. Not even invited to eat lunch with the two men, Lee was immediately sent back to New Orleans on an empty stomach and was home before nightfall. He only had a chance to grab a snack from a vending machine at the airport. This lack of respect made Lee even more wary of "Bishop." Although "Bishop" gave Lee information on where he could meet some important contacts in Mexico City, the CIA man's dismissive treatment remained a nagging concern.

---

[256] When I first spoke out, I thought "Benson" and "Benton" might be real people.

[257] Johnson placed a video on YouTube and has spoken at two JFK Conferences as of this writing. He is a competent mathematician. He does speculate about his girlfriend's role. Veciana acknowledged the couple's presence in his book, *Trained to Kill*.

Then, shortly after returning to New Orleans, Lee was told to go to Baton Rouge, where he was questioned by a military officer prior to the officer's entering a big meeting, where Lee was stationed outside the door.

Other officers, as they entered, viewed him. It made him feel uncomfortable. Lee knew that anybody could have been a security guard for this off-the-record meeting between military officers and unknown men in suits, so why was he chosen?

After that meeting, some kind of insurance account was guaranteed for Marina and the children, so Lee could leave her behind, if he had to, without worry. Lee was ordered by a military contact – not by Ochsner-- to keep nice and quiet in New Orleans, in contrast to his recent activities publicly touting Cuba and Uncle Fidel — a great relief. Basically, he was to stay low until the prisoner(s) died, at which time he had to be ready to travel at once.

Lee had already purchased the requisite bus ticket the same night he dropped me off, based on the fact that I had told him the prisoner would die. There had to be as much time as possible between the purchase of the ticket to Houston and the prisoner's death. However, Lee still attended a few impromptu meetings, requiring quick trips, such as to Baton Rouge and Sulphur, Louisiana (a small town with its own airport outside of Lake Charles). Lee may also have made a flight to Florida, but I wasn't privy to everything Lee did before we were in contact again through the Mafia's racing line. The rest of the time, Dave said Lee usually sat quietly reading on the porch, on watch for any hostile anti-Castro visitors. Unemployment checks and some American Express checks[258] met his family's basic needs: he didn't dare take a job. During this time of peace, Lee still made it clear to Marina that she must go to Texas without him when the time came. Lee's staying behind was in order to conduct a "job hunt"-- even though Lee had not actively searched for a job since leaving Reily's.

Ruth Paine, currently visiting her CIA-employed relatives out east, would come for her. Our split-up was a mere sham. I kept a packed suitcase under the bed. This was fine with Robert, who thought I was protecting my garments from getting infested with roaches. From time to time, Dave kept me and Lee informed about each other's lives. There are three interesting things about Lee's application. First, Lee, who did not like his middle name, had only placed a capital "H" on the application, and was rebuked for it. Rather than rewrite the form, Lee squeezed in the word "Harvey" that he disliked so much. Second, Lee placed "Catholic" as his religion on the application. Even though he had been raised a Lutheran. Even though Fidel Castro was kicking priests and nuns out of Cuba and was persecuting Catholics.

[258] Lee told me about American Express checks that came sporadically for extra expenses.

The official story is that Lee was 'desperate' to get into Cuba. This wasn't true; placing 'Catholic' on his application is another bit of evidence. Lee had no problem writing 'Catholic' because he could use a copy of the document to "prove" he was 'Catholic.'

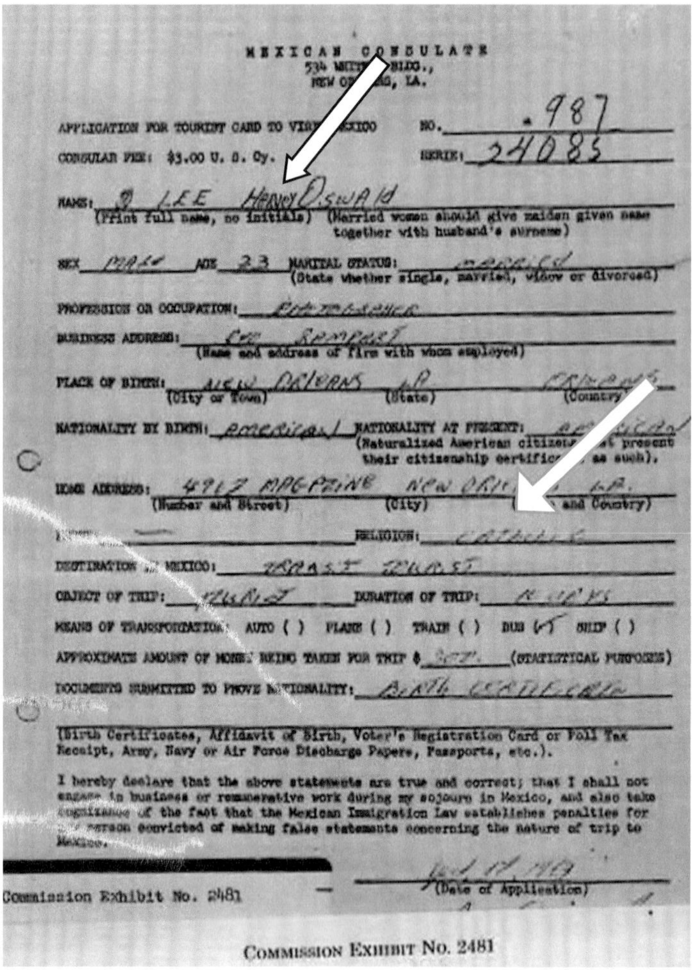

MEXICAN CONSULATE
534 [illegible] BLDG.,
NEW ORLEANS, LA.

APPLICATION FOR TOURIST CARD TO VISIT MEXICO NO. 987
CONSULAR FEE: $3.00 U. S. Cy. SERIE: 24085
NAME: O. LEE HENRY OSWALD
(Print full name, no initials) (Married women should give maiden given name together with husband's surname)
SEX MALE AGE 23 MARITAL STATUS: married
(State whether single, married, widow or divorced)
PROFESSION OR OCCUPATION: [illegible]
BUSINESS ADDRESS: [illegible] Rampart
(Name and address of firm with whom employed)
PLACE OF BIRTH: New Orleans La. [illegible]
(City or Town) (State) (Country)
NATIONALITY BY BIRTH: American NATIONALITY AT PRESENT: American
(Naturalized American citizens at present their citizenship certificate as such).
HOME ADDRESS: 4907 Magazine New Orleans La.
(Number and Street) (City) (State and Country)
RELIGION: Catholic
DESTINATION IN MEXICO: [illegible]
OBJECT OF TRIP: Tourist DURATION OF TRIP: [illegible]
MEANS OF TRANSPORTATION: AUTO ( ) PLANE ( ) TRAIN ( ) BUS (✓) SHIP ( )
APPROXIMATE AMOUNT OF MONEY BEING TAKEN FOR TRIP $ [illegible] (STATISTICAL PURPOSES)
DOCUMENTS SUBMITTED TO PROVE NATIONALITY: Birth Certificate
(Birth Certificates, Affidavit of Birth, Voter's Registration Card or Poll Tax Receipt, Army, Navy or Air Force Discharge Papers, Passports, etc.).

I hereby declare that the above statements are true and correct; that I shall not engage in business or remunerative work during my sojourn in Mexico, and also take cognizance of the fact that the Mexican Immigration Law establishes penalties for any person convicted of making false statements concerning the nature of trip to Mexico.

[redacted]

Sept 17 1963
(Date of Application)

Commission Exhibit No. 2481

COMMISSION EXHIBIT No. 2481

A simple priest in Mexico, seeing the word on an official-looking document, would agree to marry us. Priests in Mexico didn't like to marry Catholics to non-Catholics and such a document would be helpful.

Lee's Mexican Tourist Visa Application

"On 9/17/0 Oswald visited the Mexican Consulate in New Orleans where he was issued 15-day tourist card #24085. The man whose tourist card was apparently issued directly before Oswald was William George Gaudet, who told the F.B.I. ...that he was a former employee of the C.I.A.(C.D. 75, Pg. 588) Comparing information garnered from Oswald's and Gaudet's tourist card applications(CE 2078, CD 75, pg. 588), two things are possibly significant. First, all the 19 people who appeared at the Consulate on 9/17 had their names listed in C.D. 75 in the order first name, middle, last name except for Oswald and Gaudet..." [259]

As for Marina, Lee told his "I want to live in Cuba" story to her so many times that she was convinced it was true. Lee helped along the idea by inviting her, according to her testimony, to assist him in hijacking a plane to get there. Lee's incredible sense of humor was again evident.

[259]http://jfk.hood.edu/Collection/Weisberg%20Subject%20Index%20Files/O%20Disk/Oswald%20Lee%20Harvey%20Mexico/120.pdf

When Lee told Marina she could assist him by aiming a gun at the passengers to keep them obedient, as he forced the pilot to make the plane land in Havana, Marina – heavily pregnant then—told the Warren Commission that she thought Lee had lost his mind.

If only they could have seen Lee's Cheshire Cat smile, and the twinkle in his eye! By now, we had decided we would probably leave Mexico after a month or so and hide in the Cayman Islands for a year. Lee knew a trusted friend who had a small cottage we could use. [260] Going to Cuba—maybe even by hijacking a plane-- was just Lee's cover story for Marina, even though, in the end, a plane would be involved As September progressed, Lee transformed himself into a quiet homebody. Neighbors noticed that he spent many hours reading on his porch. At night, he was often still reading by lamplight. Mrs. Garner, the apartment manager, would testify that Lee couldn't possibly be working, as he was spending all his time reading books on the hot porch, clad only in yellow beach shorts and wearing flip-flops.

Finally, Dave had set things up so we could talk to each other again by phone. He used a "black box" arrangement going through a Mafia racing line between Florida and a Mafia betting station in Covington.

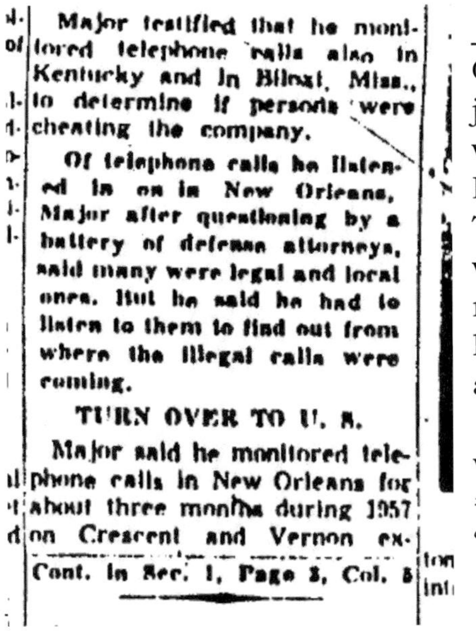
Major testified that he monitored telephone calls also in Kentucky and in Biloxi, Miss., to determine if persons were cheating the company.

Of telephone calls he listened in on in New Orleans, Major after questioning by a battery of defense attorneys, said many were legal and local ones. But he said he had to listen to them to find out from where the illegal calls were coming.

TURN OVER TO U. S.

Major said he monitored telephone calls in New Orleans for about three months during 1957 on Crescent and Vernon ex-

Cont. in Sec. 1, Page 2, Col. 5

Free Mafia Calls, and The Call Wheel

Our first few calls were short, limited to just a minute. We practiced the "call wheel" so we'd be able to use it properly. Dave set up a call wheel with me, too. This used N,S,E,W, as compass points with a phone number at each point. One number might be for work, another for home, the 3rd at a payphone, the 4th in a laundromat, etc.

A date and time would start up the wheel at, say, North, such as, phone #1(N) was Monday at 8 pm. If I said, "Call me again tomorrow an hour later,"

[260] In 1987, I was approached while training for a position in the Florida Social Service Child Protection system in Tampa when an old gentleman asked if I was "Miss Baker, Lee's girlfriend." I was shocked that he did so. He said he had found me at last, and wished to sign over ownership rights to a small house on his property, on one of the Cayman islands, if I wanted it. If I did not want the house, he said he planned to sell it. With four children yet to care for, who were ranked high for scholarships to universities, I thanked him but declined the offer. This man was almost as short as I was, tanned, and looked Cuban. I told my oldest son about the encounter: years later, he only barely remembered it. The incident deeply moved me. Lee had got us a house!

that meant call to the South phone next, but "one hour later" at South was 4 pm instead of the usual 3 pm.

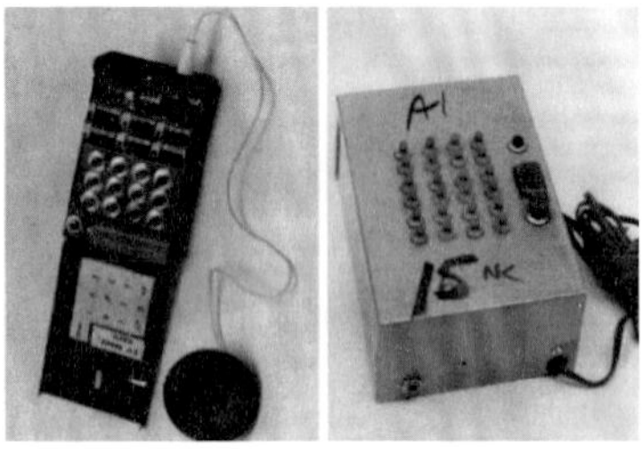

Telephone operators were paid to use boxes such as these to plug in "free" long distance calls. The news story here (excerpted) shows such racing lines were used in New Orleans by 1957. Calls on the line to anywhere were free, if you knew the code to give the operator, with no payments to any phone companies.

Of course, we also used code terms, such as "Have to go!" meant to skip the next compass point and to use the next one. And so it went. It was important not to miss a call because a "re-set" had to work for both of us, which could take two or three days.

Since we could add or delete phone numbers as well, the call wheel was impossible for anyone listening in to be able to figure out where or when we would call next.

Our plans became firmer: as soon as Lee dropped off the bioweapon to the contact in Mexico, he would "disappear," and I'd join him.

Lee's disappearance would be a known fact to his handlers: his plan to drop out of sight for up to a year and to emerge with a fake name and a new wife was acceptable if he worked in Latin America for the CIA. To escape involvement with the Mafia, his unhappy marriage and his damaged past in the USA as an "exposed" former defector who praised Castro would require a new identity; Lee was led to believe it was OK with them. There were few people that Lee fully trusted. David Ferrie was one, but they were not meeting face-to-face now, to ally all suspicions. But the best news was that Lee had reached a truce with Marina. Determined to make his last days with Marina good ones for her, Lee said, "We don't even argue anymore."

Back in Gainesville, we stayed away from our little roach-infested mansion as much as possible: Robert attended day and night classes at UF and I worked at the Craft Shop in UF's student union all day while attending a load of classes at night. We saw little of each other. Since Robert had zero interest in my life, beyond mutual access to our bed, all went well. As we entered well into September, I knew time was short now, and I purchased a gun. I had visions of being picked up by traitors who might dump me in the Gulf of Mexico on the way to the Yucatan Peninsula. At the same time, Lee awaited Ruth Paine's arrival in New Orleans with increasing concern. Ruth had promised to return by mid-September, but she had extended her stay. Lee wanted Marina to get the best medical care he could manage, which the CIA had promised.

The compliant Quaker lady – The Pain --would ever-so-conveniently drive his pregnant wife and daughter back to Dallas-and-Irving. Above all else, Lee wanted them out of New Orleans before he had to leave. The fading condition of the prisoner was a hard fact. It was now only a matter of days.

If Ruth didn't come in time, Marina would have to use Charity's emergency ward to have her baby. During this tine, Ruth was writing very affectionate, compassionate letters to Marina, and he wanted to trust her. The new date to pick up Marina and little June in New Orleans was now September 20th. That was close to the estimated death of 28 days assigned to the prisoner. When the prisoner died, Lee would have to leave, even if Ruth Paine didn't show up. Ochsner was only communicating with Lee, now, through David Ferrie, who pretended neutrality.

Waterloo (Iowa) Daily Courier
October 7, 1962

Radiation and Genetics Is Luther Topic

(COURIER NEWS SERVICE)

DECORAH—Dr. H. Warner Kloepfer, specialist in human genetics, will be on the campus of Luther College on Monday and Tuesday as a Danforth Visiting Lecturer.

He will give the first of two public lectures at 8 p. m. Monday at Valders Hall on "Radiation and Human Genetics." Tuesday morning, he will speak on "Genetics in the Service of Man" at an all-school convocation in Valders Hall.

In two informal meetings with students and faculty, he will discuss "New Horizons in Medical Genetics" and "Should Human Genes Be Synthetized Artificially?"

The Danforth Visiting Lecturers project, under which Dr. Kloepfer comes to this campus, is now in its sixth year. It is sponsored jointly by the Danforth Foundation and the Association of American Colleges.

Dr. Kloepfer, associate professor of anatomy at Tulane University's School of Medicine, is one of 16 outstanding scholars and specialists from this country and abroad selected by the Foundation and the Association's Art Program for campus visits during the 1962-63 academic year.

<u>**Friday, September 20, 1963**</u> When The Pain failed to arrive by mid-afternoon, worried about these issues, Lee contacted Dr. Warner Kloepfer for help. Dr. Kloepfer, a Quaker minister and professor on the faculty at Tulane, agreed to arrange medical care for Marina, should she go into labor. The Quaker Connection was hard at work here.

I think Lee said Werner spoke Russian, as well as one of his daughters. Dr. Kloepfer, of course, had enough power in his household to arrange for his family to visit 4905 exactly on the 20th, so they could meet Marina again, which would make caring for her, if necessary, seem the act of concerned friends. Whether Ruth Paine came today or not, backup arrangements for Marina could not wait any longer. This is why the real reason the Klopefers showed up at 4905 for a nice, friendly evening at Lee Oswald's apartment. Dr. Koepfer would be expected to offer friendly Quaker help if Ruth Paine didn't show up. So it was that the Kloepfers were enjoying a slide show about Russia when Ruth arrived that evening.

Dr. H. Warner Kloepfer Jan 4, 1958 P 23 *Times-Picayune*: "Tulanians Get Research Cash Polio Foundation Grants Pair $99,749 Dr. H. Warner Kloepfer…" (Dr. Ochsner was now fully engaged in polio research after the Cutter Incident).

Ruth immediately came inside with her two small children. Her car remained quite visible for the next few days, as it was slowly packed up.As the Oswald family items accumulated, nobody took anything. The last evening, Lee sent the two women and their little ones to the French Quarter by themselves[261]. As for Lee, he was all but glued to the apartment, in case the apartment manager's phone rang with news of the prisoner's death. He was also unwilling to be seen in the company of Marina and Ruth in the French Quarter. Ruth would insinuate that this is when Lee, left alone to pack, sneakily slipped the killer rifle into her car. But Ruth could never explain why neither she nor her husband could recall unpacking that bulky item. Marina, heavily pregnant and always tired, didn't unpack anything. Michael Paine admitted that he probably unloaded the bundle (with its obvious rifle butt easy to feel through the blanket) which he dismissed as "camping equipment," but neither he nor Ruth could explain why they left the "camping equipment" (inside Junie's favorite blanket)[262] on the floor of their garage, where it was underfoot for the next 55 days. Ruth Paine claimed she routinely stepped over the bundle lying on the sawdust-littered floor

of their garage. Michael Paine said more: he told The Warren Commission:

"The garage was kind of crowded and I did have my tools in there and I had to move this package several times in order to make space to work, and the final time I put it on the floor underneath the saw where the bandsaw would be casting dust on it and I was a little embarrassed to be putting his goods on the floor..."

The Warren Commission never asked why Lee Oswald, who visited there most weekends in the months ahead, let the package lie there underfoot, in full sight, to be stepped on, moved and allowed to be left under a band saw that threw sawdust all over it, all those weeks.

---

[261] Records vary as to who came first to 4905: Ruth, or the Kloepfers. I think it was the Kloepfers.

[262] Marina testified that the blanket was Junie's favorite. Intimidated by the Secret Service, CIA and FBI, she did not volunteer the obvious: would not Junie, who Ruth Paine said played in the garage with Ruth Paine's two young children, notice her blanket and want it back? Also, Lee knew that the Paines --Quakers—were anti-gun.

Not only that, but the children also played on boxes in the garage. The band saw was used often and *"would be casting dust."*
The blanket should have been covered with sawdust – Ruth Paine told the W.C. she, too, had used the saw, to make "children's blocks" (toy-boxes two feet long).

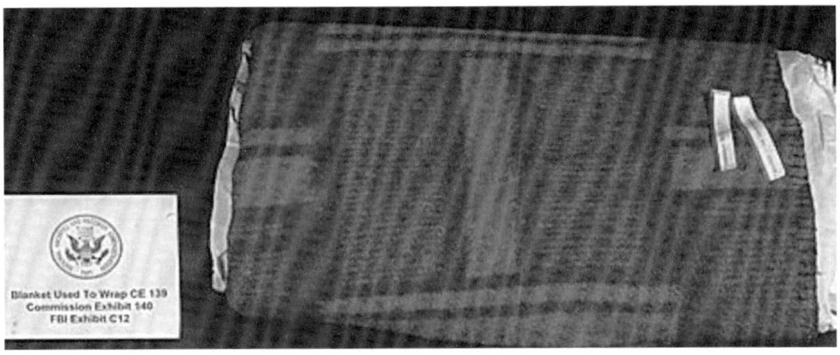

Not a speck of sawdust can be seen on the spotless blanket, though the FBI said Lee Oswald's pubic hairs (along with hairs belonging to unidentified persons) were found, "proving" the blanket was his. But let us return to New Orleans, where after three days of packing, Marina, Ruth and the children were ready to depart.

<u>Monday, September 23, 1963</u> Lee finally got his phone call. The prisoner had died; he must soon leave for Mexico City with the bioweapon. Marina and Junie would now have to go, freeing Lee to go to Mexico City. Despite Lee's and Marina's copious problems, they both saw this as a watershed moment. Neither thought they would ever see the other again. Their goodbyes were sorrowful.

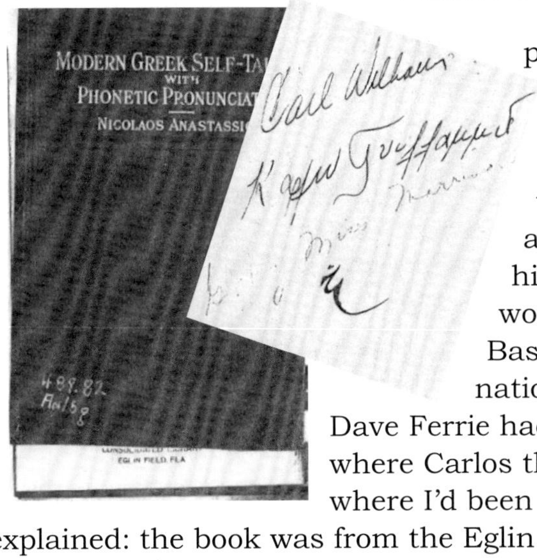

As for me and Lee, our planned escape and reunion seemed imminent. From this moment on, I could be required to disappear at any time, and fly to join him in Mexico. Alex Rorke, a trusted friend with a long history of reliable work for the CIA, would pick me up at Eglin Air Force Base. Even I knew how to get to the nation's largest air force base! Earlier, Dave Ferrie had sent a book to the Craft Shop, where Carlos the Cuban was still working, and where I'd been re-hired. By phone, Dave explained: the book was from the Eglin Field Library. Inside was a name: 'Carl Wilhaus' with 'Gift of Miss Morrison' written under it. I would be directed to Eglin AFB's library at the Base by showing the library book to the guard, in order to return the book.

I was then to proceed to the library to meet Rorke and his pilot. The book would be the contact signal. Because I didn't trust anybody and did not want to be dumped out of a plane over the Gulf of Mexico, I loaded my new revolver with bullets for the trip.

Tuesday, September 24, 1963 Lee walked out of his apartment at 4905 Magazine Street for the last time and began a historic journey.

Within 72 hours, he would be in Mexico. Much of what we know about these three days comes from U.S. Government files. The records they collected from offices in the public transportation system should have been fairly accurate concerning Lee, because no one should have understood their significance. But there are some problems and gaps that researchers have identified, especially in The Warren Commission's "official story."

Time gaps, omissions and false reports abound, puzzling researchers for decades, mainly because the official story isn't true.

In brief, the Warren Commission says on that Sept. 25, Lee took a Trailways (not Greyhound) bus from New Orleans to Houston, and then from Houston to Laredo, where he crossed the Mexican border about 2:00 P. September 26th. But was it true? First, numerous witnesses saw Lee on the *second* leg of the bus trip (Houston to Laredo), but *nobody* saw him on the *first* leg (New Orleans to Houston). The Warren Commission and FBI admitted they had no witnesses, nor any direct evidence, to support the idea that Lee Oswald was on the bus the first leg of the trip. They also admitted they only inferred that Lee was on that bus, because it was the only one going from New Orleans to Houston during the time period in question. But Lee was not on any bus from New Orleans to Houston, even though he did have a Trailways ticket. Even though it seems his suitcases were checked as luggage. The second problem was that two witnesses reported seeing Lee in Austin, Texas, and a third reported meeting him in Dallas, that same day, at the same time Lee was supposed to be on the bus between New Orleans and Houston. Austin is about 500 miles west of New Orleans. It takes over 8 hours by car. Atop that, Dallas is several more hours to the north.

It's generally agreed that Lee got on the bus in Houston that evening, as witnesses saw him and talked to him. So, if Lee was in Austin and Dallas, and if he went to Mexico City, then how did he reach Houston in time? There was a missing detail, which the Warren Commission and FBI avoided mentioning. Just as they claimed Lee could not drive, now they claimed that Lee would not have had the money or connections to use a private plane. Lee Oswald must look always broke, always friendless and always helpless. In fact, Lee had plenty of connections with private planes in The Big Easy.

David Ferrie owned two planes that had recently been refurbished. He had access to a friend's Cessna and other planes; Banister's business partner was Hugh Ward, a pilot; Carlos Marcello and his brothers owned a fleet of planes. His uncle Dutz was a Mafia "wise guy," according to "Mr. New Orleans" Frenchy Brouillette, who knew them all.[263]

The plane for Lee's use was not some puny single-engine job with a small gas tank. His trips that day required a larger, faster plane. It had to have a long-range capacity to complete the triangle of New Orleans-Austin-Dallas, and from there to Houston, in one day. But there were plenty of such airplanes in Louisiana. They provided logistical support to the oil exploration industry and could make this trip easily. In fact, such planes moved people and equipment across the oil belt of Texas and Louisiana routinely. Any company, like Schlumberger or Halliburton, that provided logistical support for oil exploration could easily accomplish this task if directed to do so. So, the question was not if could it be done, but if the "poor, stupid and friendless" Lee Oswald could *ever* get such a ride. All Lee's ties to such resources were denied. He was proclaimed unknown to David Ferrie, unknown to the oil barons, unknown to Ochsner, unknown to the Mafia, and unknown to Guy

Banister. As for Dr. Ochsner, On "7 Jan 67...right-wing columnist Henry J. Taylor (revealed) INCA's Dr. Alton Ochsner as a "consultant to the surgeon general of the U. S. Air Force **on the medical side of subversive matters.**" (#76, Human Events, 7 Jan 67, 2 pp.) Lee and I knew exactly what "the medical side of subversive matters" was all about: Lee would be taking it to Mexico City imminently. Those who foolishly claimed something than what was the "official version" were discredited, killed, ruined or ignored. I am a survivor of their perfect storm, willing to tell you what Lee told me about his trip. I will combine it with what has been established by other sources, where my knowledge had gaps, to complete the picture.

We begin with Eric Rogers, who lived in the 4907 apartment, brought in to keep a protective eye on Lee's family. In return, his rent and utility bills were paid until Lee left town. He saw Lee's family depart with Ruth Paine on Sept. 23. Then he saw Lee leave 4905 Magazine Street and board the Magazine Street bus, late on the afternoon of the 24th, carrying two suitcases, a blue zippered bag, and some goggles.

[263] *Mr. New Orleans,* Frenchy Brouillette & Matthew Randazzo V. 2009, p. 198

The Warren Commission determined that Lee waited until at least 5:30 AM to get his unemployment check on Sept. 25. Since Eric Rogers saw Lee leave 4905 Magazine St. late in the day on Sept. 24, with his suitcases, where did Lee spend the night?

The time between the afternoon of Sept. 24th and the night of Sept. 26th, when Lee boarded a bus in Houston headed for Laredo, Texas, and was seen by witnesses, has been a blank in one of the most closely-investigated timelines of a human being ever written. But Lee told me, and I told *Sixty Minutes* in 2001, though at the time, there was no way to show how everything had been set up. I tried to draw a chart. Lee's saga began when he left 4905 Magazine and dropped off his suitcases at the Trailways bus station, where David Lewis was the likely person to have made sure the suitcases were ticketed to go to Houston. Then Lee went to Ochsner's International House, where he was kept busy in tactical meetings. He slept there that night. Lee also called his uncle Dutz that night to say goodbye. He was getting ready to travel.

On **Wednesday, September 25, 1963**, before dawn, Lee, Guy Banister, Hugh Ward (Banister's partner and pilot), and an envoy from Texas met for an early breakfast at the International House. Banister explained that the envoy represented "Mr. Le Corque" who was "in tight" with Lyndon Johnson. Guy Banister described Le Corque's impressive ties, and how he was also connected to Dr. Ochsner. It all began with a heroic American fighter pilot named Claire Chennault.

Richard Nixon, Anna Chennault ("The Iron Butterfly") and Henry Kissinger

Chennault went to China in the late1930's to help Madame Chiang Kai-shek re-organize the Chinese air force in preparation for war with Japan. The result of Claire Chennault's efforts was a legendary band of American guerilla pilots called the "Flying Tigers," which fought the Japanese military in air-to-air combat on a daily basis, but claimed no association with the U.S. Government. Along the way, Chennault acquired the title of General,

though he had only been a Captain in the U.S. Army Air Corps.

The secret was that 'Le Corque' was actually Thomas G. Corcoran, a member of FDR's inner circle, who helped organize the Flying Tigers as a clandestine operation for the U.S. government. Le Corque was Chennault's main benefactor inside the U.S. Government and managed their covert relationship for years. Le Corque became General Chennault's close friend. After World War II, Chennault relocated his airplane fleet to Lake Charles. There, he worked with the oil industry in south Louisiana and southeastern Texas. A few years later, Chennault developed terminal lung cancer. Dr. Ochsner, his good friend, was a world expert in lung cancer, so it was logical that Chennault and his wife turned to him for help. As he lay dying in Ochsner's clinic, with his Chinese wife Anna Chan and Dr. Ochsner at his side, Taiwan's Madame Chiang Kai-shek, accompanied by Tommy Le Corque came to visit him, to thank him for all his heroic efforts. After Chennault's death, Corcoran's efforts to console Anna developed into romance, with Corcoran ending up owning half of Chennault's substantial airplane fleet before it was taken over by the CIA.

Dr. Ochsner now had a close relationship to Vice President Nixon, Anna Chennault and Tommy Corcoran, and was cleared for a "sensitive" role with the CIA. Anna would continue to be a valued asset to Ochsner and Nixon, including during his Presidency. In 1967-1968, Anna played a key role in Nixon's election, using her considerable influence to topple the South Vietnam Peace talks and thus extending the Vietnam War. But first, she met with Dr. Ochsner to get his advice. The interplay of these powerful people reached all the way into the ranks of those who wanted John F. Kennedy dead. [264]

Back in New Orleans, Hugh Ward, the pilot who would be flying Lee around that day, complained about having to drop the plane off at the Chennault Airfield in Lake Charles instead of flying it back to Houma, the **blimp station** where they'd soon board the plane to start the day's

long journeys. He wasn't thrilled about having to take a bus from Lake Charles to New Orleans after spending the entire day flying. But the others at the table were not sympathetic. There was pressure on the mission to commence as soon as Clay Shaw came to finalize details; it was too late to change anything so trivial. Though it was so early, Shaw arrived with a zippered blue bag like the one Lee owned. It held two thermoses: one contained the deadly cancer cells. The other thermos contained sterile water. When the medium in the first thermos that nourished the cancer cells became too acidic, it had to be changed.

[264] Ref: *Alton Ochsner, Surgeon of the South,* John Wilds and Ira Harkey, 1990.

Otherwise, the waste products from the cancer cells would kill them. There were chemicals in white packets marked "sugar" to mix with the sterile water to make an emergency medium, if necessary. Crackers and bananas were included in the bag to make it look like a lunch that would pass a simple border check. If inspected visually, the liquid feeding the cancer cells would look like and taste like weak chicken broth. When Shaw arrived, he was all business. After opening the blue bag and showing its contents to Lee, Shaw handed "Le Corque's" representative an envelope, saying, "This goes to Austin, too." Shaw also gave Le Corque's envoy a stack of files to take to LBJ's lawyers in Austin. He shook hands with everyone, commenting that he had a personal interest in making sure Lee's trip was successful. When Hugh Ward told Lee to grab something to eat off the table, because it was time to "hit the road," Lee said he loaded up a bag with warm cinnamon rolls. Nobody loved cinnamon rolls more than Lee Oswald, so of course, he told me that little detail! Everyone left International House at the same time. Banister drove Le Corque's envoy to the Lakefront Airport, where a plane waited to fly him to the Texas capital. Shaw himself said he might go on to Hammond to spend the day with his ailing father. That would distance him from the day's events.

A car and driver were also waiting outside the International House to take Lee and Hugh on a couple of errands, after which they would be taken to the "blimp station" at Houma's Terrebonne Airport. [265]

Sometime after 5:30 AM, Lee stopped at his downtown post office box, where he picked up his last unemployment check. It had just arrived in the morning mail. He endorsed it and cashed the check at a grocery store. Next, Lee stopped at the Eli Lilly building to pick up a package for St. Edward's University in Austin. Then they headed to the "the blimp station" -- the Houma-Terrebonne airport, where a twin-engine plane was waiting on the tarmac, a Hispanic man in the co-pilot's seat.

The De Havilland "Dove" was supplied by Schlumberger of Houston, TX

The plane was a De Havilland 'Dove,' a work plane used by the oil field logistics teams in south Louisiana and Texas. This one was owned by

[265] Lee could have kept the luggage on the plane and checked it in at Houston.

Schlumberger, the largest oil field services company in the world. It had just flown in from Hull Field in Sugarland, Texas on the west side of Houston. Normally equipped to carry two crew members and eight passengers, in this Dove half of the passenger seats had been removed to make room for cargo. The Dove had a range of 1,000 miles, with a top speed of over 200 MPH. It could make the 450-mile trip from Houma, Louisiana to Austin, Texas comfortably in two-and-a-half hours on a half tank of gas. Its engines were warm, its fuel tanks were topped off, and it was ready for take-off. Young Hugh, trained to fly by David Ferrie, confidently took position in the pilot's seat, and Lee got busy securing his cargo.

Just then, an alert message came over the plane's radio. It was sent by a ham radio operator who worked with the Cuban underground. It said that Alex Rorke and his pilot had "run into some trouble," having failed to report their positions while close to dangerous waters near Cuba. Many ham radio operators were CIA informants. If the report was true --if something had happened to Rorke-- the CIA already knew about it. Not only was Alex one of Lee's trusted friends who knew Lee's secret anti-Castro stance, but he was a CIA asset with a lot of experience. Alex and Geoffrey Sullivan, his pilot, were supposed to fly me from Florida to Mexico as soon as Lee dropped off the bioweapon.

They were going to help Lee and me disappear. After an anxious discussion, Hugh said they had to get in the air to stay on schedule. He encouraged Lee to lie down and get some rest. Lee, tired from days of stress, curled up in Ward's bedroll, the blue zippered bag and its insulated contents safely taped to an empty seat near him.

The Dove flew at top speed all the way to Austin. It arrived well before lunchtime. A rental car awaited the team on the tarmac; as Hugh rested, Lee and the Latino entered the car which was driven by another Latino-- destination downtown Austin near the state Capitol. There Lee went to a lunchroom near the Texas governor's mansion.

The series of events that has perplexed researchers more than fifty years will now become clear and logical -- just as clear and logical as the string of events in Lee's Clinton-Jackson saga. Despite the precautions taken to secretly fly him to Austin while he was supposed to be on a bus headed to Houston, Lee now walked ostentatiously into the U.S. Government's Selective Service office in Austin and loudly complained about the status of his Marine discharge. This was an illogical act, on the surface. Why? Because on July 25, all avenues of appeals on Lee's status were now legally closed. Lee had already addressed this issue with attorney Dean Andrews in New Orleans. So, what was Lee's true purpose? To the lady behind the desk, Lee said he was just passing through town, but *soon would be moving to Dallas*. So why did he make a complaint now?

As with many of Lee's actions, another motive was at play. The most important was to prove to anyone interested that Lee was not thinking about going to Mexico City, or living in Cuba.

Instead, he was inside a state office representing himself as someone who planned to stay in the USA. After he vanished in Mexico, as planned, what would an investigation reveal? That Lee planned to live in Dallas, meaning foul play may have occurred in Mexico City. Lee's show-up occurred far from any bus traveling to Houston from New Orleans. The timeline was being scrambled. Soon, the timeline would be scrambled even worse.

Just as he had done on our trip to Jackson, a report of Lee's presence in *Austin* would conflict with any sightings of him that same day in *Houston*. Scrambling up the timeline of his journey to Mexico would enhance our safety. But I am guessing as to motive, as Lee largely described his actions, assuming I understood his motives.

Retracing his steps, it seems that Lee went to the Selective Service office in Austin first, telling the woman there that he had *already been* to the governor's offices -- backwards from what really happened. Then Lee gave his name as "Harvey Oswald," for her to do a records search. When the frustrated clerk could not find his Selective Service card, Lee abruptly left, creating an indelible memory that "Harvey Oswald" was a weird fellow. Next, Lee waited for a courier, who soon arrived with an envelope full of cash. The courier told Lee that "nobody knew" where the money had come from, but they wanted to make sure who had it now, so Lee had to sign a receipt for the cash. Lee said he counted the bills twice. Lee was aware that he was in LBJ territory, complicated by the presence of anti-Kennedy fanatics. The two Latinos, meanwhile, were eating lunch with some anti-Castro friends and had promised to seek news about Alex Rorke. When they met again, they told him that a second report had come in. Rorke's plane was now considered missing.

This caused Lee to suspect that his plans involving Rorke in Mexico had been anticipated, possibly by an enemy in the CIA.

Or could it be an action taken by James Jesus Angleton, who was upset that Lee had not returned in a coffin, saving everybody many inconveniences? After all, Lee had not been treated with respect, or with any thought for his future by "Bishop," or by anybody else recently. And he felt uncomfortable being responsible for delivering a manila envelope full of cash to unknown contacts.

Next, the Latinos dropped Lee off at the Trek Café on South Congress Avenue to get some lunch, where he waited for about forty-five minutes while they took the package from Eli Lilly to St. Edward's University.[266] As Lee waited, he worried that Rorke and his pilot Geoffrey Sullivan had

[266] I have been unable to find any link between "Eli Lilly" and St. Edwards University.

been killed. He would have to let me know that I wouldn't be able to join him as quickly as we had planned. If there was conspiracy involved, would it be safe for me to get on a commercial plane? I'd be watched, followed. And I'd be alone, unless Lee could find somebody he trusted to protect me. Tonight, he was supposed to call me for the first time on the Call Wheel. To do so, Lee had to calculate which phone I would be at, late tonight, using Dave Ferrie's call wheel.

While pondering these things, Lee ordered several cups of coffee as he drew what I presume was our call wheel on some napkins. Lee was the only person in the café, and there was only one waitress, so she couldn't help but notice how nervous he was. She tried to strike up a bit of conversation, but Lee did not respond. After the Kennedy assassination, the waitress would report that "Oswald" was in the Café and drew on some napkins. Since the official version was that Lee was on a bus headed for Houston at the time, the waitress' report had to be ignored.[267]

When the Latinos returned, they remained in the car instead of coming inside. Lee, in his super-alert state, briefly wondered why they didn't come in. Was it because the waitress would see their faces, and would be a witness after they assaulted him and took the envelope full of cash? Lee's paranoia was justified because he had never been given their names. He was now separated from Hugh and nobody knew his whereabouts. These thoughts went through Lee's head because there was something in the attitude of these Latinos that made him distrust them. He finally left the café, taking the napkins with him. Because the waitress said Lee used more than one napkin, I suggest that Lee probably wrote out another wheel in order to reach Dave and tell him about Rorke. As for the Latinos, they turned out to be harmless.

---

[267] FBI AIRTEL TO SAN ANTONIO...RE: LEE HARVEY OSWALD Refer to page 18... Ronnie Dugger is reported as having stated he developed no information indicating Oswald was in Austin other than information furnished by Mrs. Lee Dannelly [Selective Service]. ... Stella Norman... reported she believed she saw Oswald in Trek Cafe some two months prior to [Dugger's] interview and that he had been informed by L. B. Day that he claimed to have seen the man referred to by Norman and that he was convinced this person was Oswald. Submit amended page 18 resolving obvious inconsistency. Handle immediately ...NOTE: We believe Oswald may have been in Austin afternoon 9-25 and we are trying to establish if during his trip to Mexico he traveled in round-about fashion from NO to Austin, thence east to HO and from HO by bus to Laredo. We know he boarded bus at HO 2 am, 9-26 and that he telephoned a woman in HO between 7 and 9 pm on the 26th. Mrs. Dannelly of State Selective Service Headquarters, Austin, believes he was in her office at 1 pm, 9-25-63...": http://jfk.hood.edu/Collection/Weisberg%20Subject%20Index%20Files/F%20Disk/FBI/FBI%20Headquarters%20Tickler%20Files%20Received%20by%20Mark%20Allen%204-25-85/Item%2005.pdf

They took Lee back to the plane, where he dined on cinnamon rolls. Next, they flew to Dallas. Before they landed, Hugh said Marcello's people had radioed in that Lee had to meet with Jack Ruby. I had heard Jack Ruby's name from the strippers at the YWCA in New Orleans, but had no idea that Lee knew him. I was still unaware that Sparky Rubenstein and Jack Ruby were one and the same person. Lee and Dave had forgotten to tell me!

Due to Lee's connections with Marcello, Ruby's request for 'laetrile' did not surprise me. It seemed Ruby needed Lee to get him some of the controversial cancer drug. Laetrile was legal in Mexico, but illegal in the U.S. Lee also said he had to make a reservation on an apartment in Dallas. If things didn't work out for Marina at Ruth Paine's place, due to the pressures of the new baby, Lee wanted to make sure Marina would have an apartment of her own to move into. [268] He planned to use the apartment himself for a quick return trip, if possible, to see his new baby before he vanished for an unknown length of time. The plane next flew him to Dallas, landing late in the afternoon. Lee met Ruby in a nearby restaurant. Ruby, after making his request, mentioned that he had done gun-running with David Ferrie in Miami against Castro. The Dallas airport was so close to Ruth Paine's residence that Lee insisted on being driven past her house to see if Marina and Junie had safely arrived. There was still plenty of time to reach Houston, so Lee, concerned that The Pain's heavily-packed, travel-worn station wagon might have made it from New Orleans to Dallas without breaking down, accepted Ruby's offer to have "a couple of friends" help out. In half an hour, two Latinos who knew the Dallas area arrived. They offered to drive Lee past the Paine's home in Irving to see if the blue-green station wagon was sitting in the driveway. It was. The car had already been unpacked. Now that Lee felt better about his family's safety, Ruby's Latino friends invited him to meet Sylvia Odio, a woman active in the anti-Castro community: she might have even received updated news about Rorke. Lee never told me the woman's name, but I believe it had to be **Sylvia Odio**. She is the one who told witnesses and investigators

that two Latinos introduced her to a 'Leon' Oswald. 'Leon' happened to be Jack Ruby's middle name. Lee said they spoke in Cuban-style Spanish, too rapidly for him to follow. Odio told several persons *before* Kennedy's assassination that she had met 'Leon' and that she later received a call from one of the Latinos saying Leon was 'loco' and would as soon kill Kennedy as Castro.

[268] I do not know if this information ever reached any authorities or researchers.

Many researchers consider Lee's meeting with Sylvia Odio as the first overt attempt to frame Lee for Kennedy's murder. If so, Jack Ruby may have been involved. By setting up his meeting with Lee, he could have maneuvered him into meeting with Odio. That means Lee was already being set up as a patsy before he reached Mexico City, which raises serious questions about the real purpose behind sending Lee to Mexico City.

In hindsight, any number of trusted, Spanish-speaking lab techs could have been trained instead of him, then sent to Mexico City to hand off the bioweapon. Instead, Lee was carefully groomed to be the courier. Further, Alex Rorke's plane crashed the same day Lee left for Mexico City, after leaving Cozumel. Alex and his co-pilot, Geoffrey Sullivan, were supposed to fly to Kankun / Cancun to check it there. Instead, the plane was either shot down, was sabotaged to crash, or was hijacked into Cuba.[269]

"On September 23rd , 1963, in Waterbury, Connecticut, 28-year-old Geoffrey Sullivan, a former Air Force pilot, prepared to depart on a secret mission. Sherry Sullivan is his daughter: *"The way my mom relates it, my father was supposed to come back in five days... he gave her his St. Christopher medal which he wore all the time. He explained to her that this would be his last trip. And not because he wasn't coming back, but because he didn't want to be involved in this type of operation anymore. He took off that morning, and that was the last time she ever saw him. He never came back."* Four days later, the plane disappeared. With no help from Sylvia, who had been busy packing to move and hadn't been involved with anybody else that day, Lee and the two Latinos left. Their business in Dallas finished, the Latinos took Lee back to the Dove.

---

[269] https://unsolved.com/gallery/geoffrey-sullivan/ On Oct. 6, eleven days later, Gerry Hemming took his Interpen members to hunt for the downed plane and bodies. Lee and I found the timing of the Rorke-Sullivan disappearance troubling. I agreed with Lee that it was possible that the plane had been sabotaged to make it crash. Geoffrey Sullivan's daughter, age five when her dad was shot down, eventually filed a lawsuit against the Castro regime. Quote: "Geoffrey Sullivan and New York newspaperman Alexander Irwin Rorke Jr., who was believed to be a CIA operative, took part in numerous anti-Castro operations in the three years leading up to their disappearance...The last known sighting of the pair was when they took off from Mexico on Oct. 1 (sic), 1963, in a twin-engine Beechcraft..." ... In 2009, Sullivan's daughter was awarded $21 million in damages, as she had proof her father had been kept alive in Castro's prisons for over a decade, then executed. Alex died in the plane crash (sic: other reports is that he was jailed in Cuba with Sullivan). https://bangordailynews.com/2009/08/19/news/maine-woman-wins-lawsuit-against-cuba/

There, Hugh was waiting to fly him to Houston. They landed at Hull Field in Sugarland, on the west side of Houston, where, again, car was waiting. At Hull Field (later called Hull Airport) a peculiar event occurred. Lee's blue zippered bag was "switched out" for a new one. Lee was told the new bag contained fresh cancer cells. That would give The Product an extra day of shelf life. Later, this swap would concern us because of what happened in Mexico City.

When Dave called and said, "Hector (Lee's code name) is in Houston," I knew Lee would call me soon, so I went to the designated pay phone at the designated time and waited for Lee's call. I was full of excitement: I thought I was going to be told when to meet Alex Rorke and his pilot at Eglin Air Force Base. As for these late-night calls, Robert was no problem: he was a workaholic at his studies. He wanted to pass his geology GRE, even as he labored to finish his English degree. In fact, when Robert took the GRE, he achieved an almost perfect score, though he'd only taken a few geology courses. His amazing score would gain the attention of several big oil companies, who at once offered him full scholarships, mostly to the University of Texas at Austin. By now, I was carrying nine hours of night courses myself and working at the Craft Shop during the day. When Lee finally called from Houston, around 10 pm my time, he began by telling me that Alex Rorke had gone missing.

Suburbia, June 15, 1977, Page

Hull Airport

First-class treatment at a first-class establishment

by Judy Baker

Hull is married, with two planes gleam and glitter in and laid out by the

In June, 1977, I wrote a news story about Hull Field to get the information about its government connections and Mexico saved in print (see next page).

Of the planes, 75-80 per cent are owned by businesses in Fort Bend County. But the airport also has a great deal of use by government agencies.

The Department of Public Safety, the Major Crime Task Force, the State Department of Health, and the State Attorney General, among many others, use the airport facilities at no charge.

Security personnel with guard dogs patrol the airport regularly. Hull has two sniffer dogs which can detect contraband and illicit drug shipments. Many aircraft from Mexico and South America land at Hull Airport. "We believe in prevention," said Hull, who's never had a drug or contraband incident at his airfield.

Cancer patients from a number of countries and states are brought here en route to M.D. Anderson Hospital. And resident doctors are flown in to the Richmond State School to give the children there good medical care.

The Air Ambulance Service can handle four persons on stretchers or

I could sense the stress in Lee's voice, despite his calmness. The plan had been for Alex to meet Lee in Mexico City, take him to Cancun, and to fly from there to pick me up at Eglin Air Force Base. As it now stood, Lee said he would try to find out more about Alex's fate.

In the meantime, I should be ready to go to Eglin AFB. He would try to find another pilot. If not, I could take a commercial flight out of Tampa or Miami if Dave didn't dare fly me over. Our hopes were still high, but the call was short. With no time to talk, Lee said he loved me and hung up. Later, Lee told me he had to hang up so fast because he had to call someone at a certain time, to say he was *flying* to Mexico City. The call was to a "Mr. Twiford."

Lee said his call was calculated to generate a rumor that he had flown to Mexico City from Houston, when actually, he took a bus. It was more timeline-mess-up in action. Mr. Twiford, a lowly seaman who sent out literature for his far-left Socialist Labor Party, took a plane himself from New Orleans to Houston to visit his wife, but the Warren Commission declared that the impecunious Oswald could not have afforded to do so. [270] In hindsight, maybe Lee called Twiford to help establish his *bona fides* as a leftist, as Twiford, was connected to the FPCC.

Also, the CIA would know that he was about to cross the border, since Twiford's home phone was tapped. Lee made the "Twiford call" around 9:00 pm Houston time, soon after his call to me at 10 pm, Gainesville time.

That weekend, I took many short walks to the local grocery store, pacing back and forth near their pay phone at certain times. If Lee called, I'd head for Eglin Air Force Base. If he didn't, plans had changed. In between, I pored over the newspapers in The Student Union for anything being said about Mexico, Cuba and the USSR. After the Kennedy assassination, some witnesses claimed Lee made statements such as, "I'd like to shoot JFK." If he ever did, he had good reasons for doing so. It was an easy way to learn who hated JFK.

---

[270] Sections of the affidavit of "Horace Elroy Twiford, 7018 Schley Street, Houston, Texas, being duly sworn say: 1.... I am a merchant seaman. I am a member of the Socialist Labor Party... 5. I recollect having flown home to visit my wife on September 27, 1963, from New Orleans, Louisiana, where the S.S. Del Monte, the ship upon which I was working, was docked... at this time or on October 1, when the S.S. Del Monte reached Houston, my wife told me that a L. H. Oswald had called.... My wife had written his name and the words "Fair Play for Cuba Committee" on a piece of paper... 6. I recollect that my wife told me that this telephone call had taken place during the week preceding my visit home...." Twiford's name and address was in Lee's address book.

Chapter 25
Mexico City

Friday, September 27, 1963

Lee arrived in Mexico City sometime before 10 am. The Warren Commission claims Lee checked into a cheap traveling salesmen's hotel near the bus station, some four blocks away. But Lee told me he took a taxi to a Quaker hostel, "**Casa de los Amigos**," where he quashed unwanted friendly approaches by the students there, who were mostly Quaker, by claiming he was a drug dealer. He planned to drop off the bioweapon ASAP, without any delay, then "vanish." Since he believed he would be staying at the hostel only overnight, Lee spread the word that he wanted to purchase some illegal drugs.[271] This blunt statement seems to have terrified everyone, so they completely avoided him, which is what Lee intended.

Immediately after checking in (the Warren Commission and FBI never checked the registration records at the *Casa*), the big moment finally came: the handover of the bioweapon. It was to be a swift drop-off, timed and precise. Lee went to the designated drop-off — a souvenir shop – before lunch hour, expecting a swift transfer to the designated medical tech who had the skills to keep the cells alive. Lee had memorized a set of instructions to give the contact. He waited, ready to hand over the lunch sack with its precious thermoses, but the tech failed to show.

Since the drop-off was supposed to be perfectly timed, after half an hour, Lee, worried that the contact had been harmed, tried to contact his handler. Told that "Bishop" had flown to Washington, DC. some days earlier without leaving any orders for him, Lee was both angry and frustrated. With Rorke and Sullivan missing, his contact failing to show up, and his handler ignoring him, he now believed he was in danger himself. His fears escalated: obviously, he could not leave Mexico City by Saturday, as planned. Instead, he would have to find a backup contact. "There is always a Plan B," Lee had told me. But a lot had gone wrong.

---

[271] Lee was seeking laetrile. Thus, he mentioned that he was seeking a drug forbidden in the U.S.

Lee now had justifiable visions of being arrested, interrogated, maybe even tortured by the Mexican police, if anyone at the Quaker Casa reported him. He had jokingly passed himself off as a drug dealer to the kids there,[272] thinking he'd only be staying overnight. Lee also realized I could not join him until he understood what was going to happen next.

The FBI and CIA had their own canned version of what Lee was doing in Mexico City. They would tell the world that when Lee left the bus, he registered at a cheap hotel nearby–'El Comercio'—as 'Lee, Harvey Oswald.' But that wasn't Lee's style. When Lee defected to the USSR, he stayed in one of Moscow's most expensive hotels. In his trip through Europe by train with his family, upon leaving the USSR, Lee lodged them in a fancy B & B in Rotterdam, Holland to await boarding the ocean liner that would take them to the USA. The B & B had crystal chandeliers, expensive furnishings, and a gold-plated drinking fountain which I viewed with my own eyes before everything was remodeled.

For their overseas portion of the trip, Lee and his family berthed in a bigger-than-average suite with a sea view on the classy Dutch ship Maasdam. Upon landing, they stayed at the Times Square Motor Hotel at 8th and 43rd in New York City. The hotel was an affordable choice in the heart of Times Square, with a magnificent lobby. And Lee and I never once went to a cheap hotel. At the el-cheapo 'El Comercio' the sign-in sheet also had a space for 'occupation,' where the word 'photo' was written in, in seriously compressed letters. Someone not knowing English very well might have written it, as well as transposing Lee's name. However, Lee himself could have registered at two hotels to confuse anyone tracking him. Lee was an intelligent agent, still hiding his activities and messing up the timeline. He was not a passive stooge in Mexico City. The CIA in Mexico City reported on only some of Lee's activities and the FBI and Warren Commission only published information about two of Lee's five days there. The HSCA found more information, but were stymied by George Joannides, the 'retired' CIA agent who was sent to tell the HSCA as little as possible about the real Lee Oswald, though Joannides knew Lee was running a fake FPCC branch and was in contact with anti-Castro Cubans. Lee, realizing he'd have to move at once, probably left the Casa before he owed a payment.

---

[272] See Bill Kelly's blog post, "Philadelphia Quakers - With Oswald in Mexico City" at https://ratical.org/ratville/JFK/BillKelly/QuakerandLHO.html

He would have checked into a hotel with security. That would have been his style. The Warren Commission and Dallas police always assumed Lee was "broke," using a cheap, sleazy camera for the "backyard photos,", a cheap mail-order rifle for a weapon, a cheap revolver that broke after being used to kill Officer Tippit, buses (not planes) and that he'd only eat cheap food and sleep in cheap hotels. Their version of Lee Oswald's habits, possessions, personality and intelligence kept investigators from discovering the truth. Thus, there has been astonishment to learn that Lee owned excellent cameras, had access to planes, had funds for good hotels.

The guest register at the cheap hotel. Note #23 and #27 are blank. #18 could have been blank, too, and filled in later. The signature for Lee looks fake to me. The "L" before the 'D" on 'Oswald' is atypical, as is the name 'Harvey' written up-in-the-air. Lee would not have written his middle name. he would have used the initial "H."

Though Lee was facing an incredible dilemma, he knew some important facts. First, his handler had abandoned him, leaving no special instructions. That told Lee that he might not be carrying a valuable bioweapon. Perhaps he had handed it over to M. D. Anderson in Houston, which put the bioweapon in the hands of the CIA and out of Ochsner's control. That meant that he was possibly carrying a dummy. Whether that was true or not, he knew too much. Perhaps he was being used as a lure, to see who would try to take the bioweapon from him, or who might approach him, to convince him to hand over the bioweapon. The idea that he was almost certainly being watched was especially unnerving. There were other possibilities: perhaps Castro's people or the Russians had captured his contact, and they had extracted information. They could be watching him now, to see who he'd try to reach as a backup. That could expose the backup to danger. Or they could kill him at an opportune moment and take the bioweapon for themselves. Then there was a chance that the contact was a traitor. If so, Lee had already shown up at the souvenir shop, had been identified, and was now known by sight. The bioweapon could then be taken from him by force at any time. Furthermore, if he was contacted by anybody now, how could he trust that contact? In fact, he could not. With this, and more, on his mind, Lee told me that he was absolutely stymied. If he tried to enter Cuba himself with the bioweapon, he'd still have to locate an alternate medical contact. Nor could he simply leave Mexico City. Not with all that he knew. It was chilling to realize that the CIA itself could decide to kill him themselves, rather than let the knowledge he had get into the wrong hands. They would never take the risk of allowing him to fall in the hands of either the Russians or the Cubans.

That's when Lee decided to play it stupid. If he pretended to try to enter Cuba himself, as if it were a real life-or-death situation, making himself loud, visible and noxious, in no way could he be considered an agent trying to sneak something into Cuba. Nor would any 'contact' want to approach such an unstable individual. Having made up his mind as to what he would do, Lee went to the Cuban Consulate, possibly arriving around 1:00. Lee, if nothing else, could move swiftly and efficiently. He would return again soon with passport photos for his Cuban visa application, at about 2:30 - 3:00 pm. This was a new idea on Lee's contingency list. He had flirted with pretty Silvia Duran, the Cuban Consulate's secretary, so she was happy to tell the guard to let him back in, even though the Consulate was now closed. She had just begun working there in August and the CIA hoped to recruit her for her connections.

Lee had previously operated as a lover of attractive, high-paid Japanese hostesses. In Tokyo, Lee had been a regular at the pricey Queen Bee Lounge, not to be confused with a sleazy "Queen Bee' Close to his base. He had even been given nice suits with his name embroidered into them. It had been one of his most enjoyable assignments for the CIA. Lee then went on to conquer a number of Russian girls in Minsk, too. In other words, Lee had the skills and endearing ways, which I knew for myself, to bring a lady to bed in a short space of time, if he had to. But let's start at the beginning.

First, Lee did not go alone to Mexico City. I have always stated that. The project was too important to leave in the hands of one person, who might get into an accident or be robbed. There are some dubious candidates the CIA and FBI have offered for this honor. A CIA disinfo artist, anti-Castroite and assassin, Bernardo Gonzales De Torres, claimed that a 'Rene Carbello' (a fictitious character) said 'El Mexicano' – Francisco Rodriguez Tamayo —a leader of the Lake Pontchartrain training camp—rode with Lee on the bus from Nuevo Laredo to Mexico City. That would link Lee with a fervent anti-Castro leader who later defected to the United States. Then there was 'Albert Osborne,' also known as 'John Bowen' who claimed to be a world-traveled missionary.

As 'John Bowen,' he supposedly told at least one credible person that he rode to Mexico City with Lee Oswald on the Red Arrow bus. However, he denied it to the FBI and to everyone else. Osborne was probably a longtime UK spy who had been given trivial assignments in his declining years, to travel the border towns between Texas and Mexico and to inform on suspicious activities. [273] That would link Lee to the Russians. Whatever his connections, Osborne returned to Great Britain only nine days before Kennedy's assassination --his first visit to his native England in decades. Osborne may have been the source of a phone call only 25 minutes before JFK's murder, to the British press, to be alert for important breaking news. I have described Lee going to Mexico City from Houston by bus, but Lee never told me that part of the story. Researchers told me. I know how Lee got to Austin from Houma, LA, how Lee got to Dallas, and how he got to Houston. As for the miles Lee traveled between Laredo and Mexico City, I doubt Lee ever told me. All he said was that that *he did not go to Mexico City alone.* I wonder if an Oswald imposter rode the bus to Mexico City, knowing Lee would be arriving by car, or having been told that he flew in. At every city, a car had been waiting for Lee. Lee could have had a car at Laredo because he told me he left money and possessions there. It is fascinating for me to see how Lee handled the surprise that left him saddled with the unwanted bioweapon, wondering what to do next. He was faced with a dilemma. Without orders, and with an undelivered biological weapon on his hands, he couldn't just vanish. Years later, CIA double agent **Richard Case Nagell** told journalist Dick Russell some shocking news.

He had been ordered to assassinate Lee, but in September,1963, Nagell, who had a mental disorder from a severe head injury, shot bullets into a wall 7 ft high, inside a bank, instead. He said he did it to get himself arrested -- to be kept out of the Kennedy-Oswald assassination saga. There is evidence behind his statements: Russell reported that among Nagell's possessions were found fake ID cards for "A. J. Hidell," just as were found in an "Oswald" wallet that

[273] Lyman Erickson was director of the Christian Servicemen's Center in San Antonio Texas. This is where Osborne stayed before he died.[67] Erickson knew him as Bowen. He said Osborne had told him "... '*I traveled to Mexico with Lee Harvey Oswald,* and I was called in and questioned about it.'" [emphasis added] Erickson did not quote him as saying, "'I just happened to sit next to Oswald,' ..." Ref: https://kennedysandking.com/john-f-kennedy-articles/the-dual-life-of-albert-osborne

mysteriously appeared as police investigated the sudden death by gunfire of Officer J.D. Tippit, in Dallas, only 35-45 minutes after JFK was killed there. The wallet supposedly belonged to Lee Harvey Oswald.

The problem was that when police arrested Lee in the Texas Theatre, fought with him, then hauled him into a squad car, they removed another wallet from his pants pocket. That's when we hear and see no more about the "Oswald wallet" found at the Tippit murder scene. This was just more "so-called evidence" as Lee himself called it, planted to incriminate him. Nobody carries two wallets.

It's possible that Nagell was ordered to kill Lee, after plans to make Lee a patsy had been nixed. Lee, after he delivered the bioweapon into the proper hands, simply knew too much to keep walking on Planet Earth. Hindsight is so convenient, and these are only speculations, but they should be explored.

What I know is that Lee, burdened with the bioweapon, which had a short shelf life, decided to tell officials at the Cuban Consulate an outrageous story. He started by declaring his problems to 26-yr-old Silvia Duran, who easily swooned over young American men with blue eyes, it was whispered. Lee's mysterious blue-gray eyes would have amazed her.

He had come to Mexico City, Lee told Silvia, to get a Cuban transit visa so he could visit Cuba while waiting for his Russian visa to be approved. He showed her documents and papers supporting his self-identification as pro-Castro. So, could he get a Cuban transit visa *right away*? It was an outrageous proposition. It reminds us of how Lee dared to try to register to vote in front of Palmer, the soon-to-be Grand Cyclops of the KKK, with ID from the wrong parish. Maybe a powerful friend could pull some strings to help Lee get in, was Silvia's hint. But Lee, the so-called 'communist,' had no such connections. The outrageous part is that Cuba's transit visa was only good for two weeks, while Moscow was in no hurry to process Lee's visa request "separately" from

Marina's. Silvia, based on a willingness to please, gave Lee an application form. But he had no passport photos for it. Had Lee originally planned to go to Cuba, as some argue, seasoned traveler that he was, he would have brought passport photos with him. When he returned with the required photos, I can imagine Lee expressing great gratitude to Silvia for letting him inside the compound again.

Some say the passport photos were pre-made in the USA. However, Lee's hair looks plastered down with sweat and his tie is a little crooked. And if they'd been pre-packed, why didn't he have the photos with him? Oh, that's right. This young man can't drive. Can't stay employed. Can't run a decent FPCC that never holds meetings, never has a lecture. And of course, he is too stupid to remember that visas and passport applications require passport photos. But in fact, Lee and I had planned to vanish. We had passports and did not need visas for the countries we intended to enter. Lee had expected the CIA to provide us with fake ID's, so of course he would not have been prepared to apply for a visa to Cuba. The photos were likely made in a hurry at a tourist shop. Of course, secret photos were taken of Lee's comings and goings by the CIA's omnipresent surveillance cameras. Everybody got photographed.

The CIA would lie about that, too, claiming their surveillance cameras were not working the two days Lee visited the Russian Embassy, the Cuban Consulate and the Cuban Embassy. We were speaking on what was supposed to be a safe Mafia racing line, but Lee was not dropping names, so I must fill in some blanks with best guesses. To complicate matters, Lee said he did not go to the Cuban Consulate by himself. With no name given, I can only guess.[274] It's possible that Lee and his companion were photographed so close together that the companion could not be removed from any of the photos. In the final analysis, before Kennedy was dead a week, Lee was being portrayed as a "lone nut" –friendless, dumb and weird—unaided by Russia or Cuba, despite early attempts by the CIA to promote Cuba, then Russia, as accessories in the assassination.

There are conflicting reports as to whether the 'real' Lee ever went to Mexico City. The answer is 'yes.' We can confidently use that answer to discern who is lying and who is not about Lee's trips to the Cuban consulate, his trips to the Russian Embassy, and his single trip to the Cuban Embassy. And let's use common sense. We have no record of Lee going to any employment agency in any city during that time period. We have no record of anybody claiming Lee applied for a job in any city during that time period. While there were imposters involved, they would have been easy to dismiss if Lee had started handing out FPCC flyers in Baltimore or Philadelphia, or if he'd gone to ACLU or John Birch meetings in some American city. Instead, we have plenty of people who claimed they saw the real Lee Oswald in Mexico City. Lee's whereabouts and activities were known. And Lee knew he was being watched.

---

[274] Anti-Castroite Rene Carballo told Carlos Bringuier that "El Mexicano" headed the training camp at Lake Pontchartrain and "same also accompanied L.H.O. to Mexico City." See CIA Doc ID 32270995, p 2, handwritten notes. 12/2/67

It explains some of the bizarre things he did next. Told he would have to get his Soviet visa before he could his get his Cuban visa, Lee next went to the Soviet Embassy. There he met Kostikov, who turned him over to Nechiporenko, who learned Soviet Embassy in Washington had turned Lee down for a visa. Lee was told he could make a new application for a visa there in Mexico, but the papers would still have to be sent to Moscow, and the reply from there would go to Oswald's US address. This process could take 4 months. They reported that Oswald got upset at this news, shouting, *'This won't do for me!'* At that, he was escorted from the premises.[275] Lee did not make any trips back to the Cuban Consulate after the next scene I am about to describe, though Silvia Duran would eventually be induced to claim that on Saturday, when the Cuban Consulate was closed all day, 'Oswald' returned yet again, merely to make a pointless telephone call to the Russian Embassy. While doing so, he used terrible Russian with a Spanish accent. That was not 'our' Lee Oswald. And it possibly wasn't Silvia Duran's voice, either. If indeed she assisted with the call and wasn't impersonated herself, she'd likely been coerced.[276] But Silvia may have found it wise to say anything the CIA wanted her to say, finally, to avoid a third session of torture under the hands of the Mexican police. Poor Silvia ended up arrested and beaten not once, but twice by the Mexican police, compliments of the CIA, soon after the Kennedy assassination. Any claim that she'd slept with Lee would thus be discredited as a result of interrogation under torture.

Remember, Lee had no real desire to go to Cuba. But making a public show of trying to get in, acting as fractious and inept as he could, Lee showed his handlers that he was loyally (and stupidly) trying to deliver the bioweapon himself, while making himself a nuisance.

Carlos Lechuga, UN

---

[275] http://www.blather.net/theblather/2013/10/oswald_and_the_cia_part_three/

[276] "Newman reasons that this is a Durán impostor, and an Oswald impostor who does not know what transpired between Yatskov and Oswald, and is 'trying to keep the conversation going' by talking about addresses, but does not realize that the real Oswald was not interested in visa application forms (which would involve address information), but immediate help from the Soviets. The mysterious circumstances under which this recording and the later 1 October recording went missing after the JFK assassination indicates a possible CIA or DFS operation to impersonate people in Mexico and phone up the Soviet Embassy." http://www.blather.net/theblather/2013/10/oswald_and_the_cia_part_three/

With all the surveillance and bugging going on, the CIA knew that Lee was also turning on all his charms to seduce Senora Silvia. Lee had a good reason to do so. The former Cuban ambassador to Mexico, **Carlos Lechuga**, then serving as Castro's ambassador to the United Nations, was deeply in love with Silvia. Lechuga twice wrote his wife in Nov. 1962 that he wished to divorce her and marry Silvia. He would continue his amorous pursuit of Silvia until at least 1967. This made Silvia an attractive connection for Lee to cultivate for the CIA. Lee told me up front that he slept with her. So it happened. But Lee (and I) had been labeled "expendable." By gaining Silvia as a lover, Lee made himself more valuable to the CIA.

Jefferson Morley in his book *Our Man in Mexico*, wrote: *One pressing question for [CIA's] Win [Scott] was, <u>What did Sylvia Duran know about Oswald?</u> The station already had a "substantial interest" in her before the assassination, [David] Phillips later admitted, not the least because surveillance had revealed that she had had an affair with Carlos Lechuga, the former Cuban ambassador in Mexico City, who was now serving as Castro's ambassador to the United Nations. At least one Mexican source on the CIA payroll had told his case officer that "all that would have to be done to recruit Ms. Duran was to get a blonde, blue-eyed American in bed with her."*

[I dare say, brown hair and blue-grey eyes would also suffice!] As for Lee, after he filled out a Cuban transit visa application, and had Silvia affix the passport photos to the original and to a copy, which they both signed, after visiting the Soviet Embassy and being told his visa application had not been approved, and that a new try, from the present Embassy, would take four months, Lee subsequently presented his application to Senor Eusebio Azcue Lopez at the Cuban Consulate later that afternoon.

Seeing that the Russian visa was missing, Azcue reasonably declined to proceed. That's when Lee put on a classic hissy-fit. Lee's vociferous shouts of despair and anger, aimed at the two Consuls, only made them despise him, which was exactly what Lee wanted. Keep in mind the true situation involving his predicament with the bioweapon, to keep context. The last thing Lee really wanted was a transit visa to Cuba. The show he put on was to prove to the CIA that he had tried, while his emotional and irrational harangue would make sure he'd be turned down. Of course, researchers, not knowing the back story, would think Lee was acting like a fool (Where have we heard that before?).

There happened to be just enough time to get the transit visa before his Mexican tourist visa expired (in fact, his Cuban transit visa was stamped on the 10th of October,). But by then, the bioweapon would be dead.

Lee made such an ass of himself that Eusebio Azcue, the recently resigned Consul, and his replacement, Alfredo Mirabel, never wanted to see him again. But that's not the way Silvia thought about it. Their vivacious, pretty assistant gave Lee her hand-written phone number, which she always did, she said, for those awaiting approval of their visa requests. By phoning her, Lee could ask about the visa approval anytime. And he could also invite her for tea in a nice restaurant. Whatever magical words and gestures Lee used, in person or on the phone, Silvia met Lee again under pleasant circumstances that became more and more pleasant. Lee spoke of it as a necessity.

We had long reconciled ourselves to having to sleep with our respective mates, and to treat them well. This was just another bump in the road.

Lee even worried if Silvia would get in trouble for her generosity. Indeed, she would. But consider Lee's position. He was carrying a bioweapon. It had to be passed on to a Cuban medical contact before it expired. As a backup, Lee had been told to memorize a list of highly trusted techs, medical students and doctors that Ochsner had assembled. If he could reach any one of them who could be trusted... of course, that would now be highly unlikely. Still, Lee had been told to hand off the bioweapon --even if it was a dummy. That was not his problem.

There were two more ways that might work to find a backup contact, presumably possible after Lee finished entertaining Senora Duran (after she left the Consulate Friday and Saturday). An "emergency visa" could be issued for itinerant foreign artists, musicians, actors, photographers and writers involved in cultural studies and events, if they appealed to the right person. The right person was Raul Aparicio, the Cultural Attache for Cuba. [277] Meanwhile, Lee's application to get a transit visa remained in Silvia's hands. With all her many connections, it seemed just natural, I'm sure, for the two of them to meet at Sanborns, not too far from the Cuban Consulate, to discuss the problem while dining in one of the city's finest restaurants.

Sylvia herself told Liring/3 (see Appendix) a love-struck unwitting informant who reported it to a trusted CIA agent—concerning Lee, that "I liked him from the beginning." [278] Silvia also told Liring/3 that she had not only dated Lee Oswald, she also slept with him. That was after Lee had freshened up from his trip and his hissy-fit, no doubt. Silvia also told a relative that she "dated" Lee and that she also ate at "Sanborns" with him.

---

[277] I once obtained such a visa in The Netherlands, good for six months instead of a mere 90 days, so I could create oil paintings, which take more than 90 days to properly dry.

[278] Ref: Phillip Shenon's interviews with Duran's relatives and "The LIRING-3 Operation. [A] document from June 1967 discussed informant LIRING-3's conversation with Sylvia Duran, in which Ms. Duran reportedly "admitted that she had sexual relations with him (Oswald) but insisted she had no ideas of his plans... CIA Station Chief Win Scott commented "The fact that Sylvia Duran had sexual intercourse with Lee Harvey Oswald on several occasions ... is probably new, but adds little to the Oswald case."

Richard Case Nagell had described Sanborns as a meeting-place for agents and informants. There were five Sanborns, but one was in the right section of the sprawling city. Researcher Mary Ferrell said it was "near" the US Embassy.[279] That was an understatement: in 1963, the American Embassy was still located in the upper stories of the same building as Sanborns! A new, separate US Embassy would open in 1964.[280]

How many Russian communist agents would agree to meet a Cuban Consulate official in the bowels of the U.S. Embassy? But that's where Lee met Silvia. The restaurant was surely bugged by not only the Americans, but by the Soviets. The Cubans and Mexicans might have had it bugged, too. [281] ,[282] No wonder Silvia was arrested the day after the Kennedy assassination by the Mexican police, by order of the CIA! Whatever happened at dinner, and that night, it was pleasant enough that other "dates" were arranged. Friday night is my best guess as to when Silvia probably gave Lee the information that her best friend, **Teresa Proenza**, worked with **Raul Aparicio**, the Cultural Attache' in the Cuban Embassy. This was the man that Lee needed to see, and the Embassy was open Saturday, whereas the Consulate was not. Since Lee had registered as a "photographer," an artistic profession, it was

---

[279] from Dick Russell, *The Man Who Knew Too Much*, Carroll & Graf, 1992, p. 354),

[280] There were four other Sanborns in Mexico City, but this one was the most . Donald Petterson, visa and welfare officer at the US Embassy, described the elegant Sanborns restaurant and how the American Embassy was embedded in it: "The embassy in those days was housed in the Sanborn Building. Sanborn's famous Mexican restaurant was on the ground floor, and some commercial offices occupied the next few floors. The consular section was on the fourth floor. The rest of the embassy didn't begin till the sixth floor..." https://adst.org/wp-content/uploads/2012/09/Mexico1.pdf

[281] https://www.maryferrell.org/pages/Sylvia_Durans_Interrogation.html

[282] There were four other Sanborns in Mexico City, but this one was the most . Donald Petterson, visa and welfare officer at the US Embassy, described the elegant Sanborns restaurant and how the American Embassy was embedded in it: "The embassy in those days was housed in the Sanborn Building. Sanborn's famous Mexican restaurant was on the ground floor, and some commercial offices occupied the next few floors. The consular section was on the fourth floor. The rest of the embassy didn't begin till the sixth floor..." https://adst.org/wp-content/uploads/2012/09/Mexico1.pdf

possible that Aparicio could quickly approve an artist's visa to Cuba for him, since Lee had classified himself as a "tourist" on his Mexican Visa application, instead of as a businessman. Lee could claim he wanted to go to Cuba to create the base for an artistic event in photography. Aparicio was known to be generous about granting such quick, short-term visas. He was indeed the man to see. It's likely that Silvia gave Lee that information. Aparicio's office was in the Cuban Embassy, next to the Cuban Consulate. Lee would have no trouble finding it. According to CIA records released in 2017, Aparicio's office was bugged for at least the years 1961,1962, 1963 and 1964, even though Aparicio's records for 1963 – an estimated 50 pages of transcript—are missing. But from other records, we know the CIA ordered Aparicio's phone to be tapped that Saturday, the same day Lee came to the Cuban Embassy meet him. Teresa Proenza, who had recommended 26-year-old Silvia Duran to her secretarial position at the Consulate, was Aparicio's assistant. She ran his office in his absence.

A staunch Communist, an art afficionado with connections to the famous Diego Rivera, and a lesbian, she too was attracted to Silvia, even though Silvia had a young child and a 40-year-old husband, Horatio. While Lee had scant hope that the debonaire Aparicio would grant him a visa, Lee knew that he was the best source for medical contacts who could get into Cuba. [283] Aparicio was the go-to man for doctors, scientists and medical students who wanted work, tech or lecture in Cuba. He was an affable man who would probably give him some leads.[284] Aparicio was also a CIA contact person, witting or unwitting. Lee only described to me as someone willing to share information who was chronically unwell.

The CIA tapped Aparicio's phone that day. Was it to pinpoint when Lee would be there, so that the imposter who showed up at the same time at the Cuban Consulate, would not be caught in the act? It makes sense, because that same morning an unpleasant event occurred inside the Cuban Consulate, aimed at framing Lee Oswald. Aparicio, due to a high blood sugar event from his uncontrollable diabetes, went to the hospital that morning. That meant his assistant, Teresa Proenza, would be handling his visitors until he returned. After the Kennedy assassination, when Proenza came under scrutiny, she said Lee "had come in cold," and that she directed him to the proper authorities at the Cuban Embassy.

---

[283] https://www.archives.gov/files/research/jfk/releases/2018/104-10102-10145.pdf

[284] See CIA File #104-10189-10028: 518 pages on Aparicio, using MKTRAP, an audio bug, before and after 1963, with 1963 missing. On July 17, 1964, Aparicio explained his job to a visitor: "I am the Cultural Advisor here but my main job is to contribute in forming technical and scientific groups because at present that's what we need."

With the bugging and phone tap going on, the CIA knew this was a lie. Lee told me Aparicio wasn't there, but his assistant was. Proenza was waiting for him.[285] But no amount of masculine charm would work on Silvia's lesbian friend. To recap, about the same time the real Lee Oswald was inside the Cuban Embassy, trying to get information at Aparicio's office, an imposter pretending to be Lee was inside the Cuban Consulate (which was closed), where he called the Soviet Embassy, with either the real Silvia Duran or someone pretending to be her, facilitating the call. The imposter had a Spanish accent but insisted on speaking in Russian so bad he could hardly be understood: The CIA telephone surveillance transcript of the call to the Soviet Embassy at 11.51am has *'Durán' putting an American on the line to them. He speaks in bad Russian and says he had visited the Soviet Embassy, now has 'his address' from the Cuban Consulate and agrees to come to the Soviet Embassy now to 'leave' his 'address' with them...The transcriber of the tapped phone would go on to claim that the American speaker 'is identical with the man who would, in a telephone call three days later, state "My name is Oswald"'* [286]

The Second Call by the Imposter :*Caller*: *(again in very poor Russian) Hello, this is LEE OSWALD speaking. I was at your place last Saturday and spoke to a Consul, and they say that they'd send a telegram to Washington, so I wanted to find out if you have anything new? But I don't remember the name of that Consul.* ***Soviet guard**: KOSTIKOV. He is dark?* ***Caller:** Yes. My name is OSWALD.*

Since Lee was proficient in Russian, this lack of skill in Russian would become a sticking point. In Nov. 1993, a *Washington Post* story by CIA assets Lardner and Pincus said FBI's J. Edgar Hoover himself told President Lyndon Johnson that the caller was not Lee Oswald: "The morning after the Nov. 22, 1963, assassination of President John F. Kennedy, his successor in the White House, Lyndon B. Johnson, was told by FBI Director J. Edgar Hoover that the bureau had *"the tape and the photograph"* of a man who *"claimed"* to be Lee Harvey Oswald visiting the Soviet Embassy in Mexico City less than two months before the murder. *"That's one angle that's very confusing,"* Hoover said. *"That*

---

[285] This excerpt from the 2017 CIA doc. dump (104-10189-10028) shows Aparicio was the #1 person who could get Lee Oswald the names of medical contacts. It reads: **"... I am already preparing another group... not only for medicine but for...especially engineers, chemists, biologists, etc....[who] can go there for 15 days, I month or 1 year to give courses...as engineers, biologists, or whatever they may be, to work there...So, you give me a list of those persons showing whether he is a chemist, or whatever he is, and whether he is honest and has progressive ideas, but above all, that he is honest –he doesn't necessarily have to be a Communist –but...he must be, above all, an honest person."**

[286] http://www.blather.net/theblather/2013/10/oswald_and_the_cia_part_three/

picture and the tape do not correspond to this man's {Oswald's} voice, nor to his appearance. In other words, it appears that there is a second person who was at the Soviet Embassy down there."[287]

So much for CIA agent Bob Baer's "Tracking Oswald" TV documentary with his false claim that it was "Lee" who made the call ![288] Silvia Duran would meet Lee again, with intimate results, but was she forced to work with the imposter with poor Russian skills? Was she ordered to date Lee, to learn more about him? Silvia is still alive at this writing, but she doesn't respond to such inquiries.

As for meeting Aparicio Saturday, as hoped, a problem arose for Lee. Lee said Aparicio not only had diabetes but may also have "had a shunt." Shunts – to drain fluid from the brain or to help the heart--were uncommon in 1963. It helped me pin down Aparicio as the person Lee described. It was Silvia's friend, Teresa Proenza,[289] who met Lee in Aparicio's office instead. She would be sorry she did. After the Kennedy assassination, Proenza described Lee to investigators as behaving calmly, rationally and quietly when she saw him. Unfortunately for her, a depiction of a calm, rational Oswald was the opposite of the CIA's preferred version. The preferred version was that Lee went on a scream-fest at the Embassy, yelling that he wanted to kill Kennedy. CIA was already setting her up, and now there were additional reasons to get Proenza deported and arrested. She was imprisoned on charges trumped up by the CIA and later placed under house arrest, safely out of the way for the next three years (See Appendix). Proenza was a witness to the fact that the real Lee Oswald offered no threats against Kennedy. Former CIA agent John Newman tells us that "The Proenza deception was associated with the Agency's AMTRUNK and AMROD anti-Cuban operations, part of a general CIA strategy to 'split the Castro regime' and sour relations between Moscow and Havana. Proenza, the vice minister, the vice minister's wife, and a subordinate of the vice minister were all arrested, tried for treason, and jailed for various terms. They were all innocent."

---

[287]https://www.washingtonpost.com/archive/politics/1993/11/16/feeding-persistent-suspicions/c2d3f186-19d0-4a6e-bca2-6e65fb5c1057/

[288] A book reviewer described former CIA agent John Newman's opinion: *"scandalous it is that the CIA had known in October that Oswald met with a KGB assassination expert and they didn't tip off other agencies (p.429). The FBI that same month took Oswald off their espionage watch list (p.630)."* But Newman knows there was no evidence that Kostikov was a genuine KGB assassin, so how much of what he reports can be trusted? Is former CIA always CIA? Maybe not, for Bob Baer and John Newman.

[289] An example of Aparicio's inside knowledge [2017 CIA doc. dump 104-10189-10028: Apr. 15, 1964]: a "student of medicine" is at the door, followed by a woman who says Raul Roa asked her to send him "two reactors for his laboratory at the University."... Aparicio says that while Cuba needs writers, painters, artists, "It is vital for them to have doctors go to Cuba to help them in training other doctors..."

The Three-Day Time Limit As Saturday dawned, Lee realized that in three days, if he couldn't hand off the bioweapon, the cancer cells would die from neglect. There was a dwindling hourglass of time left to pass it on, whether it was a dummy or not. Without Aparicio's help, who might have directed him to a possible contact, Lee next headed to "the university." He soon located pro-Castro medical and tech students there. Remember: *Lee never had any original intention to go to Cuba.* It is essential to keep this in mind.[290] It seems the CIA's true plan was simply to make sure Lee Oswald showed up in Mexico City. What he did there hardly mattered, for he would be confused, disappointed and suspicious, which would play into their game. Imposters to fit their narrative would be used to frame him. Flying Lee to various Texas cities would have assured Lee of the high importance of his mission. By making Lee a courier to deliver the bioweapon, the trip itself was all the CIA needed to claim that Lee had come to involve the Soviets and/or Cubans in evil plans kill Kennedy.[291]

Mission accomplished to set the stage, the CIA would soon order Lee back to Dallas, where Michael and Ruth Paine, who had control of his wife and baby, would act to manipulate Lee again. He would end up working in the proper building to qualify as the one and only suspect in Kennedy's murder, thanks to Ruth Paine. He would attend far-right meetings replete with anti-Kennedy fanatics, thanks to Michel Paine. But the "three-day time limit" tells us of the existence of the bioweapon, for which Lee had been made responsible. The three-day time limit cannot be logically explained any other way.

John Simkin (*Spartacus*) wrote: "Oswald was told it would be *at least seven days* before his transit visa could be issued. *Oswald replied that*

[290] Books have been written whether Lee went to Mexico City or not, the CIA ultimately denying that Lee had ever been there until the History Channel used CIA agent Bob Baer to declare, in the TV series "Tracking Oswald" that Lee did go to Mexico City after all, saying Lee tried to involve Russia and/or Cuba in his evil plans to kill Kennedy. Lee's trip to Mexico City to get help to kill JFK –twisted as it was as to motive -- was revived after Russia lost US favor, charged with interference in the 2016 Presidential election.

[291] "The CIA's Mexico City Station sent cables to headquarters in early October, reporting on the Oswald visit. But these cables described a person who is clearly not Oswald, and instead matches a different person picked up on photo surveillance cameras. In response, officers at CIA headquarters in Washington sent a cable back to Mexico City correcting the description, while within hours these same officers passed on the *incorrect* description to the FBI, State Department, and Navy. When questioned about this in 1994, CIA officer Jane Roman said, "I'm signing off on something I know isn't true." Ref: https://www.maryferrell.org/pages/Oswalds_Visits_to_the_Cuban_and_Soviet_Embassies.html

he could only stay for three days."[292] To the outside world, Lee's Mexican tourist visa was good for two weeks. So why did Lee say he could only stay three more days? [293] Because of the bioweapon's short shelf life. Furthermore, Lee had applied for only a two-week Mexican visa, since after handing off the bioweapon, he was originally told he could immediately assume a new identity in Mexico. We knew we might have to go into hiding for a year in The Cayman Islands until things cooled down, but Lee was led to believe that we could eventually get our educations while serving America as CIA informants.

Dr. Mary had promised to help us get into a Mexican university behind Ochsner's back. Lee was a patriot. Lee knew there were other young CIA agents like him out there,[294] so Lee still had some faith that the CIA was not corrupt from head to foot. To be at Lee's side, I was to have been given a new identity too, as Lee's wife. Instead, Lee had an expensive, dangerous bioweapon left smoldering in his hands. He had enough sterile water and ingredients to refresh the cancer culture's liquids one time, but the new medium wasn't as good as the original. It would keep the bioweapon alive only three or four extra days. Ideally, the bioweapon would have been in a lab somewhere—soon to go to Cuba --instead of languishing in the dark interior of a thermos. What difference would a few more days make? *It would die.*

The changing stories of witnesses also obscured the truth. Did Cuban Consul Azcue know Lee was impersonated at the Russian Embassy? Yes. Both he and Silvia saw the real Lee Oswald – at the same time-- but Azcue would later claim it wasn't—maybe—Oswald. Too short, too blond, too thin a nose. Earlier, Silvia had also claimed, along with Azcue, that she had seen a shorter man with blond hair and a thin face. However, the HSCA's Lopez Report demonstrated that Silvia had been involved with the real Oswald. She eventually said she met the real Lee. That weekend, Lee attended a twist party hosted by Silvia's family. The CIA devalued the witnesses-- family members who panicked when they saw Lee on TV, under arrest for killing Kennedy-- but more than fifty years later, their story remained unchanged. He was there. "Oswald-did-it" researcher Philip Shenon even found a new family member who verified that Lee had been at the "twist party."

---

[292] Author's emphasis. https://spartacus-educational.com/JFKduranS.htm

[293] As questioned for the Lopez Report.

[294] We are asked to believe that for some reason, Lee Oswald, who told his wife goodbye in tears, because they might not ever see each other again, was now so anxious to go to the Soviet Union by himself, knowing Marina would never leave the USA, that he will make himself a pest at the Cuban Consulate! Anti-Oswald writer George Lardner reported *"...to New Orleans district attorney Jim Garrison, Azcue repeated under oath his statements in Havana earlier this summer that he thinks "there were two Oswalds."*

Lee had attended with what looked like some left-wing 'Beatnik' students. And yes, several family members reiterated that Silvia and Lee had dated. Then there were the pro-Castro university students that Lee contacted (we know why), who were surprised that Lee knew they were pro-Castro leftists. Remember, Lee had memorized a list of contacts.

Lee didn't tell me everything about Mexico City. I have put together a timeline that best fits what I know, versus what the government has told the world. Lee related what happened in reference to his attempts to find a substitute contact and his growing concern about being manipulated.

As these critical days passed, we could feel a kind of webwork tightening around us – a pressure — an unknown force of evil —and we did not know where we could turn to escape it. Even so, Lee and I tried to hold on to each other. Others had their problems as well. John Simpkin summarized the fate of Silvia Duran and her associates, soon after JFK's assassination: *"Silvia Duran, her husband and five other people were arrested. Duran was "interrogated forcefully" (Duran was badly bruised during the interview).Luis Echeverria reported to Winston Scott that Duran had been "completely cooperative" and had made a detailed statement.*

Solicitud de visa No.: 779
Fecha:
Nombre:
Ciudadania
Fecha y lugar de nacimiento:
Pasaporte No.
Ocupación
Estancias anteriores en Cuba ---
Motivos de las estancias anteriores ---
Familiares o personas conocidas residentes en Cuba
Con qué objeto? ---
Cual es el motivo del viaje propuesto
Fecha propuesta de llegada a Cuba
Dirección en Cuba:
(Firma del Interesado)
PARA USO DE LA MISION
OBSERVACIONES

This statement matched the story of the surveillance transcripts, with one exception. The tapes indicated that Duran made another call to the Soviet embassy on Saturday, 28th September. Duran then put an American on the line who spoke incomprehensible Russian. This suggests that the man could not have been Oswald, who spoke the language well."

Maybe Silvia wanted us to know about the fake Lee. Early on Saturday, before the imposter got on the phone line, and after Lee saw Teresa Proenza in Aparicio's office, and before he attended – perhaps[295]-- a bullfight, or at least visited a bullfight ring, the real Lee returned a final time to the Russian Embassy.

[295] Lee visited an arena and lamented the 'sport' of bullfighting, but he didn't tell me if he saw a bullfight. Herb Alpert was very popular at this time, and Lee asked me to listen to "The Lonely Bull."

He was there ostensibly to check on the status of his long-standing visa application to the USSR – and of Marina's.

Perhaps the Russian visa had been issued in the eleventh hour. Lee had to make a show of hope that it had come through. If it had, he could use that as an excuse to demand an expedited Cuban transit visa. But it hadn't, of course -- just as Lee expected. Tired of having to deal with Lee's rant, however adequate Lee's Russian was, the "KGB assassin" – Kostikov — one of three Consuls working at the Embassy (all three were KGB officers) quickly passed Lee on to an associate, Oleg Nechiporenko.

Barry Kavanaugh says former CIA agent John Newman asked "*...what if Oswald was being manipulated by 'handlers'? After all, his tourist visa to Mexico was issued next in sequence to the visa of William Gaudet, who worked for the CIA... [Since] On the surface, Oswald's trip to Mexico City made no sense at all... Oswald was doing and saying things 'that were not in his interest' (p.615). He could have been prosecuted for going to Cuba, while the State Department in the summer of '63 had already given him permission to travel to the USSR, which he could easily have done via Europe not Cuba.*"[1]

So there it is, in plain English.

Insisting on entering Cuba was against Lee's best interests.

Only by knowing the back story about the bioweapon can we logically explain Lee's actions. On Lee's second and final visit to the Soviet Embassy, we can see Lee playing this deadly game. He does not want to go to Cuba, but must make it seem that he does, while sabotaging any chance, and possibly saving his life. Lee now put on a show that should have given him an Academy Award.

Use Occam's Razor and common sense, consider why Lee Oswald suddenly wants to go to Russia *through Cuba,* when for months, he'd told Marina, his wife, that he only wanted to go to Cuba. Somethin g else was going on, folks.

When told he'd have to wait up to four months for his USSR visa to get processed, Lee pretended that he still wanted it immediately, and could use its unavailability as an excuse to become angry and upset at the truly helpless consuls. Lee was still nurturing the hope that I would be able to meet him safely (perhaps in Merida) and we'd just vanish. The act Lee put on was based on an extension of that idea. Lee even told the Russians that he would have to flee – *and vanish* --to save his life, because "the FBI" was after him. That created a setting where he could later become an informant to the CIA, since it made him look like a political refugee from America.

If the Russians viewed him as a refugee trying to escape the FBI, while half-mad with terror, disappearing "due to fear of the FBI" would allow Lee to drop out of sight, far from Mexico City. He'd tell me where to meet him in Mexico. Of course, we didn't have to meet at Cancun. That was just our first idea, until we lost Rorke. The money I would bring with me would be enough for us to live on for a long time in rural Mexico, or in any other remote place where an American dollar would be accepted.

---

[1] http://www.blather.net/theblather/2013/10/oswald_and_the_cia_part_three/

Then, after things cooled down, Dr. Mary Sherman would surely step in to help us get into a university, with our Spanish in good shape by then. The CIA needed informants in small towns. So, Lee had incentives to produce Act One, which seems to have occurred during his second visit to the Soviet Embassy. Here's the version written by anti-Oswald CIA assets George Lardner, and Walter Pincus:

"...At the Soviet Embassy [on Sept. 27]... *Oswald met with a consular official named* ***Valeriy Kostikov****, in reality a Soviet KGB officer whose specialties included assassination. [JVB: Most researchers realize there is no proof that Kostikov was a KGB assassin.] One of the first things Kostikov recalled of this initial meeting was that* ***Oswald ... kept repeating*** *that* **"the FBI is after him."** *...When Nechiporenko told Oswald that he could only get a visa in Washington in a process that would entail a four-month wait, Oswald shouted,* "**This won't do for me! This is not my case! For me, it's all going to end in tragedy**." *At that point, Nechiporenko, who was head of foreign counterintelligence at the embassy's KGB station, said he decided Oswald was not worth further attention. "{He} did not have any interest for us," Nechiporenko wrote."It was perfectly clear that our own internal counterintelligence back home had already studied him. Now that he was under FBI surveillance, let him be their headache, I thought."* What Lee did next was to put on Act Two at the Cuban Consulate.

"Oswald... went back to the Cuban Consulate, where he claimed to have gotten a Soviet visa and now wanted a transit visa to Havana.

The employee he spoke with, Silvia Duran, called to double-check.

Kostikov told her the Soviets had promised Oswald nothing.

The upshot was another shouting match, this time between Oswald and Cuban consul Eusebio Azcue. Duran told Mexican police after the assassination that Azcue informed Oswald that people like him "were doing harm to the Cuban revolution" and ordered him to leave the consulate."

Oleg Nechiporenko in old age

Lee's Act Three was about to follow. It would guarantee that he would look like an utter nut job. *"The next morning, Saturday, Sept. 28, Oswald returned to the Soviet Embassy while the KGB men were suiting up for a soccer game with their rivals in military intelligence, the GRU.*

This time, he was brought to [the] third consular official and KGB officer, Pavel Yatzkov, who remembered, according to a CIA report, that ***Oswald "was nervous and his hands trembled."*** *Within minutes they were joined by Kostikov, who spoke English. Oswald told his story again about his 2 1/2 years in the Soviet Union and his return to the United States in 1962.*

According to Kostikov, Oswald even dropped hints that he had ***"supposedly carried out a secret mission"*** without specifying what it was or who it was for." Lee then blamed the FBI for every problem he could think of, from persecution to ruining his jobs. "In recounting all this, ***he continually expressed concern for his life,"*** Kostikov said. He described Oswald as ***"extremely agitated and clearly nervous, especially whenever he mentioned the FBI."*** It was at that point that Oswald pulled out the revolver and put it on a table, saying, ***"See? This is what I must now carry to protect my life."*** Yatzkov grabbed the gun, took the cartridges out and put them in a drawer. When the meeting was over, Oswald picked up the gun again, put it in his pants, and Yatzkov gave back the bullets."[297]

The fake Lee Oswald in Mexico City "The 'real' Lee was photographed at least four times entering and leaving the Soviet Embassy, but a false description of another visitor there was offered in place of those photos. We know this from the following information:
"On 9 October, a few days after the photographs were taken, the station alerted CIA headquarters to the visit of the man claiming to be Oswald: "Have photos male appears be American entering Sovemb 1216 hours, leaving 12:22 on 1 Oct. apparent age 35, athletic build, circa 6 feet, receding hairline." Headquarters consulted the genuine photographs and personal information in its file on the defector. It replied by cable the next day, stating that, on the contrary, the ***23-year-old "Oswald is five feet ten inches, one hundred sixty-five pounds, light brown wavy hair, blue eyes."*** This was "the reply from CIA headquarters: [NARA RIF 104-10015-10048] but, ***"Despite sending this truthful description to Mexico City, CIA headquarters passed on the incorrect description to the FBI, the Navy, and the State Department."*** [298]

There are two problems about the "imposter" compared to the real Lee Oswald. The first has to do with the passport

[297] "TO KGB AGENTS, OSWALD WAS 'EXTREMELY AGITATED'"
By George Lardner Jr. and Walter Pincus November 16, 1993
pOST.https://www.washingtonpost.com/archive/politics/1993/11/16/to-kgb-agents-oswald-was-extremely-agitated/4089867a-47b4-4245-a2df-9560e805d1c4/
[298] See Newman, op. cit., pp.398f. In a nutshell, this information comes from the article "A Little Incident in Mexico City," Among speculations was this statement: "The destruction of evidence and the transmission of false evidence could only have been organised by people with inside access to the CIA station in Mexico City."
http://22november1963.org.uk/a-little-incident-in-mexico-city#fn07_017

photo, which some researchers try to say is not Lee. One researcher said the neck was "too thick," forgetting that this man had conquered boot camp in the Marines at only age 17, and that he had a strong, wiry body and a strong neck. The "Kostikov" call, spoken in terrible Russian, was supposed to put Lee in cahoots with the so-called KGB assassin. But even CIA asset George Lardner wrote, *"Claims that only the transcript of this incident*[299] *remained and that the recording had been 'routinely destroyed' fell flat when* ***files turned up showing that in Dallas, the voice on the recording had been compared to Lee Oswald's voice.*** *"* The CIA had Lee's voice from New Orleans, and on TV from his Dallas arrest. The recorded voice with the Spanish accent didn't match Lee's voice. Remember what Richard Helms, CIA Director, told the courts: the CIA will lie, commit perjury, or deny, to protect the Agency. Lardner's CIA-backed article went on to say "Azcue said that at some point after the Nov. 22, 1963, assassination, when he was back in Havana, he saw the film of Jack Ruby shooting Oswald and concluded this was not "the Oswald who visited the consulate" in late September.

Former CIA Director of Intelligence, Richard Helms

Recalling an argument he had with the "discourteous" Oswald he remembered, Azcue said he had "a clear picture" in his mind of a man over 30... "very thin-faced. He had cold, hard eyes. His cheeks were thin. His nose was very thin and pointed." The Oswald on film, he said, seemed younger and heavier." But too much truth had come out for Azcue's "second Oswald" to be conflated with the man Sylvia Duran now admitted to the Committee that she had seen:

"*In a taped interview with the committee staff,* ***Sylvia Tirado [Duran], by contrast, identified Oswald's pictures from Dallas as those of the man who came to the consulate.*** *"* And Mirabel echoed Sylvia Duran: "**Mirabal said, *"I believe he is the same person,"* too**."

Lardner then added, *"A copy of Oswald's original visa application, examined by committee staffers in Havana, contains the real Oswald's photo. Chief Committee counsel G. Robert Blakey added that committee handwriting experts have confirmed that the real Oswald signed the visa application..."* Recall how Lardner said, "Although he spoke no English, Mirabal signed the application for a visa."

Azcue made his version less credible when Lardner added, "He said *he never even looked at the visa photos to see if they matched with the man presenting them,* until this past April when the committee staff showed one to him... Azcue also said he was sure that the Oswald who visited

[299] https://spartacus-educational.com/JFKduranS.htm

the consulate spoke to no one other than him, Mirabal and [Silvia]Tirado..."

When the CIA offered Lee to the public as pro-Castro, not choosing to defend him as one of their own, hundreds of thousands of files about Lee disappeared, were rewritten, were sanitized or remained classified. Untold numbers of files were altered to hide Lee's true identity. A sleazy, sneaky, stupid "LHO" template was offered to the media and the public. It was to make Lee qualify as President Kennedy's assassin.[300].

Cropping photos of the mystery man, so the photo wouldn't show that it was secretly taken at the Soviet Embassy, raised questions about the CIA's tampering with evidence. The CIA said the photo blooper was due to "an effort to develop information on the assassin under pressure."

The Presumed Fate of the Bioweapon Once available, the seed material migrated at least as far as to M.D. Anderson --made clear when the Product switch-out occurred. By then, the Product was out of our control. The following document shows us that M.D. Anderson almost at once obtained CIA funding to handle radiation, and deadly cancer cells. The document you are about to read, released in 2017, describes the set-up: It reads, "*A study program to determine the effects in diverse Biological systems from exposure to high intensity coherent radiation was contracted with the M.D. Anderson Hospital and Tumor Institute, University of Texas, Houston, Texas in* ***October 1963...*"** The project was put on hold in April 1964 with the CIA asking why it should have to pay "the whole cost of the contract." But "in May, 1967," the project was again underway as "classified work for the Agency," with "no record of a clearance issued." We must conclude that M.D. Anderson and the CIA were involved in serious business, big enough to have the CIA complain about the cost. Another CIA document shows M. D. Anderson's cryo-lab conducted an inventory at the same time, proving M.D. Anderson had the means to keep cancer cells indefinitely in deep freeze.

---

300 CIA asset George Lardner of *The Washington Post*, slanted the story. This "gatekeeper" continued into the 21st century, until his retirement. My parents knew his family. His uncle, Ring Lardner was tagged a communist during the McCarthy era. George was determined to prove he was a Pure Patriot. He would write what the CIA wanted. https://www.washingtonpost.com/archive/politics/1978/09/19/ex-diplomat-denies-oswald-told-cubans-he-might-kill-jfk/a9d6eb9b-f76d-48ff-a657-b7cc72383e5e/

Removed from their icy prison, these mutated cancer cells could spring back to life, to multiply in thousands of test tubes.

So, we must ask, was the expensive bioweapon, developed in New Orleans, discarded? We should look into cancer cases among the enemies of the state. We should look into M.D. Anderson's records.

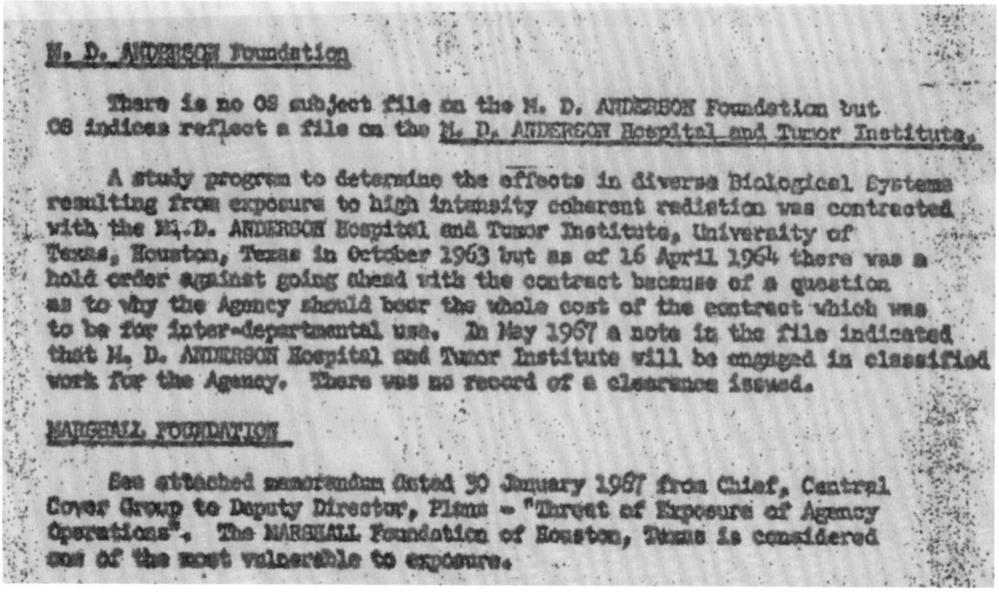

M. D. ANDERSON Foundation

There is no OS subject file on the M. D. ANDERSON Foundation but OS indices reflect a file on the M. D. ANDERSON Hospital and Tumor Institute.

A study program to determine the effects in diverse Biological Systems resulting from exposure to high intensity coherent radiation was contracted with the M.D. ANDERSON Hospital and Tumor Institute, University of Texas, Houston, Texas in October 1963 but as of 16 April 1964 there was a hold order against going ahead with the contract because of a question as to why the Agency should bear the whole cost of the contract which was to be for inter-departmental use. In May 1967 a note in the file indicated that M. D. ANDERSON Hospital and Tumor Institute will be engaged in classified work for the Agency. There was no record of a clearance issued.

MARSHALL FOUNDATION

See attached memorandum dated 30 January 1967 from Chief, Central Cover Group to Deputy Director, Plans - "Threat of Exposure of Agency Operations". The MARSHALL Foundation of Houston, Texas is considered one of the most vulnerable to exposure.

Lee shared most of what happened to him, and what he did, in several long conversations between us on the Mafia racing line.[301] Was the line secure? We thought it was because of the call wheel set-up. We had fourteen or fifteen conversations after the Mexico City fiasco, most of them lengthy. Lee had been aware, ever since July 26, that he could easily be framed for Kennedy's murder, exacerbated by the fact that New Orleans was rife with rumors about who was going to 'get' JFK first. Lee suspected that he could be made a patsy for either Castro's or Kennedy's murder.

Why invest in somebody you're going to discard? To save himself – and us—Lee made himself seem an easily-duped idiot, or a willing tool, if necessary.[302] By acting like a lunatic in Mexico City, Lee believed that he

---

[301] Until recently, I feared that files would be destroyed if I gave out Aparicio's name. However, much has now come to the fore, even if the public is unaware. Competent, honest researchers can find files released in 2017 dealing with Aparicio, the bugging of his office on the day Lee was supposed to meet him, what happened to Proenza, and related matters pointing to Lee's true activities which were covered up at the Cuban Embassy and Cuban Consulate with malicious, even ridiculous tales, such as Lee shouting in the Embassy that he wanted to kill Kennedy. Evidence of Cuba's cultural advisor Aparicio's relationship to the CIA needs to be assembled.

[302] https://www2.latech.edu/~bmagee/louisiana_anthology/texts/warren/warren--appendix_13.html

might be written off as not even worth surveillance or silencing. Lee, playing the "nut job" role, also showed his seductive skills when he went on to sleep with Silvia Duran to get as much information as he could about his situation (and likely, to increase his value to the CIA).

Lee had long suspected that his usefulness was over, making his knowledge of names, faces and events a bad combination. Lee was now convinced that Mexico was too dangerous for us. He said the government was too corrupt to be trusted. Decades later, the excellent researcher Larry Rivera published an astonishing essay about Mexico's succession of presidents in the 60's and 70's. While Lee knew that the Mexican government was deeply embedded in the CIA, including Mexico's President Adolof Mateos (his CIA code name was LITENSOR), did he know how bad it was?

Lee (R) in USSR; he enjoyed the girls!

Sometime after the party, Lee received instructions from Mexico City's CIA station. He was told not to be upset about the failed hand-off. A deadly hurricane was approaching Cuba and the hand-off had been canceled. He must return to Dallas, but not to worry—he'd be back in Mexico City before Christmas! But Lee didn't believe a word of it.

The hurricane had been no threat on the 26th. With a sense of impending doom, Lee was forced to leave. Everything had gone wrong in Mexico City, except Señora Duran. Unwilling to be caught with a thermos holding rotten cancer cells at the border, Lee left it at the souvenir shop in a safe place, though he kept the zippered bag. In Laredo, Lee said he deposited one of his two suitcases "in a locker" so he would have some nice clothes to wear when he returned to Mexico. He also placed some funds for us in a bank there (that's all I know).[303] Then, after leaving a message at the US Public Health Service border office about the location of the thermos, Lee told me he returned to Dallas by car (The Warren Commission claimed Lee returned to Dallas by bus). I later discovered there were rumors that Lee had checked about "quickie divorces" in some border towns, for which the FBI found

[303] The FBI later raided both Laredo banks' safety deposit boxes, but said they found nothing.

an 'explanation' in one case, while claiming another border town was too difficult to reach due to bad roads.

The Corruption of the Mexican Government Lee could not have known that Mexico's next two presidents in a row would also be CIA assets, with code names of their own. All three men were so close to **Win Scott**, the CIA Station Chief in Mexico, that together they attended Scott's 1962 wedding, with **President Mateos** serving as Scott's "best man." Rivera tells us it's *"now common knowledge that Win Scott (Willard Curtis) was very well connected with these Mexican Government presidents... screen captures from a very rare video of the reception shows not only how close Scott was with López Mateos, but also with both his successors, Díaz Ordaz and Echeverría Álvarez... The importance of this arrangement suggests that during the crucial months leading up to and after 22 November 1963, these men were in a perfect position to aid and abet the CIA and FBI in their quest to make Lee Oswald the patsy for the murder of JFK."*

In our naïve idealism, we thought there were options still out there in October, 1963. Lee still had some trusted CIA contacts. We now planned to hide in the Cayman Islands. After a year or so, we thought things would cool down. In all of this, Dr. Mary was a key to our hopes. We didn't factor in that Mary would be brutally murdered July 21, 1964, the day the Warren Commission came to New Orleans to get unsolicited (free will) testimonies. The day after Dr. Mary was murdered, Ed Haslam learned that Dr. Ochsner a letter about

the dangers of Communism to a friend. He did not mention Dr. Mary's murder. After such a close association for over ten years, his silence speaks oceans.

Dallas, Texas, early Oct., 1963: I only know that Lee checked in at the YMCA as ordered. He did not tell his wife he was in town until after he'd been debriefed. With his drop-off of the thermos, Lee's work on the Project was over. That meant no more posing as pro-Castro, no more publicity as a "Marxist." From the moment of his return to Dallas, Lee never mentioned going to Cuba again for the rest of his life. Marina would spread the story that Lee's "obsession" with Cuba was over because "bureaucracy" got in the way.[304]

Lee's Cuban transit visa was supposedly approved in almost record time. It was stamped Oct. 10, but Lee ignored it. The mission to kill Castro was over. Lee's attention was now focused on what would happen to John F. Kennedy, a matter into which he seems have been inserted. After his debriefing at the YMCA, Lee was able to set up his end of the "call wheel" and then he was able to call me often.

One of the first things Lee told me was how they'd used Hurricane Flora as an excuse to call everything off, after all the labor, expense and planning. "They said every demmed safe house was wrecked, and most of our contacts were scattered," he told me, in the clipped way he would talk when irritated. Lee said that later, he was shown photos of Hurricane Flora's rampage in the Caribbean. Several days before hitting Cuba, Flora hit Haiti, where it killed 5,000 people. The approach of the Category IV storm, with wind gusts over 200 mph, prompted Castro to watch it. He was expected to send out his medical teams to deal with the hurricane, if necessary. This was the excuse Lee was given for the mission's cancellation, even though Flora wasn't anywhere near Cuba when the hand-off was scheduled. But Lee had entered Mexico City on the morning of September 26th, while Hurricane Flora did not hit Cuba

---

304 Larry Rivera's research on the CIA in Mexico reveals that the Mexican government was totally under the CIA's thumb. Rivera also writes: "Indeed, in Echeverría's case, not only was he the Mexican Government's liaison to the CIA during the Sylvia Durán affair, his henchman and enforcer Captain Fernando Gutierrez Barrios, (LITEMPO4), Assistant Director of Federal Security Police, was directly in charge of the interrogations of Sylvia Duran and Gilberto Alvarado Ugarte, the Nicaraguan Intelligence agent who lied about witnessing Lee Oswald receiving a $6,500 payment in large denomination bills from a Castro agent as a supposed payment for the assassination." https://merdist.com/wp/2020/04/23/mexican-presidents-at-the-1962-winston-scott-wedding/

until October 4th. The other point was Alex Rorke, who with his pilot Geoffrey Sullivan indeed disappeared on September 25th.

In our imagination, we believed a deliberate effort had been made to keep me in Florida, though Rorke's loss may have been a coincidence. With Lee's involvement in the bioweapon project over, he was now assigned to spy on gun-running, and oh, by the way, please look into a band of right-wing nuts interested in killing President Kennedy.

Lee next attended an unknown number of various political meetings. In addition, Michael Paine, Ruth's estranged husband, chauffeured Lee to additional meetings on both sides of the aisle. Meetings we know Lee attended in late October, as mentioned in chronologies, include:

Oct. 23: "USA Day Rally": Gen. Walker, speaker, Dallas Memorial Auditorium. (Michael Paine told the Warren Commission that a "...right-wing rally was held in Dallas the night before Stevenson appeared in Dallas...)

Oct. 24: "UN Day": Adlai Stevenson, speaker, Dallas. Mem. Aud. (Michael Paine and others, witnesses)

Oct. 25: John Birch Society meeting (with Michael Paine?) Lee self-reported being at the meeting when he spoke up at an ACLU meeting.

Oct. 26: ACLU meeting with Michael Paine.

Thursday, October 3, 1963 This was the day that Dave called to tell me that "Hector" was back in Dallas. Soon, we'd have our own private call wheel as Lee acquired his three or four call points. Then Dave told me how his work with Carlos Marcllo's fake birth certificate and passport got him to thinking about my birth certificate. I needed to order a new birth certificate at once, he told me. If anyone looked at my Indiana birth record, Dave explained, the last known address would show "New Orleans," for I had ordered the certificate when living there. That had to be covered up, by ordering another worthless "female infant Vary" birth certificate right away. The new certificate was sent to Gainesville, Florida. It was dated October 7, 1963, one day after Lee and

MINISTERIO DE GOBERNACION
REPUBLICA DE GUATEMALA C. A.
DEPARTAMENTO DE MIGRACION
Nº 375
SIN DERECHOS

El Departamento de Migración, de conformidad con lo dispuesto por la Ley de Pasaportes vigente, contenido en el Decreto gubernativo número 2039, concede la presente licencia especial a favor de CALOGERS MINACORE.- - -

para que por cualquier vía pueda salir del país con destino a EE. UU. - - - - - - - -

La presente licencia es válida para salir en el término de QUINCE días de la fecha y para reingresar en Guatemala hasta el 15 de septiembre de 1961.-

Guatemala, 15 de marzo de 1961.

FILIACION
Edad 50 años.-
Estado civil Casado.-
Profesión Comerciante.-
Nacionalidad Guatemalteco.-

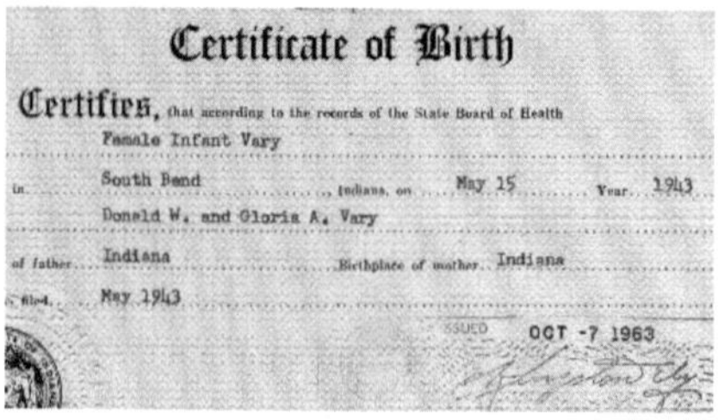

Certificate of Birth

Certifies, that according to the records of the State Board of Health
Female Infant Vary
in South Bend, Indiana, on May 15 Year 1943
Donald W. and Gloria A. Vary
of father Indiana Birthplace of mother Indiana
filed May 1943
ISSUED OCT -7 1963

I talked on our own call wheel for the first time. **(see color pages)**

Sunday, October 6, 1963 We talked two hours. Lee had plenty to say about what had happened in Mexico City.

He finished by saying that Alex Rorke and his pilot were probably dead. Rorke's plane was believed to have been shot down over Cuba after taking off from Cozumel.

Dave had promised to find another pilot to get me to Mexico when the time was right. Meanwhile, we had a new fantasy to consider: maybe we could crash the movie set of *Night of the Iguana* when filming was finished there. We'd pick up souvenirs and items left behind. Meanwhile, a reporter had inquired at the University of Florida about my cancer research. Something had to be done to hide New Orleans as the place where I stopped being involved in cancer research. Using this as an argument, Dave believed he could influence "the powers that be" to hire me at Peninsular Chem Research.[305]

Founded by UF's two top chemists, Drs. Butler and Tarrant, the lab analyzed the compositions of unusual compounds and created rare fluorochemicals and polymers for NASA and medical research laboratories. Tarrant would end up synthesizing the famous anti-cancer drug 5-fluorouracil there. Dave would arrange for me to hired as a research assistant, despite my official record, which still hadn't been adjusted (It showed I had only a "D" in general chemistry)![306]

GEN CHEM & QUAL ANAL CY 217 4 D
PHYSICAL FITNESS 1

My 'D' in Chemistry

That would be no problem, Dave insisted. Pen Chem would be provided with glowing recommends from CIA-approved sources. All the skids

---

[305] An example of research accomplished at Peninsular Chem Research is this 1966 Patent notation: United States. Patent Office · 1966 · Patents
3 [239] , Butler , George B. , to **Peninsular Chem Research** , Inc. 1 : 5 020 . diene linear copolymers. In the late 60's, Pen Chem perfected copolymer membranes to use in reverse osmosis, converting seawater to fresh. (http://www.worldcat.org/identities/nc-peninsular%20chem%20research%20inc/); in 1972, highly-fluorinated polyurethanes for NASA; "Paul Tarrant was chairman of the organic division of the University of Florida chemistry department. He had 58 pioneering papers and 11 patents to his credit, and was cofounder of Peninsular Chem Research Inc., which developed a commercially viable synthesis for the cancer-fighting drug 5-fluorouracil."

[306] I received a letter of congratulations from the Dean for the high grades I actually did receive that semester. but I never tried to excel again in any subject until late in life, when my education no longer mattered to anybody. **See Appendix**.

would be greased. I was thrilled with the idea. Such a job could substitute for some of the training I'd need to be admitted into medical school in Mexico.

Monday, October 13, 1963 I asked Robert to drive me to a pay phone located on a high curb near a row of older homes so I could "take a call about getting a job. The phone rang as I approached it. It was Dave. He said I had been hired at Peninsular Chem Research and should report to "Mr. Van May." This sophisticated laboratory was located just outside Gainesville. I would help create and test exotic "designer chemicals" for purity and composition. The slogan was that there was not a molecule they could not make. Robert never asked how I could get a paying job at such a high-level lab with only one college chemistry course on my official record, when dozens of top graduate students from UF's prestigious chemistry department would gladly have worked there for nothing, just to get that lab's name on their resumés. "You'll be working a lot of hours," Dave warned me. "So what?" I mused, thinking I'd be happy creating exotic chemicals for esoteric scientific projects. Dave had told me I'd make a few to send to New Orleans via such routes as Mound Park (a Veterans' Hospital in St. Petersburg, FL), Eastman Kodak, and our familiar chemical supplier, Eli Lilly. One glycerol I created was similar to antifreeze, which could be used to **more** safely deep-freeze deadly cancer cell lines. *Ugh.* Dr. Ochsner finally conceded that I needed something to do in Gainesville so no questions might arise about what made me abort my "holy mission" to defeat cancer. I had stubbornly registered for several night classes and would now work fulltime. This heavy schedule provided a handy excuse as to why I was seen no more in any of UF's labs.

A gas chromatography setup similar to Pen Chem's, except ours wasn't wall-mounted.

Wednesday, October 16, 1963 Once again, Lee and I started our new pre-arranged jobs on the same day. It was an incredible coincidence. Another mathematical improbability. Lee played up his connections to Marcello, bragged on his marksmanship, and exaggerated a grudge against Connally to "get invited into "a particular group." Just as in NOLA, Lee's new job at the Texas School Book Depository (TSBD) was across the street from federal buildings. Lee stayed in a "safe house" on Beckley, with no plans to resume life with Marina, though he didn't tell her that, of course. He visited her and Junie on the weekends. Lee called me most often at my University contact numbers. He gave me two contact numbers. Lee said he was a special hire, just as at Reily's. He was a clerk who located and retrieved school-book orders from stacks of boxes, but this was October, when the big schoolbook rush was over. Most school textbook orders were finished for the year, and there were already other two clerks handling orders, but Lee was made an order clerk anyway. What Lee liked was that the job was temporary. The building had been purchased recently by **Harold "dry well" Byrd**, a close friend of LBJ and his oil baron cronies. **Harold Byrd & LBJ, 1973 football game** They were refurbishing the place. The sixth floor was presently getting new flooring. With workers coming and going, it was easy for Lee to "come and go" as well.[307]

Mr. Truly, his boss, was told Lee was "working undercover" for the FBI.

Lee said soothingly, "I'll have the same kind of job freedom that I had at Reily's, but even better, because there's no time clock... Don't give up on me!" he said. "I'll be sent back to Mexico City before long. Things are working out, Juduffki!"

Then he cautioned me about his appearance. "I've lost some weight," he warned me. "So don't be worried when you see me. I haven't been sick

— I've just tried some self-discipline, like T. E. Lawrence." Lee and I had been absolutely fascinated with Lawrence. His abilities as a spy and leader were legendary, but he also demonstrated remarkable self-control and calm, no matter what he faced. Lawrence had trained himself to go without food or water for long periods of time in the Arabian deserts, and now Lee told me that he had just broken a series of fasts, and long periods of meditation. Not to worry! He was now drinking lots of milk, and devouring hamburgers, apples, cinnamon rolls, and Dr. Peppers! I told him I was happy at Pen Chem. At the very least, this had not been taken from me—the chance to work in a great organic chemistry lab, gaining skills and knowledge. With Dr. Mary's help, I daydreamed about getting back

[307] Many of Lee's weekday clandestine activities, which included meetings at safe houses, were after work. Big windows in his small room hint as to how Lee seemed to stay in his room all night.

into cancer research south of the border. I therefore saved all my Pen Chem check stubs (see Color Plates) to prove my abilities. Every so often, I was asked to make "something special" requiring a little overtime work. One time, it was to create a treatment for gonorrhea for David Ferrie!

Saturday, October 19, 1963 Friday had been Lee's 24th birthday. When I heard his strained voice on the phone, I realized that something was wrong again. It began when Lee told me that he cried when Marina and Ruth gave him a little birthday cake. Then he would say no more, until I begged him to confide in me. Reluctantly, he warned me that what he had to say was not pleasant. "I won't live to see another birthday cake," he said quietly, "unless I can get out of here. And if I don't do it right, we'll all get killed."

To my gasp of horror, he added, "I'm sorry. You had to hear it." He had pledged, after all, to confide in me, and I had a scar in my mouth as proof. I now learned that upon his return to Dallas, Lee was invited to participate in talks that hinted of assassination plans. "You know what that means," he warned me. I did. "So, you're going to go through with it?"

"I'm going to have to," he said. He said he was in a position where he might be able to do something. "The bad part is that they know I'll try to stop it..." he said. He paused to let that sink in.

"I've tried to pretend that Kennedy isn't my favorite President, but they're not buying it." An 'insider' told him that it was too late for Lee or himself to leave– they'd both be killed if they tried. So, "when the time came" the "insider" would refuse to act, and so by inaction he "...might save the President." As I realized that Lee had put on a show of stupidity that his CIA handlers would probably not believe, I started to cry, feeling both hopeless and helpless. "Don't cry," he said. "It's killing me! I can't stand your crying like that." I suddenly felt faint, and accidentally dropped the phone. When I picked up the phone again, we tried to comfort each other. Then Lee revealed that he had decided to send on any information he could about the assassination ring to those he felt he could trust, such as to "her" (Dr. Sherman). Lee said he was in deep, getting closer to identifying the tyrants who would stop at nothing to gain more power. They might even be able to blame it on Castro, impelling Americans to go to war against Cuba, and thus killing two big birds with one big stone. Lee and I both believed that an invasion of Cuba could trigger World War III, if Russia moved in to defend her Communist ally in the Caribbean. The stakes were too big to run like a coward, he said.

"I know you think I'm a good shot," he told me. "Truth is, I'm not that good. So why did they recruit me?" Lee made a bitter laugh. "They'll set me up again. You see how they hung me out to dry in Mexico City," he went on. "Now they've put off my returning to Mexico until 'a little after Christmas.'"

"Is there any way you can warn the President?" I asked. Lee said he had learned that a campaign of threats and warnings had been created to overwhelm the FBI, Secret Service and White House. Everywhere Kennedy went now, dozens of threats and warnings erupted, to the extent that neither the FBI nor the Secret Service could keep up with them. "I'm going to be snuffed, just as I told you, way back," he said. I needed to be prepared for that, he said. In fact, he would have thought it immoral of me to ask him to save himself at the expense of President Kennedy. Touching, to me, was another statement he made: "Marina hasn't had the baby yet. At least I'll be allowed to see my new son, before it's over. That's something, you know."

"How do you know it's going to be a boy?" I asked him.

"Marina says it feels different," he replied. "So, I think it's a boy." We talked on, trying to lighten the fear and paranoia that from this time on filled our days with darkness and dread.

<u>Monday, October 21, 1963</u> Little Audrey Rachel was born on the 20th, one day earlier than Marina's original doctors had calculated. Rachel weighed almost seven pounds, and the birth was quick and easy. Lee called me soon after, to tell me that he had another little girl, and that he was delighted. But I knew Lee well enough to sense that he had more to say. He finally told me. After Marina went into labor on Saturday afternoon, Ruth Paine said she would drive Marina to Parkland Hospital, but she would "appreciate it" if Lee would stay home.

That way, her two small children and little Junie wouldn't be stuck in the hospital waiting room, for who knew how long? Her argument was convincing.

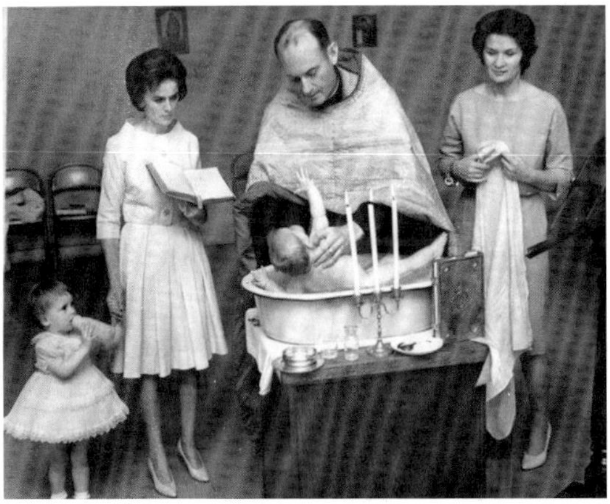

Rachel was secretly baptized into the Russian Orthodox Church against Lee's wishes.

Ruth had kindly arranged a payment plan, and best of all, since Ruth spoke Russian and was a woman Marina trusted, the hospital would let her go into the delivery room with Marina. At that time, men had problems if they wanted to be with their wives. Besides, Lee had no ride to work from Parkland Hospital. If he stayed with

Marina, how would he get to work in the morning? Hitch-hike? And how would Junie feel, having to go back with Ruth, leaving both her mother and daddy at the hospital? Junie had never been without both her daddy and her mother before. Because she wasn't seeing her daddy now except on weekends, Junie was especially anxious to be with him. Lee, recalling how June had screamed and wept every time he left for work the first two weeks in New Orleans, reluctantly agreed. He forlornly watched The Pain drive his wife away to Parkland Hospital a few hours later. Then, to his shock, Ruth soon returned. She got Marina admitted to a labor room and then drove home, leaving Marina alone, with nobody to speak Russian in her time of need. The Pain had deceived him. Lee said he was so angry that he offered some verbal insults, then "went to bed," refusing to speak to her again. He overheard enough from a phone call she made to Parkland to know that Marina had given birth to a daughter and was okay. He had to go into Dallas to work the next morning but had to return to the Paine house for Junie's sake. She was alone, without either parent, for the first time in her life. "The Pain then drove me to the hospital to see my new baby," Lee said. "I didn't want to be in the same car with her," he added, "but I wanted to see Marina... And I wanted to see Rachel. She's very pretty."

It was obvious to both of us that Ruth Paine's so-called "affection" for Marina was only skin deep. Lee had nothing good to say about Michael, Ruth's estranged husband, either. Convinced that Marina should have a car and learn how to drive, so she could be independent, Lee said he arranged for the Paines to find a used car, which they could offer as a present celebrating Rachel's birth. News of the used car thrilled Marina. She didn't know Lee was paying for the car 'under the table' — a fact he didn't reveal to her because it would indicate he had other funds. At the beginning of November, Lee had bigger things on his mind: he had obtained information that would save Kennedy's life in Chicago.

Chapter 25
The Big Event

The plot against President Kennedy thickened in November. By now, Lee had convinced me that Kennedy was a great President who sought peace, and I shared Lee's fear that his life would soon end. Lee had been recruited in the Baton Rouge meetings into the Dallas plot. He had penetrated the ring. Now, he was meeting with one or more of the plotters on a regular basis. "But I'm meeting too many new people," he told me. He was given tasks to do, as if they trusted him, but he was never certain who was who.

A Secret Service agent sought his help in assessing the possible ambush sites that might be used when the President came to Dallas. Presumably, this was to afford protection for Kennedy, but of course, such work would also reveal which sites were best for murder. One meeting in particular disturbed Lee: he called it the "trophy" meeting. It was held at the posh **3525 Turtle Creek** address. Lee had not attended that meeting, but he'd been told about it. "Kennedy won't be killed on Turtle Creek Boulevard," Lee revealed, "because Mayor Cabell, Senator Tower, and the Murchisons all have apartments right there, at 3525 Turtle Creek." General Walker happened to live on Turtle Creek, too, Lee said, but farther away. Lee said the motorcade would turn at the 3600 block "because the plotters want to show their power ... that they are in charge of their trophy."

They would also be taking trophy photos of the assassination. At this time, Lee believed the kill site would probably be the Dallas Trade Mart — if Kennedy wasn't terminated earlier in Chicago or Miami. Sickening to me and Lee was their plan to circulate a photo of JFK's head, "dead, with his eyes left open." They wanted the photo to look like a beheading.

Today, I wonder if Lee's contacts were fake agents, going through the motions to properly position him for his role as patsy — a possibility never far from Lee's mind since our showdown at Katzenjammer's. Was Lee thus kept from interacting meaningfully in Dallas with persons who might have been able to save the president? Or worse, did Lee give a fake Secret Service agent good advice on possible ambush sites, hoping to save Kennedy from execution, only to have them turn it around, and use it to kill the president more easily? These are questions that still haunt me.

Saturday, November 16, 1963 Lee met – probably late at night --with an FBI contact at a location unknown to me, revealing that a militant right-wing group was planning to assassinate President Kennedy during his visit to Dallas on November 22nd. Someone in the FBI took the information seriously and I believe he allowed Lee to send out a Teletype message, as if from J. Edgar Hoover himself, to a few key field offices that night.[308] The spelling on the original Telex, which finally emerged as evidence, is typical of Lee's spelling when in a hurry, for he was dyslexic. Lee, who had an excellent memory, had memorized several important Telex numbers that had been posted at Guy Banister's own Telex machine in his office in New Orleans. William Walter, a clerk in the FBI office in New Orleans, saw the Telex the following morning and later affirmed he sent a copy of this document to Jim Garrison when Garrison. investigated JFK's assassination. The FBI claimed it could find no copies of such a document. Is that a surprise? Lee did not specifically tell me that he sent a Telex, but he said he had sent out warnings at the risk of his life. We also have the informant "Lee" alerting the FBI in Chicago. The Telex of concern has Lee's fingerprints all over it. It is full of typos, showing a hurried composition. This is not a "handwritten copy" of the Telex. It is a typed Telex. There are many

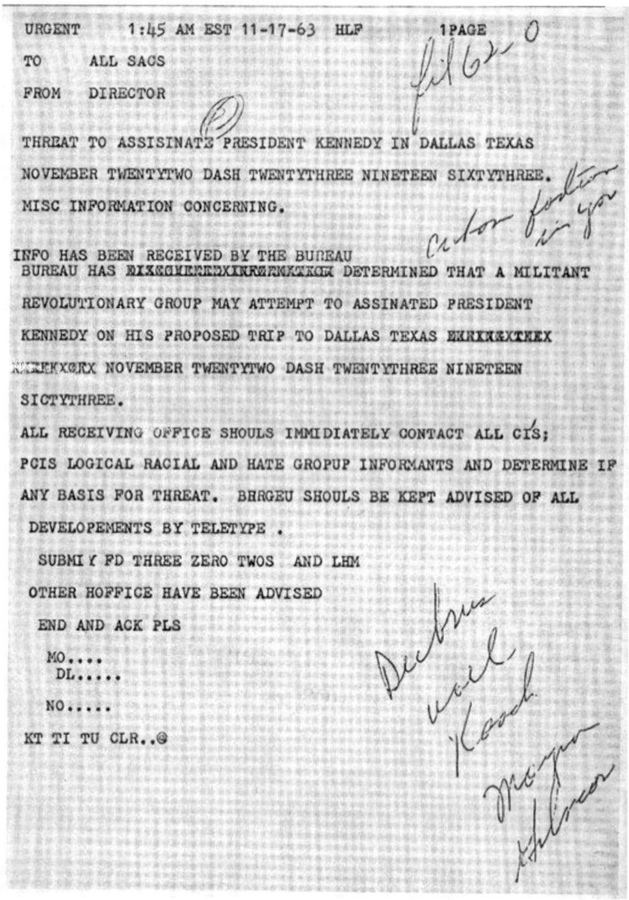

URGENT 1:45 AM EST 11-17-63 HLF 1PAGE

TO ALL SACS

FROM DIRECTOR

THREAT TO ASSISINATE PRESIDENT KENNEDY IN DALLAS TEXAS NOVEMBER TWENTYTWO DASH TWENTYTHREE NINETEEN SIXTYTHREE. MISC INFORMATION CONCERNING.

INFO HAS BEEN RECEIVED BY THE BUREAU
BUREAU HAS [illegible] DETERMINED THAT A MILITANT REVOLUTIONARY GROUP MAY ATTEMPT TO ASSINATED PRESIDENT KENNEDY ON HIS PROPOSED TRIP TO DALLAS TEXAS [illegible] NOVEMBER TWENTYTWO DASH TWENTYTHREE NINETEEN SICTYTHREE.

ALL RECEIVING OFFICE SHOULS IMMIDIATELY CONTACT ALL CI'S; PCIS LOGICAL RACIAL AND HATE GROPUP INFORMANTS AND DETERMINE IF ANY BASIS FOR THREAT. BHRGEU SHOULS BE KEPT ADVISED OF ALL DEVELOPEMENTS BY TELETYPE .

SUBMI[illegible] FD THREE ZERO TWOS AND LHM

OTHER HOFFICE HAVE BEEN ADVISED

END AND ACK PLS

MO....
DL.....
NO.....

KT TI TU CLR..@

---

308 The Teletype was reported seen at Mobile and New Orleans.

things that Marina and I might disagree on, but we agree on this issue. Marina wrote a bold letter to the Chairman of the U.S. Government's JFK Assassination Records Review Board [ARRB], saying, "I now believe that my former husband met with the Dallas FBI on November 16, 1963, and provided informant information on which this teletype was based."[309] I came to the same conclusion based on what Lee himself told me. Researcher John deLane Williams quotes **William Walter**, the student who was the FBI's night clerk: "*William Walter also appeared on the Oprah Show, November 22, 1996. He related that the original of the Teleype regarding a possible assassination attempt in Dallas was on the desk of the Special Agent in Charge's office in New Orleans. Walter also said that he had seen a file on Lee Harvey Oswald, who was an FBI informant. It was Walter's opinion that Oswald was the probable source of the warning regarding the threat to President Kennedy."*[310]

Then there is a note that Lee was supposed to have given to a secretary at the FBI office in Dallas to **FBI Agent Jim Hosty** -- a note that said he was 'going to blow up the FBI office' if Hosty didn't leave Marina alone. The note was in the FBI's hands while Lee was under arrest and still alive, at a time when outrageous planted evidence was being assembled against Lee, such as "Oswald's wallet" that was "found" where Officer J.D. Tippit was allegedly shot, to implicate him. Such a note as described by Hosty could have been used to 'prove' that Lee had violent tendencies. But it wasn't. That suggests Hosty lied. The clue is the paper trail. Something in the note was useful to the FBI's case while Lee was still alive, but was dangerous to keep after he was dead.[311] A simple complaint that Hosty was harassing his wife is the best explanation. The note could be used in a court case to prove Lee Oswald had no connection to the FBI in Dallas. On the other hand, with Lee Oswald dead, the note, if seen by

---

[309] Marina Oswald Porter, April 19, 1996, letter to Mr. John Tunheim, Chairman, JFK Assassination Records Review Board, 600 E Street NW, Second Floor, Washington, D.C. 20530, (Certified Mail No. P 271 942 632)

[310] https://johndelanewilliams.blogspot.com/2010/10/dealey-plaza-echo-2005-8-2-46-52.html

[311] A description of Lee's action by FBI secretary Nanny Lee Fenner, claiming Lee had a "wild look" in his eyes, was nervous, and kept taking the 'note' in and out of its envelope before handing the open envelope to her sounds like another attempt at character assassination. Nobody else claimed to see Lee Oswald hand the note to Fenner, and she never mentioned it until questioned years later. Gordon Shanklin, Hosty's boss, lied, denying the note ever existed until forced to testify in 1975.

the public, would look like the FBI ignored Oswald, who went on to shoot JFK. We can speculate that would make the note a candidate for its destruction. I was now in near-daily telephonic contact with Lee, who had tried to work with trusted agents in the FBI. [312]

He took this risk, even though Lee knew that J. Edgar Hoover was compromised by his relationship with the Mafia. Dallas FBI agent James Hosty, an overworked agent with a heavy caseload, had been assigned to keep track of Lee. The heavy caseload guaranteed that Lee would not be watched closely by Hosty, and we have plenty of evidence that Hosty had no real concerns about Lee. His concerns were about Marina, Lee's Soviet wife. Hosty wanted information about her and was getting it, through Ruth Paine. "[Hosty] worries me," Lee told me. I knew "the FBI" was keeping tabs on Marina. And the CIA wanted her profile kept low. The poor woman went nowhere anymore, for her own safety. She was all but locked up at the Paine residence.

At work, Lee felt pretty safe. Roy Truly, Lee's closest supervisor, had been told that Lee was an FBI informant. Only on November 22 would the Dallas Police tell him that Lee was an assassin.

I remember Lee telling me that when Ruth welcomed Agent Hosty into her home and started talking to him about Marina, Marina was not called to participate. She finally came out, worried that maybe the police were investigating her. In the Soviet Union, such visits meant trouble, and Marina was frightened. For that reason alone, Lee now saw Ruth Paine as a real danger, for failing to comfort her. He had also caught Ruth snooping through his things in New Orleans. He always knew about her CIA connections, ever since she had been a pen-pal, writing to Russian students (and I've been told, even to him) when he was living in the USSR. The pen-pal contacts had occurred through some Quaker peace outreaches, if I remember correctly. After the assassination, Marina would be advised by the Secret Service to stay away from Ruth Paine, telling her "Ruth was CIA."

Beyond all these troubles, Lee's most important achievement —saving Kennedy's life early in October — was an accomplishment he only mentioned obliquely, understating what he had done. I knew that Dr. Mary Sherman had trusted contacts in Chicago, but I didn't know how that linked to Lee's successful warning until James Douglass sent me his book, *JFK and the Unspeakable — Why He Died and Why It Matters.*

---

[312] It's possible that the note was handed over by an imposter, since we have, by hearsay, that "Lee 'Harvey' Oswald" signed it. This simple fact –that Lee disliked his middle name, which even caused him to get into fights if kids called him "Harvey" on the playground-- disqualifies unofficial notes and forms signed with Lee's full name.

Only then, reading it, did I realize how important Dr. Sherman's role had to have been in the attempt to save Kennedy.

I knew she must have been frustrated by our failed get-Castro project, which she had hoped would help save the President's life. Knowing Dr. Mary as I did, she would have continued to work with Lee behind Ochsner's back. Nor had she cut me completely off: she had promised to arrange entry for me into a medical school in the Americas. But I did not realize that Dr. Sherman's role — assisting Lee — had probably extended beyond New Orleans, back to her familiar territory in Chicago. That took courage.

On July 21, 1964, only a few hours before the Warren Commission met in New Orleans to hear unsolicited witness testimonies, Dr. Mary was murdered. The probable cause—murder via a linear particle accelerator "malfunction"--has been described by both Edward T. Haslam and by **Dr. James Stewart Campbell**, a well-known neurosurgeon[313]. Dr. Campbell had a special interest in the case: he had known Dr. Sherman since childhood. His father was Dr. Sherman's friend and colleague at the University of Chicago. Both Dr. Campbell and Mary Sherman's family have released many new photos of her to the public.

Lee reported that he was concerned because in the past few weeks, he was allowed to see *too many faces*.[314] To Lee, that meant he was slated to be killed. He wasn't expected to be around long enough to expose any of them. Worse, Lee said, too many people were allowed to see him, and would be able to recognize him if told to apprehend or kill him. Imagine the tension and stress! Lee indicated that he had some trusted contacts, but did he include New Orleans' Special Agent Warren de Brueys of the FBI, as a trusted contact? DeBrueys had followed Lee to Dallas a few weeks ago. He would prove to be one of Lee's most dire enemies.

On **Sunday, November 17, 1963**, the unexpected happened. Lee hung up in such a hurry that I knew he feared discovery. But that meant he was unable to give me one of our normal-sounding sentences to tell me when he could call again, or if I should call him, using the call wheel.

---

[313] Dr. Campbell presented his analysis to the 7th Annual JFK Assassination Conference in Dallas in 2019. His family personally knew Dr. Sherman.

[314] Asked if Lee mentioned James Files, or reported being involved with just one person for several days the week prior to JFK's assassination, the answer is no. Files said he killed David Ferrie (no). See my book ***David Ferrie:Mafia Pilot.***

For example, "I'll call back in a few days," really meant the same night and the same phone, but three hours later in our code system. To miss a call "broke" the wheel, meaning I'd have to wait for my turn.

Because we took risks to be at a particular phone, and because Lee had never failed to code us before now, I became frightened. I waited, hoping Lee might call again, before we would have to 'reset' the call wheel, risking Robert's imminent return home from the university library. I reviewed what Lee managed to tell me before he was forced to suddenly hang up. In the flat tone of an undertaker, Lee had said that he'd been lured inside a real assassination ring. He knew he was being fed bits of information on purpose, to make him feel 'connected' to The Big Event. [315] Lee knew the police were essentially corrupt. He knew the FBI was a mixed bag of good and bad guys. He had some ONI connections he trusted. That may have been a mistake.[316] was now convinced that an attempt to kill Kennedy would be made at one of three possible places: Love how Field Airport, the Trade Mart, or Dealey Plaza. Each site had its problems.

Love Field was without good natural cover, making escape difficult for the perpetrators, but the large crowd expected there would provide some cover. The Trade Mart had good sniper positions available inside and out, but would be so heavily guarded that escape would be difficult. That left Dealey Plaza, where several tall buildings surrounded what was essentially a fishbowl. However, the Dallas Police headquarters were located there. Unless the police were also involved, it would be difficult to kill JFK at the Plaza. What we didn't know in 1963, and still didn't know until 2017, was that Earle Cabell, the Mayor of Dallas and the former Dallas Police Chief, was CIA! Just as his brother, Gen. Charles Cabell. General Cabell was the CIA's #2 officer. He was fired by JFK after the Bay of Pigs debacle. His hated for the President can only be imagined. At his side, the Number One CIA officer—Allen Dulles, was also humiliated by JFK and was fired. Imagine the two most powerful men in the CIA, kicked out by their president, but retaining enormous

---

[315] The argument is made that Lee was clueless and kept in the dark. But can you control a clueless patsy? What if he decided not to go to work on Nov. 22? By bringing Lee into a place of "inside knowledge" the conspirators could manipulate him to be where they wanted him to be. They also gained insight on who was trusted by Oswald. They just had to make sure he'd die.

[316] Peter Dale Scott brilliantly shows how files on Lee Oswald were handled by the various departments such as ONI, Marines, navy, and FBI, and how deceptions were employed to keep Lee Oswald's records from getting to the public or even to each other. Lee had complained that his mother, Marguerite, had interfered with his effectiveness as a spy for the US in the USSR, which is well understood by carefully reading Peter Dale Scott's research. For important insights on Lee's records and why they were suppressed and even destroyed, see http://jfk.hood.edu/Collection/Weisberg%20Subject%20Index%20Files/S%20Disk/Scott%20Peter%20Dale/Item%2002.pdf .

power within the CIA, behind the scenes. Who was the CIA really obeying? Kennedy's new CIA Director?

Lee was immersed among Kennedy's worse enemies. When he failed to call back by 1 am-- and I knew that Lee would move heaven and earth to call me if he could -- I was terrified. What if somebody had come to do him harm? What if they'd killed him?

The call wheel was now disrupted, and Dave, who usually called Fridays and Sundays, wasn't slated to contact me again until after Friday, which Lee had called the day of "The Big Event." Before that, I would have to use the emergency number Lee had given me to reach him at the Texas School Book Depository (TSBD). It would be a person-to-person call, using the code word "janitor." My first two initials, **"J"** and **"A"** would tell him it was me. Very few occupations begin with those two letters, nor could be applied to a job at the TSBD, so it was a safe code to use. I had previously used "J. A." in the newspaper ad that Lee had seen when we first met, in the newspaper he picked up when I dropped it on the floor at the NOLA post office. Lee would refuse the person-to-person call, but according to when I called him, he would know which phone and at which time we could connect again.

Wednesday, November 20, 1963

Eddie Piper, the real janitor at the TSBD, Lee's workplace.

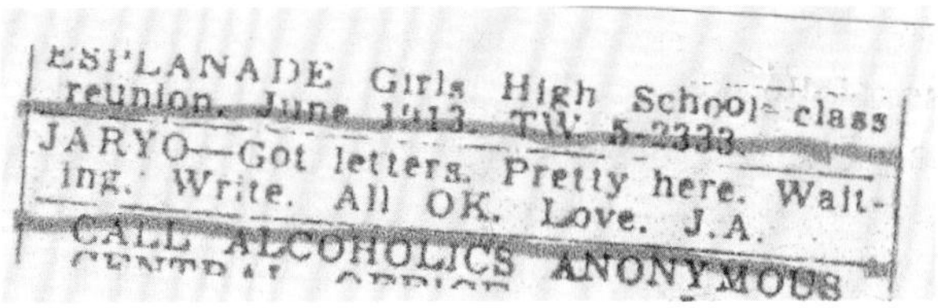

ESPLANADE Girls High School class reunion, June 1913. TW 5-2333.

JARYO—Got letters. Pretty here. Waiting. Write. All OK. Love. J.A.

CALL ALCOHOLICS ANONYMOUS

Waiting for my turn to call seemed to make time stand still. Finally, during my afternoon break at Pen Chem, on Wednesday afternoon, I called the TSBD, person-to-person, asking if Lee Oswald, the 'new janitor' was available to take the call. I hoped he would come to the phone, but I knew he got my message when the call was refused by "Mr. Oswald." I had some trouble with the operator, who was not the regular one who patched through the free call. She would later remember that a woman "with no accent" had made a person-to-person call for Lee Oswald, "the new janitor."

Later, someone would pencil in, above the operator's statement, Lee's middle name of "Harvey," which I never used. Having made the connection, I could scarcely bear waiting for Lee's return call. "The Big Event" was scheduled to happen in less than 40 hours when Robert picked me up late Wednesday night after a long, hard day at Pen Chem, where I worked late most Wednesdays and Fridays. He dropped me off at our cottage.

Then, as he'd done all week, he returned to the University library to study at his carrell for final exams. The university library was open until 2 AM during Finals Week. Waiting for my turn to call seemed to make time stand still. Finally, during my afternoon break at Pen Chem, on Wednesday afternoon, I made the call.to the TSBD. I gave the special code to the operator, who after a bit of hesitation, patched me through. When it connected, I asked if Lee Oswald, the 'new janitor' was available to take the person-to-person call. I hoped Lee would come to the phone, but I knew he got my message when the call was refused by "Mr. Oswald." The operator, who was not our regular one, would later remember that a woman "with no accent" had made a person-to-person call for Lee Oswald, "the new janitor." Later, someone would pencil in, above the operator's statement, Lee's middle name of "Harvey," which I never used. Having made the connection, I could scarcely bear waiting for Lee's return call. "The Big Event" was only about 40 hours away when Robert picked me up late Wednesday night after a long, hard day at Pen Chem, where I worked late most Wednesdays and Fridays. He dropped me off at our cottage, and then, as he'd done all week, returned to the University library to study at his carrell for final exams. The university library closed at 2 AM during Finals Week.

He wouldn't return until about 2:30 A.M. I always talked to Lee at UF's Craft Shop, or at a payphone, never at our home. We had a home phone now, since I had to call Robert if Pen Chem made me stay late. But Lee wanted no calls traced to that number. So now I waited a dark and anxious hour near a payphone by the 7-11 store. At about 11:00 p.m., Dallas time, Lee called, apologizing for not calling me back on Sunday. He'd never had enough privacy to do so. For the next hour and a half, we talked our hearts out. It was fraught with omens.

Lee's Call and the Washateria

From: wim dankbaar Sent: zaterdag 19 juli 2003 11:3
To: elect63@xs4all.nl; martin Shackelford; howpl@aol.com
CE 3000 is an FBI report of an interview with Leslie Lawson, the owner and manager of Gray's Cleaners, 1209 Eldorado, Oak Cliff on 5th December 1963...Lawson... stated that he had seen Oswald on several occasions at Sleight's Speed Wash, 1101 North Beckley. This establishment had, in fact, changed its name to Reno's Speed Wash in August 1963. A former Reno's employee, Joseph Johnson, was interviewed by the FBI on 28th July 1964 and stated that on the evening of 20th or 21st November 1963, Lee Harvey Oswald was 'washing laundry at Reno's Speed Wash.' Oswald, he said, remained there, reading magazines, until midnight. (CE 3001)
http://spot.acorn.net/jfkplace/09/fp.back_issues/25th_Issue/myth.html

"How much can you say?" I asked, worried that Lee might have to suddenly hang up again.

"We're safe," he said, "but I have meetings[317] tonight, in two different places." Earlier that evening an event perturbed Lee; he called it the "trophy" meeting --held at the posh 3525 Turtle Creek high rise, where Gov. Connally, the Murchisons, Earle Cabell (Dallas' Mayor) and other luminaries lived or enjoyed superior leisure time with friends and select women in privacy.

" General Walker happened to live on Turtle Creek, too, Lee said, not far away. Lee had not attended this meeting, but he used binoculars and pretended to feed ducks, while he got license plate numbers of those who showed up. He was on a steep slope, where he couldn't be seen, on the banks of Turtle Creek. It was an early evening meeting, where certain plans may have been finalized. I would one day hear reports of other meetings, mostly held on Thursday night, where these plans may have been revealed and accepted.[318]

"Kennedy won't be killed on Turtle Creek Boulevard," Lee said. Those who were not in the motorcade itself, who knew what was planned, could choose to watch the motorcade slow down and make a tight turn at 3600 Turtle Creek. That was a good spot for an assassination, Lee said, with few witnesses and many hiding places, but it was too private. Kennedy's enemies wanted a public execution. Lee once thought the kill site would be the Dallas Trade Mart. But now, he wasn't so sure.

---

[317] "Meeting" was a code word for "phone call." "Two different places" meant he had up to two hours we could spend on this phone call.

[318] In the 1st edition of *Me & Lee*, details of this meeting were held back so I could try to prove what Lee did, using witnesses. For four consecutive years, I brought groups of 5-20 people to 3525 Turtle Creek. They took photos, even entering the gorgeous lobby. These groups heard the history of 3525 for themselves, through the managers or security guards who told them of the important people who had lived there. We also crossed the street and walked down the steep incline to Turtle Creek's "Duck Pond" so everyone could see for themselves that Lee was able to use binoculars to get license plate numbers of cars entering there. With someone posing as Lee, kneeling on the steep slope at the duck pond where Lee had pretended to be feeding ducks as these cars drove up, we proved that nobody at the entry, including the security guard there, could have seen Lee, though Lee had a clear view of every car.

He said there was a drunken joke to circulate a photo of JFK dead, with his eyes left open."[319] They wanted it sent around as a "trophy" photo, like a hunter would use to display an animal that they shot.

"Even though they're going to try to kill him again," Lee said, "I've sent out information that might be able to save him." He said it in his cheery Scarlet Pimpernel voice. "That's worth dying for, you know!" he finished.

I could close my eyes and imagine him smiling at me as he said that, full of bravado. But he meant it. This was the moment he had lived for. The chance to make a real difference with his life. But it was no death wish. Informed that he was now 'part of the group' that would assemble in Dallas to make sure the President never left alive, and secretly the member of an abort team that would try to intervene, Lee said he would be required to obey orders from both sides.

Wm. "Tosh" Plumlee, longtime CIA contract pilot, with Antonio Veciana, head of Alpha 66. Plumlee told researcher Jim Marrs about the abort team.

When I told Jim that Lee was on an "abort team," he was shocked. Only a few knew about Plumlee's unpublished assertion, and he had no witnesses until I spoke up. My knowledge impelled Marrs to investigate me thoroughly. He ended writing the Afterword for *Me & Lee.* We were close friends to the day he died.

The abort team members planned to stake out Dealey Plaza, which had been identified as JFK's least protected area, where the greatest danger was. They would "innocently" get in the way of potential snipers, blocking lines of fire. There was no way he could provide an excuse, Lee said, for not showing up if he might be needed. [320] He was in too deep. "Why don't you make yourself sick, by taking a laxative or something?" I suggested, as if escaping the plot to murder the President would be like playing hooky from school!

We had a grim laugh over the absurdity of that one. "Juduffki!" he said, then, "Minnie-Mouse!" (my code name).

---

[319] They got their wish. The wide availability of JFK's graphic autopsy photos shows how little respect JFK's enemies had for him.

[320] William "Tosh" Plumlee, whose testimonies before Congressional committees are well-known, has verified that Lee Oswald was a member of it.

Hearing those pet names he loved to call me, I wanted to die with him.
"I want to come!" I begged. "I want to be there — with you!"
"No!" he replied. "You'll have to wait for the call from Dave."
"I want you to call me!" I told him. "I don't trust anybody anymore. And from all you're saying, it's too late to help Kennedy any more than you have. So just *go*!" I urged him.
"Even if I wanted to, which I do not," Lee said, his voice trembling, "I couldn't. We've talked about this before, Juduff. They'd not only do me in, they'd come after my family. They'd find you. You'd all die..."
What could I say? Lee was up against ruthless professional killers who followed the code of vendetta. If they were prepared to kill the President of the United States, anyone who got in their way would die, and if they couldn't kill Lee, they'd kill everyone he cared about.
At some point in this call, Lee then confided to me, in his typical way of understating things, some amazing words. "I believe I saved the president's life about three weeks ago," he told me. A thrill of pride electrified me. When I tried to get details from him, he only said that he'd bought the President three more weeks to live, and so he was content that his life had been worthwhile, after all.[321] Because time was so short now, Lee said there wouldn't be another call from him unless he reached Laredo.
"Lee," I said slowly, "you didn't say 'until.' You said 'unless.'"
"I apologize," he answered. I heard him suck up his breath. We were both very close to tears. Then he asked if my packed suitcase was still ready, under the bed. He reminded me of all the wonderful places and things we wanted to see, and had dreamed about.
"You'll get on the plane," Lee said. "I'll make sure you'll be okay... I'll be there, if ..." We both feared the end of his sentence and froze in silence. "... if I don't make it out," he finished, solemnly, "Then you'll have to go on ... without me."
"How?" I asked. "Who could ever replace you, in my heart?"
"You love babies," he said. "Promise me that you'll have babies."
"I don't want to have babies with anyone but you!" I protested.
"Oh yes, you will," he answered. "You take home baby birds and feed them. So I know you'll want to have your own babies. Promise me."
I knew in my heart that he was right, so I promised. Then Lee said he had one more wish for me to fulfill, which is why I had to stay alive. "Please tell my little girls," he said, "that their daddy was a good guy."

---

[321]Ref: Douglass, James: *JFK and the Unspeakable: Why He Died and Why It Matters*, p. 200-201, 213-217, as reported by Abraham Bolden and his wife, and corroborated by official records.

So little to ask, from a man facing death at only age 24! "I'll never forget you, as long as you live!" I blurted out.

"That might only be until tomorrow," he said, with a tense laugh, as I realized that I had meant to say, "as long as I live," but my emotions were overwhelming me and my speech was getting sloppy. "How much more can you tell me?" I asked. "Who are you up against?"

"I'll be talking to them tonight," he said softly. "Then I'll go to bed and miss you."

"And tomorrow?"

"Tomorrow, I'll go say goodbye to Junie, and Rachel, and Marina..." Lee took a gasp of air, as if he struggled to breathe. Warm tears started streaming down my cheeks again. Soon we were both crying. I wanted to hold him, but the only thing I could do was squeeze the phone tighter.

"They are calling it, 'The Big Event'" Lee said, with a voice of finality.

"Oh, my God! Lee!" I cried, feeling weak, helpless, and incredibly small.

I leaned against the pay phone with the midnight of the world spinning over me. I felt like Lee and I were standing at the flaming gates of Hell.

"Know how we wondered who my handler was?" Lee whispered. "Mr. B? Benson, Benton, or Bishop? I may be wrong..." Lee hesitated, then said firmly, "...but he's from Fort Worth, so it has to be Phillips. He is

the traitor. David Atlee Phillips is behind this. I need you to remember that name." He repeated it with cold anger. Lee then said there were two other names I had to remember: Bobby Baker and Billy Sol Estes. He said the assassination itself was not their doing, but it was *because of them*, and I was never to forget their names. I did not know, then, that Lyndon Baines Johnson, the Vice President, was likely to go to prison due to corruption charges concerning the Mafia, Estes and Baker, based on testimony being given to an investigative committee on November 22, the same day Kennedy was shot! But all of that would change with the "three" shots that were fired that same hour, in Dealey Plaza.

With Lee's words resonating in my heart, my thoughts racing every direction at once, I was frantically seeking a solution. "Is there any way you could get out of this? Something you haven't thought of?" I asked.

"They'd just get another gun to take my place," Lee said. "If I stay, that will be one less bullet aimed at Kennedy." His words seared into my soul: *"If I stay, that will be one less bullet aimed at Kennedy."*

"Maybe I can still do something," he added, grasping at a straw. "But what bothers me the most is – is –" he broke off, then hurriedly said, "they-- they're going to say *I did it.* They're going to pin it on me. And what will my babies think of me, when they grow up?"

"I hate the human race!" I wailed. This corruption was evil itself. The unmasked face of human hatred.

"Stop it!" he commanded. "I can still do something. Maybe I can fire a warning shot. The Secret Service will react," he said. "The Chief might react. Even the driver." The thought of Lee firing a warning shot, only to have the many guns of the President's Secret Service team turned on him, terrified me into silence.

Then Lee said: "I'll love you as long as my heart is still beating."

He told me that when he came to me, he would be wearing the brown shirt I had bought for him, and that he would not be wearing "that demmed wedding ring." The ring that had clinked against mine as we had walked hand-in-hand, reminding us of the unhappy marriages in which we were trapped... "Humans should live as long as oak trees!" I mourned, recalling a poem Lee had read to me about an oak and a lily.

"But lilies are beautiful, too," he countered. "Besides," Lee went on, "I'm no dummy. As you said, yourself, I still have some tricks up my sleeve."

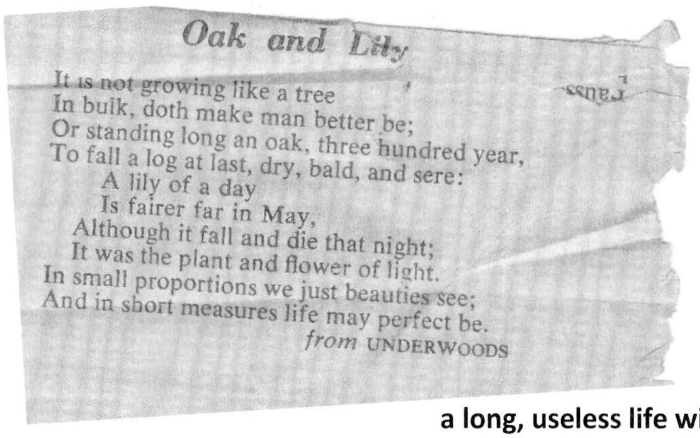

Oak and Lily

It is not growing like a tree
In bulk, doth make man better be;
Or standing long an oak, three hundred year,
To fall a log at last, dry, bald, and sere:
A lily of a day
Is fairer far in May,
Although it fall and die that night;
It was the plant and flower of light.
In small proportions we just beauties see;
And in short measures life may perfect be.
from UNDERWOODS

Ben Jonson's "Oak and Lily" poem compares a long, useless life with a short, but noble one.[322]

I was surprised when Lee asked me to pray for him. As I started praying the "Our Father," Lee suddenly broke in and we said it together.

---

[322] I'm going into detail here, because these were some of Lee's last words to me, and the idea of the "Lily" was important to him. QUOTE: "The poet, Ben Jonson, in the poem 'The Noble Nature', talks about what makes a man noble. He compares man to a sturdy oak and to a delicate lily in order to do this. Growing physically like a bulky tree or living long like a sturdy oak does not make a man a noble being. [It]..become[s] a lifeless, 'dry' and withered piece of log. So too ... [the]man who is only blessed with long life and physical and material well-being. The lily plant has a short life. It blooms in May and is very beautiful. Although the flower has the life span of a day and falls and dies by nightfall, it spreads beauty and delight in that short period. ...a meaningful life like the lily flower, though short, is what makes a man noble..." https://karnatakaeducation.org.in/KOER/en/index.php/The_Noble_Nature Lee read the poem to me from *The Norton Anthology of English Literature*, my college English textbook. On Nov. 22, 1963, I ripped the poem out and kept it the rest of my life.

When it was finished, he said, "I'm satisfied. It's a very old cry to God. Maybe He will hear it."

"I love you, Lee," I whispered, as I pressed myself against the pay phone, trying to get inches closer to the man I loved, as he spoke the last words I would ever hear him say to me. "Goodbye, Juduffki. I love you," he said.

Then he hung up the phone, and the silence began.

It was around 1:30 A.M.[323] as I walked back home alone, oblivious to the darkness around me, worrying only about the dangers that Lee faced. Thursday would be full of more worry, but void of any incident worth mentioning here. I went to work and classes as usual and played wife for Robert at home. As Friday dawned, I lay in bed sleepless, as a dark tension in the fabric of my senses deepened, as if something was being torn asunder in the very halls of the natural world. It was so evil, and so wrong, that only divine intervention, decades after the Big Event, could ever bring justice for John F. Kennedy back into the equation.

Friday, November 22, 1963 I went to work at Pen Chem, as I'd done every day for the previous six weeks. I tried to act normal, though I knew this was no ordinary day. _At lunch time, I sat down in the laboratory to eat. Cabinets and shelves lined the walls. Sleek, stainless steel counters were stacked with sophisticated equipment and orderly rows of test tubes. Imitating my boss, Van May, I had brought a Sego diet shake to eat for lunch. I dipped my milky diet drink into one of the large Dewar jars that held gallons of sub-zero liquid nitrogen and it froze in seconds, yielding a nice ice cream. I ate it with a spoon.

For some reason, our hour-long lunch break started later than usual. Van Mays, my boss, who was an excellent organic chemist, and Nancy, his equally competent main assistant, greeted several chemists who came into our lab area for lunch. They came rather late and seated themselves on tall stools at the counters to watch the news on a television we had up on the wall near the door to the right. It was rarely turned on, but today it was. Other employees came in, too. It was unusual to see so many people crowded into our small lab. I wondered why so many people came in to watch the TV when there was a volleyball game in progress outside. Besides, the entire lab seemed to be filled with people who disliked JFK. Perhaps I was just being paranoid, with so many dreadful secrets held in my heart, for every minute that crawled by increased my anxiety. Would President Kennedy die today?

---

[323] Here I show the time as it was in the original manuscript, for when our call ended. The earlier time mentioned, as to when the phone call began, was an error, for our call lasted 1 ½ hours, not 3 ½ hrs!

Would Lee? I felt so helpless.

Anyone who thinks I would have had any power to try to 'warn" the President must remember where I was, as well as the limited means to report available then, and the danger it could mean for Lee. I was a nobody. The only real information I had was the name of a high-ranked CIA officer. To whom would I report this? The FBI? After what Lee told me about them? To the police? To the White House? The CIA killed heads of state, so what would they do to Lee and me if we got in their way? There was an 'abort team' out there. Perhaps Kennedy was already safe — perhaps the assassins had been located and arrested! After all, Lee had sent information and warnings in the past, and JFK had been saved. Just as it turned 1:15 or so, I began to hear several men in the lab whispering tensely about Kennedy. One expressed his hope that somebody in Dallas would shoot him. That reminded me that I was in anti-JFK territory. I kept my mouth shut, feeling so paranoid and suspicious that I wondered if some of the people in the lab could be in on the plot. Moving away from the others, I started working on the logbooks. We had lots of bead color tests to record, and then I had some halogen laser polymerization tests to run. Finishing recording the bead test data, I returned to the logbook, occasionally glancing over at the TV which was playing clips of JFK, Jackie and Air Force One on a new channel.

A halogen laser. We used a more advanced one.

Some of the chemists and technicians were still unaccountably sitting in our lab, discussing Kennedy. I heard somebody tell my boss that the president had arrived in Dallas and that his motorcade was currently parading through the city. I reminded myself how important it was to show no interest or emotions, and to maintain my veneer of calm, but inside I was on fire. President Kennedy may have been the most charismatic leader in America, but in the Deep South, he was hated by the segregationists, the KKK and anti-Catholics. Stories kept circulating about the president being soft on Communism and "a puppet of the Pope." It seemed everyone I worked with at Pen Chem showed open disdain and even hatred for the "Yankee President." I gazed out the window, where the volleyball game was still in progress under some pine trees. I reviewed the lab schedule for the afternoon: optical analysis of a few test compounds with a ruby laser and an alkaline-halide crystal.

By now, I could do that work with my eyes shut.

A half-dozen scientists and technicians still congregated in the lab, chatting and listening. What kept them here, near the TV set?

Did they know something about the plans in Dallas? After all, my job at this facility had been arranged by people like Dave Ferrie and Dr. Ochsner. Was there a connection?

Shortly after 1:30 pm Florida time (12:30 pm Dallas time), the television erupted with an announcement that chilled my bones.

The President had been shot! He had been seriously wounded by gunfire in Dallas. Soon, the network cut away from its regular programming. I can't remember the words; I only remember my horror. About a half-hour later, we heard news that a priest had given last rites.

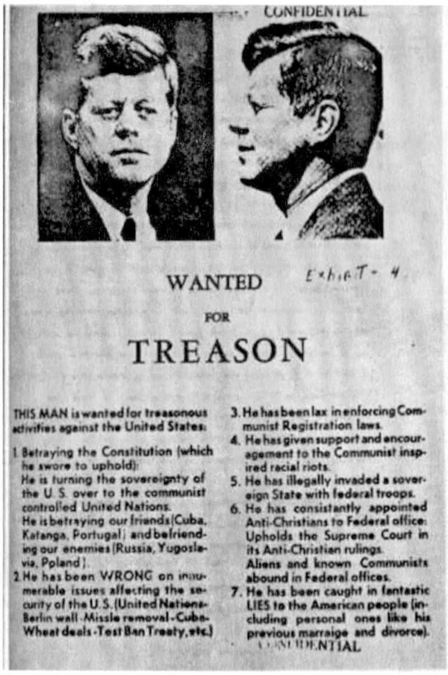
CONFIDENTIAL

WANTED Exhibit - 4

FOR

TREASON

THIS MAN is wanted for treasonous activities against the United States:

1. Betraying the Constitution (which he swore to uphold):
He is turning the sovereignty of the U.S. over to the communist controlled United Nations.
He is betraying our friends (Cuba, Katanga, Portugal) and befriending our enemies (Russia, Yugoslavia, Poland).
2. He has been WRONG on innumerable issues affecting the security of the U.S. (United Nations-Berlin wall-Missle removal-Cuba-Wheat deals-Test Ban Treaty, etc.)
3. He has been lax in enforcing Communist Registration laws.
4. He has given support and encouragement to the Communist inspired racial riots.
5. He has illegally invaded a sovereign State with federal troops.
6. He has consistantly appointed Anti-Christians to Federal office: Upholds the Supreme Court in its Anti-Christian rulings.
Aliens and known Communists abound in Federal offices.
7. He has been caught in fantastic LIES to the American people (including personal ones like his previous marraige and divorce).

CONFIDENTIAL

The fact was greeted with cheers and whistles of approval in the lab. Tears started running down my cheeks, despite my efforts to hide them.

"Good!" Mr. Mays said, slapping his big hand against his big thigh.

"For God's sake!" I exploded, "This man is fighting for his life! What's the matter with you?!" Seeing the expressions on the faces around me, I realized the terrible political error I had just committed. That was my boss! I'd forgotten where I was, and who I was supposed to be. This was Florida! And I was a mere lab assistant.

I shrank under the malevolent glares, wiped my tears, and lowered my head. I had not only exposed myself as a Kennedy sympathizer, I could have jeopardized those who had sent me here. The poisonous whispers and sidelong glances at me continued, so I went to the sink, washed my face, put my lab coat up on a hook, and fell into a seat at the records desk so I could face away from the others.

After a while, it was announced that President Kennedy was dead. I started crying again as I opened the logbook and tried to look busy. Maybe Lee had not been caught in the middle of this mess. As I wiped my eyes, I noticed my hands were shaking. OK, Kennedy was dead, but could Lee make it out of Dallas alive? Or would he be found dead in the Depository with a rifle in his hands? Lee had told me they could shoot him, and then say they killed him after he shot Kennedy... that could happen to him! I preferred to hope that Lee was heading toward a small plane waiting for him at some small airport. He had mentioned that if he could escape, he would fly to Alief Field near Houston, and from there, he would go to nearby Hull Field, and be flown to Laredo.

At least, no arrests had been announced. But then, things changed drastically. It was now about 2:00 PM in Dallas. My imagination ran wild. In another half-hour, Lee could be safe! Dave still had connections to Schlumberger's planes there. He would fly Lee to Laredo, if Lee could reach Houston from Dallas. Soon after, I could meet him in Mexico. We'd have our marriages annulled, change our names, and hide until it was safe to emerge again. But then the cursed TV interrupted my daydream. A man hiding in a movie theater had been arrested. He had killed a Dallas police officer. He had also tried to shoot the police who caught him, but was now in custody. The slain officer, J.D. Tippit, had been shot in Oak Cliff. Hearing this, my fears escalated. Lee's rooming house was in Oak Cliff.

Soon, the media's speculations began. Could the arrested man also be the President's assassin? My hopes began to dim, remembering how Lee had said he went to tell his family goodbye on Thursday evening. Then I heard the words I feared: *"Lee Harvey Oswald... suspected of killing the policeman... and of killing the president..."*

I flashed on Lee's comments from less than 40 hours ago, telling me they were going to blame it on him.

Lee in custody at midnight. Police would claim he refused legal representation when he was arraigned in two separate sessions for two murders. But twice, on TV, Lee said he was denied legal representation and asked for someone to come forward to assist him.

By 4:00 P.M., the TV and radios all around Pen Chem were repeating the name "Lee Harvey Oswald" over and over. I shuddered, realizing Lee was being set up as the scapegoat, just as he had predicted. Everyone from the half-dozen lab rooms next to ours had come into our lab now, to stand there glued to the tube. I also noticed that the news announcers constantly used Lee's middle name, like it was a mantra. What was Walter Cronkite's middle name? Why did they have to say, "Lee *Harvey* Oswald" with the same solemnity as when they identified President Lincoln's assassin as "John *Wilkes* Booth."

It had a sound of finality about it. As if they were pronouncing a death sentence, writing an obituary, or engraving a tombstone. Suddenly I began to worry about my own safety. What if the local police or federal agents burst into the lab and hauled me away? What could I say? Who would believe our government was being taken over from the inside?

While Dave, Lee and certainly Ochsner had done everything possible to eradicate all traces of my involvement, I realized that my conduct now would be remembered by the wrong people if I did not get more control of myself. I told myself: *Remember where you are. Stay calm. You have to survive!* Finally, I saw Lee's picture flash on the screen. With horror, I could see he had been beaten, and I gasped. Mr. Mays noticed. "Are you a God-damned Communist?" he shouted at me.

His assistant, Nancy, looked at me like I had lost my mind. Well, I had. It was puzzling to them. First, I had cried because President Kennedy was killed, and now I was upset because they had "caught the man who shot him." But I had lost more than they could understand.

Yes, I knew that I had lost their esteem, my job, and my future with Pen Chem, but more important, I had lost all hope for Lee. As long as he lived, he could talk. But those who knew what Lee knew would not want him to talk. Lee was a dead man walking. He wasn't dead yet. But that only meant that they could make him suffer, would try to make him confess to the murder of the man he had tried to save. Would the mob of reporters and TV cameras help protect him? Would being in the public eye help provide him a shield against those who wanted to silence him?

The lab looked like a dreamscape to me, unreal, while I worked under some kind of remote control, numb and afraid.

Malcolm Kildulf, JFK's press secretary, said Kennedy was killed by a simple shot through the temple. This photo shows the gesture he made as he announced Kennedy's death to the world. I would not see this gesture, indicating a shot from the front, again, in any of the replays of Kildulf's announcement. That's how tight the control was.

About 5:00 P.M., my colleagues began getting into their cars to go home. I had no car: I had to call Robert for a ride. There was a pay phone outside, close to a row of highly-flammable compressed liquid gas tanks, under some pine trees. I reached the phone and called Robert, who was at home studying. When I told him President Kennedy had been killed, he had little to say, and he said it in his own unflappable way, without much emotion: "That's bad news," he told me. "What a shame. It's because he was for integration, you know." I told Robert the lab was closing down, and everybody was going home. I asked him to come pick me up, even though I was scheduled to work late tonight on overtime. But Robert, always practical, reminded me that if I worked an extra hour or two, as I usually did, then we wouldn't lose money today.

"But I just want to go home!" I told him sadly, with no strength to work and no desire to fight. But Robert argued that I wouldn't feel any better at the house than I did there, so I might as well earn time-and-a-half. I began to feel resentful again towards Robert. Why wasn't he bothered by the shocking news that the president had been murdered? With no way to get home, I sat in the lab and watched the relentless news as it rolled out across the screen. The same scenes of Lee in custody were being shown over and over. It made me feel literally sick to my stomach. By now, it seemed everyone had jumped to the conclusion that Lee had killed Kennedy.

The images of the next two days are embedded in my memory, as they were in the memories of millions of others who are now mostly dead. The police paraded a rifle for all to see, announced that Lee had lived in Russia, and reported on his pro-Castro activities. I was appalled when I heard them refer to him as "the assassin," instead of "the accused assassin." What happened to "innocent until proven guilty?" Why did the media presume Lee was guilty *immediately*? Why weren't they hunting for more shooters? They kept repeating that "three shots rang out in Dealey Plaza" when some of those interviewed claimed more than three shots were fired. As the sun set and it got dark, I just sat there.

Lee didn't kill JFK! It was impossible! Lee thought Kennedy was our best hope for peace! But what about Officer Tippit? While I couldn't imagine Lee actually shooting anybody, maybe Tippit had tried to shoot him, and Lee had to defend himself. Such is the weight of an accusation. Suddenly, I gasped with the shock of remembering-- *the call wheel!* David Ferrie was supposed to call me—*now*! I always worked overtime on Fridays. If I'd gone home, I would have missed Dave's call! I checked the call-wheel schedule. Yes, it was time! I headed to the pay phone under the pine trees near the compressed gas tanks. Surely, Dave would have some inside news. The phone rang right on time, but as soon as I answered, Dave exploded at me with unexpected anger. "Do you have my library card?" he demanded. "Jackass Martin called the police and told them Hector had my library card!" Then it struck me. Dave wasn't talking about his card for the New Orleans Public Library; he was talking about his card for the Tulane Medical School library --his "TMS" library card, issued by Ochsner's Clinic.

It had a number that referred to a register of names at Ochsner's Clinic. Dave and I would be listed as research associates on the same card! If Lee was carrying that card, as Jack Martin had stated, it would lead the police not only to Dave Ferrie, but straight to me and to Ochsner.

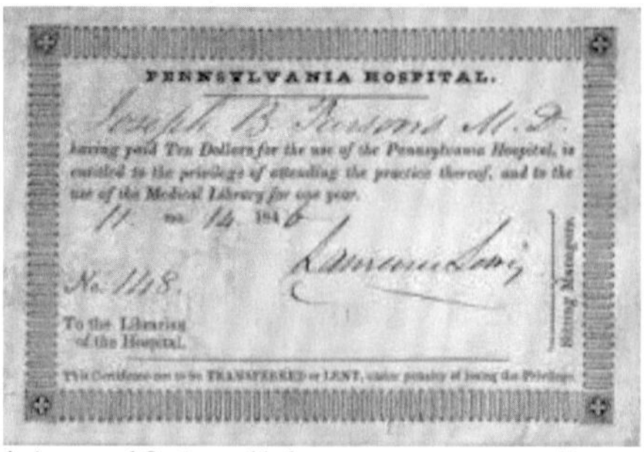

An example of a Medical Library card.

Ochsner would do anything to protect himself. It all began, as earlier described, when Dave lent me his medical library card so I could check out medical journals. At one point, I had given David Ferrie's medical library card to Lee in David Lewis's presence, so Lee could return some medical journals for me. Lewis must have told Jack Martin about it. Lee gave the card back to me later, but David Lewis (and therefore Jack Martin) didn't know that. By claiming Lee had David Ferrie's library card, Jack Martin would be able to wreak more havoc in Dave's life. He would continue to add malicious charges to this one, in the next few days, which caused the FBI to focus their attention on Dave. For example, he claimed Dave had taught Lee how to shoot a high-performance rifle with a scope on it, when all Dave had in his house were some basic, generic rifles for CAP teens to learn how to handle. I had planned to give the card back to Dave the last time I saw him, but that was the same night that I had the disastrous exit interview with Ochsner. I was simply too upset to remember to give Dave's Tulane Medical School library card back to him before he took off from 1032 for the last time, screeching his tires and blowing his horn. The card had remained lost and forgotten somewhere in the depths of my cavernous black purse.

2 of 4 basic "CAP" rifles Dave had in 1963.

"Do you have it?" Dave was now demanding, frantic. "I've even been to Hector's apartment, and it wasn't there!" I have it," I replied.

"I want you to burn it! Right now! While I'm on the phone!" Dave ordered. Here I was, standing in between a liquid nitrogen tank and a liquid oxygen tank, with "No Smoking" signs posted all around. I described the scene to Dave over the phone. "Then dissolve it in sulfuric acid!" he commanded. I agreed to do that, but I ripped the card into tiny pieces instead, and buried it in the sand under a pine tree.

A liquid nitrogen tank, horizontal orientation, such as at Pen Chem (ours was a longer tank).

"Thanks, J," Dave said, sounding a bit more relieved. "I'm okay now. I'll deny knowing anything about that card." Indeed, after acting frantic and terribly upset, a new, calm version of David Ferrie told the FBI that the police had confiscated his public library card some time ago, which he could get back, but it was an expired card, and of course, he never met Lee Oswald in his life. [324]"

Dave then told me, "I'm going over there (to Texas). The boys will be driving all the way. The good news is, we'll talk to Marcello's people at dinner to make sure Lee's going to get some high-powered legal help."

Dave had spent the afternoon in court with Carlos Marcello. It was the conclusion of a long trial. Bobby Kennedy had tried to deport him.

But the (bribed) jury "believed" that Marcello had indeed been born in Guatemala and had not lied about his fake birth certificate. At almost the same moment RFK lost his long battle to deport Marcello, the court heard that JFK had been shot, to shouts of joy from Marcello's people. David Ferrie said he was certain the timing of the verdict of 'not guilty' and JFK's death was no accident. Bobby Kennedy would hear of both events at the same time. Marcello was rubbing Bobby's nose in it.

Marcello had even brought in his favorite girlfriend, named Shasta,[325] from Mobile, Alabama to help celebrate his certain victory over Bobby Kennedy. As part of Marcello's inner team, Dave was required to attend Marcello's victory party, but he soon slipped away. Now Dave told me he was convinced that Marcello, to show his power, would also get Lee released on bail, just to make Bobby Kennedy squirm.

"We'll get Lee sprung!" Dave exclaimed.

"Sprung?" I could hardly believe my ears.

"He's not the only one who got arrested," Dave said. "He's just getting all the publicity right now. You have no concept of how powerful the mob is in Dallas. Marcello's lawyers are on top of it right now. I give you my oath –" I think he said "on a stack of Bibles" as my head began to spin, my heart grabbing onto a tiny bit of hope.

---

[324] Mrs. Garner at 4911 Magazine reported Dave's search of Lee's apartment to the FBI. Dave even asked next door at the Eames,' to see if they knew anything about a missing library card.

[325] Note #9: https://johndelanewilliams.blogspot.com/2010/10/dealey-plaza-echo-2005-8-2-46-52.html I heard Marcello brought in a girl from out of town, and this name fits.

"We'll get him out," Dave declared, "or somebody will pay, big time."
I was used to Dave's hyperbole, so when Dave said he'd call back tomorrow when he knew more, I put it on the Call Wheel. It would be to a different phone and very late. Meanwhile, he suggested that I pray to St. Jude, the Saint of Lost Causes.

.

Saturday, November 23, 1963 The wait for Dave's phone call seemed like forever. Fortunately, Robert became sleepy watching the news with our friends the Zieglers, and had returned to our little roach palace, but the Zeiglers were still up.

They liked the idea that I volunteered to get some cokes at the Seven-Eleven. As I walked to the pay phone, I was on edge. The hair on the back of my neck raised at every sound in the dark night. I hoped my watch was in synch with Dave's, so I wouldn't have to wait around for his call. The phone rang as soon as I reached it. It was a sorry mess of a call. Dave was as jumpy as a cat trapped inside a burlap bag. He apologized for calling a few minutes early. I told him I was glad he did. Then I heard Dave make a sound as if he were choking. I realized he was swallowing back his tears. "Oh, my God, J," he said to me. "I won't hide it from you." Then Dave began crying, and I started to cry, too.

I didn't think I had any tears left, but there they were, stinging my eyes. "It's hopeless," Dave said, with a croaking, cracked voice. "If you want to stay alive," he warned me, "it's time to go into the catacombs." Then he said, "Promise me you will keep your mouth shut! I don't want to lose you, too! If there is any chance to save him, we'll get him out of there, I swear to you. So, play the dumb broad. Save yourself. Remember, Mr. T will watch every step you make."_Dave meant I was being watched by "Santos" Trafficante, the Godfather of Tampa and Miami. He was also the good friend and ally of Carlos Marcello. Fortunately, Marcello liked me, which is why I believed I had a chance to survive any threats from that direction._ "I'll call you one more time,' Dave said. "I told you I would stick out my neck for you. After that, I can't call anymore... And now," he said, softly, as if giving me a benediction, "I have other calls to make. So, *Vale, Soror.*" ("Be strong, sister.")[326]

I returned to the Zieglers' house with four soft drinks from the coke machine (one for Robert later). Nobody had moved from the TV set. I felt that the whole nation was suspended, hour upon hour, on the wings of

---

[326] "Catacombs" was Dave's religious reference to the early days of Christianity where Christians hid due to persecution, and buried their dead, in underground tunnels. The Latin word "vale" is a farewell, like "take care" or "be strong."

TV and radio broadcasts. What would happen next?

When **Sunday, November 24** dawned, I was still awake. The fear and stress was unbelievable, and I couldn't sleep. Robert was surprised that I couldn't even cook. "I had no idea you liked Kennedy so much," he said. Luckily, all of America was transfixed by the tragedy, and everyone was watching their televisions. The Zieglers were no exception, and I was welcome as always. As lunchtime approached and we watched the non-stop coverage of the JFK assassination, Robert suddenly announced that he'd seen enough. He was going to go back to finish an important English paper. We had heard the broadcasts that Lee was to be transferred from the city jail to the county jail. That information was first given out the night before, then was being repeated. I was, of course, anxious for more information about Lee. I influenced my friends to watch the channel that announced it was going to cover the jail transfer. But there was delay after delay. We were subjected to continuous replays of interviews and endless discussions of the President's funeral. In this mix, there were also brief clips of Lee saying "I didn't kill anybody ... I didn't shoot anybody" and interviews of police, sometimes with some scrap of evidence that was supposed to prove Lee killed the President. "I do request someone to come forward to give me legal representation," Lee asked, more than once. I was afraid of what might happen after Lee was transferred, because he would no longer be in the public eye. He would basically vanish from real time coverage, and I well knew that the police would have no mercy on Lee Oswald, once he was removed from the TV cameras that had been giving us glimpses of him being moved from place to place inside the jail.

Lee under arrest. They had removed his shirt, and were parading him around in his undershirt, even for line-ups where others wore shirts.

I knew how corrupt the Dallas police were. To them, Lee was a cop-killer. They would make him pay I also knew there was anger out there over the murder of the president, and much of it was being directed at Lee. I didn't dare leave the set, or rest my eyes, though I hadn't had a bit of sleep. My heart ached, as I realized that millions of people saw a face they recognized only as the man who shot a beloved president. I saw the so-called "killer rifle" they claimed he used.

But Lee had told me he didn't even like rifles! Now the time had come for Lee's transfer out of the public eye.

I feared that soon he would be tortured to force a confession from him, but I knew Lee would never confess to such a thing. He would die first! With immense concern, forced to hide my true feelings about the man I loved, I stayed silent as two tall men in cowboy hats finally appeared with Lee, between two rows of men wearing suits. I saw no armed guards protecting Lee. At first, I was relieved. They had given him a sweater that covered his undershirt. Back then, it was demeaning to be in public in just an undershirt.He was being treated better, was my first thought. Then I realized Lee was now dressed all in black, like a villain or a hit man. How crowded the place was! It was practically a mob scene. My eyes were fixed on Lee. You could hear a sensation of excitement rippling through the crowd and the mob of reporters as Lee came into their view. Now I could see Lee, too, handcuffed, flanked by two tall Texas marshals who tightly gripped his arms. His face that I knew so well showed the strain of hours of interrogation.

A horn honked, distracting everyone's attention for a split second. I held my breath Lee was brought forward, now in full view, emerging from the double row of men in suits through which he had been steered. As the cameras flashed, Lee glanced briefly to his left as if he saw someone he recognized. Then suddenly, a dark, hulking figure lunged forward. He came from the direction Lee was looking and threw himself against Lee. I heard a gunshot--I saw a bit of Lee's face, his mouth twisting with pain as he gasped, and then he collapsed under a pile of thrashing bodies.

The place exploded into chaos. There were shouts and a wild scramble of camera shots. Pandemonium broke out. As police and reporters scrambled forward, I could hear myself scream. It was the most terrible moment of my life.

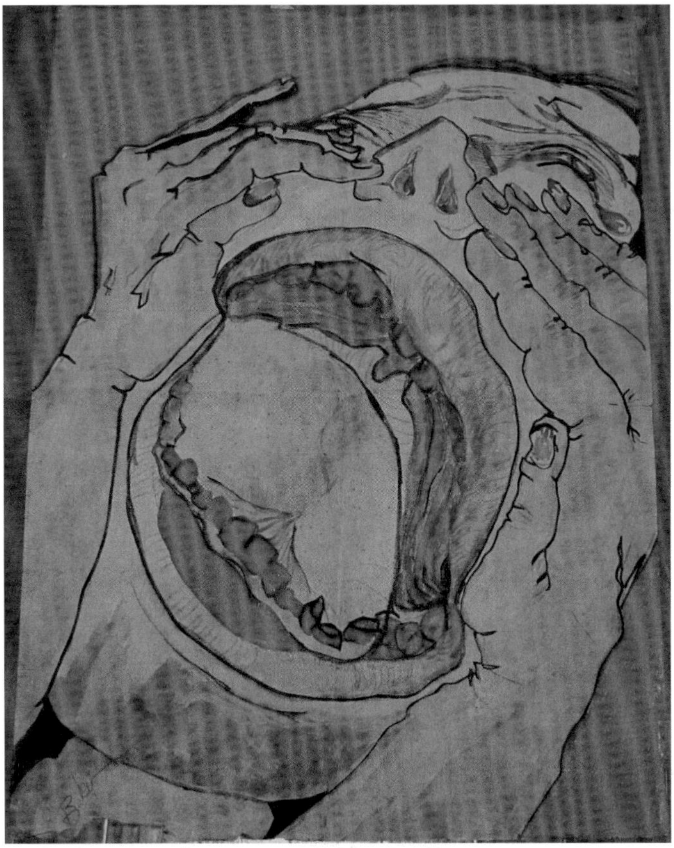

My drawing, "My Scream, Nov. 24"

I can't remember a thing after that, except vomiting in the bathroom. Then everything blanked out. I can't recall how I conducted myself. I remained that way for hours, if not days. I recall only a deep and relentless presence of anger, horror and outrage that kept me on my feet, even when I went to work the next day, despite overwhelming grief.

No, Lee did not confess during his long ordeal, in those hard hours of interrogations. Nor did he confess as he lay mortally injured, urged to admit to a crime he didn't commit. He was in that small room, helpless and bleeding, for about five minutes before the ambulance came.

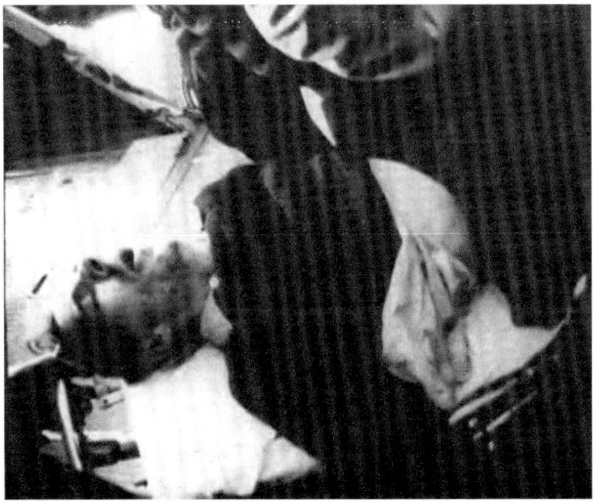

Photo shows Lee's sweater and shirt pulled up: he had been given "artificial respiration" by the police medic in the ambulance, though gunshot wounds to the abdomen must not be subjected to any pressure—a well-known fact.

Lee was given no oxygen in the ambulance, though photos show a tank of oxygen was hanging on the right-hand side of the vehicle, above his stretcher.

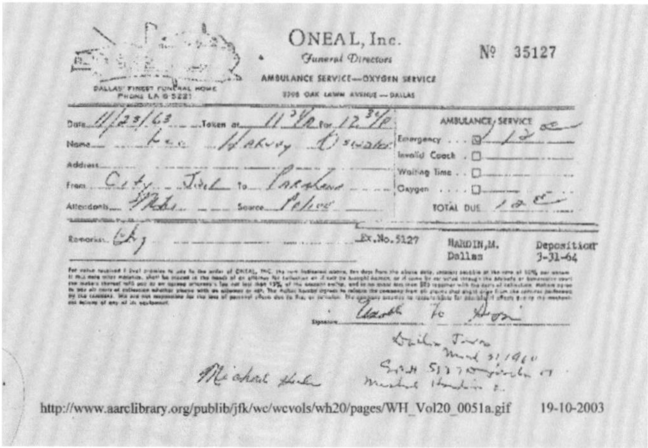
ONEAL, Inc.
Funeral Directors
AMBULANCE SERVICE—OXYGEN SERVICE
3206 OAK LAWN AVENUE—DALLAS
DALLAS' FINEST FUNERAL HOME
PHONE LA 6-5221
№ 35127

Date 11/23/63 Taken at 11 2/3 for 12 3/4
Name Lee Harvey Oswald
Address
From City Jail To Parkland
Attendants Mike Source Police
Remarks City

AMBULANCE SERVICE
Emergency ☒ 12
Invalid Coach ☐
Waiting Time ☐
Oxygen ☐
TOTAL DUE 12

Ex. No. 5127 HARDIN, M. Dallas Deposition 3-31-64

Signature

Michael Hardin

http://www.aarclibrary.org/publib/jfk/wc/wcvols/wh20/pages/WH_Vol20_0051a.gif 19-10-2003

Even there, they tried to extract a confession from him. But he shook his head 'no.'

To his last gasp, Lee showed the world the truth. An ambulance took him Parkland Hospital, where his President had died. He was even wheeled into the same room. But objections arose. JFK had died there! A few precious minutes were lost as they moved Lee to a different room. Yet the doctors claimed Lee was given treatment without prejudice. [327] Then Lee was cut wide open without any anesthesia. Clamps were placed, trying to stem the loss of blood. His lung, liver, aorta, kidney, spleen, and a blood vessel to the lung had been cut by the single bullet, a dum-dum that didn't quite exit his back. Very little blood had escaped to the outside, inciting claims by oddball theorists that Lee's death had been faked, though his blood had flooded his abdomen.

LBJ called, while Lee lay dying. In April, 1992, **Dr. Charles Crenshaw**, one of the doctors operating on Lee who took the call, told the world what LBJ had to say: "All of a sudden this voice like God comes across. 'This is Lyndon Johnson.' And he said, 'How is the accused assassin doing?' I said, 'Well, he's holding his own. He's critical. He's lost a great amount of blood. We hope we can save him.' He said, 'Would you take a message to the operating surgeon?' I said, 'Sure.' He said, 'I want a deathbed statement from the assassin.' And all of a sudden the line was broken." Dr. Crenshaw [said] he looked at Mr. Kennedy's wounds before "we placed him in the coffin, "And the rest of my life I will always know he was shot from the front."[328] But after 45 minutes of traumatic physiological stress, Lee's blood-deprived and overburdened heart finally faltered. Then it stopped beating. The man I loved more than anyone in the world was dead.

---

[327] Dr. Charles Crenshaw and a corroborating telephone operator said Pres. Johnson called Parkland's ER, seeking Lee's deathbed confession. ("The Smoking Guns," The Men Who Killed Kennedy Ep.#7). Jim Leavelle (in the 'don't shoot at me' light-colored suit) said Lee refused to confess when told he was dying and should do so.

[328]https://www.baltimoresun.com/news/bs-xpm-1992-04-02-1992093146-story.html

Chapter 26
The Big Chill

They killed the love of my life in front of the whole world. They did it in a police station, where law and order should prevail. In front of more than 70 Dallas police. I would never see him again. Never hear him again. Never touch him again. Never have his babies. Never look into his blue-gray eyes again. The perverse irony of it all was only overshadowed by my anguish. I would never be able to face Nov. 24 again without psychological torment.

The muffled rolling of the drums, the majestic pace of the horses drawing the caisson with Kennedy's body, the black-shrouded figure of Jackie Kennedy with her two small children, the mourning rows of somber witnesses, and the skittish black horse that was led riderless to Kennedy's grave, were burned into my brain, alongside the mournful cries of officer J. D. Tippit's wife at her husband's funeral.

There were glimpses of the funeral of Lee Oswald, attended only by his mother, wife and brother, with smiling reporters for pallbearers. The public was turned away. Police would not even allow John Pic, Lee's own half-brother, to attend.

If I was going to live, I had to leave the past behind. But the emotional trauma I experienced watching the murder of the man I loved paralyzed me. Thoughts of suicide flooded my head. I barely had the energy to fight them off. The joy had been sucked out of my life. What life? What was left of it? My promising medical career and my dream to cure cancer was reduced to ashes. The only man I ever truly loved was murdered before my eyes. I could say nothing of what I knew, just to survive.

I gradually unpacked the suitcase under the bed; there would be no sudden departure to a new life with a precious soul-mate. My life was now with Robert, a man who for weeks failed to notice my condition. Robert would never buy me begonias, nor yearn to read my poetry, nor would he want to climb Chichen-Itza with me.

As I combed my hair, I remembered how Lee had caressed it. He had loved it long and free. I could not bring myself to cut it. I let it grow long for ten years, then saved one of the braids, because Lee's hands had touched it. I easily convinced Robert to get his geology degree at the University of Florida, citing how expensive it would be to move to New Orleans. I needed to keep Robert out of New Orleans! No longer having a will to live, after the assassination I went to a doctor. He agreed that my health was precarious: the university gave me "H" grades. I did not register for the spring trimester. At work, I was unable to concentrate on new material,

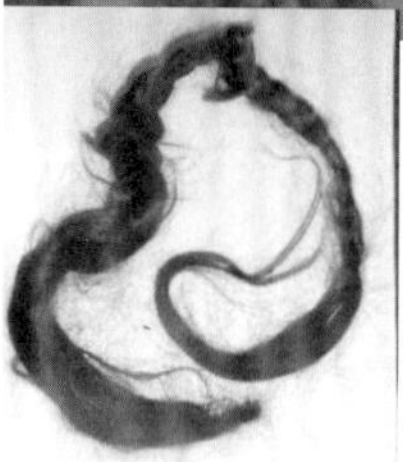

and the quality of my work suffered. It mattered little: they told me I would be terminated on December 31st. anyway. Any mention of Lee's name or the JFK assassination, or even accidental encounters like news on the radio made my heart race. And I had nightmares.

I decided to guard what was left of my sanity by refusing to watch, read or listen to anything about the Kennedy assassination. I kept that promise for 35 years.

But it was impossible not to hear that they had blamed it all on Lee, and that they had identified his killer as Jack Ruby. I knew that powerful elements of the government were involved on too many fronts and that the media was controlled to blindly accept the government line. The American citizenry was likewise a naïve and unwitting accomplice. They swallowed the lie that Lee killed JFK in a solitary act of insanity.

I believed I would be murdered if I spoke out. And, if I died, how would Lee's children ever learn the truth about him? They had the right to know that their father had not killed Kennedy, that Lee had lost his life trying to save the President. They needed to know that when Lee had a chance to flee and save himself, he stood his ground to protect them from retaliation by the monstrous forces he faced. I resolved to go on with my life, in hopes that one day I might be able to set the record straight, at least for Lee's children.

The best smile I could manage for this 1964 portrait.

But my emotions remained raw, my mood despondent, for a long time. Each smile was an effort. Dave Ferrie called one last time, to deliver a message. He was adamant: we must never, ever, speak to each other again, for our own good. He warned me that from now on, I must be "a vanilla girl." My maiden name must never appear in the papers. I must keep my head down and forget about being a science star. Forever! We were all in danger, he let me know. "I've stuck my neck out by calling you," Dave said. "But Lee would have wanted me to. Goodbye, J." He hung up. I listened to the silence and realized that my privileged contact with Lee's clandestine world was over. I was no longer part of their world and, if I kept my mouth shut, maybe they would stay out of mine.

By October, 1964, my sister Lynda had moved in with us after a terrible fight with our parents. I brought her to Gainesville with me.

On November 24, 1964 — the anniversary of Lee's death — overwhelmed with sorrow, I told my dear sister that I'd had an affair with a man I dearly loved, even though we were both married. I prayed she would not judge me. She didn't.[329] Her letter, revealing our secret, written in 2000, is in the Appendix. I've been asked to write the story of my life. It would be the story of those few evil beings who harmed me and the many, many wonderful people who helped me survive. It is in our treatment of others, our prayers and acts of kindness, our writings, art, music, bigness of heart and love, where we can make a true impact for good, and that's all I hope for. I became a Christian when Jesus Christ appeared to me in the most stunning experience of my life.

---

[329] Her letter verifying my confession to her is in the Appendix, below.

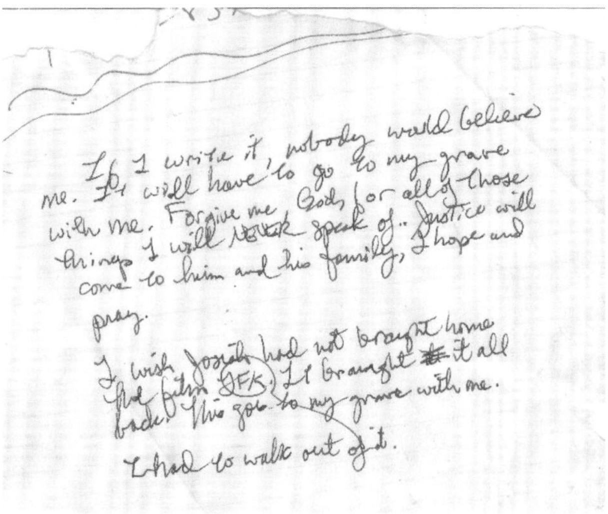
If I write it, nobody would believe me. I'll have to go to my grave with me. Forgive me, God, for all of those things I will never speak of. Justice will come to him and his family, I hope and pray.

I wish Josiah had not brought home the film (JFK). It brought it all back. This goes to my grave with me.

I had to walk out of it.

It transformed me into a creature with hope. Once more, I would someday try again to trust people. Maybe even dare to take a chance to love again. Jesus Christ powered me with strength, happiness and faith. All that happened after Him – how my love for life was reborn and my broken heart began to heal-- is worth a book in itself. In 1992, my son—home from college at Thanksgiving-- brought the film *JFK* for his brothers, sister and all their friends to watch. Though I was the chaperone for the Saturday night movie party, I had to walk out and flee to my church. This is the note I wrote there to myself, bitter and frustrated. Fast forward to **December 26, 1998**.

Finally, my youngest child, a daughter, married and went on her honeymoon. *I was alone!* The very next day I rented ***JFK.*** *At last!* Watching Joe Pesci's dramatic portrayal of Dave Ferrie and Gary Oldman's depiction of Lee was a surreal experience for me. I noticed odd things, like Joe Pesci's voice had a higher pitch than Dave's, and 'Lee' stuttered too much. But beyond trivialities, it was a reasonable re-creation of the world Lee and I had known. Still, what struck me most was the inscription at the beginning of the film. It seared into my brain: ***"To lie by silence when we should protest makes cowards of men."***

Where had the years gone? I was now 55 years old! My oldest child was 30! Lee's children had grown up, never hearing the truth about their father!

I had failed him. I had "lied by silence." But there was more. I loved Lee. I had never stopped loving him. And I had promises to keep. No matter what the consequences, before it was too late, I had to start writing.

No fool, I steeled myself to bear the punishment that was sure to come for doing so. Lee had sacrificed everything to do what was right. *Now it was my turn.* It was Winter Break from teaching. I spent it writing, night and day. I wrote everything I knew and remembered, in a series of letters to my oldest son. Numbers, data, dates, descriptions and quotes came pouring forth from my memory. I covered sheet after sheet of paper, writing deep into the night, for almost two solid weeks. I'd recall a name --it would lead to three. An address—then I'd recall the event. When it was done, I assembled all the evidence and documents I had and laid it all on the bed. Was there enough? I knew there was, so I started trembling all over. Then a calm came over me. There would be no turning back. Later, I begged researchers to ask me questions, to trigger memories I hadn't tapped. I could not believe how many lies they had been fed. The real Lee Oswald had been demonized and transformed into a weirdo, a freak, a monster. Hundreds of books had been published, with a wide range of theories. But in the beginning, I knew none of that.

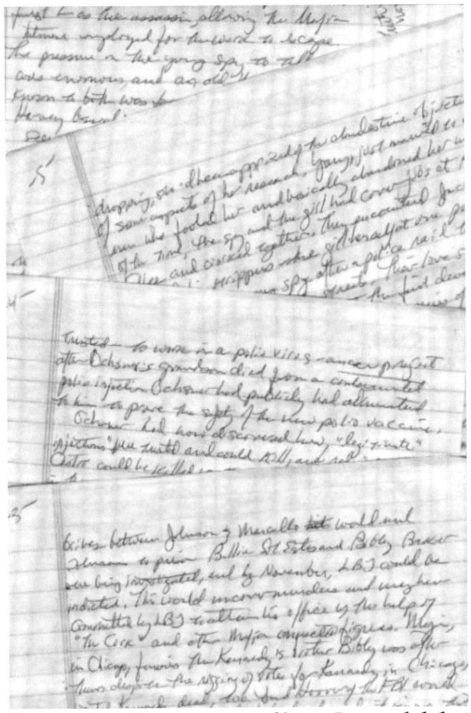

I did not wish to expose my secrets to anyone at the university where I taught, so I mostly avoided using the university's library, which was also under construction. Besides, the elevators rarely worked. At this time, I had injured my back and was on crutches.[330] So I went to the Lafayette Public Library instead, where I selected two popular books about Lee: *Oswald's Tale* and *Marina and Lee.* It didn't take long to be utterly shocked at the lies, especially regarding the startling distortions about Lee's personality. I could hardly recognize Lee in the twisted caricature of him that they presented. There was also a shock when I learned who Jack Ruby really was. He was not just the man who had murdered Lee. His real name was Jacob Rubenstein, and in his youth, his old mob buddies from Chicago called him "Sparky" because of his short temper. Jack Ruby was "Sparky" Rubenstein! *Lee's friend!* The man whom I had met at Dave Ferrie's apartment in New Orleans! Could life really be this perverse? It was Sparky who told me that he had known Lee since he was a child. It was Sparky who had given me a $50 bill as an apology for losing my rent due to the police raid at Mrs. Webber's whorehouse. It was Sparky who had taken us to dinner at Antoine's (and to Clay Shaw's House) the night Lee saved us from the menacing sailor. And it was Sparky who had hosted our evening at the

[330] At first, I confided to Dr. Joe Riehl, my Dissertation Director, but because he led me to a hostile newsgroup online (I sought honest researchers, not John McAdams' trolls!) I became afraid and lost trust in him. He never saw my original manuscript, just the teaser book. Needless to say, he was deeply offended and broke contact.

500 Club with Carlos Marcello. Sparky was Carlos Marcello's friend Jack Ruby — the one the strippers at the YWCA told me about!

That same Sparky had marched into the basement of the Dallas Police Station, pulled out his .38 caliber Cobra, and killed Lee. When I realized Lee had been murdered by a friend he had known since he was a child, my eyes were opened as to the depth of the corruption that rules our nation. I recalled that in his last phone call to me, Dave had tried to explain why Jack Ruby had to kill Lee — that Lee would have been tortured to extract a confession, or they would kill him in the attempt, once they got him out of the public eye. Dave had forgotten that neither he nor Lee had ever told me Sparky's new name. Dave had tried to convince me that Lee's murder was a mercy killing. He wanted me to accept that, so I wouldn't tell anybody what I knew about Lee's killer, and his knowledge of the Project. Of course, I never did. Learning that Jack Ruby had died of cancer while awaiting re-trial, perhaps even due to the same cancerous bioweapon that Lee and I helped develop, gave me no satisfaction. No one deserves to die like that. The hour had come. I wanted the world to know the truth. I would have to record it all. Leave my memoirs for my children, and for Lee's children. I would have to go back, and see who was still alive. I needed to see if any of the old places were still there. I called my sister and asked her to go with me to New Orleans. After more than 35 years, I was ready to confront the pain. With our friend Debbee in tow, we headed to New Orleans to visit the places burned into my brain by the events I had lived through.

One of my hand-written maps from 1963 that I drew so I wouldn't get lost. The other side had names, addresses and phone numbers. Such scraps from the past helped me remember many details.

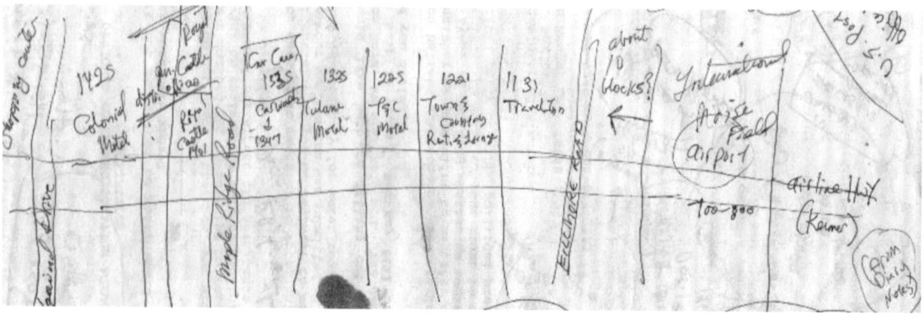

When we did, I had vivid and painful flashbacks. Some were overwhelming. At one point, when we were riding on a streetcar down St. Charles Ave., I was suddenly overcome and burst into tears. I had to get off the streetcar. I was experiencing flashbacks, like a traumatized soldier who returns to a battlefield. I was followed by a puzzled and worried sister and friend. It terrified me to realize how much pain was still locked inside.

Now I knew that the very act of speaking up would be difficult for me emotionally. Would I break down and start crying in the middle of interviews? Could I maintain my composure enough to get my story out? Nevertheless, I was determined to break my silence. But how? Where do you go to tell a story like mine? And to whom? On **<u>Jan. 13, 1999,</u>** I contacted ABC's "48 Hours" and they asked producers at *60 Minutes* to interview me.

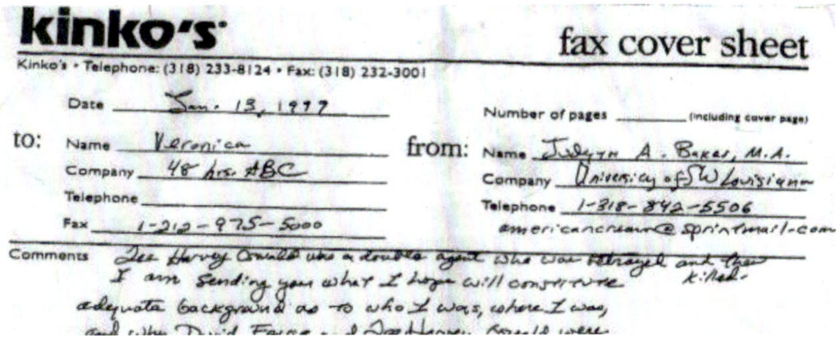

kinko's

fax cover sheet

Kinko's • Telephone: (318) 233-8124 • Fax: (318) 232-3001

Date Jan. 13, 1999

Number of pages ______ (including cover page)

to: Name Veronica
Company 48 hrs. ABC
Telephone
Fax 1-212-975-5000

from: Name Judyth A. Baker, M.A.
Company University of SW Louisiana
Telephone 1-318-842-5506
americancream@sprintmail.com

Comments Lee Harvey Oswald was a double agent who was betrayed and then killed. I am sending you what I hope will constitute adequate background as to who I was, where I was, and why David Ferrie and Lee Harvey Oswald were ...

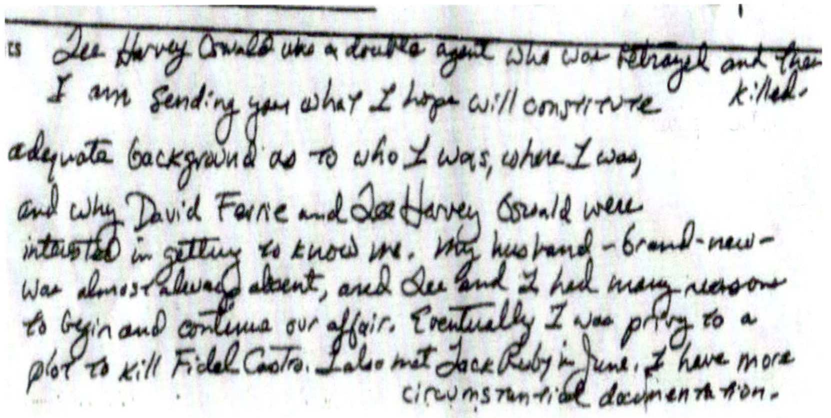

Lee Harvey Oswald was a double agent who was betrayed and then killed. I am sending you what I hope will constitute adequate background as to who I was, where I was, and why David Ferrie and Lee Harvey Oswald were interested in getting to know me. My husband - brand-new - was almost always absent, and Lee and I had many reasons to begin and continue our affair. Eventually I was privy to a plot to kill Fidel Castro. I also met Jack Ruby in June. I have more circumstantial documentation.

Everyone was shocked that a major witness was still alive.

Telephone interviews followed. While they were being conducted, I obtained a literary agent and gave him a teaser book, for I was afraid of who might sue me or try to hurt me. I told him that later I'd give more accurate information to any publisher who was sincerely interested. I also sent for a reporter in Baton Rouge, the state capital, to come look at my REAL manuscript. He came down and photographed it to document its existence, so I had proof the "teaser book" would never be considered the "first" book. I did not anticipate the absolute viciousness of the vile personal attacks that trolls hurled at me from Day One. I finally gave up trying to defend myself after ten long years.

They were not there to learn and listen. They were there only to destroy. They drove me away from their websites, but not from my goal of getting the truth out about Lee. What surprised me was the volatile reaction of many pro-conspiracy JFK researchers, some of whom were heavily invested in their own theories (and in their book sales). Lee Oswald's involvement in a bioweapon project forced them to rethink everything. It radically challenged everything they had been taught about Lee Oswald, which from the beginning was distorted and limited.

The David Lifton Interference Campaign I am particularly concerned about researcher David Lifton's intentions, who since 1999 has spread that I "inserted" myself into the record. Many researchers believe him, based on Lifton's reputation as a good researcher. Therefore, they have refused to interview me. They also accepted CIA asset John McAdams' claims that I 'embellished" or changed my story. Not so. I added details, when asked to do so, over a period of more than 20 years, to questions asked of me. For example, in 2013 I was asked to draw the layout of 1032 Marengo, which I did in detail. They declare that "adding details" is "embellishment." My drawing was checked against an original property record by a diligent researcher, Brian Kelshaw, who was able to prove that Lee's sketch in his address book could not have referred to Lee's apartment in Minsk, as falsely claimed by another researcher.

It is not "embellishment" to provide additional details when asked. I was asked to reconstruct my conversations with Lee, as I had done my best to memorize every word that Lee spoke. I did so using my diary notes and my having memorized everything possible that Lee had told me, in his own words. I reluctantly decided to reveal even our intimacies, thanks to researcher Harrison E. Livingstone insisting that it must get into the record. He called it "pillow talk," but in fact, it took considerable effort on my part to get Lee to disclose his secrets. He did so, at last, because I was his "Portia" to his "Brutus," who had earned that right.

In these pages, Lee's legacy, his courage and his heart are revealed, in contrast to the official version—that Lee was cruel, was stupid, was a liar, a braggart and a murderer.

The damage Lifton and CIA asset John McAdams did remains on the Internet, I guess forever. They refused to meet me. Ignored my witnesses. Spread gross lies. I must write these things because the information I have about the Kennedy assassination must not be discarded simply because an angry little man's book didn't get published. Publishers didn't publish Lifton's "life of Oswald" book because they met me and saw the evidence. While they didn't have the courage that publisher Kris Millegan Trine Day has, to publish *Me and Lee*, they knew I had witnesses, evidence and logical explanations for the so-called "mysteries" –mysteries that have been revealed to you. On the other hand, Lifton had blanks, or explanations that did not match the logical and plain truth, once pointed out. Since then, more files and more witnesses have emerged, all in support of what I've written. (Read more comments about this matter in the footnote.[331]) I learned, rather late in the game, that some people will say almost anything on the Internet. One respected researcher, Jack White, claimed I changed my name from 'Avary' to 'Vary' because I did not like my family name! Another one claimed that I had been diagnosed with a serious mental illness by a psychologist who had never met me.

---

[331] Mr. Lifton wanted to destroy me as a witness. First, he was angry when *Sixty Minutes* canceled his interview and began investigating me instead. His reaction was to call *Sixty Minutes* and trash me. When he gloated that Sixty Minutes wasn't flying me in to New York, first class, as they would have done for him, they responded by flying me in first class! Next, his book was canceled after his enemy, the eminent researcher Harold Weisberg, saw my evidence files and called Lifton's publisher. Weisberg told the publisher that "Lifton has New Orleans all wrong" and that "a new witness has the answers." In response, Lifton began his decades-long campaign to destroy me. He began by claiming I could not have met Lee on April 26, 1963 because I described Lee wearing ordinary clothes and saying Lee was living at the YMCA, when he declared Lee was seen wearing a suit at 1:30 PM that day, had not been in New Orleans on the 25th as I had claimed, and was living with his aunt and uncle. His "correction" was spread everywhere, but he was wrong. First, Lee and I met at the post office no later than 9:30 am, after I finished working at Royal Castle at 8:00 AM. We talked about an hour and a half, which gets us to 11:00 AM. Lee had plenty of time to change to a suit for his job interview at 1:30. Lifton himself "discovered" that Lee indeed had to arrive before April 26, with a bus ticket dated April 24, adding that "nobody" knew where Lee spent his nights in town until the following Sunday, when his aunt testified that Lee *finally* moved in. But, Lifton declared, there was no evidence that Lee was staying at the YMCA, though that's exactly where Lee went after his trip to Mexico City. Lifton also spread the lie that I claimed to have been doing "cancer research in a coffee factory." And not long after September 11, 2001, he claimed (as a joke) that Osama Bin Laden taught me how to fly, but not land. I received a death threat over that stupid "joke." The really bad guys working with John McAdams spread McAdams' statements that Dr. Mary Sherman was not a cancer researcher—just an orthopedic surgeon—and that cancer could not be given to mice. As of July, 2021, they still declare I have no witnesses and no evidence. McAdams' 'researcher' Dave Reitzes spread around, for example, that I claimed In an email to him that Lee had not been circumcised. At the same time, that these people claimed I did 'deep research' to "insert' myself into Lee's life, they claim I could not have looked at Lee's autopsy online (!) Reitzes took my email and altered it, adding the single word 'not' to my statement that Lee was circumcised.

I learned that the groups and forums on the internet, whether pro-conspiracy or anti-conspiracy, were led by only a few people, who had often judged me based on lies and altered emails supplied by John McAdams and David Lifton. Worst of all, when I attempted to correct the lies, I was accused of changing my story, or of "making excuses."

Then there were the "experts" whose theories had become a belief system. If they 'liked' a new witness, it was because the new witness supported their belief system, much of what was often based on falsehoods promulgated by the CIA and FBI. They said that if the CIA had no record of me, then I never worked for them – even though the CIA had sanitized and destroyed countless records on the case. Worst of all, I didn't claim small things. I claimed big things. They demanded photos of me and Lee together—something we had deliberately avoided.

But slowly, things began to change. I have been consistent and new files and witnesses keep backing up all my original statements. Computers could now search through files using key words-- and found a lot. I was not the only ignored or invisible witness. What I had to say began to take on relevance. Slowly, some researchers started to listen. While some of them still try to ignore my existence, time is on my side, because truth, once exposed, cannot be overcome by the old lies out there that never did make sense. The truth makes sense. The truth leads to more truth.

Jim Marrs The change began when Jim Marrs decided to interview me

in person after *Sixty Minutes* was blocked from filming me three times.

He interviewed me in person and on camera, followed by researchers such as Dr. Jim Fetzer, John deLane Williams, Dr. John Hughes, Wim Dankbaar, Phil Singer, Robert Groden and Harrison E. Livingstone.

Peter Devries, a Dutch investigator who uncovered frauds and criminals, also investigated me to either 'bust' me or endorse me. He endorsed me. I also obtained the support of other witnesses and researchers such as HSCA's Robert Tanenbaum, Dick Russell, Dennis David and Abraham Bolden, with input from Gerry Patrick Hemming, Col. Dan Marvin and others who understood Lee's covert world and its rules and rhythms. But it was *60 Minutes* that introduced me to author Edward T. Haslam, who had been doing ground-breaking research into the death of Dr. Mary Sherman, her connections to David Ferrie and his cancer research project for over a decade.

Sixty Minutes flew me to New York, Washington DC and New Orleans. They interrogated me for many hours. They tried three times to film me over a period of fourteen months, but CBS higher-ups forced them to shut it down. I learned of scurrilous attempts to discredit me, behind my back, such as by Brian Duffy of *US News & World Report*. Hewitt, Scheffler, Wallace, Liebengood, Platzman and their producers fought to get the story aired. These good men, who were about to retire, saw the story as a crowning achievement of their careers, if they could get CBS to let them do it. Don Hewitt told C-Span "The door was shut in our Faces." But Dan Rather had always had his hooks *in Sixty Minutes*, and now he used them.

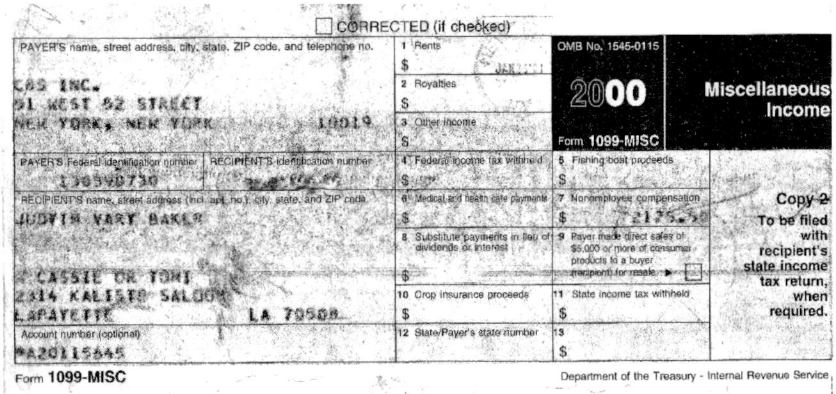
CORRECTED (if checked)

PAYER'S name, street address, city, state, ZIP code, and telephone no.
CBS INC.
51 WEST 52 STREET
NEW YORK, NEW YORK 10019

1 Rents $
2 Royalties $
3 Other income $

OMB No. 1545-0115
2000
Form 1099-MISC
Miscellaneous Income

PAYER'S Federal identification number: 1305VD730
RECIPIENT'S identification number

4 Federal income tax withheld $
5 Fishing boat proceeds $

RECIPIENT'S name, street address (incl. apt. no.), city, state, and ZIP code
JUDYTH VARY BAKER
C/ CASSIE OR TONI
2314 KALISTE SALOOM
LAFAYETTE LA 70508

6 Medical and health care payments $
7 Nonemployee compensation $ 2125.50
8 Substitute payments in lieu of dividends or interest $
9 Payer made direct sales of $5,000 or more of consumer products to a buyer (recipient) for resale ▶
10 Crop insurance proceeds $
11 State income tax withheld $

Account number (optional): *A20115645

12 State/Payer's state number
13 $

Copy 2
To be filed with recipient's state income tax return, when required.

Form 1099-MISC — Department of the Treasury - Internal Revenue Service

$2,125.50

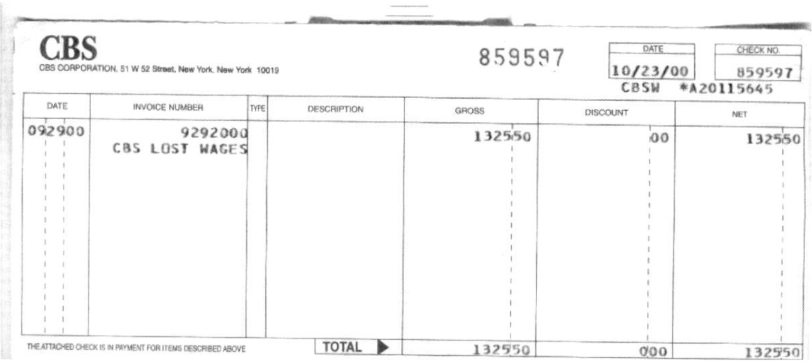
CBS
CBS CORPORATION, 51 W 52 Street, New York, New York 10019

859597

DATE: 10/23/00 — CHECK NO.: 859597
CBSW *A20115645

DATE	INVOICE NUMBER	TYPE	DESCRIPTION	GROSS	DISCOUNT	NET
092900	9292000 CBS LOST WAGES			1325 50	00	1325 50
THE ATTACHED CHECK IS IN PAYMENT FOR ITEMS DESCRIBED ABOVE			TOTAL ▶	1325 50	0 00	1325 50

Check stub for $1,325.50 shows one of two payments for lost wages from CBS.

I received compensation from CBS because I was a legitimate witness, but too hot to handle.

<u>Mike Wallace and Don Hewitt, on set</u>.

In compensation, I was told I would be awarded my lost wages – something I was told *Sixty Minutes* had never done before. The W-2 form from CBS shows what they termed "an unprecedented payment to a witness." *Sixty Minutes* had never previously extended such an honor.

The total payment was $2,126.50. That's how badly they felt about it. Mike Wallace, Phil Scheffler, Don Hewitt and researcher Howard Liebengood had promised, three times in a row, that the filming would definitely occur, that it would *never* be canceled!

Meanwhile, I had written a "teaser book" for my literary agent to shop around, anxious not to disclose details that could result in destroyed evidence or would endanger the witnesses I had located. The teaser was a pot-boiler version which the agent himself rewrote --created just to see who might bite.[332] Then, they'd get my real manuscript. That is how I met **Harold Weisberg**, possibly the greatest living researcher of all, but I didn't know who he was! He proudly told me that he had written the "definitive answer" to "Posner's book, *Case Closed* when he wrote ***Case Open.*** But I had no idea what Posner's book was—that it was the number-one best seller that claimed Lee shot JFK!

Weisberg, having seen my evidence files, got up, went into the cubicle beside mine where he had been interviewing me for a book publisher, and he called David Lifton's publisher. At the time, I had no idea who Mr. Lifton was, but soon, I would. Lifton, assisted by Debra Conway, had written a long-awaited book about Lee, and it was in pre-sales. But Weisberg was now saying that "Lifton" had "got it all wrong about New Orleans and Mexico City," and the publisher "would be sorry" if they published it. Lifton's book, Weisberg said, had it all wrong about New Orleans, but he—Weisberg—had been there with Garrison, and everything I told him about New Orleans had filled some gaping holes for him in Garrison's investigation, in which he had participated!

I overheard it all. This man was living history! He was a man who from personal experience knew that there were big mysteries and question-marks regarding Lee, David Ferrie, Guy Banister, Carlos Marcello, Jack Ruby, and all the rest of the people in New Orleans that I had personally

---

[332] Some of the teaser book was based on a short story I'd written about Lee in 1995, where one of my professors (not Prof. Pat Rushin, my favorite) had rejected a story I wrote about Lee Oswald as "the reader will never believe he was that nice a guy," and ordered me to write "the opposite of what you've written, to be acceptable to the reading public." So, I rewrote it, presenting Lee as gloomy, color-blind, weird and dull. I even wrote that Lee "next went to Dallas and killed somebody." Upset at what I'd written, I confessed to Pat Rushin and Bettie Sommers, another professor, that I had really known the real Lee Oswald, and that he didn't kill JFK. I contacted Rushin around 2010 and he recalled our conversation, but Sommers did not.

encountered. Sadly, the publishing company Weisberg represented was afraid to publish, despite his recommendation. and in the meantime, a furious Mr. Lifton became my enemy for life when his book was canceled. An avalanche of lies, distortions and fake stories about me then exploded on the internet. Lifton himself helped. For example, he posted that I claimed to have conducted cancer research "in a coffee factory." I kept copies of most of his misleading and hostile statements. He preferred to discredit a new witness rather than revise his book, which remained unpublished, as of 2021. All the big publishers I visited saw the evidence and signed non-disclosure agreements, but were afraid to publish. Meanwhile, internet trolls learned about me and began mistreating me spitefully. If I said the sun rose in the east, they said I was lying. Weisberg had pledged to help me, but he was old, and his kidneys were failing. He died about a year after we met. Next, Howard Liebengood, who had also pledged to help me as soon as he retired in 2005,[333] also suddenly died. Genial Dr. Howard Platzman had tried to write my story, using that big stack of emails Liebengood had inspected, but Lee's and my conversations were missing from his version, and he didn't interpret how we thought correctly (how could he? It was complicated!). I turned it down after vainly trying to fix it.

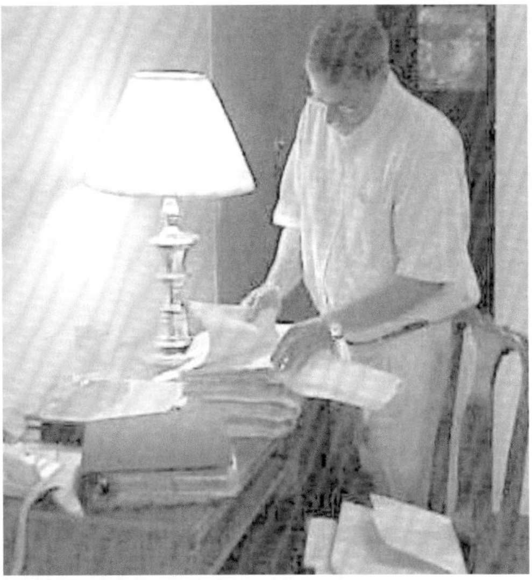

Howard Liebengood is shown inspecting hundreds of emails I sent to Martin Shackelford (and cc'd to Dr. Howard Platzman). As they asked questions, my responses were immediate as memories popped to the surface with every question. Later, I found two boxes (and later, a third) where I had kept old notes I'd written every Thanksgiving about Lee. These "souvenirs" as attorney Mark Mueller calls them, are stepping-stones to memories. (Photo by Martin Shackelford.)

[333] "Howard Scholer Liebengood was an American lawyer and lobbyist. A protégé of Senator Howard Baker, he served as Sergeant at Arms of the United States Senate from 1981 to 1983 before leaving to become a lobbyist for the Tobacco Institute. He later served as chief of staff to Senators Fred Thompson and Bill Fris. Wikipedia Born: December 29, 1942, South Bend, IN He died Jan. 13, 2005. Since he had also been born in South Bend, just months apart, we discovered we had a lot in common and had become good friends.

A fourth box, lost since Jan. 2,000, when forced to move due to vandalism, had even more material. By 2003, I had most of my evidence files in order and had found several witnesses. Then Nigel Turner showed up, sent by the legendary **Gerry Patrick Hemming**, a famous figure in the anti-Castro movement. Hemming had personally known Lee Oswald. I had flown to meet Hemming in the spring of 1998, eight months before deciding to speak out, to see how he would react to the secret information Lee had given me about him. It was information that nobody but Lee and he knew. After that, Hemming blind cc'd me when he wrote to his Interpen members. I kept copies of those emails.
Then **Nigel Turner**, learning what I had told Hemming, began

investigating me for one of his A & E History Channel documentaries. He assiduously examined and photographed my evidence files and interviewed me by tape for some 28 hours, then vanished for weeks as he researched everything and talked to witnesses. He then returned and recorded me again, this time for some 18 hours, on film, in Orlando, Florida, and New Orleans. He saw many sites in New Orleans that are no longer there, , including where the LINAC had been housed. He compared my long, intricate story on film and with the tapes and saw that my story didn't change. Impressed, instead of placing me in a section of one of his two new documentaries, he told A & E that they'd have to add a third documentary. It became "The Love Affair: Episode 8." Of course, it was only 46 minutes long (commercial breaks cut into the 'hour'), and a lot was missing, but the gist was there. When "The Love Affair" aired in November 2003, on The History Channel, along with the two other new segments in the series for "The Men Who Killed Kennedy," the LBJ family had a meltdown. Eisener of Disney, Pres. Ford and Pres. Carter, and former LBJ aide and Film Guild President Jack Valenti went ballistic, accompanied by Lady Bird Johnson and her daughters who raised up from the ashes of LBJ's legacy as vengeful Phoenixes. The whole batch of them threatened to sue everybody within reach.

I recall Nigel coming to Haarlem, The Netherlands, where I had fled in exile after being unable to endure any more hospitalizations and injuries from "accidents' --and losing jobs due to "flyers" circulating as to my "immoral conduct with Kennedy's assassin." Hang-up calls in the middle of the night, saying one of my children had died, or that I was going to "have another accident" had become unbearable burdens. Researcher Wim Dankbaar got me to Holland, for which I'll always be grateful. As Turner and I watched "The Love Affair" together in October, 2003, in my little Lee Harvey Oswald Museum there (I had plenty of security), Nigel said, "This will be shown for the next nine years! They can't take this away from you! Then, on the 50th, we'll do a sequel to "The Love Affair"!" But I knew better, and told him so. I was living in exile and had been hospitalized too many times to think the program would be allowed to stay on TV. Nigel next took the film to Marina Oswald, with whom he was friends. As she watched it, she finally commented, "Well... so, he had an affair." I heard that later, others tried to tell her it was all a hoax, but in her heart of hearts, she surely had to know.

Sure enough, after only five showings, "The Love Affair" vanished. Next, the 9-year contract vanished (I had never accepted a penny, by the way, but Mr. Turner lost income from at least 50,000 DVDs that were canceled only 3 days into sales. Next, a kangaroo court of anti-Oswald historians solemnly declared the segment "The Guilty Men" (Episode 9) a fraud (and so, by extension, the other two I the series—mine and "The Smoking Guns"). Turner was skewered. He was declared a liar and a fraudster. He was smeared as "The man who shamed the History Channel." He vanished from the scene into the black hole of censorship. Shockingly, *I never heard from him again.* I was told he was alive but that he refused to even answer the door in London. With the quashing of "The Love Affair" in 2003,[334] life became hell on earth. Terrible things happened that could be made into a movie. I was a survivor, but just barely.

What drove me overseas will give you an idea of what my life was before going into exile. Between 2000 and 2003 my life had already been ruined by vandals, burglaries, auto "accidents." hang-up calls and wrecked jobs where people would call in and say I was a convicted child abuser or was selling drugs. My son discovered drill holes in my doors, with wires inside, after finding little piles of sawdust. A gallon jug of hydrochloric acid was thrown at me while I was about to teach an English class. My English Building got a bomb threat. 21 computers were stolen from the English Building's composition lab and I was blamed, though on crutches at the time. When it was shown the computers were stolen through an opening in the roof, charges were dropped. But I had to find work elsewhere, as the English department cut back my teaching to two token classes. Even so, each place I taught, I was sabotaged. Two more auto accidents, a cut brake-line, doors ripped off my mailboxes, burglaries, and an intense internet campaign to discredit me became a relentless chain of events. After being hospitalized with my fourth concussion, which caused permanent damage to my vision, I fled overseas.

---

[334] ("The Love Affair" is currently, showing on *NewsMax*—somebody has had the power to make it so (thank you!).),

It all culminated when researcher Harrison E. Livingstone published my book behind my back, with help from researcher Martin Shackelford, who believed it was the only way it would ever get published without being relentlessly censored. They said it had to be done before my enemies published anymore lies about me. I agreed, but then Livingstone refused to let me see its final edit. Technically, I had approved the book, but when I was not allowed to see that final edit, I retracted permission. Livingstone had refused me access, arguing that if I did not like his edit, I could steal it and sell it to another publisher!

Furious at the insult, I stopped the publication after some 85 copies were sold, hoping Shackelford's brother would be paid from that income for the small loan he'd ponied up for the project.

Next, the well-regarded author Anthony Summers recommended my manuscript to his own fine agency in London. I was thrilled! But then a Dutch journalist who had recently been in a mental institution flew over to London and demanded a share of publishing rights, though I had fired him an agent. Because he was acting like a lunatic, they threw the book out. In desperation, I then sent my original manuscript to Edward T. Haslam, who I believed was the only man on the planet who could get the book into the hands of a publisher I trusted Kris Millegan of Trine Day Press. It was a scary move: Haslam had told *Sixty Minutes* he thought I was a fraud! Thank God, after reading my original manuscript, Haslam knew I was the real deal. But before he was about to recommend me, he put me through the wringer. *Why?* Because in 1972, he had met someone posing as me –claiming to be the real "Judyth Vary Baker" who had known Lee Harvey Oswald. She had encountered Haslam at a house party in New Orleans. This is why Haslam thought I was an imposter. And that's what he told *Sixty Minutes.* So now, in 2005, Haslam's attitude toward me was both suspicious and cautious. But he started reading the book. That led to interviews. In person. On the phone. By email. In the end, Haslam realized I was the missing link in his own extensive and dedicated research. In 2007, he included my story in his popular book, *Dr. Mary's Monkey,* which helped people to understand the players (like Dr. Ochsner) and issues (like anti-Communism and the SV40 Monkey Virus contaminating our polio vaccines), which are back stories to the bioweapon project conducted in New Orleans. However, when Haslam's book was released, and my own book was being handled by Trine Day, which was slowly and methodically checking things out, I received a death threat so serious was so specific that on September 11, 2007, I fled to Sweden from Hungary and applied for political asylum! Imagine, a 64-year-old woman, half-blind due to 'accidental' injuries, with a Service Dog – an American, as well- begging the Swedes to save her life! While under their temporary protection, I missed my mother's funeral.

They held my passport. I will always be grateful to the Swedish system that sheltered me for 10 ½ months, until my social security became bankable in July, 2008 and I could survive on my own. Though *Me & Lee*, the first edition of this book, was edited expertly by Haslam and other editors, who fixed a zillion typos and removed useless technical words, still, in the end, too many pages were removed, and I battled the editors for several months to get half of the pages put back in. At last, *Me & Lee* was ready to publish, but that would just be the beginning.

When the leaders of conferences about the assassinations wouldn't invite me to speak, Kris Millegan, Jim Marrs and others found ways to get me interviewed. Then, in 2013, I founded The Annual JFK Assassination Conference. It will hold its 9th annual meeting Nov. 2021. More than 300 presentations have been made at these JFK Assassination Conferences, where new and old witnesses and researchers, exposing the truth, are speaking up to destroy the lies. They have a voice, unless they claim that Lee Oswald "did it." With that simple rule, many new witnesses came forth, no longer fearing they would have to debate seasoned old warriors who had refused to give them a hearing. Today, convincing evidence continues to emerge that is exonerating my Lee.

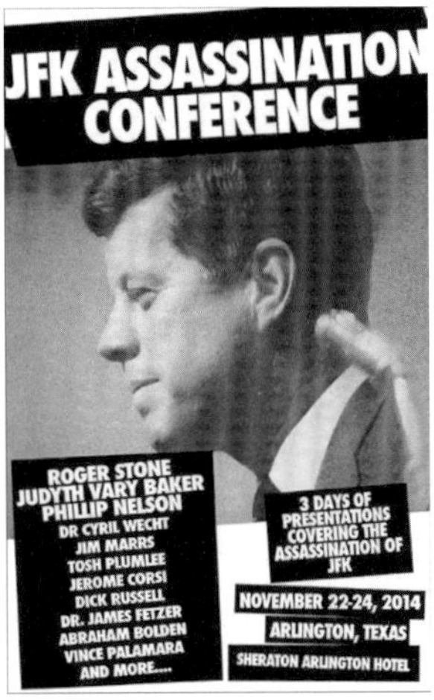

I have paid a price. I would pay it again. For my own safety, I have lived outside the United States year-round most of the time, until trapped in the US by COVID restrictions in 2020 (I had come for a mere six-day visit, with one suitcase!). By then, some members of my family were ready to welcome me back into their lives. I'm in touch with two of my children, and maybe a third will come around; though I haven't seen much of my ten grandchildren and two great-grandchildren for years, I am at peace, having done what is right. I did it for love. For the love of a man who would have done it for me. I have told his story as accurately and faithfully as humanly possible. I have agonized over every word he spoke, to get it right. All quotations have been rendered as best as my memory can recall. I memorized mnemonic poems to remember names and quotes. By rehearsing Lee's words, year after year, determined not to forget them, I was able to preserve much of what he told me in his own words. I have done what I can. June and Rachel, I now do what your father asked me to do: I tell you resolutely, firmly, honestly and sincerely: ***Your daddy was a good guy***. And I speak that statement to the whole world. Now I leave my testimony in your hands.

Judyth Vary Baker

AFTERWORD by Mark Mueller

Lee Harvey Oswald and Me is a vital contribution to our rapidly evolving understanding of the concealed history of covert assassination projects targeting domestic and foreign leaders, including John F Kennedy and Fidel Castro and many others.

I became aware of Judyth Vary Baker while researching aspects of MLK/JFK assassinations for my own book project *Breakfast in Memphis.* "Like many others, I wasn't exactly sure what to make of Judyth and her claims. She is kind of like a real-life Forrest Gump character who stumbles into a highly improbable historical scenario as both a witness and participant. Real life is indeed stranger than fiction, and the claims Judyth was viciously attacked for making have been now verified by supporting witnesses, newly discovered documents and photographs as well as the still incomplete and long delayed disclosures from the federal government.

I knew Judyth was a lightning rod for controversy, an inspiration for many and a ready punching bag for internet trolls and skeptics in the research community. I made personal contact by email and phone in the fall of 2020. We had an intersecting mission of uncovering and communicating the truth of the JFK assassination.

Her motivation was deeply personal due to her relationship with Lee Harvey Oswald and promises she made to him to inform his daughters what his real role and purpose was. Judyth and I, along with an increasing number of others too numerous to mention, saw the need to collapse the convenient yet destructive lies that form much of modern American history.

I met Judyth in person in November 2020 during her JFK conference in Dallas during the height of COVID restrictions. She somehow managed to put on a very comprehensive program (part live and part zoom) with not enough help or even a cell phone. Her persistence and drive were impressive. I was impressed that a woman in her late seventies, with no car or cell phone and with vision problems and difficulty walking due to injuries, hardship and age could accomplish this. I was at the conference as a speaker at her invitation to do a presentation from the viewpoint of a lawyer selecting a jury for Lee

Harvey Oswald's trial, had he lived. Imagine how history would have been different had a trial occurred and LBJ, J Edgar Hoover, Jack Ruby, members of the Dallas Police Department, the CIA, the mafia, and others had been subpoenaed and subject to live cross examination!

Over the course of several days Judyth and I discussed many areas of JFK research, including what witnesses were still alive and what avenues still needed exploration. It was obvious Judyth combined an almost unfathomable amount of research with a rare and freakish memory for details. Her memory is so unusual and beyond the range of normal that she has been attacked on that basis alone. Fortunately for her she kept what I will call souvenirs that support her recollections and was able over time to assemble other supporting pieces of material.

Judyth is without a doubt extremely intelligent as well as extremely traumatized by her life experiences, of which seeing Lee Harvey Oswald murdered on television was the most damaging. It is a credit to her that she has battled back against nearly impossible odds to tell her very important story.

She took me, Pastor Roy Johnson and a handful of others attending the conference to the gravesite of Lee Harvey Oswald. She told me I would feel the presence of his spirit there. As we spread roses on Lee's gravesite a wind suddenly appeared and an unmistakable presence of something otherworldly made itself known. Roy and I both developed goosebumps and looked at each other in acknowledgment. Lee was not who history said he was, he was a good Marine. I wrote the following poem to Judyth and Lee for my own book and for publishing here ...

To Judyth and Lee

Government ink
A Harsh tattoo
Branded like cattle
stained much deeper
skin to bone
Labeled
And shunned
Ridiculed and
Avoided

Scarlet and black
Flashing neon

What they say
You become

Hard choices
Roads not traveled

Art by Paul Wilson

Broken hearts and
A fallen soldier
2 Young daughters
a wife
and a lover
All
Tattooed
In government ink
False history
A convenient
And unbelievable
Story
Of lone nut
Commie ex soldiers
In all our school books
Life magazine
and TV
News reporters
Yes you too
Dan Rather
Speaking lies
For CIA bosses
The company Line
was Make Believe
You reassured a
Nation of willing fools

That 6th floor corner
window
The gun
The shells
The lone assassin
None of it was true

From a graveyard
Near Dallas
Lee is the
whisper of wind
Semper fi
Semper fi,
A good Marine
Till the end

But who and why
And what does it matter?
The credits and
characters
Scroll down like a movie
Producers
Writers
Directors
Editors
Executive /co-producers
actors
Cameos
soundtrack
Crew
Grips
Makeup
Disguises
Bullets
And
Weapons
Security
Marketing
Funding
Accounting
Distribution
Commissions
Blue ribbon panels
Congressional blessings

Blame it on the devil
So many faces
And too many
names
Johnson, Nixon, Bush
Tolson
Dulles, lawyers and cops,
secret service real and
imposters, mafia/CIA/
military gunmen and
leaders, Bay of Pigs
survivors, hit men ,
soldiers of fortune ,
Cubans, Watergate
burglars, Hoover...
McCloy,
And so many others ...
Who made the profits
Who gained the power
Who sealed the
documents...
Kept killing for silence
Buried for decades
Redacted or just gone
A nation's betrayal
We pretend we can't
See
Neutered and
Pickled
kept in a jar
A nation without
Balls ... heart...
brains
or even a mirror
Here we are now
America the great
Broken by lies
Branded by treason

I'm out of the game

From ***Breakfast in Memphis***
by Mark Mueller

Mark Mueller

Offering an umbrella of powerful protection with creative and ingenious solutions in the defense of victims of environmental, medical and industrial abuse, Mark Mueller is listed year after year as one of America's top 100 trial attorneys, as well as one of the nation's top ten environmental lawyers. As a result of Mark's longtime interest in the assassinations of JFK, RFK and MLK Jr., he has gained an expert's knowledge, which, coupled with his skill and experience as a top trial lawyer with courage to think out of the box, means we have a champion in this epic fight for justice and truth.

BACKGROUND Mark Mueller grew up in rural Wisconsin, attended Colorado College for a year, and graduated with a B.S. in psychology and a minor in philosophy from the University of Wisconsin-Madison. He moved to Texas for law school at the University of Houston Law Center (J.D. 1981). Mark has taken and passed four state bar exams (Wisconsin, Texas, Montana, and Louisiana) and has been admitted by reciprocity in Georgia, Oklahoma, and Pennsylvania.

GROUNDBREAKING CONTRIBUTIONS His work and cases contributed to groundbreaking medical publications and presentations in birth injury cases. In addition to his substantial and often precedent-setting birth injury work, Mark has handled a wide variety of cases including those involving chemical and radiation exposures, business fraud, insurance bad faith, electrocutions due to faulty products, deaths and injuries from unsafe industrial and household products, deceptive trade practices, Native American land rights, premises liability for rapes, and sexual misconduct against religious orders, therapists and counselors. He has handled high profile cases, such as the "Texas Condom-Rape" case, where his efforts led to reform of the grand jury system by using professional counselors to educate grand jurors about rape trauma and responses, leading to the successful prosecution of his client's rapist.

GIVING BACK Mark has been involved in a wide variety of environmental and progressive groups and causes. He has served as a rape crisis volunteer counselor and volunteer legal counsel for a number of public interest and non-profit organizations. He also attended and has taught for several years at the nation's finest program for trial lawyers, the Trial Lawyers College – founded by the nation's best trial lawyer, Gerry Spence of Wyoming. In 2009, Mark accepted a pro bono case involving a mother's unprecedented effort to retrieve sperm from her murdered son for future use with a surrogate mother. In that case, Mueller orchestrated a successful court hearing in less than three hours, which led to the mother's recovery of her son's sperm. These cases and others have led to appearances on Oprah Winfrey, Good Morning America, The Today Show, Montel Williams, and others as well as national front-page news coverage.

APPENDIX

HALE BOGGS, M. C.
2D DISTRICT, LOUISIANA

COMMITTEES:
WAYS AND MEANS
CHAIRMAN, SUBCOMMITTEE ON ADMINISTRATION OF FOREIGN TRADE LAWS AND POLICY
JOINT ECONOMIC COMMITTEE

Congress of the United States
House of Representatives
Washington, D. C.

FOR IMMEDIATE RELEASE
Thursday, March 15, 1962

WASHINGTON, D.C.--- President Kennedy will fly to New Orleans, La., on Friday, May 4, to deliver a major address on foreign economic policy, Rep. Hale Boggs(D.-LA.), the House Majority Whip, announced today.

The International House of New Orleans will sponsor the President's visit to the Crescent City, Congressman Boggs said.

Dr. Alton Ochsner, president of International House and an internationally famous surgeon, will be in charge of arrangements in New Orleans for the President's visit, Boggs noted.

President Kennedy probably will deliver his address in the city's Municipal Auditorium about 11:00 A.M. on May 4. Howeve further details of the visit will be determined by the President at a White House conference with Boggs and New Orleans Mayor Victor H. Schiro next Tuesday morning (March 20).

More details of the President's trip to the Crescent City probably will be announced after the White House meeting, which has been scheduled for 10:00 A.M., Boggs stated.

Shortly after his speech on foreign economic policy, President Kennedy is scheduled to depart for Eglin Air Force Base, Florida.

XCongressman Boggs said that all members of the Louisiana Congressional delegation will be invited to accompany the President on his flight to New Orleans.

(MORE)

<u>Ochsner, who despised Kennedy, was in charge of the President's 1962 visit</u> <u>to New Orleans</u>. As a doctor, he may have learned a great deal about Kennedy's health and security. Photos show us that JFK's personal physician, who usually rode in Kennedy's car in motorcades, was moved to a different car when JFK was in the Fort Worth and Dallas motorcades.

THE WHITE HOUSE
WASHINGTON

May 20, 1961

Dear Miss Vary:

The President has received your friendly letter, and he thanks you for the nice things you say about him. Your desire to be of service to your country has been noted and there are many ways you can help our country through responsible citizenship at the community, national, and international levels. I am enclosing several releases which include some of the things the President has mentioned in this respect.

With the President's best wishes,

Sincerely,

Ralph A. Dungan

Ralph A. Dungan
Special Assistant
to the President

Miss Judyth Vary
4402 Pompano Lane
Palmetto, Florida

Enclosures

Letter to President Kennedy, Feb.14, 1961, From Judyth

International Science Fair, military officers, company executives, politicians and the CIA were interested in the youthful exhibitors and their exhibits. At Eli Lilly, I was asked to sign a loyalty oath to qualify for scholarships (documented in this book as peculiar to Indiana). I was put in contact with Walter Reed Institute for Research by Sept. 1960. I was also asked to write to the President. I erred in writing that I was "asked to write to Pres. Kennedy" who did not take office until 1961, but of course, I did write to President Kennedy soon after he took office. I received a reply from Ralph Dungan, an aide and close friend of JFK.

Markings on my letter, below, were made at the White House: my letter is a copy from the National Archives.

PRESIDENT JOHN F. KENNEDY,
1600 PENNSYLVANIA AVENUE,
WASHINGTON, D.C.

ack mob 5-20-61

FEB. 14, 1961

JUDYTH VARY,
4402 POMPANO LANE,
PALMETTO, FLA.

DEAR PRESIDENT KENNEDY;

I KNOW THAT YOU HAVE RECIEVED PROBABLY THOUSANDS UPON THOUSANDS, OR MILLIONS, OF CONGRATULATIONS FOR BECOMING OUR NEW PRESIDENT. BUT I WANT TO CONGRATULATE YOU AGAIN. YOU HAVE HELPED TO PARTIALLY WAKE AMERICA FROM HER HORRIBLE AND DANGEROUS APATHY. YOU HAVE LIT THE LAMP THAT REVEALS THE RATS AND THE BROKEN WINDOWS IN OUR SUPPOSEDLY SECURE HAVEN FROM WORLD STRIFE. I HOPE YOU CAN PATCH UP THE HOLES; YOU SAID IN YOUR MOMENTOUS INAUGURAL SPEECH THAT 'ASK NOT WHAT YOUR COUNTRY CAN DO FOR YOU, BUT WHAT YOU CAN DO FOR YOUR COUNTRY'...WELL, I WOULD LIKE TO KNOW WHAT WE, THE VOTELESS, TEENAGE MINORS, WHO CARE ABOUT THEIR COUNRRY, CAN DO? I KNOW THAT MOST OF US WOULD GLADLY LAY DOWN OUR LIVES FOR OUR COUNTRY. THE VOTELESS, TEENAGED MINORS IN BOTH WORLD WARS HAVE. SIR, FRANKLY, WHAT CAN WE, AS CITIZENS AND AMERICANS, DO? IN THE LAST ELECTION, WE YOUNG PEOPLE CUT OUT PAPER DONKEYS WITH 'GET OUT AND VOTE' SIGNS ON THEM; ELEPHANTS, TOO, FOR THAT MATTER. IT WAS VERY DISAPPOINTING TO SEE HOW FEW RELATIVE TO THE POPULATION ACTUALLY VOTED. IT WAS EVEN MORE DISHEARTENING TO REALIZE THAT, WHEN CONFRONTED WITH VARIOUS QUESTIONNAIRES ON WORLD AFFAIRS, ETC., WE TEENAGERS FOUND THAT THE PEOPLE AT LEAST IN THIS AREA DON'T EVEN CARE ABOUT WHAT IS HAPPENING ABOUT THEM. ALL THEY SEEM TO CARE ABOUT IS SEGREGATION, RELIGION, AND TAXES. I THINK THAT THIS IS NOT UNIVERSALLY SO (I HOPE TO GOD IT IS NOT!), BUT SURELY SUCH APATHY AND SUCH PREJUDICES SHOULD NOT EXIST IN THIS SUPPOSEDLY PROGRESSIVE NATION. PRESIDENT KENNEDY, WHAT COULD I, AS A TYPICAL TEENAGE CITIZEN, DO? WHAT CAN MY FRIENDS DO? WE ARE VERY INTERESTED IN OUR COUNTRY'S WELFARE,--WE'RE NOT ALL JUVENILE DELINQUENTS! WE REALIZE THAT TODAY OUR COUNTRY IS BEING CHALLENGED BY SEVERAL NEW POWERS,--BEING HUMILIATED, TOO, IN SOME CASES, BEING CONFOUNDED, EVEN SCORNED. I PROMISE YOU THAT A LOT OF US DO CARE, AND WE'RE BEHIND YOU ALL THE WAY! IT TAKES COURAGE TO FACE SUCH PROBLEMS AS YOU MUST FACE NOW. IT TAKES COURAGE THESE DAYS TO EVEN ACKNOWLEDGE THE FACT THAT THEY EXIST, I GUESS. MAY GOD BLESS YOU! MAY YOU 'STICK TO YOUR GUNS'. I HOPE THAT YOU WILL LET US ENTER THE RANKS OF THOSE WHO WANT TO FOLLOW YOU INTO THE FEARFUL BUT PROMISING 'NEW FRONTIERS'! WE PROMISE TO DO WHAT WE CAN. I DON'T THINK THAT THIS NEW GENERATION 'TEMPERED' BY WAR AND DEPRESSIONS AND EDUCATED TO REALIZE AND DECIPHER THE HANDWRITING ON THE WALL, WILL LET YOU DOWN. WE'RE BEHIND YOU, MR. PRESIDENT! LET US BE YOUR VAN GUARD!

SINCERELY YOURS,
JUDYTH VARY.

PARTICIPANTS

SIXTH PRECLINICAL I SEMINAR
ORINS Medical Division
Oak Ridge, Tennessee
September 19-23, 1960

Daniel F. Beals, M.D.
University of Tennessee
Memorial Research Center and Hospital
Knoxville, Tennessee

Harry S. Brown, Jr., M.D.
Central Intelligence Agency
2430 E Street, N.W.
Washington 25, D. C.

Roy L. Byrnes, M.D.
31807 Coast Highway
South Laguna, California

James B. Matthews, M.D.
Veterans Administration Hospital
Oteen, North Carolina

William H. Murphy, M.D.
University Hospital
Augusta, Georgia

Milton W. Roggenkamp, M.D. >
Professional Building
Bradenton, Florida

Claire B. Sledge, M.D.
105 South 5th Avenue

OAK RIDGE Connections

These documents show connections to Oak Ridge involving two of the doctors on record in newspaper articles who assisted my cancer research.

PARTICIPANTS

THIRD PRECLINICAL II SEMINAR
ORINS Medical Division
Oak Ridge, Tennessee
December 7-11, 1959

).	J. G. Klemm Harvey, M.D. Mercy Hospital Muskegon, Michigan
	George J. Haslam, M.D. Bishop Clarkson Memorial Hospital Omaha, Nebraska
1.D.	W. M. Hindman, M.D. Memorial Hospital Fremont, Ohio
). tal	Menard Ihnen, M.D. University Hospital Augusta, Georgia
. Hospital nia	Russell W. Kerr, M.D. St. Joseph's Hospital Kansas City, Missouri
D. t	Werner A. Laqueur, M.D. Beckley Memorial Hospital Box 128 Beckley, West Virginia
M.D. ervice Hospital	Victor Levine, M.D. 30 North Michigan Avenue Chicago 2, Illinois
	Lee Paul, M.D. Muncie Clinic 420 West Washington Street Muncie, Indiana
).	Robert T. Rogers, M.D. St. Lawrence County Laboratories Canton, New York
. ity Hospital	John A. Shively, M.D. Manatee Memorial Hospital Bradenton, Florida

"The Indiana Biological Association" was an unofficial group at Notre Dame that backed me. ~45 yrs. later, Dr. Mirand "recalled" I was kicked out of RPMI! He recalled being angry, but it was just over renting an unapproved room. RPMI's Publicity Dept. sent glowing reports of my work to Florida newspapers and to the American Cancer Society, so upon my return a big party was held in my honor. I was attending St. Francis when Mrs. Watkins wrote, **"I did make our annual meeting of the Cancer Society and some very nice things were said about your work."**

OAK RIDGE <u>Connections</u>

I had other connections through Col. Phillip V. Doyle and retired military officers in the Sarasota area**.** Dr. Milton W. Roggenkamp learned how to grow cancer cells in test tubes at Oak Ridge in Sept. 1960 and was able to guide me. He also supervised the first X-ray treatment of my Webster-Swiss white mice and the first intraperitoneal injection into a mouse with mercaptoethylamine) (It killed it.).

Dr. Harry S. Brown, CIA, was in the same group trained to grow tissue cultures as was 'my' Dr. Roggenkamp.

Dr. John Shively at Manatee Memorial Hospital gave me access to the new oncology lab, new x-ray equipment, and the hospital's medical library, as well as guidance in sterile lab techniques needed to handle germ-free mice.

He was also trained at Oak Ridge, in 1959.

<u>Letter from Mrs. Watkins,</u> dying of kidney cancer, to me at St. Francis, October 1961.

Bx 45,1961.

My dear Judy,
Illness has made me unable to write for ever since y
you were here. I did make our annual meeting of the Cancer Society
and some very nice things were said abut your work.
C01 Doyle attended nd he told us how you got started in your
interest in c.a. Research.
When I got home tha evening your lette had come. I was so
sorry that I did not have it at the m eting.
I got a notice or two in the papers/ any publicity is a help to
the Cancer Society
I have been able to sit up long enough to gt our needed notices
or and that is abo all I have been able to do/ Howeve am better
and my tummie that ha been misbehaving is much bett .
I shall be inte ested in hearing how your paper came out before
the biological Society and how the res rch is coming along.
I am happy that you like Wayne at the College
And your work on the college newspaper. All those ets will help
ome day. It will help for you to be a good jo rnalist and I t
think you are. A researcher tha can write about his exreimants can
get it over so much better.
I do hope you are keepin well.
I have to make this short this time but hope to be able to write
more before long.
Lots of lo e, Judy and ke p w .
affectionately,

Bx 45,1961.

My dear Judy,
Illness has made me unable to write for ever since y
you were here. I did make our annual meeting of the Cancer Society
and some very nice things were said abut your work.
C01 Doyle attended nd he told us how you got started in your
interest in c.a. Research.

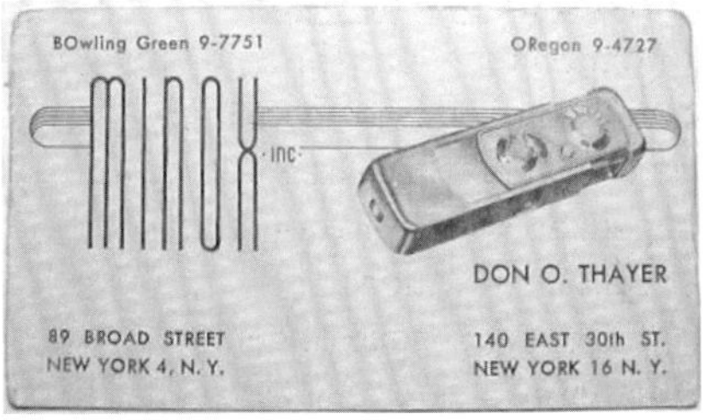

<u>MINOX:</u> My father, an inventive electrical engineer, did some classified work for Chrysler. He also owned a **Minox camera,** so I was able to easily recognize Lee Oswald's Minox. This card was in my Dad's wallet. Dad had CIA security clearance in the late 1950's.

Photo: Our father having us pose for the camera, 1
Spring, 1960

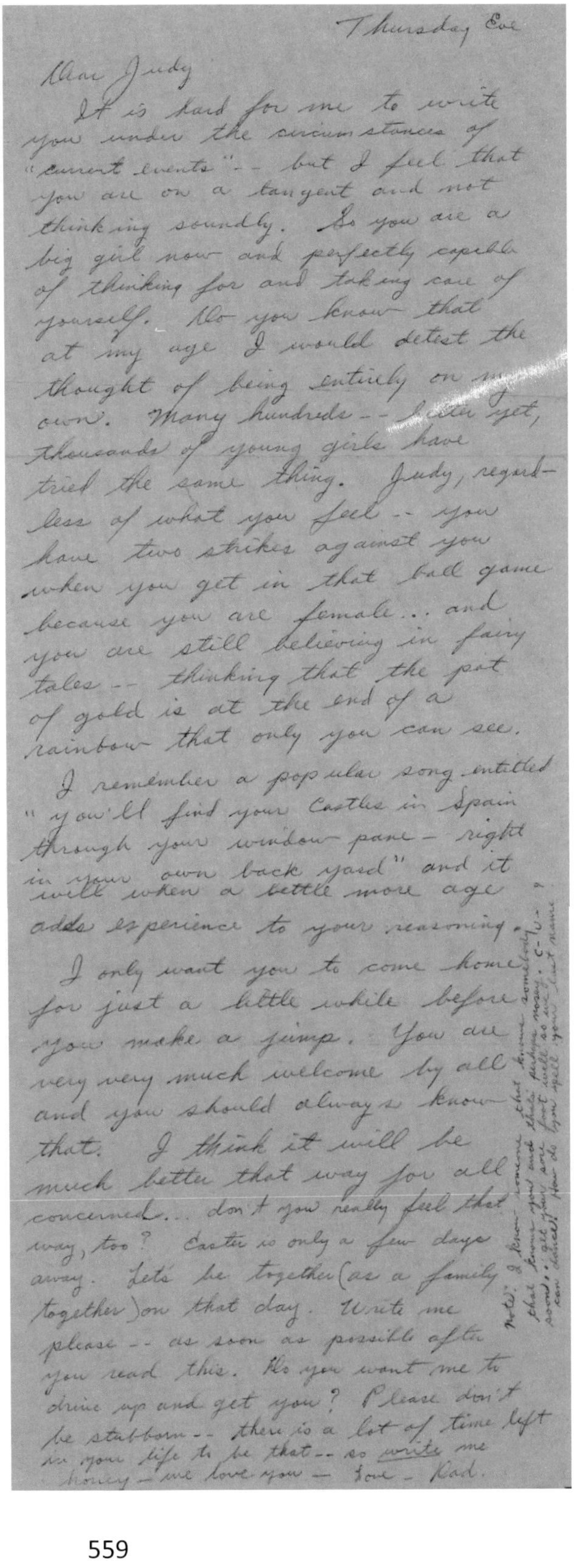

Thursday Eve

Dear Judy

It is hard for me to write you under the circumstances of "current events" -- but I feel that you are on a tangent and not thinking soundly. So you are a big girl now and perfectly capable of thinking for and taking care of yourself. Do you know that at my age I would detest the thought of being entirely on my own. Many hundreds -- better yet, thousands of young girls have tried the same thing. Judy, regardless of what you feel -- you have two strikes against you when you get in that ball game because you are female ... and you are still believing in fairy tales -- thinking that the pot of gold is at the end of a rainbow that only you can see.

I remember a popular song entitled "you'll find your Castles in Spain through your window pane - right in your own back yard" and it will when a little more age adds experience to your reasoning.

I only want you to come home for just a little while before you make a jump. You are very very much welcome by all and you should always know that. I think it will be much better that way for all concerned ... don't you really feel that way, too? Easter is only a few days away. Let's be together (as a family together) on that day. Write me please -- as soon as possible after you read this. Do you want me to drive up and get you? Please don't be stubborn -- there is a lot of time left in your life to be that -- so <u>write</u> me honey - we love you - Love - Dad.

note: I know someone that knows somebody that knows you and that's perhaps nosey. C-U-soon. get your sore foot well so we can dance! How do you spell your last name?

8. <u>Letter from my Father</u>

Written after my father unsuccessfully tried to have me arrested and returned to Bradenton. My father wanted me to leave UF to work in his office, claiming a "female" had no chance in a man's world. He also wonders if I had eloped (writing on the side of the letter), as I was now dating a lot of boys and enjoying every minute.

My parents in front of their "State Line Television" store, 1952.

Ruth Paine abandoned Marina at Parkland Hospital The documentation for this unexpectedly coarse treatment of Marina by Ruth Paine is found in Mary Ferrell's chronology: "Mrs. Paine takes Marina to Parkland where she is admitted at 8:56 p.m. and delivered by Dr. James F. Herd, 1114 N. Winnetka, of Audrey Rachel Oswald, 6 lbs, 15 oz., at 10:41 p.m. The baby is #22347. (22:230,746; CD 210, p. 5)" "**Oswald stays at the Paine house with June Lee Oswald and Mrs. Paine's two children**. Mrs. Paine says Oswald goes to bed**; she calls hospital after waiting "a proper time" and learns of the birth.** She tells Oswald the next morning. (2:404,514; 3:39; 9:361,436; 22:746; 24:694; *Dallas Times Herald*, 11/28/63, p. A-38; *Detroit Free Press*, 12/7/63, p. A-3; *Redbook*, July 1964, pp. 85, 87)" (This incident has been used to show Lee Oswald had no feelings for his wife.) Mary Ferrell says Lee Oswald 'did not want to go' to Parkland when Paine offered to drive him there the next evening.[more below] **Oct. 21, 1963 (Monday)** — "Oswald returns to Irving with Buell Wesley Frazier after work. Mrs. Michael Paine takes him to Parkland Hospital, between 7:30 p.m. and 8:00 p.m., to see the baby. (3:40; 11:291; 22:746; 24:694) Mrs. Paine says Oswald did not want to go. (3:40) (Perhaps he feared he might be asked to pay something." Thus, the subtle demonization of Lee Oswald, even in this chronology. Note that the birth occurred only an hour and 44 minutes after Marina arrived, but Ruth Paine did not stay with Marina. She left. Compare this to Ruth Paine's affectionate and generous statements in her letters to Marina. They seem utterly sincere. She even wrote a letter praising Lee and saying she liked him. She even gave blood for Marina's medical emergencies.

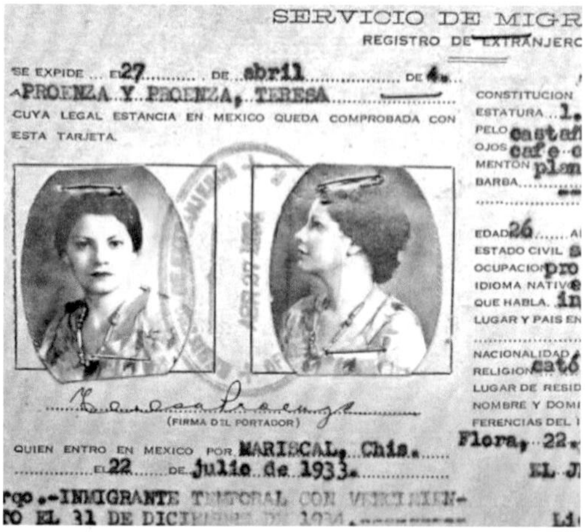

TERESA PROENZA'S Vindication: Arrested as soon as she arrived in Cuba and placed under house arrest for three years, after being framed by the CIA, in 2019 the book "Do not Forget": Teresa Proenza (1908-1989). A Cuban spy in politics, culture, and art in Mexico, by historian Xavier Guzmán Urbiola was presented in the Sala Adamo Boari of the Palacio de Bellas Artes in Mexico City. Friend of the great artist Diego Rivera, by 2019, long after her death, the truth about her exploits as a revolutionary wiped out the false allegations.

Jack Ruby –Injected with Cancer Cells **Jack Ruby, while in jail,** claimed he had been injected with cancer cells. Jack had seen our lab and knew that the injections were painful. He knew that a larger bore needle was needed (so the cancer cells wouldn't clog the needle). In 2019, full records of Jack Ruby's hospital and nurse notes were released to the National Archives, and I was privileged to be the first one to unstaple them and get them copied. That's when I learned that Ruby had been x-rayed over 375 times during his stay of less than a month, plus 8 '360 ' x-ray doses (whole body). He needed lidocaine inside his sore mouth because of so many x-rays; the resultant diarrhea, vomiting and increasing weakness was killing him. He died from a blood clot in his thigh that had grown so large it could not have been missed. He was hospitalized two days after a new trial was scheduled. The document below shows _most, but not all_ the x-rays Ruby received in less than a month. A few others can be found in nurses' notes. Ruby's body was ravaged by classic symptoms of radiation poisoning atop his cancer condition. Even when he no longer had strength to be taken to the x-ray room, a portable x-ray machine was rolled to his bedside in his last days, to give him more doses. He remained shackled to his bed at all times, which encouraged blood clots. **QTY** = quantity **360 =** whole body x-rays Note how many times Ruby is given x-rays on day two! He had **30** x-rays, **plus a 360**, on day three! He had a total of **8 360 x-rays.(each 360 is a whole-body dose)**

33 x-rays 12/10
28 x-rays 12/11
30 x-rays 12/12
32 x-rays 12/13
32 x-rays 12/14
(note credit)
32 x-rays 12/16
34 x-rays 12/17
08 x-rays 12/19
52 x-rays 12/21
26 x-rays 12/22
26 x-rays 12/23
26 x-rays 12/24
4 x-rays 12/25
4 x-rays 12/27
(+ a 360!)

Ruby received at least 375 recorded x-rays

RELEASED PER P.L.-102-526 (JFK ACT)

DALLAS COUNTY HOSPITAL DISTRICT

5201 HARRY HINES BLVD. PHONE ME 1-5050, EXT. 661 DALLAS, TEXAS 75235

PARKLAND MEMORIAL HOSPITAL WOODLAWN HOSPITAL

Patient: RUBY JACK

CASE NUMBER	UNIT NUMBER	STMT. MO. DA. YR.	INS. CODE	F.C.	ADMISSION MO. DA. YR.	DISCHARGE MO. DA. YR.
12545	318801	01 01 67		98	12 09 66	01 03 67

GUARANTOR: (NAME AND ADDRESS)

STATEMENT OF CHARGES

SERVICE DATE	DESCRIPTION			AMOUNT	REF.
12 15 6	0360	X-RAY	74891	$10.00	
12 15 6	0360	X-RAY	74891	$35.00	
12 15 6	0360	X-RAY	74891	$15.00	
12 13 6	0360	X-RAY	73024	$30.00	
12 18 6	0360	X-RAY	77943	$15.00	
12 20 6	0360	X-RAY	79677	$20.00	
12 21 6	0360	X-RAY	81159	$15.00	
12 27 6	0360	X-RAY	92466	$15.00	
		RADIOLOGY		$290.00	TOT
12 10	1240		QTY 01	$.25	
12 10	1229		QTY 12	$18.00	
12 10	1225		QTY 20	$10.00	
12 12 6	1229		QTY 10	$15.00	
12 11 6	1226		QTY 22	$16.50	
12 14 6	1226		QTY 20	$15.00	
12 12 6	1225		QTY 20	$10.00	
12 11 6	1229		QTY 06	$9.00	
12 14 6	1229		QTY 12	$18.00	
12 14 6	1229		QTY 12	$18.00CR	
12 18 6	1229		QTY 06	$9.00	
12 17 6	1225		QTY 22	$11.00	
12 16 6	1229		QTY 12	$18.00	
12 17 6	1229		QTY 12	$18.00	
12 16 6	1226		QTY 20	$15.00	
12 13 6	1225		QTY 20	$10.00	
12 13 6	1229		QTY 12	$18.00	
12 19 6	1229		QTY 08	$12.00	
12 21 6	1225		QTY 20	$10.00	
12 21 6	1226		QTY 20	$15.00	
12 21 6	1229		QTY 12	$18.00	
12 23 6	1229		QTY 04	$6.00	
12 24 6	1225		QTY 22	$11.00	
12 27 6	1229		QTY 04	$6.00	
12 23 6	1226		QTY 22	$16.50	
12 25 6	1229		QTY 04	$6.00	
12 24 6	1229		QTY 04	$6.00	

In ***CROSSFIRE,*** Jim Marrs addresses "The Mysterious Death of Jack Ruby" (p. 429) and notes that on October 5, 1966 the Texas Court of Appeals overturned Jack Ruby's conviction and on December 7, 1966 ordered a new trial to be held outside of Dallas. Two days later, Ruby became acutely ill (he had been congested and coughing before this -jvb) and entered Parkland. Doctors initially thought he had pneumonia, but quickly changed their diagnosis to lung cancer. Before the week was over, the Parkland doctors announced that Ruby's lung cancer had advanced so far that it could not be treated (meaning it had spread to other parts of the body — Stage IV). The median survival time of a patient with Stage IV lung cancer is eight months, but twenty-seven days after the onset of his initial symptoms of cough and nausea, Jack Ruby was dead. Deputy Sheriff **Al Maddox** was Ruby's jailer at the time. He later told researchers that Jack Ruby told him of being injected with cancer and handed him a note making that claim. Maddox also remembered what he described as a "phony doctor" had visited Ruby shortly before he became sick. A second law enforcement officer said Ruby had been placed in an x-ray room for about 15 minutes with the x-ray machine running constantly, an action that would have certainly compromised his immune system. " end quote.

More About the Chicago Plot and Lee Oswald's Intervention to Save Kennedy

Quotations from James W. Douglass' ***JFK and the Unspeakable: Why He Died and Why It Matters*** **(2008):** "…On **Wednesday, October 30, 1963,** the agents at the Chicago Secret Service office were told of the Chicago plot by Special Agent in Charge Maurice Martineau**. Abraham Bolden** was one of the agents present. Bolden had left the White House detail voluntarily two years before in protest against the poor security being given to the President. Special Agent in Charge Martineau's announcement to his Chicago Secret Service Agents about a plot against Kennedy came in the context of their preparations for the President's arrival at O'Hare Airport three days later on **Saturday, November 2 at 11:30 AM** (**https://www.facebook.com/groups/newjimcrowmoving/permalink/10154196679300027/**) (emphasis by author, JVB) … **At 9:00 AM Wednesday morning**, Martineau told the agents the FBI had learned from an informant that four snipers planned to shoot Kennedy with high-powered rifles. Their ambush was set to happen along the route of the Presidential motorcade, as it came in from O'Hare down the Northwest Expressway and into the Loop on Saturday morning. **The FBI had said "the suspects were rightwing para-military fanatics". The assassination "would probably be attempted at one of the Northwest Expressway overpasses". They knew this from an informant named "Lee".** …**It was an FBI informant named "Lee"** whose alert disrupted the more critical four-man sniper team that represented the real threat to Kennedy and thus to potential patsy Vallee as well. …When [Abraham Bolden] raised the possible connection between the November 2 Chicago plot and the Dallas assassination to his fellow Secret Service agents in Chicago, to which most of them agreed, Martineau shut down the discussion and told his staff that Lee Harvey Oswald was a lone gunman, that there was no connection to Chicago, and that they should forget November 2nd. [Bolden would be framed and incarcerated for raising these objections.] **Three decades later, in January 1995, the Secret Service deliberately destroyed its records of the Chicago plot when the Assassinations Records Review Board (ARRB) requested them**.

SECRET

CIA's "last official contact" w/ Ochsner Clinic, Nov. 3, 1963.

CIA: Ochsner a 'former' contact and a "cleared source" in New Orleans

b. Dr. OCHSNER is Director of the Ochsner Foundation, head of the Ochsner Clinic, and President of the Information Council of America. He is a world-famous surgeon.

c. Dr. OCHSNER was of contact interest in October 1947 and November [illegible]. He has been a cleared source since 13 May [illegible]. The last official contact with Dr. OCHSNER personally occurred on [illegible] January 1962 and with the Ochsner Clinic on 3 November 1963.

Dr. ALTON OCHSNER is a prominent physician and surgeon connected with the Ochsner Clinic and Ochsner Foundation Hospital at New Orleans. Dr. OCHSNER is a former New Orleans Division SAC contact.

MORE INFORMATION ON MARY MORGAN JENKINS, JOAN MELLEN'S TAMPERING WITH EVIDENCE, AND THE JACKSON TRIP In 2004, Joan Mellen claimed NOLA resident **Gladys Palmer was in the old car** seen by Jackson barber Lea McGehee and by State Rep. Reeves Morgan and his daughter Mary Morgan. She claimed Gladys was Lee's 'real' girlfriend. [though Gladys was in her forties] She also said a black Cadillac linked to Palmer picked Lee up at Reeves Morgan's house that night – denied by his daughter Mary Morgan Jenkins in 2014 to the author in the presence of witness Kris Millegan. Mellen said Palmer's car was the Clinton -Jackson black Cadillac, but **witness Tom Williams** learned that Palmer (once employed by Jack Ruby in Dallas) drove to Jackson in a black **Lincoln Continental, not a Cadillac,** and checked into the State Hospital for alcoholism two weeks before JFK was shot. Ref: Claude B. Slaton, "Further Feliciana Research," "The Truth Is Redacted" Website (http://www.redacted.com). **In 2013, Mellen dumped Palmer as Lee's girlfriend and offered Gloria Wilson as Lee's girlfriend instead** (she was murdered, said Mellen). She also stated that Lee got into a black Cadillac after seeing McGeHee (what? leaving 'Gladys' or 'Gloria' all alone? **Why would 'Gladys' or "Gloria' drive Lee Oswald to the barber shop, to have him be picked up there in a Cadillac?)** Then a story was made up that the lady in the car sat there while laundry was being done, when **McGeHee originally said the car left as soon as Lee Left**—a period of only 20 minutes. The nonsense created by Mellen is based on her belief that Lee Oswald couldn't drive, though many witnesses have stated otherwise). McGeHee said in the presence of witness Kelly Thomas, that Mellen pressured him to add a 'Cadillac' story **– never mentioned in his Garrison testimony years earlier**– to his story, that Oswald was laughing as he passed by in a black Cadillac. **Even so, she could not eliminate me from the same old car where I was spotted by Reeve Morgan's daughter, Mary, later the same day**. Dr. Howard Platzman penned an essay exposing the gymnastics involved in trying to dismiss my testimony. Reeves Morgan and his daughter Mary never forgot Lee's visit. **Mary, then in high school, didn't recall telling Garrison's Moo-Moo Sciambra on June 3, 1967 that she saw a woman sitting in the old car, but she did vividly recall the car.** She said, **"there was never a Cadillac there."** She agreed with her father that the visit occurred at the end of Aug- early Sept. (Clay Shaw trial, pp. 45-49, official transcript) and that her father was indeed burning trash in the fireplace. In 2014, Mary met me (Judyth Baker) with Kris MIllegan as a witness. After asking many specific questions, Mary agreed I had to have been in the old car. Over the years she'd forgotten me, but after I told her **(1)** the color of the house back then, **(2)** the direction the car was oriented, **(3)** its color, **(4)** described the unusual crescent driveway, **(5)** the original length of the porch's steps, and that there was a large, reddish object on the porch, to the left, Mary then said she knew I'd been there. The large, reddish object on the porch was an old, rusty freezer. She had come onto the porch to retrieve something from it when she saw the old car. Her brother Van, she said, was easily led to agree with interviewers. She said he was too old to be climbing trees in 1963. **The final nail in Mellen's coffin is the fact that *Mellen never interviewed Mary Morgan Jenkins*!**

18. CANCUN and DR. WYLLYS ANDREWS, AUG. 1963: A Kubark memo (below) refers to Wyllys Andrews of Tulane as "former OSS/CIA employee # 2769" ... Andrews and his son excavated a midden on the isle of Kankun /Cancun, living on a small, isolated coconut plantation there. Their work ended in August, 1963, and an exhibit went on display at Tulane's Latin American library, with maps and details. Lee and I realized we could meet there safely. This is the "Cancun" critics lambasted me over, claiming "nothing" existed there in 1963.

Cancun mid-1960's

4. With reference to Willard ANDREWS, Security indices contain no record. I believe the individual referred to is Wyllys ANDREWS, (Edward) Wyllys ANDREWS IV, #2769, a former OSS/CIA employee who has lived in Mexico for many years and has continued to have social contacts with representatives of this Agency in Mexico as well as with Agency employees from Headquarters who visit him from time to time. ANDREWS, like CAIN, was born in Chicago of parents who also were born in the general area of Chicago.

Email, 2003: "I urge you to consider this carefully"... "**From: wim dankbaar Sent: zaterdag 19 juli 2003 11:30 To: elect63@xs4all.nl; martin Shackelford; howpl@.....com**
CE 3000 is an FBI report of an interview with Leslie Lawson, the owner and manager of Gray's Cleaners, 1209 Eldorado, Oak Cliff on 5th December 1963...Lawson... stated that he had seen Oswald on several occasions at Sleight's Speed Wash, 1101 North Beckley. This establishment had, in fact, changed its name to Reno's Speed Wash in August 1963. A former Reno's employee, Joseph Johnson, was interviewed by the FBI on 28th July 1964 and stated that on the evening of 20th or 21st November 1963, Lee Harvey Oswald was 'washing laundry at Reno's Speed Wash.' Oswald, he said, remained there, reading magazines, until midnight. (CE 3001)

20. My sister's letter about my confession to her about Lee, Nov. 1964:

My sister wrote a long letter describing what I told her:**Subj: memories Date: 05/16/2000 1:29:29 AM Central Daylight Time From: bxxxxxxx) To:** electlady63@aol.com **(Judyth V. Baker)** Dear Judy, I am sorry for not writing you sooner, but with my new job and school, it has been quite hectic. I don't need to tell you about hectic because I think you wrote the book on that already. Speaking of books, I told you I would write to you about what we shared in conversations many years ago... I believe in the fall of 1964 when I lived with you and Bob in Flavette at U of F. I remember on one particular evening, we were reminiscing about our past and what we hoped would be in our future lives, and that was the night when our conversation turned to even more serious talk about you. I remember we stayed up very late, and you were quite concerned about whether or not you should tell me something so serious in nature that you weren't sure if we should continue our discussion. But, you know me, I egged you on to tell me what was so important that you couldn't share it with me. I remember you told me that if I wanted to know what you were keeping to yourself, I had to swear to secrecy and never tell anyone about this. You said if anything ever happened to you.... such as an early or premature death, then I should tell anyone that would listen about what you were about to tell me. I swore to you I would keep your secret, and up until this day I have done that. Now, because of the writing of your book, and with your permission, I will repeat what you told me so many years ago. You told me you were afraid for my well-being, but felt I needed to know what had transpired in your life at that time. Here goes..... You told me that you had a love affair with a man who was trying to help our country and he was involved in very secret and covert activities for our country. You said you met him when Bobby left you all alone after you were married and you fell in love with each other. You told me if anything ever happened to you, I was to look for a green glass that he had given you as proof of what you were telling me. You said that my life might be in danger if I ever mentioned this to anyone and made me promise that I would never speak of this conversation again unless something happened to you. I was full of questions, and you were very hesitant to give me many details, other than you and he had shared a common interest in saving our country and the President, and that you were both very much in love. You said you wanted to be buried next to him some day, and someday you would tell me the whole story about the two of you. You said you worked closely together and had some close friends who were also working with you. You said the friends were also in danger and you wouldn't tell me much more. You said someday I would know everything, but it would mean you probably would not be alive if that knowledge came to me. I remember I was frightened for you and didn't understand what it was all about, but I also knew you were in pain and hurting over this man you loved so much. You ...wanted me not to think badly of you for being in love with another man when you were already married to Bobby. I told you I would never judge you, Judy, and I never have. I have kept this secret all these years, including how you and he had loved each other so much and how you wanted to be buried next to him when you die. I now know why you wanted to protect me and not tell me the details of you and Lee... and I also know why you feared for your life for all of these years and wanted to protect me and your children from any danger. I know what you told me was the truth back then, and I still remember the fear and at the same time the love in your voice when you told me this information. I hope people will believe you and me as well, because I swear what I have just written is true. I love you honey, with all of my heart. **Your sister, Lynda**

LIRING/3 AND SILVIA DURAN'S AFFAIR WITH LEE OSWALD:

"LIRING/3" as a reliable source. Look at these files: **FROM FILE 1**: 104-10015-10027: LETTER CONCERNING CONTACT WITH SILVIA DURAN. 7/5/67 letter from Thomas Lund (C/WH William Broe) to Willard Curtis (COS Mexico City Win Scott), stating his desire to follow up on the report of the alleged relationship between Duran and Oswald. Notes that appear to be Anne Goodpasture's state that a longer investigation may be needed "beginning with as much as we know re time of day & where OSWALD was from LIENVOY". That notation means that Lee was photographed by cameras. ... Also see 7/3/67, 104-10176-10000: From LIFEAT: "SAN-34 (19 June) reveals that LIRING-3 is continuing his meetings with Sra. Silvia Duran... it appears that L-3 is developing a romantic attachment with Sra. Duran.)"

FROM File # 104-10431-10003: HSCA FILM **: [IDENTIFICATION OF LIRING/3:]** Re 1968: "LIRING-3 identified as **Carlos Delmar Jurado,** 201-798301. Also see 180-10144-10236:...Rex Bradford

("History Matters" site) writes that Jurado was imprisoned in Guatemala. REF: **104-10176-10222, p. 107**, dated **1/15/69**: "On 29 October Rowton met LIRING-3 after his release from jail...The results of the initial debriefing were cabled in Mexico City-7900...LIRING-3 has been meeting relatively frequently with LIRING-9, who has been debriefing him on his incarceration in Guatemala (See Mexico City-8159 and -8228).

AND FINALLY, **Bradford writes, re:** 104-10176-10006: LIRING-3 **"The famed poet Roque Dalton (201-215097) saw LIRING-3 as a hero for the time in jail that LIRING-3 did in Guatemala during 1968 - and wrote about him** - ...debriefing of LIRING-3 conducted by Rowton can be read, starting at p. 106. A good summary is at p. 177.

"Harvey Lee" does not mean George deMohrenschildt knew a "Harvey" as separate from a "Lee" (Armstrong "Harvey and Lee" theory) It is a linguistic artifact. Fluent in Belarussian-style Russian, George de Mohrenschildt, born near Minsk, Belarus, where Lee lived, called Lee "Harvey Lee," avoiding using 'Lee' as a first name, as did most Russians, who thought of 'Lee' as a Chinese word, or perhaps as a nautical term (подветренная сторона). This does not mean George thought Lee was "Harvey" and that "Lee" was yet another person George may have known. Marina also avoided calling Lee by his name and used "Alek". "Lee" was really "Lee" and not "Harvey" [for "Harvey and Lee afficionados] which is evident when Lee's first daughter's name is shown in full: **June Lee Oswald**. In Russian tradition, the father's first name is the child's middle name**.** After Lee's death, George betrayed out of fear, but in his last days, he wrote about Lee with affection and respect. Regarding Lee's ability to speak and read Russian, George stated "Lee spoke it very well, only with a slight accent." For no reason George could comprehend, Marina would make fun of Lee for the errors he made, speaking Belarussian-style Russian. George was one of the few educated people Lee encountered, besides myself, who appreciated his character, intellect and political knowledge. A couple of years after finishing his book, the Baron would end up "committing suicide" with a shotgun in his mouth — scant hours before an interview he was to have with Gaeton Fonzi, an intrepid HSCA investigator.

The Training Film **At least two important people, (HSCA investigator Bob Tanenbaum and CIA hitman Colonel William Bishop, viewed the training film before it vanished from the HSCA's safe**. Tanenbaum stated that it had been found at Georgetown University and ceded to the HSCA. It vanished from the HSCA safe sometime after Tanenbaum viewed it. Tanenbaum and I used a third party to compare notes on what we recalled about the film, after which we became good friends and have supported each other's statements about the training film's contents and existence ever since. **Tanenbaum** went on to speak at three of my JFK Assassination Conferences in a row.

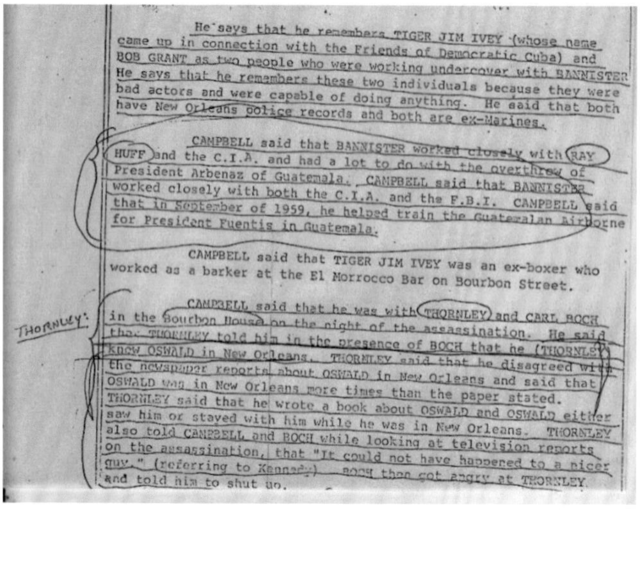

He says that he remembers TIGER JIM IVEY (whose name came up in connection with the Friends of Democratic Cuba) and BOB GRANT as two people who were working undercover with BANNISTER. He says that he remembers these two individuals because they were bad actors and were capable of doing anything. He said that both have New Orleans police records and both are ex-Marines.

CAMPBELL said that BANNISTER worked closely with RAY HUFF and the C.I.A. and had a lot to do with the overthrow of President Arbenaz of Guatemala. CAMPBELL said that BANNISTER worked closely with both the C.I.A. and the F.B.I. CAMPBELL said that in September of 1959, he helped train the Guatemalan Airborne for President Fuentis in Guatemala.

CAMPBELL said that TIGER JIM IVEY was an ex-boxer who worked as a barker at the El Morrocco Bar on Bourbon Street.

CAMPBELL said that he was with THORNLEY and CARL BOCH in the Bourbon House on the night of the assassination. He said that THORNLEY told him in the presence of BOCH that he (THORNLEY) knew OSWALD in New Orleans. THORNLEY said that he disagreed with the newspaper reports about OSWALD in New Orleans and said that OSWALD was in New Orleans more times than the paper stated. THORNLEY said that he wrote a book about OSWALD and OSWALD either saw him or stayed with him while he was in New Orleans. THORNLEY also told CAMPBELL and BOCH while looking at television reports on the assassination, that "It could not have happened to a nicer guy." (referring to Kennedy) BOCH then got angry at THORNLEY and told him to shut up.

KERRY THORNLEY: On May 14, 1969, Andrew Sciambra reported on his interview of witness Al Campbell for Garrison, concerning Kerry Thornley. Al Campbell, who was David Ferrie's friend and an investigator for Guy Banister, said that Kerry Thornley told him "he knew Oswald in New Orleans"

.

The Slaughter of Mice and Its Effects on Lee: Lee conducted the slaughter of hundreds of cancerous mice to help me. What effect did it have on him? I quote from McMillan's book. She implies that Lee's symptoms (see below) were due to mental instability, offering no concrete reason In fact, Lee and I were dealing with a project that gave us nightmares. In the first sentence after mentioning that Lee obtained his passport, coinciding with our first big mouse killing, McMillan next describes Lee having nightmares: *"...Lee was having trouble in his sleep again — the first time since February. One night he cried, yet when he woke up he could not remember what his dream had been about. He started having nosebleeds... and one night toward the very end of June he had four anxiety attacks during which he shook from head to foot at intervals of half an hour and never woke up."* (p. 417**)** Because I loved Lee, reading this sentence (even in 1999) caused me to say out loud, **"She didn't wake him up?" What caring wife, witnessing her husband suffering in his sleep, from not one, but four anxiety attacks, would not have wakened him, would not have tried to comfort him?** I then understood what a hard heart Marina had toward Lee, if McMillan told the truth. Then — a harsh assessment from McMillan — *"Just as in the period when he was making up his mind to shoot General Walker,"* the CIA affiliate wrote*, "these attacks appear to have presaged a decision that was causing him pain."* McMillan tries to convince the reader that Lee is about to make yet another horrific decision — perhaps involving ´another´ murderous attempt on somebody — such as President Kennedy — and says this is giving him nightmares. **McMillan inadvertently gives some proof as to what Lee did with us there, for she mentions nose bleeds**. Most adults do not suffer from nose bleeds, but some of us who worked in laboratories in the 1960s did, for volatile chemicals such as isopropyl alcohol and acetone were used liberally to cleanse dangerous areas, the fumes of which dried out mucous membranes, making us **prone to nosebleeds**. My family remembers my nosebleeds when I was in high school, while working with my mice. Such nosebleeds no doubt contributed to my anemic state. -- Quotes from *Marina and Lee*, 1st Edition, McMillan-Johnson.

Pete Tusa –knew everything and everybody in the upper quarter from Esplanade to St. Philip St. I talked with him a few times and he told me that he even talked with Oswald. He first noticed him around the French Market looking for baskets of fruit or vegatables at bargin prices. Some of the merchants told Pete that Oswald was a pain always wanting to bargin about the price. They did not know what he was trying to get for what price etc. They asked Pete to see if he could keep Oswald from coming around and trying to bargin in the busy time of the day. He said he made contact with Oswald and asked him if he was buying for a resturant or grocery store and that he could arrange for him to get some wholesale prices on the stuff. At first Oswald said OK but then changed and said he was not buying for a resturant or grocery. So Pete had him followed with the baskets of stuff he bought and found he was bringing them out to the wharf and to ships. Pete just thought he was working some kind of deal with the ships and told the merchants who wound up giving him wholesale prices. He said Oswald did this for a few weeks. He also noticed Oswald hanging around the old Men's Mission on Esplanade and Bourbon. He never saw him go in, but noticed that he talked to a couple of different people outside. (Shaw lived around the corner but never saw him with Shaw). He told me that Oswald also talked to a friend of his whose name he would not give me. Said he talked to him about renting an automobile From the guys business. Said the guy refused.

He said Oswald was known to be around a Latin American that was not a Cuban and sometimes would go into Lala's restaurant with him. The restaurant was owned by Pete's cousin. Some of Pete's other relatives were in business with the Bannistellas and the Ferreras who ran most of the seafood markets at that part of the quarter. He said Oswald would sometime ask them about contacts to fishing boats. Don't know if they gave him any information. He talked to some other people after the assasination and said that none of them like

A Planned Meeting with Layton Martens:

I believed Layton would remember me, despite the briefness of our acquaintance, and therefore tried to find him after speaking out. I finally located him, through a musician who knew both him and musician/Marcello bouncer and possible hitman, witness Mac McCullough. Layton was still living, and in fine health, in Louisiana, with a band of his own. I called him, and we arranged to meet on Saturday, March 25. But Martens suddenly died of a heart attack (age 57) exactly one week before our meeting, on March 18, 2000.

Did Lee Oswald Sell Fruit on the Docks Because of the Arms Shipment?

I asked researchers, would there be any trace of the Caracas gun shipment? In fact, new files show that rifles were indeed being smuggled in from Caracas in 1963, years after I reported it. , In fact, a trace remains, fueled by negative knowledge that Lee was “an assassin.,”: a respected independent investigator, “Cal” plodded the streets of New Orleans, kindly providing information to me and others. For example, he talked to Reily employees who remembered me, though none could remember Lee working there. “Cal” sent us the results of what he was able to learn about Lee, the docks, and selling fruit, upon being asked to look into it. Also, he was asked if anyone saw Lee visiting any bars where old retirees hung out, as I hoped somebody might have remembered Lee looking into the Huey Long murder case. ...The informant’s name was freely given. By purchasing fruit and selling it to ships along the docks, Lee set up a temporary reputation as a ‘fruit seller.’ Then, when it was time to be rid of the bananas and oranges removed from the crates to hide the rifles, Lee and others sold fruit, and nobody noticed. This is probably how I ended up with bananas at lunch time! Cal mentions Lee visiting “the old Men’s Mission on Esplanade.” Lee told me he asked “old men” about the slain doctor Weiss in the Huey Long murder case. About the car, Lee tried to obtain a late model car for us, when we had to make a momentous quick trip to Jackson’s mental hospital, at the end of August. I found it remarkable that a trace of Lee’s attempt to find a better car, rather than the old one we were forced to use, survived.

<u>The 2 ½-dollar bills found on Lee Oswald</u>: . Found in Lee’s pockets when he was searched after his arrest: a box-top and two halves of two different dollar bills with serial numbers that belonged to a cache of money captured in a Federal raid. The Dallas Police photo shows the serial numbers recorded from the two half-dollar bills. For contact purposes, if a person Lee sat next to had offered a one-half dollar bill, Lee would have responded with one of the matching halves.

SEARCHING THE SHADOWS: A LAYMAN'S INVESTIGATION INTO THE ASSASSINAT

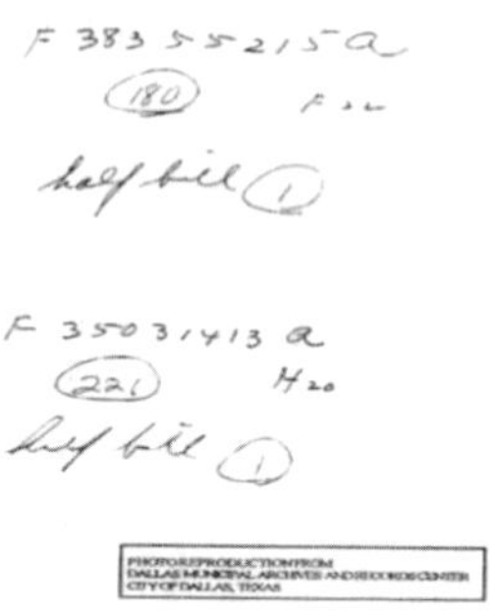

Found in Oswald's wallet when he was arrested were two halved dollar bills with different serial numbers. Were these designed to be used as a contact with the owner of the other two halves? What possible explanation could be used to determine their reason for being in Oswald's possession?

<u>The Girl in the Car: from Opening Statement, Clay Shaw Trial: Jim Garrison (I was in the car)</u>

JFK Collection: HSCA (RG 233)

110

a young lady in the automobile.

Now I want to at this time make it abundantly clear that the State does not claim that it identified that woman at all. The State is certainly not coming before this Jury and saying that it was Marina Oswald, now Marina Oswald Porter, that drove him. I wish we could have identified her, I wish we could have brought her into the courtroom and presented her to you. But nevertheless he did appear on that occasion.

Clay Shaw Trial, New Orleans . Also, from a memo by Andrew Sciambra, May, 1967: "Morgan said that his daughter, who is presently attending Southeastern Louisiana College in Hammond, was also in the house at the time and later on, after the President was shot, she remarked to her daddy that if she remembers correctly, that when OSWALD was in the house talking to her father, there was a woman sitting in the automobile waiting for him. (Mary Morgan will be home from school this week and I will talk to her to see if she remembers any of the details, Sciambra wrote. **[Morgan would not allow his daughter to testify.].**

Lee H. Oswald's Reily Time Cards and "J's" **Cards shown below are from scans like this one at left, made at The National Archives, signed and authenticated, and have not been altered, unlike the time cards in the Mary Ferrell Foundation's Archives as of June, 2021, where in one instance two "J's" and two "Made 40"'s were erased --marks made the author, Judyth Baker, as Reily VP Sec. Lee's first clock-in, clock-out is for FRIDAY, MAY 10, at bottom of first time card to left, at 7:53, with clock-out at 4:30. This was the ONLY clock-in Lee Oswald ever made at the ordinary working hours at Reily, which were 8:00 – 4:30. Lee clocked in at 7:59 and Judyth clocked him out at 4:30 precisely. His other clock-ins for his first week were 8:24, 8:18, 8:23, and 8:29, whereas Judyth clocked Lee out precisely at 5:00, 5:00, 5:00, and 5:00. Oswald's 3rd week is the most erratic, with clock-ins at 9:53, 8:50, 9:45, 9:00 and 9:59. Judyth, trying to adjust to Oswald's erratic clock-ins, makes clock-outs at 6:35, 5:31, 6:30, 5:30 and 6:30.**

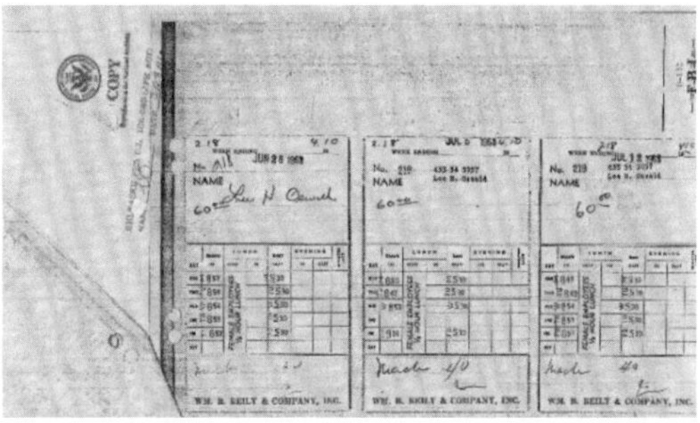

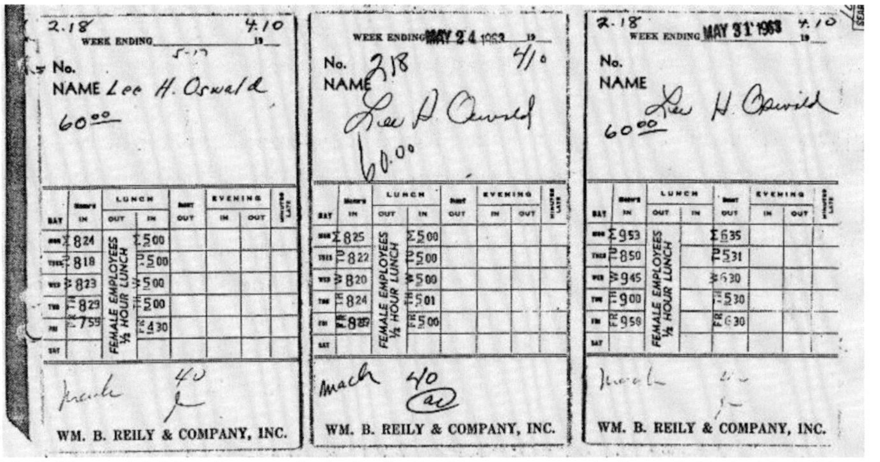

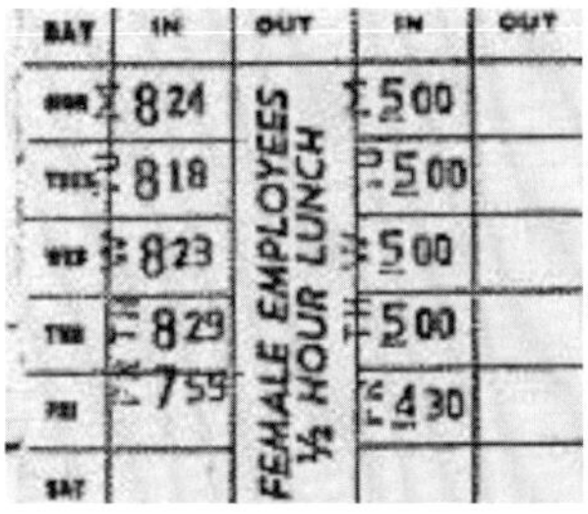

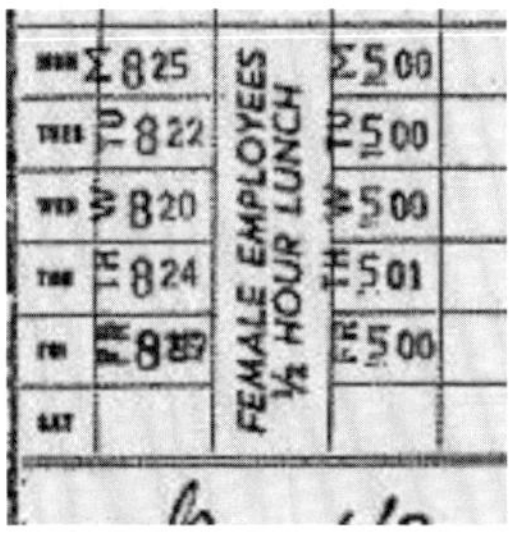

LEE CLOCKED IN TWICE, ONCE AS A 'STANDARD' EMPLOYEE, AT ABOUT 8:25, AND THEN AGAIN AS A 'REILY' EMPLOYEE, AT ABOUT 8:57, ON FRIDAY, MAY 17, WHEN HIS LAUNDERED RECORDS WERE TRANSFERRED FROM STANDARD TO REILY.

HIS CHECK WAS CUT FAST ENOUGH ON FRIDAY THAT HIS FIRST CHECK WAS ISSUED BY REILY ('O' WAS CUT LATER THAN 'B' SO JUDYTH'S ('BAKER') HAD HER FIRST CHECK ISSUED BY STANDARD, BUT OSWALD, AS AN 'O' GOT HIS FIRST CHECK ISSUED BY REILY, AS THERE WAS MORE TIME TO SWITCH IT OVER TO REILY FILES.
(Judyth and Lee rode the bus together daily for 11 wks of Reily paychecks for Lee.)

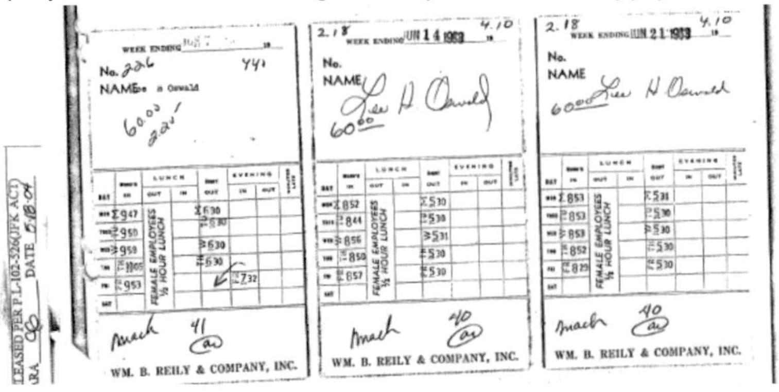

Lee's 4th, 5th and 6th weeks at REILY. Here, <u>all three weeks of Lee's work are accepted by Personnel</u>, who marked "Made 40" and approved the time cards with the usual circled initial.

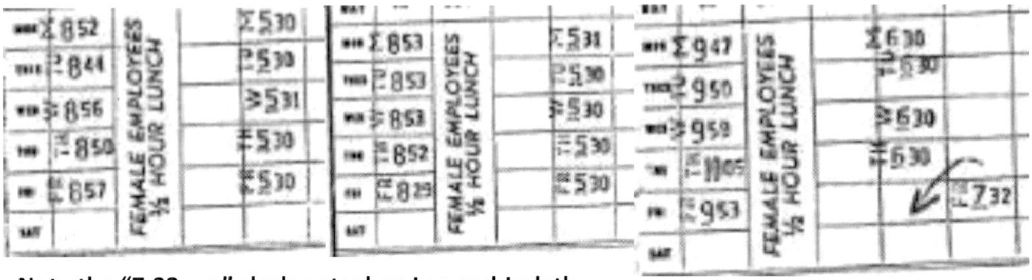

Note the "7:32 pm" clock-out when Lee and Judyth went on a double date with David and Anna Lewis and did not get back in time to clock Lee out at 6:30. Judyth clocked Lee out precisely at 6:30 the other days of this week, while Lee clocked in at 9:47, 9:50, 9:59, 11:05 and 9:53. Personnel will soon get complaints that Oswald is often "missing. They will be sending more time-cards for Judyth to approve and sign as the weeks pass, such as the three weeks in a row, below:

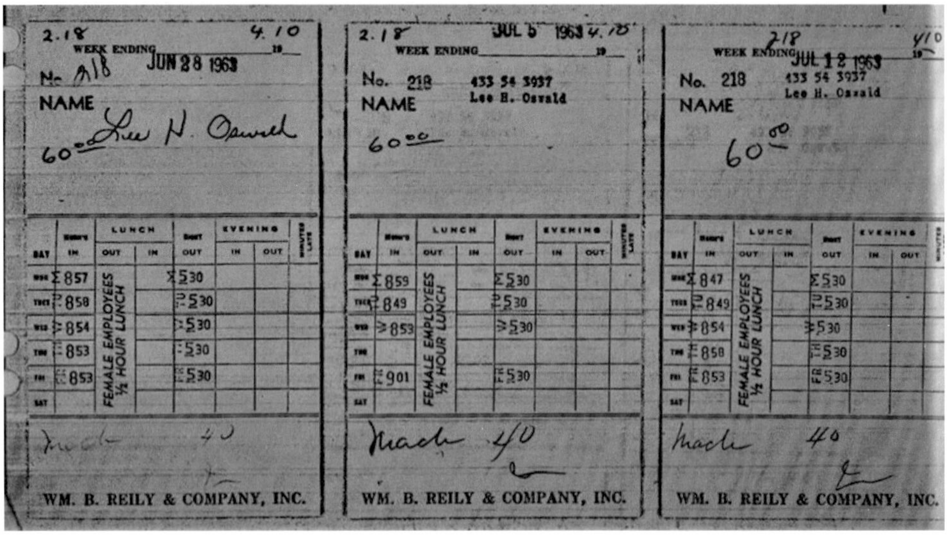

. Judyth made <u>12 precise clock-outs of 5:30 and 3 "5:31" clock-outs in this 3-week span</u>. Lee had 6- 8:53 clock-ins, 3- 8:52 clock-ins, and 2- 8:29 clock-ins, the rest being 8:44, 8:50, 8:56 and 8:57. Marina Oswald told the Warren Commission that Lee was always home by 5:00, which never happened. Had Lee worked normal hours, and had gone straight home, he might have arrived by 5:00 every day if traffic wasn't too bad, slowing down the bus.

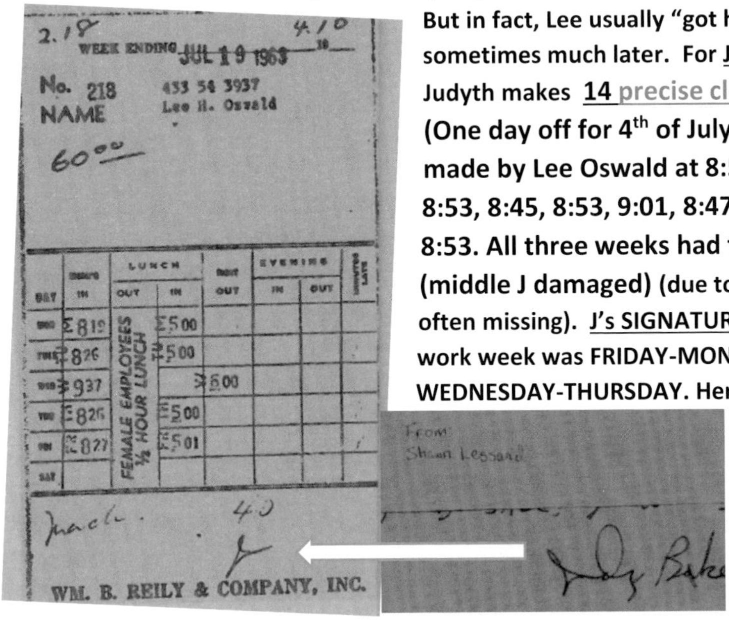

But in fact, Lee usually "got home" at about 7:00, and sometimes much later. For <u>JUNE 28, JULY 6, JULY 12</u>: Judyth makes <u>14 precise clock-outs at exactly 5:30.</u> (One day off for 4th of July.) Clock-in times were made by Lee Oswald at 8:57, 8:58, 8:54, 8:53, 8:53 8:53, 8:45, 8:53, 9:01, 8:47, 8:49, 8:54, 8:58 and 8:53. All three weeks had to be initialed by Judyth (middle J damaged) (due to complaints that Lee was often missing). <u>J's SIGNATURES AND INITIALS:</u> Reily's work week was FRIDAY-MONDAY-TUESDAY-WEDNESDAY-THURSDAY. Here, on Lee's last week of work at Reily's,_Friday, July 19th began the 11th week for Lee Oswald as a Reily employee. The last time card shows the Friday, July 19 clock-out of 5:01, the day Lee was fired. The 10th work week began the previous Friday. Judyth clocked Lee out this week at 5:00, 5:00, 6:00, 5:00. Lee clocked in at 8:19, 8:26, 9:37 (family emergency), 8:26, and 8:27.

<u>Similar J's</u>

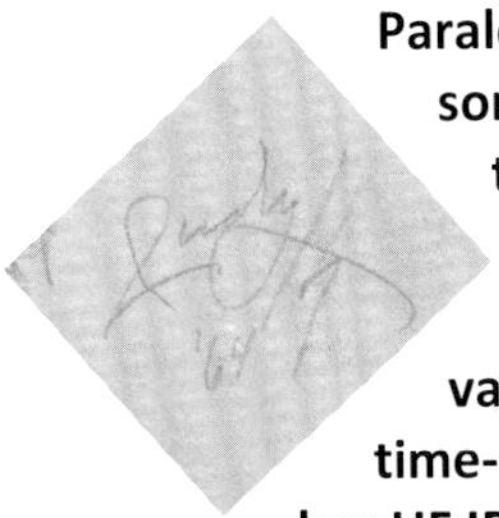

Paralegal <u>Shawn Lessard</u>, going through a box of old papers with Judyth's son, found one of Judyth's signatures on a poem from 1964. The "J" there resembles the "J" on Lee Oswald's last timecard that Judyth initialed. Lessard signed the paper as a witness and sent it to Judyth, who was living in Sweden. Below are examples of Judyth's various "J's" showing how they differ. Those who say the "J's" on Lee's time-cards mysteriously differ from each other need to view the "J's" on her UF ID cards, especially for 1965.

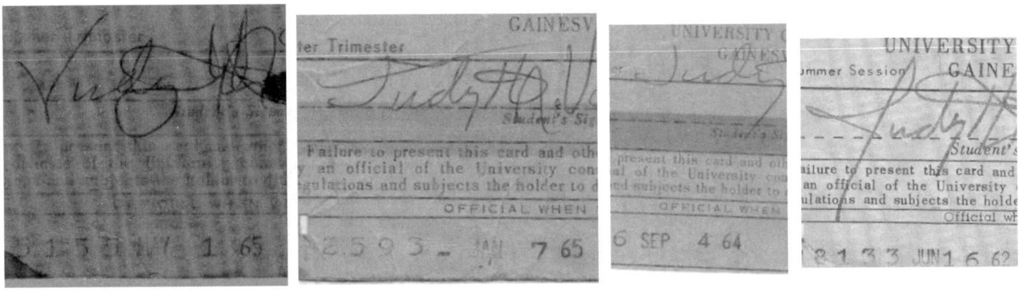

LEE's FAKE BACKGROUND REPORT: 1. Has no signature 2. Desmare's (Superintendent) initials are typed in, but Desmare didn't remember writing the report. 3. Says aunt has known Lee only 1-1 ½ yrs.(!) 4. No mention of Russia, jobs in Texas, Russian wife, etc. 5. Misspells 'effects' in this supposedly professional financial report. 6.'Savings' 'estimated' -no mention of a bank account. Read paragraph 1 (the only paragraph numbered) . Note the word "favorable" used three times. Ask yourself if a professional wrote it. No mention of unfavorable discharge, former employment in Texas .

RETAIL CREDIT COMPANY
CHARACTER—FINANCIAL REPORT

CONFIDENTIAL

New Orleans, La. OFFICE

Dist. Agcy., File or Fed. & Br. Cl. #: ns

Acct. No. 6605

REPORT FROM (If not city in heading) (State whether former addr., etc.)

5-16-63 16
OSWALD, LEE HARVEY
New Orleans, La. 757 French St.
Maintenance-Standard Coffee Co

Transaction: –
Amount $ –
Mo. Notes $ –

IDENTITY:	1. How long known to you and informants?	1. You – Informants 1½yrs-2y Intv Aunt
	2. How long has applicant resided at present residence address?	2. 2wks-Prev U.S. Marines
	3. About what is his age? (If around 21 verify if possible.)	3. 23
	4. Is he married? Number of dependents including wife?	4. Yes Number of Dependents? 2
	5. Show racial descent	5. AS
BUSINESS:	6. Show name of present employer.	6. Standard
	7. In what line of business is applicant engaged?	7. Coffee Business
	8. What position does he hold?	8. Maintenance Man
	9. How long with present employer?	9. one week*prev U.S. Marines
STABILITY:	10. Is he employed FULL TIME? (If not, show how many days per week he works, etc.)	10. Yes
	11. Are prospects for continued permanent employment good?	11. Yes
	12. Is he steady, progressive and does he live within his income?	12. Yes
FINANCES:	13. Estimate applicant's net worth.	13. 2,500(Est)
	14. Of what does worth consist principally?	14. Personal affects and Savings
	15. Does he own or rent his home?	15. rent
	16. What is applicant's ANNUAL EARNED income?	16. $ 3,500(Est)
	17. Estimate added ANNUAL income from pensions, rents, investments, disability, etc. Show source.	17. $ none Source
	18. If wife employed, by whom? Her ANNUAL income.	18. No $
	19. Do you learn of any foreclosures, suits, judgments, failures, encumbrances, bankruptcies against him? (If so, which, give details.)	19. No
CHARACTER—HOME SURROUNDINGS:	20. Are home surroundings favorable? (If not, explain.)	20. Yes
	21. In what type neighborhood does applicant live? (Show middle class, wealthy, low industrial, etc.)	21. middle class
	22. Any criticism of honesty, fair dealings, character or reputation? (If any, cover fully.)	22. No
	23. Do you learn of any criticism due to illegal activities, domestic trouble, morals or habits? (If so, cover below.)	23. No
	24. Do you recommend doing business with applicant?	24. Yes

REMARKS: 25. BUSINESS: Cover former and present business connections, success and general business reputation; prospects for future and general stability.
26. FINANCES: Comment on present and past financial standing, record for living within means, any illness or physical impairments that might affect his earning capacity.
27. CHARACTER-HOME SURROUNDINGS: Comment on character, habits and morals, home surroundings and class of associates. Give type of neighborhood, stability and class of residents in the section.

1. Lee Harvey Oswald is employed as a Maintenance Man for the Standard Coffee Company, and has been so engaged in this occupation for the past one week, and enjoys a favorable business reputation. Previous to this, he was in the U.S. Marines for some three years. He enjoys a favorable business reputation, and his prospects for the future appear to be favorable.

FINANCES: His present and past financial standing is good, and he is regarded as an individual who lives within his means. Learned of no illiness or physical impairments that might affect his earning capacity.

CHARACTER-HOME SURROUNDINGS: His character, habits, and Morals are good, and he is known to keep good associates, and well regarded. He resides with his wife, and child. They live in a middle class residential section with frame homes that are well kept, and living conditions are adequate. Stability and class of residencts in this section is good.

RCD lcc

MAY 2 1963

RETAIL CREDIT COMPANY
Form 1630—10-52 PRINTED IN U.S.A.

Signature of person making report ________

CHARACTER—FINANCIAL REPORT

Read paragraph 1 below (the only paragraph numbered) . Note the use of the word "favorable." Ask yourself if a professional wrote it:

stability and class of residents in the section.

1. Lee Harvey Oswald is employed as a Maintenance Man for the Standard Coffee Company, and has been so engaged in this occupation for the past one week, and enjoys a favorable business reputation. Previous to this, he was in the U.S. Marines for some three years. He enjoys a favorable business reputation, and his prospects for the future appear to be favorable.

MARY SHERMAN: CANCER EXPERT

Woman Expert in Cancer Slain In Burned Louisiana Apartment

NEW ORLEANS, July 21 (UPI) — The police answered a fire call today and found the badly burned and repeatedly stabbed body of a woman expert in bone cancer.

The body of Dr. Mary S. Sherman, 51 years old, was on the floor of her apartment on St. Charles Avenue, a prosperous area. Neighbors had smelled smoke and called the police to investigate a fire.

A coroner's investigator, Sam Moran, said Dr. Sherman's body had apparently been set on fire in the bed and rolled off on the floor. She had been stabbed eight times in the left arm, chest and stomach.

The front door of the apartment had been forced and Dr. Sherman's purse looted. Her car was missing but was later found about eight blocks away.

Dr. Sherman did cancer research work at the Ochsner Foundation Hospital in New Orleans.

She was a widow and lived alone. Her apartment was the target of burglars several times in the last few years, and she had a burglar alarm installed. It was apparently not working last night.

Her maid said she last saw the doctor yesterday afternoon. She said she had been in good spirits and talked of a woman friend who might arrive for a visit.

Dr. Sherman was born in Evanston, Ill., and held two degrees from Northwestern University and a medical degree from the University of Chicago. She taught there before joining the Ochsner group in New Orleans 12 year ago.

She was a partner in the Ochsner Clinic and was director of the bone pathology laboratory of the Ochsner Medical Foundation.

A spokesman for the clinic described her as "an internationally recognized authority in bone and joint pathology." Much of her work dealt with cancer of the bone.

John McAdams disputed my claim that Dr. Mary Sherman was an expert in cancer, claiming that Sherman never did cancer research and was only an orthopedic surgeon. He also claimed that mice could not be given cancer, according to a biologist at his university (Marquette). His statements went everywhere, harming my reputation, when I first spoke out, influencing researchers to ignore me. VIZ: *Wall Street Journal:* "Woman Expert in Cancer Slain…"

By the way, we put our little pink pills away a month and a week ago, and the doctor says it takes three months before we can really try to start a family, since the pills put you all out of whack, especially since I've been on them for almost four years. But maybe we'll surprise everybody. I feel VERY fertile! to say nothing of Bob!

Which reminds me, our best friend had a miscarriage. She was on pills two years, and it took them six months before she was properly in tune, and then she got Placenta Praev(i and needed a D&C, poor thing. She has our doctor, and she said he was very good indeed through the whole thing (to the tune of $130.00, he should have been!).

So, anyway, PLEASE PLEASE PLEASE PLEASE WRITE TO YORE LONELY RELLATIVS. WE NEED HELP! WE NEED YUR ENCURAGEMUNT AND MORE THAN THAT WE NEED TO KNOW THAT AMERICA IS STILL THERE, SO PUTTY PUTTY PEAS, PLEASE LET US KNOW HOW YOU ARE, and some --*%$#JUICY GOSSIP,TOO!!!!

<u>Ignorant about Clay Shaw trial—Geology Research in Rural Mexico</u> in <u>1967-1968</u>, with a native-style rented apartment in Saltillo, Coahuila, spending months in the mountains for Robert's research and dissertation. Note "almost four years on the pill" and plea for news –"We need to know that America is still there…" I wrote… baby Susie was born May 28, 1968. By then, I refused to endanger my baby.

Saint Francis College
Fort Wayne, Indiana
June 23, 1961

Miss Judyth Vary
4402 Pompano Lane
Palmetto, Florida

Dear Miss Vary:

Thank you for your letter of June 10. We regret the delay in answering, but my absence from campus for some time has resulted in belated correspondence.

We are happy to know that you have selected Saint Francis as the college of your choice, and we are pleased to renew our original full-tuition scholarship offer of $350.00. This scholarship is renewable each year (provided that you maintain the required scholastic index), amounting to a total of $1400.00.

Since our college is comparatively small, we do not have facilities for extensive laboratory research at present. Some experimentation with white mice or other small animals will be possible. We have plans for a new science building in the near future and will begin construction of a new residence hall and a new classroom building this [illegible]

You may be interested in [illegible] instructors have [illegible] ships [illegible]

In reference to several of your questions, we do have advanced placement in languages. There are opportunities for "overloads" for students who maintain a 3.5 cumulative average. We are cognizant of originality of thought, and we feel that we are reasonably (sometimes extremely) strict.

Distance may prohibit your visiting Saint Francis College, but we do want you to know that you are most welcome any time. We wish you and your family could meet some of the faculty and students and also see the residence hall with its attractive accommodations for the girls. You will like the truly Franciscan spirit of joy and friendliness that prevails on the campus in both classroom and extra-curricular activities, welding the students into just one big family.

We would appreciate hearing from you soon to learn about your plans. May the Holy Spirit guide you in the choice of a college suited to your needs and interests. God bless and love you always.

Sincerely in St. Francis,

Sister M. Veronica

Sister M. Veronica, OSF
Director of Admissions

DECLARATION OF INNOCENCE
CONCERNING OFFICIAL CHARGES AGAINST
LEE HARVEY OSWALD, FALSELY ACCUSED OF MURDERING
PRESIDENT JOHN F. KENNEDY NOV. 22, 1963

Whereas, the findings of the FBI, the Warren Commission and the HSCA were based on extreme prejudice regarding Oswald, and
Whereas, these findings are considered obsolete, in view of masses of new and exculpatory evidence, as well as the statements of ignored or formerly silent witnesses who felt threatened due to extreme prejudice,
The Undersigned, who themselves are witnesses, experts and/or independent researchers in the matter, hereby declare, with confidence, that Lee Harvey Oswald did not murder President John F. Kennedy.

Hence, we set our hand to this "Declaration of Innocence," of Lee Harvey Oswald, urging all nations and governments to recognize the validity and importance of our collective decision in the case.

Name Qualifications/Expertise Date

AUTHOR 10-16-15
Dr. Mary's Monkey
Retired FBI
CONSULTANT – "THE GUILTY MEN" – HISTORY CHANNEL 2003
author – CIA – drugs –
Journalist/author 10-17-15
Professor 10-17-15
WITNESS son of E. Howard Hunt 10/17/2015
AUTHOR – 10-17-15 WITNESS
10-17-15
Sulzer – I saw Lee in 1963 at the ... Apts – questions of Dr. Mary
– researcher 10/18/15

Ed Haslam -Author- Dr. Mary's Monkey Roger Stone – Author - Witness'Zack'
Shelton - Retired FBI Victoria Hawes Sulzer – "I saw Lee …"
Daniel Hopsicker -CIA – drugs Romney Stubbs - researcher
Jim Marrs – journalist/author
David Denton – Professor
Saint John Hunt – witness- son of E. Howard Hunt (1 of 3 such collections)

<u>The Cullen Moore Horoscopes</u> in *The Times-Picayune*

Cullen Moore, an astrologer and horoscope writer located in New York, had syndicated columns called *Stars and Lovers* (Sundays) and *Moon Messages* (weekdays).[335] Oswald was Libra and I was Taurus. Oddly, some horoscopes Oswald read to me when we rode the Magazine Bus to work at Reily's resonated with intrigue. I saved the dates of some intriguing entries and in 2002, was able to find and Xerox them. The May 23, 1963 entry for Libra, for example, reads: **"Venus, the planet of love, strongly invites you. Avoid the clandestine."** At that time, Oswald and I had commenced a love affair. A few of the interesting bits of advice from the horoscopes that Oswald (Libra) read:

May 25: "**Keep quiet about financial arrangements. Do not reveal confidences. If you are dealing with underground or behind scenes affairs, do prevent interference."**

May 30: "Quiet behind scenes maneuvers will gain more ground than airing your views."

May 31: (at the same time that I was engaged in clandestine cancer research efforts, with Oswald beginning to learn certain lab techniques as well), the column was headlines with "Today's Rays Splendid for Research Scientist"

THE TIMES-PICAYUNE, NEW ORLEANS, LA., FRIDAY MORNING, MAY 31, 1963

MOON MESSAGES FOR YOU

Today's Rays Splendid for Research Scientist

By CULLEN MOORE

Today's Moonrays are splendid for the student, the research scientist, and all who try to discover things not apparent on the surface. Mysteries in human conduct also may be revealed.

ARIES (March 21-April 20)—Try not to irritate one who works with you (or who is connected in employment matters).

TAURUS (April 21-May 21)—Luck with those who depend on you and admire your skill. Popularity with subordinates.

GEMINI (May 22-June 21)—Some clashes in matters around

July 1st**:** Column Headline: "Rays favorable Today: Detectives May Benefit" **"Today's Moonrays are favorable for detectives, investigators, all who deal in behind-scene activities. Medicine, science, may also benefit. The sensitivity of the atmosphere should reveal many strange things."**

Aug. 1st**: "A walk or sudden visit is revealing. You should use the telephone, telegraph, or send important messages."**

Aug. 11: "**...Beware of subversives...**" **"Your temper is too high. You could cut off your greatest benefactor or lose a loyal friend unless you calm down. See things from more unbiased view."**

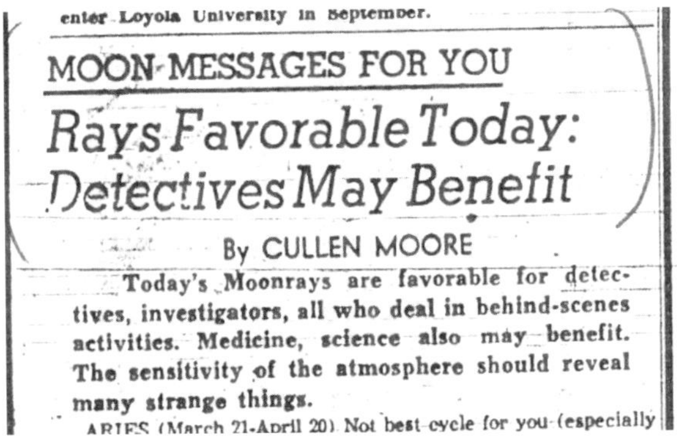
enter Loyola University in September.

MOON MESSAGES FOR YOU

Rays Favorable Today: Detectives May Benefit

By CULLEN MOORE

Today's Moonrays are favorable for detectives, investigators, all who deal in behind-scenes activities. Medicine, science also may benefit. The sensitivity of the atmosphere should reveal many strange things.

ARIES (March 21-April 20) Not best cycle for you (especially

Aug. 20: "**A secret matter could take a surprising twist. Be sure you are open-minded, tolerant.**

(Interestingly, Oswald was surprised on Aug. 21 when his status as a returned defector from the USSR was made public during the Latin Listening Post radio "debate" on WDSU).

---

335 "Now It Can Be Foretold" Ann Bayer(assistant editor of *Life Mag.*) , *Life Magazine*, Sept. 26, 1969

<u>**Oswald Innocent and Framed**</u> **The accused assassin. Question: Does this look like a gloating killer? What was his motive? The Warren Commission said he wanted to make his mark in history. If so, why did he resolutely deny killing the President? Photos were selected and retouched to make Lee look like he was "smirking"— taking advantage of a natural conformation of the shape of Lee's mouth. <u>The frown on Lee's lips was retouched to look like a "smirk."</u> His chin was retouched to look more "square" to better match the infamous "backyard photo."**

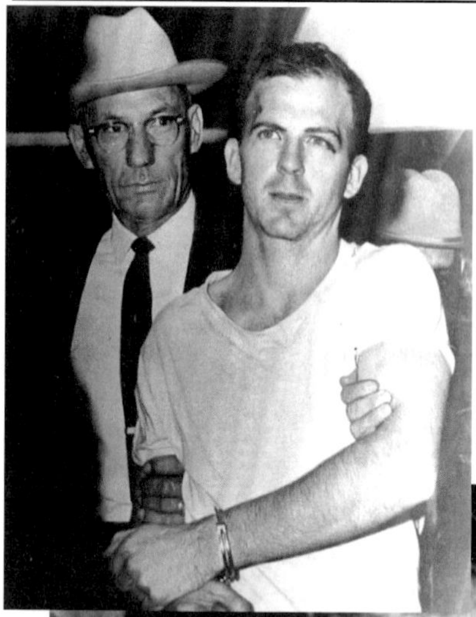

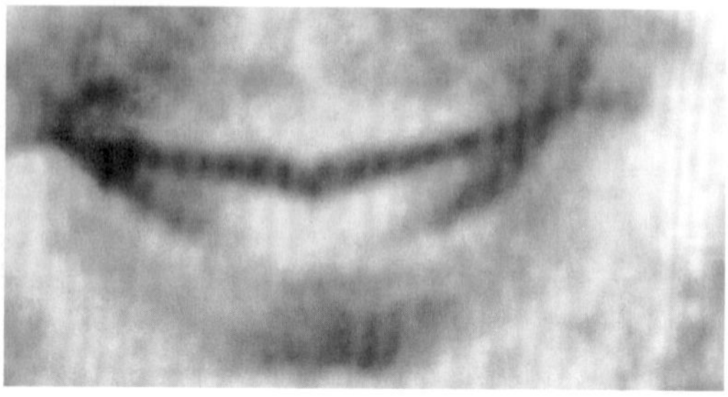

Retouched Lips, drawn to make a smirk.

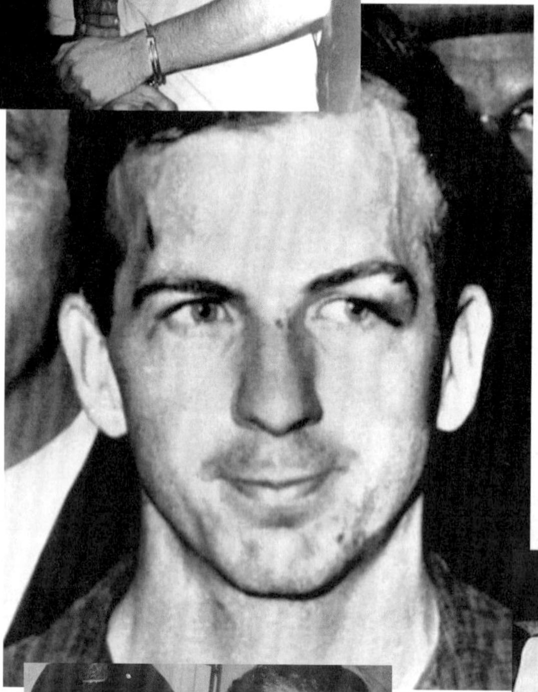

A frown was turned into a 'smirk'

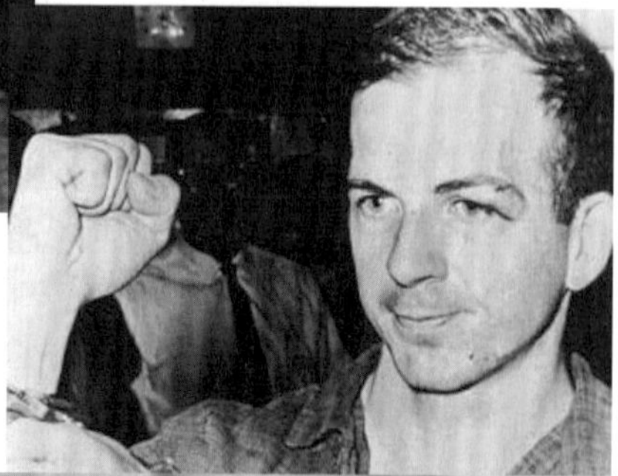

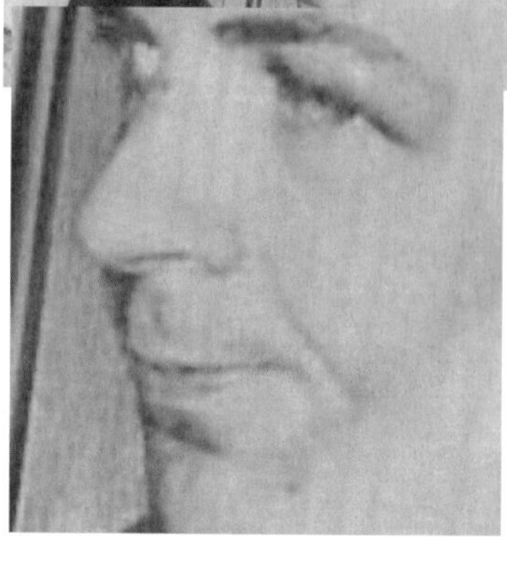

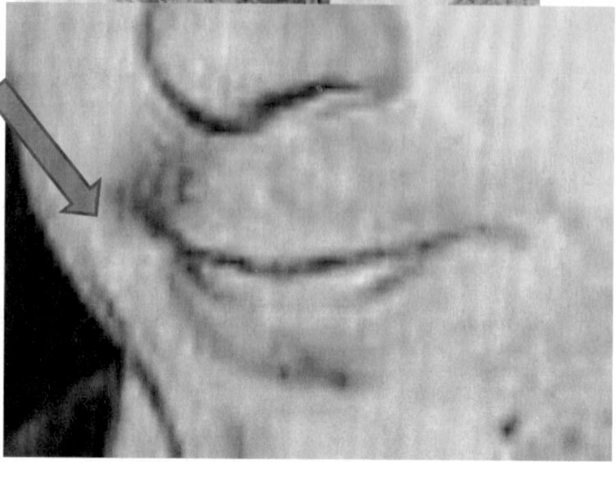

WALTER REED ARMY INSTITUTE OF RESEARCH
WALTER REED ARMY MEDICAL CENTER
WASHINGTON 12, D. C.

IN REPLY REFER TO: MEDEC-ZOA 2 September 1960

Miss Judyth A. Vary
5607 18 Street, West
Bradenton, Florida

Dear Miss Vary:

We are very pleased to learn of your interest in protecting against radiation injury.

I am arranging for two chemicals to be sent to you under separate cover. These chemicals are mercaptoethylamine as the hydrochloride. This material should be administered to mice intraperitoneally in a concentration of 13 milligrams of free base per milliliter about fifteen minutes before irradiation. A solution of greater concentration may be used. The solution is prepared by dissolving the chemical in distilled water and adjusting the pH to 7.4. This should be done relatively soon before you use it, since air will tend to oxidize the compound to the disulfide, in which case it will have somewhat less protective activity. This chemical as well as the other one I am sending to you is hydroscopic; that is to say, it will take water from the air and turn into a liquid. You should therefore, keep it inside a desiccator so that the material will remain dry. The chemicals that I am sending to you are packed in a jar with desiccator around them. If the desiccator turns pink you can put the desiccator only in the oven to regenerate its original blue color. The second compound is aminoethylisothiourea bromide hydrobromide. This should be given intraperitoneally in a dose of 350 milligrams per kilogram as a double salt, i.e. as it comes from the bottle. The solute injected should not exceed more than half a milliliter in volume and it also must be adjusted to a pH of 7.4. If it is injected at a pH of around 1 or 2 it will have an irritant effect in the mouse. If it is injected around pH 4 to 5 then the compound will rearrange to a structure which is not quite as useful as that which is injected around pH 7.4.

The protective activity of these two compounds is somewhat different. The aminoethylisothiourea is somewhat more effective in protecting mice against radiation then is mercaptoethylamine. However, we think the mechanism of the isothiourea derivative is appreciably different from the mercaptoethylamine

MEDEC-ZOA 2 September 1960
Miss Judyth A. Vary

I am enclosing both in case you wish to use two sets of mice for protection studies. My thought is you should use the isothiourea initially; if you have good luck then use the mercaptoethylamine.

I am interested in your studies on hypothermia and in the work that you are doing with the stearates. We have some similar work going on in tissue culture with hypothermia which I would be very pleased to talk over with you sometime. Furthermore, if you have difficulty in obtaining some of the stearates let us know what you're interested in. We will be pleased to send them to you if we have them available.

We look forward to hearing from you again as to the results of your studies. And look forward to facilitating your work on this interesting experiment.

Very sincerely yours,

David P. Jacobus

DAVID P. JACOBUS, M.D.
Chief, Department of

THE WRAIR LETTER

Judge Jim Botelho's Assessment of Lee Oswald. Botelho, who lived in the same quonset hut with Lee Oswald at El Toro, said he and Lee were close friends. He was only asked negative questions about Lee by the FB I, he said. They purchased classical music LP's together, he said, pooling their money, then would play the classical music loudly to drown out "the country music" playing in the Quonset hut next to theirs. Of Kerry Thorney, who claimed he was close friends with Lee, Botelho was filmed saying that they considered Thornley to be "a jerk" and that he was a mere acquaintance. He presented his opinions, which were filmed and recorded, at two JFK Assassination Conferences in Dallas, and despite his affliction with Parkinson's, wrote out the following notes, from which he read, which displayed Lee's character. "I thought Lee was training to become a spy," he also said. "I saw him go regularly into places where you couldn't go unless you had a high security clearance, which the Warren Commission claimed he didn't have." Jim kindly signed over all five of the cherished classical records that he had kept so many years, into my care, writing "To Judyth with love from Lee and Jim." Parkinson's Disease has harmed his handwriting ability.

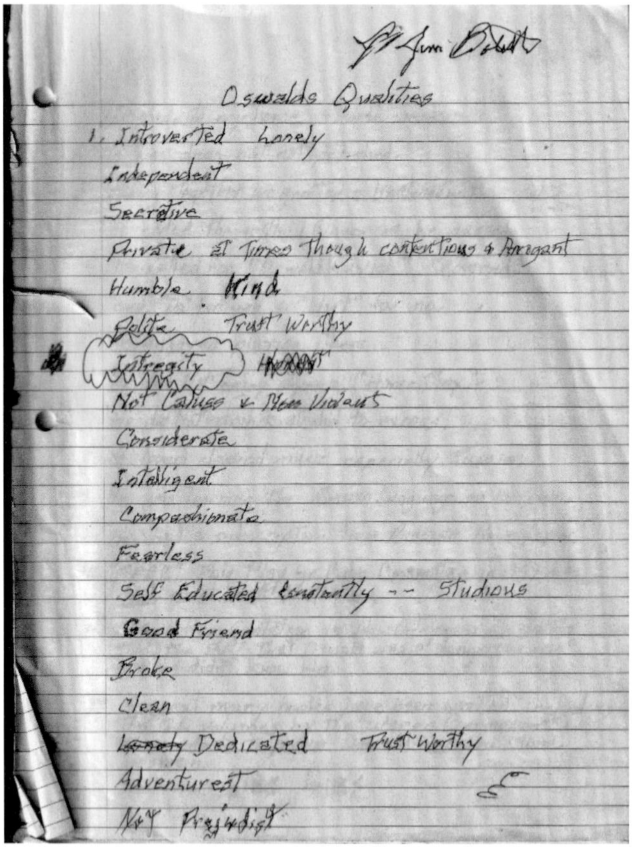
Oswalds Qualities
1. Introverted Lonely
Independent
Secretive
Private at Times though contentious & Arrogant
Humble Kind
Polite Trust Worthy
Integrity
Not Callous & Non Violent
Considerate
Intelligent
Compassionate
Fearless
Self Educated Constantly -- Studious
Good Friend
Broke
Clean
~~Lonely~~ Dedicated Trust Worthy
Adventurest
Not Prejudist

Jim started his list about Lee with "the negatives" to show he wasn't being biased.

Spelling corrected:
Introverted Lonely

Secretive

Private at times though, contentious and arrogant

Humble Kind
INTEGRITY (circled)
Not Callous / Non Violent / Considerate / Intelligent / Compassionate / Fearless /Self-educated / Constantly Studious / Good Friend Clean /Dedicated / Trustworthy / Adventurous / Not Prejudiced

INDEX (limited to major items)

Comments & Apologies

To obtain more important files and records, researchers, please
correlate this book with available material in my books ***David Ferrie: Mafia Pilot*** (for best timeline and vital facts about Ferrie) and ***Kennedy & Oswald: the Big Picture*** (esp.concerning the Michael and Ruth Paine and the Backyard Photos) -JVB
N.B. **TYPOS and Evidence files:** This book was released unedited in 2021 to avoid censorship and deletions. It is a labor of love, updating the original Me & Lee, which has evidence files not included here (and vice-versa). Between both books, most evidence files are now in print. There will be typos, as the author's eyesight is poor. Please accept my apologies! *-JVB*